JERUSALEM
THE CENTER OF THE UNIVERSE

JERUSALEM
THE CENTER OF THE UNIVERSE

Its Archaeology and History (1800–100 BCE)

Israel Finkelstein

SBL PRESS

Atlanta

Copyright © 2024 by Israel Finkelstein

All rights reserved. No part of this work may be reproduced or transmitted in any form or by any means, electronic or mechanical, including photocopying and recording, or by means of any information storage or retrieval system, except as may be expressly permitted by the 1976 Copyright Act or in writing from the publisher. Requests for permission should be addressed in writing to the Rights and Permissions Office, SBL Press, 825 Houston Mill Road, Atlanta, GA 30329 USA.

Library of Congress Control Number: 2024939897

Contents

Original Publications ix
Figures xi
Abbreviations xiii
Chronological Periods xvii

Part 1. Introductions

1. Introduction: The Center of the Universe 3
2. The Mound on the Mount: A Solution to the "Problem with Jerusalem"? 9

Part 2. The Bronze Age and the Iron I

3. Middle Bronze Jerusalem 29
4. The Shephelah and Jerusalem's Western Border in the Amarna Period 33
5. Saul and Highlands of Benjamin Update: The Role of Jerusalem 49

Part 3. The Iron IIA and the Early Iron IIB: The First Leap Forward

6. Jerusalem and the Benjamin Plateau in the Early Phases of the Iron Age 63
7. Has King David's Palace in Jerusalem Been Found? 71
8. The Large Stone Structure in Jerusalem: Reality versus Yearning 95

9. The Iron Age Complex in the Ophel, Jerusalem:
   A Critical Analysis 109

10. Geographical and Historical Realities behind the Earliest
    Layer in the David Story 127

11. Kirath-jearim: Israel's Impact on Jerusalem in the First Half
    of the Eighth Century BCE 147

Part 4. The Iron IIB: The Largest City in the Levant

12. The Emergence and Dissemination of Writing in Judah 167

13. Epigraphic Evidence from Jerusalem and Its Environs at
    the Dawn of Biblical History: Facts First 195

14. Migration of Israelites into Judah after 720 BCE: An Answer
    and an Update 203

15. Temple and Dynasty: Hezekiah, the Remaking of Judah,
    and the Rise of the Pan-Israelite Ideology 221

16. The Settlement History of Jerusalem in the Eighth and
    Seventh Centuries BCE 245

17. The Finds from the Rock-Cut Pool in Jerusalem and the
    Date of the Siloam Tunnel: An Alternative Interpretation 261

18. Comments on the Date of Late Monarchic Judahite
    Seal Impressions 271

19. Mozah, Nephtoah and Royal Estates in the Jerusalem
    Highlands 281

20. The Unique Specialized Economy of Judah under Assyrian
    Rule and Its Impact on the Material Culture of the Kingdom 293

Part 5. The Iron IIC

21. The Acts of Solomon: The Impact of Jeroboam II of Israel
    and Manasseh of Judah 315

22. The Sites of Mordot Arnona and Armon HaNatziv on the
Southern Outskirts of Jerusalem: An Alternative Archaeological
and Historical Interpretation 325

Part 6. The Dark Age and Recovery

23. Jerusalem and Judah 600–200 BCE: Implications for
Understanding Pentateuchal Texts 343

Part 7. Conclusions

24. Jerusalem and Empires: Long-Term Observations 359

Works Cited 375

Ancient Sources Index 435
Place Names Index 439
Personal Names Index 446
Subject Index 448

Original Publications

2. 2011. "The Mound on the Mount: A Solution to the 'Problem with Jerusalem'?" *JHS* 11, doi.org/10.5508/jhs.2011.v11.a12. Coathored with Ido Koch and Oded Lipschits.
4. 2014. "The Shephelah and Jerusalem's Western Border in the Amarna Period." *Egypt and the Levant* 24:265–74.
5. 2020. "Saul and Highlands of Benjamin Update: The Role of Jerusalem." Pages 33–56 in *Saul, Benjamin, and the Emergence of Monarchy in Israel: Biblical and Archaeological Perspectives*. Edited by Joachim J. Krause, Omer Sergi, and Kristin Weingart. AIL 40. Atlanta: SBL Press.
6. 2018. "Jerusalem and the Benjamin Plateau in the Early Phases of the Iron Age: A Different Scenario." *ZDPV* 134:190–95.
7. 2007. "Has King David's Palace in Jerusalem Been Found?" *TA* 34:142–64. Coathored with Ze'ev Herzog, Lily Singer-Avitz, and David Ussishkin.
8. 2011. "The 'Large Stone Structure' in Jerusalem: Reality versus Yearning." *ZDPV* 127:1–10.
9. 2022. "The Iron Age Complex in the Ophel, Jerusalem: A Critical Analysis." *TA* 49:191–204.
10. 2013. "Geographical and Historical Realities behind the Earliest Layer in the David Story." *SJOT* 27:131–50.
11. 2020. "Archaeological Excavations at Kiriath-jearim and the Ark Narrative in the Books of Samuel." Pages 313–31 in *The Mega Project at Motza (Moẓa): The Neolithic and Later Occupations up to the Twentieth Century*. Edited by Hamoudi Khalaily, Amit Re'em, Jacob Vardi, and Ianir Milevski. Jerusalem: Israel Antiquities Authority. Coathored with Thomas Römer and Christophe Nicolle.
12. 2020. "The Emergence and Dissemination of Writing in Judah." *Semitica and Classica* 13:269–82.

13. 2017. "Epigraphic Evidence from Jerusalem and Its Environs at the Dawn of Biblical History: Facts First." *NSAJR* 11:21–26. Coathored with Benjamin Sass.
14. 2015. "Migration of Israelites into Judah after 720 BCE: An Answer and an Update." *ZAW* 127:188–206.
15. 2006. "Temple and Dynasty: Hezekiah, the Remaking of Judah and the Rise of the Pan-Israelite Ideology." *JSOT* 30:259–85. Coathored with Neil Asher Silberman.
16. 2008. "The Settlement History of Jerusalem in the Eighth and Seventh Centuries BCE." *RB* 115:499–515.
17. 2013. "The Finds from the Rock-Cut Pool in Jerusalem and the Date of the Siloam Tunnel: An Alternative Interpretation." *Semitica et Classica* 6:279–84.
18. 2012. "Comments on the Date of Late-Monarchic Judahite Seal Impressions." *TA* 39:203–211.
19. 2015. "Mozah, Nephtoah and Royal Estates in the Jerusalem Highlands." *Semitica et Classica* 8:227–34. Coathored with Yuval Gadot.
20. 2022. "The Unique Specialized Economy of Judah under Assyrian Rule and Its Impact on the Material Culture of the Kingdom." *PEQ* 154:261–79. Coathored with Yuval Gadot and Dafna Langgut.
21. 2021. "The Acts of Solomon: The Impact of Jeroboam II of Israel and Manasseh of Judah." Pages 475–84 in *Essays on Biblical Historiography: From Jeroboam II to John Hyrcanus*, by Israel Finkelstein. FAT 148. Tübingen: Mohr Siebeck.
22 2023. "The Sites of Mordot Arnona and Armon HaNatziv on the Southern Outskirts of Jerusalem: An Alternative Archaeological and Historical Interpretation." *RB* 130:225–42.
23. 2016. "Jerusalem and Judah 600–200 BCE: Implications for Understanding Pentateuchal Texts." Pages 3–18 in *The Fall of Jerusalem and the Rise of the Torah*. Edited by Peter Dubovský, Dominik Markl, and Jean-Pierre Sonnet. FAT 107. Tübingen: Mohr Siebeck.
24. 2023. "Jerusalem and Empires: Long Term Observations." *HeBAI* 12:31–47.

Figures

1.1. The Old City of Jerusalem and environs	4–5
1.2. The City of David ridge and the Temple Mount	7
1.3. Aerial photograph of the Temple Mount, City of David ridge, Ophel excavations, and Givati Parking Lot excavations	8
2.1. Map of the City of David	12
2.2. Map of Jerusalem	18
3.1. Middle Bronze remains above the Gihon Spring	31
4.1. Sites mentioned in the chapter	35
7.1. Plan of the Large Stone Structure	75
7.2. Schematic plan of the Stepped Stone Structure	81
7.3. Aerial view of the Stepped Stone Structure	83
7.4. General view of the excavation area	87
7.5. Alternative interpretation of the Large Stone Structure	88
7.6. Suggested reconstruction of the remains	89
8.1. Actual remains associated with the Large Stone Structure	98
8.2. Stepped Stone Structure before and after restoration	103
9.1. Architectural elements in the Ophel	111
9.2. Iron Age remains in the western sector of the Ophel	113
9.3. Western Ophel, Section a–a	115
9.4. Western Ophel, Section f–f	117
9.5. Storage jars found in L12-223c	123
10.1. Map of the Shephelah, Hebron Hills, and Beersheba Valley	134
11.1. Map showing the location of Kiriath-jearim	148
11.2. Aerial view of Deir el-Azar (Kiriath-jearim)	148
11.3. View of the site, looking south	151
11.4. Massive terrace outlining the summit of the hill in the east	152
11.5. Massive terrace outlining the summit of the hill in the west	152
11.6. Digital elevation model of the hill of Kiriath-jearim	153
11.7. Aerial view of the site, 1918	154

11.8. Orthophoto of the hill of Kiriath-jearim	155
11.9. Massive retaining wall in Area B	156
11.10. Orthophoto of Area A	157
11.11. Digital elevation model of the hill, showing the outline of the Iron Age raised platform	158
12.1. Hebrew ostraca from Arad	169
13.1. The Ophel inscription	198
17.1. The Rock-Cut Pool near the Gihon Spring	262
17.2. Area of the Gihon Spring	264
17.3. Cross-section through Rock-Cut Pool and Round Chamber	264
17.4. Map of Iron Age Jerusalem	265
18.1. Judahite, Yehud, and Judean seal impressions	273
19.1. The Jerusalem highlands	282
19.2. Map of the vicinity of Tel Moza/Qaluniya	285
20.1. Geographical units and vegetation zones in Judah	295
20.2. Iron Age winepress in the Jerusalem highlands	301
20.3. Winepress I and Building II at Khirbet er-Ras	301
20.4. Harvesting of grapes in soil pockets	302
20.5. Simplified pollen diagrams of the Dead Sea record	304
22.1. Map indicating the location of the sites discussed	326
22.2. The Mordot Arnona stone heap	329
22.3. Mordot Arnona, the monumental building of Period 3	329
22.4. Monumental architectural elements from Armon HaNatziv	333
23.1. Expansion of Jerusalem during the Iron Age	346

Abbreviations

Primary Sources

A.J.	Josephus, *Antiquitates judaicae*
b.	Babylonian Talmud
B.J.	Josephus, *Bellum judaicum*
Bibl. hist.	Diodorus Siculus, *Bibliotheca historica*
C. Ap.	Josephus, *Contra Apionem*
Geogr.	Strabo, *Geographica*
Hist.	Herodotus, *Historiae*; Tacitus, *Historiae*
Hist. Phil.	Pompeius Trogus, *Historiae Philippicae Epitoma*
Hist. plant.	Theophrastus, *Historia plantarum*
Mat. med.	Dioscorides Pedanius, *De materia medica*
Nat.	Pliny the Elder, *Naturalis historia*

Secondary Resources

AASOR	Annual of the American Schools of Oriental Research
ÄAT	Ägypten und Altes Testament
ABD	Freedman, David Noel, ed. *Anchor Bible Dictionary*. 6 vols. New York: Doubleday, 1992.
ABS	Archaeology and Biblical Studies
ADPV	Abhandlungen des Deutschen Palästina-Vereins
AIL	Ancient Israel and Its Literature
ANEM	Anxcient Near East Monographs
AOAT	Alter Orient und Altes Testament
ASOR	American Schools of Oriental Research
BA	*Biblical Archaeologist*
BAR	*Biblical Archaeology Review*
BASOR	*Bulletin of the American Schools of Oriental Research*

BEATAJ	Beiträge zur Erforschung des Alten Testaments und des antiken Judentums
BETL	Bibliotheca Ephemeridum Theologicarum Lovaniensium
BetM	*Beit Mikra/Beth Mikra: Bulletin of the Israel Society for Biblical Research*
Bib	*Biblica*
BibEnc	Biblical Encyclopedia
BJRL	*Bulletin of the John Rylands University Library of Manchester*
BJS	Brown Judaic Studies
BN	*Biblische Notizen*
BZAW	Beihefte zur Zeitschrift für die alttestamentliche Wissenschaft
CBQ	*Catholic Biblical Quarterly*
CHANE	Culture and History of the Ancient Near East
ConB	Coniectanea Biblica
COS	Hallo, William W., and K. Lawson Younger Jr., eds. *The Context of Scripture*. 4 vols. Leiden: Brill, 1997–2016.
CRAI	*Comptes rendus des séances de l'Académie des Inscriptions et Belles-Lettres*
DMOA	Documenta et Monumenta Orientis Antiqui
EA	El-Amarna tablets
EBR	Klauck, Hans-Josef, et al., eds. *Encyclopedia of the Bible and Its Reception*. Berlin: de Gruyter, 2009–.
EncBib	*Encyclopedia Biblica* [Hebrew]. 9 vols. Jerusalem: Bialik Institute, 1952–1982.
ErIsr	*Eretz-Israel*
ESI	*Excavations and Surveys in Israel*
FAT	Forschungen zum Alten Testament
G.R.	Grid Reference
HAT	Handbuch zum Alten Testament
HBAI	*Hebrew Bible and Ancient Israel*
HKAT	Handkommentar zum Alten Testament
HSS	Harvard Semitic Studies
IAA	Israel Antiquities Authority
IEJ	*Israel Exploration Journal*
JAJSup	Journal of Ancient Judaism Supplement
JAOS	*Journal of the American Oriental Society*
JCS	*Journal of Cuneiform Studies*

JESHO	*Journal of the Economic and Social History of the Orient*
JHS	*Journal of Hebrew Scriptures*
JNES	*Journal of Near Eastern Studies*
JQR	*Jewish Quarterly Review*
JSJ	*Journal for the Study of Judaism*
JSNTSup	Journal for the Study of the New Testament Supplement Series
JSOT	*Journal for the Study of the Old Testament*
JSOTSup	Journal for the Study of the Old Testament Supplement Series
LHBOTS	Library of Hebrew Bible/Old Testament studies
NEA	*Near Eastern Archaeology*
NEAHL	Stern, Ephraim, ed. *New Encyclopedia of Archaeological Excavations in the Holy Land*. 5 vols. Jerusalem: Israel Exploration Society and Carta, 1993, 2008.
NRSVue	New Revised Standard Version Updated Edition
NSAJR	*New Studies in the Archaeology of Jerusalem and Its Region*
OBO	Orbis Biblicus et Orientalis
OJA	*Oxford Journal of Archaeology*
OLA	Orientalia Lovaniensia Analecta
ORA	Orientalische Religionen in der Antike
OTL	Old Testament Library
OtSt	Oudtestamentische studiën
PEF	Palestine Exploration Fund
PEQ	*Palestine Exploration Quarterly*
PJb	*Palästinajahrbuch*
PNAS	*Proceedings of the National Academy of Sciences*
Qad	*Qadmoniot*
RB	*Revue biblique*
SBT	Studies in Biblical Theology
SBLStBL	Society of Biblical Literature Studies in Biblical Literature
Sem	*Semitica*
SHANE	Studies in the History (and Culture) of the Ancient Near East
SJOT	*Scandinavian Journal of the Old Testament*
SWBA	Social World of Biblical Antiquity
SymS	Symposium Series
TA	*Tel Aviv*

Transeu	*Transeuphratene*
TTKi	*Tidsskrift for Teologi og Kirke*
UF	*Ugarit-Forschungen*
VT	*Vetus Testamentum*
VTSup	Supplements to Vetus Testamentum
ZAW	*Zeitschrift für die alttestamentliche Wissenschaft*
ZDPV	*Zeitschrift des deutschen Palästina-Vereins*

Chronological Periods

The chart below summarizes the chronology of periods discussed in this book; dates are approximate. Middle Bronze I to Iron IIA dates are dictated by radiocarbon results: Iron IIC to Hellenistic dates are determined according to archaeological and historical considerations. All dates are BCE.

Middle Bronze I	2000–1750
Middle Bronze II	1750–1650
Middle Bronze III	1650–1550
Late Bronze I	1550–1400
Late Bronze II	1400–1200
Late Bronze III	1200–1130
Early Iron I	1130–1050
Late Iron I	1050–950
Early Iron IIA	950–880
Late Iron IIA	880–780
Iron IIB	780–680
Iron IIC	680–586
Babylonian	586–539
Persian	539–332
Early Hellenistic	332–167
Late Hellenistic	167–37

Part 1
Introductions

1

Introduction: The Center of the Universe

Jerusalem is the center of the universe, the hub of the three great monotheistic religions and the heart of major concepts of Western civilization. How did this happen? Geographical conditions were far from ideal. The city was located in the relatively godforsaken and arid southern highlands, which had little tillable land; to its east was desert, which could support mainly an animal economy. No major road to the south, north, east, or west passed through its gates. It was far from the sea and had no economic resources to speak of. The temple was an outcome of many generations of development and hence cannot be seen as the raison d'être of the Jerusalem phenomenon. So how can we explain the city's rise to centrality and dominance? How is it that in certain periods it expanded to become the largest and most important city in the Levant?

My aim in this book is to provide the answer to this riddle. I will do so by critically looking at the archaeological finds (in fact, the interpretation of the finds); accordingly, drawing the settlement history of Jerusalem; and putting these data on the background of the history of Judah and its relationship with the empires of the ancient world.

Jerusalem's history stretches over many millennia, so I will obviously not deal with this entire framework. The chronological limits of this book are from the Middle Bronze Age to the late Hellenistic period (ca. 1800–100 BCE). Much of it is devoted to the period when biblical texts were produced in Jerusalem and other places, roughly 800–100 BCE. In this book relative chronology (e.g., Iron IIA, Iron IIB) is based on the common understanding of ceramic typology. Absolute chronology is dictated by radiocarbon studies at sites such as Megiddo and Tel Reḥov, which present the best conditions for sampling: short-lived items from sequences of superimposed floor accumulations related to architectural remains and accompanied by

Fig. 1.1. The Old City of Jerusalem and environs, marking the main locations discussed in the book, looking north (courtesy of the City of David archive, by Copterpix air photos).

1. Introduction: The Center of the Universe

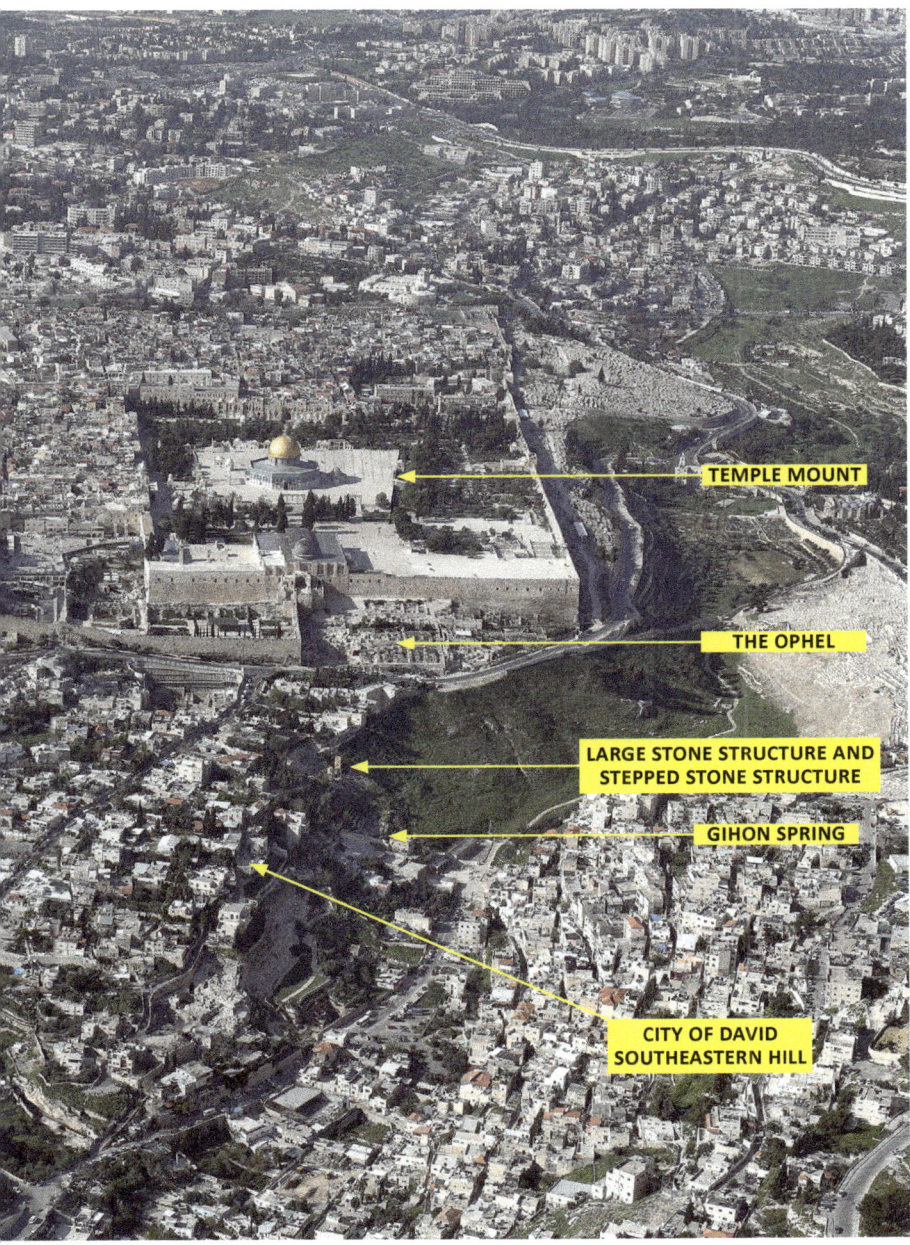

high-quality pottery assemblages. In Jerusalem, the nature of the site hinders reliable radiocarbon dating, as most samples come from fills, make-up for floors, brick material, plaster, and mortar components. Such contexts introduce "old-date effects": dates older than the given layer ostensibly associated with them. They may be helpful only in dictating *termini post quem*, that is, the oldest possible dates for a given context.

The geographical backdrop of the book is the old part of the city of Jerusalem, which is composed of three components: the Temple Mount; the City of David ridge to its south, with the Gihon Spring on its eastern slope; and the southwestern ridge, mainly the Armenian and Jewish Quarters of today's Old City (figs. 1.1–1.3). In some of the chapters, especially the ones on the economy of Iron IIB–C, I divert to the outskirts of the city. Terms such as City of David and Ophel are used in their archaeological connotation, with no attempt to identify them in the field.

Jerusalem is one of the most excavated places in the world. It has been investigated for over two centuries, at times with one dig area just meters away from another. Field research has dramatically intensified in recent years. The problem is that the city is populated, with the Bronze to Hellenistic remains mostly covered by later occupations, to say nothing of the more recent urban structure of the Old City. As a result, little remains available for modern excavation, which puts this book in a good place to summarize the results in the field.

Another issue that needs to be dealt with is the tension between archaeology and text or, better yet, archaeology and faith. In fact, throughout the history of research in Jerusalem, good archaeologists have tended to ignore the meaning of their own finds and follow textual ideology instead. Many of the chapters presented in this volume deal with this surprising phenomenon. Needless to say, I adhere to the finds and interpret the texts rather than the other way around.

This book presents a collection of articles published over the past two decades. I took several steps to bring its divergent parts together as a continuous story. In some articles—mainly older ones—I added addenda in order to update readers on developments in the field and on recent publications. To connect the articles into a coherent flow, I also wrote what might be termed "promos" at the beginning of each chapter. In some places I erased repetitions; where the paragraphs in question were essential for the broader story in the chapter, this was not always possible. Andrea Garza prepared the indexes, for which I offer my gratitude.

1. Introduction: The Center of the Universe

Fig. 1.2. The City of David ridge (southeastern hill) and the Temple Mount, showing the main sites and areas of excavations, looking north. Area G includes the Large Stone Structure and Stepped Stone Structure (photograph courtesy of Duby Tal, Albatros).

Fig. 1.3. Aerial photograph of the Temple Mount, the northern tip of the City of David ridge, the Ophel excavations, and the Givati Parking Lot excavations, looking north (courtesy of the City of David Archive; photograph by Yair Izbotski).

2

The Mound on the Mount: A Solution to the "Problem with Jerusalem"?

Unlike other central south Levantine Bronze and Iron Age sites, such as Hazor, Megiddo, Samaria, and Lachish, where the exact location and size of the ancient site is well known, in the case of Jerusalem, the location of the ancient mound is elusive at best. This chapter presents my view on the matter and serves as background for the entire book.

Introduction

The conventional wisdom regards the City of David ridge[1] as the original mound of Jerusalem. Yet intensive archaeological research in the last century—with excavations in many parts of the roughly 6 hectares ridge (see the map in Reich and Shukron 2008b), has proven that, between the Middle Bronze Age and Roman times, this site was fully occupied during only two relatively short periods: in the Iron Age IIB–C (between ca. the mid-eighth century and 586 BCE) and in the late Hellenistic period (starting in the second half of the second century BCE). Occupation in other periods was partial and sparse—and concentrated mainly in the central-eastern sector of the ridge, near and above the Gihon Spring. This presented scholars with a problem regarding periods for which there is either textual documentation or circumstantial evidence for significant

---

This chapter was coauthored with Ido Koch and Oded Lipschits.

1. We are using the term City of David in its common archaeological meaning, that is, the ridge to the south of the Temple Mount and west of the Kidron Valley, also known as the southeastern hill. For the biblical term, see Hutzli 2011.

occupation in Jerusalem; we refer mainly to the Late Bronze Age, the Iron IIA, and the Persian and early Hellenistic periods.[2]

Scholars attempted to address this problem in regard to a specific period. Na'aman (2010c) argued that the Late Bronze city-states are underrepresented in the archaeological record in other places as well; A. Mazar (2006b, 2010) advocated the "glass half full" approach, according to which, with all difficulties, the fragmentary evidence in the City of David is enough to attest to a meaningful settlement even in periods of weak activity; one of us (Lipschits 2009) argued for enough spots with Persian period finds on the ridge; another author of this paper (Finkelstein 2008b) maintained that the weak archaeological signal from the late Iron I–early Iron IIA (the tenth century BCE) and the Persian and early Hellenistic periods reflects the actual situation in Jerusalem, which was only sparsely populated in these periods. Still, one must admit that the bigger problem of many centuries in the history of Jerusalem with only meager finds has not been resolved.

In what follows we wish to put forward a solution to this riddle. Following the suggestion of Knauf (2000) regarding the Late Bronze Age and Iron Age I, we raise the possibility that, similar to other hilly sites, the mound of Jerusalem was located on the summit of the ridge, in the center of the area that was boxed in under the Herodian platform in the late first century BCE. Accordingly, in most periods until the second century BCE, the City of David ridge was outside the city. Remains representing the Late Bronze–Iron I–Iron IIA and the Persian and early Hellenistic periods were found mainly in the central part of this ridge. They include scatters of sherds but seldom remains of buildings and hence seem to represent no more than (usually ephemeral) activity near the spring. In two periods—in the late eighth century and in the second half of the second century BCE—the settlement rapidly (and simultaneously) expanded from the mound on the Temple Mount to both the southeastern ridge (the City of David) and the southwestern hill (today's Jewish and Armenian Quarters).

The theory of "the mound on the Mount" cannot be proven without excavations on the Temple Mount or its eastern slope, something that is

---

2. The intensive archaeological work in the City of David in the last century (probably unparalleled anywhere else in the region) renders the "absence of evidence is not evidence for absence" argument irrelevant in this case.

not feasible in the foreseen future. Indeed, Na'aman (1996, 18–19) stated that, since "the area of Jerusalem's public buildings is under the Temple Mount and cannot be examined, the most important area for investigation, and the one to which the biblical histories of David and Solomon mainly refer, remains *terra incognita*," and Knauf (2000, 87) maintained that "Abdi-Khepa's and David's Jerusalem lies buried under the Herodian-through-Islamic structures of the Temple Mount, thus formulating a hypothesis which cannot be tested or refuted archaeologically."

We, too, regard our reconstruction below as a hypothesis. In other words, for clear reasons—the inability to check it in the field—we cannot present a well-based solution for the "problem with Jerusalem." Rather, our goal is to put this theory on the table of scholarly discussion.

Settlement History of the City of David

What follows is a brief discussion of the City of David's settlement history, a summary rather than a thorough description of every parcel of land excavated. The ridge should be discussed in three sectors: north, south, and center (fig. 2.1 below).

By *north* we refer to excavations between the southern wall of the Temple Mount and the City of David visiting center (E. Mazar's "palace of King David").

In E. Mazar and B. Mazar's (1989) Ophel excavations, Hellenistic remains were found superimposed directly on Iron IIB–C remains, which were founded, in turn, on bedrock. Kenyon's Sites R and S revealed remains from the Roman period and later (Kenyon 1974). Recent excavation in the Givati Parking Lot by Reich and Shukron and by Ben-Ami and Tchekhanovets revealed remains from medieval times down to the late Hellenistic period and, below them, on bedrock on the slope to the Tyropoeon, late Iron II and some Iron IIA remains (Ben-Ami and Tchekhanovets 2008, 2010). The latter should be understood, in fact, together with the remains in the central sector of the ridge (below). Remains unearthed nearby by Crowfoot (Crowfoot and Fitzgerald 1929) were interpreted as a Bronze Age, Iron Age, and Persian period western gate to the City of David (e.g., Alt 1928; Albright 1930–1931, 167); in fact, they comprise a substructure covered by a fill for a large late Hellenistic or early Roman building (Ussishkin 2006a).

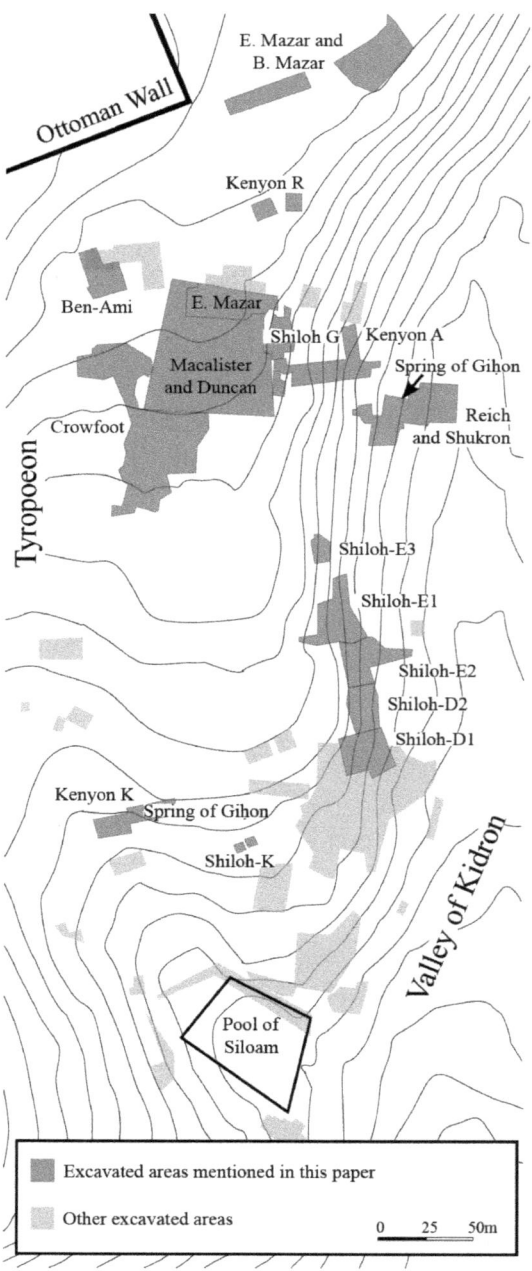

Fig. 2.1. Map of the City of David indicating main excavation areas mentioned in the chapter.

2. The Mound on the Mount

In sum up this evidence, no remains of the Middle Bronze, Late Bronze, Iron I, Persian, or early Hellenistic periods have thus far been discovered in the northern sector of the City of David. It is also significant that, apart from a few pottery sherds and some other scanty remains, finds from these periods were not reported from B. Mazar's (1971) excavations near the southwestern corner of the Temple Mount. On the other hand, rich Iron IIB–C remains were unearthed near the southern wall of the Temple Mount.

By *south* we refer to all soundings south of Shiloh's Area D1. Here, too, the Middle Bronze, Late Bronze, Iron I, Iron IIA, and Persian and early Hellenistic periods are absent. In Area A1, early Roman remains were found over late Iron II remains (De Groot, Cohen, and Caspi 1992). In Kenyon's Site K, located on the southwestern side of the City of David, circa 50 meters to the north of the Pool of Siloam, late Iron II sherds were found on bedrock, superimposed by late Hellenistic finds (Kenyon 1966, 84). Shiloh's Area K, in roughly the same line as Kenoyon's Site K, was excavated to bedrock; the earliest remains date to the early Roman period. In this case, a large-scale clearing operation, which could have destroyed earlier remains, seems to have taken place in the Roman period (see also Kenyon 1965, 14; 1966, 88 for her excavations nearby).

The central part of the City of David—between the visitors center/Shiloh's Area G and Shiloh's Area D1—should in fact be divided into west and east. Only a few, limited-in-scope excavations have been carried out in the former; they did not reveal early remains. The eastern part of the central sector includes mainly the Macalister and Duncan dig/E. Mazar's visitors center excavations (Macalister and Duncan 1926; E. Mazar 2007, 2009); Kenyon's Area A (Steiner 2001), Shiloh's Areas G, E, and D (Shiloh 1984); and Reich and Shukron's work near the Gihon Spring (e.g., 2004, 2007, 2009). Iron IIB–C and late Hellenistic remains were found here, too. In addition, this is the only sector of the City of David that produced finds from the "missing periods." These include the impressive Middle Bronze fortifications near the Gihon Spring and remains of this period in Kenyon's Area A and Shiloh's Area E1; Late Bronze pottery in Shiloh's Areas E1 and G and in E. Mazar's excavations in the area of the visitors center; Iron I finds under the terraces on the slope and in the visitors center excavations; Iron IIA, Persian, and early Hellenistic finds between Shiloh's Area D1 and G and in E. Mazar's excavation.

Still, even in the central part of the City of David ridge, the finds from the missing periods are fragmentary: not a single building, in fact, not a single floor of the Late Bronze Age or Persian period has been found thus far, and only one structure of the early Hellenistic period has been unearthed (in Shiloh's Area E1). Actual building remains of the Iron IIA exist in only two places:

(1) The Stepped Stone Structure (Cahill 2003a; A. Mazar 2006b; in fact, only its lower part: chs. 7 and 8 below) is a stone mantle that covers terraces constructed in order to stabilize the steep slope. Its dating is circumstantial: it may belong to the late Iron IIA or to the Iron IIB (ch. 8 below).

(2) Several walls in E. Mazar's excavations in the area of the visitors center may date to the Iron IIA (Finkelstein, Fantalkin, and Piasetzky 2008; ch. 8 below). E. Mazar (2009), A. Mazar (2010), and Faust (2010) reconstruct a major complex that constituted a revetment on the slope (the Stepped Stone Structure) and a fortress or a palace on the ridge. Although this is possible, evidence for a large edifice on the ridge is meager, and physical connection between the two structures is nonexistent (ch. 8 below).

Late Iron IIA (or transitional Iron IIA/B) finds—pottery and bullae—were retrieved from a fill deposited in the rock-cut pool near the Gihon Spring (Reich, Shukron, and Lernau 2007; Reich and Shukron 2009; De Groot and Fadida 2010).

To sum up this short review of the settlement history of the City of David: in the Late Bronze, Iron I, Iron IIA, and Persian and early Hellenistic periods, activity—sparse in nature and with little building remains—was concentrated in a strip on the center-east part of the ridge, mainly its slope, from the Gihon Spring to Shiloh's Area D about 200 meters to its south.

The Problem with Jerusalem

In recent years, a formidable Middle Bronze fortification and elaborate water system have been unearthed near the Gihon Spring (Reich and Shukron 2004, 2009). These finds, however, are not accompanied by habitation remains, which raises a question about the location of the Middle Bronze settlement of Jerusalem.

The Amarna letters indicate that in the fourteenth century BCE Jerusalem was one of the most influential city-states in Canaan. Jerusalem dominated a vast territory in the southern hill country (Finkelstein 1996c; for a somewhat different view, see Na'aman 1992a; 2010d, 45–48), and its political sway reached large areas in the lowlands. Pointing to the meager finds also in sites of other Late Bronze city-states in Canaan, Na'aman (2010c, 167–69) linked this situation to the general decay of Canaan at that time. Still, the question is whether a few pockets of pottery in the center of the City of David—without evidence for the construction of a single building—can represent Jerusalem of the Amarna period.

Difficulties regarding the Iron IIA emerge from both archaeology and text. Archaeologically speaking, the first fortifications in Judah, in the Shephelah (Lachish IV and possibly Beth-shemesh 3) and Beersheba Valley (Arad XI and Tel Beersheba V) date to the late Iron IIA in the mid- to second half of the ninth century BCE (Finkelstein 2001; Herzog and Singer Avitz 2004; for absolute dating, see Finkelstein and Piasetzky 2009, 2010). The Great Wall of Tell en-Naṣbeh (Mizpah) seems to have been built at that time on the northern flank of Judah (Finkelstein 2012b). No fortification has thus far been found on the western side of the City of David (see Ben-Ami and Tchekhanovets 2010, 72), and the Iron Age fortifications along the eastern slope of the ridge date to the Iron IIB (Shiloh 1984; Reich and Shukron 2008a). It is illogical to assume that Judahite countryside towns were strongly fortified in the late Iron IIA while the capital was left unprotected.

From the text perspective, 2 Kgs 14:13 relates how Joash king of Israel (who reigned in 800–784 BCE, that is, in the end phase of the Iron IIA) "broke down the wall of Jerusalem" (see Na'aman 2010c, 169–70). No wall that can be associated with this account has been found. The Tel Dan Inscription supports the biblical testimony that Judah participated in the struggle against the Arameans in the days of Hazael. According to 2 Kgs 12:18–19, Jehoash paid tribute, probably as a vassal, to the Damascene king. This source seems to be reliable historically, mainly because of the reference to Gath, which has recently been supported by the results of the excavation at Tell eṣ-Ṣafi (Maeir 2004). The meager late Iron IIA finds near the Gihon Spring can hardly account for Jerusalem of that time.

Jerusalem of the Persian period has recently been a focus of debate between two of the authors of this article (Finkelstein 2008b; Lipschits 2009). Setting aside the disputed issues of the nature and date of the description of the city wall in Neh 3, it is clear from an Elephantine letter (Porten 1996, 135–37) that mentions priests and nobles in Jerusalem and seemingly also from the distribution of the early *yhwd* stamp impressions, that during the Persian period Jerusalem was the center of the province of Yehud (Lipschits and Vanderhooft 2007). Early Hellenistic sources such as Ben Sira testify for the importance of Jerusalem in the Ptolemaic and early Seleucid periods. Finally, scholars suggest that a significant number of biblical texts were compiled in Jerusalem in the Persian and early Hellenistic periods. Some of these works are of special importance, such as the Priestly material in the Pentateuch, prophetic works, a late redaction of the Deuteronomistic History, and at least parts of Ezra and Nehemiah and Chronicles. The ridiculously poor finds in the City of David ridge can hardly account for a town that produces such a large and varied number of literary works.

A Solution: A Mound on the Temple Mount?

Over a decade ago, Axel Knauf proposed that Late Bronze and early Iron Age Jerusalem had been located on the Temple Mount. Knauf rightly argued (2000, 76) that from the strategic point of view a town covering the southeastern hill would have been indefensible without commanding the top of the ridge: the Temple Mount. In what follows we wish to elaborate on Knauf's proposal, adapt it to what we know about the archaeology of Jerusalem today, and interpret it in view of the textual evidence for the missing periods in the City of David.

To start with, it should be noted that major Bronze and Iron Age towns in the central hill country were located on relatively small mounds. Shechem (Tell Balatah) and Hebron (Tell Rumeida) covered an area of 4–4.5 hectares each, the mound of Bethel covers an area of circa 3 hectares (Kelso 1968, 2), and most other mounds are smaller. Even ninth-century Samaria, the center of a relatively large and powerful kingdom that competed with Damascus for hegemony in the Levant, covered an area of no more than 8 hectares (Finkelstein 2011b). Hence one should not expect Late Bronze to Iron IIA Jerusalem to have covered a much larger area.

There can be no question that the ruling compound of Iron Age Jerusalem—the temple and the palace of the Davidic kings—was located on the Temple Mount. But scholars seem to evaluate Iron Age Jerusalem with the notion of the Herodian Temple Mount and current Haram al-Sharif in mind. In Herodian times, when the city covered a very large area of some

180 hectares, the Temple Mount featured substantial open areas—somewhat similar to the situation today. Yet there is no reason to telescope this situation back to the Bronze and Iron Ages. Bronze Age city-states in the Levant such as Megiddo and Lachish were the hub of territorial entities. They accommodated a palace, temple(s), and other buildings that served the bureaucratic apparatus, as well as residential quarters for the ruling class. Most members of other sectors of the society lived in smaller settlements in their hinterland. The same holds true for the hubs of Iron Age territorial kingdoms in the southern Levant, such as Samaria and Hama. Jerusalem probably looked the same: the Temple Mount must have accommodated the temple, the palace, other buildings related to the administration of the kingdom as well as habitation quarters for the kingdom's bureaucrats; one should not envision large open spaces in its midst.

How big could have been a mound located under the Temple Mount? Had there been such a mound, the huge construction project that had taken place on the Temple Mount in Herodian times, including major leveling operations, must have eradicated much of its remains. Still, one could have expected to find pottery representing Bronze and Iron Age activity (as well as finds from the Persian and Early Hellenistic periods) in, for example, B. Mazar's excavations near the southwestern corner of the Temple Mount and in E. Mazar and B. Mazar's excavations to the south of the Temple Mount. The fact that no such remains have been found may be linked, among other reasons, to intensive later construction activities, which cleaned these areas down to bedrock, or to intensive post–Iron Age erosion or accumulation of debris. However, there may be another explanation: The current Temple Mount is made up of the rectangular Herodian platform; had there been an ancient mound on the hill, it could have covered a smaller area, with its lower slopes located dozens of meters away from the current boundaries of the platform. Judging from the situation in other hilly mounds, if one walks a few dozen meters away from the slopes, the ancient sherds diminish in number and then disappear. This factor, together with erosion, leveling, and accumulation of debris, could have resulted in the absence of Bronze and Iron Age debris on the slopes of the hill.

The Herodian platform covers an area of circa 470 × 280 meters (about 13 hectares). Subtracting 50–60 meters on each side—to account for the paucity of Bronze and Iron Age as well as Persian and Hellenistic pottery around the hypothetical tell—one gets a mound of circa 350 × 180 meters, that is, an area of about 5 hectares (fig. 2.2), equivalent in size to or bigger

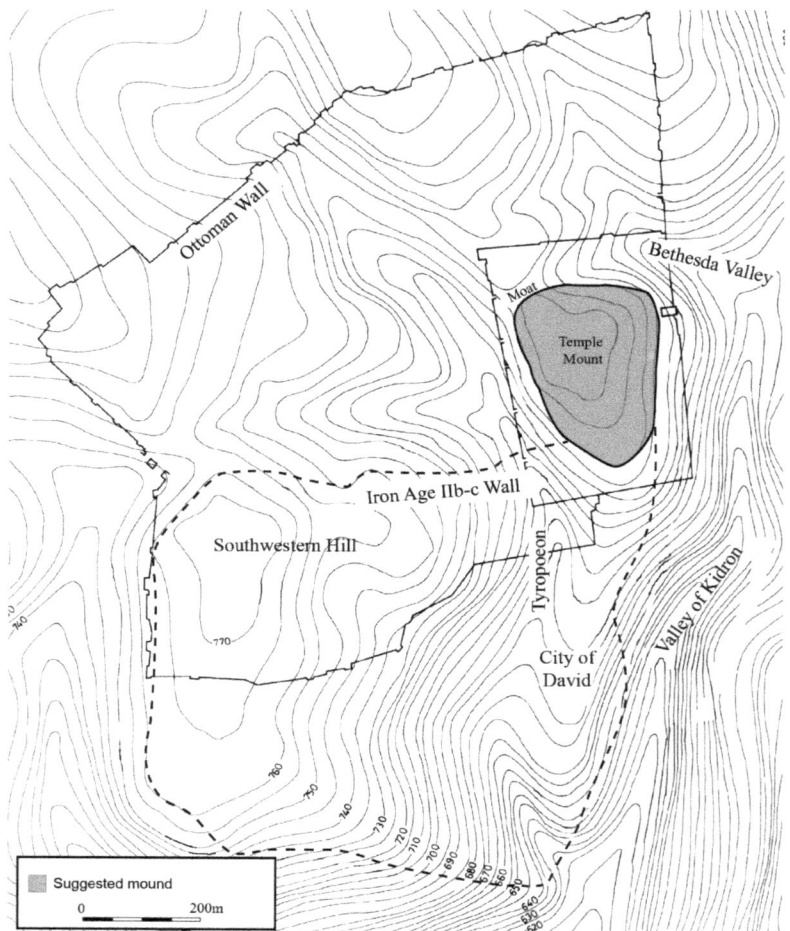

Fig. 2.2. Map of Jerusalem showing the possible location of the supposed mound on the Temple Mount, the City of David, and the line of the Iron IIB–C city wall.

than Tell Balatah (Shechem). This is a meaningful mound size even in the lowlands, taking into consideration that Iron Age Megiddo (the top of the mound) covered just under 5 hectares and that Iron Age Lachish stretched over an area of 5.7 hectares. According to this reconstruction, an ancient mound was completely "trapped" under the Herodian platform.[3]

---

3. Somewhat similar to the ancient mound of Atlit or the Moabite site of ancient Kerak, which seem to have been boxed in under the large medieval castles.

Such a mound would be well defended topographically on almost all sides: by the steep slope to the Kidron Valley in the east, by the relatively steep slope to the Tyropoeon in the west (which, according to results of excavations, was much deeper in the Iron Age than today; see e.g., Ben-Ami and Tchekhanovets 2010, 68; section in B. Mazar 1971, fig. 1), and by the steep slope to the Valley of Bethesda under the northeastern sector of the current Temple Mount (see topography of the Temple Mount in Hubbard 1966, fig. 1). The vulnerable sides would be the northwest and the south.

In the northwest, a moat must have been cut in the saddle that separates the hill from the continuing ridge. Warren (Warren and Conder 1884, 136ff.; and see Hubbard 1966, fig. 1) mapped the natural rock around and inside the Temple Mount by digging shafts alongside the Herodian supporting walls and by examining the subterranean chambers within the Haram al-Sharif compound. While doing so, he investigated the saddle that connects the Temple Mount with the northeast hill and reported on two ditches there: one to the north of the Temple Mount and another inside its limits. The latter is a 6-meter ditch that disconnects the Temple Mount from the ridge (Warren and Conder 1884, 215; see also Wilson and Warren 1871, 13). This trench in the rock, which was identified as a fosse or a dry moat, was also documented by Vincent (1912: section K-L; see also Bahat 1980, 11a; Ritmeyer 1992, 32–33) and was dated by Hubbard (1966, fig. 3), Ottosson (1979, 31; 1989, 266), Oredsson (2000, 92–95), and Ussishkin (2003a, 535; 2006b, 351; 2009, 475) to the period of the Judahite monarchy.

If one envisions the temple on the highest point of the hill, the ruling compound could have been located on the edge of the ancient mound, in approximately one third of the site in its northwestern sector, with the palace possibly behind the temple (e.g., Ussishkin 2003a, 535; 2006b, 351–52; 2009, 473; see also Wightman 1993, 29–31). This leaves the entire southern and eastern parts of the hill for the rest of the city.

According to this proposal, during the second millennium and the early first millennium BCE—until the great territorial expansion of Jerusalem in the Iron IIB—as well as during most of the second half of the first millennium, after the 586 BCE destruction and until the late Hellenistic period, Jerusalem had been located on a mound that was later leveled and boxed in under the Herodian platform.[4] This area could have

---

4. Another clue for the location of Bronze and early Iron Age Jerusalem

been fortified in the late Iron IIA, in parallel to the fortification of major Judahite towns such as Lachish, Tel Beersheba, and possibly Mizpah. This means that, until the Iron IIB, the southeastern hill (the City of David) was an open area outside of the city that probably featured agricultural installations, sporadic activity areas, and several buildings, mainly near the spring. It was only during the late eighth century BCE that the southeastern ridge, together with the southwestern hill, was incorporated into the city and fortified. In other words, in both the Iron IIB and the late Hellenistic periods the expansion of Jerusalem to the south (the City of David = the southeastern ridge) and the southwest (the southwestern hill) took place at approximately the same time. This, in turn, is the reason why no fortification of these periods has ever been found in the west of the City of David: simply, there was no period when this was the outer line of the city; therefore, there was no need to fortify it (Ussishkin 2006a, 153).

The only ostensible difficulty with this scenario is the location of the spring: outside and relatively far (over 300 meters) from the city. This could have been compensated by water cisterns on the Temple Mount. Those mapped by Warren (Waren and Conder 1884, 163ff.; Gibson and Jacobson 1996) probably represent later periods in the history of Jerusalem, mainly in Herodian times; however, as indicated by Tsuk (2008, 114), at least some of them had first been cut in earlier days. In any event, it is noteworthy that Samaria likewise is far from a spring and must have subsisted on rock-cut cisterns on a daily routine.

Discussion

In what follows we suggest a brief reconstruction of the extent of Jerusalem from the Middle Bronze Age to the late Hellenistic Period.[5]

---

comes from the distribution of burials: the two more significant Middle and Late Bronze tombs found close to the Old City are located on the Mount of Olives, to the east of the Temple Mount (map in Maeir 2000, 46), whereas the late Iron II tombs surround the large city of that period (Barkay 2000). We wish to thank Ronny Reich for drawing our attention to this issue.

5. The sifting of the debris taken from the southern part of the Temple Mount by the Islamic *Waqf* has revealed a small number of sherds representing early times, except for the Iron IIB–C and the Hellenistic periods (Barkay and Zweig

The situation in the **Middle Bronze** is perplexing. The massive, monumental stone walls uncovered near the Gihon were erected in order to protect the spring and provide a safe approach to the water from the ridge (Reich and Shukron 2009, 2010); this includes the segment of the wall unearthed by Kenyon (1974, 81–87; Reich and Shukron 2010). The key area is E1, where Shiloh (1984, 12, fig. 14) uncovered a stretch of a fortification with fills carrying Middle Bronze pottery on its inner side. More important is a floor with Middle Bronze vessels that ostensibly abuts the fortification. No fortification has been unearthed on the western side of the City of David; as mentioned above, the "gate" dug by Crowfoot is probably a substructure for late Hellenistic or early Roman building (Ussishkin 2006a). No Middle Bronze finds have been detected in the northern sector of the City of David. Accordingly, E. Mazar (following Macalister and Duncan 1926, 15) proposed that the Middle Bronze city was limited to the southern part of the City of David, south of Shiloh's Area G and the visitors center, with the fortifications near the spring located in its northeastern corner (E. Mazar 2006b; 2007, 16–17, 28, 52; 2009, 24, 26). This idea is also based on Macalister and Duncan's assumption (1926, 15) that a depression (labeled by them the Zedek Valley) ran in this place from east to west across the ridge. However, Rock Scarp A (Macalister and Duncan 1926, fig. 39 and pl. I)—probably the reason for this theory—seems to be no more than an ancient quarry. Indeed, Kenyon indicated the obvious, that the bedrock along the crest of the ridge rises toward the north (Steiner 2001, fig. 4.18). Also, there is no parallel to a town built on the lower slope of a ridge dominated by higher grounds immediately outside its walls.

We would suggest that the Middle Bronze city was located on the supposed mound under today's Temple Mount. If the fortification in Area E1 indeed dates originally to the Middle Bronze, then the city of this period could have stretched over a bigger area, comprising both the Temple Mount and the north-center sectors of the City of David. This scenario raises three

---

2006, 219–220; 2007, especially table in p. 59). As a result, Barkay and Zweig (2007, 59) reject the possibility of an ancient mound on the Temple Mount (ibid.). We do not agree and do not incorporate this information into our discussion, because: A) the debris was taken from the southern end of the Mount, away from the supposed mound; B) much of the debris there was not in situ and there is no way to know where it had come from and for what reason it was deposited there in antiquity.

difficulties: first, Middle Bronze finds are absent from the north of the City of David ridge; second, no other Middle Bronze city in the hill country, not even Shechem, covered such a large area; third, no fortification has thus far been unearthed on the western side of the City of David. The other possibility, that the fortification in Area E1 is later than the Middle Bronze (this can be checked only when detailed sections are published), also raises difficulties: in this case, the city was located on the mound in the north, with a separate fortification near the spring—an arrangement unknown in any other city in the Levant. In any event, since no connection between the mound on the Temple Mount and the fortification near the spring has to date been discovered and no finds from this period were unearthed in the northern part of the City of David, the nature of at least some of the Middle Bronze remains in the City of David ridge, as well as the extent of the Middle Bronze city, remains a riddle.

The **Late Bronze** city was located on the mound under today's Temple Mount (Knauf 2000). The small quantity of Late Bronze pottery found here and there in the City of David above the Gihon Spring probably represents ephemeral presence outside the city, near the water source.

Activity near the spring intensified in the **Iron I**. Remains of buildings were uncovered under the terraces on the slope (Steiner 1994) and in E. Mazar's excavations in the area of the visitors' center (2009, 39–42). Poor finds—mainly pottery—were retrieved by Shiloh from his Areas D1 and E1 (1984, 7, 12). The quantity of Iron I pottery in the brown deposits found under E. Mazar's "palace of King David" (2007, 48) is also significant. All this seems to indicate that activity near the spring intensified. However, the area between the spring and the mound in the north remained uninhabited.

In the Shephelah and the Beersheba Valley, the **Iron IIA** can be divided stratigraphically and, in the case of large enough assemblages of finds, ceramically into two phases: early and late Iron IIA (Herzog and Singer Avitz 2004). The results of excavations in Jerusalem, as well as in other sites in the highlands, do not provide enough data for such a distinction. Still, it seems that both the original Stepped Stone Structure and the early walls in E. Mazar's excavations date to the later phase of the period (Finkelstein 2001; chs. 7 and 8 below; Finkelstein, Fantalkin, and Piasetzky 2008). At that time the main settlement, which was probably fortified by a massive wall similar to the Great Wall of Tell en-Naṣbeh (Mizpah), was still located on the Temple Mount. Assuming that the chronistic notes in

2 Kgs 14:13 are historically sound, this could have been the wall that was breached by King Joash of Israel in the early eighth century. It is possible that the Stepped Stone Structure was erected outside of the city to support a large building on the eastern flank of the ridge, possibly a fortress (A. Mazar 2010 and Faust 2010 suggested the existence of such a fortress but dated it to the Iron I) that protected the approach to the water source. However, there is no link between the Iron I rooms and the large walls around them, and the connection between the stone revetment and the walls on the ridge is impossible to verify today (ch. 8 below).

The turning point in the settlement history of Jerusalem came in the **Iron IIB**, in the mid- to late eighth century BCE. Prosperity in Judah as an Assyrian vassal and demographic changes—whether sharp and quick following the fall of the Northern Kingdom (ch. 15 below; Finkelstein 2008b) or slow and more gradual (Na'aman 2007, 2009a)—brought about a major urbanization process in Jerusalem. For the first time the settled area expanded to the entire City of David ridge, which was now densely occupied. During the same time, the city expanded to the southwestern hill (today's Jewish and Armenian Quarters). The new quarters were surrounded by a city wall, which must have been connected to the older (probably Iron IIA) fortification on the mound under the Temple Mount (Ussishkin 2009, 473). In the City of David, the new city wall is known only along the eastern side, above the Kidron Valley (Steiner 2001, 89–92; Shiloh 1984, 8–10, 28, figs. 30, 33; Reich and Shukrun 2000, 2008a). Segment of this fortification, already noticed by Warren, was excavated by E. and B. Mazar (1989) in the Ophel. On the southwestern hill it has been uncovered in the modern-day Jewish Quarter (Avigad 1983, 46–60; Avigad and Geva 2000; Geva and Avigad 2000b) and possibly also under the western wall of the Old City (near Jaffa Gate; Geva 1979; 1983, 56–58) and in HaGai (el-Wad) Street (Kloner 1984). There was no need to fortify the western side of the City of David (Ussishkin 2006a, 153).

In the **Persian** and **early Hellenistic** periods the settlement shrank to the original mound on the Temple Mount. The City of David was again an open, desolate area. Pockets of pottery found in the center of the ridge testify for some activity in the vicinity of the spring and possibly on the eastern slope to the south of it. According to Finkelstein, the detailed description in Neh 3, which represents an insertion into the original text (e.g., Torrey 1896; 37–38; 1910, 249; Mowinckel 1964, 109–16), probably relates to the long Hellenistic fortifications that encircle the southeastern ridge and the southwestern hill. According to Lipschits, the verses in Neh 3 that describe the construction of six gates are unique in their sentence structure, word order, and verbs used; they differ from the usual formula deployed to describe the construction of the wall itself (see already Reinmuth 2003, 84, who pointed out the different sources of the verses, and Lipschits 2007, who demonstrated that the gates verses are part of two different later additions to the original list of people who supported the building of the wall). Without the burden of the many gates, the original account described the course of the city wall of the small mound of Jerusalem on the Temple Mount.

The entire City of David ridge was settled again in the **late Hellenistic** (Hasmonean) period. Similar to the situation in the Iron IIB, the city expanded in parallel to the southeastern and southwestern hills, and hence in this period also there was no need to fortify the western side of the City of David.

Summary

There are two solutions for the "problem with Jerusalem," that is, the fact that archaeology does not supply enough data for several periods in the second and first millennia BCE that are well-documented by textual material. According to the first, the acropolis, with the temple and the palace only, was located on the Temple Mount, and the town itself extended over the ridge of the City of David. This means that in the Late Bronze, Iron I, Iron IIA, and Persian and early Hellenistic periods, Jerusalem was a small, sparsely settled settlement.

In this article, we suggest a second solution to the quandary: the original mound of Jerusalem—that is, the acropolis *and* the settlement—which had been located on the Temple Mount, was boxed in under the Herodian platform in the late first century BCE. This theoretical mound could have covered a significant area of ca. 5 hectares, the size of the larger Bronze and Iron Age mounds in the hill country. It was probably fortified in the Middle Bronze Age and again in the late Iron IIA in parallel to the fortification of important towns in the countryside of Judah, mainly Lachish, Tel Beersheba, and Mizpah. This mound on the Temple Mount was the sole location of the town in the Middle Bronze, Late Bronze, Iron I, Iron IIA, and Persian and early Hellenistic periods. In all these periods activity in the City of David was meager and restricted to the central part of the ridge, mainly its eastern side near the Gihon Spring. In two periods—the Iron IIB and the late Hellenistic—the settlement expanded to include the southeastern ridge (the City of David) and the southwestern hill; the new quarters were fortified, but there was no need to build a city wall on the western side of the City of David, as this line ran in the middle of the city.

Addendum

1. Iron IIA remains have recently been found in the eastern sector of the Ophel (see ch. 9 below).

2. We now know that the expansion of Jerusalem began in the late Iron IIA, from the mound on the Temple Mount southward, in the direction of the Gihon Spring (chs. 9 and 14). This extension—unfortified—was limited to the area sloping down to the Givati Parking Lot and the visitors center excavations.

Part 2
The Bronze Age and the Iron I

3
Middle Bronze Jerusalem

I have chosen to start my chronological journey with a short chapter on the Middle Bronze. I do so because this is the first period in the history of Jerusalem for which there are significant finds, which influence the discussion on the layout of the settlement in later periods. In addition, this is the first period in which one can securely reconstruct Jerusalem as the hub of a city-state in the southern highlands.

The layout of Middle Bronze Jerusalem remains a riddle, especially in relation to two locations: the monumental walls near the Gihon Spring and the remains on the southern tip of the City of David ridge. Here I wish to comment on both issues.

Ussishkin (2016) reviewed the evidence for Middle Bronze fortifications along the eastern slope of the City of David ridge and proposed that all elements in fact date to the Iron IIB–C. I agree with some of his conclusions and oppose others.

I agree with Ussishkin (also Reich and Shukron 2010, 150) that Wall 3 (Kenyon's Wall NB; Steiner 2001, 10–12) in mid-slope above the Gihon Spring should probably be understood as a terrace or revetment rather than a fortification (for the phenomenon of terraces on the eastern slope of the City of David ridge, see Bocher 2021). I also agree that the sherds retrieved from the narrow trench between Wall 3 and the rock scarp to its west provide only a *terminus post quem* for its dating. I oppose the idea that the wall can be dated (to the Iron II) according to the pottery found

---

The Middle Bronze is essential to set the stage for the layout of Jerusalem in its entire history, so I decided to enter here this subchapter from my "Jerusalem's Settlement History: Rejoinders and Updates" (Finkelstein 2023).

in the debris thrown against its eastern face, on the side of the slope. This debris could have been put there to support the wall when it was built or added to an existing wall in order to reinforce it; it only provides this operation with a *terminus post quem*. All that can be said is that the wall abuts Wall 108 (rather than is incorporated into it; contra Gadot and Uziel 2017, 129), the northern of the two parallel cyclopean walls that run from west to east and connect to the Spring Tower (Reich and Shukron 2010, 149; Ussishkin 2016, 5; more below). Despite the few large boulders (Gadot and Uziel 2017, fig. 4), the quality of Wall 3 is inferior to Wall 108 (Reich shukron 2010, 149). Wall 3 is "trapped" in a time slot between the construction of Wall 108 in the Middle Bronze (see below) and Wall 1 (which was built over it) of the Iron IIB (all this contra Wightman 2022).

Shiloh (1984, 26; De Groot 2012, 147) described Wall 285 in Area E as a city wall that was reused in the Iron Age (Wall 219). Ussishkin is correct to see both as terraces on the slope and to propose that the former is later than the Middle Bronze remains to its west (contra Wightman 2022; see Reich 2011, 260–61, who interpreted the two as one architectural element).

I do not agree with Ussishkin's proposal to date Walls 108 and 109 and the Gihon Spring Tower to the Iron Age. Reich and Shukron (2010) dated this monumental construction (fig. 3.1) to the Middle Bronze. They interpreted the two parallel walls as a fortified passage leading to the spring and the Spring Tower as a system aimed to defend the water source. The pottery found in relation to Walls 108 and 109—even if originating from fills—dates to the Middle Bronze. To differ from the case of Wall 3, there are enough find spots there to argue that, if the wall had been built in the Iron Age, a few sherds from this period would have been found. No less important, the construction with cyclopean boulders is similar to at least two other sites in the highlands: Shechem and Shiloh (for the latter, see Finkelstein and Lederman 1993); I am not aware of Iron II construction of this type, certainly not in the highlands.[1]

A year after Ussishkin's article, Regev, Uziel, Szanton, and Boaretto (2017) published radiocarbon determinations for samples extracted under the eastern wall of the Spring Tower. The two latest results fall in the ninth century BCE. The authors raised two possible interpretations for these

---

1. Note how different the construction method of the Gihon walls is from that of the Iron Age fortification unearthed just a few meters to the south (Vukosavovic, Chalaf, and Uziel 2021, fig. 4).

Fig. 3.1. Middle Bronze remains above the Gihon Spring (courtesy of the Ronny Reich and Eli Shukron expedition to the City of David, Photo: V. Naikhin).

results: (1) construction in the Middle Bronze and repair of the wall in the Iron II; (2) construction in the Iron II. The former solution is the one to accept, because repair of the original wall can in fact be observed in the area from which the samples were taken (Regev et al. 2017, figs. 3–4; for other arguments against the second option, see Reich 2018). The two radiocarbon determinations that fall in the ninth century provide the earliest possible date for the repair.[2]

To sum up, the hub of Middle Bronze Jerusalem was located on the Temple Mount, probably surrounded by massive cyclopean wall similar to that known at Shechem. In fact, this is the period when the power in the central highlands emerges in two areas—the north and south—a situation that will prevail in the entire history of the region. The only other remains are the big walls on the slope, leading in the direction of the Gihon Spring. There was no built-up area between the Temple Mount and this section of the ridge, probably meaning that the monumental walls emerged from a fort that existed on the ridge, in the vicinity of the Givati Parking Lot excavations. The remains there must have been removed in later generations, in the Iron Age II and perhaps even more so the Hellenistic period and later. The few remains, not associated with fortifications, in the southeastern tip of the ridge can be added as some sort of activity areas. As far as I can judge, there is no proof for construction of tunnels to carry water from the Gihon Spring to the southern end of the ridge in the Middle Bronze.

Addendum

A large set of radiocarbon results from Middle Bronze contexts in Jerusalem has recently been published (Regev et al. 2021). The results point to continuous human activity in the area of the Gihon Spring and to its south. The context of most of the samples (fills and collapse debris, rather than sets of floors) and their nature (charcoal, single seeds, bones) do not allow for a comprehensive reconstruction of the settlement history and urban development in the City of David (the southeastern ridge) in the first half of the second millennium BCE.

---

2. The date of the Gihon complex is indirectly related to the nature and date of the rock-cut depression unearthed immediately to the south of Wall 109; I discuss this issue in chapter 17 below.

4
The Shephelah and Jerusalem's Western Border in the Amarna Period

---

The scope of Late Bronze finds in Jerusalem is limited, but the textual data in the Amarna tablets of the fourteenth century BCE are relatively rich. The most important details can be found in letters sent from Jerusalem itself and neighboring city-states. Especially important material deals with the relationship between Jerusalem and city-states in the lowlands to its west. Dealing with this issue is significant for two reasons: it sheds light on the transformation of Jerusalem from a hub of a city-state to a capital of a territorial kingdom; and it illuminates the later expansion of Judah from the highlands to the Shephelah.

I have already shown the paucity of Late Bronze remains in Jerusalem, but the Amarna archive of the fourteenth century BCE testifies for the importance of the city at least on the southern Canaanite scene. The archival information on the involvement of the city in the west indeed indicates that Jerusalem was an important hub of a highlands city-state, with connections beyond the hill country.

Several issues related to the Shephelah in the Amarna period have recently been addressed. First and foremost among them are the territorial disposition of the region at that time (Na'aman 2011; see before Finkelstein 1996c; Na'aman 1997) and skirmishes between the highlands and Shephelah polities along the border between them in the early phases of the Iron Age, as depicted in the Hebrew Bible, compared to parallel situations described in the Amarna letters (Na'aman 2010b; ch. 10 below). The petrographic study of the Amarna letters (Goren, Finkelstein, and Na'aman 2004) and the growing archaeological evidence for the Late Bronze IIA in southern Canaan, at sites such as Beth-shemesh and Jaffa (Ziffer, Bunimovitz, and Lederman 2009; Burke et al. 2017, respectively) shed new light on this period. Being an adherent of the *longue durée* concept of territorial history, I believe that the situation in the Shephelah in the Late Bronze Age indeed holds a key to understanding the processes that took place in this region in the Iron Age (for this line of thought, see, e.g., Finkelstein and Na'aman 2005; Na'aman 2010b). This is especially true regarding the Amarna period, which supplies detailed textual information about city-states, settlements, and political maneuvers in this area.

In what follows I wish to deal with three connected issues: (1) the number and location of the city-states of the Shephelah as depicted in the Amarna letters; (2) tensions and skirmishes in the eastern Shephelah, along the boundary of the lowlands polity with Jerusalem, compared to similar situations in the area of Shechem farther to the north; these affairs may testify to expansion attempts of Jerusalem to the west; and (3) destruction layers at sites in the south and the status of Egyptian rule in Canaan in the Amarna period.

The Number of Late Bronze City-States in the Shephelah

This topic has recently been discussed in detail by Na'aman (2011; see already Na'aman 1975), who sought the minimal number of Canaanite city-states in the Shephelah according to the Amarna tablets. Na'aman listed three main (the first three below) and five conjectured city-states (fig. 4.1):

(1) Gazru = Gezer, with its three rulers—Milkilu, Yapaḫu, and Ba'ludanu—who sent twelve of the Amarna letters.
(2) Gimtu = Gath (Rainey 1975), with two rulers—Shuwardata and Abdi-Ashtarti (for the location of the latter, see Na'aman 1979; Goren, Finkelstein, and Na'aman 2004, 283–86)—who sent eleven letters.
(3) Lakisha (= Lachish), with three rulers—Zimreddi, Shipṭi-Ba'lu, and Yabni-Ilu—who sent six Amarna letters.
(4) Beth-shemesh, where Na'aman identifies the seat of the queen mother Belit-labi'at, the author of EA 273–274, and Yaḫzib-Hadda, who wrote EA 275–276 and probably also 277 (Goren, Finkelstein, and Na'aman 2004, 290–91).

4. The Shephelah and Jerusalem's Western Border

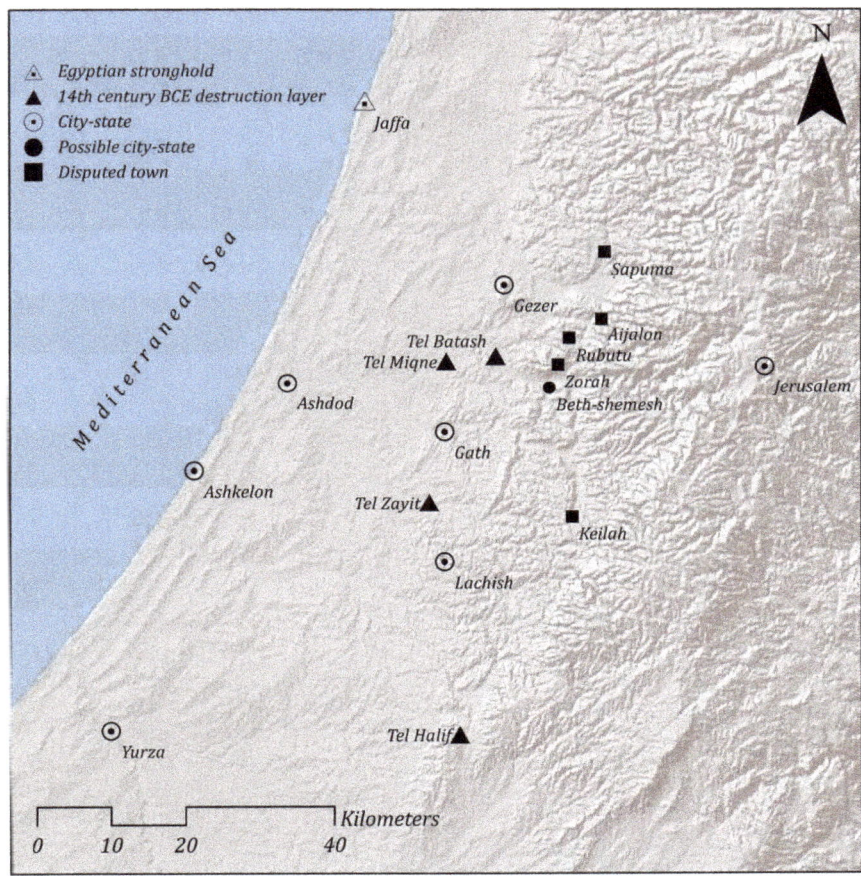

Fig. 4.1. Sites mentioned in the chapter.

(5) Murashti, mentioned in EA 335, where Na'aman suggests placing Shipṭi-Baʻlu mentioned in EA 333 and Turbazu mentioned in EA 288 and 335. Na'aman identifies this place with Tel Zayit, south of Tell eṣ-Ṣafi.

(6) [xx]shiki of EA 335, according to Na'aman possibly the seat of Yaptiḫ-Hadda, referred to in EA 288 and 335.

(7) The seat of Abdina, the sender of EA 229, which Na'aman suggests locating somewhere in the longitudinal valley that separates the highlands and the Shephelah.

(8) Aḫṭiruna of EA 319, whose vocabulary fits a scribe of southern Canaan. The location of this place could not be identified in the

petrographic study of the Amarna letters because the tablet was probably sent from Gaza (Goren, Finkelstein, and Na'aman 2004, 302–3).

Na'aman, then, identifies up to eight city-states in an area circa 35 × 20 kilometers. When one thinks about issues of agricultural output and manpower (for the latter, see Bunimovitz 1994), this is unlikely, not to mention that no area in Canaan features a similar density of polity. For instance, the fertile Jezreel and Beth-shean Valleys had four to five polities, and the entire coastal plain south of Beirut had ten city-states. The task is therefore to separate the explicit evidence from the conjectured, in other words, to verify how confident one can be that all the above sites indeed served as hubs of Amarna petty rulers and to check whether Amarna rulers with no named seats can be "added" to the main hubs of city-states in the Shephelah and southern coastal plain.

Of the two letters of Belit-labi'at, one (EA 273) was checked petrographically and was found to have probably been sent from Gezer (Goren, Finkelstein, and Na'aman 2004, 276–77). In it this queen or queen mother reports events that took place at Ayyaluna (= biblical Aijalon[1]) in the Aijalon Valley and Ṣarḥa (= biblical Zorah) on the ridge overlooking the valley of Nahal Soreq. Accordingly, she could have been located at Beth-shemesh, which would have her reporting about events to her north; however, putting her at Gezer is an equally strong option (discussion in Goren, Finkelstein, and Na'aman 2004, 277; see also Rainey 2012, 137, who sees her as the widow of Milkilu). In fact, the link made by Belit-labi'at between the sons of Milkilu and Aijalon and the town of Zorah hints that Aijalon and Zorah belonged to Gezer.

Based on the petrographic investigation, the three letters of Yaḫzib-Hadda could have been sent from Beth-shemesh, but they could also have been dispatched from a town on the eastern flank of the Gath territory (because of the petrographic similarity to EA 278 of Shuwardata; Goren, Finkelstein, and Na'aman 2004, 290–91). In fact, one may wonder if Yaḫzib-Hadda was not another ruler at Gath; his letters do not disclose his time during the Amarna correspondence, and Na'aman's notion (2011,

---

1. The first mention in the article of a place which is identifiable with a biblical toponym is in its Amarna form, with the biblical name in parenthesis. Following references are usually only to the biblical name.

4. The Shephelah and Jerusalem's Western Border   37

283) that there is no slot for a third ruler there (in addition to Shuwardata and Abdi-Ashtarti) is inconclusive. This is so because: (1) according to Na'aman EA 366 is the only Shuwardata letter still within the time of Labayu (e.g., Na'aman 1975, 120, 122, 128), while Abdi-Ashtarti ruled after Shuwardata, so another ruler is possible in the early days of the correspondence; (2) the similarity between EA 278, an early letter of Shuwardata, and EA 275–276 of Yaḫzib-Hadda (Knudtzon 1915, 1329; Campbell 1964, 112–13; Na'aman 1975, 131) puts the latter early in the correspondence; and (3) the three letters of Yaḫzib-Hadda may have been dispatched at one time from a single place during a specific event (Goren, Finkelstein, and Na'aman 2004, 291), which means that he could have ruled for a very short period of time. Note in this connection the instability in the other city-states of the Shephelah, with three mayors at Gezer and in Lachish during the period of the archive.

The letters of the three Lachish rulers also leave a slot for another mayor in the early days of the correspondence, before the death of Labayu (see Na'aman 1975, 133). A "space" in the early days of the correspondence can also be found in the cases of Yurza and possibly Ashkelon (Na'aman 1975, 228), as well as in Ashdod (for the latter being a seat of a Canaanite ruler, see Goren, Finkelstein, and Na'aman 2004, 292–94).

The text of EA 335 does not say that Murashti (biblical Moresheth-gath, that is, in the Iron Age a place located in proximity to Gath) and [xx]shiki were seats of Canaanite rulers. They could have been towns in the territories of Lachish or Gath or on their western border with city-states of the coastal plain (similar to Aijalon and Zorah in the territory of Gezer in EA 273). Note Na'aman's proposal (2011) to identify Murashti with Tel Zayit, situated circa 8 kilometers south of Tell eṣ-Ṣafi and 7 kilometers north of Lachish. The possibility that [xx]shiki is mentioned (as Nentishi) in a hieratic inscription on a Lachish bowl (Sweeney 2004; Na'aman 2011, nn. 4, 9), strengthens the prospect that it was a town in this city's territory.

Turbazu and Yaptiḫ-Hadda are mentioned together with Zimreddi of Lachish. They may have been rulers of city-states on the southern coastal plain, such as Yurza and Ashkelon. Note that only one ruler of Yurza (Pu-Ba'lu in EA 314–316) is mentioned in the archive, probably in its later days. Two rulers of Ashkelon are known: Yidia and Shubandu (the latter put in Ashkelon according to the petrographic study of his letters; Goren, Finkelstein, and Na'aman 2004, 294–99).

Shipṭi-Baʿlu of EA 333 is not identified by Naʾaman with the individual of the same name who ruled at Lachish, probably because he is mentioned in the tablet together with Zimreddi of Lachish. But could they have been father and son?

Petrographically, the letter of Abdina (EA 229) is similar to EA 64, which was probably sent by Abdi-Ashtarti of Gath from somewhere in the eastern flank of the latter's territory (Goren, Finkelstein, and Naʾaman 2004, 284–86). Abdina could indeed have ruled somewhere in the eastern Shephelah or could have been another short-time ruler at Gath.

Finally, Aḥtiruna is associated with the south because of the vocabulary of the letter (EA 319). The petrographic investigation shows that it was probably sent from Gaza (Goren, Finkelstein, and Naʾaman 2004, 302–3). It could have been a city in the Shephelah (and then some of the above-mentioned rulers, e.g., Abdina, could also have ruled from there). Naʾaman's proposal to equate the name with the biblical name Ataroth (Goren, Finkelstein, and Naʾaman 2004, 302) would point to the highlands (rather than the Shephelah), the location of all biblical sites carrying this name on both sides of the Jordan. Elsewhere I have raised the possibility, remote as it may sound, that this place was located in Transjordan, in the vicinity of Amman (Finkelstein 2014b).

My proposals above may be somewhat probable or not probable at all; what I have tried to show here is that the real minimal number of city-states in the Shephelah is three: Gezer, Gath, and Lachish. Beth-shemesh is indeed a possibility, also because of the results of excavations there, which seem to underline its importance in the Amarna period, as is a (still-unidentified) place in the southeastern Shephelah: Tel Eton (for this site having been a significant Late Bronze settlement, see Faust and Katz 2012, 178). These notions can change the number of city-states in the Shephelah from three to five; however, given the data at hand even these cases cannot be proven, and this is not to mention the other alternatives listed above.

Skirmishes on the Border between the Jerusalem Highlands and the Shephelah

Six Disputed/Fought-Over Towns

Na'aman (1979) laid the foundation for understanding the turmoil in the south in the Amarna period. Several Amarna letters mention skirmishes over towns located on the border between the territories of Jerusalem and city-states in the Shephelah. Table 4.1 summarizes this information.

Table 4.1. Amarna letters referring to clashes over towns located on the border between the highlands of Jerusalem and the Shephelah

EA no.	Sent by (ruler and city)	Town in question	Main information in the text
279	Shuwardata, Gath	Qeltu (= biblical Keilah)	Shuwardata goes against the traitors in Keilah.
280	Shuwardata, Gath	Keilah	The king of Egypt permitted Shuwardata to wage war against Keilah, and he did. The town was restored to him. Abdi-Heba wrote to the men of Keilah to bribe them. Labayu is dead; Abdi-Heba, accused of being the new Labayu, took Shuwardata's town.
287	Abdi-Heba, Jerusalem	Keilah	Milkilu and Tagi (?) brought troops to Keilah against Abdi-Heba.
		Aijalon	Abdi-Heba sent gifts with a caravan, but it was stopped near Aijalon.
289	Abdi-Heba, Jerusalem	Rubutu Keilah	Milkilu and Tagi took Rubutu. Milkilu, Tagi, and the sons of Labayu helped Keilah in order to isolate Jerusalem.

290	Abdi-Heba	Rubutu	Milkilu and Shuwardata brought troops from Gezer, Gath, and Keilah and took Rubutu. Ginti (probably the capital of Tagi) was also involved on their side.
		Bit-NIN.URTA	Bit-NIN.URTA, a town of Jerusalem, went over to the side of the men of Keilah.
273	Belit-labi'at, Beth-shemesh or Gezer	Aijalon and Zorah	The Apiru wrote to Aijalon and Zorah, and the two sons of Milkilu barely escaped being killed
274	Belit-labi'at, Beth-shemesh or Gezer	Ṣapuma	Ṣapuma is taken

Six towns are mentioned in these letters. It is essential to first fix their location and territorial affiliation.

Qeltu, biblical Keilah, is identified with Khirbet Qila (G.R. 150113). The mound is located in the longitudinal valley of the eastern Shephelah, below the sharp drop of the Hebron Highlands to the west. The town—disputed between Shuwardata's Gath and Abdi-Heba's Jerusalem—probably changed hands more than once during the time of the correspondence. From its geographical position—in the Shephelah and far from Jerusalem—there can be little doubt that it originally belonged to Gath. Perhaps the fact that it was slightly isolated tempted Abdi-Heba to try to capture it (for comparison between the events in the Amarna period and the biblical narrative of David and his men at Keilah, see Na'aman 2010b).

Rubutu was a town near the border of Gezer and Jerusalem (B. Mazar 1957, 60–63; Aharoni 1969; Kallai and Tadmor 1969, 143–44; Kitchen 1973, 434–35; Ahituv 1984, 165–67). The most common identification is with Khirbet Hamideh (Bir el-Hilu) near Latrun (Aharoni 1969). Na'aman (2000a) suggested identifying it with the Rubutu mentioned in Ta'anach tablet TT 1:26, *Rbt* of the Thutmose III and Sheshonq I lists, and the city of Aruboth, the center of the Solomonic third district (1 Kgs 4:10). Accordingly, he sought Rubutu in the Dothan Valley. Na'aman's suggestion cannot be accepted for two reasons: (1) the two Amarna tablets clearly show that Rubutu was disputed between Gezer and Jerusalem; (2) this is also the location of *Rbt* mentioned by Thutmose III and Sheshonq I (in the order Gezer → Rubutu → Aijalon; e.g., B. Mazar 1957, 60; Aharoni 1979, 325; more recently Finkelstein and Fantalkin 2012). Originally

4. The Shephelah and Jerusalem's Western Border

this place must have been in the territory of Gezer. It was probably taken over by Abdi-Heba and then restored to Gezer with the help of Tagi and Shuwardata. Originally Shuwardata was an ally of Jerusalem (EA 366); his involvement in the Rubutu affair hints that it took place close to the time of the Keilah dispute.

Locating **Bit-NIN.URTA** depends on the identification of the West Semitic deity that is veiled by the Mesopotamian name Ninurta (e.g., Na'aman 1990b, 252–54; Rainey 2012) and on its association in EA 290 with Keilah. Abdi-Heba complains that Bit-NIN.URTA, his town, was taken over by men of Keilah, possibly a group of Apiru based there. This could have been in retaliation against Abdi-Heba's attack on Keilah. Several locations have been suggested for Bit-NIN.URTA: Beth-horon (Kallai and Tadmor 1969; Rainey 2012, 136), Beth-zur (Singer 1993, 136), and an unidentified Beit 'Anat (Na'aman 1990b, 252–54; see detailed review of different proposals in Kallai and Tadmor 1969, 139). From the archaeological point of view, Beth-horon and Beth-zur are preferable candidates, since they revealed Late Bronze finds (Beit Ur el-Tahta and Khirbet et-Tubeiqah, respectively; Finkelstein 1988, 48, 177). Identification with Beth-zur would fit better the association with Keilah, as Khirbet et-Tubeiqah is only 8 kilometers to the east-southeast of Khirbet Qila. But in the microtopography of the region, Beth-zur in the highlands is a world apart from Keilah in the lowlands. It is therefore better to seek a place in the Shephelah close to Keilah. In this regard one is reminded of two names hinting at a cult place mentioned in Josh 15 in the Lachish-Eglon-Makkedah district of the Judahite Shephelah, that is, possibly close to Keilah, to its south: Beth-dagon (15:41) and Migdal-gad (15:37); however, apart from the fact that they represent a period many centuries later than the Amarna correspondence, in both cases the identification of the West Semitic deity with the Mesopotamian Ninurta is improbable.[2] Still, any of the Late Bronze sites in the vicinity (Finkelstein 1996b) could have had a temple called after a deity that can be identified with Ninurta.

Ayyaluna and Sarha are biblical Aijalon, identified with Yalo in the east of the Aijalon Valley (G.R. 151138), and biblical Zorah, identified at Sarha, on the ridge overlooking the Soreq Valley from the north (G.R. 148131). The queen mother Belit-labi'at writes that the Apiru wrote to

---

2. Personal communication from Ran Zadok.

these towns and that the two sons of Milkilu were almost killed as a result. Both places were located on the eastern flank of the territory of Gezer (Na'aman 1992a). In the case that the Apiru referred to by Belit-lebi'at is Abdi-Heba, this may indicate another attempt of westward expansion by Jerusalem.

Zadok (1986, 180) suggested that Ṣapuma may be the same as Sappho of Josephus (*A.J.* 17.10.9 §290; *B.J.* 2.5.1 §70), identified at the village of Ṣaffa (G.R. 155146) in the foothills near Late Bronze Gezer's eastern border. For lack of Late Bronze remains there, Zadok proposed to seek Ṣapuma at a nearby site. The relatively large multiperiod mound of el-Burj (Horvat Tittora), located only 3 kilometers west of Ṣaffa, could fit this identification (Na'aman 2011, 292; for Late Bronze finds there, see Gophna and Porath 1972, 235, though later surveys of Shavit [1992, 90] and Hizmi [1993, 109] failed to retrieve similar finds). In EA 274 Belit-labi'at reports that the town of Ṣapuma has been taken by the Apiru. Being in the foothills, it must have been a town in the territory of Gezer. In this case, too, it is possible that the attack came from Jerusalem.

Jerusalem's Expansion Attempts?

Plotting the contested towns on a map (fig. 4.1) makes it clear that at least five of them—and possibly all six—are located in the eastern Shephelah, along the eastern flank of the territories of Gezer and Gath, bordering on the territory of Jerusalem in the highlands. In fact, the five towns form a straight line from Ṣapuma in the north to Keilah in the south. As explained above, Bit-NIN.URTA could have been located in a similar geographic setting south of Keilah.

Jerusalem—either explicitly or under the disparaging title Apiru—is related to the affairs in all these places. Based on this and on comparison to the Shechem and Amurru Amarna dossiers (Finkelstein and Na'aman 2005; Goren, Finkelstein, and Na'aman 2003, respectively, and see below), it is only logical to assume that these were attempts by Abdi-Heba to expand his territory to the lowlands in the west and subjugate towns located on the eastern flanks of Gezer and Gath (possibly also Lachish in the case of Bit-NIN.URTA). The rulers of Gezer and Gath, probably backed by Egypt (Na'aman 2000b on Abdi-Heba's conflict with the Egyptian authorities) and assisted by Tagi of Ginti-kirmil (Jatt in the Sharon Plain; Goren, Finkelstein, and Na'aman 2004, 256–59) and at a certain point probably also by the sons of Labyau of Shechem (EA 289), fought back.³ The construction of "a house," possibly a fort, in the service of Egypt in a place named Manḫatu in the land of Gezer (EA 292) may also be related to the unrest in the eastern territory of this city-state.⁴

One can speculate that the assassination of three southern rulers—Zimreddi, Yaptiḫ-Hadda, and Turbazu—described in EA 288 (from the viewpoint of Jerusalem) and EA 335 (from the viewpoint of Gath) is connected to the struggle in the eastern Shephelah. Zimreddi was the ruler of Lachish, probably the southernmost city-state of the Shephelah, which bordered on the southwestern flank of the Jerusalem territory. As I suggested above, Yaptiḫ-Hadda and Turbazu could have ruled in two cities on the southern coastal plain, such as Yurza and Ashdod.

I would also speculate that the three rulers may have cooperated with Jerusalem in putting pressure on southern and western towns in the territory of Gath. This situation may be depicted in EA 281 and 283, in which Shuwardata complains that his towns are hostile to him and the war against him is severe (see also EA 271, in which Milkilu reports on the war against him and Shuwardata; on all this, including other references in the letters, see Na'aman 1979). In EA 335 Abdi-Ashtarti of Gath complains that Lachish is hostile and that Murashti has been seized. This town may be identified somewhere south of Tell eṣ-Ṣafi (Gath), for instance, at Tel Zayit (Na'aman 2011, 285), about midway between Gath and Lachish. The other place mentioned with Lachish is restored "Jerusalem" by Moran (1992, 358) and [^{URU}x-x]-shi-ki by Na'aman (2011, 284), who proposed to equate it with a town named Nentisha, referred to in an inscription on a bowl from Lachish (Sweeney 2004).⁵ This may also hint at a town on the border of Lachish and Gath. The town of Silu, where

---

3. This period of unrest characterizes an advanced stage in the Amarna correspondence; earlier, Shuwardata was an ally of Jerusalem (EA 366).

4. The stationing of an Egyptian garrison in Jerusalem may also have been connected to these affairs.

5. Another town that may be connected to these events is Tianna of EA 284, 298, and 306, identified by Na'aman with Ashdod and by myself with a town on the border between Gezer and Ashdod (see discussion in Goren, Finkelstein, and Na'aman 2004, 292). The reading Tianna was dismissed by Rainey 2003.

the three kings were killed (EA 288.42, 46), could have been located in a similar geographic setting.[6]

All this may hint at the existence of two coalitions in the south. One, led by Jerusalem, included Lachish[7] and two additional city-states on the coast, possibly Yurza and Ashdod;[8] the other, backed by Egypt, consisted of Gath, Gezer, and, seemingly, Ashkelon (see EA 287). The three rulers may have been assassinated by agents of the anti-Jerusalem coalition in order to relieve the pressure on Gath.

Jerusalem, Shechem, and Attempts at State Formation

The fact that at a certain point Shechem may have helped the city-states of the Shephelah against Jerusalem seems to hint at a struggle in the highlands, too. But this should not veil the similarities in the policies of the two polities and the fact that the core of unrest in southern Canaan was in the central highlands. Both Jerusalem and Shechem attempted to expand to the lowlands, possibly with the same goals in mind, and they did so by taking their own aggressive steps and seemingly also by establishing broad anti-Egypt coalitions.

This is certainly true for Shechem. Its maneuvers have been dealt with in detail elsewhere (Finkelstein and Na'aman 2005), hence a short summary will suffice. The Shechem coalition included Gezer, Ginti-kirmil, the city-state that was located at Tel Yokneam, Shimon, Anaharath, and Pihilu (= Pehel), while the Egypt-supported anti-Shechem coalition included Megiddo, Rehob, Achshaph, Acco, and possibly Hazor. Shechem's goals seem to have been to establish access to the Mediterranean trade, command over important trade routes, and domination over the fertile lands of the Jezreel–Beth-shean Valleys. Shechem apparently managed to extend its rule to the southern part of the Jezreel Valley (EA 250), and its coalition attempted to encircle the Jezreel Valley entities: the Egypt-supported city-states of Megiddo and Rehob and the Egyptian

---

6. For its location in the southern lowlands of Canaan, possibly near Lachish, rather than on the eastern border of the Nile Delta, see Na'aman 1979.

7. Assuming that EA 287 does not name Lachish (Na'aman 1975, 40 n. 38).

8. Especially if the latter was involved with the Muḫḫazu affair, mentioned in EA 298; see note 9 below.

4. The Shephelah and Jerusalem's Western Border 45

center of Beth-shean. At the peak of its maneuvers, the Shechem coalition dominated large and important parts of Canaan, from the Bashan in the northeast through the northern sector of the central highlands to the Sharon and the coastal plain south of the Yarkon River in the southwest. It controlled the port of Dor (also Acco), important sections of the international road leading from Egypt to Syria and Mesopotamia along the coastal plain and the Bashan, and a section of the King's Highway in Transjordan.

The steps taken by Abdi-Heba, as described above, seem to have been somewhat smaller in scope and ambition and appear to have started somewhat later, possibly as a result of what looked at the time like a success by Shechem and a weak reaction on the part of Egypt. As in the case of Shechem, Jerusalem's maneuvers included two components: subjugation of towns in the lowlands near its territory and establishment of a coalition with lowlands city-states. Jerusalem may have aimed at forming a hold in harbors along the coast and some sort of domination on the international road on the southern coastal plain.[9] No wonder that in both cases the anti-central highlands coalition was supported by the Egyptian authorities—a minimal step taken in order to maintain control in the region.[10]

What we see here are early attempts to establish territorial formations ruled from the central highlands.[11] With no historical documentation,

---

9. The Muḫḫazu incident, mentioned in EA 298, may be part of this. Yapaḫu, the ruler of Gezer, mentions how his brother became his enemy, entered Muḫḫazu, and "pledged himself to the Apiru." I have already noted that, in the case of several complaint letters from southern Canaan, the disparaging title Apiru may be understood as referring to Jerusalem. Muḫḫazu should probably be identified with the port site of Yavneh-Yam in the territory of Gezer, south of Jaffa (Goren, Finkelstein, and Na'aman 2004, 270).

10. The expansion of Abdi-Ashirta and Aziru of Amurru from their original stronghold in Mount Lebanon to the western foothills and then to the coastal plain, and the establishment of a large territorial polity that stretched over part of the Orontes Valley, too, was also treated in detail elsewhere (Goren, Finkelstein, and Na'aman 2003). Although this affair took place in a different geopolitical scene—on the northern border of Egyptian rule in Canaan—and on a larger scale, it features several striking similarities to the affairs in southern Canaan.

11. This phenomenon is known from different periods in the history of the Levant. To mention only the sedentary parts of the region, and to start with recent centuries, it resembles the eighteenth-century CE expansion of Dahr el-Umar in

there is no way to know if these were the first such attempts and whether they were the only such episodes in the Late Bronze and early Iron Ages. It is clear, though, that full success in such maneuvers was difficult as long as Egypt ruled Canaan and hence came only two centuries after New Kingdom Egypt withdrew from the region, with the emergence of Israel and Judah. Similarities between the case of Shechem of the Amarna period and the rise of the Northern Kingdom include expansion attempts to the coast in the west and the Jezreel Valley in the north (Finkelstein and Na'aman 2005; somewhat different version in Finkelstein 2013b). Parallels between the policies of Jerusalem of the fourteenth century BCE and the emergence of Judah are featured mainly in the expansion attempts to the Shephelah in the west (for Judah, see, e.g., Fantalkin and Finkelstein 2006; Fantalkin 2008; Sergi 2013; a somewhat different view in Na'aman 2013a).

Egyptian Rule in Canaan in the Amarna Period

The Amarna archive covers a relatively short period of about twenty-five years. The question arises if the situation of unrest, expansion of highlands polities, and deterioration of Egyptian rule depicted in the letters was specific to this period or endemic to the Egyptian province of Canaan in the Late Bronze Age. In this case, too, with no similar records for other phases of the period, the textual material can hardly provide an answer.

Archaeology may shed light on this issue. Recent excavations have revealed evidence for fourteenth-century BCE destruction layers at a surprisingly large number of sites, especially in the area in the southern lowlands as discussed in this chapter (fig. 4.1).

Beth-shemesh. The city of Level 9, which dates to the Late Bronze IIA in the fourteenth century BCE, came to an end in a dramatic destruction by fire, characterized by hundreds of collapsed mudbricks, which were baked in heavy conflagration (Ziffer, Bunimovitz, and Lederman 2009; Bunimovitz, Lederman, and Hatzaki 2013, 53).

---

the Lower Galilee and the ca. 1600 CE politics of Fakhr ed-Din in the Chouf Mountains of Lebanon. The Hellenistic period provides at least two examples: the Ituraean kingdom that emerged in Mount Lebanon (see, e.g., Marfoe 1979, 23–25) and the Hasmonean kingdom that began its expansion from a modest settlement in Jerusalem.

Tel Zayit. The earliest of the Late Bronze II layer at the site, which apparently dates to the Late Bronze IIA, features a large public building that was destroyed by fire. The accumulation of the collapsed remains reaches circa 2 meters (Tappy 2008).

Tel Batash. Stratum VII at this site, which features a large, well-planned, multistoried building, was destroyed by a fierce conflagration that left destruction debris up to 2 meters high. The assemblage in this layer dates to the fourteenth century BCE (A. Mazar 1997b, 1:58–71; Panitz-Cohen 2006, 130–32).

Tel Miqne/Ekron. The final phase of Stratum IX in the *sondage*, which apparently dates to the fourteenth century, ended in fire (Dothan and Gitin 1993, 1052).

Tel Halif. The early phase of Stratum IX, which dates to the Late Bronze IIA, ended in what is described as a "general destruction" (Seger 1993, 556).

An interesting clue for the situation in Canaan in the Late Bronze IIA comes from the Egyptian center of Beth-shean, which may have suffered destruction during the Amarna period. The evidence comes from Stratum R-1a (Level IX of the University of Pennsylvania excavations) of the Late Bronze IIA in the fourteenth century BCE (Mullins and Mazar 2007, 196). The situation in other Egyptian strongholds—for instance, in Jaffa (preliminary report in Burke et al. 2017)—is not clear yet. But the Beth-shean results seem to show that even an Egyptian center of power was not immune in this period of unrest; in other words, there were forces in Canaan that did not hesitate to act against the heartland of Egyptian rule.

Whether all the destructions in southern Canaan were caused by local strife or whether some of them were inflicted by Egyptian punitive campaigns is not known. It is noteworthy that no similar wave of destructions has thus far been revealed until the late thirteenth century or even later, in the mid- to late twelfth century BCE, the end phase of Egyptian rule in Canaan. From this one may obtain a glimpse into the gravity of the situation in the fourteenth century BCE. On the other hand, this may hint that the Egyptian military campaign referred to in EA 367 and 370 and other letters succeeded in pacifying the country.

Conclusion

The Amarna letters provide detailed information on the territorio-political situation in southern Canaan in the fourteenth century BCE. Three dominant city-states—Gezer, Gath, and Lachish—ruled in the Shephelah. To these one may add Beth-shemesh and an additional, yet-unknown seat of one or more local rulers. The letters seem to disclose a progressive attempt by Jerusalem to expand to the west by conquering towns on the eastern flank of the Shephelah polities. Comparison to the case of Shechem hints that, in order to advance its territorial (and probably economic) goals, Jerusalem may have tried to establish an anti-Egypt coalition with some lowlands city-states. All this, and a series of destruction layers at fourteenth-century BCE sites, including Egyptian forts, demonstrates the gravity of the situation in Canaan from the viewpoint of the Egyptian administration.

The Jerusalem and Shechem portfolios in the Amarna archive draw a picture of early attempts by the highlands polities to establish territorial kingdoms that include areas in the lowlands. They provide an enlightening comparison for the first steps in the emergence of Judah and Israel several centuries later.

But before dealing with this question, I wish to present my views on the end phase of the Iron I.

5
Saul and Highlands of Benjamin Update: The Role of Jerusalem

The Iron I was a vital phase in the history of Jerusalem, as it bridged what we know from the Amarna letters about the city-state of the Late Bronze Age and the rise of Judah as a territorial kingdom in the Iron IIA. At this point, it becomes necessary to study the biblical text, to evaluate whether the material on King Saul in 1 Samuel preserves a memory of the situation in the southern highlands before the rise of the Davidic dynasty.

Introduction

In recent years, I have published a number of works on the highlands of Benjamin.[1] They have dealt with two main issues: the territorio-political affiliation of the highlands of Benjamin with Israel or Judah (Finkelstein 2011c; contra Na'aman 2009b) and the rise of a north Israelite territorial entity in the tenth century BCE, which I associated with the biblical tradition on the house of Saul (Finkelstein 2006a). These issues are fundamental to understanding the emergence of the two Hebrew kingdoms and the background of several "historical" descriptions and historiographical concepts in the Bible. The fragmentary nature of the sources of information makes research on these themes difficult. First, in order to "reach" the old, pre-Deuteronomistic Saul tradition in the books of Samuel, one needs to peel off later layers (e.g., Edelman 1991; Scheffler 2000; Nihan

---

1. By "highlands of Benjamin," I refer to the geographical term, which is not necessarily fully similar to the biblical tribal one.

2006; Kaiser 2011, 2012), especially the strong Deuteronomistic one, not to mention that the scope of the old material is debatable. Second, there is only one extrabiblical source: the Egyptian account of the Sheshonq I campaign to Canaan. Being a list, rather than annals, it gives a somewhat vague testimony; also, the exact date of Sheshonq's reign and the date of the campaign (or campaigns) during his reign are disputed (more below). Third, much of the archaeology of the highlands of Benjamin in the period under discussion—the late Iron I and early Iron IIA—leaves much to be desired from the perspectives of both chronology and interpretation of the nature of the remains.

In this chapter I take a fresh look at both issues: the geographical and historical background to the Saul narrative and the question of territorial affiliation of the highlands of Benjamin. The discussion below leads me to comment on other themes: the circumstances of the contemporaneous rise of the two Hebrew kingdoms and the origin of the united monarchy concept in the Bible. Let me say in advance that the missing parts in the puzzle are far more considerable than those that exist. Hence, I offer my observations as a platform for discussion—a background stage setting for what may be cached behind the biblical text, the Sheshonq list, and the fragmentary archaeological data.

My Former Reconstruction

I start with a short summary of my former views.

1. I have argued that Israel and Judah were in dispute over the land of Benjamin. Until the decline of the Omride dynasty, it was part of the north. Then, in a period when Israel was weakened as a result of the pressure of Hazael, it was taken over by Judah in the time of King Jehoash, who seems to have acted under Damascene auspices. The area was probably controlled again by Israel in the days of Joash and Jeroboam II. Renewed Judahite domination of the region is clearly attested starting in the late eighth century, as result of the fall of the north and of Judah becoming an Assyrian vassal.

2. I have proposed the existence—in the tenth century BCE—of a north Israelite polity that was centered in the plateau of Gibeon-Bethel. This entity is hinted at by shreds of pre-Deuteronomistic Saul royal tradition in the book of Samuel and by the list of towns taken over during the

campaign of Sheshonq I to Canaan. These sources refer to the same territories in the highlands and the Gilead around the outlet of the Jabbok River, in approximately the same period (the tenth century BCE). A late Iron I/early Iron IIA (in terms of absolute chronology, this, too, translates to the tenth century BCE; see Finkelstein and Piasetzky 2010) polity in this region is also insinuated by the unique concentration of casemate-fortified sites; together with Khirbet Qeiyafa (more below) these are the only contemporary fortifications known in the sedentary areas west of the Jordan River.

3. Scholars are in dispute regarding the seat of Saul. This stems from the Geba/Gibeah confusion in the biblical texts.[2] There are two possibilities here. According to the first, Geba/Gibeah of Saul/Gibeah of Benjamin refers to the same place, which should be identified with the village of Jaba on the desert fringe. Contra many scholars (Na'aman 2014a), Tell el-Ful is not an option, as the archaeological evidence for activity there in the period under discussion is meager at best (Finkelstein 2011e). Another option is to locate the seat of Saul more centrally, at Gibeon (Blenkinsopp 1974; Ahlström 1993; Edelman 1996; Van der Toorn 1993; Knauf 2001b).

4. I argued (Finkelstein 2017) that the pre-Deuteronomistic Saul story includes parts of the following materials:[3]

- Saul's search for his father's mules (Edelman 1988);
- His coronation in an unnamed place by an unnamed man of God;
- The root of the story on the rescue of Jabesh from the city-state of Ammon;
- The battle of Geba and Michmash;
- Seemingly the opening of the narrative on the battle in the Valley of Elah;
- Additional clues in the early layer of the David story (ch. 10 below);

---

2. For the possibility that the confusion stems from Israelite and Judahite pronunciation/spelling, see Arnold 1990, 37–38, 42.

3. On this matter, see different views in, e.g., Na'aman 1992b; Edelman 1996, 151–56; Dietrich 2007, 155–57; White 2000.

- The root of the story on the battle of Gilboa; the geography and the link with the former Egyptian center of Beth-shean are too specific to be invented by later authors.

5. I assumed that the territory of the Saul polity included the highlands north of Jerusalem and the western slopes of the Gilead, with possible extension to the northeastern Shephelah in the Valley of Elah (Finkelstein and Fantalkin 2012). At least part of this territory may be echoed in the summary of the regions ruled by Ishbaal in 2 Sam 2:9 (Edelman 1985; Na'aman 1990a). This seems to be a northern-derived text used by a Deuteronomistic author, who may have added the term "all Israel."

6. The penetration of Sheshonq I into the highlands is an exception in the history of Egyptian campaigns to Canaan. There is hardly a way to explain this risky maneuver other than as a reaction to a menace posed to renewed Egyptian interests in Canaan by a highlands polity. I would refer mainly to expansion attempts of such highlands entities to the lowlands in the west and north (compare the case of Labayu of Shechem in the Amarna period; Finkelstein and Na'aman 2005). With no historical great united monarchy, a contemporary northern polity in the central highlands is the only option for such a threatening entity. Sheshonq I took over the heartland of the Saulide territory in the plateau of Gibeon and its extension in the area of the Jabbok in the Gilead.

7. This issue is related to the territorial affiliation of the much-discussed site of Khirbet Qeiyafa. The layout of the site hints at a highlands origin of the builders. Alexander Fantalkin and I proposed that the site belonged to the north Israelite Saulide polity and that it was destroyed/abandoned as a result of the Sheshonq I campaign (Finkelstein and Fantalkin 2012). A north Israelite affiliation of the site fits the references to the (otherwise geographically odd) presence of Saul in the Valley of Elah and the area of Adullam. In another article, Fantalkin and I (2017) showed that material culture characteristics of the site are better understood as representing a northern (rather than Judahite) association.

8. A Saul royal tradition, which is the source of the pre-Deuteronomistic Saul material, was composed in Israel in the days of Jeroboam II, that is, in the first half of the eighth century BCE—just slightly more than a century and half after the events (Finkelstein 2017).

9. The written royal Saul tradition was brought to Jerusalem by Israelites who moved to the south after 720 BCE. The archaeological evidence

is unmistakable: a dramatic demographic transformation in Jerusalem in particular and Judah in general in the Iron IIB (ch. 15 below). This transformation can in no way be explained as the result of natural population growth, economic prosperity, or intra-Judahite movement of people. Appearance of Israelite material culture in Judah starting in the late eighth century supports this historical reconstruction (ch. 14 below; contra Na'aman 2014a). The Israelite Saul tradition was later incorporated into Deuteronomistic writings. The ratio of northerners in the population of Judah prevented the authors from dismissing it; rather, it was contained (McCarter 1980b; Halpern 2001, 73–103) and put to the service of Judahite royal ideology (ch. 15 below).

Difficulties in My Former Historical Reconstruction

This reconstruction was not free of difficulties.

1. The central highlands were traditionally divided between two territorial entities, one located at Shechem or its vicinity and the other in Jerusalem. Ostensibly, a territorial formation with its hub in the Gibeon Plateau is an exception in this long-term situation.[4]

2. One should ask: At the time of the Gibeon Plateau polity, who ruled in the nearby, traditional southern hub of Jerusalem? The biblical answer—using the term Jebus/Jebusite—is an enigma; it resonates as stemming from a late polemic or a pun, more than depicting a memory of a historical situation.

3. A pre-Deuteronomistic layer in Samuel contains stories about David as a leader of an Apiru band that was active on the southern fringe of the highlands of Judah. A pivotal part of the story deals with his maneuvers between the rulers of the highlands (Saul) and the Shephelah (the king of Gath; Na'aman 2010b; ch. 10 below). Saul is referred to as acting in the area of the Valley of Elah and probably also the southern Hebron Highlands (e.g., 1 Sam 23:19; 24:1–2; it is difficult to separate Saul from the David story here). Was this possible without control over Jerusalem?

---

4. *Ostensibly* because et-Tell ("Ai") of the Early Bronze (together with Tell el-Far'ah North) is a similar case.

4. Related to the question of Jerusalem, two pre-Deuteronomistic references in Samuel mention Philistine garrisons stationed in the highlands—in Geba or Gibeon (1 Sam 10:5, 13:3)[5] and Bethlehem (2 Sam 23:14, one of the heroic stories that appear in two groups in 2 Sam 21:15–22 and 23:8–21; Isser 2003). This raises a number of questions. There was no Philistine united military force in the tenth century; the main Philistine city-states that bordered on the highlands were Gath (though we know relatively little about its archaeology in this phase) and Ekron (until the end of Stratum IV there). Were they strong enough to put garrisons in the highlands? If not, are the references to Philistine garrisons ahistorical, or does "Philistine" stand for Egypt? Obviously, the two garrisons were established to the north and south of Jerusalem; if they were meant to control it, one must ask when they were founded and who ruled in Jerusalem at that time.

Below I try to deal with these difficulties and offer a reasonable reconstruction of the history of the region in the tenth century BCE.

An Updated Reconstruction

Here I wish to propose a more elaborate, three-stage scenario for the history of the Saulide territorial entity.[6]

Stage I: The Beginning

Saul came from a well-to-do rural family in or near the town of Geba/Gibeah, identified in the present-day village of Jaba on the eastern fringe of the Gibeon-Bethel Plateau,[7] or from Gibeon, which features a (late?) Iron I fortification system (Finkelstein 2013b, 40; for reasons to prefer this or that site, see below). The *core* territory of his rule is probably referred to

---

5. Deciding about the location of this garrison depends on resolving the confusion Geba/Gibeah/Gibeon.

6. For the immense literature on Saul, see Dietrich 2007, 162–64; different studies with bibliographies in Ehrlich and White 2006; more recently, Bezzel 2015. I will concentrate on questions of territorial expansion and historical background.

7. For survey results, see Feldstein, Kidron, Hanin, Kamaisky and Eitam, 1993, 177–79.

5. Saul and Highlands of Benjamin Update 55

in the story about the search for his father's asses (1 Sam 9:4–5): the lands of Shalishah, Shaʿalim, Zuph, and Yemini. That Yemini equals Benjamin is obvious. For the land of Shaʿalim/land of Shual, see 1 Sam 13:17, associated with Ophrah, northeast of Bethel. Zuph may be related to Ramathaim (1 Sam 1:1)—seemingly Ramathaim of 1 Macc 11:34 and Arimathea of Matt 27:57 and John 19:38. If so, better than Ramah, it should probably be identified in or near Rantis in the western sector of the biblical land of Ephraim (Kallai 1976). These toponyms seem to cover the areas of Benjamin and southern Ephraim. Their ancient origin is hinted by the fact that they do not appear in Deuteronomistic writings. Indeed, the reference to the hill country of Ephraim (הר אפרים) in 1 Sam 9:4a is a Deuteronomistic addition. However, the author did not fully understand the term *hill country of Ephraim* any longer, because Deuteronomistic authors use it to delineate the *entire* central highlands area of the Northern Kingdom (Josh 19:50; 21:21; Judg 4:5, 10:1; 1 Kgs 12:25).

In his early days, Saul's seat of power must have been his hometown. This is the straight-forward meaning of the text, which speaks about Gibeah of Saul. With no firm rule in the highlands, a strongman could have wrested a small territory for himself between the two traditional hubs of Shechem and Jerusalem. Somewhat comparable situations could be Jeroboam I in Zeredah, in the southwest of the biblically described inheritance of Ephraim (Kochavi 1989), and the family that sat in the village of Ras Karkar, which dominated the same area in the late Ottoman period. An early hub on the desert fringe—rather than Gibeon—would be more logical and less threatening to nearby Jerusalem.

I have already mentioned that sites in the heartland of the Saulide territory feature casemate fortifications. I refer to Tell en-Naṣbeh, et-Tell (Ai), Gibeon, and Khirbet ed-Dawwara; the fortifications in these places date to the late Iron I and/or early Iron IIA, in the tenth century (Finkelstein 2013b, 38–40). Casemate-fortified sites seem to hint at the rise of territorial entities in other parts of the southern Levant as well, that is, Moab near the Arnon (Finkelstein and Lipschits 2011) and Ammon (Finkelstein 2011d).

Stage II: Expansion to the South

Naʾaman (2014b) suggests that Jerusalem was "one of Saul's power bases." I, too, think that at a certain stage Saul became strong enough to take control of Jerusalem, the center of power near him. In the later phases of the Late Bronze and the early Iron I, the city-state of Jerusalem must have continued to rule over the southern part of the central hill country, similar to the situation in the Amarna period. The takeover of a seat of power by a neighboring strongman is not unfamiliar in these periods, as seen, for instance, in the rise to power of Aziru in Amurru of the fourteenth century BCE (Singer 1991; Goren, Finkelstein, and Na'aman 2003). Parallels from other periods are Dahr el-Omar in Acco and Fahr ed-Din in Lebanon in the late Ottoman period.

The takeover of Jerusalem (impossible to know from whom) enabled Saul to expand to the south as far as the Hebron Highlands and to the border with Gath, the major city-state of the Shephelah. At a certain stage, he seems to have managed to extend his activity to the upper Shephelah. Khirbet Qeiyafa could have been built as a stronghold facing Gath (Finkelstein and Fantalkin 2012). This transitional Iron I/early Iron IIA site shows affiliation with material culture characteristics of sites in the northern part of the central highlands and the northern valleys rather than nearby sites in Judah (Fantalkin and Finkelstein 2017). The building of Khirbet Qeiyafa could have led to confrontation with Gath, vaguely memorized in the old tradition on the battle in the Valley of Elah (I refer mainly to 1 Sam 17:1–3). Originally (before the account was usurped by the Deuteronomistic David story and authored in Greek ambiance) it commemorated the hero Elhanan (2 Sam 21:19; Isser 2003, 34–37).

The expansion to the south must have put Saul in conflict with another contender to the regional seat of power, David of Bethlehem, who was pushed to the southern fringe, to maneuver between Saul's Jerusalem, Philistine Gath, and the southern "copper chiefdom" of Tel Masos (ch. 10 below). The story of the conquest of Jebus by David is etiological, based on the phenomenon of rock-cut tunnels near the Gihon Spring known to the late-monarchic inhabitants of Jerusalem. Whether it is based on an old conquest tradition, and who was the conqueror, is difficult to say. The Deuteronomistic reference to pre-Davidic Jerusalem as Jebus possibly refers to a group settled there and at the same time mocks its ancient inhabitants (Na'aman 2014b).

Once conquered, Jerusalem could have been fortified like the sites in the Gibeon Plateau. As the ancient mound is located on the Temple Mount (see ch. 2 above), this issue cannot be investigated.

Stage III: Expansion to the North

At a certain point, Saul may have taken advantage of the decline of Shechem a short while earlier and expanded to the north, too.[8] This is evident from the Gilboa tradition (why would a later author invent this?), from the reference to Bezek in 1 Sam 11:8 (here probably only the toponym is old; why would a later author invent a link to a place not important in his time?) and to Jabesh, and from 2 Sam 2:9, which was discussed above. This means that the area ruled by Saul in his peak prosperity stretched over the entire central highlands all the way north to the border of the Jezreel Valley, if not into the valley itself, covering the territories of the two traditional city-states of the highlands: Jerusalem and Shechem combined.

Saul's expansion to the margins of the Jezreel Valley and the coastal plain, that is, close to the strategic international road to the north, brought about his demise, as it collided with the renewed ambitions of Egypt of the late Twenty-First and early Twenty-Second Dynasties regarding Canaan. Once again, this situation was not new, being comparable to the confrontation between Labayu of Shechem with Egypt of the Eighteenth Dynasty in the Amarna period and, if one looks for more recent history, to the clash of Dhahr el-Omar with the Ottomans following his takeover of Acco.

A United Monarchy of Saul?

The Saul polity created the peculiar situation of a leader considered to be northern ruling from a southern hub. An oral memory of this situation could have been committed to writing in the north in the time of Jeroboam II, when scribal infrastructure for such an endeavor already existed. Other northern royal foundation and heroic traditions (in the latter, I refer to the savior stories in the book of Judges) could also have been assembled and put in writing at that time (Finkelstein 2017). Domination of Judah by Israel in the days of Joash and Jeroboam II is evidenced from the chronistic part of 2 Kgs 14:11b–13 and is hinted at by the finds at Kuntillet ʿAjrud (Ahituv, Eshel, and Meshel 2012) and Kiriath-jearim

---

8. The destruction of Shechem Stratum XI was probably contemporaneous with the devastation of Shiloh in the second half of the eleventh century BCE. For Shechem, see Finkelstein 2006b; for Shiloh, Finkelstein and Piasetzky 2006b.

(ch. 11 below). Hence the Saul story could have been considered in the north to be a forerunner of the idea of a great united monarchy ruled by a northern king. The written Saul royal tradition—of a northern king ruling over a united monarchy from Jerusalem—reached Judah with Israelites after 720 BCE and could have served as a model for the idea of a united monarchy ruled by Davidic kings from Jerusalem.[9]

Egypt and the Highlands

Sheshonq I, the founder of the Twenty-Second Dynasty and seemingly the more assertive of the Egyptian rulers of the time, reacted to the north Israelite challenge. He campaigned into the highlands and took over the Saulide power bases in the Gibeon Plateau and the area of the Jabbok River in the western Gilead. The fortified sites of Khirbet Qeiyafa, Khirbet Dawwara, et-Tell, and Gibeon were destroyed or abandoned. Sheshonq reorganized the territory of the highlands back to the traditional situation of two city-states[10] under his domination. He may have chosen adversaries of the house of Saul to rule over these polities: David in Jerusalem and Jeroboam I at Shechem (on chronology, see below). For the latter, the possible reference to association with Egypt in the Jeroboam I Masoretic Text and in the alternative history in the Septuagint (if the latter includes pre-Deuteronomistic materials)[11] may mean that Jeroboam's rise to power could also have been associated with these events: as a vassal of Egypt. Jeroboam, a local (perhaps Apiru?) strongman from the highland northwest of modern Ramallah, may have opposed Saul's expansion to the north, fled to Egypt as a result, and returned in coordination with Sheshonq I.

To pacify the highlands and prevent future trouble, Sheshonq I could have established garrisons in certain key places. This may be the background to the references to Philistine garrisons on both sides of Jerusalem:

---

9. On northern texts arriving in Judah after 720 and incorporated into the Bible, see, e.g., Van der Toorn 1996, 339–72; Schniedewind 2004; Schuette 2016; references to additional studies in Edenburg and Müller 2015b.

10. They became territorial kingdoms later, Israel in the first half of the ninth century and Judah in the second half.

11. For a positive answer, see Schenker 2000, 2008. For a different view, seeing the Septuagint addition as a midrash, see Talshir 1993; Sweeney 2007.

Bethlehem, hometown of David (2 Sam 23:14); and Geba or Gibeon, hometown of Saul (1 Sam 13:3; on this the centrally located Gibeon is preferable). Gath, the major city-state of the Shephelah, seems to have associated with the pharaoh: not only was it not damaged by him, but following his campaign Gath grew in size and influence. People from Gath could have been in the service of Sheshonq in these strongholds, providing the background for the reference to *matzav* and *netziv Plishtim* (rather than Egypt) in these two places. When the stories were committed to writing, Egypt in the highlands was a fading memory, while the Philistine city-states were still a menace to Judah. We know about the two garrisons near Jerusalem because of the Judahite connection. Obviously, Sheshonq must have put similar garrison forces near Shechem and in the Jezreel Valley (for the latter, note the Sheshonq stela at Megiddo).

A major question is whether this reconstruction can work chronologically. The answer is positive. According to the Bible-free chronology for the Third Intermediate Period suggested by Thomas Schneider (2010), the reign of Sheshonq I is dated 962–941 BCE. The most probable radiocarbon date for the destruction of Khirbet Qeiyafa is 956–942 BCE (Fantalkin and Finkelstein 2017). The number forty being typological, the forty-year reign of David and the same length for Solomon mean no more than "long time"; the accession of David can fall in the early years of Sheshonq I's reign. Finally, assuming that the information in the book of Kings on the length of reign of the northern monarchs is based on a north Israelite text that was composed in the early eighth century (Robker 2012), calculating back from the secure date of the death of Joram in 841 puts the accession of Jeroboam I circa 940 BCE. All this should be evaluated with two additional notes: (1) the traditional date given by Kitchen (1986) to Sheshonq I, 945–924 BCE, can also work, especially noting that Ishbaal ruled for a number of years after Saul; (2) Sheshonq may have undertaken more than one campaign to Canaan (Redford 1973, 1992; Dodson 2000), starting early in his reign (Ben-Dor 2011). Finally, zooming out from details, it seems historically illogical to consider all these events and processes that apparently took place during the period and in the same geographical arena separately.

Since I am reconstructing history from just a few vague sources, it should not come as a surprise that my updated scenario still faces at least two difficulties. (1) If Jerusalem had been the seat of Saul, why does it not appear in the Sheshonq I list? Was the name mentioned in a blurred part of the relief? Or, perhaps following the campaign and the placing of David there, Jerusalem was considered a vassal rather than an adversary of Egypt; note that there is no reference to Shechem (the seat of Jeroboam I) either. (2) If 2 Sam 2:9 is considered an authentic pre-Deuteronomistic source, why is Judah not mentioned? Perhaps this source was reshaped by a Deuteronomistic author.

Conclusion

In this chapter I offer a more nuanced, three-stage process for the geographical expansion of the Saulide entity in the tenth century BCE. In the peak of its rule, the house of Saul could have ruled from Jerusalem over the entire central highlands, that is, over the territories of the two traditional Bronze Age city-states of Shechem and Jerusalem. The memory of this early "united monarchy," which was ruled by a northern king from the southern hub, may have served as a model for the idea of a great united monarchy ruled by a northern king in the time of Jeroboam II and, no less important, for the Deuteronomistic concept of a united monarchy ruled from Jerusalem by a Davidide. Though admittedly hypothetical, this reconstruction is in line with the few fragmentary sources of information on the highlands in the tenth century BCE. It also provides a reasonable scenario for the otherwise rather enigmatic contemporaneous rise of Israel and Judah.

Part 3
The Iron IIA and the Early Iron IIB: The First Leap Forward

6

Jerusalem and the Benjamin Plateau in the Early Phases of the Iron Age

Having discussed the situation in the late Iron I, in the tenth century BCE, I now advance to the Iron IIA and the first expansion of Jerusalem from the original mound on the Temple Mount in the direction of the City of David ridge, in the ninth century BCE. I deal with this in the next four chapters. Discussion of this period is related to the biblical traditions on Jerusalem of the days of the "united monarchy." I begin by confronting a theory according to which the expansion of Jerusalem had already commenced in the late Iron I.

In a 2017 *Zeitschrift des deutschen Palästina-Vereins* article, Omer Sergi suggested a novel reconstruction of the archaeology and history of Jerusalem and its countryside in the Iron I and early Iron IIA. Sergi argued that Jerusalem emerged as a dominant highlands stronghold as early as the late eleventh/early tenth century BCE and that it ruled over the Benjamin Plateau. His chain of reasoning is as follows:

- The Stepped Stone Structure, located on the eastern slope of Jerusalem's southeastern ridge (commonly referred to as the City of David), dates to the late eleventh/early tenth centuries BCE.
- This is a monumental structure. Building it could be achieved only by recruiting people from Jerusalem's countryside.
- Jerusalem of the time was a "highland stronghold."
- The Jerusalem countryside can be delineated according to results of archaeological surveys; it included the territory between Bethlehem/Beth-zur in the south and Bethel in the north.

In what follows I take a critical view at Sergi's theory by scrutinizing the archaeological validity of each of these arguments. I then offer a different interpretation for the elements discussed by Sergi as well for other finds in Jerusalem and Judah.

Dating the Stepped Stone Structure

Let me start with a preliminary comment. Under the title "Stepped Stone Structure" (for a photograph, see fig. 7.3), Sergi lists several components of construction on the slope above the Gihon Spring (see also E. Mazar 2009). This listing confuses a rather simple situation. There are basically two elements of construction here: stone terraces and/or support walls on the slope, which were covered in one place by a stone mantle (below I use the better description stone coating). These elements have drawn undue attention from scholars (in recent years, e.g., Steiner 1994; Cahill 2003a; A. Mazar 2006b, 2010; E. Mazar 2009; Faust 2010) because they date to pre-eighth-century BCE phases of the Iron Age and can ostensibly be used to illuminate the nature of the city in the tenth century BCE. Accordingly, the task of the researcher is to carefully sort out facts from arguments meant to keep the glass "half full" (A. Mazar 2006b), that is, to confirm the biblical description of a glamorous Solomonic Jerusalem.

The facts regarding the date of construction of the elements on the eastern slope of the "City of David" ridge are as follows:

1. In Kenyon's Square A/I, the terraces were built over "transitional period of the Late Bronze Age and the Iron I period" (Steiner 2001, 24; description on 24–28); the pottery drawing (Steiner 2001, fig. 4.5) looks to me more Late Bronze than Iron I.
2. The fill in the terrace system in Kenyon's Squares A/I–III and Trench I yielded mainly Late Bronze and possibly also Iron I pottery (Steiner 2001, fig. 4.16).
3. In Shiloh's Area G, Iron IIC buildings were constructed over the stone coating, which covers the terraces (Shiloh 1984, 29; Steiner 2001, 58–77). Cahill's early "floors" in one of these building, which she dates to the Iron IIA (2003a, 56–66), are no more than construction fills (see ch. 7 below).

4. There is more than one phase of construction in the stone coating (ch. 7 below).
5. The latest sherds retrieved from between the stones in the "massive terraces" (part of the Stepped Stone Structure) were described as possibly dating to the tenth century BCE, in terms of the time meaning the Iron IIA. Indeed, a few items published by Steiner (2001, fig. 5.11, left column) seem to date to that period (a few items described as originating from under the "massive terraces" may even date slightly later; fig. 5.11, middle column, items 16, 56).

We are facing two possible chronological scenarios:

Scenario A: All components of the Stepped Stone Structure—terraces and stone coating (except renovation of the latter)—are contemporaneous. In this case the structure is indeed impressive and should be dated to an advanced phase in the Iron IIA, if not slightly later (contemporaneous or later than the latest sherds in number 5 above). The broader logic—the possible relation with the early phase of construction in the Large Stone Structure immediately above the slope (E. Mazar 2007, 2009; for the architectural elements belonging to it and the question of dating, see ch. 7 below) and appearance of monumental architecture in other places in Judah—points to the later phase of the late Iron IIA in the late ninth century BCE (date for the Iron IIA according to radiocarbon measurements; Finkelstein and Piasetzky 2010; Toffolo et al. 2014).

A new, important piece of information regarding activity on the eastern slope has recently been added: radiocarbon dates of short-lived samples extracted from below the eastern face of the Gihon Spring Tower (Regev et al. 2017). The results clearly show that we are dealing with an accumulation, as the dates range between the early second millennium and the ninth century BCE. The drawing published by the authors (2017, fig. 4) seems to show that this section of the eastern wall of the Spring Tower is a renovation of the original Middle Bronze tower, possibly after it had collapsed. If so, the latest radiocarbon date puts the renovation in the late ninth century. It is possible, then, that the entire treatment of the slope, including the construction of the Stepped Stone Structure, dates to the late ninth century BCE. The goal was to prevent collapse and damage to the area of the spring (more below).

Scenario B: The Stepped Stone Structure is part of a support system that functioned for many centuries in a spot where the slope is especially steep (more below) and collapse may risk the area of the spring. In this case one would assume a beginning of operations in the Middle Bronze, with the construction of the fortifications around the spring, and continuous activity until the Iron Age if not later. Dating one spot of the terracing according to pottery below or within the fill is meaningless, because the situation may change a short distance away. In any event, in this scenario, too, the combination of the radiocarbon dates from below the Spring Tower and the latest pottery in the fills on the slope point to the late Iron IIA, in the (late?) ninth century BCE. Considering all pieces of information from the slope and the area of the spring, this scenario is the more reasonable.

In both scenarios A and B there is no validity to Sergi's dating of a single monumental structure in the late eleventh/early tenth century BCE.

Monumentality

As described above, the terraces/support walls and the stone coating were meant to reinforce the steep slope in its most vulnerable spot: to prevent collapse and possibly support construction on the rim of the ridge. Assuming that some treatment of the slope must have started in the Middle Bronze Age, maintenance of the system in later generations must have been an annual routine. With terrace-construction knowledge in the highlands, this endeavor did not call for recruiting a large population from the countryside. Moreover, during renovation of the system in the late Iron IIA, in the late ninth century, the population of Jerusalem had already grown significantly (more below), to allow enough manpower to deal with stabilizing the slope above the spring.

In any event, comparing the construction of Jerusalem's eastern-slope terraces to the creation of Middle Bronze "fortifications" (for placing this word in quotation marks, see Finkelstein 1992b; Bunimovitz 1992) in the highlands (Sergi 2017a, 7) is certainly not adequate, as the latter involved surrounding sites with massive stone walls, with thousands of boulders, and laying massive earth revetments (Finkelstein 1992b). Moreover, the Middle Bronze construction must have been executed in a shorter period of time than maintenance of the slope during centuries of activity.

Jerusalem as a Highland Stronghold

The Stepped Stone Structure is a support system on the slope. But where is the "stronghold"? There is no late eleventh- or early tenth-century BCE fortified town/village on the ridge above the terraces—not even a single building. If the Stepped Stone Structure and the Large Stone Structure excavated by E. Mazar above it (2009; also more than a single-period building; see ch. 7 below) were connected, something that cannot be verified today (ch. 8 below), such a stronghold could have existed—in the Late Iron IIA, in the (late?) ninth century BCE.

This assertion fits the bigger picture of the archaeology of Jerusalem in the early phases of the Iron Age. For reasons specified elsewhere, the southeastern ridge (the City of David) cannot be considered the mound of ancient Jerusalem, meaning that the ancient tell must have been located on the Temple Mount (ch. 2 above, following Knauf 2000). Jerusalem started expanding from the ancient mound to the south, in the direction of the spring, in the Iron IIA, in the ninth century BCE. This is testified by finds in three locations: the Givati Parking Lot near the Dung Gate (Ben-Ami 2014), the area immediately to the south of Al-Aqsa Mosque (E. Mazar 2015, 459–74; ch. 9 below) and the visitors center above Shiloh's Area G (E. Mazar 2009; ch. 7 below).

To summarize this point, had there been a stronghold in Jerusalem in the late eleventh/early tenth century BCE, it was located on the Temple Mount and beyond the reach of modern research. And had there been a stronghold above the spring, it was constructed in the Iron IIA, in the ninth century BCE.

The Jerusalem Countryside

Sergi asserts that the area between Bethlehem and Bethel was densely settled in the eleventh/early tenth centuries, while the hill country to its north remained uninhabited or thinly settled; hence he associates the sites located between Jerusalem and Bethel with Jerusalem. This idea does not conform with the data.

The area south of Shechem was densely settled in the Iron I (Finkelstein, Lederman, and Bunimovitz 1997, 894–96, 949). The absence of sites in the few kilometers between et-Taiyiba and the valley of Shiloh is meaningless; due to environmental factors, this area was not settled even in the peak periods of activity in the highlands (compare, e.g., to the Iron II; Finkelstein, Lederman, and Bunimovitz 1997, 951), and, in any event, there is no such void immediately to its west. As for the Iron IIA, identification of habitation in this period during the surveys was difficult for two reasons: first, diagnostic sherds for subdivision within the Iron II are not easy to come by in the case of sites that yield just a few Iron Age items; second, in the early 1990s, when the results of the survey were prepared for publication, identification of such sherds had not yet been fully established. Still, if one looks at the list of pottery types with today's knowledge in mind, the map of the "Iron Age I–II" represents, in fact, the Iron IIA (Finkelstein, Lederman, and Bunimovitz 1997, 29, 950). Clearly, the area between Bethel and Shechem was densely settled. Hence there is no reason for Sergi to question the ability of Shechem to rule 30–40 kilometers to its south. The settlement patterns are simply mute regarding the question of the northern border of Jerusalem's rule.

However, there may be a clue in the biblical text. I differ from Sergi in the interpretation of 1 Kgs 15:16–22 (Finkelstein 2012b), but one thing is quite clear: this tradition, even if based on an etiological story and reinforced by events in the eighth century BCE (Finkelstein 2012b), preserves a memory that in the early days of the kingdom of Judah the Benjamin Plateau was ruled by Israel.

Conclusion

All pieces of archaeological information converge on the late Iron IIA, in the ninth century BCE:

- renovation of the Gihon Spring Tower (above);
- appearance of a large number of uninscribed bullae near the spring (Reich, Shukron, and Lernau 2007);
- renovation of the support system on the slope above the tower (the Stepped Stone Structure);
- expansion of Jerusalem from the mound on the Temple Mount to the south, in the direction of the Gihon Spring;
- first construction in the area of the Large Stone Structure, above the slope;

- intensification of settlement activity in the southern highlands, especially in the area of Hebron and south of it (ch. 23 below).
- expansion of Judah to the Shephelah and the Beersheba Valley (Fantalkin and Finkelstein 2006; Sergi 2013).
- construction of the Great Wall in Tell en-Naṣbeh to the north of Jerusalem (Finkelstein 2012b).

But when in the ninth century? Only a historical scenario can provide an answer. It seems to me that all the above reflects a given geopolitical situation in the second half of the ninth century: prosperity in Judah as a vassal of Damascus, following the temporal decline of the Northern Kingdom and the destruction of Gath by Hazael.

7

Has King David's Palace in Jerusalem Been Found?

> In the next three chapters I focus on three specific locations with Iron IIA remains: the Large Stone Structure and Stepped Stone Structure above the Gihon Spring and the Ophel immediately to the south of the Temple Mount.

Recent excavations at the City of David have revealed the remains of a set of massive walls constructed of large undressed stones. The excavator, Eilat Mazar, has presented them as the remains of a single, substantial building, which she labeled the Large Stone Structure (E. Mazar 2006a, 2006c, 2007). Mazar dated her Large Stone Structure to circa 1000 BCE and, inspired by the ideas of the late Benjamin Mazar (E. Mazar 2006a, 20), identified it as the palace of King David. Eilat Mazar's archaeological, chronological, and, in fact, historical conclusions have unreservedly been endorsed by Amihai Mazar (2006b, 269–70). The ostensible importance of this discovery and the media frenzy that has accompanied the excavation demand discussion, which is based on the preliminary publications and on our own observations made during our visits to the site in both excavation seasons.

History of Research

Eilat Mazar's excavation field, which in 2005 covered an area of circa 25 by 5–14 meters, is located on the crest of the City of David ridge, directly to

---

This chapter was originally coauthored with Zeev Herzog, Lily Singer-Avitz, and David Ussishkin.

the west of Shiloh's Area G. This field (and the adjoining eastern slope of the ridge) has been explored extensively. It falls within the northern side of Macalister and Duncan's Field No. 5 (Macalister and Duncan 1926, map in back pocket). Macalister and Duncan exposed most of the area down to bedrock, including several cisterns and a rock-cut "olive press" (1926, pl. I; compare also the photograph at 1926, fig. 20, with that at E. Mazar 2007, 31). They also uncovered the Jebusite Ramp along the upper edge of the eastern slope (1926, Pl. V), commonly known today as the Stepped Stone Structure, as well as the two towers adjacent to the ramp: the southern Great Tower, which they attributed to the "Early Hebrew period"; and the northern Maccabean Tower (1926, map in back pocket). This fortification system has been widely identified as part of the late Hellenistic, Hasmonean first wall of Jerusalem (e.g., Geva 2003a, 529–34; Wightman 1993, 88–94).

In the 1960s, the area was explored by Kenyon (for the final report, see Steiner 2001). On the eastern slope (in her Area A, with subareas AI–XXVIII), Kenyon exposed parts of the Stepped Stone Structure with domestic units built over it and investigated the set of the underlying terraces. In the late 1970s and early 1980s, Shiloh continued the exploration of the eastern slope (his Area G, Shiloh 1984; for additional data on Shiloh's excavations, see Cahill 2003a), studying, in the main, the same structures dealt with by Kenyon and their extensions.

The extensive exploration of the site, and the fact that certain areas were later backfilled, has affected the state of preservation of the ancient buildings. Modern restorations and additions are also evident. In the case of the southern tower, this can easily be traced by comparing Macalister and Duncan's photographs (1926, fig. 46) with what currently exists. Shiloh described a massive revetment that supports the northern tower as a "modern retaining wall" (no. 6 in Shiloh 1984, pl. 27:1), and Steiner noted that "part of the northern ramp had been restored with cement by the Department of Antiquities of Palestine" (2001, 51).

The Finds according to Eilat Mazar

Eilat Mazar did not present the various elements in her excavation according to numbered strata; rather, she referred to them in terms of labels (e.g., the earth accumulation, the Large Stone Structure) and periods. In what follows we summarize her finds from bedrock to the Byzantine period (see E. Mazar 2007 in general; photograph on 31 for the stratigraphy of the first four elements):

(1) In several spots, the excavation reached bedrock with rock-cut cupmarks that were dated to the Chalcolithic period.

(2) Next there is a whitish, leveled surface that fills crevices in the bedrock and creates a flattened surface with plots of even bedrocks. It was dated between the Chalcolithic period (the cupmarks below it) and the Middle Bronze Age (the earliest pottery in the layer above it; see below). Eilat Mazar (2006b, 21; 2006c, 12) suggested that in one place the area had been flattened in order to prepare for activity in the next phase.

(3) Atop the whitish, leveled surface lies the brown earth accumulation. Pictures published thus far show its thickness to range between circa 10 centimeters and a few dozen centimeters. A large number of pottery sherds dating to the Middle Bronze, Late Bronze, and the Iron I was found in it. Eilat Mazar compared the Iron I sherds from this layer to the Giloh and Shiloh V assemblages (2006c, 11–12). She interpreted the brown earth accumulation as an accumulated layer of debris representing centuries of activity in an open space (2006c, 11; 2007, 48), located outside the limit of the second-millennium city. Following Macalister and Duncan (1926, 15), she believes that the Bronze Age city was situated farther to the south on the ridge of the City of David (E. Mazar 2006b; 2006c, 12; 2007, 16–17, 28, 52).

(4) Remains of massive walls constructed of big stones were built over the brown earth accumulation. Eilat Mazar interpreted these remains as belonging to a *single* building that she labeled the Large Stone Structure (fig. 7.1). According to Mazar, the main wall of this building (Wall 107), described as "slightly curved," runs from west to east and is 28.4 meters long and 2.5–3.0 meters wide. Walls oriented perpendicularly to Wall 107 and bonded to it were unearthed along its southern side. The walls found on the northern side of the excavated area adjoin Wall 107 but are not bonded to it. Mazar (2006c, 12–13; 2007, 60) argued that the latter walls belong to a later phase of construction of the Large Stone Structure. The eastern wall of Mazar's Large Stone Structure (Wall 20) runs along the eastern edge of the crest of the ridge, above the steep slope, immediately to the west of the Stepped Stone Structure. Macalister and Duncan's northern Maccabean Tower adjoins the outer, eastern side of Wall 20. No floor levels related to the Large Stone Structure have been uncovered. Fragments of

several Iron IIA vessels were found in a narrow slot between walls in the northeastern sector of the excavation area (Locus 47).

Mazar dated the construction of the original building to circa 1000 BCE (2007, 17–18, 63; see also A. Mazar 2006b, 269–70) and identified it with the palace that, according to 2 Sam 5:11, the Phoenicians built for King David. She interpreted the additions on the northern side of the building as a reinforcement carried out prior to Pharaoh Sheshonq I's attack on Jerusalem (2007, 61–62; for the foundations of Mazar's dating, see below).

According to Mazar (2007, 67), the Large Stone Structure continued to be in use during Iron Age IIB, until the destruction of Jerusalem in 586 BCE. Iron IIB pottery was found in two locations (Loci 39 and 47), both unconnected to floors. No remains were assigned to the Persian period.

The city wall built on top of the eastern slope and the two towers adjoining it were late Hellenistic and identified with the Hasmonean fortification (E. Mazar 2007, 71). This includes the segment of the city wall to the north of the northern tower, which Kenyon identified (1974, 191) with the fortifications built by Nehemiah. According to this view, Wall 20, which marks the eastern limit of the Large Stone Structure, was reused by the Hasmoneans in their fortification system (E. Mazar 2007, plan on 73). Among the remains of the Second Temple period, Mazar describes a cistern with two compartments and a stone-built arched roof, first exposed by Macalister and Duncan (1926, 93–96, fig. 80). According to her observation, an "arched cistern is located at the western end of our excavation area, its arch having been built into W107 of the Large Stone Structure.... The impression already received is that the cistern was hewn in the earliest stages of human activity in this area. Once the Large Stone Structure was built [… the Iron Age IIA] *the cistern was incorporated into the structure*, and would subsequently be used continuously in the preceding periods of activity" (E. Mazar 2007, 73, emphasis added). A ritual bath (*mikveh*), first exposed by Macalister and Duncan (1926, pl. VI), is also attributed by Mazar (2007, 75) to the Hasmonean period on the basis of coins of Alexander Jannaeus discovered within its walls. The ritual bath did not cut any of the walls of the Large Stone Structure.

An Early Roman (Herodian) vaulted chamber was built over and into the walls of the Large Stone Structure (E. Mazar 2007, photograph on 74).

7. Has King David's Palace in Jerusalem Been Found?

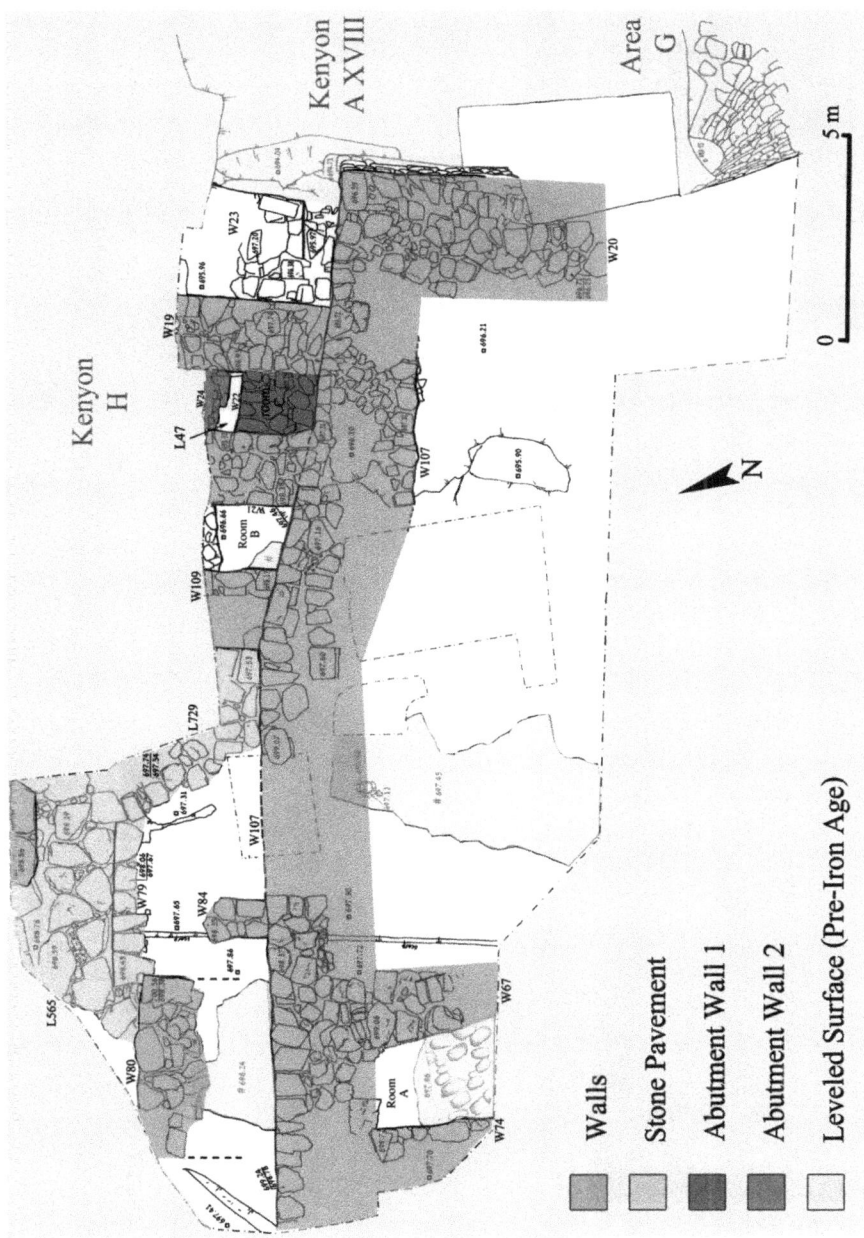

Fig. 7.1. A plan of the Large Stone Structure (courtesy of E. Mazar; after E. Mazar 2007, 59).

All the remains described above were sealed by the so-called House of Eusebius, which extended over a large part of the area; it was excavated by Macalister and Duncan (1926, 105–19) and now partially by Mazar (2006a, 23; 2007, 77).

The Finds: An Alternative Interpretation

Below the Large Stone Structure

Eilat Mazar dated the cupmarks in the bedrock on the basis of their similarity to cupmarks at other Chalcolithic sites, as well as the discovery of Chalcolithic sherds by Shiloh and by Reich and Shukron in their excavations on the eastern slope (E. Mazar 2007, 21–22). It seems, however, that the earliest sherds found by Mazar in this specific area date to the Early Bronze Age (2007, 23). Therefore, although the dating of the cupmarks to the Chalcolithic period is possible, it is not the only possibility.

The whitish, leveled surface, which had been laid in order to flatten the area, did not yield pottery (E. Mazar 2006b, 21; 2007, 29–30). It was dated between the Chalcolithic period (the cupmarks in the bedrock) and the Middle Bronze (the earliest pottery in the overlying brown earth accumulation; 2007, 20–21). The latter argument holds only if the brown earth accumulation indeed represents an accumulation of in situ activity rather than a fill or a make-up for construction (see below).

The brown earth accumulation discovered below the walls assigned to the Large Stone Structure yielded Middle Bronze, Late Bronze, and Iron I pottery. Mazar interpreted this layer as representing long-term activity in the second millennium BCE in an open space outside the city (2006c, 11; 2007, 48). Accordingly, she argues (following Macalister and Duncan 1926, 15) that the Bronze Age city was located farther to the south on the ridge of the City of David (E. Mazar 2006b, 22, fig. on 26; 2006c, 12; 2007, 16–17, 28, 52). We find both suggestions difficult to accept.

The brown earth accumulation seems to be too thin for an accumulation of several centuries. This and the lack of inner stratification suggest that it could have been laid here as a fill or a make-up for construction. In other words, it could have been brought here from another location.

The idea that the Middle Bronze fortified settlement was restricted to the southern part of the ridge is ostensibly based on Macalister and Duncan's assumption that a depression ran in this place, oriented from east to west across the ridge, which they labeled the Zedek Valley (1926, 15). However, Rock Scarp A (1926, fig. 39 and pl. I)—probably the reason for this theory—seems to be no more than an ancient quarry. Indeed, Kenyon indicated the obvious, that the bedrock along the crest of the ridge rises toward the north (Steiner 2001, fig. 4.18).[1] Mazar's theory seems to have been affected by her own interpretation of the biblical verses rather than based on factual data (see discussion below).

Regarding the time when the brown earth accumulation was laid in this spot, the latest sherds found in it were compared by Mazar to the pottery of Giloh and Shiloh V (2006c, 11–12; Early and Middle Iron I, respectively; see Finkelstein and Piasetzky 2006b). The published drawings (E. Mazar 2007, 50) show only cooking pots with everted rims, in the Late Bronze tradition. But the accompanying picture (2007, 47) shows cooking pots with erect rims as well and at least one rim that seems to date to the late Iron I or early Iron IIA. Indeed, in one place Mazar (2006a, 25) acknowledges that the latest Iron I sherds from the brown earth accumulation date to the very end of the Iron I. In low-chronology terms this means the tenth century BCE.

Two olive pits and one bone from the brown earth accumulation were radiocarbon dated (E. Mazar 2007, 49). One olive pit was measured 3545±50, which gives a calibrated 1 σ date of 1950–1770 BCE. The bone was measured 2960±50, which translates into a calibrated 1 σ date of 1270–1080 BCE. The second olive pit from this layer was radiocarbon dated to 2780±50, which provides a 1 σ calibrated date of 1000–890 BCE (58.9 percent) or 870–840 (9.3 percent). The latter sample translates into the late Iron I/early Iron IIA in low-chronology terms. To sum up this issue, the latest pottery and the latest ^{14}C date from the brown earth accumulation point to the tenth/ninth century BCE.

The Large Stone Structure

As mentioned above, the assumption that the walls of the Large Stone Structure are all segments of a single monumental structure forms the

---

1. Finkelstein and Herzog find it difficult to accept that a fortified Middle Bronze stronghold was constructed on a slope, dominated by the higher ground on the continuation of the ridge to the north.

basis of Mazar's stratigraphical and chronological analysis. Mazar's dating of the Large Stone Structure to circa 1000 BCE is based on her interpretation of the biblical text and three archaeological arguments:

(1) It was built on top of the brown earth accumulation, the latest pottery of which dates to the Iron I.

(2) The Large Stone Structure and the Stepped Stone Structure are in fact parts of a single architectural complex (E. Mazar 2007, 46, 64). The latter dates between the Iron I (pottery found by Kenyon under the terraces, located, in turn, under the Stepped Stone Structure; Steiner 1994) and the tenth century (Shiloh's Stratum 14 pottery found according to Cahill [2003a, 57–61, fig. 1.13] in the earliest surface in a house built into the Stepped Stone Structure on the slope).

(3) Locus 47, a 25- to 70-centimeter narrow slot between walls in the northeastern section of the excavated area, yielded large fragments of several late Iron IIA vessels, including a Black-on-Red juglet (E. Mazar 2006c, 14, fig. 4; 2007, 66). Mazar interpreted the construction of this room as a second phase in the history of the building.

Regarding argument 1 above, we have already shown that the latest sherds in the brown earth accumulation under the building date as late as the tenth to ninth century BCE (low chronology; late eleventh to ninth century according to the conventional chronology) and that it seems that this is not an in situ accumulation but rather a fill-debris that was brought to this location from somewhere else on the crest of the ridge or its slope.

As for argument 2, Mazar's interpretation, according to which the Stepped Stone Structure and the Large Stone Structure belong to one Iron IIA complex, is based on circumstantial considerations that are open to alternative interpretations. Although the Large Stone Structure reaches close to the top edge of the Stepped Stone Structure, no clear-cut, physical connection between the two structures has been established. Also, it is doubtful whether such a connection—if it existed at all—can be established, as the present top of the Stepped Stone Structure seems to be a modern restoration. As will be discussed below, the Stepped Stone Structure seems to represent more than one phase of construction, with its upper part probably dating to the Hellenistic period, if not later.

Regarding argument 3—the late Iron IIA pottery in Locus 47—the following observations are pertinent:

(A) It is difficult to establish the date of the walls in the northeastern sector of the excavated area (see below).

(B) With no floor in Locus 47, it is difficult to know if the Iron IIA pottery found there belongs to the original room (Room C). The picture of this location (E. Mazar 2007, photograph on 61, right) seems to indicate that the relevant vessels were found in stone and pottery rubble. The fact that they are all broken (two "half" bowls, one "third" of a bowl, a fragment of a krater, a "quarter" or "third" of a jug, and about "half" of a juglet) is a clear indication that they were *not* found in situ. Significantly, the excavator herself doubts whether the pottery in Locus 47 was found in situ and suggests that it is part of a fill that had been brought here from elsewhere: "The state of preservation of the vessels suggests that they were at some nearby location prior to the construction of W22 and W24, and somehow were deposited at this spot when the walls were built" (E. Mazar 2007, 61).

(C) The upper part of the same locus (Locus 47) yielded Iron IIB pottery (E. Mazar 2007, 61 n. 121, fig. on 70, nos. 6, 7, 10). The loci numbers from this place apparently disclose that at least one Iron IIB item (fig. on 70, no. 7, from Locus 678) was found under four (of the seven) Iron IIA items (from Locus 661)! The division between lower Iron IIA and higher Iron IIB material within Locus 47 is therefore questionable, as is the idea that this is an in situ assemblage.

(D) Iron IIA pottery was found *under* two elements in nearby Room B (E. Mazar 2007, 61).

(E) A bone found in Locus 47 was radiocarbon dated to 2725±70. The calibrated 1 σ date is 930–800 BCE 67.4 percent.

To sum up this point, the Iron IIA pottery in Locus 47 cannot be used to date the surrounding walls.

On the other hand, there are strong indications that some or all parts of the Large Stone Structure may have been built later than the Iron IIA.

(1) Much activity took place in this general area during the Iron IIB. Macalister and Duncan (1926, 179–91, pls. XIX–XX) published typical pottery, *lmlk* seal impressions, figurines, and even a Hebrew ostracon dating from this period, all of which were uncovered in their excavations. Their finds fit the situation in other parts of the City of David, where the Iron IIB period is well represented, including Shiloh's Area G immediately to the east of the area under discussion (Shiloh 1984, 4) and the so-called Ophel area to the south of the Temple Mount (Mazar and Mazar 1989). The Iron IIB period is hardly represented in Mazar's excavations, but this could have been the result of the clearing of this area

by Macalister and Duncan (or in antiquity, by the builders of the Large Stone Structure; see below).

(2) Several of Mazar's finds indicate the possibility that walls of the Large Stone Structure were built in post–Iron Age times: a late Iron II bulla was found "tucked away among the masonry of the Large Stone Structure" (E. Mazar 2007, 19); Herodian pottery was found between and under some of the boulders that covered the Large Stone Structure (2007, 56), and, in fact, the debris in the spaces between the walls yielded similar pottery. However, these finds could have reached these places as the result of back-filling activities by Macalister and Duncan.

(3) The walls of the Hasmonean ritual bath (*mikveh*) and Wall 107 of the Large Stone Structure were built in the same orientation and approximately at the same elevation, including the bottom level of their foundations (compare plans in E. Mazar 2007, 59, 73).

(4) A Byzantine wall was built on a flattened part of a wall that, according to Mazar, belongs to the Large Stone Structure (see photograph in 2007, 31).

The Stepped Stone Structure

Before continuing, we must take a closer, fresh look at the Stepped Stone Structure. A discussion of its nature and date is relevant for understanding the nature and date of the walls unearthed on the crest of the ridge to its west. Various structural elements have been associated with the Stepped Stone Structure, having been uncovered in several excavations and analyzed by various scholars. Amihai Mazar has divided the Stepped Stone Structure into five "components" (2006b, 257–59; see fig. 7.2 below); for the sake of convenience, we shall use his division. Here we are concerned in the main with his Component 2, that is, the Stepped Stone Mantle—defined as the "mantle wall" by several scholars (see 2006b, 258)—extending over the upper part of the slope and reaching the city wall located at the top. The Stepped Stone Mantle of the Stepped Stone Structure extends above a system of terraces (Component 1) whose structural relationship to the Stepped Stone Mantle and their dates do not concern us here. Further remains uncovered by Kenyon in her Trench I, and defined by A. Mazar as Components 3, 4, and 5, are not physically connected to Components 1 and 2 and are different in character; their relationship to the latter is not clear.

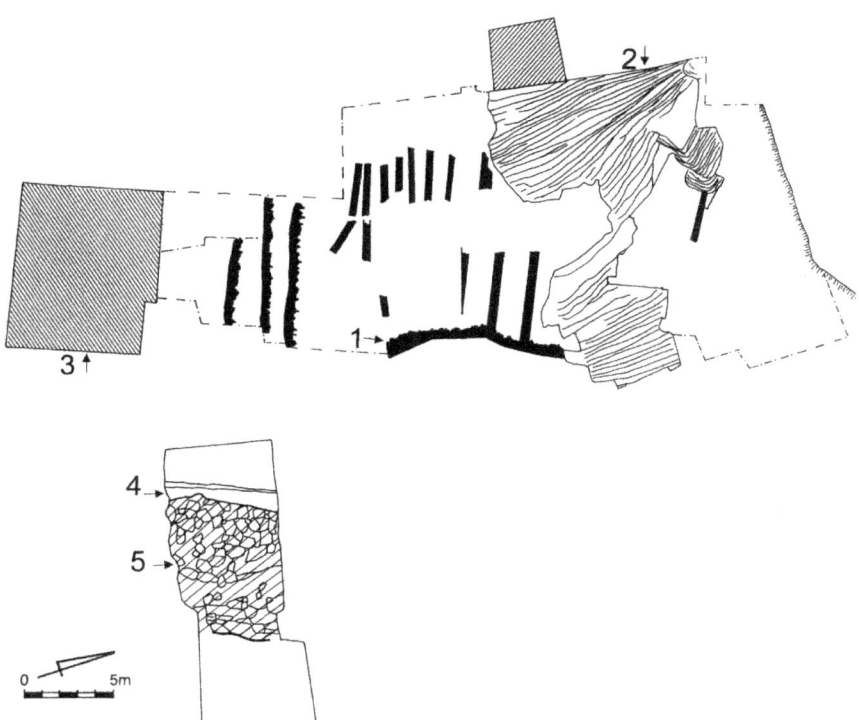

Fig. 7.2. Schematic plan of the Stepped Stone Structure with Components 1–5 marked (after A. Mazar 2006b, fig. 1).

The common view assumes that the Stepped Stone Mantle (Component 2) had been erected in a single construction effort, not later than the Iron IIA, and was in use for a long period. A fresh examination by us in the field and a reassessment of the published data lead us to conclude that there are significant structural differences between the lower and upper parts of this complex Stepped Stone Mantle and that it represents more than one building activity. The recurrent need for a revetment in this spot was first observed by Duncan, who discovered a fissure in the rock scarp: "The hollow or fissure referred to is filled up with great boulders, as far inwards as I could see, and for a considerable distance under the foundations of the great Jebusite Eastern Rampart" (in Macalister and Duncan 1926, 52).

The different phases in the Stepped Stone Mantle are evident in the size of the stone blocks used for construction (see fig. 7.3; E. Mazar 2007, photograph on 45). The blocks in the lower courses are significantly smaller than those in the upper third of the structure. Such arrangement negates the ordinary method of constructing retaining walls, which regularly consist of larger stone blocks at the bottom and smaller ones at the top.[2] The orientation of the two parts also differ: the lower courses, of smaller stone blocks (uncovered by Shiloh 1984, fig, 16, pl. 29:1), run in a south–north orientation, while the upper courses are oriented toward the northwest.

Two pieces of information possibly indicate the date of the lower part of the Stepped Stone Mantle. First, the latest sherds retrieved from between the stones in Components 3, 4, and 5 date to the Iron IIA (Steiner 1994, 19; 2001, 50; 2003, 358). However, as the connection of these structures to the Stepped Stone Mantle is not firmly established, this datum should be used with reservation. Second, Iron II houses were built over the lower part of the Stepped Stone Mantle. Cahill argued that pottery from Shiloh's Strata 14 and 13 (tenth and ninth century BCE according to the traditional dating system) was found on the two lower-floor levels in the Burnt Room House, which was built over the Stepped Stone Structure (Cahill 2003a, 56–66, figs. 1.11–1.14). However, only sherds, rather than complete vessels, were uncovered here, and they are registered as originating from ten different loci. Quite possibly, the sherds described by Cahill are associated with fills supporting the "upper" floors of the Burnt Room House (which was built on a steep slope) rather than from earlier, lower floors. It is noteworthy that neither Kenyon nor Shiloh observed any tenth- or ninth-century occupational layers in these houses and that they both dated them to the second half of the seventh century (Kenyon 1974, 137; Shiloh 1984, 28). To sum up this issue, the lower part of the Stepped Stone Mantle could have been built in a later phase of the Iron IIA (pottery of this period was found nearby between the stone courses in walls of Components 3, 4, and 5) or the early phase of the Iron IIB (before the construction of the Burnt Room House in the late Iron II). In both low-chronology and modified-conventional-chronology' (A. Mazar 2005) terms, this means the ninth–eighth centuries BCE.

---

2. A good parallel is the retaining wall of the stairwell of the Tel Beersheba water system (Herzog 2002b, 92).

7. Has King David's Palace in Jerusalem Been Found?

Fig. 7.3. Aerial view of the Stepped Stone Structure. Note the differences in the size of the blocks and orientation between the lower and upper courses.

Regarding the upper part of the Stepped Stone Mantle, it seems that its upper courses are incorporated into the late Hellenistic, Hasmonean city wall. In other words, it must have been constructed—or at least rebuilt—in the late Hellenistic period. This date was originally suggested by Kenyon (1974, 192–94). Shiloh also observed the association of the upper part of the Stepped Stone Mantle with the Hellenistic fortification system: "the line of the 'First Wall' and its towers integrated the top of the stepped stone structure" (Shiloh 1984, 30). Most likely the upper part of the Stepped Stone Mantle was built (or rebuilt) in order to stabilize the slope and support the city wall; the entire slope was then covered by a thick earthen glacis (1984, 20–21, figs. 17, 28).[3]

Discussion

With the absence of floors, and taking into consideration constructional disturbances in the Roman and Byzantine periods and disturbances as a result of modern research, the walls of the Large Stone Structure cannot be accurately dated. The straightforward archaeological data indicate only that these walls should be dated to after the latest pottery in the brown earth accumulation (late Iron I/early Iron IIA) and before the Herodian period (the date of the vaulted chamber built over and incorporated into Wall 107). In the Persian and early Hellenistic periods, activity in the entire City of David was sparse, and most of it was concentrated to the south of this spot (Finkelstein 2008b). Three options for the construction of the walls of the Large Stone Structure should therefore be considered: the Iron IIA, the Iron IIB, and the late Hellenistic, Hasmonean period.

One can argue, with Eilat Mazar, that the original Stepped Stone Structure (more accurately termed above as the Stepped Stone Mantle) was constructed in order to support the slope and prepare for the construction of the Large Stone Structure. The large building blocks and the Proto-Ionic capital found by Kenyon (1963, 16, pl. VIIIB) in the bottom of her Square A XVIII immediately to the east of the Large Stone Structure

---

3. The upper, flat course of the Stepped Stone Mantle is a modern reconstruction.

7. Has King David's Palace in Jerusalem Been Found?

and to the north of the Stepped Stone Structure could have collapsed from the building on the crest of the ridge (E. Mazar 2007, 54).

However, dating all the walls of the Large Stone Structure to the Iron IIA raises serious difficulties, all presented above: a late Iron II bulla was found between stones of one wall; early Roman pottery was found between and under its boulders and in the spaces between the walls; a Hasmonean ritual bath (*mikveh*) was built in the same orientation and elevation as the walls of the Large Stone Structure; and a Byzantine wall was built directly on top of a wall of the Large Stone Structure. Each of these problems can be explained away individually, mainly as resulting from the severe damage inflicted on this area in Roman and later periods and by modern researchers; as a *set* of difficulties, however, they cannot be easily dismissed.

Dating the walls of the Large Stone Structure to the Iron IIB would not resolve the problems listed above. In fact, this option would add another obstacle: the nearly total absence of Iron IIB finds, even in isolated pockets, in Mazar's excavations.

This leaves us with the third alternative, according to which the walls of the Large Stone Structure were built in the Hellenistic period. But first one needs to examine whether the elements uncovered by Mazar indeed belong to a single structure.

The plan of the Large Stone Structure consists of three distinguishable elements (fig. 7.1 above): two described by Mazar as one feature (Wall 107), forming the northern end of the building, and one labeled Wall 20, marking its eastern end. As far as we can judge, Wall 107 in fact represents two separate structures: a well-built western part and flimsy remains on the eastern side of the area (fig. 7.4). The two could not have belonged to a single building (see photographs in E. Mazar 2007, 17, 57). The western part of Wall 107 is built in a straight line and is made of carefully laid large stone blocks, mostly placed as headers along the face of the wall. The eastern part of Wall 107 is constructed with less care, forming a winding line that runs diagonal to the western part of the wall. It is built of smaller stone blocks, mostly laid with their long side facing the edge of the wall. The single place that allegedly presents the full width of the wall (E. Mazar 2007, 59) shows a heap of stones rather than a carefully built wall. Indeed, the two "faces" of this section are not parallel. Moreover, a few stones in the eastern part of Wall 107 were placed *above* the northeastern corner of Wall 106 of the large cistern dated by Mazar to the Second Temple period (2007, photograph on 74).

Wall 20 of the suggested Large Stone Structure (fig. 7.1 above) is clearly part of the late Hellenistic, Hasmonean city wall (also E. Mazar 2007, plan on 73). In Mazar's opinion, the wall was originally constructed in the Iron IIA—when it was connected to the Stepped Stone Structure—and was reused in the late Hellenistic period. As we argued above, the upper part of the Stepped Stone Structure should be assigned to the late Hellenistic period, and thus the assumption that Wall 20 was originally built in the Iron Age IIA remains without basis.

The well-built western section of Wall 107 is evidently part of a large structure (fig. 7.5). An examination of the plans of the lowest remains recorded by Macalister and Duncan (1926, pl. V) in this area reveals the presence of a thick wall running from east to west, parallel and to the south of the western section of Wall 107. They labeled it the Inner Wall and attributed it to the Jebusite Stratum. When the Inner Wall and the western section of Wall 107 are drawn together, they form a rectangular structure, with a possible entrance in the southern side (fig. 7.6).

An additional unit that seems to belong to this structure is the ritual bath (*mikveh*). This structure, too, was first exposed by Macalister and Duncan and assigned by them to the Hebrew Stratum (1926, pl. VI). Both the orientation and level of the walls (including foundations) of the ritual bath perfectly fit the plan of the western part of Wall 107 and should probably be attributed to the same layer (fig. 7.5).

Figures 7.5–6 show the above three elements restored together as a single building. The possible date of this building in the late Hellenistic period is indicated by the Alexander Jannaeus coins found in the walls of the ritual bath. Other elements in this area that should be attributed to this phase of construction are the city wall, with the two towers extending along the eastern edge of the ridge, and the upper part of the Stepped Stone Structure. All these elements—the rectangular building with the ritual bath, the city wall, and the upper part of the Stepped Stone Structure—make one coherent plan.

Dating the main construction operation in this area to the late Hellenistic (Hasmonean) period would eliminate all the difficulties raised above. The later finds, including the Early Roman pottery found in the spaces between the walls, comply with this dating. This option may also supply a partial explanation for the absence of Iron IIB remains in Mazar's excavations: these remains were removed in preparation for construction in the Hellenistic period. It also explains why the rectangular building in

Fig. 7.4. General view of the excavation area, looking east. Note the carefully built western section of Wall 107 and the flimsy eastern section, oriented diagonally to the former (courtesy of E. Mazar; after E. Mazar 2007, 57).

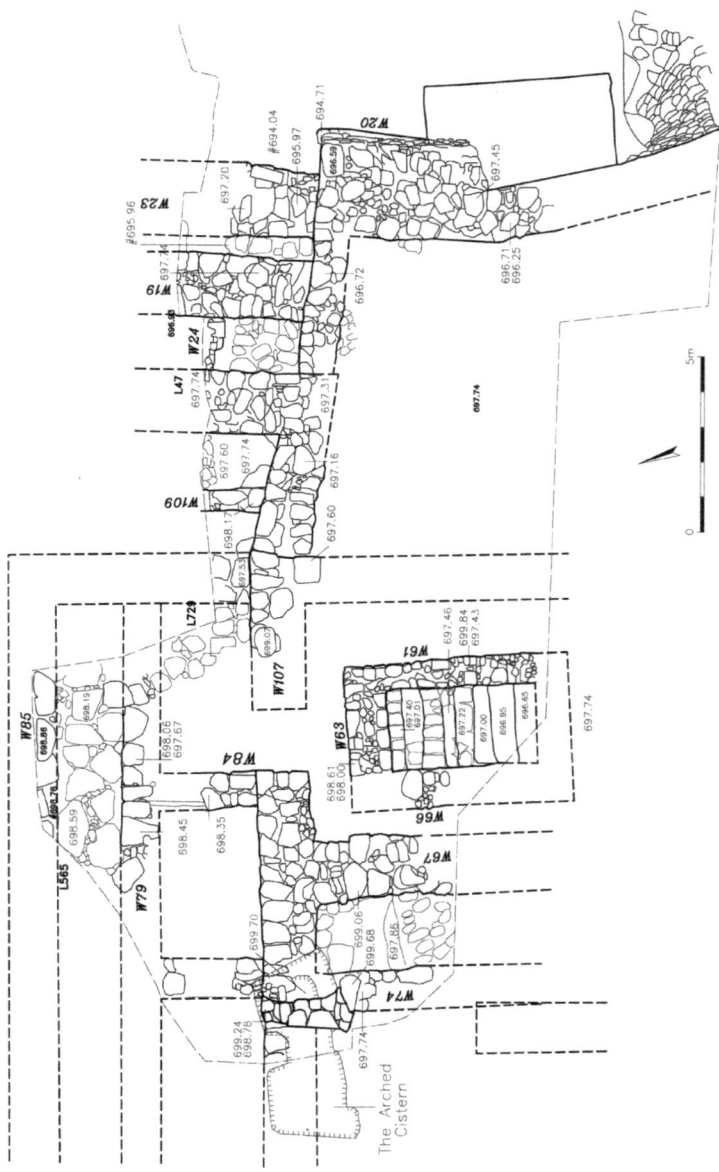

Fig. 7.5. Alternative interpretation of the Large Stone Structure and other remains (prepared by Ze'ev Herzog).

7. Has King David's Palace in Jerusalem Been Found?

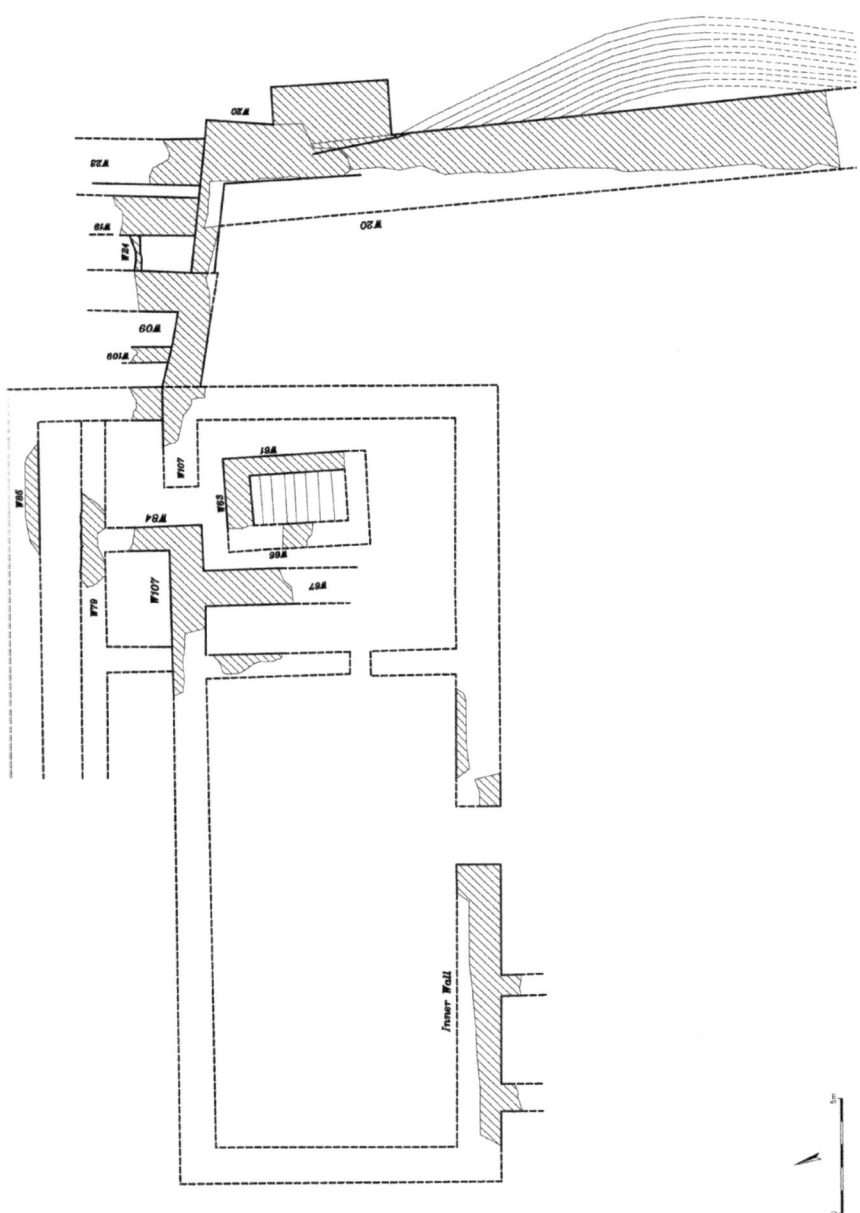

Fig. 7.6. A suggested reconstruction of the remains (prepared by Ze'ev Herzog).

the west seems to be incorporated (through a set of walls) with a segment of the Hasmonean city wall in the east.

Ostensibly, a late Hellenistic option for the dating of these elements faces two difficulties: (1) The construction method of Wall 107 is somewhat different from that of the city wall. This can be explained as representing the different functions of the two elements. (2) The entire history of this part of the City of David in the Bronze and Iron Ages would be reduced to an accumulation of less then one meter (the brown earth accumulation). But this is not a unique case in the City of David. Structural remains of the Bronze and Iron Ages have completely been eradicated in other locations, such as Kenyon's Site K (1965, 14), Shiloh's Area K (Ariel and Magness 1992), and the area excavated by Crowfoot in the Tyropoeon Valley (Crowfoot and Fitzgerald 1929, 7–58) as interpreted by Ussishkin (2006a, 154–59).

Eilat Mazar's "Historical" Interpretation

Though historical interpretation is not the goal of this chapter, it is worth citing Mazar's arguments, because they illuminate her views on biblical archaeology and biblical history and provide the background for her interpretation of the above-discussed remains: their function and their date.

Mazar follows two principles: (1) biblical data are accepted without criticism as the basis for archaeological interpretation; (2) therefore, biblical information takes precedence over archaeological data. Mazar's discussion of the "Solomonic city wall" in the so-called Ophel area to the south of the Temple Mount (E. Mazar 2006d) is a case in point. As she admits, the chronological data recovered in her excavations indicate that the *sole* Iron Age fortification system extending in this area was in use during the eighth–seventh centuries BCE. However, according to the biblical sources the Solomonic city wall must have passed here, hence the fortification system in question must be Solomonic in date.

Turning back to the area of the Large Stone Structure, we see that Mazar reads the biblical references to Jerusalem in a sequential, literal way. Ignoring thirty years of research on the book of Genesis and the patriarchal narratives (e.g., Van Seters 1975; Thompson 1974), she interprets Genesis as reflecting Middle Bronze Age realities, referring to Melchizedek king of Salem (Gen 14:18, a late, probably postexilic source; e.g., Gunkel 1901,

288–90; Astour 1966, 67–74; Van Seters 1975, 119–20; Soggin 1995; Carr 1996, 163–66) as the king of Middle Bronze Jerusalem (E. Mazar 2007, 14). Disregarding decades of research on the conquest traditions (e.g., Noth 1938b; Alt 1939; Weippert 1971; Van Seters 1990; Na'aman 1994), Mazar reads the typically Deuteronomistic book of Joshua as an early account of the conquest of Canaan. She therefore dates Adoni-zedek king of Jerusalem of Josh 10 to the Late Bronze Age (E. Mazar 2007, 14, 37). In her opinion, Jerusalem does not appear in the detailed description of the conquest of the Shephelah and the southern highlands (Josh 10) because its huge Middle Bronze fortifications, which continued to be in use in the Late Bronze Age, deterred Joshua from assaulting the city (2007, 37; we should note that there is no clue in the archaeological record for a Late Bronze reuse of the Middle Bronze fortification).

Mazar proposes reading the story of the conquest of Jerusalem by the tribe of Judah in Judg 1:8, "after the death of Joshua," against an Iron I background (E. Mazar 2007, 37 n. 71). Traces of fire in one spot (under Room B of the Large Stone Structure) should, in her opinion, be associated with this tradition (2007, 47–48). "The Jebusite city conquered by King David was strong and well-fortified. Although no considerable architectural remains that can be confidently attributed to this period … have been uncovered, the biblical descriptions in 2 Sam 5:6–9 and 1 Chr 11:4–7 accord with what we know of Jerusalem in previous periods—an important capital city surrounded by massive fortifications." After "his takeover David let the city's king … and inhabitants live (1 Chr 11:4–8), and even hastened to incorporate them into his regime, as indicated by the story of Uriah the Hittite, one of David's warriors" (E. Mazar 2007, 44–45). The latter two citations are most telling for Mazar's method, as indicated above: there is no archaeological evidence, but the biblical story, including references to the fourth-century BCE book of Chronicles, is sufficient for historical reconstruction of events that ostensibly took place circa 1000 BCE.[4]

Mazar was driven to dig in this spot by the idea that the palace of King David must have been located here (E. Mazar 1997; 2007, 7–8). She follows 2 Sam 5:11, according to which the artisans of Hiram king of Tyre built a

---

4. Elsewhere E. Mazar (2007, 19, 64) uses toponyms mentioned in Neh 3 to identify buildings in tenth-century BCE Jerusalem.

palace for King David. She identifies the location of the palace according to 2 Sam 5:17 (E. Mazar 2006a, 18–20; 2007, 52): "When the Philistines heard that David had been anointed king over Israel, all the Philistines went up in search of David, but David heard about it and went down to the stronghold" (NRSVue). Mazar believes (following Macalister and Duncan 1926, 15) that the Bronze Age city was located farther south on the ridge of the City of David (E. Mazar 2006b; 2006c, 12; 2007, 16–17, 28):

> It appears as though David was residing in his new palace at the time of the Philistine attack, and thus was forced to leave the palace and go down to the fortress, where he would have felt more protected. It follows that the city fortress stood to the south of the palace. Since it can be reasonably assumed that this fortress had been built at the northern edge of the Canaanite city ... the new palace, consequently, must have been built just to the outside of the city wall. (E. Mazar 2007, 52; also 2006a, 18–20)

As we have already shown, there is no archaeological or topographical evidence to support the view that the Bronze Age stronghold was restricted to the southern part of the ridge. This settlement could have included the area excavated by Mazar and even areas farther north. Needless to say, we do not accept such a literal reading of 2 Sam 5:17.

Summary

Eilat Mazar's excavations in the City of David add several points of information to what we know about the history of this problematic site. Yet, the main find—the Large Stone Structure—was not properly interpreted and dated. First, it seems to consist of several elements, mainly a rectangular building in the west and the city wall in the east. Second, all one can safely say is that its various elements postdate the late Iron I/early Iron IIA and predate the Roman period. Circumstantial evidence seems to suggest dating at least some of the elements to the late Hellenistic period.

Beyond archaeology, one wonders about the interpretation of the finds. The biblical text dominates this field operation, not archaeology. Had it not been for Mazar's literal reading of the biblical text, she never would have dated the remains to the tenth century BCE with such confidence. This is an excellent example of the weakness of traditional, highly literal, biblical archaeology—a discipline that dominated research until the 1960s, that was weakened and almost disappeared from the scene in the later years of the twentieth century, and that reemerged with all its attributes in the City of David in 2005.

Addendum

1. For a more nuanced, updated interpretation of the remains discussed here, see chapter 8, where I suggest that some of the remains belong to the Iron IIA while others date to the Hellenistic period. See also the summary in the addendum to chapter 8.

2. On the rock-cut depression that runs across the City of David ridge, see recently Gadot et al. 2023, who argue that "by the Late Iron IIA, the ditch served as a moat between the acropolis—possibly including the Temple Mount—and the city" (140).

(a) This depression does not look like a defensive feature. Iron IIA moats (for instance, those uncovered at Jezreel and Khirbet Atarus in Moab) are a few meters wide with vertical rock-cut sides, rather than a very broad (35 meters!) depression, as is the case in Jerusalem. Several researchers suggested that this feature is a result of quarrying operations.

(b) The data at hand do not allow dating this operation.

8

The Large Stone Structure in Jerusalem: Reality versus Yearning

---

This is a more advanced and neuanced treatment of the finds above the Gihon Spring: both the Stepped Stone Structure and the Large Stone Structure. In chapter 7 I dealt with the results of Eilat Mazar's 2005 excavations. Here I include the results of the second season of excavations in this area in 2006–2007 and relate to articles that appeared after the publication of the original article appearing here as chapter 7.

Two opposing interpretations of recent finds in Eilat Mazar's excavations in the City of David have now been presented to the scholarly community. The first was published by the excavator herself (E. Mazar 2007, 2009) and is fully supported by Amihai Mazar (2010, 34–45). Much of the Eilat Mazar–Amihai Mazar analysis is now backed by Faust (2010). The second interpretation of the finds, based on the results of the first season of excavation at the site in 2005, was presented by Herzog, Singer-Avitz, Ussishkin, and me (see ch. 7 above).

The Mazar–Mazar–Faust interpretation of the finds is based on three pillars:

1. Massive walls built of large boulders uncovered by E. Mazar belong to one large building, labeled the Large Stone Structure (see also A. Mazar 2010, 40; Faust 2010, 118).
2. The Large Stone Structure and the Stepped Stone Structure (referring to the stone mantle over the terraces on the slope; see Cahill 2003a, 33–54; A. Mazar 2006b, 257–65; ch. 7 above, with refer-

ences to previous research) form one architectural complex (E. Mazar throughout; A. Mazar, e.g., 2010, 45; Faust 2010, 117).
3. The construction of this complex should be dated to the Iron I or the Iron IIA, in any event no later than the tenth century BCE.[1]

According to the second analysis of the finds (ch. 7 above; see also Finkelstein, Fantalkin, and Piasetzky 2008):

a. The remains interpreted by E. Mazar as belonging to a Large Stone Structure do not form a single building. Some of the walls may date to the late Iron IIA (in radiocarbon terms, the mid- to second half of the ninth century BCE),[2] while other walls probably belong to the Hellenistic period.
b. The Stepped Stone Structure cannot be considered a monolithic construction. There was an ongoing need to support the slope here, as this is the narrowest point on the ridge of the City of David. Therefore, the terraces on the slope and the stone mantle (the Stepped Stone Structure) had to be renovated time and again. In all probability, the lower part of the Stepped Stone Structure dates to the Iron IIA, while the upper part seems to date to the Hellenistic period; the latter was most likely built as support for the late Hellenistic First Wall (the Hasmonean fortification).
c. There seems to be a connection between the upper (Hellenistic) part of the Stepped Stone Structure and the Hellenistic city wall. Theoretically, there could have been a similar connection between the original, Iron Age Stepped Stone Structure and supposed Iron IIA structures that were erected on the crest of the ridge (the so-called Large Stone Structure), though such a connection does not exist today.

---

1. The main difference within the Mazar–Mazar–Faust interpretation is that E. Mazar ascribes the construction of the Large Stone Structure to King David, while A. Mazar (2010, 45) and Faust (2010, 127) identify it with the Jebusite fort conquered by King David.

2. Herzog, Singer-Avitz, and Ussishkin suggested dating all elements to the Hellenistic period, while I accept the possibility that some of the remains may date to the Iron IIA (Finkelstein, Fantalkin, and Piasetzky 2008).

8. The Large Stone Structure in Jerusalem

Faust (2010, 121) argues that the second season of excavations at the site rendered much of the second interpretation (ch. 7 above) obsolete. This is not so. In what follows I wish to examine the results of the second season in the City of David (2006–2007) and take issue with the Mazar–Mazar–Faust analysis of the finds.

General Comments on the Area of Excavations and the Remains

As a starting point, I wish to emphasize the problematic nature of the excavation area under discussion—as a caution of what can and what cannot be deduced from the remains unearthed there.

1. The architectural remains are fragmentary; almost no wall has been fully preserved.
    a. Comparing what was actually found (stone-by-stone drawing in E. Mazar 2009, 64; fig. 8.1 below) to the reconstructions (E. Mazar 2009, 65; A. Mazar 2010, 36; Faust 2010, 117) is revealing. In his plan, Faust makes an attempt to distinguish between finds and reconstruction. However, his drawing of the *actual remains* goes far beyond what was found, including some crucial points: the full eastern line of Wall 20 in his plan does not exist in E. Mazar's plan (this includes the critical point of connection between the Stepped Stone Structure and Wall 20); Wall 107, which has an angle in its northern face (an angle that makes it difficult to accept its full length as belonging to a single wall), appears in Faust's plan as a straight-line wall; Faust's drawing of the northwestern corner of the area also shows more than what was actually found.
    b. The main contribution of the second season was the uncovering of "Rooms" D and E in the eastern sector of the area. E. Mazar and Faust reconstruct a line of four rooms here, while A. Mazar draws two rooms. However, Room D is reconstructed according to two stones, each in a different wall (E. Mazar 2009, 59, plan)! So in reality, only one half of a room (Room E) can be safely reconstructed here.
2. Secure dating of a building in archaeology can be done mainly according to assemblages of finds retrieved from its floors. No such assemblage has been found in this excavation. With the pos-

Fig. 8.1. The actual remains associated with the Large Stone Structure (E. Mazar 2009, 64). Comparison to Faust's plan (2010) shows how changes in small details in the latter (e.g., the northern line of Wall 107) opens the way to an overstated reconstruction.

sible exception of Room E (but see below), not a single floor with finds exists in the entire area.

3. Structures from the Hellenistic, Roman, and later periods penetrated deep, sometimes down to bedrock, and destroyed earlier remains (E. Mazar 2009, 86). Some of these walls were oriented with earlier walls and used them as their foundations; in fact, "in many cases it was difficult to distinguish by sight the Herodian walls from the Iron Age ones" (2009, 84).

4. In many places late Hellenistic and early Roman pottery was found as deep as the massive walls interpreted as belonging to the Large Stone Structure[3] (details in ch. 7 above). In one spot a com-

---

3. Here and below I use this Mazar–Mazar–Faust term even though I do not think that evidence for such a structure exists.

plete Herodian cooking pot was found among the large boulders (E. Mazar 2009, 86); in another place a late Iron II bulla was found between the stones (E. Mazar 2007, 19).

5. The entire area under discussion had been excavated in the early twentieth century and than backfilled (Field 5 in Macalister and Duncan 1926, 2, fig. 1; see photograph at 1926, 8, and detailed map in the pocket at the end of the volume). In several places this excavation reached bedrock (1926, pl. I). As a result of this operation, many of the finds collected by E. Mazar cannot be considered as retrieved in situ. Another result of this old excavation, as well as disturbances in antiquity, is that centuries in the history of the City of David may be missing from the accumulation.

6. Modern restoration work was carried out in the upper part of the Stepped Stone Structure and the Hasmonean city wall. A. Mazar diminishes the importance of this point, saying that these works were done to the south of the current dig area, but adds an illuminating sentence: "except for some reinforcement with cement of several existing stone courses" (2010, 38). The latter includes the crucial sector of connection between the Stepped Stone Structure and Wall 20 of the Large Stone Structure; as I will show below, significant restoration work was carried out here.

Under these circumstances, stratigraphic and chronological observations are based on little solid evidence, and every reconstruction is highly hypothetical. Declaring that we are now "in possession of significant finds from what appears to be good archaeological contexts" (Faust 2010, 121) demonstrates overconfidence, to say the least.

Having pointed out the severe problems facing those who wish to deal with the architecture, stratigraphy, and dating of the remains in the area excavated by E. Mazar, I can now turn to the three foundations of the Mazar–Mazar–Faust interpretation: one Large Stone Structure, connected to the Stepped Stone Structure, and dating to the Iron I or the Iron IIA.

Do the Remains Belong to a Single Large Stone Structure?

Faust says that the "highlight of the excavations is a large and massive stone structure, which covered the entire excavation area and seems to have extended even far beyond its limits" (2010, 117). As I already mentioned above, the remains of the Large Stone Structure are fragmentary, with the reconstructions of both E. Mazar and Faust going far beyond the evidence on the ground (compare Faust 2010, fig. 1, with E. Mazar 2009, 65, and fig. 8.1 in this chapter). Moreover, much of Wall 20—the eastern and best-preserved wall of the reconstructed building—is the late Hellenistic (Hasmonean) city wall (even according to E. Mazar, 2009, 77, upper drawing; see also Shiloh 1984, pl. 27.1 and fig. 27).

No less important, nowhere does a floor connect to half Room E on one side and to massive walls that can theoretically be associated with the Large Stone Structure on the other side (see plan in E. Mazar 2009, 64). E. Mazar describes a chalk floor that ostensibly makes this connection (2009, 62), yet in the west the picture (2009, 62) seems to show that the floor goes *under* Wall 214 (incidentally, note that the questionable "connection" is in an area of two stones!), while in the east the floor ends before half Room E (2009, 64, plan; E. Mazar's suggestion that the floor was cut by a robbers trench there cannot be proven, as the edge of the floor is patchy [2009, 59, plan]). In other words, there is no way to safely associate "Rooms" D and E and their finds with the massive walls that ostensibly belong to the Large Stone Structure.

To this one should add two more observations. (1) The main "wall" of the reconstructed Large Stone Structure—Wall 107—does not form a straight line, and most of it lacks the southern face. The wall is made of two sections, with different orientation and quality of construction (ch. 7 above). (2) According to the plan (E. Mazar 2007, 59) the foundations of the walls that ostensibly belong to the Large Stone Structure drop dramatically from west to east: from 698.78 at the western end of Wall 107 to 696.25 in Wall 20. In fact, the foundation level of the western end of Wall 107 is circa 1.3 meters higher than the chalk floor (which supposedly belongs to the building) roughly 9 meters to the east (level 697.45); moreover, it is half a meter higher than the patch of floor located only about 1.5 meters from this point (level 698.24; these patchy floors, which appear in the first published plan as "pre–Iron Age" [E. Mazar 2007, 59], are taken as belonging to the Large Stone Structure in the second publication [2009, 64, text on 62]). Monumental edifices were not built like this. Had the builders wanted to construct a Large Stone Structure on the edge of the slope, they would have had either to level the bedrock or to lay a proper fill.

To sum up this point, the possibility that the remains form parts of one large structure is slim. The remains probably belong to different structures, built in at least two periods of activity (below).

The Connection between the Large Stone Structure and the Stepped Stone Structure

Following E. Mazar, A. Mazar says that the "'Stepped Structure' in Shiloh's Area G and the 'Large Stone Structure' … to its west, should be defined as part of one and the same architectural complex" (A. Mazar 2010, 34). Faust adds that "in the recent season the connection between the Large Stone Structure and the stepped stone structure in Area G seems to have been substantiated beyond reasonable doubt" (2010, 121). Whether these statements are to be trusted depends on the connection between the uppermost part of the Stepped Stone Structure and the north–south wall that runs along the crest of the ridge (E. Mazar's Wall 20). Following are five comments that shed light on this issue.

(1) It is agreed by all authorities that the South and North Towers exposed by Macalister (Macalister and Duncan 1926) date to the late Hellenistic period and are part of the First Wall of Hasmonean Jerusalem (e.g., Geva 2003a, 529–34; Wightman 1993, 88–94). Regarding the wall that runs between the two towers, it is quite clear that its side sections, that is, the parts that connect to the towers, belong to the same fortification system as the towers (e.g., Shiloh 1984, pl. 77:1). We are left, then, with the few meters of the wall in the center of the section between the towers—the spot that is related to the uppermost part of the Stepped Stone Structure (the area of the five large stones seen in the plan in E. Mazar 2009, 64).

(2) While the lower part of the Stepped Stone Structure must predate the late Iron II (ch. 7 above),[4] the upper sector is built with different stones, and at least part of it was set in a different orientation. The sections of the

---

4. A. Mazar states that the material with Iron IIA pottery below the late Iron II floor in the building over the Stepped Stone Structure must be regarded as an early floor and not as a constructional fill because it does not show a mixture of pottery (2010, 38). No such floor exists, and the content of a fill reflects the place (usually a dump) where it was taken from—no more and no less. Thus the Iron

Stepped Stone Structure under the Hellenistic part of the wall between the two towers (picture in Shiloh 1984, pl. 27.1; see also fig. 27) seem to fit in with the same construction effort and hence probably belong to a renovation of the Stepped Stone Structure in the Hellenistic period (ch. 7 above).[5] In this regard, one should note the similarity in the style of the stones between the upper, northern part of the Stepped Stone Structure and the eastern face of Wall 20, as well as the difference between these two sections and the lower part of the Stepped Stone Structure (E. Mazar 2009, 58, photograph).

(3) The uppermost part of the Stepped Stone Structure is a result of modern restoration work. This becomes clear when one compares the pictures published by Macalister and Duncan (1926, fig. 47; see fig. 8.2 top, taken from the Matson collection) to the pictures taken during Shiloh's excavations or a short while thereafter (e.g., E. Mazar 2009, 37; fig. 8.2 bottom). The latter has two or three more courses than the former (counting from a sort of a hole seen in both pictures in the upper, right-hand side of the Stepped Stone Structure). This is why today the uppermost part of the Stepped Stone Structure seems to be "wrapped" around the city wall (see, e.g., picture in E. Mazar 2007, 45). A. Mazar's statement that the restoration involves no more than "reinforcement with cement of several existing stone courses" (2010, 38) is therefore inaccurate. This restoration is located in the only place where a connection between the Stepped Stone Structure and a hypothetical Iron Age section of Wall 20 could have been theorized.

IIA pottery there only tells us that the floor of the building could not have been laid earlier than this period.

5. A. Mazar (2010, 39) argues that the earth glacis with Hellenistic pottery found by both Kenyon (e.g., Steiner 2001, 26 in the background of the picture, 84) and Shiloh (e.g., 1984, pl. 36) on top of the Stepped Stone Structure negates the possibility that the latter was renovated in the Hellenistic period. The opposite is true. The Hellenistic builders had two goals: to prevent erosion on the slope and to prevent an easy approach to the fortification. Accordingly, the old, Iron Age Stepped Stone Structure was renovated in order to serve, yet again, as a support on the deteriorating slope; the glacis was then thrown on top of it (and on top of the late Iron II structures constructed on its lower part), in order to create a steep slope and prevent an attacker from reaching the fortification by climbing the Stepped Stone Structure.

8. The Large Stone Structure in Jerusalem

Fig. 8.2. The Stepped Stone Structure before (top: 1926) and after (bottom: E. Mazar 2009, 37) restoration. Readers should count from the black line up: two or three courses were added at the top.

(4) The excavator presents evidence showing that the layer of debris of Iron I metal industry (east of Room E) abuts the inner face of Wall 20 (E. Mazar 2009, 59, picture and plan). However, the foundation of the Hellenistic fortification could have been constructed over earlier walls. Indeed, according to E. Mazar's own testimony, boulders of the Large Stone Structure were used as massive foundations for later walls, and "in many cases it was difficult to distinguish by sight the Herodian walls from the Iron Age ones" (2009, 84). The layer with remains of Iron I metal industry may abut such an early, pre-Hellenistic, prefortification wall.

(5) If the eastern face of the central part of Wall 20 dates to the Iron Age, where is the Hellenistic fortification?

To sum up this point, the statement that "the eastern wall of the 'Large Stone Structure' is also the upper part of the 'Stepped Stone Structure'" (A. Mazar 2010, 40) is erroneous. The only architectural connection that exists on the ground is between the upper part of the Stepped Stone Structure—probably Hellenistic in date—and the Hellenistic city wall. A connection between the original, Iron Age Stepped Stone Structure and possible Iron IIA walls unearthed by E. Mazar (some of the walls of her Large Stone Structure) could have existed in antiquity, but they cannot be proven today. Those who claim that the "magnitude and uniqueness of the combined 'Stepped Structure' and the 'Large Stone Structure' are unparalleled anywhere in the Levant between the twelfth and early ninth centuries BCE" (A. Mazar 2010, 45) or that "the combined building was the main structure in Iron Age I Jerusalem … and is indeed the most impressive building from this period throughout the region" (Faust 2010, 128) speak about a structure that cannot be seen today and that may have never existed.

The Date of the Remains

The accumulation between bedrock and the stone pavement or installation in the southeast corner of "Room" D (in fact, between bedrock and "Rooms" D and E in general) is minimal: 10–20 centimeters (E. Mazar 2009, 34, photograph). This compact debris includes, from bottom up, the earth accumulation with Late Bronze and Iron I pottery, the metal industry of the Iron I, a layer with Iron I collared-rim jars (2009, 34–35, 59–62), and several Iron IIA sherds under the pavement (2009, 35). A hand-burnished bowl found with the latter (2009, 61) is compared by E. Mazar to the material in Locus. 47; the latter dates to the late Iron IIA, as it includes a Black-on-Red vessel (for its appearance in the Levant, see Herzog and Singer-Avitz 2004, 215). The late Iron IIA should be placed in the mid- to second half of the ninth century. All this shows that at least the pavement/installation in the southeast corner of "Room D" cannot predate the ninth century BCE (for the dates of the two phases of the Iron IIA, see Finkelstein and Piasetzky 2010; Boaretto, Finkelstein, and Shahack-Gross 2010). The fact that remains of metal industry were found under the pavement/installation as well as over it (E. Mazar 2009, 61) demonstrates the stratigraphic problems in this area.

In a previous work I raised the possibility that the latest pottery in the earth accumulation under the massive walls associated with the Large Stone Structure dates to the beginning of the Iron IIA (ch. 7 above). E. Mazar now accepts that this earth accumulation may include material from the early Iron IIA (2009, 38, contra her own words later [51] that the latest sherds in this accumulation date to the Iron I). It seems that A. Mazar's demand that, in order to date the Large Stone Structure to a post–Iron I date, we should expect to find "at least a few post–Iron I sherds in these layers" has now been fulfilled. This means, again, that the massive walls can hardly antedate circa 900 BCE.[6]

E. Mazar (2007, 63; 2009, 51–52), A. Mazar (2010, 43), and Faust (2010, 122) all emphasize the importance of the Iron IIA material found in Locus 47 as indicating a second phase in the history of the Large Stone Structure, insinuating that it was originally built earlier. However, in this locus Iron IIB pottery was found *below* the Iron IIA items (ch. 7 above). A. Mazar tried to resolve this problem by saying that "the sherd might have come from an upper level of this locus" (2010, 43). However, E. Mazar now raises the possibility that these sherds "were introduced into the material of the lower part of the locus during the excavation" (2009, 53 n. 127). There are two possibilities here: if there were, indeed, in situ Iron IIB sherds under the Iron IIA pottery, the entire deposit cannot be regarded

---

6. The latest radiocarbon date from the earth accumulation under the massive walls is 2780+/-50 (E. Mazar 2009, 39 n. 88), which translates to a calibrated date of 997–850 BCE (68 percent). Contra Faust (2010, 122), this determination cannot help in dating the construction of the walls; it only means that the walls were not built before circa 1000 BCE.

as in situ material; and if the Iron IIB sherds were "introduced" into this spot during the excavation, the reliability of the entire dig is shattered. In any event, and at the very least, the Iron IIA pottery in this locus cannot be used to date the construction of E. Mazar's Large Stone Structure.

This is as far as the evidence for dating goes. The only thing that can be said regarding the date of the supposed early walls in this area is that they were laid during or after the Iron IIA. Both E. Mazar and Faust (e.g., 2010, 127) adhere to the old notion that the Iron IIA dates to the tenth century BCE. However, as I have shown time and again (see, e.g., Finkelstein 2010a), this dating is based on circular arguments that come from a literal reading of the biblical text. Radiocarbon investigations put the Iron IIA between the second half of the tenth century and circa 800 BCE (Finkelstein and Piasetzky 2009, 2010). Faust's statement that the results of the 2006–2007 excavation seasons "solve the issue of the date of the structure in an almost final manner" and that we are now "in possession of significant finds from what appears to be good archaeological contexts,[7] which clearly indicate that the Large Stone Structure should be dated to the Iron Age I" (Faust 2010, 121; also 124: "securely dated to the Iron Age I") may be true only for half Room E, which covers an area of circa 4 × 3 meters. In fact, even this is far from certain.

Summary

As things stand today:

1. There is no single Large Stone Structure. There is no physical connection between half Room E, which may date to the Iron I or to the Iron IIA, and the massive walls associated by E. Mazar, A. Mazar, and Faust with the Large Stone Structure.
2. There is no connection today between massive walls possibly dating to the Iron Age on the ridge (E. Mazar's Large Stone Struc-

---

7. My understanding of "good archaeological context" is, e.g., a destruction layer with an assemblage of pottery, such as Shiloh V, Megiddo VIA, Reḥov IV, Tell eṣ-Ṣafi 4, Lachish III, or the destruction layer investigated by Faust at Tel Eton. The entire area of Mazar's excavation does not have a single "good archaeological context"; this, of course, is not the fault of the excavator.

ture) and the Iron Age part of the Stepped Stone Structure. The only physical connection is between the Hellenistic part of the Stepped Stone Structure and the Late Hellenistic fortification.
3. Some of the massive wall stabs unearthed by E. Mazar may date to the Iron IIA in the ninth century BCE; others may date to the Hellenistic period.
4. Based on solid archaeological arguments alone, that is, without relying on the biblical text, no seasoned archaeologist would have associated the remains in question with monumental architecture of the tenth century BCE.

Addendum

Ben-Ami and Tchekhanovets (2016) have recently suggested identifying remains of fortification uncovered in the Givati Parking Lot in the northwestern sector of the City of David ridge with the western side of the Seleucid fortress, the Acra. They proposed that the fortifications above the Gihon Spring, dealt with in this chapter, belong to the other (eastern) side of the same fortress. If so, there are two stages of construction in the latter: the first may belong to the early second-century BCE Acra, and the second represents the incorporation of this fortification into the Hasmonean city wall in the second half of the second century BCE.

9

The Iron Age Complex in the Ophel, Jerusalem: A Critical Analysis

In this chapter I turn to the Ophel, slightly to the northeast of the area discussed in the two previous chapters. Remains here, dating to the different phases of the Iron II, are better preserved. They are of crucial importance for the study of the settlement history and layout of Iron Age Jerusalem.

Remains in the Ophel[1] are among the most impressive Iron Age monuments in Jerusalem and Judah—and, in fact, throughout the southern Levant. Located immediately to the south of the Herodian Temple Mount, they are of major importance for reconstructing the layout and settlement history of Jerusalem, including the location of the ancient mound—the hub of the Bronze and Iron Age town. There is no doubt that these structures functioned over a long period of time, at least some of them until the Babylonian destruction of the city in 586 BCE. The major question is the date of their construction. According to excavator Eilat Mazar (2011, 2015, 2018; see also A. Mazar 2020), they were built in the tenth century BCE and demonstrate the greatness of the city in the days of the united monarchy. In this chapter I examine this assertion, as well as the nature of the finds. Although the remains cover a single continuous area, I divide the discussion into two: the western Ophel, excavated by Benjamin Mazar and Eilat Mazar between 1968 and 2009 (Mazar and Mazar 1989; E. Mazar

---

1. I am using the terms Ophel and City of David only in their modern context of archaeological research (in contrast to their biblical connotations; for the City of David in the Bible, see Hutzli 2011).

2011); and the eastern Ophel, dug by Eilat Mazar between 2009 and 2013 (E. Mazar 2015, 2018).

Two introductory comments are warranted:

1. In order to avoid confusion, I generally use relative chronology terms based on ceramic typology considerations, that is, early and late Iron IIA, Iron IIB, and Iron IIC. There is a consensus regarding the absolute dating of the latter two to the eighth and seventh (and early sixth) centuries BCE, respectively (although for the *beginning* of the Iron IIB, see different views in Finkelstein and Piasetzky 2011; A. Mazar 2011). In cases where it is difficult to distinguish between them, I use the undivided term Iron IIB–C. Eilat Mazar dated the Iron IIA, especially its early phase, to the tenth century BCE. However, a massive body of radiocarbon results from numerous strata in Israel shows that the Iron IIA covers the second half of the tenth century and the ninth century BCE (e.g., Finkelstein and Piasetzky 2010, 2015). The transition between the early and late phases within this period occurred circa 900 BCE or in the early years of the ninth century (Finkelstein and Piasetzky 2011; A. Mazar 2011 for a slightly different view; see, recently, Finkelstein and Kleiman 2019).
2. Here I deal only with the archaeological evidence; I do not engage Mazar's treatment of biblical texts (for this, see ch. 7 above).

The Western Sector of the Ophel

The complex excavated in the western sector of the Ophel (fig. 9.1) was described in the final report (Mazar and Mazar 1989) as a royal building and a gate constructed in the ninth century and destroyed in 586 BCE. Later, Eilat Mazar (2006d) suggested redating the remains to the tenth century BCE. Additional work in this area was carried out in 2009. In a book summarizing the excavation, Eilat Mazar (2011) presented her reasoning for the new dating.

Following the 2009 excavations, she divided the remains into five components (fig. 9.1; plan in E. Mazar 2011, 145): The Royal Structure (Building D in Mazar and Mazar 1989), the Gatehouse (Building C in Mazar and Mazar 1989), the Extra Tower and Straight Wall, the Large

Fig. 9.1. Architectural elements in the Ophel (adapted from E. Mazar 2015, 462; 2011, 145): (1) the Royal Structure; (2) the Gatehouse; (3) the Outer Gate; (4) the Casemate Wall; (5) the Large Tower; (6) the Extra Tower; (7) the Straight Wall; (8) the Far House; (9) the Great Projecting Tower (Mazar's terminology; attention should be given the actual remains rather than the reconstruction in gray).

Tower and Outer Gatehouse, and "what may have been a casemate wall" (E. Mazar 2011, 145).[2]

---

2. To avoid confusion, I am using Mazar's terminology for the structures, without committing myself to her interpretations (e.g., regarding the Gatehouse) or identification with biblical references, some (in Nehemiah) probably dating to the Hellenistic period.

The Excavator's Description of the Remains

Below is a summary of Mazar's description and interpretation of the remains, which I divide, for the sake of clarity, into three, rather than five, segments.

The Royal Structure

An assemblage of vessels, mainly storage jars, was found crushed on the floor of the two southern[3] rooms in the Royal Structure (Mazar and Mazar 1989, 29–48; E. Mazar 2011, 56–59). The vessels date to the Iron IIC, and the destruction should be affiliated with the 586 BCE Babylonian assault on Jerusalem (evidence for this destruction has recently been found in the nearby Givati Parking Lot; Shalev et al. 2020). The Royal Structure had a lower, older, floor (Mazar and Mazar 1989, sections in plans 16–18, 27; photos in E. Mazar 2011, 68, 112–13), which Mazar dated to the Iron IIA on the basis of the pottery—including a complete black juglet—found in a fill below it (for the fill, see Mazar and Mazar 1989, 34; E. Mazar 2011, 67–69).[4] This fill rested on a foundation platform made of large stones (called plinth stones in Mazar and Mazar 1989).

The Gatehouse, Large Tower, and Casemate Wall

The walls to the west of the Royal Structure were interpreted by Mazar as a four-chambered gatehouse (Mazar and Mazar 1989, 59; E. Mazar 2011, 85–89). The southwestern room of the structure (23041; fig. 9.2) was found filled with over forty storage jars as well as many other vessels, all dating to the Iron IIC (Mazar and Mazar 1989, 14–17, pls. 2–7; E. Mazar 2011, 44). An earthen floor with Iron IIC pottery lying on it was uncovered in what Mazar interpreted as a passageway of the Gatehouse, circa 1 meter above bedrock (E. Mazar 2011, 82–83; sections in Mazar and Mazar 1989, 14, 28–29; E. Mazar 2011, 82). The fill below the floor in the southwestern room (section in Mazar and Mazar 1989, plan 13; photo in E. Mazar 2011,

---

3. The complex is oriented southwest–northeast. For the sake of simplicity, I refer to its orientation as west–east.
4. This juglet—with the handle reaching the middle of the neck—dates to the Iron IIA. However, the date of the fill is dictated by the latest items retrieved from it.

9. The Iron Age Complex in the Ophel, Jerusalem

Fig. 9.2. Iron Age remains in the western sector of the Ophel; in front, the southwestern room (no. 2 in fig. 9.1), looking northeast.

91) yielded Middle Bronze sherds, with "a few sherds from the First temple period," including "several burnished bowl fragments that were too small to indicate the method of burnishing" (Mazar and Mazar 1989, 20; citation from E. Mazar 2011, 93). Nevertheless, Mazar dated the latter to the Iron IIA. A stone platform similar to the one found in the southern rooms of the Royal Structure was unearthed in the southwestern chamber of the Gatehouse, under this fill (E. Mazar 2011, 92). The lower part of the fill below the floor of the passageway, close to bedrock, yielded a small number of sherds, not slipped or burnished, assigned by Mazar to the Iron IIA (2011, 108). According to her, these sherds date the construction of the Gatehouse.

Earth debris found in 2009 abutting the outer side of the Gatehouse's southern wall was interpreted as a fill inside the Large Tower (the latter investigated by Warren in the nineteenth century). The latest sherds in this fill date to the Iron IIA (E. Mazar 2011, 128–34, with photographs; pottery plates on 131–32). For Mazar, this pottery dates the construction of both the Gatehouse and the Large Tower.

According to Mazar, the Large Tower supported a plaza that was located on the inner side of an outer two-chambered gate (plan in E. Mazar 2011, 145). She raised the possibility that a casemate wall ran from the Gatehouse to the west (2011, 142–43).

The Extra Tower and the Straight Wall

The Extra Tower, which had been investigated previously by both Warren and Kenyon (1974, 115–16), lies to the south of the Royal Structure. The Straight Wall continues the Royal Structure's southern wall to the east. The Extra Tower provided additional strength to the entire system. No floor was found inside it. The platform of large stones found under the southern part of the Royal Structure was also detected within the Extra Tower (E. Mazar 2011, 78–79). Kenyon excavated earth debris abutting the outer face of the Extra Tower's eastern wall and dated it to the eighth century BCE (1974, 115–16). Consequently, Mazar argued that the Extra Tower was added to an earlier complex (E. Mazar 2011, 118–19). More of this debris was found in 2009 a few meters to the northeast, abutting both the southern wall of the Royal Structure and the western end of the Straight Wall (2011, 117–18, 122–23, 124–25). According to Mazar, this debris should be divided into two, with the upper part consisting of refuse with late Iron II material thrown from the Royal Structure to the slope

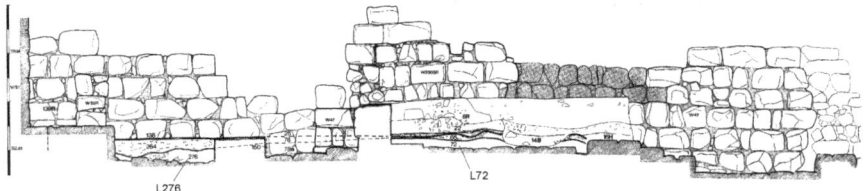

Fig. 9.3. Western Ophel, Section a–a, view to the southeast (based on Mazar and Mazar 1989, 178, plan 17; for the axis of the section, see 166, plan 2); note the location of Loci 276 and 72 (reproduced with the permission of the Institute of Archaeology, The Hebrew University of Jerusalem).

and the lower part consisting of original fill laid on bedrock in the Iron IIA (2011, 122).

Critical Analysis

The Royal Structure

A close look at the color photographs taken in 2009 (E. Mazar 2011, 68, 112–13) raises doubts about the existence of a lower floor in this building. The debris between the Iron IIC floor and bedrock indeed has several components of different colors, but this could be the result of the construction method. More important is the information that can be gleaned from the full report on the results of the excavations in the 1970s and 1980s. In the southeastern room of the Royal Structure, what was considered the lower floor can be clearly seen in Sections a–a and e–e (Mazar and Mazar 1989, plans 16–17, 177–78). Locus 276 is sealed debris, described as the "fill of the lower floor ... down to the plinth stones ... absolutely unlike the upper fill both in color and in nature of the finds" (Mazar and Mazar 1989, 34; see fig. 9.3 above). It seems to have yielded Iron IIB–C sherds (e.g., Mazar and Mazar 1989, pl. 13:19, 21; see 35 for the mention of wheel-burnished sherds in this context). Locus 78a also represents a fill below the ostensible lower floor, down to the big stones of the platform (Section b–b; Mazar and Mazar 1989, plan 18, 179). This locus, too, yielded Iron IIB–C sherds, including the typical open flat-rimmed bowls and wheel-burnished bowls (Mazar and Mazar 1989, pl. 16). In the adjacent room to the west, Locus 72 stands for the fill below the ostensible lower floor, down to the large stones of the platform (fig. 9.3; see also Section c–c in Mazar and Mazar 1989, plan

27 on 187). A significant number of the sherds in this locus, some of them of wheel-burnished bowls, date to the Iron IIB–C (Mazar and Mazar 1989, pl. 22); especially noteworthy are open bowls with a flat rim (e.g., pl. 22:1–5).

Apparently aware of this obstacle to her dating of the building to the Iron IIA, Mazar asserted that "it was still possible to distinguish the tenth century BCE pottery found in the fill beneath it [the lower floor], despite the fact that it was mixed with the pottery from the floor above it" (E. Mazar 2011, 70). In other words, it was not possible to distinguish between an Iron IIB–C floor above and an Iron IIA floor below; the distinction was made according to the date of the sherds, not their location in the stratigraphy.

The evidence is therefore clear: Iron IIB–C sherds were found in the entire fill, including its lower layer. If there had been a lower floor in the Royal Structure, it, too, would have dated to the Iron IIB–C. There is no indication of any pre–Iron IIB construction here.

The Gatehouse and the Large Tower

Interpreting Building C as a Gatehouse is problematic for several reasons:

1. The ostensible two eastern gate chambers are reconstructed from very little evidence in the field.
2. There is no threshold at the entrance to the supposed passageway, nor is there a drainage channel under the passageway—both well-known features in Iron Age gates.
3. The large number of vessels (including over forty storage jars) found in Room 23041, which is 2.8 × 2.4 meters in area (Mazar and Mazar 1989, 14–17, pls. 2–7; E. Mazar 2011, 44), makes its identification as a gate chamber unlikely (as indeed suggested to Mazar by Avigad, who compared the Gatehouse to the Ostraca Building at Samaria; Mazar and Mazar 1989, 59; E. Mazar 2011, 88).
4. The topography here is the steepest anywhere in Iron Age Jerusalem (see map in E. Mazar 2011, 144, photograph on 35) and is therefore not suitable for a gate.[5]

---

5. The topography does not pose an obstacle in interpreting the Gatehouse as an entrance into an inner compound in the city (Wightman 1993, 41–42; Herzog 1997, 237).

Fig. 9.4. Western Ophel, Section f–f, view to the southwest (Mazar and Mazar 1989, 174, plan 13; for the axis of the section, see 166, plan 2); note location of Locus 68 (reproduced with the permission of the Institute of Archaeology, The Hebrew University of Jerusalem).

A close look at the detailed plan (Mazar and Mazar 1989, plan 7) reveals a more probable option: the Gatehouse is simply the continuation of the Royal Structure. They incorporate one spacious Iron IIB–C building, large parts of which served for storage (see also Geva 1993, 5–6; Reich 2000, 99).

Locus 68 represents the fill below the floor in the southwestern "chamber" (Room 23041), down to the stone platform (fig. 9.4). This locus produced Bronze and Iron Age sherds (Mazar and Mazar 1989, 20), including Iron IIB–C items (e.g., 1989, pl. 9, see especially no. 22). In the final report these sherds were described as wheel burnished (see also 1989, 20; note a change of wording in the later publication: "too small to indicate the method of burnishing" [E. Mazar 2011, 93]). In other words, contrary to the claim that the date of construction of this room within the Iron II cannot be accurately established (Mazar and Mazar 1989, 20, 59), the wheel-burnished sherds found in the fill under the floor indicate that it could not have been laid before the Iron IIB in the eighth century BCE.

Pottery from the fill below Floor 303 of the passageway was not presented in the 1989 report. In any event, since there is no lower floor here even according to Eilat Mazar, the entire body of the fill must be evaluated together. The small number of finds included a seventh-century rosette impression and two eighth-century scarabs (E. Mazar 2011, 107–8).

A full description of the pottery found in 2009 in the fill abutting the outer face of the Gatehouse's southern wall (inside the Large Tower) has not yet been published. If the latest sherds in this fill indeed date to the Iron IIA, they are in contrast to the latest sherds from the fill below the Gatehouse. Indeed, the earth for the fill in the Large Tower could have been brought here at a later phase of the Iron Age from a dump-debris with Iron IIA sherds.

Finally, it is important to note that the casemate wall—as well as the outer gate ostensibly built over the Large Tower—are reconstructed by Mazar according to the situation in other Iron Age sites in Israel (Mazar and Mazar 1989, 59; E. Mazar 2011, 145); they do not exist in the Ophel.[6]

The Extra Tower and the Straight Wall

Since no floor was found in the Extra Tower and its inner space was disturbed by post–Iron Age remains, the only dating information for the structure comes from debris found abutted to the outer side of its eastern wall, from which Kenyon retrieved eighth-century pottery (1974, 115–16). In 2009 Mazar reexamined this debris and indeed found Iron IIB–C finds down to its lowest layers (E. Mazar 2011, 118; 2018, 177–85; Mazar and Lang 2018; Mazar and Livyatan Ben-Arie 2018; Mazar and Morgan 2018). This evidence is in line with the data from the fill under the "lower floor" in the Royal Structure. Mazar argued that the lower 20 centimeters of the debris found a few meters to the northeast, abutting the southern wall of the Royal Structure and the southern face of the Straight Wall, yielded Iron IIA pottery (E. Mazar 2011, 122). If this is the case, this earth, too, could have been taken from a dump-debris with early pottery.

Discussion

The large administrative building (the Royal Structure and the Gatehouse) was erected on a moderate slope at the edge of the steeper slope into the Kidron Valley. There was a need, therefore, to establish a flat area for construction. This was done by means of earth fills and the large stone platform that was built against the sloping bedrock (see image in E.

---

6. Moreover, the Iron Age city wall of Jerusalem is a solid wall. No indication for a casemate wall has ever been found in Jerusalem—not even the short segment of two parallel walls excavated by Kenyon near the Gihon (1974, 14–15, fig. 37).

Mazar 2011, 114). Such a large building, constructed on an artificial fill, needed to be supported on the side of the slope. This was facilitated by the Large and Extra Towers and the fills placed inside them. In fact, even this was probably insufficient. The towers, the southern wall of the Royal Structure, and the Straight Wall must have been supported by a glacis-like fill on their outer side. Without such support, the heavy pressure of the fills in the towers and under the building would have endangered the entire complex.

The Straight Wall did not function as a city wall; it may have formed the outer line of another elaborate building, similar to the complex of the Royal Structure and Gatehouse. The Iron IIB city wall was found in several places in the middle of the eastern slope of the City of David ridge. In the northeastern sector of the ridge, this fortification must have passed somewhere near the complex under discussion here, either at the top of the steep slope or, more likely, somewhat downslope (see, e.g., Wightman 1993, 41–42)—in a location similar to the segment of the wall recently unearthed near the Gihon Spring (see Vukosavovic, Chalaf, and Uziel 2021).

The pottery evidence from the fills indicates that the complex described here was constructed in the late Iron II, probably in the eighth century BCE (Ussishkin 2003a, 534, includes the Ophel remains in his description of the eighth-century fortifications), possibly even later, in the Iron IIC; the pottery evidence available is not sufficiently conclusive to determine a date. This is in keeping with the general picture that emerges from the archaeology of Iron Age Jerusalem: the City of David ridge and the south-western hill were surrounded by a city wall for the first time in the second half of the eighth century BCE. This city wall is known from several locations on the eastern slope of the City of David ridge and the southwestern ridge (for the latter, see summary in Geva 2003a). No trace of a city wall dating to an earlier phase of the Iron Age is known anywhere in Jerusalem. Judging from the broader picture (Iron IIA city walls at Lachish and Beersheba) and the chronistic verse in 2 Kgs 14:13 referring to a wall in Jerusalem circa 800 BCE, such a city wall may have existed in the core of Iron Age Jerusalem—the proposed mound on the Temple Mount (see ch. 2 above; Finkelstein 2023).

The Eastern Sector of the Ophel

The eastern sector of the Ophel was excavated in 2009–2013, and the results were published in two volumes (E. Mazar 2015, 2018). The pottery from the dig has recently been treated by Ariel Winderbaum (2021). Although described as final reports, Mazar's volumes do not provide full information on the results of the excavation: there is no orderly discussion of the remains; there are no proper final plans; and much of the information is given as description of loci (Mazar and Lang 2018). Moreover, the constant mix of archaeology and biblical references renders comprehension difficult.

The Excavators' Description of the Remains

The structures in the eastern sector of the Ophel were found in a lesser state of preservation than the Royal Structure and Gatehouse to their west. Mazar interpreted these fragmentary remains built on bedrock as belonging to two complexes (see fig. 9.1 above): the Far House (Buildings Ia and Ib) and the Great Projecting Tower (Building II; see plan in Mazar 2015b, 462). Two rooms in the southeastern area of the Far House (Building Ib) were explained as belonging to a casemate fortification (E. Mazar 2018, 320). Mazar referred to two phases of activity—the earliest remains in the Ophel—and dated both to the early Iron IIA (2015b, 464–65[7]).

Winderbaum (2021) adhered to Mazar's dating of the remains. Following a meticulous study, he concluded that the first monumental construction at this site belongs to "Horizon IIIb," which dates to the end phase of the early Iron IIA. Winderbaum acknowledged that this horizon is mainly composed of fills and that it is not clean of later intrusions. Nevertheless, he asserted that this monumental phase "refutes … the claims that Jerusalem of the Early Iron Age IIA was a small and unimpressive village" (2021, 1:450).

Critical Analysis

The fragmentary remains were constructed on bedrock; there is no stratigraphy in this area in the sense of a set of layers found one on top of

---

7. Her Phase III refers to the western Ophel.

another. The walls of the Far House and the walls of the Great Projecting Tower were built in different orientation from one another and in different orientation from the adjacent Straight Wall and Royal Structure in the western sector of the Ophel. In fact, the two clusters of walls of the Far House (Buildings Ia and Ib) were also constructed in somewhat different orientation from one another. Two clusters in different orientations can also be seen in the Great Projecting Tower (for all this, see Mazar 2015b, plan on 462). This means that there are three or four systems of walls here, of different construction quality, and there is no reason to assign them to two major building efforts. The architectural and therefore chronological relationship between these groups of walls is impossible to verify, except for the fact that the western part of the Great Projecting Tower cuts into Building Ib of the Far House (Mazar and Lang 2018, plan on 335).[8] Finally, there is no reason to interpret the walls in the southeastern area of the Far House as a casemate wall; these appear to me to be simple rectangular rooms in a building.

The Straight Wall, which runs immediately to the south of Building Ib and connects (?) to the westernmost wall of the Great Projecting Tower, is part of the monumental construction in the western sector of the Ophel. As already noted above, it was probably built in the Iron IIB. The question is how to date the fragmentary remains of the Far House and the Great Projecting Tower. This leads us to Winderbaum's study of the pottery.

Let us start with a methodological comment: the end phase of the early Iron IIA (as per Winderbaum's dating of the first "monumental" remains) features no trace of monumental building activity in Judah. The first attestation in this direction comes from well-dated late Iron IIA layers of the ninth century BCE (Lachish IV, Beth-shemesh 3, Beersheba V, and Arad XI). The same holds true for Israel (the Northern Kingdom: the Megiddo VA–IVB horizon[9]). A *uniqum* in Jerusalem—the capital of the demographically depleted and culturally marginal Judah—is possible but unlikely. In order to consider this possibility, a strong case must be

---

8. Regarding the relationship between the Straight Wall and the Great Projecting Tower, Winderbaum raises two possibilities: that the former connects to the latter or that it is cut by it.

9. But see early appearance of significant architecture in Level Q-5, which dates circa 900 BCE (Finkelstein and Kleiman 2019).

presented. I refer to clean pottery assemblages of complete pottery vessels (or at least a significant sherd collection) on floors, which can be affiliated with a secure relative ceramic horizon, and these floors must be clearly connected to the monumental architectural features. Furthermore, the system must be pegged to well-stratified sites in Judah, especially Lachish.[10]

The above secure stratigraphy-ceramic typology-architecture connection does not exist in the Ophel:

1. The Ophel exhibits only patches of floors that are difficult to associate with the main architectural elements.
2. Winderbaum refers to seven horizons (eleven subphases; 2021, 1:58), but nowhere have they been unearthed in a stratigraphic sequence; in fact, the reader gets the impression that these horizons were decided on the basis of pottery analysis.
3. There are no pottery assemblages of restorable vessels on floors; in fact, with the exception of one locus (see further below), there are not even collections of sufficiently large sherds. Most of the pottery fragments are small and sometimes even tiny.
4. Drawing a distinction between the early and late Iron IIA is difficult even in an assemblage of complete vessels (e.g., Herzog and Singer-Avitz 2004, 210), let alone in collections of tiny sherds.
5. Most of the pottery assemblages originated from fills. Even in cases of patches of plaster with no tight stratigraphy, one can barely establish if the sherds belong to the floor or to the fill laid above it in preparation for later construction. The following quotation summarizes the situation: "very few floors were found with pottery lying upon them, with the few floors that did have in-situ pottery on them yielding only small amounts of indicative pottery" (Winderbaum 2021, 1:8).
6. In any collection of small sherds, especially in fills, the *latest* items determine the date of the assemblage, as old sherds may originate from earlier debris: bricks and the like (note Middle Bronze to Iron I sherds in the Ophel debris; E. Mazar 2015b, 463). This is well demonstrated in several cases:

---

10. It is difficult to accept that the pottery repertoire in Jerusalem is different from that of Lachish, located only 40 kilometers to the southwest.

9. The Iron Age Complex in the Ophel, Jerusalem

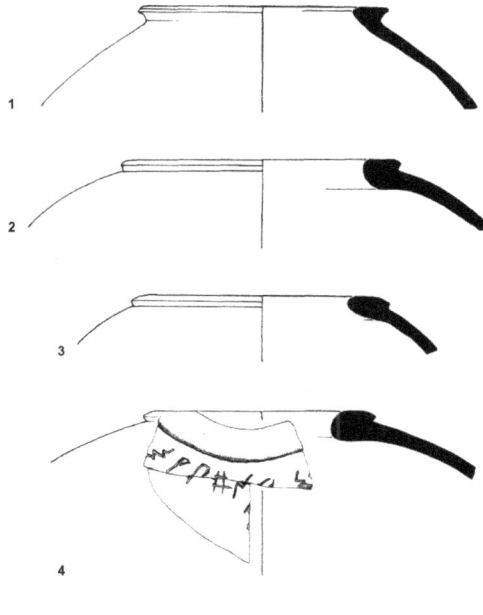

Fig. 9.5. Storage jars found in Locus 12-223c (Mazar 2015b, 468; used by permission).

a. The holemouth jar in figure 7.9:2 is described as representing Horizon II (Winderbaum 2021, 1:380, 2:235), dated to the Iron I/II transition. As far as I can judge, this item cannot date earlier than the later phase of the late Iron IIA, preferably slightly later.

b. The only locus with large parts of vessels is 12-223c, a concentration of broken storage jars found immediately on bedrock (Winderbaum 2021, 2, pl. 4). Winderbaum affiliated this assemblage with Horizon IIIA, which in his opinion dates to the early phase of the early Iron IIA. However, four of the pithoi (fig. 9.5) appear only in the later phase of the late Iron IIA (see detailed discussion in Kleiman 2021). In other words, what looks like an early context on bedrock cannot date before the late ninth century BCE (the broken vessels could have been part of a fill brought to this place; E. Mazar 2015, 467).

c. The cooking pot in Winderbaum's figure 6.8:10 represents Horizon IIIB, dated to the second half of the early Iron IIA.

This typically Iron IIB vessel may appear in the final phase of the late Iron IIA but not in the early Iron IIA.

d. The cooking pot in Winderbaum's figure 7.2:19 is described as representing Horizon III of the early Iron IIA. There are no such cooking pots in this phase of the Iron Age; they appear for the first time in the later phase of the late Iron IIA and are typical of the Iron IIB.

To summarize, it is reasonable to date the earliest structures in the eastern sector of the Ophel to the Iron IIA but impossible to give them a precise date within this period. Moreover, it is impossible to brush aside a slightly later date (note that four of the glyptic items from the eastern Ophel are described by Keel 2015 as "Iron IIA–early IIB"). Still, placing these remains—or at least most of them—within the late Iron IIA, probably in the later phase of this period, seems the most reasonable option. The structures in the western sector of the Ophel were added in the Iron IIB. The buildings in the west continued to function until the destruction of Jerusalem in 586 BCE. The poor preservation of the structures in the east does not allow us to trace their exact history.

Conclusions

The Ophel area developed gradually. The structures in its eastern sector seem to represent more than one construction activity. They were probably built in the late Iron IIA, some perhaps added slightly later, in the early phase of the Iron IIB. The structures in the western part of the Ophel date to the Iron IIB–C.

The Bronze and Iron Age mound of Jerusalem was located on the Temple Mount (ch. 2 above; Finkelstein 2023; contra Geva and De Groot 2017). The late Iron IIA construction in the eastern Ophel represents the first expansion of the settlement to the south, in the direction of the Gihon Spring. Apart from the Ophel, this expansion is represented in the western sector of the Givati Parking Lot excavations (Ben-Ami 2014), in the early phase of the Large Stone Structure and Stepped Stone Structure above the spring, and in the repair of the Spring Tower (ch. 8 above; Finkelstein 2023). Based on historical logic, I would place this expansion phase in the second half of the ninth century BCE (Finkelstein 2023).

Earlier sherds should be interpreted as representing fill debris brought here in preparation for construction; these include the entire sequence from the Early Bronze to the Iron I (Mazar 2015b, 463) and the (possible) early Iron IIA finds.

The monumental part of the construction in the Ophel includes the Royal Building and its western part (Mazar's Gatehouse), the Extra Tower, and the Straight Wall, all built in the Iron IIB.

There is nothing in the Ophel that can be conclusively interpreted as a fortification—a gate or a city wall, either casemate or solid—which means that in its early history, this new quarter of Jerusalem was not fortified. Late Iron IIA towns in Judah, especially Lachish and Beersheba, were fortified by massive walls. It makes no sense to envision the capital of the kingdom as an unfortified settlement. It is reasonable, therefore, to theorize that the mound on the Temple Mount was fortified. This is also hinted at in the chronistic verse in 1 Kgs 14:13, which refers to King Joash of Israel breaching the wall of Jerusalem. The Ophel was fortified together with the entire City of David ridge and the Southwestern Hill in the Iron IIB. The city wall must have passed along the upper eastern slope or at midslope and should probably have looked like the fortifications excavated at midslope south of the Gihon Spring.

Needless to say, the final verdict on this issue could only be given if a sectional trench on the eastern slope of the Ophel were dug, a venture that would be difficult to achieve because of an old Jewish cemetery located there.

Addendum

In a recent article, Regev et al. (2024) report the first systematic project of radiocarbon dating Iron Age remains in Jerusalem. I have already commented on the methodological problem of radiocarbon dating in Jerusalem (ch. 1 above). Regarding the settlement history of the site, the authors offer two observations that relate to this chapter, in fact, to chapters 5–8 as well.

1. Evidence for continuity of activity in the southeastern ridge throughout the Iron Age. Although, for the periods before circa 800 BCE, the ^{14}C results come from samples that cannot be considered as originating from clean contexts, they support what we know archaeo-

logically. Construction (to differ from fills) in the Iron I, for instance, is evident in Eilat Mazar's excavation in the Visitors' Center (under the Large Stone Structure) and in remains unearthed by Kenyon under the terraces on the eastern slope.

2. Jerusalem expanded in the ninth century BCE. In this case, too, the ^{14}C results come mainly from fills, and they support what we already know. Traditional archaeology points to significant Iron IIA (ninth century BCE) activity in the northern sector of the southeastern ridge: the construction of the Large Stone Structure (the visitors center) and part of the Stepped Stone Structure on the upper part of the slope (chs. 7–8); the earliest buildings in the eastern sector of the Ophel (ch. 9); and simpler structures on the western slope of the Givati excavation compound. I should add that the ^{14}C dates do not provide evidence of pre-eighth-century building activity in Area E south of the Gihon Spring and that the ostensible evidence of the construction of Building 100 in the Givati compound as early as the ninth century is based on samples from fills and make-up debris, which provide only a *terminus post quem*.

10

Geographical and Historical Realities behind the Earliest Layer in the David Story

Although the composition of the earliest layer in the David story cannot be dated before the late eighth century BCE (see chs. 12, 14, and 15), the realities depicted in it must be sought before circa 840 BCE. Hence, I incorporate the following chapter into this part of the book.

The historical and territorial situation in the southern part of the hill country and the Shephelah in the late Iron I and Iron IIA (ca. 1050–800 BCE)[1] have been thoroughly discussed in recent years in regard to several issues: the nature of Apiru activity on the boundary between the Hebron hill country and southern Shephelah (Na'aman 2010b); territorial extension of the early north Israelite polity that was centered in the area of Gibeon-Gibeah (e.g., Finkelstein 2006a; see further in ch. 5 above); the course and targets of the Sheshonq I campaign to Canaan in the second half of the tenth century (Finkelstein and Fantalkin 2012); the territorial affiliation of the fortified site of Khirbet Qeiyafa in the Valley of Elah (e.g., Garfinkel, Ganor, and Hasel 2011; Na'aman 2012b; Koch 2012; Finkelstein and Fantalkin 2012); the date and circumstance of the expansion of Judah to the Shephelah and the Beersheba Valley (Fantalkin and Finkelstein 2006; Sergi 2012); and the reality behind the list of towns that received the spoil of Amalek in 1 Sam

---

1. For relative chronology, see Herzog and Singer-Avitz 2004; for absolute dates, Finkelstein and Piasetzky 2010. Note that much of this chronological scheme is now broadly accepted; the main remaining disagreement is about the late Iron I/early Iron IIA transition; but there, too, the gap is narrowing; see Finkelstein and Piasetzky 2011; A. Mazar 2011.

30 (Na'aman 2010a). These works call attention to the detailed geographical information in the books of Samuel regarding the activity of David and his band on the southern fringe of the hill country and their confrontation with the Philistines. In what follows I propose that the early layer in this material reflects genuine historical memories that portray settlement and demographic patterns in the south that are earlier than the middle of the ninth century BCE. I also try to reconstruct the territorial situation in the south in this early phase of the Iron Age. Although in places admittedly somewhat speculative, the discussion below may shed light on the geographical and historical background of the early David narrative.

The Evidence

The different layers in the books of Samuel have been discussed in detail by a substantial number of biblical scholars; delving into this issue again is not the goal of this chapter. I wish only to delineate briefly the texts that in my view represent the earliest Judahite layer, in order to look at them geographically, chronologically, and historically.

Most scholars agree that the books of Samuel contain significant pre-Deuteronomistic materials (e.g., Noth 1981a, 77, 86; McCarter 1980a, 26–27; Na'aman 1992b, 2010a; Römer and de Pury 2000, 123; Dietrich 2007). Several years ago Neil Silberman and I proposed that the original pre-Deuteronomistic story of the rise of David to power with the apologia at its center (for this, see McCarter 1980b; Halpern 2001, 73–103) was written down in the late eighth century in connection with the reorganization of Judah following the dramatic demographic transformation experienced by the kingdom after the fall of the Northern Kingdom (ch. 15 below). However, this material also seems to include several blocks and layers. I refer mainly to early stories about David and his band (Isser 2003) and positive early northern stories about Saul,[2] which must have been transmitted orally, and to the apologia, which represents the ideology of Judah at the time of the actual compilation.

My position regarding the earliest Judahite layer can be summarized as follows:

---

2. Now embedded in the Judahite story; see, e.g., Dietrich 2007, 278–84.

1. It is difficult to peel off the layers in the narrative of David's rise to power according to a strictly literary study without considering the geographhical, archaeological, and historical contexts.

2. Because of the complex system of blocks and layers, even the original early stratum cannot be read as a continuous, single story.

3. The initial southern layer contains stories about David as a leader of an Apiru band that was active on the southern fringe of the highlands of Judah.[3] A pivotal part of the story deals with David's maneuvers between the rulers of the highlands (Saul) and the Shephelah (the king of Gath). This manner of territorial and political behavior is described in detail in the Amarna letters in relation to Keilah (Na'aman 2010b) and other towns located on the border between the Judean Highlands and the Shephelah: Ayyaluna = Aijalon, Ṣarḥa = Zorah, and Sapuma (EA 273–274; see ch. 4 above). Despite the centuries-long chronological distance, the reality of the Late Bronze Age is constructive for understanding the situation described in the biblical text (more below).

4. The heroic stories in 2 Sam 21:15–22 and 2 Sam 23:8–21 (Isser 2003) also belong to the early southern layer. They preserve folktales of daring actions undertaken by David's warriors in the course of their confrontation with the Philistines.

5. Being part of the stories of David's life as an outlaw on the southern fringe of the highlands and his dealings with the king of Gath, the material about his sojourn in Ziklag (1 Sam 27:6; parts of 1 Sam 30) and the spoil of Amalek (1 Sam 30:26–31) probably belongs to the early southern layer.

6. The early David stories are folktales that have no theological stance (Isser 2003, 53). Sections regarding questions posed to YHWH, as well as David's dealings with priests and prophets, seem not to belong to this layer (e.g., 1 Sam 23:2, 4, 10–12; 30:7–82; 2 Sam 5:17–25). The stories about the cave at Adullam and the rescue of Keilah well demonstrate this; as far as I can judge, the original narrative includes 1 Sam 22:1–2, 5b; 23:1, 3, 5, 13 (or 13a), 14–15.

7. As noted above, the apologia—the northern accusations against David and the Judahite response—does not belong to the original material. It should be read against the background of demographic changes in Judah

---

3. I do not mean to return to the simplistic equation Apiru = Hebrew; for a connection from a socioeconomic perspective, see Rowton 1976; Na'aman 1986.

in the late eighth century and later, after the fall of the Northern Kingdom, when the population of the Southern Kingdom was transformed into a mix of original Judahite and Israelite groups; the latter, some of whom originated from the highlands of Benjamin and southern Samaria, carried with them anti-David sentiments (ch. 15 below).

8. The early David story includes a memory of a confrontation between Israel and the Philistines in the Valley of Elah (1 Sam 17:1–4 [also 8–11?]).[4] Originally, this story could have been connected to the heroic act of David's warrior Elhanan (1 Sam 21:19) or to a parallel, early story about the young David. Evidently, much of the story as we have it today dates to much later days.[5]

The Date of the Early David Layer

In attempting to date the reality depicted in the early David layer as delineated above, the following issues should be taken into consideration:

1. In terms of the stratigraphy of the text, the early layer is older than the written version of the rise of David to power with the apologia. The latter was probably written down circa 700 BCE or somewhat later (ch. 15 below; Na'aman 2010a). Writing in Judah commenced in the late ninth century but at that time was sporadic and did not include complex texts; scribal activity gained prominence only in the late eighth century and more so in the seventh century BCE (Finkelstein and Sass 2013). Therefore, materials prior to the late eighth century must have been transmitted orally.

2. The early David layer mentions place names that do not appear in the distinctive Deuteronomistic writings, first and foremost in the detailed list of towns of Judah in Josh 15, which dates to the late seventh century BCE (Alt 1925; Na'aman 1991). I refer to Gob (2 Sam 21:18, 19, possibly also 16), Horesh (1 Sam 23:15, 16, 18, 19), the hill of Hachilah (1 Sam

---

4. This is regardless of the latest redaction of the story, e.g., Rofé 1987. Note that the toponyms Azekah and Socoh, as well as the Valley of Elah, appear in the shorter LXX version of the story, which is considered to be the original; see Tov 1985; Auld and Ho 1992.

5. Finkelstein 2002b; A. Yadin 2004 and bibliography. For a different view on these issues, see, e.g., Millard 2009; Zorn 2010.

23:19; 26:1, 3), the forest of Hereth (1 Sam 22:5), Siphmoth (1 Sam 30:28), and Athach (1 Sam 30:30, if not garbled). It seems that these places (e.g., Gob, Siphmoth) did not exist and were no longer known in late monarchic days. Interestingly, at least some of them refer to elements in the landscape (grove, hill, forest, high place); they may represent a period when the countryside of southern Judah was still sparsely settled.

3. The antiquity of the reality behind the early layer of the narrative on David's rise to power is evident from the description of David and his people as a band of Apiru active on the southern fringe, playing their cards between the kingdoms of Saul and Gath. The late Iron IIA saw two important processes in the settlement history of Judah. The first was the intensification of settlement activity in the highlands in general and south of Hebron in particular. In the latter area, the number of sites grew from three in the late Iron I to sixteen in the Iron IIA (Ofer 1994). The second is the expansion of Judah into the Beersheba Valley. In the early phase of the Iron IIA and probably the beginning of the late Iron IIA (= late Iron IIA1, first half of the ninth century), this area was ruled by the Masos chiefdom.[6] Judah penetrated into the valley where it established two forts—Arad XI and Beersheba V—as a vassal of Hazael of Damascus in the second part of the late Iron IIA (= late Iron IIA2, the second half of the ninth century BCE).[7] The intensification of settlement activity south of Hebron and the construction of fortresses in the Beersheba Valley brought an end to the settlement reality that enabled the activity of Apiru bands in the southern Hebron hill country. In other words, starting in the second half of the ninth century, the authorities in Jerusalem were probably able to control the entire Judean Highlands. Thus a story about the ploy of an unruly Apiru band in the Hebron Highlands must depict a reality earlier than the late ninth century BCE.

4. Gath (together with Ekron) was probably one of the two most important cities in Philisia in the Iron I and the largest and leading city in the south in the Iron IIA (Uziel and Maeir 2005; Maeir 2012, 26–49).

---

6. Finkelstein 1995, 103–26; for the date, see Boaretto, Finkelstein, and Shahack-Gross 2010.

7. Fantalkin and Finkelstein 2006. The division of the late Iron IIA into two is a historical judgment rather than an archaeological one: the late Iron IIA1 covers the time of the Omride dynasty in Israel (ca. 880–840) and the late Iron IIA2 the period of Damascene hegemony in the region (ca. 840–800 BCE).

It was violently destroyed by Hazael in the second half of the ninth century (Maeir 2004; 2012, 26–49) and never fully recovered from this event. According to the Great Summary Inscription of Sargon II, in the late eighth century Gath was probably a subordinate of Ashdod (Younger 2003). It does not appear among the Philistine cities in early seventh-century Assyrian sources and in late seventh-century prophetic works (e.g., Schniedewind 1998, 75). The dominant role of Gath in the early David material must therefore represent a pre-840/830 BCE reality.

5. The expansion of Judah to the Shephelah and the construction of Judahite administration centers at Beth-shemesh (Stratum 3) and Lachish (Level IV)[8] also took place in the second half of the ninth century. It was made possible by the destruction of Gath (Fantalkin and Finkelstein 2006; Fantalkin 2008). Indeed, the early David story does not include any indication of Judahite rule in the Shephelah and the Beersheba Valley; it must reflect an earlier historical reality.

To sum up these points, the early layer in the David story probably reflects a situation before the late ninth century BCE in the south. The archaeological finds in places mentioned in this layer are discussed below. They seem to indicate that this biblical material reflects a very late Iron I and mainly an Iron IIA situation, in absolute terms, the period of time between circa 950 and 850 BCE.

Geography and Archaeology

Having delineated the components of the early layer in the David story, I can now turn to the geography and territorial history depicted in it. The discussion is divided into three units: the territory of Gath in the Shephelah; the theater of operations of David and his band in the highlands south of Hebron; and the area described in the list of cities that received the spoil of Amalek.

The Kingdom of Gath

Only a handful of sites in the Shephelah are mentioned in relation to the early David story. They include Gath, Adullam, Keilah, and Ziklag; if the

---

8. For the finds in these sites, see Bunimovitz and Lederman 2009; Ussishkin 2004e, respectively.

Valley of Elah story preserves an early memory, one can add Azekah, Socoh, and Gob (fig. 10.1). The locations of most of these sites are well known, and there is no need to repeat them here. Na'aman (2008) and then Finkelstein and Fantalkin (2012) suggested placing Gob at Khirbet Qeiyafa, overlooking the Valley of Elah, but this is far from a certainty. Ziklag should be sought in the southwestern corner of Gath's territory, the most widely accepted identification being Tel Sera (Oren 1982). Putting Ziklag aside, the sites are restricted to the Valley of Elah and the section of the longitudinal trough valley that separates the Shephelah and the highlands immediately to its south. This is the central sector of the eastern flank of Gath's territory. It is noteworthy that other parts of the Shephelah are not mentioned. I refer to the northern Shephelah, that is, the Aijalon and Soreq Valleys (Aijalon, Zorah, Eshtaol, Beth-shemesh), including places that are prominent in the ark narrative (Ekron and Beth-shemesh); and the southern Shephelah—in the area of Lachish, Mareshah, and Libnah—which was of great importance in the late eighth century, during the campaign of Sennacherib against Judah.

Turning to archaeology,[9] to date Iron I Gath has only been partially explored. Preliminary finds (Maeir 2012), however, and the concentration of early alphabetic inscriptions in its territory, some of which seemingly date to this period (Finkelstein and Sass 2013), attest to its status. In the Iron IIA, Gath was the largest and most important city in the southern lowlands (above).[10]

Although the narrative mentions only the cave of Adullam and not the town itself, it is worth looking at the finds of esh-Sheikh Madhkur, the location of this biblical site. It was surveyed by Dagan (Dagan 1992, 149–50), who collected Late Bronze and Iron II sherds (the latter undivided into subperiods). No Iron I pottery was reported.

---

9. In this chapter the review of finds retrieved at the different sites in excavations and surveys is restricted to the Iron I and the Iron IIA.

10. In the Iron I, Ekron was the most important city in the southern lowlands (possibly together with Gath), stretching over a large lower mound 20 hectares in size. It probably ruled over the area of the Soreq Valley. Ekron declined at the end of this period. In the Iron IIA it was a relatively small and unimportant town that covered the upper mound only (Dothan and Gitin 2008, 1955). Note that 1 Sam 17:52, if meaning to refer to important Philistine cities, must preserve a tenth-century memory—the last time when both Ekron and Gath were of significance.

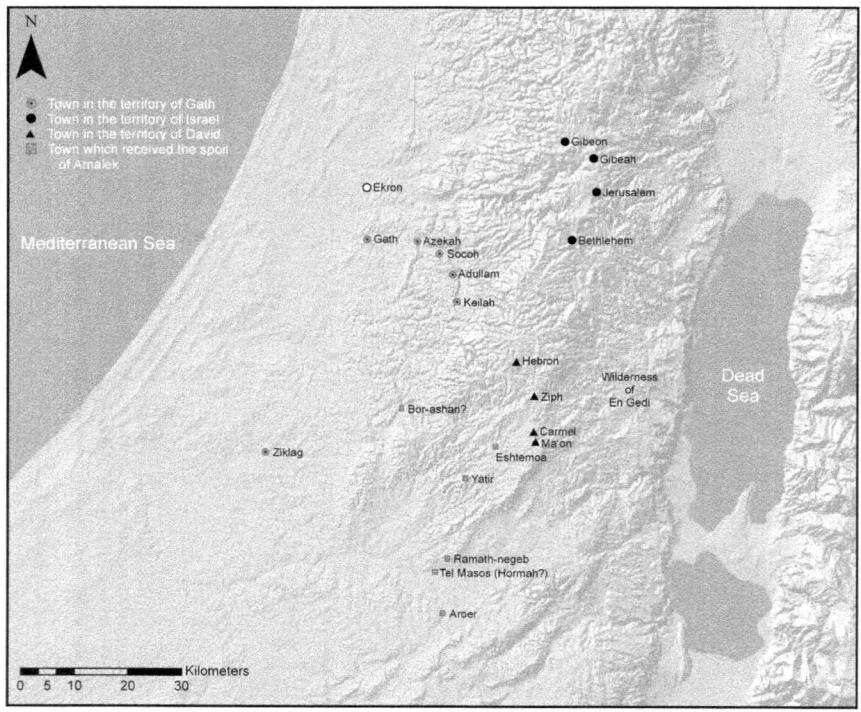

Fig. 10.1. Map of the Shephelah, southern Hebron Hills, and Beersheba Valley indicating places mentioned in the chapter.

Keilah was surveyed twice. Both Kochavi (1972, 49) and Dagan (1992, 161) reported Late Bronze and Iron II pottery but no Iron I sherds. Azekah was excavated twice. Bliss and Macalister retrieved Late Bronze, Iron I, and Iron II finds (summary in Dagan 2011, 83–84). The first season of the renewed excavations at the site yielded Late Bronze, Iron IIA, and Iron IIB finds (Lipschits, Gadot, and Oeming 2012). Socoh was surveyed by Dagan, who reported Late Bronze and (undivided) Iron II finds (Dagan 1992, 134). Tel Sera, possibly the location of Ziklag, covers the entire Iron I–IIA sequence (Oren 1993).

All in all, if one is looking for a single period to fit the reality of Gath and its territory as depicted in the early David stories (which, admittedly, is not necessarily the case), the Iron IIA before circa 840/830 seems to be the most adequate.

There was no large city-state south of Gath in the Iron I (ca. 1130–950 BCE), which means that the city ruled over the entire territory from the southern margin of the Soreq Valley in the north to the northwestern margins of the Beersheba Valley in the south (Singer 1993) and from the longitudinal valley below the hill country in the east to the borders of the coastal cities in the west. During the early Iron IIA and late Iron IIA1 (ca. 950–840 BCE), Gath seems to have ruled over the entire Shephelah, growing to be the most important city in the south (below).

Keilah and Adullam were towns on the eastern border of Gath, facing the highlands. Both are mentioned in connection with skirmishes with David and his people (Adullam indirectly, 2 Sam 23:13). The situation in Keilah is similar to the one described in the Amarna tablets (Na'aman 2010b); at that time it was a city in the eastern territory of Gath that was taken over, for a while, by Jerusalem. Ziklag was located in the southwestern sector of Gath's territory, facing the pastoral nomadic land to its south.

The Highlands South of Hebron

Adhering to the long-term idea and to the Amarna model of rivalry between Gath and Jerusalem, one must ask: In the period discussed here, who was Gath's rival in the highlands? Jerusalem was hardly an option. Archaeologically, the Iron I and the early phases of the Iron IIA are poorly represented (chs. 7 and 8 above). Textually, no place in the highlands of Judah, Jerusalem included, is mentioned in the Sheshonq I list.[11] However, several places in the highlands immediately to the north and northwest of Jerusalem do appear in the list (see, e.g., Aharoni 1979, 325; Kitchen 1986, 298, 435; Finkelstein and Fantalkin 2012). Elsewhere I have suggested that the house of Saul materials in 1 Samuel preserve a memory of an early north Israelite territorial polity that was ruled from the area of Gibeon-Gibeah.[12] This area was densely settled, and several of its sites were fortified at that time—the only such group west of the Jordan River (Fantalkin and Finkelstein 2006). The Gibeon-Gibeah polity dominated the entire territory of the central highlands to the north of Jerusalem up

---

11. Attempts to harmonize this fact with the biblical text, such as the proposal that the treasures of the temple were handed over to the pharaoh at Gibeon (e.g., Kitchen 1986, 447), contradict the logic of ancient Near Eastern military campaigns accounts.

12. E.g., Finkelstein 2006a. For a discussion of whether this area should be described as north Israelite, see Finkelstein 2011c, contra Na'aman 2009b.

to the margins of the Jezreel Valley and the western slopes of the Gilead (Edelman 1992, 997; Knauf 2001b, 16; Finkelstein 2006a), and it may have been responsible for the demise of the late Iron I "New Canaan" city-states in the Jezreel Valley (Finkelstein and Piasetzky 2009). Expansion attempts by the north Israelite polity to the lowlands in the north and southwest could have endangered the renewed interests of Egypt of the Twenty-Second Dynasty in Canaan. The campaign of Sheshonq I targeted this polity; Sheshonq penetrated into the highlands in the area of Gibeon and also attacked the area of the Jabbok River. His campaign brought about the decline of this early north Israelite polity. A group of sites in the Gibeon plateau, among them Khirbet Raddana, et-Tell (Ai), and Khirbet ed-Dawwara, were abandoned at the beginning of the early Iron IIA, that is, in the late tenth century BCE.

For the discussion here, the important question is how far south the Gibeon polity ruled. The answer can come from the biblical text, possibly also from archaeology. The sole logic in the tales of Saul's presence in the Valley of Elah (an area not particularly important at the time of authors of later phases of the Iron Age) and the tradition regarding his pursuit of David in the remote, off-the-beaten-track southern highlands is that the north Israelite polity ruled at least as far south as the vicinity of Hebron. The straightforward interpretation of the geography of the confrontation in the Valley of Elah is that the Philistines camped to the south of the valley, somewhere between Socoh and Azekah,[13] while the Israelites camped to its north, with the valley itself separating them. This would raise the possibility that Khirbet Qeiyafa, located on the northern side of the valley, was a north Israelite border fort and that its abandonment is connected to the campaign of Sheshonq I (Finkelstein and Fantalkin 2012). It is difficult to say whether the tale regarding a Philistine garrison at Bethlehem, which appears in the heroic stories (2 Sam 23:14), preserves a genuine memory. If it does, such a garrison could mark the southern limit of the Saul territory or a Philistine (or possibly Egyptian?) attempt to delineate the southern extent of this polity. In other words, it could have been established as a

---

13. Ephes-dammim/Pas dammim (see 1 Sam 17:1; 1 Chr 11:13), read by many as a toponym (e.g., Driver 1913, 138; McCarter 1980a, 290; Na'aman 2008, 3), probably means "before blood was shed," that is, before the beginning of the battle (interpretation of Ran Zadok, cited in Finkelstein and Fantalkin 2012).

bulge between the north Israelite territory to the north and the relatively sparsely settled area ruled by one or more groups of Apiru to the south.

The area to the south of Bethlehem was sparsely settled in the late Iron I; archaeological surveys have recorded about fifteen Iron I settlements between Jerusalem and Hebron but only three to the south of Hebron (Ofer 1994). This isolated, arid area was locked between three polities: Gath in the west, Israel in the north, and the Masos chiefdom (below) in the south.[14] It provided an ideal landscape for the activity of a group of Apiru: away from central rule, in an area that would be treacherous for maneuvers of an organized military force.

This was the theater of operations of David's Apiru band (fig. 11.1 above). The identifiable places mentioned in the text are Ziph (= Khirbet Ziph), Maon (= Khirbet Main), and Carmel (= Khirbet Kirmil)—all south-southeast of Hebron—plus the wilderness of Ein Gedi, meaning the desert area west of the oasis. Whether Hebron was the hub of this group from the outset or was taken over by it at a certain point is impossible to say. In any event, this remote sector of the highlands was the base from which the David group maneuvered between the other forces in southern Canaan and from which it finally managed to take over Jerusalem—the traditional government center in the southern highlands.

Archaeologically, the area south of Hebron was surveyed twice. Kochavi reported Iron Age sherds in all three sites without providing a breakdown into subphases of the period (Kochavi 1972, 68, 76–78). Ofer retrieved in them Iron IIA finds but no Iron I sherds.[15] In this case also, then, archaeology supports an Iron IIA reality behind the David tradition.

The Towns That Received the Spoil of Amalek

The places mentioned in the list of towns that received the spoil of Amalek (1 Sam 30:26–31) that can be safely identified are (fig. 11.1 above):[16]

Eshtemoa is identified with the large village of es-Samuʿ south-southwest of Hebron. The site yielded three jugs, each bearing the Hebrew

---

14. For the latter, see Finkelstein 1995, 103–26, and below.
15. Ofer 1993b, fig. 2A/43–44, sites 49 Tell Zif, 147 Khirbet Main, and 73 Khirbet el-Karmil east.
16. See discussions in, e.g., Fritz 1975; Kallai 1986, 350–53; and Naʾaman 2010a.

inscription *ḥmš*; their date is probably the late Iron IIA or Iron IIA–B transition (Finkelstein and Sass 2013). The survey of this site produced Iron I and Iron IIA sherds (Ofer 1993b, fig. 2A/19, site 25).

Yatir. The large ruin of Khirbet Yatir is located 7 kilometers to the southwest of es-Samuʻ. Limited excavations (Eshel, Magness, and Shenhav 2000) did not reveal pre–Iron IIC finds, but the large Byzantine ruin probably covers much of the early settlement.

Ramath-negeb is commonly identified at Tel ʻIra, located on a hill on the northern margin of the Beersheba Valley (e.g., Lemaire 1973; Rainey 1976). The earliest remains here date to the Iron IIA (Beit-Arieh 1999, 170).

Aroer. Late monarchic Aroer (LXX for the MT's Adadah of Josh 15:22) should certainly be identified with the mound of Khirbet ʻArʻara, or Arair, on the southern margin of the Beersheba Valley, between modern Dimona and Beer Sheva. This place did not reveal pre–Iron IIB finds (Thareani 2011). It is reasonable to accept Kochavi's (1969, 45) proposal to identify Aroer of 1 Sam 30 with Tel Esdar, located 2.5 kilometers north of Khirbet ʻArʻara. Kochavi dated the two Iron Age strata that he uncovered at the site to the late Iron I and Iron IIA, while Herzog and Singer-Avitz (2004, 225) date both of them to the early Iron IIA; I endorse the latter view.

Hebron. Ending a list of twelve places, the mention of Hebron may be a later addition. The mound of biblical Hebron (Tell Rumeida) is located on a hill in the middle of the modern town. Three different excavations were carried out here by Hammond, Ofer, and Eisenberg. They revealed remains dating to the Iron I and Iron IIA (Ofer 1993a, 1994).

Negev of the Kenites. The Kenites are associated with Arad (Judg 1:16), and hence this term probably refers to the eastern sector of the Beersheba Valley.[17]

Bor-ashan is probably Ashan of Josh 15:42, which must have been located in the southeastern tip of the Shephelah, possibly at Tell Beit Mirsim (Kallai 1986, 357).

Other identifications, for example, Bethel = Tel Beer-sheva and Atach = Tel Eton (Naʾaman 2010a), are highly hypothetical, hence not discussed here.

Two place names that appear in the list deserve further discussion:

---

17. Aharoni 1968b. The exact location of the Negeb of the Jerahmeelites is difficult to establish.

10. Geographical and Historical Realities

Racal. The LXX[B] renders this name Karmelo, that is, Carmel. Whether the original is indeed a distortion of Carmel or the LXX entered a name known in the Hellenistic period is difficult to say.

Hormah. This place is also mentioned in the lists of the towns of Simeon and the Negev district of Judah (Josh 19:4; 15:30, respectively) and in several references in the wandering and conquest narratives. Its location has been debated. Na'aman's proposal to identify it at Tel Halif (Na'aman 1980, 2010a) is good geographically but difficult, if not impossible, archaeologically, because the site seems to have lain abandoned in the late seventh century (Seger 1993), the time reflected in the lists of Simeon and Judah. Tel Masos (Aharoni 1976) fits archaeologically, as it yielded both Iron I–IIA and Iron IIC remains, though the latter are seemingly restricted to a single building: a fort (Kempinski et al. 1981, 165–68).

In this case, too, then, if one is looking for a single pre-850 BCE period to represent the reality behind the biblical narrative, the Iron IIA is the best fit.[18]

Plotting the towns that received the spoil of Amalek on a map shows that, except for the questionable Racal = Carmel (above) and Hebron (which may be an addition to the original list), they are all located to the west and southwest of David and his band's theater of operations and to the south and southeast of the territory of Philistine Gath. Before 840 BCE, this was the location of the Tel Masos desert polity, which also encompassed the Iron IIA sites in the Negev Highlands (Finkelstein 1995, 103–26) and which profited from participating in the mining of copper in the Arabah and the transportation of copper to the west (Fantalkin and Finkelstein 2006; Martin and Finkelstein 2013). Recent radiocarbon results from two of the Negev Highlands sites hint that this desert system operated between the second half of the tenth century and the middle to late ninth century BCE, that is, in the very late Iron I, the early Iron IIA, and at least the late Iron IIA1 (Boaretto, Finkelstein, and Shahack-Gross 2010; Shahack-Gross et al. 2014). In the Bee-sheba Valley it was replaced in the second half of the ninth century (late Iron IIA2) by the Judahite forts of Beersheba V and Arad XI (Fantalkin and Finkelstein 2006).

---

18. Na'aman (2010a) noticed that the 1 Sam 30:26–31 list must depict a pre-Sennacherib 701 BCE campaign reality. Several points hint at a yet earlier date, mainly the description of David as an Apiru and the reference to Ziklag as a city in the territory of Gath.

Discussion

The early layer in the narrative of David's rise to power in 1 Samuel seems to shed light on the territorio-political situation in the south in the tenth and early ninth centuries BCE. In order to understand this situation, one needs to start with the relatively well-documented Late Bronze Age. At that time the central hill country was divided between two territorial polities: Jerusalem and Shechem. Jerusalem ruled over the entire southern part of the central highlands, probably from the area of Gibeon in the north to the Hebron hill country in the south.[19] The Shephelah to its west was governed by three main city-states: Lachish, Gath, and Gezer.[20] The border between Jerusalem and the Shephelah city-states passed along the longitudinal trough valley that runs from north to south immediately to the west of the steep slopes of the Judean hills. The highlands to the south of Jerusalem were sparsely inhabited and probably thickly forested; excavations and surveys recorded approximately ten small settlements in the entire area (Goren, Finkelstein, and Na'aman 2004, 354–55). These environmental conditions enabled the activity of unruly Apiru bands that maneuvered between the highlands and Shephelah polities. The Keilah incident referred to in the Amarna correspondence depicts this situation: the town, which is located in the longitudinal trough valley, belonged to Gath. It was occupied for a while by Jerusalem and then returned to Gath; the Apiru played an important role in this affair. Other confrontations along the highlands–Shephelah border mentioned in the Amarna letters—in Rubutu, Ayyaluna (= Aijalon), Ṣarḫa (= Zorah), and Sapuma—seem to depict the same type of affairs (see ch. 4 above). The situation portrayed in the Amarna letters probably endured until the end of Egyptian rule in Canaan in the late twelfth century BCE and beyond.

We do not possess historical information for the early phase of the Iron I, in the late twelfth and early eleventh centuries BCE. Archaeologically, the situation south of Jerusalem did not change much during this period, but there was dramatic growth in the number of settlements in the highlands north of Jerusalem, including the area of Gibeon-Gibeah-

---

19. For a somewhat different reconstruction, see Na'aman 1992a.
20. For a possible additional polity, see Na'aman 2011.

Bethel. In the late Iron I and the beginning of the early Iron IIA—the late eleventh to late tenth centuries BCE—in circumstances that are undetectable, the latter area became the hub of an early north Israelite territorial entity, hinted at by both archaeological and historical sources (Finkelstein 2006a). Archaeologically, a group of sites in this area was fortified—the only such concentration of fortifications in the entire area west of the Jordan River. Historically, the Sheshonq I list and the northern biblical materials on the house of Saul refer to the very same area. It seems that this polity had taken over Jerusalem and ruled in the highlands of Judah as far south as Bethlehem or even the vicinity of Hebron and possibly expanded to the northeastern sector of the Shephelah, around the Elah and Aijalon Valleys. This was the only time in the Bronze and Iron Ages that we know of in which the entire central highlands was ruled by a single territorial polity.

The rest of the Sphelelah was ruled by Ekron (which was the largest city in the region in the Iron I) and Gath. Ekron dominated the Soreq Valley. In the Iron I, following the demise of Late Bronze Lachish and the collapse of the settlement system around it, Gath ruled over large parts of the southern lowlands, covering the territories of Late Bronze Lachish and Gath combined (Singer 1993). Ekron declined in the late Iron I, which left Gath as the leading power in the Shephelah in particular and the southern lowlands in general in the Iron IIA. Indeed, at that time Gath was the largest city in the south (Uziel and Maeir 2005), one of the two most important cultural centers in the country.[21]

The sparsely settled and remote area to the south of Hebron probably continued to serve as an ideal retreat for Apiru bands. This was the theater of operations of the David band, which maneuvered between the north Israelite highlands polity and the dominating Philistine kingdom in the southern Shephelah. The incident at Keilah (1 Sam 23) well demonstrates this (Na'aman 2010b). The text describes David as coming to the rescue of the town; in fact, his Apiru group may have taken it over from Gath in order to plunder its agricultural output (Singer 1993). The David band probably shifted alliances between Saul and Gath to its advantage: economic gains and rule in the south Hebron Hills as a base for further expansion. But the ambiance of the story, as well as the conclusion, seems

---

21. Together with Reḥov in the north (Finkelstein and Sass 2013).

to indicate that in the final act David and his band cooperated with Gath and the Egyptians against the north Israelite polity.

Sheshonq I's intervention in the area of Gibeon and the Jabbok River brought about the demise of the early north Israelite polity and its replacement—probably at his initiative—by two new, emerging polities in the central highlands: the Northern Kingdom centered in Shechem and then Tirzah; and the Southern Kingdom concentrated in Jerusalem. These were probably the circumstances under which Jerusalem regained its old status as the center of a south highlands polity. Jerusalem, under David's rule and Egyptian hegemony, inherited at least some of the territories of the north Israelite polity, including the Gibeon-Bethel Plateau and possibly areas farther to the north. A vague memory of this situation—of Jerusalem's short-term rule over areas in the highlands that were not included in its territory in late monarchic times—may be the source of the tradition in Judah of a great united monarchy in the days of the founders of the Davidic dynasty.[22]

This reconstruction emphasizes the crucial role played by Sheshonq I in shaping the territorio-political situation in Canaan in the second half of the tenth century: both Judah and the Northern Kingdom Israel emerged as vassals of the Egyptian pharaoh. In fact, the Sheshonq I intervention restored the second millennium BCE territorial order in the highlands: the two-polity rule centered in Jerusalem and the vicinity of Shechem.

In the Shephelah, Ekron declined at the end of Iron I. This was possibly also connected to the new order imposed by Egypt, which promoted Gath as the main power in the southern lowlands.

The Sheshonq I campaign also had a strong impact to the south of the highlands. The prosperity in copper mining in Wadi Feinan to the south of the Dead Sea (Levy et al. 2004, 2008) brought about the rise in the late Iron I of a desert polity in the Beersheba Valley and the Negev Highlands, with its hub at Tel Masos (Fantalkin and Finkelstein 2006). It seems that one of the targets of the Sheshonq I campaign to Canaan was the monopolization of the Wadi Feinan copper industry and the redirection of its transportation: from the north via the Transjordanian plateau to the northwest, in the direction of Egypt. As a result, following the Sheshonq I campaign,

---

22. In the late tenth and early ninth centuries BCE, the area of Gibeon-Bethel was again ruled by the north Israelites (Finkelstein 2011c; contra Na'aman 2009b).

the Tel Masos chiefdom reached its peak prosperity in the early Iron IIA and the late Iron IIA1—in the late tenth and first half of the ninth centuries BCE. This situation seems to stand behind the list of towns to which David sent the spoil of Amalek; groups living in the southwestern tip of the Hebron Hills and the Beersheba Valley were probably clan-related to the inhabitants of the area of Hebron. Their relation to Judah became more obvious in the second half of the ninth century BCE, when the Beersheba Valley was incorporated into the territory of the Southern Kingdom.[23]

In its early days, then, Judah ruled over the same territory that was dominated by Late Bronze Jerusalem: the southern highlands. It did not yet extend to the Shephelah, which was ruled by powerful Gath and to the Beersheba Valley, which was dominated by the Masos polity. Judah's expansion into these areas came a century later, as a result of another new order imposed on the region, this time by Hazael. In the west, the destruction of Gath (Maeir 2004, 2012) opened the way for Judah, as a vassal of Damascus (2 Kgs 12:19), to take over the eastern sector of the Gath territory. In the south, too, Judah served the interests of Damascus; the construction of the forts of Arad and Beersheba was probably connected to the attempts of Hazael to monopolize copper trade in the Levant by ceasing production in the Arabah and promoting trade with Cyprus (Knauf 1995, 112–13; Fantalkin and Finkelstein 2006).

Above I noted that the geographical reality depicted in the early David story best fits the Iron IIA before 840 BCE, in the sense that this is the period when most of the sites mentioned in the text were inhabited. Chronologically, this suggests two alternative interpretations. According to the first, the days of the rise of David to power parallel the very beginning of Iron IIA. This seems difficult to accept, as it leaves only roughly

---

23. This brings about the question of the identification and location of Amalek of 1 Sam 30. Most references to Amalek in the Hebrew Bible belong to later layers in the text, but it is difficult to reconstruct the Ziklag story without the name of this group (though the reference to camels may also belong to a later layer). Amalek is not mentioned in the detailed Assyrian references to nomadic groups in the south and hence either characterizes an earlier period (Na'aman 2010a) or, better, was of local importance only. The text puts them in the desert to the west and southwest of the Beersheba Valley. At least in the Ziklag story they may correspond to the inhabitants of the Negev Highlands and the area of (modern) Nahal Besor (for Iron IIA sites in this region, see Gazit and Gophna 1993; Knauf 1988, 93–94; Mattingly 1992; Na'aman 2010a and bibliography).

two decades for the rule of the founders of the Davidic dynasty. According to the second interpretation, the David stories developed over a longer period of time: in the end days of Iron I and the early phases of Iron IIA (the tenth and early ninth centuries). In other words, they developed and turned into important tales in Judah in the first several decades of its existence, but still before the expansion of the kingdom to the west and south following the new arrangements imposed on the region by Hazael circa 840 BCE or a short time thereafter.

Summary

Read against the background of archaeological research, the geographical information embedded in the early David story in 1 Samuel depicts pre-Deuteronomistic reality that can be dated to the tenth and/or early ninth centuries BCE—in any event, before circa 840 BCE. The text delineates the existence of three territorial units: an early north Israelite polity that ruled as far south as the area of Bethlehem-Hebron, with a possible extension to the northeastern Shephelah; the kingdom of Gath, which ruled over much of the Shephelah as far south as the boundary of the Beersheba Valley; and the desert formation of Tel Masos in the Beersheba Valley and farther to the south. The text describes David as a leader of an Apiru band with a base in the sparsely settled, unruly highlands south of Hebron, who maneuvered between these units.

The territorial set up depicted in the early David story portrays several long-term conditions in the south in the second millennium BCE, before the consolidation of the territorial kingdoms of the Iron Age, among them attempts of highlands polity to expand to the Shephelah and Egyptian reaction on the side of the Shephelah kingdoms, which served their objectives. The territorial situation in the south changed as a result of the Sheshonq I intervention in the region. His campaign brought about the rise of the two Hebrew kingdoms of the highlands, the hegemony of Gath in the lowlands, and the prosperity of the Tel Masos polity in the Beersheba Valley and the Negev Highlands. The next change in the territorial setting in the south came with the campaign of Hazael of Damascus in the second half of the ninth century BCE, when Judah, as a vassal of Damascus, expanded to the Shephelah and the Beersheba Valley, inheriting territories from Gath and replacing the Tel Masos polity.

Addendum

Several topics dealt with in this chapter have been treated by me and colleagues in more recent publications:

1. Khirbet Qeiyafa, its date and territorio-political affiliation in particular and the chronology of the Shephelah in general (Finkelstein and Piasetzky 2015; Fantalkin and Finkelstein 2017).

2. The archaeology and history of the south in the early phases of the Iron Age, including the Negev Highlands, the Beersheba Valley, and the Arabah, with reference to the Tel Masos desert formation (Finkelstein 2014d).

3. The possible expansion of the Gibeon-Gibeah territorial formation (the house of Saul in the biblical memory) to the southern part of the hill country (ch. 5 above).

In recent years I have changed my mind on several issues dealt with in this chapter:

1. I now think that the united monarchy concept in the Bible originated in Israel in the first half of the eighth century BCE (Finkelstein 2020d).

2. Today I would not assign 1 Sam 17:8–11 and 17:52b to the early layer of the David narrative. Both belong to a later phase in the history of the tradition.

Additional archaeological information is now available for several sites. The newly added data confirm with the views expressed in the chapter.

1. Azekah was inhabited throughout the Iron II; there is no evidence for activity in the Iron I (Lipschits, Gadot, and Oeming 2018, 96).

2. Socoh, too, was apparently settled throughout the Iron II (Hasel, Garfinkel, and Weiss 2017, 223).

3. Hebron was inhabited throughout the Iron Age, with the Iron I and Iron IIB–C more prominently represented than the Iron IIA (Eisenberg and Ben-Shlomo 2017, 13–14, 441).

11

Kiriath-jearim:
Israel's Impact on Jerusalem in the
First Half of the Eighth Century BCE

There are few finds in Jerusalem that can be dated securely to the early phase of the Iron IIB, that is, in the first half of the eighth century BCE. The results of my excavations at Kiriath-jearim, a few kilometers to the west, shed light on this period in the history of Jerusalem and Judah. Read against the background of the ark narrative in the Bible, they hint that in this period the Northern Kingdom dominated Jerusalem and that the roots of the united monarchy ideology should be sought in eighth-century BCE Israel.

Identification of Kiriath-jearim

The site of Deir el-Azar is located on a dominating hill, 13 kilometers west of Jerusalem (figs. 10.1 and 10.2), commanding a vast panorama over the coastal plain to the west and the Judean Highlands to the east and southeast. At its summit stands the Convent of the Ark of the Covenant, built at the beginning of the twentieth century over the ruins of a Byzantine monastery or church. The size of the site can be estimated at 4–5 hectares, which makes it one of the largest mounds of the Bronze and Iron Ages in the highlands of the southern Levant.

The identification of Deir el-Azar with the biblical town of Kiriath-jearim is based on the following considerations:

This chapter was originally coauthored with Christophe Nicolle and Thomas Römer.

148　　　　　　　　　　Jerusalem the Center of the Universe

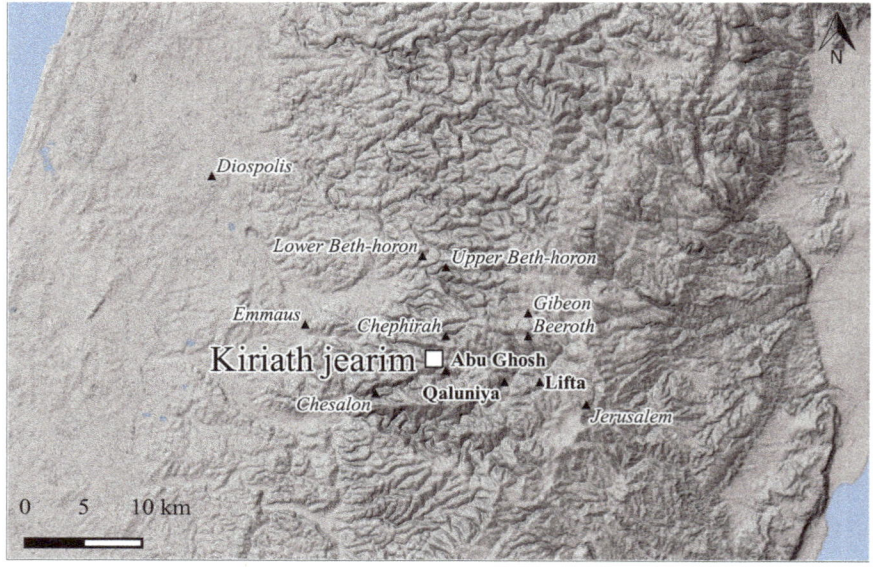

Fig. 11.1. Map showing the location of Kiriath-jearim.

Fig. 11.2. Aerial view of Deir el-Azar (Kiriath-jearim), looking south.

1. The description of the boundary between the territories of the tribes of Judah and Benjamin in Josh 15:9–10; 18:14–15, respectively.
2. Eusebius's description of a village named "Kariathiareim" at a distance of 10 Roman miles from Jerusalem on the road to Diospolis (= Lod; *Onomasticon* 48.24).
3. The name of the village located at the bottom of the hill, Qaryat el-ʿInab (Abu-Gosh) that preserves the term Kiriath from the ancient name.
4. The Arabic name of the site, Deir el-Azar, seemingly a corruption of "Monastery of Eleazar," which was probably the name of the Byzantine building that commemorated the priest Eleazar, who was in charge of the ark when it was kept at Kiriath-jearim (1 Sam 7:1).

Kiriath-jearim is mentioned a number of times in the Bible under different names (for details, see Finkelstein and Römer 2019b), mainly in the chapters on the tribal territories and towns in the book of Joshua and in the ark narrative in 1 Sam 4:1b–7:1 (to be discussed below). Regarding its location as a border town, in the older texts it apparently appears as belonging to the territory of Benjamin, while in later passages it is referred to as located in Judah. The texts relating to the town can be dated from the eighth century (the original ark narrative; see below) through the seventh century (1 Sam 6) to the fourth or third centuries BCE, if not slightly later (references in Chronicles).

The Name of the Site

Of special interest is the association of Kiriath-jearim in some texts with the name Baalah (Josh 15:9–10; 2 Sam 6:2 according to 4QSam and the parallel text of 1 Chr 13:6) or with Kiriath-baal (Josh 15:60; 18:14). It has often been thought that Kiriath-baal had been the ancient name of the town and that it was changed in late monarchic times due to negative connotations of the term Baal. In fact, in places where both names appear together, Kiriath-jearim always comes second, as an explanation. An alternative theory would be to understand Baal or Kiriath-baal as a polemical designation, appearing in texts dated to times when the site was considered a rival of Jerusalem. One may recall, for instance, the name Beth-aven, which is a polemical name given to Bethel in the book of Hosea (4:15, 10:15; also Amos 5:5). Nevertheless, unlike Hosea, our texts do not show any clear indication of a polemical objective. Some scholars proposed to understand Baalah (or Kiriath-baal) and Kiriath-jearim as two different sites located in proximity to each other (Fritz 1994, 160; Noth 1938a, 62–63; de Vos 2003, 321–23). However, all biblical texts mentioning these names point to one location. Besides, there is no archaeological evidence for two Iron Age sites existing side by side at Deir el-Azar or its vicinity. That sites may have had more than one name is attested elsewhere, for instance, Bethel and Luz, Hebron and Kiriath-arba. The name Kiriath-baal could have been given to this site because of the presence of a temple to Baal. One can wonder if this Baal was a title for YHWH or whether it was ascribed to another storm deity.

The best solution for these different names is the following. According to 1 Sam 7:1, the ark was brought to Kiriath-jearim and then onto the "hill" (*gibʿāh*; see also 2 Sam 6:3). We read in 1 Chr 13:6 that "David and all Israel *went up* to Baalah, that is, to Kiriath-jearim, which belongs to Judah" (NRSVue, emphasis added). The MT of Josh 18:28 uses the expression "the hill of Kiriath." All this may suggest that Kiriath-baal (or Baalah) was the name of the summit of the hill, where the shrine stood, while Kiriath-jearim was the name of the town, which included both the summit and the slopes. This would fit our topographical observations regarding the existence of an elevated platform on the summit (the Gibeah [and Kiriath-baal?]), which accommodated a shrine (more below).

The Excavations

A salvage excavation at the summit of the hill in the mid-1990s (McKinny et al. 2018), as well as two intensive field surveys (one carried out in the 1980s and the other more recently), together with our current project, offer a coherent picture of the history of the site (Finkelstein et al. 2018, table 1): continued activity, although of low intensity, from the Early Bronze through to the Iron IIA (from the third millennium through to the end of the ninth century BCE); first peak of prosperity during the Iron IIB–C (from the early eighth century to the beginning of the sixth century BCE); a phase of low activity during the Persian and early Hellenistic periods;

11. Kiriath-jearim

Fig. 11.3. View of the site, looking south, showing the flat, elevated, constructed summit.

renewal of intensive activity in the late Hellenistic period (second century BCE), with a third peak in the early Roman period (first century CE); and, finally, the construction of a monastery during the Byzantine period and some presence in the early Islamic period.

The most striking element of the site is its topography. The summit of the hill is exceptionally flat and, seen from afar (fig. 10.3), seems to have been artificially shaped. In order to understand this, one should pay attention to two massive terraces that outline the summit of the hill: (1) a long terrace 5.5 meters high in the east, oriented north–south (fig. 10.4); (2) a long and even higher terrace in the west, parallel to the one in the east (fig. 10.5).

These two terraces are clearly visible on our digital elevation model of the site (fig. 10.6) and in aerial photographs taken at the beginning of the twentieth century (fig. 10.7). The latter apparently presents another terrace in the north, oriented east–west, which was at least partially built over when the modern convent expanded. These terraces seem to outline an elevated platform of rectangular shape, erected on the summit of the hill. Establishing such a monumental platform must have required the building of massive retaining walls and the undertaking of a substantial filling operation. Investigation using seismic and geodetic equipment by Amotz Agnon of the Institute of Earth Sciences in the Hebrew University and his team indeed indicates the presence of major fills, several meters

Fig. 11.4. The massive terrace outlining the summit of the hill in the east, looking northwest.

Fig. 11.5. The massive terrace outlining the summit of the hill in the west, looking northeast (the cement wall was built in the 1980s).

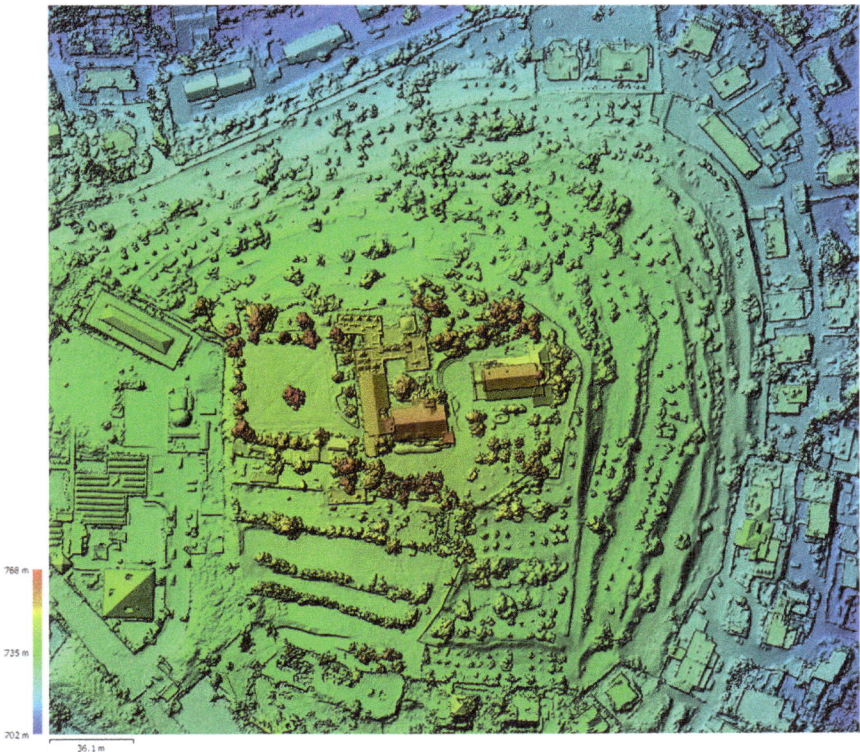

Fig. 11.6. Digital elevation model of the hill of Kiriath-jearim. Note the straight outlines of the massive north–south terraces in the east and in the west.

high in some places, laid between the inner faces of the terrace walls and the natural bedrock slope of the hill. Our assumption was that the old retaining walls, which created the platform, must be hidden in the massive terraces—otherwise the latter would not have survived the erosion of many centuries.

Verifying the theory of the raised platform was one of the main goals of the excavation. Two other considerations dictated the decision regarding the excavation areas: (1) it is impossible to dig in the inhabited parts of the convent; and (2) the fact that, in the highlands, summits are generally eroded, meaning that bedrock is expected to appear close to the surface (this is indeed what had been noticed during the salvage excavations carried out at the summit in the 1990s).

Fig. 11.7. Aerial view of the site looking north, photo taken by the Bavarian Air Force in 1918. Note the large terraces in the west and in the east. The modern construction is the building of the convent (the church had not yet been constructed).

Thus, three excavation areas were chosen for the first season (fig. 10.8); all three were extended during the second season.

- Area A, immediately to the north of the convent. Its goal was to check if an east–west retaining wall was constructed here.
- Area B on the southeast slope. The goal here was to verify the hypothesis of a massive retaining wall hidden in the eastern terrace.

Fig. 11.8. Orthophoto of the hill of Kiriath-jearim with the three excavation areas, looking north.

- Area C at the bottom of the eastern slope. The objective was to understand the nature of the site's slopes beyond the area of the alleged elevated platform on the summit.

In what follows, I discuss only the finds in Areas A and B. The excavations confirmed the hypothesis that the summit of the hill is artificially constructed. Massive stone walls directly erected on bedrock were exposed in the north and in the east. In the east (fig. 10.9), the massive wall constitutes the core of the long terrace visible on the surface, as well as on the digital elevation model and in the old aerial photos (figs. 10.6–10.7). In the north, two parallel massive walls were unearthed, the older—probably the original retaining wall—running slightly to the north of the convent (fig. 10.10, photograph taken at the end of the 2019 excavations season). Hence it is also clear that the western terrace, which has not been excavated, hides the western retaining wall of the platform. The southern retaining wall seems to have been identified in magnetometer and ground-penetrating radar investigations undertaken by Agnon and his team under the parking lot of the convent. Thus it seems that the raised platform was rectangular

Fig. 11.9. The massive retaining wall in Area B (southeast section of the site) at the end of the 2017 excavation campaign. The wall was first built in Iron IIB, then repaired in the late Hellenistic and early Roman periods.

in shape, measuring 110 × 150 meters and oriented exactly north–south/east–west (fig. 10.11).

Dating the construction of these support walls and thus the erection of the platform is not an easy task. Traditional archaeological dating based on ceramic assemblages is impossible; due to erosion, no floor directly connected to the inner face of the retaining walls could be detected. In addition, the retaining walls had been repaired twice, during the late Hellenistic and early Roman periods, meaning that the fill layers on their inner sides have produced mixed pottery assemblages. In Area B in the southeast, for instance, most pottery sherds inside of the support wall and all the way down to bedrock date to the Iron IIB and Iron IIC (from eighth to the beginning of the sixth centuries BCE), but late Hellenistic (second century BCE) and early Roman (first century CE) pottery sherds are also present; they probably indicate periods of repairs of the walls (see Finkelstein et al. 2021, fig. 17). Repair operations in the massive wall in Area B

Fig. 11.10. Orthophoto of Area A at the end of the 2019 excavation campaign, looking north and showing two massive walls. The southern wall (bottom of the picture), which dates to Iron IIB in the first half of the eighth century BCE, is the original retaining wall of the raised platform. The northern wall is a fortification dating to the late Hellenistic period; it was repaired in the early Roman period.

are noticeable also architecturally, first and foremost in the incorporation of drafted stones in second use. Needless to say, with no floors and clean contexts related to the platform, there were no samples suitable for radiocarbon dating.

Faced with these difficulties, we turned to two other methods in order to date the massive support walls. (1) In 2019 we dismantled sections of the two massive parallel walls in Area A (fig. 10.10) in order to retrieve pottery sherds from between their courses; the latest of these sherds were expected to shed light on the date of construction. The pottery sherds recovered from between the stones of the southern (and more massive) of the two walls date to the Iron I and Iron IIA, with only one sherd belonging to the Iron IIB. This implies that the wall was built at the beginning of the Iron IIB (had it been constructed later in the Iron IIB, more sherds of this period would be expected here). This date is supported by another piece of evidence. A kind of an earthen glacis, leaning against the outer face of the retaining wall and probably aiming at stabilizing it, produced mainly Iron IIB items and one possible Iron IIC sherd, which indicates that it was

Fig. 11.11. Digital elevation model of the hill, schematically showing in white lines the suggested layout of the retaining walls that supported the Iron Age raised platform.

added to the wall in a later phase of Iron IIB or the very beginning of Iron IIC, that is, at the end of the eighth century or in the beginning of the seventh century BCE. The latest sherds in the dismantled part in the northern of the two massive walls in Area A yielded early Roman sherds, possibly representing repair of a slightly earlier, late Hellenistic fortification.

(2) Samples for Optically Stimulated Luminescence (OSL) dating were taken in both seasons (2017 and 2019). Ten OSL results were obtained for samples extracted in the first season (for details, see Finkelstein et al. 2018, table 2), most of them from the massive retaining wall in Area B (fig. 10.9) and from the northernmost of the two massive walls in Area A (fig. 10.10; the southern of the two had not yet been exposed in 2017). The original construction phase is represented by three results from the base of the inner face of the southeast massive wall in Area B. They provided the following results: 1110–770, 1320–960, and 1140–780 BCE. They present a broad time span covering the Late Bronze II through to the early Iron IIB. However, when one considers the settlement history of the site, the only appropriate option for the construction of these massive retaining walls within this time span is the early Iron IIB in the first half of the eighth

century BCE. This is so because the construction of such a monumental platform could have been undertaken only during a period of intensive activity at the site. Other OSL results, from the upper part of the massive wall's inner face in Area B and from the northern of the two massive walls in Area A, fall in the Hellenistic and Roman periods. Evaluating them together with the pottery evidence from the fills on the inner side of Area B's massive wall and from Area A, they seem to hint at construction/renovation activities in the late Hellenistic and early Roman periods (more in Finkelstein and Römer 2019a).

Taking into account the evidence from the dismantled walls, the OSL results, differences in construction methods of the massive wall in Area B, the pottery from the layers exposed on the inner face of the massive wall in Area B, and the settlement history of the site, we can tentatively reconstruct the history of the raised platform at the summit of the hill: an original construction phase in the early Iron IIB followed by two later phases of reconstruction in the late Hellenistic and early Roman periods (Finkelstein et al. 2018; Finkelstein and Römer 2019b). At the end of two excavations seasons, all three building phases were clearly observed in the sole massive wall exposed in Area B, whereas in Area A they are represented in the two parallel massive walls that we uncovered: the southern one built in the early Iron IIB and the northern one constructed in late Hellenistic times and repaired in the early Roman period (fig. 10.9).

As far as the identity of the early Iron IIB builder is concerned, one may first note the location of the site on a commanding hill guarding an important road from the coast to Jerusalem and hence dominating the city, as well as the biblical tradition placing Kiriath-jearim on the border between the tribes of Judah and Benjamin, meaning the border between Judah and Israel, at least during part of their history. Three candidates for the construction of the platform come to mind: Judah, Assyria, and Israel.

To start with Judah, no raised platform of this type is known in its territory, and, in any event, in the beginning of the eighth century Judah did not command the personnel and economic resources necessary for undertaking such a monumental construction project. Regarding the possibility of an Assyrian stronghold, a relatively similar raised platform apparently existed at Buseirah in Edom (aerial photograph in Bienkowski 2002, 38); it was probably constructed by the Assyrians as an administrative and control center along the Arabian trade route. One could suggest that a similar administrative center had been built at Kiriath-jearim for controlling Jerusalem after the Sennacherib campaign in 701 BCE. However, both the pottery evidence from Area A and the OSL results are too early for such an Assyrian endeavor. We are left with the third option, that of an Israelite construction.

Indeed, raised platforms of this type are known in the Northern Kingdom, east of the Dead Sea (Finkelstein and Lipschits 2010), and in various sites in Cisjordan, including its capital Samaria (Finkelstein 2011b). We therefore suggest that the Kiriath-jearim platform was constructed by Israel after the subjugation of Judah by King Joash, hinted at in 2 Kgs 14:11–13. Taking into account the pottery evidence from Area A and the OSL results, which point to the early eighth century, the project must have been undertaken in the days of Jeroboam II (788–747 BCE). Both archaeology and biblical texts indicate that he was probably the most powerful of the Northern Kingdom's monarchs.[1] During his reign, Israel reached its peak territorial and demographic expansion, as well as economic prosperity. It seems that the platform at Kiriath-jearim was built on the border between Israel and Judah as an Israelite administrative complex with the purpose of controlling the vassal kingdom of Judah and its capital Jerusalem.[2] This administrative center may have included a sanctuary: the temple presupposed in the ark narrative.

The Ark Narrative and Kiriath-jearim

The ark narrative consists of two blocks in the book of Samuel. The first, 1 Sam 4:1–7:1, relates the capture and return of the ark. In the beginning of the narrative, the ark of YHWH stands in the sanctuary of Shiloh. The Israelites bring it to the battlefield, where it is captured by the Philistines,

---

1. See several articles in *Hebrew Bible and Ancient Israel* 6, 2017.

2. Thanks to its commanding position over the road leading from the coastal area to Jerusalem, the site of Kiriath-jearim played a similar role—controlling Jerusalem—in two later historical circumstances. In the middle of the second century BCE a fortress was apparently built here by the Seleucids, when they attempted to suppress the Hasmonean revolt (Finkelstein and Römer 2019b). Later, circa 70 CE, a Roman military unit was posted here, in the context of the unrest during the First Jewish Revolt (cf. the inscriptions discovered at the site and in its vicinity in Cotton et al. 2010, 11, 25–26, 38–39).

who carry it to the temple of their god, Dagon, at Ashdod. The ark inflicts calamities on the Philistines, so they decide to return it to the Israelites. After it leaves Philistine territory, it first goes to Beth-shemesh, where YHWH, for unclear reasons, strikes the people of the town. It then arrives at Kiriath-jearim, in the house of Abinadab, where a priest named Eleazar is put in charge of it. The second block, 2 Sam 6, then relates how David transferred the ark from Baalah (Kiriath-jearim) to Jerusalem.

The idea of an ancient tradition related to the ark is due to Leonhard Rost's (1982) notion of an independent ark narrative in 1 Sam 4:1b–7:1 and 2 Sam 6. According to Rost, the story aimed at explaining the arrival of the ark in the temple of Jerusalem after the destruction of Shiloh and its captivity in Philistia. The narrative would have been written by a priest in charge of the ark during David's or Solomon's reign. YHWH is presented as a God who fights Israel's enemies and brings victory to his people.

Rost's hypothesis was first widely accepted, but soon after questions arose, especially as to the problem whether 2 Sam 6 (the transfer of the ark to Jerusalem) belongs to the original story (e.g., Schäfer-Lichtenberger 1995). First, the story in this chapter is quite different from the narrative in 1 Sam 4–6. Second, had 2 Sam 6 been part of the original ark narrative, one would have expected David to be introduced by the narrator from the beginning. Third, in 1 Sam 4–6, the ark is somehow identified with YHWH, while in 2 Sam 6 it appears more as a kind of cultic symbol. Fourth, 1 Sam 4–6 does not hint at Jerusalem as the final destination of the ark; one could have expected some kind of preparation of the reader if the story had been, from the start, the *hieros logos* for the ark in Jerusalem.

For these reasons, one should follow scholars who propose that the original story ended in 1 Sam 7:1, with the ark arriving at Kiriath-jearim (e.g., Miller and Roberts 1977; Porzig 2009). We suggest that the first narrative was written in order to legitimize Kiriath-jearim as the new venue of the ark, after Shiloh. Taking into consideration the archaeological evidence, the best candidate for the construction of the sanctuary at Kiriath-jearim, on the border of Israel and Judah, is Jeroboam II, who also built Bethel, Penuel, and other sanctuaries, apparently in order to commemorate important northern foundation and cultic traditions.[3] Moving

---

3. The story in 1 Kgs 12, which attributes the construction of Dan and Bethel to Jeroboam I, actually reflects realities of Jeroboam II's time (see Römer 2017).

the ark to Kiriath-jearim on the border between Israel and Judah and close to Jerusalem could have been connected to an Israelite ideology of a united monarchy ruled by a northern king over the territory of the two Hebrew kingdoms "from Dan to Beersheba" (this was probably the origin of the united monarchy concept of Judah in the late seventh century BCE; for both, see Finkelstein 2019).

The question remains regarding the identity of the redactor of the part describing the transfer of the ark from Kiriath-jearim to Jerusalem by David. The answer to this question depends on one's view regarding the question of when the ark actually arrived at the temple of Jerusalem. The fact that the books of Kings do not say anything about the ark after it was placed in the temple by Solomon (1 Kgs 8) is puzzling. A rather simple explanation could be that the ark arrived at the temple of Jerusalem only in the days of King Josiah. This would mean that the authors of 2 Sam 6 and 1 Kgs 6–8 were the scribes of the late seventh-century Judahite monarch. Had the ark been brought to Jerusalem by Josiah in the context of his reform, only fifty years before the destruction of the temple, one could understand why the books of Kings do not say anything about the ark in Jerusalem. Indeed, a puzzling verse in 2 Chronicles may attest that Josiah was the one who placed the ark in the temple of Jerusalem: "He [Josiah] said to the Levites who taught all Israel and who were holy to the Lord, 'Put the holy ark in the house that Solomon son of David, king of Israel, built; you need no longer carry it on your shoulders. Now serve the Lord your God and his people Israel'" (2 Chr 35:3 NRSVue).

We have seen earlier that Kiryath-jearim is located at the border between the tribal territories of Judah and Benjamin, an area often disputed by the kingdoms of Israel and Judah.[4] Josiah could have annexed the territory of Benjamin and then, within the framework of his centralization policy, have brought the important symbol of YHWH from Kiriath-jearim to Jerusalem. The fact that Josiah did not destroy the ark but brought it to Jerusalem can be explained by its old (north Israelite) Yahwistic character.

But how could the Josianic authors tell a story about the transfer of the ark by David, when the people of Jerusalem knew that this had been done in their own time by Josiah? Indeed, another possibility is that the ark was transferred from Kiriath-jearim to Jerusalem by King Hezekiah, after the

---

4. For biblical texts mentioning Kiriath-jearim, see above and Koch 2017.

fall of the Northern Kingdom. In this case enough time had passed until the days of Josiah to allow his authors to claim that the ark was brought to the temple by David. Still, as recent history teaches us, historical "inventions" can be assimilated even if people should know better.

Conclusion

(1) The first version of the ark narrative in 1 Sam 4:1–7:1* was probably written under Jeroboam II, who made Kiriath-jearim—on the border between Israel and its vassal kingdom Judah—the new sanctuary of the ark, instead of the holy place at Shiloh. The sanctuary of the ark was established in a monumental compound that could have had other functions, among them guarding the road to Jerusalem and hence dominating Judah's capital. Placing the ark on the border between the two Hebrew kingdoms could have also been related to a "united monarchy" ideology in Israel.

(2) The original ark narrative, which ends in 1 Sam 7:1 was therefore the *hieros logos* of the shrine of Kiryath-jearim.

(3) The ark was transferred from Kiriath-jearim to Jerusalem probably during the reign of King Josiah, who, in the framework of his centralization policy, had it set in the temple of Jerusalem. Josiah's scribes edited the ancient text and composed the story in 2 Sam 6. They also rewrote the story of the construction of the temple in 1 Kgs 6–8 in order to "prove" that the ark was part of the temple ever since its construction. Another possibility is to date the transfer of the ark from Kidiath-jearim to Jerusalem somewhat earlier to the days of Hezkiah. This would mean that enough time had passed between the actual event and the composition of 2 Sam 6 to allow the Josianic scribes to argue that the ark was brought to the temple by David.

Part 4
The Iron IIB: The Largest City in the Levant

12

The Appearance and Dissemination of Writing in Judah

The next two chapters are devoted to the crucial issue of the beginning of significant scribal activity in Jerusalem and Judah. They formulate the essential questions regarding composition of biblical texts and in turn the subject of historicity in biblical traditions. In my opinion, the only way to explore this theme is by analysis of the archaeological finds, that is, by detecting securely dated inscriptions in the archaeological record.

Introduction

Establishing the beginning of scribal activity and the later dissemination of literacy in Judah is essential for reconstructing the history of the kingdom and tackling questions such as the historicity of the united monarchy and the history of composition of biblical texts. In the past, discussions of these issues were based on information ostensibly provided by the biblical text, such as the reference to scribes in the court of David and Solomon (e.g., 2 Sam 8:16). Needless to say, this is a circular argument that can hardly be accepted in modern scholarship, as many of the narratives related to David's reign may represent later and even north Israelite realities (for the latter, e.g., Na'aman 2017; Sergi 2017b; Finkelstein 2020b). Reaching conclusions on Judah based on analysis of all inscriptions from the southern Levant, Proto-Canaanite and Hebrew, and from good contexts or not dateable contexts (e.g., Lemaire 2015; Rollston 2017), can also be misleading.

I wish to thank Benjamin Sass for reading the manuscript and providing me with important remarks.

Archaeology provides independent evidence on writing in Judah; I refer to the relatively large number of ostraca found in Judahite sites, especially in the Negev (the Beersheba Valley), as well as other media of writing, that is, incised pottery sherds (or vessels), seals, seal impressions, bullae and (the very few) monumental inscriptions. However, the archaeological record also needs to be interpreted critically, especially regarding stratigraphic context and hence date of the finds.[1] Moreover, treating the entire corpus of inscriptions from Iron Age Judah (and elsewhere) under the same umbrella is a methodological error; it is clear that the production of ostraca, for instance, reflects a higher level of literacy than inscribing one's name on an object.

Evidence for widespread dissemination of writing in Judah in the Iron IIC, in the late seventh century BCE, is abundant (fig. 12.1). This is obvious from the sheer number of finds and their distribution (e.g., Ahituv 2008; Na'aman 2015) and from recent algorithmic and forensic studies on the number of authors in the Arad ostraca (Faigenbaum-Golovin et al. 2016; Shaus et al. 2020). Writing in Judah, at least in administrative and royal circles, is also evident in the late eighth century, as manifested by the Siloam Inscription,[2] the early *lmlk* seal impressions and "private" seal impressions on *lmlk* storage jars (for the latter two, see Lipschits, Sergi, and Koch 2010). But what was the scope of writing at that time, for instance, in ink on ceramic sherds (ostraca)? Further, what about the period before the late eighth century? I refer to the early Iron IIB, in the first half of the eighth century, and to the late Iron IIA, in the ninth and early eighth centuries. The latter is relatively well recorded thanks to exposure of layers such as Lachish IV and Beersheba V (for radiocarbon-established absolute chronology in the south, see Finkelstein and Piasetzky 2015). The former is more difficult to isolate but is now known from the destruction of Beth-

---

1. Two preliminary comments on the scope of the chapter are in place here: (1) I will deal only with inscriptions that originated from excavations; all market items are excluded for reasons of authenticity (and, in any event, they do not come from dateable contexts). (2) Apart from a short comment on Moab, I am not dealing here with appearance of writing in the Transjordanian kingdoms.

2. Reich and Shukron (2011) suggested an earlier date for the Siloam Tunnel and thus the Siloam Inscription, in the early eighth century. I believe that the traditional date, in the very late eighth century BCE, should be retained (ch. 17 below).

12. The Appearance and Dissemination of Writing in Judah

Fig. 12.1. Hebrew ostraca from Arad, circa 600 BCE.

shemesh 3 (renewed excavations), radiocarbon-dated to circa 765–745 BCE (Finkelstein and Piasetzky 2009).

The key site for dating these early phases of writing in Judah has conventionally been Arad, with its corpus of Hebrew ostraca (fig. 12.1). Yohanan Aharoni (1981) assigned one ostracon from Arad (no. 81) to Stratum XII of the early Iron IIA in the late tenth to early ninth century and four ostraca (nos. 76–79) to Stratum XI of the late Iron IIA—in the case of Arad in the second half of the ninth century (and/or the early eighth century BCE).³ These have been considered the earliest Hebrew inscriptions recorded in Judah. In addition, Aharoni assigned thirty-nine ostraca and incised inscriptions to Strata X–VIII of the Iron IIB in the second half of the eighth century—a large number that ostensibly points to widespread writing (for the relative dates of the Arad layers, see Herzog and Singer-Avitz 2004, 231; Singer-Avitz 2002; for absolute dates, Herzog 2002a, 14).

According to this broadly accepted order (e.g., Naveh 1982, 66; Finkelstein and Sass 2013, 169; Na'aman 2015; Sergi 2020), writing in Judah is evident in 800 BCE at the latest. However, several pieces of evidence seem to challenge this notion.

1. It is evident today that the use of the Proto-Canaanite script continued into the ninth century BCE (Finkelstein and Sass 2013). This is demonstrated by the Kefar Veradim inscription (found with a Late Iron IIA ceramic assemblage; Alexandre 2002a), the lingering Proto-Canaanite tradition in the short Megiddo inscription (Sass and Finkelstein 2016), and, most importantly for Judah, by the Ophel inscription (Mazar, Ben-Shlomo, and Ahituv 2013). Based on the form of the pithos on which it was incised, the latter cannot date much before the middle of the ninth century BCE (Kleiman 2021). This would mean that the latest evidence for the Proto-Canaanite script and the earliest Hebrew script date to the same period.⁴

2. The latest Tell eṣ-Ṣafi/Gath inscriptions, including one painted, are well dated to the late Iron IIA before the destruction of Gath by Hazael in the 830s (Maeir 2012, 47–49) or later, circa 810 BCE (Lipinski 2000, 386–87; Kleiman 2015). Their script can be described as "supra-regional" cursive, before the appearance of Hebrew and other local scripts (Finkelstein and Sass 2021). This observation puts the Hebrew of Arad 76 automatically later than the late ninth century BCE.

---

3. Unstratified ostracon no. 80 was associated by Aharoni (1981, 100) with Stratum XI, based on paleographic consideration, but in the list at the end of the volume it is assigned to Stratum X (184). Note that only three or four letters are readable and that a similar *yod* appears in several Level II Lachish inscriptions (Lemaire 2004, 2119).

4. For a full discussion of the date of these inscriptions, see Finkelstein and Sass 2013 (Kefar Veradim and Ophel); Sass and Finkelstein 2016 (Megiddo).

12. The Appearance and Dissemination of Writing in Judah

3. No Hebrew inscription—ink, incised, or impressed—has been found in any other Iron IIA Judahite layer. Especially noteworthy are Beer-sheba V, Lachish V and IV, and Beth-shemesh 3.

4. Associating Ostraca 81 and 76–79 at Arad with Strata XII and XI, respectively, means that Hebrew ink writing is evident in Judah earlier than the far more developed Israel, where the earliest such inscriptions date to the first half of the eighth century: the Samaria ostraca and the Kuntillet ʿAjrud inscriptions.

These observations call for a fresh look at the provenance of Arad Ostraca 76–79 and 81. In view of the meager number of ostraca and incised inscriptions found in all other late eighth-century Judahites sites (more below), the inscriptions assigned by Aharoni to Strata X–VIII should also be carefully reexamined.

The Date of the "Early" Arad Inscriptions

Ostraca 76–79 and 81

To start with a general comment, Aharoni's stratigraphy of the fortress of Arad has been challenged by many authorities (Y. Yadin 1965; Mazar and Netzer 1986; Ussishkin 1988; Herzog 2002a, 5, 7). Among other issues relating to this old dig, with ostensibly tight stratigraphy, note that no floors are marked on the plans published by Herzog (2002a) and that activity in the Hellenistic period damaged the older remains, sometimes in a significant way (e.g., Herzog 2002a, 12–13). It is clear, then, from the outset that Arad cannot serve as an anchor for the archaeology and history of Judah.

Turning to the ostraca (details in the appendix below, table C), number 81, which was assigned by Aharoni to Stratum XII, cannot be securely dated. It was found in Locus 432F, 70 centimeters higher than another locus that was assigned to this layer, in an open space with no floor (Aharoni 1981, 184; Herzog 2002a, fig. 5). Also note that the excavation of Locus 432 commenced in the elevation of Stratum VIII or even higher (Herzog 2002a, Fig. 16).

As for the four ostraca assigned to Stratum XI, number 78 was found in Locus 778D, located below the room that yielded the Eliashib seals and three other inscriptions (nos. 31–32 and 34). This context was affiliated by

Mazar and Netzer (1986, 87–87) with Stratum VI. Its excavation began, more or less, in the level of Stratum VIII (Locus 778A, 74.80 m). Number 79 was discovered in an area disturbed by both the collapsed water cistern and the northwestern corner of the Hellenistic tower.

It is clear, then, that attention should be given first and foremost to Arad 76, the longest (at least seven lines) with the largest number of letters (sixteen read by Aharoni 1981, 98–99) in this group, and to Arad 77, which was found in the same locus (Locus 949, Square K/16). Stratigraphically, these inscriptions were found 30–35 centimeters above the lowest level of Locus 949 (Square K/16, 73.00 m), which was assigned to Stratum XI. This is certainly not a secure location such as accumulation resting on a clearly identifiable floor. Indeed, another inscription found in this locus (no. 74) was defined as unstratified (Aharoni 1981, 97). Therefore, these items cannot constitute the anchor for fixing the earliest evidence for writing in Judah.

Additionally, looking at the photo and facsimile of Arad 76 in the original publication, it is obvious that Aharoni reconstructed some of the characters from vague traces. This is true also when looking at the recently taken multispectral images of this inscription (Na'aman 2021). Even the *ṣade* in line 4 is not clear enough to be securely reconstructed. Moreover, visible characters in Ostracon 76 do appear in Iron IIC Arad inscriptions, such as the *qoph* in line 5, the clearest letter in this inscription (compare to table in Aharoni 1981, 133–34), and the *zayin* in line 6, which apparently appears in Ostracon 17 of Stratum VI. The only letter that looks old in Aharoni's facsimile is the *mem*, which appears twice (lines 1 and 3). However, the two are drawn from extremely eroded signs and are probably reconstructed according to Aharoni's understanding of how a Stratum XI *mem* should look, and a somewhat similar *mem* to the one drawn by Aharoni apparently appears in Ostracon 13 of Stratum VI and Ostracon 60, which Aharoni assigned to Stratum IX (late eighth century; more below). The latter was found in a nearby square (Locus 1036).

Inscriptions Assigned by Aharoni to Strata X–VIII

Thirty-nine inscriptions were assigned by Aharoni to Strata X–VIII of the Iron IIB, which date to the second half of the eighth century BCE. Na'aman (2015) accepted Aharoni's stratigraphic affiliation of these inscriptions and explained the unique proliferation of writing at Arad as representing the military role of the site. This is not a convincing argument. First, no secure eighth-century BCE ostracon was found at the fort of Kadesh-barnea, located approximately 85 kilometers to the north of the contemporary site of Kuntillet ʿAjrud; the latter site, affiliated with the Northern Kingdom, yielded a large number of inscriptions. Second, Tel ʿIra and Tel Malḥata certainly played an important role in the administration and military affairs of Judah in the south (for ʿIra, see Ostracon 24 from Arad, accepting that this is the location of Ramath-negeb).

With no final and detailed report on the results of the excavations at Arad, it is difficult to scrutinize the exact stratigraphic affiliation of Aharoni's Strata X–VIII inscriptions. Still, the appendix below shows that only four (!) of the thirty-nine items—Ostraca 45, 60, 87, and 90—can perhaps be associated with Strata IX and VIII (hoping that the contexts in which they were discovered will be shown in the future to signify floors).[5] Note the case of Ostracon 40, assigned by Yohanan Aharoni to Stratum VIII (1981, 74) but probably belonging later, as it "shares with no. 24 of Stratum VI its script, contents, and author's name" (Naʾaman 2003; 2015, 50; Dobbs-Allsopp et al. 2005, 69–70). Further support for the dating of Arad 40 comes from the fact that the inscription was found 1.05 meters above the lowest level of the locus with which it was associated (compare the elevations in Aharoni 1981, 182, with those that appear in Herzog 2002a, fig. 16). Locus 469, in which numbers 50–52, were found, was reassigned by Herzog (2002a, fig. 17) to Stratum VII, meaning that their association with Stratum VI cannot be excluded. Also to be noted is the fact that other late eighth-century layers in the Beersheba Valley did not yield ostraca; the only exception is Stratum II at Beersheba, with two finds (more below).

To summarize the discussion on Arad, as evidence exists for appearance of ostraca in Judah in the late eighth century (two from Beersheba and seemingly two from Lachish; see below), it is possible that a few Arad ostraca also originated from Strata X–VIII, though with the data at hand this cannot be proven.

---

5. In the Hebrew edition of *Arad Inscriptions*, Aharoni (1986) assigned incised number 93 to Stratum XI in the text but to Stratum IX in the list. In the English edition both the text and the list put it in Stratum IX; indeed, the locus (841) appears in Herzog's plan of Stratum IX (2002a, fig. 15).

The inevitable conclusion from the above discussion is that Arad cannot serve as a basis for discussing the emergence of Hebrew writing (and literacy) in Judah.

Ostraca from Other Sites

Having dismissed the affiliation of Ostraca 81 and 76–79 with Arad XII–XI and noting the problematic nature of the stratigraphy of Arad also for the Strata X–VIII items, for pre-seventh-century layers we are left only with Stratum II at Beersheba. Na'aman lists three ostraca with this layer, noting that "Stratum II was destroyed by the Assyrians in about 701 BCE and following that destruction, it was abandoned for hundreds of years" (2015, 59). However, the recently published final report of the excavations at Beersheba sheds different light on this matter. Herzog (2016, 26) notes that, after the destruction of the city of Stratum II, "the site was resettled, apparently as a local undertaking by what seems to have been a private rather than state initiative.... the project was never completed and the settlers moved away. This endeavor may have lasted between a few months to a year or two at most" (see also Singer-Avitz 2016, 658). This activity, listed as Stratum I, is also described as squatters settling into the ruins of Stratum II (Herzog 2016, table on 29). The pottery repertoire (Singer-Avitz 2016) indeed lacks the typical forms of the Iron IIC, such as lamps with high base, holemouth jars with horizontal flat rims, and cooking pots with grooved everted rim. However, today we know that the Iron IIB/IIC transition took place in the first half of the seventh century, if not the middle of that century (ch. 18 below; this is the essence of Lipschits, Sergi, and Koch 2010), meaning that the activity of the Stratum I squatters could have lasted well into the first half of the seventh century. Having said this, we need to look more carefully at the three ostraca from Tel Beersheba (Aharoni 1971).

There is no reason to doubt the stratigraphic affiliation of Beersheba Ostracon 1 to Stratum II, as it was found in an exterior hall of one of the storehouses (Aharoni 1971, 71). Ostracon 3 also seems to come from a secure Stratum II context (74). But Ostracon 2, found in a "robbers trench of the casemate wall" (73), may belong to the Stratum I activity, in the early seventh century.

Outside of the Beersheba Valley, Lachish is the most important site to consider. As is well known, a large number of ostraca were retrieved from

Level II there, dated to the late seventh century (Lemaire 2004). At least for the three first expeditions (Starky's, Aharoni's, and Ussishkin's), only two ostraca should be discussed in relation to Level III.[6]

1. Number XXIII was found "in Podium A of the Judean Palace-Fort ... in the Level IV constructional fill, or what is more likely Level III debris from Palace C, eroded since the British dig" (Lemaire 2004, 2116–17).

2. Number XXXIII (Lemaire 2004, 2128–29) came from the courtyard in front of the gate (Ussishkin 2004b, 566), which is less than an ideal (that is, stratigraphically secure) context, especially noting that the Level II Lachish gate ostraca were found only 15 meters away from this spot.

An ostracon recently found at Hebron was dated to the end of the eighth century (Vainstub and Ben-Shlomo 2016, 158), though the stratigraphic description speaks about Iron IIB–C pottery in this context (153–55; "Phase 7 fill" in Vainstub 2017; Phase 7 dated to the Iron IIB–C in Ben-Shlomo and Eisenberg 2017, 14).

It is especially noteworthy that all ostraca found in Jerusalem came from seventh-century contexts (Stratum 10, e.g., Naveh 2000) or from unstratified loci (e.g., Lemaire 1978). No ostracon was uncovered in an eighth-century context, that is, in Shiloh's Stratum 12.

To summarize this point, of the roughly two hundred ostraca known from Judah,[7] almost all originated from seventh-century (mainly late seventh century) contexts; only two to four ostraca (at Tel Beersheba and possibly Lachish) can be securely dated to the late eighth century BCE. The ratio is more balanced for the incised inscriptions (more below).

Other Pieces of Evidence to Consider

The following are additional points pertinent to the discussion on the emergence of literacy in Judah.

---

6. A third ostracon, no. XXXIV "was found in Area GW, Level IV ... as this part of the outer gate is largely eroded in later periods the ostracon may well be a stray find from a later level" (Lemaire 2004, 2129).

7. Including Edomite ostraca from the territory of Judah.

1. The well-stratified and intensively excavated late Iron IIA Judahite sites of Lachish IV, Beersheba V, and Beth-shemesh 3 (which was probably established in that period) yielded no inscriptions, ink or incised. This is also true for the contemporary Stratum 14 in the City of David in Jerusalem. The three es-Samuʿ (Eshtemoa) jugs with the ink inscription ḥmš on each came from an unstratified context (Yeivin 1990). Typologically, the jugs date to either the Iron IIA or Iron IIB (for this, see Kletter and Brand 1998).

2. The first point above is especially noteworthy in view of the relatively large number of inscriptions that originated from the contemporary, nearby Iron IIA layers at Tell eṣ-Ṣafi/Gath and the countryside towns in its territory (Maeir and Eshel 2014; Finkelstein and Sass 2021).

3. The earliest Hebrew inscriptions from Judah[8]—the only securely dated Judahite Hebrew inscriptions that predate the last third of the eighth century BCE—are the two Uzziah seals purchased in the market in the late nineteenth century (Avigad and Sass 1997, 50–51). The early date of their acquisition seems to eliminate the possibility of forgery. The *yau* component in the names of the two officials (Shebanyau, Abiyau) and the king (Uzziyau) hint at north Israelite influence: perhaps these administrators were Israelites who served in Judah during a period of Israelite domination over the Southern Kingdom (more below). In this connection, note that the only other cotemporary inscribed seal (or inscribed seal impression) is the northern Shema servant of Jeroboam item from Megiddo.

4. Based on his analysis of the Arad finds (and accepting Aharoni's affiliation of finds to Strata X–VIII), Na'aman (2015) theorized that in the Negev short incised inscriptions are more prevalent in eighth-century strata, while ostraca are numerous in the late seventh-century layers. If many of these Arad finds in fact date to later strata than their original affiliation, the balance somewhat changes: in the Negev, thirteen incised inscriptions originated from stratigraphically secure late eighth-century layers versus four from seventh-century layers, to which some of the above-mentioned Arad items should be added. At Lachish only one item was retrieved from Level III (and two from Level II; Lemaire 2004).

---

8. I am not dealing here with the Proto-Canaanite Ophel inscription (Mazar, Ben-Shlomo, and Ahituv 2013). This unique find can hardly shed light on literacy in Judah. Among other reasons, though petrographic investigation pointed to its origin in the highlands, the exact location where it was made cannot be verified.

5. The *lmlk* administrative system appears in the late eighth century BCE; inscribed "private" seal impressions appear on the early *lmlk* storage jars (pre-701 BCE; Lipschits, Sergi, and Koch 2010).

6. In addition to the evidence from Level III at Lachish, which was intensively excavated and produced only two possible ostraca and one incised inscription (no. XXI-A, Lemaire 2004, 2114), attention should be given to two other intensively excavated Judahite sites in the Shephelah. Beth-shemesh (the mound), which was destroyed in 701 BCE, produced a single inscribed bowl from a late eighth-century context (Manor 2016). Tell Beit Mirsim, which was destroyed in 701 and apparently resettled for a short while in the early seventh century (Finkelstein and Na'aman 2004), yielded five incised inscriptions from Stratum A (Albright 1932, 77; photographs in Albright 1943, pl. 60). Neither site produced ostraca.

7. The uninscribed, iconic bullae form the area of the Gihon Spring (Reich, Shukron, and Lernau 2007) are dated according to the pottery found with them to the late Iron IIA (De Groot and Fadida 2011) or Iron IIB (Singer-Avitz 2012), that is, to the late ninth or eighth century BCE. Uninscribed bullae from the Ophel excavations are given the same time range (Keel 2015). Inscribed bullae appear in Judah in large numbers in Iron IIC layers, that is, starting around the middle of the seventh century (Aharoni 1975b, 19–22; Avigad 1986; Avigad and Sass 1997, 167–241; Shoham 2000; Mazar and Livyatan Ben-Arie 2015; see latest summary in Mendel-Geberovich, Chalaf, and Uziel 2020). A bulla from Lachish (Avigad and Sass 1997, 199, no. 498) was found in a Level III room (Tufnell 1953, 348); this is in line with the appearance of inscribed private seal impressions on the *lmlk* jars.

8. Plaster inscriptions—theorized to portray the existence of writing on papyri (Lemaire 1985, 275, 284)—appear in Israel in the first half of the eighth century at Tell Deir ʿAlla and Kuntillet ʿAjrud. Such inscriptions are quite rare, yet it is noteworthy that no such inscription is known in Judah, despite the large-scale excavations in many sites in the arid Beersheba Valley. Most of these excavations were carried out after the discoveries at Kuntillet ʿAjrud, so there must have been already awareness to the need to look for such finds—in situ or in small pieces in the debris.

Table 12.1 below summarizes the data for Judah.

Table 12.1: Appearance of writing in Judah by medium and date

	Iron IIA	Iron IIB, pre 701 BCE	Iron IIC
Ostraca	—	x (2–4)	x, many
Incised	—	x	x
Seals and seal impressions	—	x, mainly on *lmlk* jars	x, many
Bullae	—	x, one so far	x, many
Monumental inscriptions	—	x (Siloam)	x[9]

Discussion

The above survey, with the thorough treatment of the Arad inscriptions (details in the appendix below), shows no indication for writing in Judah until the late eighth century BCE (except the two Uzziah seals; see below). Even then evidence for writing is limited, exhibited mainly in the basic administrative system of the kingdom (the *lmlk* seal impressions and seal impressions of officials) and the court in Jerusalem (the Siloam Inscription). Ink writings are scarce: two to four short ostraca from Tel Beersheba and Lachish and perhaps a few more from Arad. Expansion of writing activity is evident only in the seventh century BCE, its scope perhaps best demonstrated by the large number of writers at Arad traced by both algorithmic and forensic investigations (Faigenbaum-Golovin et al. 2016; Shaus et al. 2020, respectively). Although future discoveries may change these observations, the data at hand seem to be broad and solid, with far-reaching implications.

Our survey puts a question mark on the very foundations of past paleographic observations regarding the Hebrew letters in the different phases of the Iron II. Evidently these (e.g., the tables in Aharoni 1981, 133–37) were based on misleading data regarding the basic information on stratigraphy and thus chronology. Even analysis of the late eighth- versus late seventh-century ink letter shapes is impossible: there is little value in describing such distinctions based on about thirteen clear charac-

---

9. Except for the sheer logic of continuity after the Siloam inscription, see a piece of unstratified monumental inscription from the City of David, which Naveh (2000, 1–2) dated to the seventh century BCE.

ters in Ostracon 1 from Tel Beersheba (exhibiting only eight letters in the Hebrew alphabet) and possibly a few more characters in Ostraca XXIII and XXXIII from Lachish. In a way, the same holds true for the Northern Kingdom. A recent algorithmic study of the Samaria ostraca by the Tel Aviv University digital epigraphy team revealed only two "hands" in the thirty-one ostraca that were investigated (Faigenbaum-Golovin et al. 2020). Apart from these two Samaria scribes, the only pieces of evidence for ink inscriptions in Israel are one inscription from Hazor (Yadin et al. 1960, pl. CLXX:6), one inscription from Beth-shean (A. Mazar 2006a), and the inscriptions from Kuntillet ʿAjrud (Ahituv, Eshel, and Meshel 2012). The latter is a short-lived, single-building site where the number of scribes must have been limited. Archaeologically (ceramic evidence for Hazor, Beth-shean, and Kuntillet ʿAjrud) and paleographically (Samaria), these inscriptions all date to the same period. They represent therefore no more than a handful of scribes and hence can hardly help in constructing a reliable paleographic system (Faigenbaum-Golovin et al. 2020).

The question of perishable papyri has often been raised to claim for writing in ancient Israel earlier than the Iron IIB (e.g., Naveh 1982, 70; Lemaire 2015, 32; Naʾaman 2015, passim). Support of this assumption has been sought in signs on the back side of late Iron IIA/early Iron IIB bullae from the area of the Gihon Spring, which were interpreted as papyri print (Reich, Shukron, and Lernau 2007). However, Baruch Brandl, an expert on this issue, suggests that these signs are prints of wooden boxes or basketry rather than papyri (pers. comm.).

Still, this is a problematic assertion on two grounds. First, had there been intensive writing on papyri, especially in the Iron IIB–C, some material evidence should have surfaced in the many excavations in the dry Beersheba Valley (also in Edomite sites of the seventh century BCE). Second, had there been widespread writing on papyri in the Iron IIA and Iron IIB, even concentrated only around the king in Jerusalem, something could be expected to leak to other media of writing: ostraca, incisions, seals and seal impressions, and bullae; this is not the case.[10] The absence of evidence for writing on plaster (possibly related to writing on papyri; Lemaire 1985, 275, 284) in Judah, even in the dry south, is seemingly

---

10. Indeed, when a papyrus does surface (in Wadi Murabaʿat—Ahituv 2008, 213–215), there is strong evidence also in all other media of writing.

another indication that writing on papyri was not prevalent in the Southern Kingdom.

Sections in the Mesha Inscription show the ability to compose texts with literary qualities as early as the late ninth century BCE.[11] Moab exhibits another ninth-century royal inscription and several items of monumental art that seem to belong to the same period (for the latter, see Weber 2017). Hence the question arises: Why Moab and not its neighbor Judah? Of course, this can also be understood as sheer bad luck in archaeological discoveries or a result of the territory of Moab being arid and not densely settled in later centuries (meaning that sites are "exposed" to the investigator's eye). But there is more here. Until its incorporation into the Assyrian-led Arabian trade in the late eighth century, Judah was isolated from the main trade arteries of the region, whereas Moab was located on the King's Highway, which led from the south, including the important Iron I–IIA copper production centers at Wadi Feinan, to Damascus and the north. Indeed, in the second half of the ninth century Moab seems to be under the geopolitical influence of Hazael of Damascus. These factors demonstrate the possibility that Moab was inspired by the culture of the northern Levant as early as the (late?) ninth century BCE; this is seen, in fact, also in its monumental art (e.g., Weber 2017).

As mentioned above, the two Uzziah seals—presenting the earliest evidence for Hebrew writing in Judah—seem to point to the importance of Israel in the appearance of writing in the Southern Kingdom. Kleiman (2017) suggested that the advent of the administration system in Judah, as manifested in the *lmlk* impressions, was also influenced by north Israelite administrative knowledge. This should come as no surprise, as other items of material culture, among them ashlar masonry with drafted stones, volute capitals, and olive oil installations, seem to have been introduced to Judah from Israel (more details in ch. 14 below).

Writing abruptly appears in Judah in several media in the late eighth century (first noticed by Jamieson-Drake 1991, 147). For now, we are dealing with the Siloam Inscription, several ostraca, a small number of incised inscriptions carrying only a few characters, the *lmlk* administration system, and private seal impressions on *lmlk* jars. One reason for this sudden development is the incorporation of Judah into the Assyrian

---

11. Lemaire (2015, 28) puts the Mesha Stele as late as ca. 810 BCE.

administration and economic system after 732 BCE. Second, Israel—and Israelites who settled in Judah after 720 BCE (ch. 14 below; contra Na'aman 2014a)—could have influenced the Southern Kingdom. Israel does not have sites in arid areas (apart from Kuntillet ʿAjrud), so the evidence there is less than that from Judah. Still, it is clear that ostraca and writing in ink on complete vessels appear in the north several decades before the south; the gap is longer if one considers that ink writing proliferated in Judah only in the seventh century. This is true not only for mundane texts; literary texts, too, appear in Israel (Tell Deir ʿAlla in its territory and Kuntillet ʿAjrud Inscription 4.2 being north Israelite culturally) over a century before the appearance of the first literary text in Judah: inscription number 1 from Horvat Uza (Beit-Arieh 2007; Na'aman 2013b). Needless to say, this reflects on the ability to compose biblical texts in the two Hebrew Kingdoms (see Finkelstein 2017).

One could argue that, in two kingdoms sharing a border, with their capitals only circa 55 kilometers apart as the crow flies (and the important northern shrine of Bethel only 15 kilometers from Jerusalem), practices such as ink writing on pottery sherds would be transmitted in a short period of time of no more than a few years. However, other factors dictated the need for writing and thus proliferation of scribal activity, such as level of administration, trade relations, and other economic endeavors (e.g., the horse and oil industries in Israel). As mentioned above, other items of material culture also appear in Israel earlier than in Judah (in the case of ashlar masonry perhaps a century and half earlier). In other words, I am distinguishing here between the ability to compose royal inscriptions, which could, indeed, be transmitted from one court to the other in a short period of time, to daily, mundane use of the medium of writing in the administrative and military systems of the kingdoms and beyond.

Summary

It is possible that writing on papyri was present in Judah at the end phase of the late Iron IIA/early Iron IIB, in the late ninth and/or first half of the eighth century. Further, although evidence is lacking, it is also possible that at that time the royal court in Jerusalem could produce a royal inscription. But there is no indication for significant writing in Judah before the late eighth century (and then, too, it is quite restricted in scope).

The earliest dateable inscriptions from Judah—the two Uzziah seals—may indicate Israelite influence on the Southern Kingdom in the early Iron IIB, the first half to middle of the eighth century. Following the defeat of Amaziah by Joash at Beth-shemesh (2 Kgs 14:11–13), Israel may have ruled over Judah. Israelite dominance is especially manifested in the days of Jeroboam II, who seems to have been the builder of an administration center at Kiriath-jearim, which controlled the approach of Jerusalem from the west (Finkelstein and Römer 2020, and see ch. 11 above).

The first step in the proliferation of writing in Judah, in the late eighth century, seems to have been influenced by two developments: the incorporation of the Southern Kingdom into the Assyrian administrative and economic systems after 732 BCE; and the migration of Israelites to Jerusalem and other places in Judah after 720 BCE. While Israel exhibits the ability to compose literary texts as early as the first half of the eighth century BCE (Finkelstein 2017), Judah reached this stage not before the late eighth century, and probably later, during the seventh century BCE. Indeed, northern biblical texts such as the Jacob cycle in Genesis and the savior stories in Judges could have been authored in Israel in the first half of the eighth century and incorporated into Judahite texts over a century later. The development of major concepts in the Judahite ideology, including the idea of a united monarchy, should be understood as part of these processes: migration of people, ideas, features of administration, and literacy from Israel to the south during the eighth century and especially after the fall of the north.

Appendix: The Archaeological Context of the Arad Inscriptions

Below we present a systematic reevaluation of the archaeological context of the Arad inscriptions based on published data (Aharoni 1981; Herzog et al. 1984; Herzog 2002a; Singer-Avitz 2002, table 12.c), especially comparison between the recorded elevations of the inscriptions (Aharoni 1981, 181–85) and the loci with which they were associated (Herzog 2002a, 5, 9, 12, 15–17, 19). Paleographic considerations are noted only in specific cases, such as Ostracon 40. In our view, the only inscriptions that can be

---

This appendix was originally coauthored with Assaf Kleiman.

12. The Appearance and Dissemination of Writing in Judah   183

considered as having originated from secure contexts are those found in undisturbed locations, close to the lowest level of the given locus, and accompanied with clear architecture.

Our analysis shows that all five inscriptions that were assigned to Strata XII–XI and most (80 percent) of the inscriptions that were affiliated with Strata X–VIII originated from dubious contexts (table 12.A). Still, some of the inscriptions of the latter group may indeed belong to their originally assigned layer, especially in light of the remarkable concentration of thirty-four inscriptions in the area of the Iron IIB sanctuary (table 12.B, cluster 1), but this cannot be proven with the data at hand. In fact, significant structures could have existed here in the Iron IIC, structures that did not survive due to the collapse of the rock-cut water cistern and subsequent (Hellenistic period) construction works (Herzog 2002a, 12–13). Note that several inscriptions exposed in this area (e.g., nos. 24 and 61) clearly belong to Stratum VI (Aharoni 1981, 46, 91; Na'aman 2003; Dobbs-Allsopp et al. 2005, 47–48, 87). In contrast, it is readily apparent that nearly all the inscriptions assigned by Aharoni to Strata VII–VI (in this case also ca. 80 percent) were exposed in well-defined contexts. This is especially clear in the case of the Eliashib Archive: eighteen ostraca and inscribed pithos (Singer-Avitz 2002, fig. 49.3) were found on the floor of Locus 637 (see, e.g., field photo in Aharoni 1981, 11).

Table 12.A: Secure/unsecure stratigraphic contexts of the Arad inscriptions

Ceramic Phase	Not Secure		Secure		Total	
	N =	% =	N =	% =	N =	% =
Iron IIA (Strata XII–XI)	5	100			5	
Iron IIB (Strata X–VIII)	29	81	7	19	36[12]	
Iron IIC (Strata VII–VI)	8	21	31	79	39	100
Unstratified Material	27	100			27	
Total	69	64	38	36	107	

---

12. Thirty-nine according to Aharoni's original list (where Locus 469 was assigned to Stratum VIII).

Table 12.B: Secure/unsecure contexts according to location in the fortress

Area	Not Secure		Secure		Total	
	N =	% =	N =	% =	N =	% =
Cluster 1 (Squares E–J/13–16, NW sector)	25	74	9	26	34	
Cluster 2 (Squares E–J/9–12, SW sector)	11	85	2	15	13	
Cluster 3 (Squares K–N/8–10, SE sector)	2	8	24	92	26	
Cluster 4 (Squares K–N/13–17, NE sector)	11	79	3	21	14	100
Cluster 5 (Squares C–D/12–14, western slope)	13	100			13	
Cluster 6 (Squares E–O/18, northern slope)	3	100			3	
Various contexts	4	100			4	
Total	69	64	38	36	107	

12. The Appearance and Dissemination of Writing in Judah   185

Table 12.C: A reassessment of the archaeological context of the Arad inscriptions

No.	Loc.	Square	Elev. of item	Elev. of Loc.	Original Stratum	Comments
1–19	637	L/9	75.75	75.70	VI	Found 5 cm above Floor 637 (Eliashib's Archive).
20	433	G/9	75.95	75.80	VI	Found 15 cm above the lowest level of the locus. For complete Iron IIC vessels from this locus, Singer-Avitz 2002, fig. 47.8-14.
21	649	K/9	75.75	75.65	VI	Found 10 cm above the lowest level of the locus. For a complete Iron IIC vessel from this context, Herzog et al. 1984, fig. 29.6. See also no. 78 (65 cm below).
22	605	E/13	75.35	75.10	VI	Found 25 cm above the lowest level of the locus. Many complete vessels assigned to Stratum VII were unearthed below it (Singer-Avitz 2002, figs. 41–42). The division between Strata VII and VI is unclear in this area. For a complete Iron IIC vessel from this locus, Herzog et al. 1984, fig. 25.15. See also no. 41 (40 cm below).
23	482	E/12	75.45	482 A = 75.15	VI	Found 30 cm above the lowest level of Locus 482A. Locus 482 is not marked on the plan of Stratum VI. The division between Strata VII and VI is unclear in this area.
24	374	C-D/12	75.25	—	US	Unstratified, found on the western slope of the fortress. Based on paleographic considerations, dated to Stratum VI (Naʾaman 2003; Dobbs-Allsopp et al. 2005, 47–48) (together with no. 40). See also nos. 25, 27, 29, 35, 58, 73, and 83.
25	374	C-D/12	72.40	—	US	Unstratified, found on the western slope of the fortress. See also nos. 24, 27, 29, 35, 58, 73, 83.
26	397	G/14	73.70	—	US	Unstratified, found in a pit with Aramaic inscriptions in the northwestern sector of the fortress (Aharoni 1981, 10, 52, 187), near the collapsed rock-cut water cistern. See also nos. 71 and 82.
27	374	C-D/12	71.20	—	US	Unstratified, found on the western slope of the fortress. See also nos. 24–25, 29, 35, 58, 73, 83.
28	730	J/18	—	—	US	Unstratified, found during cleaning (Aharoni 1981, 54) on the northern slope of the fortress.
29	374	C-D/12	72.30	—	US	Unstratified, found on the western slope of the fortress. See also nos. 24–25, 27, 35, 58, 73, 83.
30	410	G/10	75.80	75.65	VI	Found 15 cm above the lowest level of the locus.

No.	Loc.	Square	Elev. of item	Elev. of Loc.	Original Stratum	Comments
31	779	L/8	75.45	75.20	VII	Found 25 cm above the lowest level of the locus, below Eliashib's archive and together with the Eliashib seals (nos. 105–107 in Aharoni 1981). This context is contemporaneous with Room 637 of Stratum VI (Zimhoni 1985, 84–85; Mazar and Netzer 1986, 88–89; Ussishkin 1988, 153–54). For complete Iron IIC vessels from this locus, Singer-Avitz 2002, figs. 43–45. See also nos. 32 and 34 (same elevation).
32	779	L/8	75.45	75.20	VII	Found 25 cm above the lowest level of the locus, below Eliashib's archive, together with the Eliashib seals (nos. 105–107 in Aharoni 1981). This context is contemporaneous with Room 637 of Stratum VI (Zimhoni 1985, 84–85; Mazar and Netzer 1986, 88–89; Ussishkin 1988, 153–154). For complete Iron IIC vessels from this locus, Singer-Avitz 2002, figs. 43–45. See also nos. 31 and 34 (same elevation).
33	952	J/16	75.00	74.70	VII	Found 30 cm above the lowest level of the locus. For complete Iron IIC vessels from this locus, Singer-Avitz 2002, fig. 46.1–11. See also nos. 49 (same elevation) and 53 (10 cm below).
34	779	L/8	75.45	75.20	VII	Found 25 cm above the lowest level of the locus, below Eliashib's archive, together with the Eliashib seals (nos. 105–107 in Aharoni 1981). This context is contemporaneous with Room 637 of Stratum VI (Zimhoni 1985, 84–85; Mazar and Netzer 1986, 88–89; Ussishkin 1988, 153–154). For complete Iron IIC vessels from this locus, Singer-Avitz 2002, figs. 43–45. See also nos. 31–32 (same elevation).
35	374	C-D/12	72.55	—	US	Unstratified, found on the western slope of the fortress. See also nos. 24–25, 27, 29, 58, 73, 83.
36	605A	E/13	74.80	74.45	VII	Found 35 cm above the lowest level of the locus and in an open area. Excavation of this locus began in Stratum VI (Locus 605, 75.10 m; see Herzog 2002a, fig. 19). The division between Strata VII and VI is unclear in this area. For complete Iron IIC vessels from this locus, Singer-Avitz 2002, figs. 41–42. See also nos. 41 (15 cm above), 42 (same elevation), and 46 (5 cm below).
37	785	J/16	75.30	75.25	VII	Found 5 cm above the lowest level of the locus. For a photo of this context, Aharoni 1981, 66. See also no. 89 (15 cm below).
38	929	C/14	73.75	—	US	Unstratified, found on the western slope of the fortress. See also nos. 54–57.

12. The Appearance and Dissemination of Writing in Judah

No.	Loc.	Square	Elev. of item	Elev. of Loc.	Original Stratum	Comments
39	314	J/14	68.25	–	US	Unstratified, found in the northern sector of the fortress, near the northern wall of the Hellenistic tower. For a photo of this context, Aharoni 1981, 69.
40	429	G/12	74.50	73.45	VIII	Found 1.05 m above the lowest level of the locus (and 35 cm below the lowest level of Locus 422A [Str. VII; inscription originally affiliated by Aharoni with this layer]). Architecture of Stratum VIII in this square was reused in Stratum VII. For complete Iron IIB vessels from this locus, Singer-Avitz 2002, figs. 35–36; for a handle with *lmlk* seal impression, M. Aharoni 1981a, 126 (Locus 429 was defined in this publication as "dismantling baulk"). For a photo of this context, Aharoni 1981, 13. Based on paleographic considerations, Naʾaman (2003; also Dobbs-Allsopp et al. 2005, 69) dated this ostracon to the time of Stratum VI (together with the unstratified no. 24). The contradiction between the date of the inscription and the rich Iron IIB ceramic assemblage from this locus suggests mixed material (so Naʾaman). See also no. 86 (55 cm above).
41	418	E/13	74.95	74.40	VIII	Found 55 cm above the lowest level of the locus and above the lowest level of another locus in same square (605A) that was assigned to Stratum VII. Discovered close to Pit 436A and the collapsed rock-cut water cistern. For complete Iron IIB vessels from this locus, Herzog et al. 1984, figs. 22.3–4, 6, 19–20. See also nos. 22 (40 cm above), 36 (15 cm below), and 42 (15 cm below).
42	418	E/13	74.80	74.40	VIII	Found 40 cm above the lowest level of the locus, close to Pit 436A and the collapsed rock-cut water cistern. For complete Iron IIB vessels from this locus, Herzog et al. 1984, fig. 22.3–4, 6, 19–20. See also nos. 36 (same elevation), 41 (15 cm above), and 46 (5 cm below).
43	781	H/15	74.90	74.80	VII	Found 10 cm above the lowest level of the locus (assigned to Stratum VIII in Aharoni 1981 and to Stratum VII in Herzog 2002). It was found near the northern wall of the Hellenistic tower. See also nos. 47 (30 cm above) and 100 (1.8 m below).
44	418	E/13	74.45	74.40	VIII	Found 5 cm above the lowest level of the locus, close to Pit 436A and the collapsed rock-cut water cistern. Many Iron IIC vessels were discovered just above this locus (Singer-Avitz 2002, figs. 41–42, 74.80–74.50 m). For complete Iron IIB vessels from this locus, Herzog et al. 1984, fig. 22.3–4, 6, 19–20. See also no. 46 (30 cm above).

No.	Loc.	Square	Elev. of item	Elev. of Loc.	Original Stratum	Comments
45	753	L/8-9	74.30	74.50	VIII	Found 20 cm below the lowest level of the locus. If Locus 753 represents a floor, then this is one of the earliest stratified inscriptions at Arad. Note, however, that according to Aharoni (1981, 77), this ostracon was exposed under the "house of Eliashib" of Stratum VI (see nos. 1–19).
46	418	E/13	74.75	74.40	VIII	Found 35 cm above the lowest level of the locus, close to Pit 436A and the collapsed rock-cut water cistern. For complete Iron IIB vessels from this locus, Herzog et al. 1984, fig. 22.3–4, 6, 19–20. See also nos. 36 (5 cm above), 42 (5 cm above), and 44 (30 cm below).
47	963	H/15	75.50	75.10	VII	Found 40 cm above the lowest level of the locus. According to Aharoni (1981, 79), the inscription was exposed "above the floor level of Stratum VIII." Discovered near the northern wall of the Hellenistic tower. For a complete Iron IIB/C juglet from this locus, Herzog et al. 1984, fig. 22.16. See also no. 43 (30 cm below).
48	882	E–F/18	73.30	—	US	Unstratified, found on the northern slope of the fortress.
49	786 + 1010	J/16	75.00–75.15	74.90	VIII	Found 10–25 cm above the lowest level of the locus. Note the existence of Pit 952 of Stratum VII near this locus (for complete Iron IIC vessels from the pit, Singer-Avitz 2002, fig. 46.1–11). See also nos. 33 and 89 (same elevation).
50	469	E/14	74.65	74.50	VII	Found 15 cm above the lowest level of the locus (assigned to Stratum VIII in Aharoni 1981 and to Stratum VII in Herzog 2002a). According to Aharoni (1968a, 11, fig. 17; 1981, 84), the inscription was found in the sanctuary of Stratum VIII, near the holy of holies. The division between Strata VII and VI is unclear in this area. See also nos. 51–52 (5 cm below).
51	469	E/14	74.60	74.50	VII	Found 10 cm above the lowest level of the locus (assigned to Stratum VIII in Aharoni 1981 and to Stratum VII in Herzog 2002a). According to Aharoni (1968a, 11; 1981, 84) the inscription was found in the sanctuary of Stratum VIII, near the holy of holies. The division between Strata VII and VI is unclear in this area. See also nos. 50 (5 cm above) and 52 (same elevation).
52	469	E/14	74.60	74.50	VII	Found 10 cm above the lowest level of the locus (assigned to Stratum VIII in Aharoni 1981 and to Stratum VII in Herzog 2002a). According to Aharoni (1981, 84) the inscription was found in the sanctuary of Stratum VIII, near the holy of holies. The division between Strata VII and VI is unclear in this area. See also nos. 50 (5 cm above) and 51 (same elevation).

12. The Appearance and Dissemination of Writing in Judah 189

No.	Loc.	Square	Elev. of item	Elev. of Loc.	Original Stratum	Comments
53	1010	J/16	74.90	74.90	VIII	Found at the lowest level of the locus. Note, however, the existence of Pit 952 of Stratum VII near this locus (for complete Iron IIC vessels from the pit, Singer-Avitz 2002, fig. 46.1–11). See also no. 33 (10 cm above).
54	929	C/14	72.70	—	US	Unstratified, found on the western slope of the fortress. According to Aharoni (1968a, 11, fig. 17), the inscription was uncovered in "rooms bounding the temple." See also nos. 38, 55–57.
55	929	C/14	72.70	—	US	Unstratified, found on the western slope of the fortress. According to Aharoni (1968a, 11), the inscription was uncovered in "rooms bounding the temple." See also nos. 38, 54, 56–57.
56	929	C/14	71.45	—	US	Unstratified, found on the western slope of the fortress. See also nos. 38, 54–55, 57.
57	929	C/14	72.40	—	US	Unstratified, found on the western slope of the fortress. See also nos. 38 and 54–56.
58	374	C–D/12	71.35	—	US	Unstratified, found on the western slope of the fortress. See also nos. 24–25, 27, 29, 35, 73, 83.
59	68	L/16	74.55	74.25	IX	Found 30 cm above the lowest level of the locus. According to Aharoni (1981, 89), the stratigraphic affiliation of the inscription is uncertain ("… apparently from Stratum IX"). See also no. 80 (65 cm below).
60	1036	K/17	74.55	74.35	IX	Found 20 cm above the lowest level of the locus. If Locus 1036 represents a floor, then this is one of the earliest stratified inscriptions at Arad.
61	615B	E/15	74.25	615A = 74.27	IX	Found 2 cm below the lowest level of Locus 615A. Locus 615B is not marked on the plan of Stratum IX. According to Aharoni (1981, 91), this area was very disturbed. For an almost complete Iron IIB vessel from this locus, Herzog et al. 1984, fig. 19.5. Aharoni (1981, 91) and Dobbs-Allsopp et al. (2005, 87) suggested to (paleographically) reassign it to the time of Stratum VI.
62	350	G/15	74.60	74.40	IX	Found 20 cm above the lowest level of the locus. According to Aharoni (1981, 91), the inscription was exposed in a cell near the altar. Discovered near the collapsed rock-cut water cistern. Based on paleographical considerations, Dobbs-Allsopp et al. (2005, 88) suggested to reassign it to Stratum VI. See also no. 101 (1.15 m below).

No.	Loc.	Square	Elev. of item	Elev. of Loc.	Original Stratum	Comments
63	443C	H/9	74.10	73.75	IX	Found 35 cm above the lowest level of the locus. Excavation of this locus began in Stratum VI (Locus 443, 75.80 m; see Herzog 2002a, fig. 19). Aharoni (1981, 90) and Dobbs-Allsopp et al. (2005, 88) suggested to affiliate it (paleographically) with Stratum VI. See also no. 91 (60 cm above).
64	801	M/10	74.20	801A = 74.00	IX/VIII	Found 20 cm above the lowest level of Locus 801A. Locus 801 is not marked on the plan of Stratum VIII. In the Hebrew version of *Arad Inscriptions* (Aharoni 1986, 93, 224), this item was assigned to Stratum IX.
65	791	H/14	74.30	74.15	IX	Found 15 cm above the lowest level of the locus. Unearthed near the collapsed rock-cut water cistern and the northern wall of the Hellenistic tower. See also no. 87 (22 cm below).
66	38	L/15	74.75	74.40	IX	Found 35 cm above the lowest level of the locus.
67	107	K/16–17	74.00	74.00	X	Found at the lowest level of the locus. According to Herzog (2002a, 33), only one segment of the whole building in which the inscription was found survived.
68	105A	K/15–16	74.30	105 = 74.30	X	Found at the lowest level of Locus 105. Locus 105A is not marked on the plan of Stratum X.
69	365	F/12	73.50	73.10	X	Found 40 cm above the lowest level of the locus. It is an open area; no details concerning this context were given by Aharoni (1981, 94). See also no. 92 (50 cm above).
70	394	G/15	73.35	73.10	X	Found 25 cm above the lowest level of the locus. If Locus 394 represents a floor, then this is one of the earliest stratified ostraca at Arad. For a complete Iron IIB vessel from this locus, Singer-Avitz 2002, fig. 24.10. See also nos. 101 (10 cm above) and 102–103 (5 cm below).
71	397	G/14	73.15	—	US	Unstratified, found at the edge of a pit with Aramaic inscriptions in the northwestern sector of the fortress (Aharoni 1981, 10, 52, 187), near the collapsed rock-cut water cistern. See also nos. 26 and 82.
72	208	O/14	—	—	US	Unstratified, found on the eastern slope and above a wall (no number).
73	374	C–D/12	67.90/ 76.90?	—	US	Unstratified, found on the western slope of the fortress. See also nos. 24–25, 27, 29, 35, 58, 83.

12. The Appearance and Dissemination of Writing in Judah

No.	Loc.	Square	Elev. of item	Elev. of Loc.	Original Stratum	Comments
74	949	K/16	73.65	73.00	US	Unstratified. According to Aharoni (1981, 97), the inscription was found when cleaning up the walls and trench. See also nos. 76–77. See also no. 97 (1.6 m above) and 76 (30 cm below).
75	235	N/15	73.90	73.80	X	Found 10 cm above the lowest level of the locus. According to Aharoni (1981, 98), the stratigraphic affiliation of the inscription is uncertain.
76	949	K/16	73.35	73.00	XI	Found 35 cm above the lowest level of the locus. Its location was defined in relation to the sanctuary (Aharoni 1981, 98). Another inscription from this locus (no. 74) was defined by Aharoni as unstratified (1981, 97). Note the existence of a later pit here (Locus 11; Aharoni 1981, 10). See also nos. 74 (30 cm above) and 77 (5 cm below).
77	949	K/16	73.30	73.00	XI	Found 30 cm above the lowest level of the locus, its location defined in relation to the sanctuary (Aharoni 1981, 98). Another inscription from this locus (no. 74) was described by Aharoni as unstratified (97). Note the existence of a later pit here (Locus 11; see Aharoni 1981, 10). See also no. 76 (5 cm above).
78	778D	K/9	73.10	—	XI	Locus 778D is marked on the plan of Stratum XI without an elevation. Excavation of this locus began, more or less, in the level of Stratum VIII (Locus 778A, 74.80 m; Herzog 2002a, 16). It is located in an open area. According to Aharoni (1981, 100), this inscription was found below the room that yielded the Eliashib seals (nos. 105–107). See also no. 21 (65 cm above).
79	950	H/14	73.30	93.00/ 73.00?	XI	Found 30 cm above the lowest level of the locus, in an open area and near the collapsed rock-cut water cistern. Its location was defined in relation to the sanctuary ("in the southern court of the sanctuary"; Aharoni 1981, 100), later reassigned to Stratum X (Herzog 2002a). See also no. 95 (55 cm above).
80	68A	L/16	73.90	73.75	X	Found 15 cm above the lowest level of the locus. Excavation of this locus began in Stratum IX (Locus 68, 74.25; Herzog 2002a, fig. 15). According to Aharoni (1981, 100), the stratigraphic affiliation of the inscription is uncertain ("found within a wall"). See also no. 59 (65 cm above).

No.	Loc.	Square	Elev. of item	Elev. of Loc.	Original Stratum	Comments
81	432F	E/9	71.85	—	XII	Excavation of this locus began, more or less, in the level of Stratum VIII (Locus 432b, 74.45 m; Herzog 2002, fig. 16) and continued down at least to 71.85 m (i.e., 2.6 m). Locus 432F is not marked on the plan of Stratum XII (in Herzog 2002a, fig. 5, but see M. Aharoni 1981b, plan 1), where the elevation of the nearest locus (Locus 455c) is 71.15 m—70 cm below the level of the inscription. See also no. 99 (1.15 m above).
82	397	G/14	73.70	—	US	Unstratified, found in a pit with Aramaic inscriptions in the northwestern sector of the fortress (Aharoni 1981, 10, 52, 187), near the collapsed rock-cut water cistern. See also nos. 26 and 71.
83	374	C-D/12	71.75	—	US	Unstratified, found on the western slope of the fortress. See also nos. 24–25, 27, 29, 35, 58, 73.
84	613	F/14	76.00	—	VI	The stratigraphic affiliation of the inscription is uncertain (Aharoni 1981, 102). Found 20 cm below the level of the Roman period stratum.
85	905	J/15	75.90	905A = 75.30	VI	Found 60 cm above the lowest level of Locus 905A. Locus 905 is not marked on the plan of Stratum VI.
86	422	G/12	75.05	422A = 74.80	VII	Found 25 cm above the lowest level of Locus 422A. Locus 422 is not marked on the plan of Stratum VI. The division between Strata VII and VI is unclear in this area. See also no. 40 (55 cm below).
87	380	H/14	74.08	74.30	IX	Found 22 cm below the lowest level of the locus. If Locus 380 represents a floor, then this is one of the earliest stratified ostraca at Arad. For complete Iron IIB vessels from this context, Singer-Avitz 2002, fig. 30.1–4. Note, however, the existence of a nearby fill (Locus 704) and a pit from the Persian period that contained many Aramaic inscriptions (Locus 325, lowest published elevation is 74.30 m [Aharoni 1981, 10, 185–87], 22 cm above the inscription). See also nos. 65 (22 cm above) and 95 (23 cm below).
88	—	—	—	—	US	Surface find.
89	786	J/16	57.15/ 75.15?	74.90	VIII	Found 25 cm above the lowest level of the locus. Note, however, the existence of Pit 952 of Stratum VII near this locus (for complete Iron IIC vessels from the pit, Singer-Avitz 2002, fig. 46.1–11). See also nos. 37 (15 cm above) and 49 (same elevation).

12. The Appearance and Dissemination of Writing in Judah

No.	Loc.	Square	Elev. of item	Elev. of Loc.	Original Stratum	Comments
90	245	M/17	74.80	74.80	VIII	Found at the lowest level of the locus. If Locus 245 represents a floor, then this is one of the earliest stratified incised sherds at Arad. Note, however, that "this sector of the site was seriously damaged by later construction phases (mainly in the Hellenistic period)" (Herzog 2002a, 77–78),
91	443B	H/9	74.60	74.35	VIII	Found 25 cm above the lowest level of the locus. Excavation of this locus began in Stratum VI (Locus 443, 75.80 m; Herzog 2002a, fig. 19). For a complete Iron IIB vessel found in this locus, Herzog et al. 1984, fig. 22.18. See also no. 63 (60 cm below), paleographically affiliated by Dobbs-Allsopp et al. (2005, 88) with Stratum VI.
92	355	F/12	74.00	73.95	IX	Found 5 cm above the lowest level of the locus. It is an open area. See also no. 69 (50 cm below).
93	841	H/11	74.10	74.10	IX	Found at the lowest level of the locus. It is an open area, very close to the Hellenistic tower. In the Hebrew edition of *Arad Inscriptions* the stratigraphic affiliation of this decanter is confused (Aharoni 1986, 108, Stratum XI; 225, Stratum IX). For complete Iron IIB vessels from this locus, Herzog et al. 1984, figs. 18.4, 7; 19.1–2.
94	611	F/15	84.20/ 74.20?	74.10	IX	Found 10 cm above the lowest level of the locus. Discovered near the collapsed rock-cut water cistern.
95	384	H/14	73.85	73.60	X	Found 25 cm above the lowest level of the locus. Discovered in an open area, near the collapsed rock-cut water cistern. See also nos. 87 (23 cm above) and 79 (55 cm below).
96	232	N/17	—	—	US	Unstratified; no contextual information.
97	21	K/16	75.25	75.15	VII	Found 10 cm above the lowest level of the locus. Note the existence of a later pit here (Locus 11, Aharoni 1981, 10). For a handle with *lmlk* seal impression from this locus (75.40 m), M. Aharoni 1981a, 126. See also no. 74 (1.6 m below).
98	514A	H/10	73.45	514 = 74.05	X	Found 60 cm below the lowest level of Locus 514. Locus 514A is not marked on the plan of Stratum IX. The division between Strata X and IX is unclear in this area. In the Hebrew version of *Arad Inscriptions*'s list (Aharoni 1986, 220), this jug was assigned to Stratum XI, but in the text it is affiliated with Stratum X (112).

No.	Loc.	Square	Elev. of item	Elev. of Loc.	Original Stratum	Comments
99	455	E/9	73.00	72.50	X	Found in an open area, 50 cm above the lowest level of the locus (assigned to Stratum IX in Aharoni 1981 and to Stratum X in Herzog 2002a). For complete Iron IIB vessels from this locus, Singer-Avitz 2002, fig. 28.2–3. See also no. 81 (1.15 m below).
100	947	H/15	73.45	73.00	X	Found 45 cm above lowest level of the locus. For complete Iron IIB/C vessels from this locus, Singer-Avitz 2002, fig. 29.14–15. See also no. 43 (1.8 m above).
101	388	G/15	73.45	72.80	X	Found 65 cm above the lowest level of the locus, within the collapsed rock-cut water cistern. For complete Iron IIB vessels from this locus, Singer-Avitz 2002, fig. 24.1–7. Based on paleographic considerations, Dobbs-Allsopp et al. (2005, 104) suggested affiliating it with Stratum VII. See also nos. 62 (1.15 m above) and 70 (10 cm below).
102	394	G/15	73.30	73.10	X	Found 20 cm above the lowest level of the locus. According to Aharoni (1981, 115–16) and Herzog (2002a, 56, 58), this bowl was exposed on the bench at the foot of the altar together with no. 103. For a complete Iron IIB vessel from this locus, Singer-Avitz 2002, fig. 24.10. Based on paleographic considerations, Cross (1979), supported by Ussishkin (1988, 155), assigned this bowl to Stratum VI. Herzog et al. (1984, 12; see also Herzog 2002a, 69–70) argued that this area was covered by Iron IIB and Iron IIC floors. See also no. 70 (5 cm above).
103	394	G/15	73.30	73.10	X	Found 20 cm above the lowest level of the locus. According to Aharoni (1981, 115–116) and Herzog (2002a, 56, 58), this bowl was exposed on the bench at the foot of the altar together with no. 102. For a complete Iron IIB vessel from this locus, Singer-Avitz 2002, fig. 24.10. Based on paleographic considerations, Cross (1979), supported by Ussishkin (1988, 155), assigned the bowl to Stratum VI. Herzog et al. (1984, 12; also Herzog 2002a, 69–70) argued that this area was covered by Iron IIB and Iron IIC floors. See also no. 70 (5 cm above).
104	13	L/13	—	—	US	Unstratified. According to Aharoni (1981, 118), the inscription was found in the northeastern corner of the Hellenistic tower.
110	—	—	—	—	US	Surface find. Rainey (1977) suggested assigning it to Stratum VI. See also nos. 111–112.
111	—	—	—	—	US	Surface find. Rainey (1977) suggested assigning it to Stratum VI. See also nos. 110 and 112.
112	—	—	—	—	US	Surface find. Rainey (1977) suggested assigning it to Stratum VI. See also nos. 110–111.

13
Epigraphic Evidence from Jerusalem and Its Environs at the Dawn of Biblical History: Facts First

---

In chapter 12 I dealt with the entire dataset regarding the dissemination of Hebew writing in Judah, with special emphasis on the Iron IIB, the eighth century BCE. Here I focus on the ostensible evidence for scribal activity in Jerusalem in the Iron I and Iron IIA, circa 1150–750 BCE.

Introduction

Christopher Rollston (2017) has presented a broad and informative discussion of early alphabetic inscriptions in the Levant in the Late Bronze, Iron I, and Iron IIA, focusing on the question of scribal activity in Jerusalem. Both the factual details and interpretation in his discussion are debatable. Here we examine Rollston's article in a yeshiva-spirit deliberation, hoping that Chris, a good friend since his student days at Megiddo many years ago, will accept, and perhaps even enjoy, this kind of dialogue.

Let us start with Rollson's own words in the introduction to his paper:

> the most convincing constructs of human activities (including, therefore, writing) are those that are entirely data-driven.... we must make a concerted effort to analyze the data in the most sober, disinterested manner possible.... it is the data that we must put in the driver's seat, not our presuppositions. (2017, 1)

This chapter was originally coauthored with Benjamin Sass.

We cannot agree more. The study of early alphabetic writing in the Levant is all about separation of facts from suppositions that do not come from archaeology. By *facts* we mean time and location, that is, the chronology of the inscriptions and their place of discovery. Creating distribution maps according to relative (and then absolute) dates (Finkelstein and Sass 2013) is the basis for the discussion; doing this puts the inscriptions in context and avoids misinterpretations.

Facts

We presented our working paradigm's method in detail several years ago:

> The spatial and temporal distribution of the inscriptions in question illuminates the spread of the alphabet.... The dating criteria for the inscriptions are first and foremost where they exist, the archaeological context, the typological dating of the inscribed object, and only lastly the palaeographical dating of the script. (Finkelstein and Sass 2013, 149–50)

We argued for a three-step method in dealing with the dissemination of early alphabetic inscriptions:

1. Work only with those inscriptions that come from clear stratigraphic contexts.

2. Based on ceramic typology, establish the relative chronology of the layer from which the inscription emerges (or the relative chronology of the vessel, if possible).

3. Translate this relative (ceramic-based) chronology to absolute chronology only according to radiocarbon dating of the different phases of the Iron Age (Sharon et al. 2007; Finkelstein and Piasetzky 2010; Toffolo et al. 2014).[1] For the Iron I–IIA, all other absolute dating assertions are interpretative, based primarily on biblical verses that describe the past from the ideological perspective of authors who lived centuries after the alleged events took place. Needless to say, radiocarbon has a margin of uncertainty

---

1. Note that Rollston still works with the traditional, Bible-based high chronology for the Iron Age strata in the Levant; a great deal of our differences boils down to the radiocarbon-based attribution of strata such as Megiddo VA–IVB to the historically documented Omrides rather than to the biblically described Solomon.

that may be crucial for historical reconstruction, but deploying Bayesian modeling can reduce these uncertainties and establish a workable system of dating.

Regarding chronology and geographical setting, Rollston's discussion of four inscriptions—three of which play an important role in his attempts to demonstrate tenth-century BCE scribal culture in Jerusalem—reveals the chasm that separates our method from his.

Izbet Sartah: Rollston dates this inscription to the twelfth century, adhering to Naveh's paleographic assertion in an over forty-year-old article (1978). The Izbet Sartah Ostracon was found in a silo stratigraphically assigned to Stratum II, now dated to the early Iron IIA (Finkelstein and Piasetzky 2006b; Herzog and Singer-Avitz 2011). But the material in the silo was secondarily deposited after it had gone out of use; the pottery sherds represent the entire sequence of the site. If indeed there was an occupational gap at the site in the late Iron I (Finkelstein and Piasetzky 2006b), the ostracon could date from either the early/middle Iron I, late twelfth and eleventh centuries (Stratum III), or early Iron IIA in the late tenth to early ninth centuries BCE (Strata II–I). In a situation such as this, choosing between the alternatives by allowing paleographic considerations is justified; accordingly, we prefer the latter solution (details in Finkelstein and Sass 2013, 157, 159).

Kefar Veradim: Rollston says that the finds in the tomb "range from the tenth or the early ninth century BCE," and, based on "a constellation of factors," he dates them to the tenth century BCE (2017, 7–8). Typologically, the bowl has a broad range: from the Late Bronze II to the Persian period (Alexandre 2002a; Sass 2005, 36–39). However, the pottery in the sealed tomb dates to the late Iron IIA (Alexandre 2002b), meaning the ninth century BCE (Finkelstein and Piasetzky 2010). Dating the bowl a long time before the burial is unlikely (Alexandre 2002a, 67–68). Still, it is possible that it was a few decades old when deposited in the tomb, hence a date circa 900 BCE cannot be brushed aside.

The Ophel: Rollston cites the excavator, Eilat Mazar, that the inscription (fig. 13.1 below) was found in an Iron IIA context (Mazar, Ben-Shlomo, and Ahituv 2013), for Rollston covering the tenth and ninth centuries BCE (2017, 1). The shape of the vessel on which the inscription was incised, a forerunner of the Kuntillet ʿAjrud pithos, has late Iron IIA parallels, probably not dating much before the middle of the ninth century BCE (Finkelstein and Sass 2013; Kleiman 2021).

Fig. 13.1. The Ophel inscription (Mazar, Ben-Shlomo, and Ahituv 2013; reproduced with permission).

Qeiyafa: We are in agreement with Rollston on dating the Qeiyafa ostracons to a ceramic phase (in our opinion, transitional Iron I/IIA; Finkelstein and Fantalkin 2012) that falls in the tenth century BCE. But we differ with him regarding the spatial context of the finds. Rollston sees the site as belonging to the vicinity of Jerusalem and hence attesting to literacy there in the tenth century. However, Tell eṣ-Ṣafi/Gath, located only 10 kilometers to the west, produced seven early alphabetic inscriptions that date to the Iron IIA (one of them possibly to the late Iron I), and several additional inscriptions originated from sites in its immediate vicinity, including Qeiyafa and Tel Zayit. Moreover, Tell eṣ-Ṣafi and Tel Reḥov—in the Iron IIA the two largest urban centers in the southern Levant—produced circa 30 percent of the early alphabetic inscriptions known to date (eighteen of sixty). Adding sites in their immediate vicinity, the number grows to twenty-six of sixty, or 43 percent (Finkelstein and Sass 2013). To differ, Jerusalem produced a single early alphabetic inscription; speaking about "Jerusalem and its environs" is perhaps true for looking at modern maps, but it is wrong in the context of the Iron I–IIA.

To summarize this point, for the long period starting in the Late Bronze IIB and ending in the early Iron IIB (ca. 550 years, 1300–750 BCE), Jerusalem produced a single inscription—in Proto-Canaanite script. Most examples taken by Rollston as evidence for scribal culture in the tenth century in fact date to the ninth century BCE.

Interpretation

Rollston belongs to the camp of scholars who follow the traditional Albrightian (and later Cross) school of thought on the history of ancient Israel (for the epigraphy perspective, see also, e.g., Lemaire 2006; Millard 2012; Richelle 2016). A pivotal issue for this group, either directly (Millard 1989) or indirectly,[2] has been the historicity of the united monarchy of David and Solomon. Had there been such a golden age, strong scribal activity would have taken place in the royal court, and hence, even if redacted later, the Bible would include real-time evidence for the reign of these monarchs. Confirmation of scribal activity in the tenth century BCE is therefore essential for the survival of this paradigm. Being aware that there is no extrabiblical evidence for the existence of writing in Solomonic Jerusalem, Rollson turns to two circumstantial arguments. The first, referred to by him as "Jerusalem and its environs in Iron IIA," has already been dealt with above. Let us now turn to the second: the persistence of scribal activity in the southern Levant from the Late Bronze to the Iron IIA (the latter according to Rollston, against the radiocarbon evidence, in the tenth century).

We see a chain of flaws in this (originally Cross-structured, e.g., 1967) paradigm. Rollston ignores the profound difference in the sociopolitical background of the Iron I and early Iron IIA compared to both the Late

---

2. For instance, Rollston states, "The tenth century was … a period of fecundity in the world of Levantine city-states, and thus, of scribalism in the Levant as well. After all, kings and kingdoms need scribes to keep royal records, produce and maintain legal documents, and to tout the great deeds of the king" (2017, 8). He does not tell us which West-Semitic-writing kings and kingdoms between 1000 and 900 BCE he has in mind.

Bronze Age and the late Iron IIA, in fact "plucking" the inscriptions from solid archaeological and historical reality.

Rollston's Amarna example is a nonstarter because one cannot compare a system of city-states under imperial rule to the city-states of the Iron I or even the nascent territorial kingdoms of the early Iron IIA. Note that the entire Iron I did not produce a single securely dated inscription. Two early alphabetic inscriptions date to either the Iron I or early Iron IIA (Izbet Sartah ostracon, Beth-shemesh Baal sherd), one (Qeiyafa) is transitional Iron I/IIA, and two are probably early Iron IIA with a possibility of originating from the Iron I (Kefar Veradim, Ophel pithos sherd). As for the early Iron IIA, in addition to what we have just described for the Iron I, layers dating to this period produced eight inscriptions, plus two that date to either the early or late Iron IIA (data in Finkelstein and Sass 2013, table 1). It is the late Iron IIA that features the dissemination of scribal activity, and this is exactly what we are saying: scribal activity grows significantly with the prosperity of two important city-states (Rehob and Gath) and the more developed territorial kingdoms—Israel of the beginning of the late Iron IIA (the first half of the ninth century) and Judah later in the late Iron IIA (the second half of the ninth century). Royal monumental inscriptions also appear in the Levant starting in the second half of the ninth century BCE. Finally to be considered in relation to Rollston's arguments, not a single inscription that can safely be described as written in Hebrew script comes from the heartland of Israel and Judah prior to the later phase of the late Iron IIA, in the second half of the ninth century! We believe that these data put Rollston's longue durée notion in perspective.

We cannot close without a note on the Phoenician monumental inscriptions, first and foremost the Ahiram sarcophagus text, which play an important role in Rollston's argument; they should serve as a case study and warning. We do not intend to repeat the arguments put forward by Sass regarding the dates of these inscriptions (2005, 2017; summarized in Finkelstein and Sass 2013, 180–82). Suffice it to say that the Ahiram inscription has no secure date and that placing it in the early tenth century comes from adhering to Albright's craving for an archaeological backdrop for the biblical description of a magnificent united monarchy (Albright 1958, 2*). The statues of Sheshonq I and Osorkon I inscribed with early alphabetic inscriptions provide no arguments, because the Byblian kings Abibaal and Elibaal may have added their inscriptions years after the rule of the said pharaohs. In other words, Shehsonq I and Osorkon I supply nothing but a *terminus post quem* for the said inscriptions (more in Sass 2017, 132–33). Finally, the earliest monumental Byblos inscriptions display a substantial cursive-like component, providing them with a *terminus post quem* circa 900 (on the cursive script, see Sass and Finkelstein 2016). They also display a large proportion of older, precursive or Proto-Canaanite forms, but on the background of the cursive ones, the older forms are to be understood as archaizing: an assemblage of letters, like any other assemblage in archaeology, is dated by its most recent component.

Conclusion

Above we have demonstrated that all pillars of Rollston's article—the persistency of scribal activity from the Late Bronze to the Iron IIA; the dating of a large number of inscriptions to the tenth century BCE; and the insistence on significant scribal activity in the Iron IIA "in Jerusalem and its environs"—do not stand scrutiny with emphasis on temporal and spatial distribution of stratified and/or ceramically dated inscriptions. Chronologically, few inscriptions date to the tenth century BCE, and not a single inscription can be associated with Jerusalem of that time. Alphabetic writing developed slowly between the thirteenth century and the early ninth, with a first peak occurring only in the late Iron IIA, the ninth century BCE. Jerusalem produced a single early alphabetic inscription, in Proto-Canaanite script, dating to the ninth century BCE. This and other inscriptions, such as Kefar Veradim, Khirbet Qeiyafa, and Megiddo (for the latter, see Sass and Finkelstein 2016), indicate that the ninth century was a period of transition from Proto-Canaanite to cursive Hebrew and other regional West Semitic alphabets.

14

Migration of Israelites into Judah after 720 BCE: An Answer and an Update

The next three chapters are somewhat related to the previous two. They deal specifically with the demographic situation in late monarchic Jerusalem and more generally in Judah. In this chapter I return to the much-debated question of the migration of Israelites to Judah following the takeover of the Northern Kingdom by Assyria.

Introduction

The theory of migration of Israelites into Judah after the fall of the Northern Kingdom in 720 BCE emerged from biblical scholarship in an attempt to explain the impact of Israelite ideas on pivotal theological stances in the Hebrew Bible (e.g., Alt 1953, 250–75; Nicholson 1967, 57–82 and bibliography). It was then supported by archaeological work, which indicates dramatic demographic growth in Jerusalem and the various regions of Judah in the later part of the eighth century BCE (Broshi 1974; ch. 15 below; see also Van der Toorn 1996, 339–72; Schniedewind 2004). In a 2014 article in *ZAW*, Nadav Na'aman dismissed this reconstruction as invalid, based on a different interpretation of the archaeological data.[1]

This Israelites-in-Judah premise is crucial for biblical exegesis—far beyond the fields of archaeology and historical reconstruction—because

---

1. Na'aman 2014a; see also the exchange on the archaeology and history of Jerusalem in the eighth and seventh centuries BCE in Na'aman 2007 and ch. 16 below. In opposition to the theory of mass migration of Israelites into Judah, see also Knauf 2006; Guillaume 2008.

it has the potential to explain the incorporation of northern texts, including those competitive to the Jerusalem temple (e.g., Jacob at Bethel) and even hostile to the Davidic dynasty,[2] into Judahite literary works. It also explains the merging of northern and southern traditions such as the Saul and David stories and the Jacob and Abraham patriarchal sagas (Finkelstein and Römer 2014a, 2014b). Finally, it sheds light on the rise of the pan-Israelite ideology in Judah. It is essential, therefore, to carefully assess Na'aman's arguments.[3]

Na'aman dealt with three issues that are central to the dispute: the appearance of personal theophoric names in Israel and Judah; the demography of the Shephelah in the years 720–701 BCE; and the demographic situation on the southwestern hill in Jerusalem during the same time slot. In what follows I will examine each of these arguments, emphasizing both methodology and data, before presenting an update on the archaeological evidence behind the thesis of Israelite migration to Judah.

Preliminary Observations

Reconstruction of history is always about time and location. Advances in research that have occurred in the years since my original publication

---

2. The accusation against David in Samuel; for this, see McCarter 1980b; Halpern 2001.

3. I will refer to Knauf (2006) and Guillaume (2008) only in passing when addressing archaeological data. I choose not to deal with speculations such as, "Many Israelites may have left for economic reasons.... they would have moved to Philistia and, further down the road, to Egypt" (Knauf 2006, 294); or, "prior to 720 Israel did not have a standard administrative language, so there is even less reason to assume that this kingdom developed anything like a national tradition" (2006, 294). Further, I do not know how to respond to statements such as, "The flood-of-refugees hypothesis reflects modern anxieties more than ancient probabilities" (Guillaume 2008, 207). Guillaume advocates the flawed idea of replacing solid archaeological data with vague theoretical constructs: "The following will not discuss the archaeological data which is open to vastly different interpretations.... Hence I focus on the validity of the notion of refugees in the ancient world" (2008, 197); note the baseless speculation that the population growth in Judah was a result of the Assyrian policy of relocating exiles from the area of Ashdod (2008, 201).

14. Migration of Israelites into Judah after 720 BCE

regarding Israelite refugees in Judah (ch. 15 below) call for a fresh treatment of both issues.

Chronology

Treatment of the archaeological data from Jerusalem in particular and Judah in general requires good control over the subdivision of the Iron II into three ceramic typology subphases: Iron IIA, Iron IIB, and Iron IIC. In order to use finds and settlement patterns associated with these phases in a historical discussion (for instance, the time it took Jerusalem to grow to its maximal area), one needs first to translate them into absolute chronology. Especially important for the theme of this chapter are the two transitions: from the Iron IIA to the Iron IIB and from the Iron IIB to the Iron IIC. Establishing an approximate[4] absolute date for the former can be done mainly according to ^{14}C results that are now available for a large number of sites both in the north and south of Israel. Because of the Hallstatt Plateau in the calibration curve,[5] radiocarbon dating is of no help in determining the Iron IIB/C transition, which therefore depends solely on archaeological considerations.

A methodological note is in place here: it should be clear that the end of a given ceramic phase at one site does not necessarily mean the end of that ceramic phase county-wide. To give an example for an area close to Judah, the destruction of Stratum A3 at Tell eṣ-Ṣafi/Gath—a layer that features a late Iron IIA pottery assemblage—can be dated by a combination of ^{14}C results and textual arguments to circa 840–820 BCE.[6] This does not eliminate the possibility that the ceramic tradition of the late Iron IIA continued for a while in other places. Indeed, in the north of Israel the late Iron IIA pottery tradition probably continued into the beginning of the eighth century BCE (Finkelstein and Piasetzky 2009, 2010); in Judah, the end of Beth-shemesh 3, which features a pottery assemblage characterized as transitional Iron IIA/B (Bunimovitz and Lederman 2006), probably dates

---

4. *Approximate* because transitions in pottery traditions are the result of gradual processes that can take a few decades.

5. The Hallstatt Plateau is a flat sector in the calibration curve caused by variations in solar activity that prevents reaching accurate radiocarbon dates between ca. 750 and 400 BCE.

6. "After 835/832 BCE," according to the excavator (Maeir 2012, 47–49).

to the first half of the eighth century, close to its middle (Finkelstein and Piasetzky 2009, contra Katz and Faust 2014). In other words, the beginning of the Iron IIB should be dated to the middle of the eighth century or just a bit earlier, not to 800 BCE, as argued by Na'aman (2014a, 9, 10).

Scholars have tended to date the end of the Iron IIB to the Sennacherib campaign in 701 BCE because of the dramatic destruction layers with rich pottery assemblages that represent this event, first and foremost Level III at Lachish. However, destruction events should not be equated with much slower and more gradual cultural transformations, including changes in pottery traditions. Sheer logic tells us, then, that the Iron IIB ceramic traditions continued for a while into the first half of the seventh century BCE. This is difficult to prove, mainly due to the lack of destruction layers during most of the seventh century BCE (Finkelstein 1994); in fact, almost no pottery assemblage can safely be placed in the first half or middle of the seventh century BCE.[7] Nonetheless, the notion that the Iron IIB ceramic tradition continues into the seventh century is supported by stratigraphic evidence for (Iron IIB–characterized) settlement activity after the 701 destruction in several Shephelah sites (Finkelstein and Na'aman 2004) and by recent observations regarding the *lmlk* seal impressions (Lipschits, Sergi, and Koch 2010, 2011; ch. 18 below). The transition from the Iron IIB to the Iron IIC should therefore be seen as a gradual process in the first half of the seventh century (details in ch. 18 below).

To sum up this section, the Iron IIB—the focus of this chapter—lasted about one century, from the later part of the first half (or middle) of the eighth century until sometime in the first half (or middle) of the seventh century BCE.

Location of the Ancient Mound of Jerusalem

The location of the ancient tell of Jerusalem is essential for the discussion here because it is a key for estimating the size of the city before its giant leap forward in the Iron IIB. Conventional wisdom maintains that the mound of Jerusalem in the Bronze and Iron Ages was located on the southeastern ridge, known in archaeological research as the City of David. However, long periods in the history of Jerusalem—some of them well-attested in

---

7. For a possible exception, though on the coast, far from Judah, see Fantalkin and Tal 2009.

the textual record (e.g., the Amarna phase of the Late Bronze Age and the Persian and early Hellenistic periods)—are represented there only by a small number of sherds, with no evidence of building activity. In fact, even these finds are known only from the area above and slightly to the south of the Gihon Spring; the northern and southern parts of the ridge yielded no remains from these periods. Moreover, in pre-Roman times the southeastern (City of David) ridge was fully inhabited only in the Iron IIB and the late Hellenistic periods; in all other periods—even those that provide evidence for building endeavors such as the Middle Bronze and the Iron IIA—activity was limited to the area of the Gihon.

This is not the only problem with Jerusalem. First, although the eastern side of the southeastern ridge was protected by city walls in the Iron IIB and the late Hellenistic period, no trace of any fortification has ever been found on the western side of the ridge, which borders on the Tyropoeon Valley. This is not to mention that at its narrowest point the ridge is only circa 75 meters wide (a unique topographic situation unknown at other major mounds in the Levant). Second, mounds in the highlands were usually located on the highest topographical points. The southeastern ridge is lower than its surroundings; in fact, it is dominated on three sides by higher areas. Third, the idea that in the Iron Age the Temple Mount—the highest point that is the easiest to protect—was occupied only by the temple and the palace and that it featured large empty spaces is influenced by what scholars know about the situation there in Herodian times and by the landscape of the Haram al-Sharif platform of our day. The fact of the matter is that, in the Bronze and Iron Ages, no mound featured this kind of layout; rather, the temple and palace compound formed one sector of a densely inhabited mound. In short, the southeastern ridge cannot be regarded as the original mound of ancient Jerusalem (and therefore cannot be titled the City of David; for biblical texts, see Hutzli 2011).

As a result of all this, Ido Koch, Oded Lipschits, and I suggested (ch. 2 above), following Knauf (2000), that the original mound of Jerusalem was located on the Temple Mount. Similar to other hubs of Bronze Age city-states and Iron Age territorial kingdoms, this mound, which could have covered an area of 5 hectares or more (the size of the biggest mounds in the highlands, such as Shechem), included both residential and public areas; the temple and the palace were probably located in its northern sector (Ussishkin 2009). This original mound was the location of Jerusalem in most phases of the Bronze and Iron Ages. Before Roman times the city expanded to cover the southeastern ridge and the southwestern hill (the Jewish and Armenian Quarters of today's Old City and Mount Zion) only in the Iron IIB and the Late Hellenistic periods and was then surrounded by fortifications.

This theory,, which cannot be tested in the field because the Temple Mount cannot be excavated, resolves all the problems listed above: the lack of evidence on the southeastern ridge for periods well-attested textually; the fact that much of the ridge provides no evidence for phases of the Bronze and Iron Ages except for the Iron IIB–C; and the lack of fortification on its western side (because the expansion included both areas at the same time).[8]

Points Raised by Na'aman

Theophoric Components in Israelite and Judahite Personal Names

Na'aman points to the lack of evidence of the proliferation in the use of the Israelite *yw* (*yo*) versus Judahite *yhw* (*yahu*) in personal names in Judah after 720 BCE.[9] I refute this argument based on the following observations.

1. As Na'aman rightly states (2014a, 5), the number of inscriptions with personal names in eighth-century Judah is so meager that it does not allow us to reach clear conclusions (see ch. 12).

2. Na'aman compares the situation in Israel in the first half of the eighth century to that in Judah in the late eighth century and (in the case of the Iron IIB in Jerusalem, where there was no Sennacherib destruction) possibly even in the first half of the seventh century. In other words, there

---

8. For all this, see detailed discussion in ch. 2 above, with bibliography to previous studies.

9. Na'aman raises two other issues regarding script: contra Schütte (2012), he argues that the variants in the Judahite script cannot be related to the "assumed migration of Israelite scribes to Judah"; and he opposes Rendsburg and Schniedewind's assumption (2010), that the author of the Siloam Inscription was an Israelite refugee. I will not delve into these matters here because in both cases an answer in the affirmative or negative does not provide a verdict regarding the issue of Israelite refugees in Judah after 720 BCE.

is a significant gap of fifty to one hundred years between the two situations, which renders his comparison futile.

3. What we have at our disposal from seals and seal impressions (and bullae) are names of officials, probably relatively high in the hierarchy of the Judahite bureaucracy. It must have taken at least several decades for Israelites to reach this status. By then Israelites or their descendants may already have used the Judahite version of the theophoric component in their names.

4. Israelites who reached the high echelons of Judahite bureaucracy must have adopted Judahite ways of writing the theophoric name. In fact, they may have embraced local culture as a means to advance their social status.

5. Many of the Israelites who made their way south must have emigrated from southern Samaria, which bordered on Judah. We do not know how the theophoric name was written in this region.

6. When it comes to the broader set of data, most inscriptions found in Judah as well as late monarchic biblical texts date to the late seventh and early sixth centuries BCE, approximately a century after the migration of Israelites from the north. One cannot expect the Israelite manner of writing theophoric names to have survived in Judah over so long a period.

To sum up this issue, the *yw* versus *yhw* argument could have been used if we had a large database for Israel close to 720 and for Judah immediately thereafter, but even then it would not have been free of difficulties. Therefore, this argument is not pertinent to the debate.

Demography of the Shephelah

Regarding the Shephelah, Na'aman (2014a, 9) poses the following question: Is it possible that the dramatic demographic growth in the Shephelah took place in the short period of time between the fall of Samaria in 720 BCE and the Sennacherib destruction in 701 BCE?

The answer to this question, of course, lies in the details of the settlement patterns in the region. Much of what we know about the Shephelah comes from the main mounds that demonstrate habitation continuity from the Iron IIA to the Iron IIB. In fact, some of the central sites—mainly mounds—were also inhabited in the Iron IIC (Dagan 2004, 2681). And since there is evidence at several of them for post-701 BCE activity still within the Iron IIB (Finkelstein and Na'aman 2004), one wonders if some of the main mounds were not inhabited continuously throughout the Iron II; the 701 BCE crisis could have resulted in destruction and possibly short occupational gaps at many of the sites, but some of them could have recovered after a short while (Finkelstein 1994 and ch. 18 below, contra Lipschits, Sergi, and Koch 2011). Hence, although the number of new sites in the Iron IIB is remarkable, most of them are small villages and farmhouses. The twenty years between 720 and 701 BCE provide a long enough time slot for the establishment of many of these sites.

Moreover, Sennacherib's 701 BCE attack may have been directed primarily at the central urban centers. Our knowledge of the assault comes from the main mounds—first and foremost from Lachish. Almost no late Iron II villages in the region have been excavated, so there is no information on the devastation of rural sites. In other words, at least some villages or farmhouses could have survived the Assyrian attack. Furthermore, as mentioned above, since several central sites provided evidence for renewed activity after 701 BCE and still within the Iron IIB, it may be assumed that some farmhouses and villages could actually have been established in the later part of the Iron IIB, that is, in the first half of the seventh century BCE, when the Shephelah recovered from the Sennacherib devastation.[10] In other words, the growth in the number of sites in the region could have taken longer than twenty years.

Three more points are in place here.

1. Some of the rural Iron IIB sites in the Shephelah may have been established as early as the incorporation of Judah into the Assyrian economy in 732 BCE—a date that could have signaled the intensification of the olive-oil industry there.

2. Following the events in Israel in 722–720 BCE, the Shephelah seems to have become a prominent olive-oil producer under Assyrian auspices (Gitin 2003 with reference to previous works); its prosperity may have attracted a large number of people, mainly Israelite experts in olive culture and olive-oil industry.

3. As shown in the update below, the number of new rural Iron IIB sites in the region may have been somewhat smaller than previously presented.

Taking all this into consideration, I see no insoluble obstacle in connecting much of the demographic growth in the Shephelah in the Iron IIB

---

10. On the region at that time, see Finkelstein 1994.

with migration of Israelites after the Assyrian conquest of the Northern Kingdom.

Jerusalem

Na'aman (2014a, 9) argues that the population of the city before 720 BCE, as well as the number of inhabitants after 720 and before 701 BCE, cannot be determined (also Guillaume 2008, 207); consequently the theory of mass migration from the north cannot be tested. Instead, he advocates a theory of "natural growth of the city's population, combined with a steady movement of people from the Judahite highlands and the Shephelah … and the flight of refugees from the areas destroyed by Sennacherib" (2014a, 11).

Contra Na'aman (2014a, 9), it *is* possible to gauge the demographic changes in the city in the different phases of the Iron II. This can be achieved thanks to the detailed chronological information and the unparalleled archaeological data from the different parts of the city. The fortification that encircled the large Iron IIB city must have been built when a significant populace had already been settled in the new areas on the southeastern ridge and southwestern hill; it would have been illogical to invest in so immense a project in order to protect just a few farmhouses. According to almost all authorities, including Na'aman, the city wall was erected before 701 BCE (contra Knauf 2006, 293). This means that the expansion from less than 10 hectares in the late Iron IIA (see update below) to 60 hectares in the Iron IIB occurred within a period of roughly fifty years—in the second half of the eighth century, *before* the Sennacherib campaign and the destruction of the Shephelah towns. In other words, even though the possibility of immigration to Jerusalem from the Shephelah after the 701 catastrophe is valid, it does not resolve the problem of the city's growth before the Sennacherib assault. Moreover, even if the new areas of Jerusalem were not fully built up, we are dealing with a significant population increase in a matter of a few decades.[11] Where did these people come from? Theoretically, one could argue, with Na'aman, that this demographic growth represents migration from the country-

---

11. The fills cited by Na'aman (2014a, 10) as evidence for the sparseness of occupation on the northwestern hill must indicate otherwise, that buildings *were* constructed above them, or else why lay fills? These buildings did not survive the dense occupation and intense building activities of many later centuries.

side of Judah to the capital—a result of prosperity that stemmed from the incorporation of Judah into the Assyrian economic system. However, the rural sectors of Judah show the same trend of dramatic population growth (rather than depletion, which would have been the case if people moved from the villages to the capital) in the Iron IIB.[12]

To sum up this point, a post-701 BCE migration from the Shephelah cannot explain the demographic boom in the city in the second half of the eighth century, and the theory regarding "economic" migration from rural areas in the highlands to Jerusalem before 701 BCE is not supported by the evidence on the ground. The best (if not only) solution is still to equate the growth in Jerusalem (and Judah; see below) with the contemporaneous depletion of population in the highlands region of southern Samaria: the Ephraimite Highlands (ch. 15 below; for the biblical material, see Van der Toorn 1996, 339–72).

Migration of Israelites into Judah: An Update

Na'aman's statement that "no concrete evidence for the presence of immigrants of northern origin within the late eighth century kingdom of Judah" (2014a, 3) exists is surprising, as this historical reconstruction is backed by both avenues of archaeology, settlement patterns and material culture, not to mention the evidence that comes from the very existence of a large number of northern-derived texts in the Hebrew Bible. As far as I can judge, there are few notions regarding historical processes in the Iron Age that are supported by such a solid assemblage of data.

Recent developments call for an update of the data presented previously (ch. 15 below). I refer to discoveries in Jerusalem; the new premise regarding the original mound of Jerusalem (above); and fresh observations regarding settlement patterns and material culture in Judah.

---

12. Guillaume raises the question of food logistics: "since neither Jerusalem nor Judah could have fed large number of refugees" (2008, 207). This statement, too, stems from insufficient knowledge of the archaeological data. The maximal population of the kingdom in the late eighth century can be estimated, based on solid archaeological information, at not much over 100,000 (Broshi and Finkelstein 1992). A population of that size can easily be supported by the countryside of the kingdom (Finkelstein 1994).

Settlement Patterns and Population Growth

Jerusalem. During the Late Bronze, Iron I and the early Iron IIA,[13] that is, until circa 900 BCE at the earliest,[14] Jerusalem was limited to the original mound on the Temple Mount (above). The first expansion of the city from the original mound can now be dated to the next phase in its history. New excavations in the Ophel (Mazar, Ben-Shlomo, and Ahituv 2013) and in the Givati Parking Lot in the northwestern sector of the City of David (Ben-Ami 2014) revealed evidence for activity in the late Iron IIA, in the ninth century BCE: elaborate buildings in the former and simpler habitations in the latter.[15] This means that the settlement now extended to the southern slope of the Temple Mount. On the southeastern ridge, activity in the late Iron IIA is evident only in the area above and slightly to the south of the Gihon Spring.[16] The remains above the Gihon may have belonged to a fortress that protected the spring. Other parts of the ridge reveal no evidence of habitation at that time. All in all, Jerusalem of the late Iron IIA covered an area of circa 8.5 hectares, compared to my estimate of the area of the mound on the Temple Mount as having covered about 5 hectares. Judging from the fact that major Judahite Iron IIA cities in the Shephelah (Lachish, Beth-shemesh) and north of Jerusalem (Mizpah; Finkelstein 2012b) were fortified, the original mound of Jerusalem on the Temple Mount must have been surrounded by a city wall; there is no evidence that the "new quarter" on the southern slope of the

---

13. For two phases in the Iron IIA, see Herzog and Singer-Avitz 2004.
14. For the absolute dates of the early and late phases of the Iron IIA, see Finkelstein and Piasetzky 2010.
15. Broader considerations seem to indicate that the first expansion of Jerusalem, as well as the expansion of Judah into the Shephelah, the Beersheba Valley, and the area south of Hebron, took place in the later part of the late Iron IIA, in the second half of the ninth century BCE (Fantalkin and Finkelstein 2006; Fantalkin 2008; Sergi 2013; ch. 10 above).
16. E. Mazar 2007, 2009. This structure was described as one component in a bigger building effort that included the Stepped Stone Structure on the slope (E. Mazar 2007, 2009; A. Mazar 2010; Faust 2010). However, both structures probably feature remains from more than one period, and the connection between them cannot be proven (chs. 7 and 8 above). For Area E (the Iron IIA remains were found mainly in Area E North sector, which is the closest to the spring) of the Shiloh excavations, see De Groot and Bernick-Greenberg 2012.

Temple Mount was fortified (Ben-Ami 2014). Calculating approximately two hundred people per built-up hectare and taking into consideration the existence of large public areas, one can estimate the population at circa fifteen hundred people. Iron IIB Jerusalem was the largest city in the land of Israel and covered an area of 60 hectares. Assuming that Geva (2006) is correct and not all sectors of the southwestern hill were densely inhabited, this translates to approximately ten thousand inhabitants (a bit less than my original estimate of twelve thousand souls; Geva's 2014 estimate of eight thousand seems somewhat too low).

The Shephelah. Following the results of Dagan's survey (1992), I previously described a growth in the Shephelah from 21 sites in the Iron IIA to 276 in the Iron IIB. However, I failed to notice that Dagan identified Iron IIA sites only according to the pottery of Level V at Lachish (rather than V–IV) and that he lumped the pottery typical of Level IV with that of the well-known Level III, which was destroyed in 701 BCE, that is, with the Iron IIB instead of the Iron IIA.[17] His numbers, therefore, require updating. Also note that in the Shephelah some of the Iron IIB sites may have been established in the early seventh century BCE (above). Since Dagan does not provide a breakdown of Lachish's Levels IV and III sherds per site, it is difficult to establish the true number of sites. The number of Iron IIB sites should be only slightly reduced, because most of those sites that are now added to the Iron IIA group were also probably inhabited in the Iron IIB. I can only estimate, then, that the numbers should be updated from 21 and 275 to a significantly larger number than 21 (no way to estimate exactly) and, say, 250 in the Iron IIA and early Iron IIB (before 701 BCE), respectively.

The highlands south of Jerusalem. Following the results of the survey conducted by Ofer (1993b), I described a growth in the highlands of Judah from 34 sites in the Iron IIA to 122 in the Iron IIB. However, here also I am now aware of the fact that Ofer put his Iron IIB parallel to Levels V and IV at Lachish (Ofer 1993b, 23–24), which are considered today as Iron IIA. It should also be noted that his Iron IIC parallels what is described here as Iron IIB.

---

17. Dagan 1992, 253; for Level IV belonging to the Late Iron IIA, see Zimhoni 1997, 171; Herzog and Singer-Avitz 2004; Katz and Faust 2014. I am grateful to Omer Sergi for drawing my attention to this issue.

For his Iron IIB (= the Iron IIA here), Ofer lists 86 sites, "more than half of them small or very small" (1994, 105). Even a smaller number means a more moderate population growth in the Iron IIA/B transition; still, the total built-up area (to differ from the number of settlements) more than doubled. Also, in the highlands of Judah, which did not suffer from the Sennacherib assault, some of the Iron IIB sites may have been established in the later phase of the period, in the early seventh century BCE. I would therefore suggest that the number of settlements in the highlands of Judah grew from circa 80 sites, most of them small, to circa 120 sites, many of them larger, and that the population doubled.

I should note that my original description of the process as the arrival of a "torrent of refugees" may indeed be inadequate, as we are probably dealing with a process rather than a short, sudden episode.[18] Although many of the new residents in Jerusalem must already have been settled in before 701 BCE, when the city wall was erected, others could have joined in the decades that followed, in the first half of the seventh century BCE. This is also true for the process of growth in the highlands of Judah and, as mentioned above, possibly even in the Shephelah. In other words, the migration from Israel to Judah could have taken several decades, possibly half a century: a strong episode in the years following the Assyrian takeover of the north and a continuous trickle in the following decades.

Material Culture

Na'aman states that the "material culture discovered in the excavated sites [in the Shephelah] is purely Judahite. No vessels or other artifacts originating in the highlands of Samaria have been discovered in any of the ruined sites" (2014a, 9). This statement is incorrect, or at least imprecise.

Let me start with two methodological comments. First, many of the Israelites who came to Judah probably emigrated from the southern part of the Samaria Highlands, that is, from areas neighboring on Judah. This is where surveys seem to have revealed significant depletion of population after 720 BCE. Hence a priori one cannot expect these migrants to have exhibited features of material culture significantly different from that of Judah. Second, the typical material culture characteristics of the

---

18. Described by Na'aman (2014a) and Guillaume (2008) as a "flood of refugees."

different Levantine territorial kingdoms developed mainly in the late seventh century BCE, long after the fall of the Northern Kingdom.[19] In fact, in the period before 720 BCE, it is not always easy to identify material culture characteristics that distinguish between the two Hebrew kingdoms. Therefore, such a distinction depends on a limited number of features that do not always find expression in the assemblage from a given site.

The above comments notwithstanding, several typical ninth and/or early eighth century BCE elements of Israelite material culture *do appear* in Judah—in the Shephelah and elsewhere—starting in the late eighth century BCE:

- Stone installations for olive-oil extraction that are known in Israel starting in the Iron IIA (Eitam 1987) appear in Judah at sites such as Tell Beit Mirsim and Beth-shemesh only in the Iron IIB (Katz 2008, 38–42). Also noteworthy is the change in the center of olive-oil production: from Samaria in the early Iron IIB (as reflected, among other finds, in the early eighth-century BCE Samaria ostraca), and probably the Iron IIA as well, to the Shephelah in the Iron IIB–C, in the late eighth and seventh centuries BCE (Gitin 2003; Finkelstein and Na'aman 2004). Note that in Samaria sites that feature rock-cut installations for extraction of oil are known (from surveys) mainly south of Shechem (Eitam 1979).
- Pottery items that are characteristic of the Phoenician coast and the territory of the Northern Kingdom appear in Judah starting in the Iron IIB, in the late eighth century (Singer-Avitz 2010).
- Ashlar masonry, typical of elaborate Israelite structures (especially at Samaria and Megiddo) in the Late Iron IIA, appears in Judah in the late eighth century (the Beersheba altar) and later (Ramat Rahel).
- Proto-Ionic capitals, which appear in Israel in the Iron IIA, for example at Megiddo (and probably also at Samaria and Hazor, where dating is more difficult), are known in safe contexts in Judah only in the later phases of the Iron Age.

---

19. For Judah, see, e.g., Kletter 1999; for Ammon, Bienkowski 1991, 38–51.

- Longitudinal pillared buildings, which served as stables, appear at Megiddo in Israel in the first half of the eighth century (Cantrell and Finkelstein 2006) and at Lachish in Judah in Level III (Ussishkin 2004e, 86–87), which dates to the second half of the eighth century BCE.
- Rock-cut tombs that are popular in the Samaria Highlands before the Assyrian conquest appear in Judah in the late eighth century (Yezerski 2013).
- For small finds, note that square bone scaraboids, which were originally produced in Israel, arrived in Judah after the Assyrian takeover of the north (Brandl 2006).
- Ideas and cult practices are no less important than features of material culture. Beyond the theory that Deuteronomistic ideas were brought to Judah from the north (e.g., Nicholson 1967 and bibliography), as Na'aman rightly observed (2002a), the concept of centralization of cult as a tool of political and economic control, which may be traced in Israel to the Iron IIA/B transition (Na'aman 2002a; Finkelstein 2013b, 138–40), was practiced in Judah in the late eighth century BCE.[20]
- Beyond all this, one needs to consider another item of (material) culture: the introduction of a large number of northern texts and traditions into Judahite literary works.

Needless to say, caution is important here: some of these features may have appeared in Judah later than in Israel because the south developed into a prosperous kingdom later than the north. In addition, some of these features could have found their way into Judah as a result of simple cultural diffusion and trade relations. What I am saying is that one cannot argue for the lack of Israelite items of material culture in Judah in the period after the fall of the north.

---

20. For the archaeological evidence, see Herzog 2002a, 69–72; ch. 15 below.

Summary

There is no escape from the unmistakable archaeological evidence of a dramatic demographic transformation in Judah in the Iron IIB, in the second half of the eighth century and the early seventh century BCE, and this transformation can in no way be explained as the result of natural population growth, economic prosperity, or intra-Judahite movement of people. I maintain that many of the new settlers in Jerusalem, the highlands of Judah, and the Shephelah emigrated from the territory of Israel, a large number of them from the southern Samaria Highlands, where surveys seem to demonstrate deterioration of settlement activity after 720 BCE. Appearance of Israelite material culture in Judah starting in the late eighth century supports this historical reconstruction, and, no less important, none of the issues raised by Na'aman is decisive enough to dismiss it. Therefore, I indeed stand behind the Occam's razor principle (noted by Na'aman 2014a, 14): in the case of competing hypotheses on the growth of Jerusalem and Judah in the Iron IIB, the one containing fewer assumptions—the premise advocating large-scale settlement of Israelites in Judah—should be selected.

The same holds true for the competing explanations for the incorporation of Israelite traditions, including written materials, into Judahite texts. It is difficult to understand the Hebrew Bible without acknowledging that late monarchic Judah was composed of a mix of Judahites and Israelites. The number of Israelites in Judah was probably large enough to force biblical authors to be mindful of their most important foundation myths and at least some of their royal traditions. Needless to say, some of these traditions could also have reached Judah in later times; for instance, Israelite texts could have been preserved at Bethel (Knauf 2006) and found their way to Jerusalem when Judah appropriated this shrine in the late seventh century (Guillaume 2008, 204). But what would have been the need to incorporate them into the Judahite texts a century after the migration of Israelites into Judah?

The discussion on the demography of Judah in the late eighth century, the migration of Israelites to Judah after 720, and the incorporation of northern texts into Judahite biblical works reminds me of the Greek myth on the foundation of Byzantium: when consulted by Byzas of Megara about a good place to establish a colony, the Delphi oracle answered, "opposite the Land of the Blind," referring, of course, to those who cannot see the obvious.

Addendum

1. Two books published in recent years, Fleming 2012 and Schütte 2016, deal with the question of Israelites in Judah.

2. An issue of *HBAI* has recently been dedicated to "Deuteronomy: A Judean or Samaritan Composition" (Edenburg and Müller 2015a).

3. Golub (2017, 2018) has recently assembled the archaeological evidence for the use of theophoric names in Israel and Judah. The updated data do not change my analysis above.

4. Additional data on the late Iron IIA buildings immediately south of the Temple Mount have now been presented in the first final report on the Ophel excavations (E. Mazar 2015b).

5. I have recently advanced the idea that other important biblical traditions, such as the conquest and the united monarchy concepts, originated in the north (Finkelstein 2020d, 2020f). I have also dealt with the temples of Israel in the eighth century BCE and their impact on the concept of centralization of cult in Judah of the seventh century BCE (Finkelstein 2020c).

15

Temple and Dynasty: Hezekiah, the Remaking of Judah, and the Rise of the Pan-Israelite Ideology

---

Here I deal with the impact of the dramatic demographic changes that took place in Judah in the late eighth century on the cult and ideology of the kingdom and consequently on the composition of its texts.

The incorporation of Judah into the Assyrian world system and the fall of the Northern Kingdom in the late eighth century BCE stimulated momentous economic and demographic events that are crucial for understanding the early development of the biblical tradition. They shed light on the centralization of the cult in Jerusalem and on the background for the compilation of the early history of the Davidic dynasty.

The rise of the kingdom of Judah has been a major theme in archaeological and historical research in recent years (Jamieson-Drake 1991; Finkelstein 1999, 2001; Bunimovitz and Lederman 2001; Herzog and Singer-Avitz 2004). The accumulation of archaeological data points to three major phases in state formation in Judah.

1. A **formative phase** in the Iron I (mid-twelfth to late tenth centuries BCE) and possibly the early Iron IIA (late tenth or ca. 900 BCE; see Herzog and Singer-Avitz 2004; Finkelstein 2001). At

---

This chapter was originally coauthored with Neil Asher Silberman. Being the earliest article incorporated into this book, it calls for a large number of updates, for which see the addendum.

that time the situation in Jerusalem in particular and the southern hill country in general continued that of the Late Bronze Age (Na'aman 1996): Jerusalem was a small highland village covering a limited area of circa 2 hectares in the center of the City of David ridge, and the southern hill country was sparsely inhabited, with the number of sites—most of them small—not exceeding twenty, probably fewer (Ofer 1994, 102; Finkelstein 2001).

2. A **middle phase** characterized by the late Iron IIA pottery of Level IV at Lachish and its contemporary sites (Herzog and Singer-Avitz 2004). The first signs of more fully articulated state formation appear in Judah in the ninth century BCE. This can be seen at four sites: Lachish and Beth-shemesh in the Shephelah and Beersheba and Arad in the Beersheba Valley. They feature the earliest fortification systems and other significant public building activities (Finkelstein 2001).

3. A **full-blown state phase** characterized by the Lachish Level III pottery horizon. This phase, which dates to the late eighth century, features an advanced bureaucratic apparatus, a fully developed settlement hierarchy, monumental building activities, and mass production of secondary agricultural products (Jamieson-Drake 1991; Finkelstein 1999).

Past studies concentrated mainly on identifying the successive state-formation phases with their most obvious archaeological manifestations. However, the specific historical context of the rise of Judah into full statehood in the late eighth century BCE has been mentioned only in passing. In what follows we wish to present additional archaeological data, reevaluate old data, and deal with the international background, demographic developments, and sociopolitical changes related to this process that contributed to a dramatic transformation of Judah's collective identity.

The Great Leap Forward, 732–701

In assessing Judah's state formation, the determination of a date for the transition from phase 2 to phase 3 (above) is crucial for our discussion. In ceramic (and stratigraphic) terms we refer to two different and generally easy to identify phases in the pottery sequence of Judah, which have been thoroughly discussed in recent years: the assemblages of Levels IV and III at Lachish and their contemporary strata.[1] The first assemblage represents the late Iron IIA, that is, the period covering the ninth century (mainly the second part of it) and possibly the early eighth century BCE.[2] The second assemblage represents the late eighth century BCE, until the Sennacherib destructions of 701 BCE (and probably the early seventh century, which is difficult to identify for the lack of destruction layers; see Finkelstein 1994; Finkelstein and Na'aman 2004). The transition between the two should probably be put sometime in the first half to the middle of the eighth century. Ussishkin, Zimhoni, and Herzog and Singer-Avitz suggested that the stratigraphic transition from the Lachish IV to the Lachish III horizon should be related to the earthquake in the days of Uzziah and Jeroboam II, which is mentioned in Amos 1:1 and is usually dated to circa 760 BCE (Ussishkin 1977, 52; Zimhoni 1997, 172–73; Herzog and Singer-Avitz 2004). A ceramic date at that time or even a bit later around the middle of the eighth century BCE seems reasonable (Zimhoni 1997, 173).

Let us first take a close look at Judah's transition from the cultural phase of Lachish IV to the succeeding phase of Lachish III. In the early eighth century BCE, Judah was living in the shadow of the great Northern Kingdom, which at that time reached its peak economic prosperity, territorial expansion, and diplomatic dominance. The economic prosperity is manifested by the Samaria ostraca, which attest to a highly organized, bureaucratic economy; the Samaria ivories; the Megiddo horse-breeding and training industry (Cantrell and Finkelstein 2006); and the elaborate Hazor and Megiddo water systems. It is also revealed by social criticism of the eighth-century northern prophets Amos (5:11; 6:4–6) and Hosea (12:1). The superiority of Israel over Judah is accepted by the Judahite Deuteronomistic Historian in the fable about the relationship between Amaziah king of Judah and Joash king of Israel (2 Kgs 14:9–10).

At this time Jerusalem was still restricted to the ridge of the City of David. It seems reasonable to assume that it already covered the entire ridge—an area of circa 6 hectares (including the eastern slope; Shiloh

---

1. Zimhoni 1997; Herzog and Singer-Avitz 2004. Note that on this matter the two chronology-debate camps are not far from each other (compare Mazar and Panitz-Cohen 2001, 274–76 to Finkelstein 2002a, 122–24).

2. For the best collection of vessels, from Tell eṣ-Ṣafi in the Shephelah, see Maeir 2001.

1984, 3)—though this is difficult to prove in the current state of archaeological research. Excavations on both the eastern and western slopes of the ridge failed to produce evidence for a defense system predating the late eighth century, and there is good reason to argue that the city had not yet been fortified.[3] In fact, the entire territory of Judah in the highlands failed to produce evidence for a single major urban center; the hill country to the south of Jerusalem was still relatively sparsely settled. It is difficult to estimate the number of sites there, but it was far smaller than that of the late eighth century (see ch. 14). The same holds true for the Beersheba Valley. Beersheba and Arad feature ninth- and early eighth-century fortification systems, but most other sites were not yet inhabited (e.g., Aroer) or were small in size (e.g., Tel 'Ira; Beit-Arieh 1999, 170). Lachish and Beth-shemesh seem to have been the most important sites in the Shephelah, both having been fortified before the mid-eighth century (Ussishkin 1983, 171–73; Bunimovitz and Lederman 2001, respectively). But the number of sites in the Shephelah—including fortified centers—was still limited (for the survey results, see Dagan 1992, 253–56, and see ch. 14).

The most common preconditions for a fully formed state apparatus—literacy and a centralized economy—are lacking in the archaeological record. There is no evidence anywhere in Judah for meaningful scribal activity in the ninth or early eighth century. Only a few inscriptions, seals, and seal impressions can be assigned to the phase 2 period, notably among them the two Uzziah seals (Avigad and Sass 1997, 50–51); no ostraca can safely be ascribed to this period of time (see below). There is no evidence for a developed economy specializing in the mass manufacture of secondary products such as olive oil. Standardized weights had not yet appeared (Kletter 1998). Pottery was not mass produced until the time of the Lachish III phase (Zimhoni 1997, 170–72). In short, in the first half of the eighth century Judah was still in an interim phase between the

---

3. Ussishkin 2003c. The Stepped Stone Structure on the eastern slope has been described as a tenth-century BCE public work manifesting the power and prosperity of the united monarchy (e.g., Cahill 2003a; A. Mazar 1997a, 164). However, the support systems on the eastern slope of the City of David had been constructed for the first time earlier than the tenth century and were then renovated and extended during subsequent centuries (Finkelstein 2001; Steiner 2003). Pottery dating to the ninth if not eighth century BCE was found between the surface courses of the Stepped Stone Structure (Steiner 1994, 19).

Amarna-like conditions of the Iron I and early Iron IIA (phase 1 above) and the full-blown statehood of the late eighth century (phase 3). This interim phase lasted for about a century between the mid-ninth and the mid-eighth centuries BCE.

Several decades later, during the Lachish III phase in the history of Judah, the socioeconomic character of the Southern Kingdom was utterly revolutionized. Jerusalem grew to be the largest city in the entire country, covering an area of circa 60 hectares (Broshi 1974; Avigad 1983, 54–60; Reich and Shukron 2003; Geva 2003b), with an estimated population of up to ten to twelve thousand inhabitants. The city was surrounded by a system of massive fortifications: a city wall on the eastern slope of the City of David (Shiloh 1984; Reich and Shukron 2003) and a 7-meter-thick wall to the west, on the western hill (Avigad 1983, 46–53; Geva 2003b). Water was supplied to the fortified city by the Siloam Tunnel, which led from the Gihon Spring to a pool in the southern tip of the valley separating the ridge of the City of David and the western hill, a location more accessible for the many inhabitants of the new quarters in the west. Elaborate rock-cut tombs began to be hewn around the city, testifying to the existence of affluent elite.[4]

In the southern hill country, as well as on the plateau to the north of Jerusalem, the number of settlements and the total built-up area grew dramatically (Ofer 1994; Finkelstein 1994). This was also the case in the Shephelah and the Beersheba Valley (Dagan 1992; Singer-Avitz 1999, respectively). There is good reason to suggest that in the years before the Sennacherib campaign (701 BCE) Judah attained its maximal territorial expansion and unprecedented population density (Finkelstein 1994). Well-planned countryside towns such as Beersheba II and Tell Beit Mirsim A represent a highly organized state. Beersheba features a system of well-built storehouses and an elaborate water system (which had already been built before; Herzog 2002b). At Lachish, the gate, the podium of the fortress, and the system of stables first built in Level IV were extended (Ussishkin 1983, 147–54).

---

4. The precise date of appearance of monumental rock-cut tombs in Jerusalem is difficult to establish, as most tombs were found empty of finds. But the distribution of the tombs around the maximal size of the city hints at the late Iron II, from the late eighth century onward (Barkay 2000, 247; for other arguments for this dating, see Ussishkin 1993, 325–28).

The high level of organization of the Judahite state at that time is indicated in additional archaeological phenomena. Monumental inscriptions in the Siloam Tunnel and on the facades of the Siloam tombs appear at that time, and the number of seals, seal impressions, and ostraca grows dramatically (Naveh 1982; Sass 1993; Renz 1995, 38–39). Standardized weights also appear for the first time (Kletter 1998). The *lmlk* jars and seal impressions of officials found on some of the jars also attest to an advanced bureaucratic apparatus, though not necessarily representing a sudden preparation for the revolt against Assyria. It seems due, rather, to the considerable growth and increasing complexity of the economy of Judah (see ch. 24); for the first time pottery is mass-produced (Zimhoni 1997, 170–72) and Judah engages in large-scale, state-controlled olive-oil production in the Shephelah at Tell Beit Mirsim and Beth-shemesh (Eitan-Katz 1994; Finkelstein and Na'aman 2004).

To sum up, in a very short period in the second half of the eighth century BCE Judah developed into a highly bureaucratic state with a rapidly developing economy. In order to identify the specific stimuli that may have encouraged and accelerated this process, we must be more precise chronologically. In other words, we need to go beyond archaeologically derived dates, based on the Lachish IV and Lachish III pottery assemblages, and turn to history.

Two momentous events seem to have shaped the history of Judah in the second half of the eighth century BCE. The first was the incorporation of the kingdom into the Assyrian global economy, which must have started in the days of Tiglath-pileser III of Assyria and King Ahaz of Judah in the 730s. Beginning in 732 BCE, Judah's participation in the Assyrian-dominated Arabian trade was the apparent main reason for the prosperity in the Beersheba Valley, along the routes that led from Arabia via Edom to the Mediterranean ports, which were turned into Assyrian emporia (Finkelstein 1992a; Singer-Avitz 1999; Na'aman 2001a). Somewhat later, apparently after the destruction of Ashdod and the rise of Ekron in the days of Sargon II, Judahite olive oil must have been traded to Assyria and other clients, possibly through Ekron (Finkelstein and Na'aman 2004). The second major event was the fall of the Northern Kingdom in 722–720 BCE.

Demographic Upheaval in Judah

A key phenomenon, which cannot be explained against the background of economic prosperity alone, is the sudden growth of the population of Jerusalem in particular and Judah in general in the late eighth century. Assuming that the broad wall in the western hill of Jerusalem was constructed before 701 BCE (after 701 Judah was a tame vassal of Assyria, and one can hardly imagine it fortifying its capital with a huge city wall), in a few decades in the late eighth century Jerusalem grew in size from roughly 6 to 60 hectares and in population from around one thousand inhabitants to over ten thousand (estimated according to two hundred inhabitants per hectare). The population of the Judahite countryside also grew dramatically in the transition from the Lachish IV to the Lachish III horizons (phases 2 and 3 above). The number of settlements in the hill country to the south of Jerusalem swelled from perhaps 34 in the Iron IIA to 122 in the late eighth century (Ofer 1994, 104–5). In the Shephelah, the number increased from 21 in the Iron IIA to 276 in the late eighth century.[5] Beyond the increase in the number of sites, one needs also to consider that they grew bigger and were more densely inhabited. All in all, the assumption that in the late eighth century, in a matter of a few decades, the population of Judah doubled would be a modest—and probably underestimated—evaluation.

This dramatic increase in the population of Judah in the transition from the Lachish IV to the Lachish III horizons cannot be explained as the result of natural demographic growth or of a gradual and peaceful migration into Judah from neighboring areas. From a strictly economic point of view, the Judahite hill country had always been less attractive than the lowlands or even the more fertile and well-watered northern areas of the central hill country. The only reasonable way to explain this sudden and unprecedented demographic growth is as a result of a flow of refugees from the north into Judah following the conquest of Israel by Assyria. The growth probably continued in Jerusalem and the southern hill country with another torrent of refugees who arrived after the devastation of the Judahite Shephelah and the Beersheba Valley by Sennacherib in 701 BCE.[6]

---

5. Dagan 1992; for a somewhat different way of counting, see Dagan 2000, lists in volume 2. For updates on both the highlands and the Shephelah, see ch. 14.
6. The first to point out to these processes was Broshi (1974).

All this means that the economic "great leap forward" and the major demographic expansion of Judah took place in a very short period of time, between 732 (but mainly 722) and 700 BCE (or several years later). In a few decades, Judahite demography, economy, and society were totally revolutionized. Judah was transformed from an isolated, formative tribal kingdom into a developed state, fully incorporated into the Assyrian global economy. No less important, the population dramatically changed from "purely" Judahite to a mix of Judahites and ex-Israelites, who had apparently fled from the direct Assyrian control that was now imposed on the territories of the conquered kingdom of Israel. Indeed, in light of the extent of the population growth in this short period, an assumption that up to half of the Judahite population in the late eighth/early seventh century BCE was of north Israelite origin cannot be too far from reality. Likewise in Jerusalem a substantial proportion of the population may well have been ex-Israelite.[7]

Although one might have expected to find clear confirmation in the material culture for the presence of northern Israelites in Judah in the late eighth century, the evidence is not strong.[8] The reason may be that many of the refugees came from the southern part of the highlands of Israel (see below), where the material culture was quite similar to that of Judah. Yet one significant item typical of southern Samaria does appear in Judah in the late eighth century. We refer to the stone-cut olive-oil presses found in several concentrations in ninth- to eighth-century rural sites in that region (Eitam 1987). Similar installations appear in Judah in the late eighth century (Katz 2001, 46, 50), most of them in two sites in the Shephelah: Tell Beit-Mirsim and Beth-shemesh (Finkelstein and Na'aman 2004).

Can we speculate on the exact places of origin within the territory of the former Northern Kingdom of the presumed wave of refugees? The answer may be at least partially positive, and it comes mainly from survey-derived data. Pottery collected in surveys is limited in quantity and variety and therefore allows only rough chronological distinctions. In the case dealt with here, regarding the territory of the Northern Kingdom

---

7. In the absence of written material, the question of the status of the people who left their homes in the north and why they left remains elusive. But it is reasonable to assume that many of them belonged to the elite of the kingdom, people who were in greater danger of deportation than others.

8. See, e.g., Brandl 2006 and updates in ch. 14.

in the highlands, it is relatively easy to set apart late Iron II and Persian period types, but very difficult, if at all possible, to distinguish chronological phases in the late Iron II survey collections (see n. 12 below). In other words, the only way to trace demographic changes in the period under discussion is to compare the situation during the peak settlement activity in Iron II, most probably representing the mid-eighth century BCE, with the period of peak prosperity of the Persian period in the fifth–fourth century BCE. Although we are dealing with a long period of time that could have experienced periodic oscillations that cannot be traced in survey material, the data are nevertheless of great significance.

In the area of northern Samaria (between Shechem and the Jezreel Valley) the number of sites did not change dramatically between the late Iron II and the Persian periods: 238 and 247, respectively (Zertal 1993). Zertal has not provided the total built-up area for the Iron II sites, but comparing Broshi and Finkelstein's (1992) estimate for the Iron II (260 hectares) to Zertal's (1990, 11) numbers for the Persian period (170 hectares), one can get a sense of a moderate decline. The assumption of overall occupation stability in this area is corroborated by the evidence from the Shechem syncline—probably the most fertile niche in the entire region of northern Samaria—where the number of sites actually grew from the Iron II to the Persian period (Zertal 1992, 54–56). Thus the change between the two periods is more in the distribution of the settlements in the different subregions (Zertal 1990; 1996, 86–87) than in the total number of sites. Deploying the broadly accepted density coefficient of two hundred people per built-up hectare, these numbers translate into a decline (of ca. 35 percent) from approximately 52,000 people in the eighth century to 34,000 in the Persian period. In other words, even if several thousand Israelites were deported in the late eighth century to Mesopotamia and foreign groups settled by the Assyrians in their stead, this area did not suffer a major demographic crisis in the late Iron II.[9]

---

9. Zertal (2003, 396) tried to reconstruct the settlement pattern of the seventh century BCE (to differ from the eighth) in northern Samaria according to a few pottery types and argued for a significant decline in the number of sites after the fall of the north. However, most of these types can also be found in the eighth century BCE. His main, probably only, criterion was therefore the wedge-decorated bowl (Zertal 1996, 84), which he linked to the Cuthean deportees who were settled by the Assyrians in the region (Zertal 1989). Without dealing with the

The situation is utterly different in southern Samaria, the area between Shechem and Bethel. The number of sites there decreased from 238 in the eighth century to 127 in the Persian period, and the total built-up area shrank even more spectacularly, from circa 170 to 45 hectares (75 percent).[10] Translating these figures into estimated population, we face a striking reduction from 34,000 to 9,000 people. Even if the long period between these two datum points saw several oscillations, it is clear that southern Samaria suffered a major, long-term demographic blow in the wake of the conquest of the Northern Kingdom.

This is also hinted by the fragmentary evidence on the locations where the Assyrians settled the Mesopotamian deportees. The Gezer and Tel Hadid cuneiform tablets attest to the presence of Babylonian deportees in the early seventh century BCE (Na'aman and Zadok 1988, 2000). The name Avvim, which appears in the list of late seventh-century towns (Josh 18:23; on the list, see Na'aman 1991), seems to have originated from the name Avva, one of the places of origin of the Mesopotamian deportees (2 Kgs 17:24); Avvim is located in the northern group of towns in the highlands of Benjamin, together with Bethel, Zermaraim, and Ophrah, that is, in the area around Bethel. Papyrus Amherst 63 mentions deportees who were probably settled in Bethel itself (Steiner 1991).

All these archaeological and textual clues relating to the southern part of the Northern Kingdom and the vicinity of Bethel suggest that many Israelites may have fled this area in fear of deportation and that foreign groups were settled in their stead. In the eighth century BCE, southern Samaria was an important oil-producing region (Eitam 1987); by settling foreign deportees there, the Assyrians may have attempted to help recover its economic output. Settling loyal population near the border of the vassal kingdom of Judah must have been intentional, as a measure of caution against future unrest. In short, it is reasonable to suggest that many (though certainly not all) of the north Israelite refugees who settled in Judah after 722 BCE came from southern Samaria. These people must have come to

---

question of the validity of this identification, the presence or absence of a single pottery type in survey sites (some of which produce a limited number of sherds) can be random and misleading. Zertal's interpretation of the situation in the seventh century is therefore based on very shaky grounds.

10. Finkelstein, Lederman, and Bunimovitz 1997, 898–906; for sites size legend, see p. 20 of that volume.

Judah with their own local traditions. Most significantly, the Bethel sanctuary must have played an important role in their cult practices, and the memories and myths of the Saulide dynasty, which originated in this area, could have played an essential role in their understanding of their history and identity.

The presence of substantial numbers of northern immigrants in Judah, and the new demographic situation it created, must have presented a challenge to the southern leadership and created an urgent need to unite the two segments of the new Judahite society—Judahites and Israelites—into a single national entity. In other words, there must have been a necessity to reformat Judah into a new nation. The main problems that needed to be addressed were ideological: particularly the different, not to say alien and hostile, cult and royal traditions of the northerners who came to settle in Judah.

In the following sections we wish to suggest two important ways by which King Hezekiah and his Jerusalem elite attempted to forge a sense of common identity among the diverse population of Judah in the late eighth century BCE: by focusing the new nation around the Jerusalem temple and by celebrating the early members of the Davidic dynasty as the founding kings of all Israel.

Centralization of the Cult

One of the most extensively discussed events in 2 Kings' account of the reign of Hezekiah is his cult reform (2 Kgs 18:3-4). Scholars have debated the historicity of this description, some accepting it as reliable (e.g., Weinfeld 1964; McKay 1973, 15-17; Haran 1978, 132-42; Halpern 1991; Lowery 1991; Rainey 1994; Swanson 2002), while others raise doubts or reject it altogether (Handy 1988; Na'aman 1995a; Fried 2002). The literary arguments—regarding the reliability of the Chronicler's description of the same event, the relationship of Hezekiah's cult reform to that of Josiah, and its connection to the Deuteronomic law of extirpating Canaanite cult objects, among many other issues—have not led to a decisive answer regarding the historical nature of this event. The primary evidence provided by archaeology, which comes from the two southern Judahite sites of Arad and Beersheba, has also been debated. Other relevant data come from the site of Lachish in the Shephelah. A reexamination of this material offers new insights about the historicity and nature of Hezekiah's cult reform.

Arad

The construction of the sanctuary at the fort of Arad was assigned by Yohanan Aharoni to Stratum XI, which he dated to the tenth century BCE. Aharoni argued that it underwent a major alteration before going out of use: the large altar in the courtyard was dismantled in the late eighth century (Stratum VIII), in the course of Hezekiah's cult reform, while the shrine itself was demolished in the late seventh century (Stratum VI), in the course of the cult reform of King Josiah (Aharoni 1968a). After Aharoni's death, the Arad team revised his conclusions, suggesting that both the altar and the shrine were removed in the days of Hezekiah (Herzog et al. 1984, 19–22). Ussishkin (1988) challenged these archaeological interpretations and biblical associations. In his opinion, the sanctuary had been built *after* the destruction of Stratum VIII and was destroyed together with the entire fort at the end of Stratum VI. Therefore, according to his understanding, the demise of the sanctuary had nothing to do with either the Hezekianic or the Josianic cult reforms described in the Bible.

In the course of the preparation of the Arad finds for final publication, Herzog reworked the stratigraphy and chronology of the Arad sanctuary (Herzog 2001; 2002a, 35, 40, 69–72). In his opinion, the sanctuary had functioned for only a short period of time, in the days of Strata X and IX, both dated within the eighth century BCE (Singer-Avitz 2002, 114–19). The shrine, together with its altar, were dismantled at the same time and buried under a 1-meter fill at the end of Stratum IX. The incense altars of the sanctuary were laid intact on their sides and intentionally buried. Stratum VIII, which represents the fort of the very late eighth century—the one that was attacked by Sennacherib in 701 BCE—did not have a sanctuary.

Herzog presented clear stratigraphic evidence for his interpretation (2001; 2002a, 35, 40, 69–72): walls and floors of Stratum VIII were built over the sanctuary, after it had gone out of use; the pottery on the floors dates to the eighth, rather than the seventh, century (Singer-Avitz 2002, contra Ussishkin 1988), and the Strata VII–VI floors in the vicinity of the sanctuary are 2 meters higher than the floor of the *debir* of the shrine. Herzog, like Aharoni, interpreted the Arad finds as evidence for the eradication of the sanctuary in the late eighth century in the course of the cult reform of Hezekiah.

Herzog dismissed Ussishkin's seventh-century dating of the sanctuary (Ussishkin 1988) and answered much of Na'aman's criticism (1999, 405–8; 2002a, 585–92), according to which the sanctuary survived until the final demise of Stratum VIII in 701 BCE, though its incense altars went out of use.[11] Without ignoring the methodological problems related to the excavation of Arad (Ussishkin 1988; Herzog 2002a, 7) and the immense difficulties in interpreting the stratigraphy of the site, it seems to us that Herzog's reconstruction, based on a meticulous study of the excavation records, is the most convincing: the sanctuary had been built in Stratum X and continued to function in the days of Stratum IX. It then went out of use and was buried under a thick fill. The Stratum VIII fort of the last years of the eighth century BCE therefore did not have a shrine. The finds from Beersheba and Lachish present a clear parallel to this phenomenon.

Beersheba

At Beersheba, a large horned altar built of ashlar blocks was dismantled, with some of its stones buried in the Stratum II glacis and others reused in the Stratum II pillared storehouses (Aharoni 1974; 1975a, 154–56). Aharoni suggested that the altar originally stood in a sanctuary. Since no such building was discovered at the site, he proposed that it had been completely and intentionally demolished when the large Building 32 was constructed (Aharoni 1975a, 154–56; see also Herzog, Rainey, and Moshkovitz 1977; Rainey 1994). Aharoni interpreted this evidence as supporting the biblical description of Hezekiah's cult reform: when Stratum II was built early in Hezekiah's days, the sanctuary was destroyed and the stones of its altar either discarded or reused.

Na'aman (1995a, 185–87; 2002a, 593–95) raised three objections against Aharoni's interpretation: (1) the altar could have stood in an open place rather than in a sanctuary; (2) Building 32 served a military-admin-

---

11. Na'aman (2002a, 592) argued for signs of destruction in the cella of the sanctuary, while Herzog (2002a, 64–66) saw no such signs. The Assyrian-style lion weight found near the sacrificial altar (Na'aman 1999, 406–7) belongs to Stratum IX and hence could have reached the site in the 730s BCE; therefore, it cannot be used to decide the dispute between Herzog and Na'aman.

istrative purpose, and there is no need for "farfetched theories" to interpret its function; (3) there is no way to determine the original date of the altar in pre–Stratum II Beersheba. Na'aman concluded that, "in the present state of our knowledge, we should best leave the Tel Beersheba altar outside the discussion of Hezekiah's religious policy" (1995a, 187).

We do not find Na'aman's criticism to be convincing for a number of reasons: (1) whether the altar stood in an open space or in a courtyard of a sanctuary is irrelevant; (2) the original location of the altar cannot be determined and is therefore also irrelevant;[12] (3) the stones of the altar were found in only two places; the most likely explanation, if not the only logical one, is that the altar was dismantled a short time before the construction of Stratum II. We find it highly unlikely that an altar of, say, Stratum V had been dismantled and its blocks dumped or reused in Strata IV and III and then found and reused in only two places in Stratum II. Without engaging in pure speculation about the original location of the altar, the most straightforward explanation would be that an altar that had still functioned in Stratum III was dismantled and buried in the fortification and buildings of Stratum II. Every other interpretation would need to explain away this simple logic. Stratum II was built in the very late eighth century BCE and was most probably destroyed by Sennacherib.[13]

Lachish

In 1968, Aharoni unearthed several fragmentary remains near the Persian-Hellenistic "Solar Shrine," which he interpreted as a Judahite sanctuary from the days of Level V, the tenth century according to his dating. He described the sanctuary as a small, rectangular broad room, with benches along its walls. A stone altar and a few cult vessels were found inside it, surrounding what he identified as a *bamah*. Aharoni proposed that the shrine was destroyed by fire at the end of Level V (Aharoni 1975b, 26–32, pls. 3–6, 60).

Ussishkin (2003b) has recently reexamined the results of Aharoni's excavations and come to different conclusions. According to his analysis,

---

12. The idea that an altar, which stood outside of the town, was removed by the Assyrians (Na'aman 2002a, 593) has no factual basis.

13. Knauf (2003) proposed that Stratum II survived the Sennacherib assault on Judah and continued into the early seventh century. Pottery analysis cannot distinguish between 701 or twenty years later; his other arguments are not convincing.

which seems to us convincing, the elements connected by Aharoni with the Level V sanctuary actually belong to several strata in the habitation sequence of the site. Ussishkin also noted that no traces of a real destruction by fire had been distinguished in the excavation. He concluded that the whole idea of a Level V sanctuary destroyed in a conflagration stemmed from the impression left by the pile of restorable cult objects. Ussishkin proposed that the objects were lying in a pit that was probably sealed by the constructional fill laid under the floor of the Level III palace-fort courtyard. He therefore dated the vessels and the pit to the days of Level IV in the late Iron IIA (ninth and early eighth century BCE; Herzog and Singer-Avitz 2004). Ussishkin suggested that these cult vessels came from a sanctuary that had gone out of use and were dumped into a pit and covered by the Level III fill.

The cult vessels found in the pit are difficult to date typologically (Zimhoni 1997, 62). The fact that the pit was covered by the fill and floor of the palace-fort courtyard of Level III does not necessarily imply that the pit itself predates that level. Since we have no idea when exactly within the time period represented by Level III the floor of the courtyard was laid, it is entirely possible that a preexisting shrine (of Level IV) was dismantled during the Level III era and its cult objects buried in a pit that was then covered by the newly laid palace-fort courtyard of Palace C (for the latter, see Ussishkin 1996, 33–37).

Discussion

The finds at Arad, Beersheba, and Lachish therefore seem to be consistent: all three present evidence for the existence of sanctuaries in the eighth century BCE, but in all three sites the sanctuaries were dismantled or fell into disuse before the end of the eighth century. In other words, in all three, the city that was destroyed by Sennacherib in 701 did not have a shrine.[14] It is also noteworthy that none of the large number of seventh- and early sixth-century sites excavated around Judah produced evidence

---

14. The only piece of evidence that can be interpreted otherwise is the depiction of several objects in the Sennacherib Lachish relief, which may be identified as cult vessels. Na'aman (1995a, 191–93; 1999, 404–5) interpreted them as evidence that at Lachish a Judahite shrine survived until the Sennacherib campaign in 701 BCE. However, the identification of the objects in the relief is far from clear,

for the existence of a sanctuary. In sum, these data provide strong evidence for the systematic removal of countryside sanctuaries in the late eighth century BCE.

In terms of historical context, this activity must have been connected with the policies of either Ahaz or Hezekiah—the two kings who ruled in Judah in the late eighth century BCE. Archaeology cannot provide an exact date within this time frame for the removal of the countryside shrines, but an examination of the broader events (see below)—and the testimony of 1 Kgs 18:3-4—point to the days of Hezekiah. The archaeological evidence for the elimination of countryside shrines seems to mesh with the biblical report that in his days Judah went through a sweeping cult "reform." Yet this process should be evaluated from socioeconomic and political, rather than strictly religious, perspectives, probably as part of an effort to centralize the state cult in the capital Jerusalem.[15] Such a policy would have been aimed at strengthening the unifying elements of the state—the central authority of the king and the elite in the capital—and at weakening the old, somewhat autonomous clan-based leadership in the Judahite countryside (Halpern 1991, 26–27).

No less important in centralizing the authority of the state through the establishment of a single national cult center was averting the threat posed by the temple of Bethel, in the territory of the former northern kingdom of Israel, located only 17 kilometers north of Jerusalem. As we have suggested, a significant sector of the population of Judah in the late eighth century, up to half if not more, was of north Israelite origin. These people, many of whom lived in Jerusalem and the area surrounding it, may have maintained their northern cult traditions even after their resettlement in Judah. And since many originated from southern Samaria, it seems logical to assume that their most important cult place was the temple at Bethel. Indeed it is probable that ex-Israelites living in Judah continued to visit this important cult place. Located in the province of Samaria, Bethel was under direct Assyrian rule, while Judah was an Assyrian vassal; there thus should have been no political or military impediment to conducting pilgrimages from Jerusalem to Bethel, at least not until 705 BCE. This

and Ussishkin (1982, 105, 107) explained them as ceremonial symbols of state that were taken as booty from the local Judahite governor's palace.

15. For a possible similar process in the Northern Kingdom in the transition from the ninth to the eighth century strata, see Na'aman 2002a, 595–97.

situation was likely considered intolerable by the Judahite authorities, especially in view of the new demographic situation, which called for an attempt to bind together the two sectors of the Judahite population: Judahites and Israelites.[16]

Thus an obvious solution was to ban all sanctuaries—countryside shrines in Judah and the Bethel temple alike—except for the royal temple in Jerusalem. The centralization of the cult in the Jerusalem temple was a step taken to strengthen the central authority of the emerging state over the local, clan-based power hubs, which must have necessarily been connected to countryside shrines. This may be the economic and demographic background for the biblical descriptions of a cult reform in the days of Hezekiah and possibly even the reference in 2 Chr 30:1 that Hezekiah called on the people of the north to accept the dominance of the Jerusalem temple.[17]

In short, the cult reform in the days of Hezekiah, rather then representing a puritan religious enthusiasm, possibly related to cleansing Judah of Assyrian religious influence (e.g., Rowley 1962; McKay 1973, 15–17), an act of rebellion against Assyria (Lowery 1991, 151), the organization of the state before the Sennacherib assault (Handy 1988), or capitulation to Assyria (Swanson 2002), was actually a domestic political endeavor. It was an important step in the increasing power of the Davidic king and his entourage in Jerusalem, in the remaking of Judah in time of a demographic upheaval, and in the rise of Judah to full statehood.

In Chronicles, Hezekiah is portrayed as a second Solomon (Williamson 1977, 119–25), mainly because all members of the nation, southerners and northerners alike, are called to worship in one temple, in Jerusalem.[18] The temple is the focus of the plan for the reunification of Israel (Williamson 1991). This may well reflect the ideology of the Chronicler, mainly

---

16. Rainey explained the centralization of the cult in the days of Hezekiah as an attempt to reach out to the Israelite population of the north (that is, in their northern territories), after the fall of Israel (Herzog et al. 1984, 21).

17. On the possibility that Chronicles includes genuine memories on the days of Hezekiah that do not appear in the Deuteronomistic History, see, e.g., Halpern 1981; Japhet 1985; 1993, 18–23; Rainey 1997; Vaughn 1999b.

18. For a slightly different point of view, seeing Hezekiah as both a second David and a second Solomon and interpreting this as a revival of the great united monarchy ideology, see Throntveit 2003.

his attitude toward the north (e.g., Braun 1977; Williamson 1977; Japhet 1989). However, as we have already mentioned, a number of scholars have proposed that some of the Hezekiah material in Chronicles that does not appear in the Deuteronomistic History could have originated from a genuine late monarchic source (see references above). In fact, one may wonder if the original kernel of the description of the construction of the temple by Solomon in 1 Kings was not related to the reorganization of the Judahite cult by Hezekiah in the late eighth century BCE.

Compilation of the Early Hisory of the Dynasty

The biblical narrative of the early days of the Davidic dynasty and the establishment of the united monarchy of Israel (1 Sam 16–1 Kgs 2) has been divided by scholars into two main texts: the History of David's Rise to Power (1 Sam 16:14–2 Sam 5) and the Court, or Succession, History (2 Sam 9–20 + 1 Kgs 1–2; see, e.g., Rost 1982; von Rad 1966, 176–204; Keys 1996; de Pury and Römer 2000). The two stories (in which more than one source may be identified; e.g., Halpern 2001, 15–18) were supplemented by additional material and combined into a single narrative, which was then redacted, possibly more than once. Both stories contain information about the Saulides—the first northern dynasty, and neither is entirely complimentary to King David. They include hinted allegations against the founder of the Jerusalem dynasty: cooperating with the Philistines; betraying his fellow Israelites; being responsible for the death of the first king of Israel; being liable for the death of other key figures related to Saul, including Saul's son Ishbaal, his other descendants, and Abner, the commander of the northern army; and being responsible for other murders and wrongdoing in the cases of Absalom, Amasa, and Uriah, among others. It is significant that many of the most serious accusations deal with themes related to the Saulides and the north.

Two related questions have been raised regarding these epic stories: their date and motivation. Regarding the date, most scholars opted for the tenth century BCE or immediately thereafter and argued that the History of David's Rise and the Succession History were put in writing during the reign of the early Davidides or immediately thereafter, in order to legitimize David and Solomon: they aimed at explaining how David came to power and why Solomon, who was not the first in line to the throne, succeeded him in Jerusalem.[19] Regarding the motivation, if these literary works were intended as pro-Davidic legitimacy, the question can be raised why the authors and later redactor(s) would leave the negative stories and accusations against King David in the text. McCarter (1980b) and Halpern (2001) suggested that much of the material was written as an apologia: to counter the bitter northern allegations against King David, to vindicate him of any wrongdoing, and to explain what really happened according to the point of view of the Davidic dynasty.

The idea of a tenth-century compilation comes from a broader perception, that the reign of Solomon was a period of exceptional enlightenment during which great historical works were written in Jerusalem (e.g., Rost 1982; von Rad 1966, 176–204). This theory was founded, in turn, on the biblical description of a great Solomonic empire—full circular reasoning in clear conflict with the archaeological reality.

It is obvious that the stories under discussion contain some early memories, such as the portrayal of Gath as the most important city in Philistia. Gath was destroyed in the second half of the ninth century BCE and did not recover later (Maeir and Ehrlich 2001); indeed, it is not mentioned in late monarchic biblical sources and in seventh-century Assyrian records (Schniedewind 1998). In addition, the description of David's wars discloses ninth-century realities (Na'aman 2002b) quite incompatible to the tenth-century BCE scene. In any event, most important of all is the fact that the History of David's Rise and the Succession History could not have been put in writing before the expansion of literacy in Judah in the second half of the eighth century BCE.

As we have stressed above, this is closely connected with the rise of full-blown statehood in Judah, as indicated by a wide range of archaeological evidence. This includes the growth of Jerusalem into a major urban center, the dramatic expansion of the Judahite population, and the establishment of a centralized bureaucracy that required extensive literacy and scribal activity. None of this is apparent before the late eighth century BCE. Over a century of archaeological excavations in Jerusalem and at virtually every important mound in the countryside of Judah has failed to find any inscribed material before this period. And even the scribal

---

19. E.g., Rost 1982; von Rad 1966; McCarter 1980b, 495; Halpern 2001, 100–102; for a variety of other opinions, see de Pury and Römer 2000.

activity and widespread literacy that began in Judah in the late eighth century spread significantly only in the seventh century BCE (Jamieson-Drake 1991; Schniedewind 2004). Hence the dating of the appearance of historical literature in Israel and the beginning of historiography in the Western tradition (thus von Rad 1966, 176–204) to the tenth century BCE in Jerusalem should be dismissed out of hand. There is no sign of significant scribal activity in the tenth century BCE (see ch. 13); Jerusalem was no more than a remote, small village with a population of a few hundred people, and Judah had no more than a few villages with a population of a few thousand people (Finkelstein 2001; Ussishkin 2003c).

The apologia theory is also problematic on motivational as well as chronological grounds. It fails to deal with a key question: Most accusations against David deal with northern figures, not necessarily with people directly related to the Davidic dynasty or to Judahite circles, so why should the author deal with them at all? In a great Davidic/Solomonic empire, why should anyone be preoccupied with allegations relating to the small territory of the Saulides? In other words, why did the author include this material in his story? Why was it not simply eliminated, as it was in the books of Chronicles centuries later? The fundamental criterion in dating the story of the early Davidides should therefore be: What is the period that best fits a compilation of a saga that takes into account negative northern traditions about the founder of the Jerusalem dynasty? What is the period in which the author, certainly a Judahite, needed to counter these traditions with an apologia, without being able to ignore them?

These texts cannot be dated too late, because it is quite obvious that they went through a Deuteronomistic redaction in the late seventh century.[20] The only chronological span left for their initial composition is therefore the second half of the eighth century and the first half of the seventh century BCE. When we consider the broader historical situation, the most reasonable period for the initial composition of the History of David's Rise and the Succession History is the late eighth century BCE, after the fall of the north, when the population of Judah swelled dramatically to include a large number of Israelite refugees.[21] Parallel to the centralization of the Judahite cult in Jerusalem, which included the rejection of the

---

20. For the pre-Deuteronomistic realities in Samuel, see Halpern 2001, 57–72.

21. On the late eighth century as a crucial date in the compilation of biblical literature, see Schniedewind 2004.

Bethel temple, the Judahite royal family and its entourage had a significant interest in a project of strengthening the power of the dynasty by uniting southerners and northerners around the Davidic King. To that end, they needed to reconcile two conflicting traditions regarding the early days of the Jerusalem dynasty: on the one hand, the upbeat southern traditions about David, the founder of their dynasty, and about Solomon, the builder of their temple; and, on the other hand, the critical northern traditions that preserved memories of the same early period but from a distinctly Saulide perspective.[22]

As we have seen above, there is good reason to suggest that many of the northerners who lived in Judah came from southern Samaria. This was precisely the area where the first northern chiefdom emerged and where the Saulide traditions most probably retained their power. So an attempt was made to reconcile the traditions brought to Judah by a significant immigrant population with the local royal traditions of the Davidic dynasty. The History of David's Rise and the Succession History were put in writing in order to justify the rule of a royal house that was established by David and continued through the line of his son Solomon. The author(s) did not eliminate the northern traditions because they could not; they had to cater to the large northern population in Judah.[23] Instead of ignoring the northern accusations, the author(s) included them in the story but at the same time answered them in order to vindicate David from almost all of his serious wrongdoings. The great apologia was therefore an instrument for reconciliation between south and north *within* Judah and a vehicle for the rise of pan-Israelite ideology. This was the moment when the concept of the united monarchy took on unprecedented importance and its centrality was retrojected into the distant past. But its motivation was the creation of a united monarchy within the borders of Judah, certainly not in all ex-Israelite territories, which were under direct Assyrian rule.

---

22. The collection of the books of the four eighth-century prophets—two southern and two northern—may have also taken place at that time (Schniedewind 2004, 85).

23. For the need to respect the traditions of the northern refugees, see also Schniedewind 2004, 78, 191.

Conclusion

In the late eighth century Judah experienced a dramatic transformation from a sparsely settled tribal territory ruled from a small highland village into a bureaucratic state with a dense population and a large, fortified, and elaborate capital. This transformation was accompanied and advanced by the first widespread appearance of literacy and a significant rise in scribal activity. The momentous change in Judah was brought about by two processes: the incorporation of the kingdom into the Assyrian global economy and the fall of the Northern Kingdom, which sent a torrent of refugees to the south. Judah's demography, society, and economy were altered forever, as it now included a significant number of Israelites and featured a large urban center and a prosperous economy strongly linked to regional trade networks. Facing these new challenges, the Davidic dynasty sought to remake the nation by uniting the two main population groups—Judahites and north Israelites—into a single Israelite society. This, rather than a suggested appeal to Israelites living in the Assyrian province of Samaria, must have been the main stimulus behind the rise of the pan-Israelite idea in Judah.

In order to remake the nation and strengthen the authority and prestige of the royal family, the Jerusalem court engaged in two ideological projects centered on the concepts of temple and dynasty. The king, his entourage, and priestly allies eliminated the countryside shrines and centralized the cult in the Jerusalem temple, weakening the legitimacy and religious authority of the rural aristocracy. At the same time, the Davidic court sponsored the authorship of the early "history" of the Davidic dynasty, merging formerly conflicting southern and northern traditions into a single narrative of the united monarchy of Israel.

Addendum

1. For an additional treatment of migration of Israelites to Judah after the Assyrian takeover of the Northern Kingdom, see chapter 14 in this volume (originally Finkelstein 2015a). It includes updates on the archaeology of Jerusalem (including the theory that the original mound of Jerusalem was located on the Temple Mount), the settlement patterns in the Judean Hill Country and the Shephelah, and Israelite items of material culture that appear in Judah starting in the late eighth century BCE.

2. I now see the rise of the united monarchy concept as a three-stage process. The idea originated from Israel of the first half of the eighth century BCE, when a northern king (Jeroboam II) actually ruled over Judah (Finkelstein 2020d). With the fall of Israel and the arrival of large number of Israelites in the south in the late eighth century, it was inherited by Judah as a message of a united monarchy of Israelites and Judahites within the kingdom. It was finally reexpanded in the days of Josiah, after the pullout of Assyria, to promote the idea of a future great united monarchy that will stretch from Dan to Beersheba, this time ruled from Jerusalem.

3. I now think that materials in Chronicles that do not appear in Kings—including those describing the days of Hezekiah—reflect realities and needs of Hasmonean times and therefore cannot be used for reconstructing the history of monarchic Judah (Finkelstein 2015a). This does not hinder the main ideas advanced in this chapter.

4. The question of cult centralization in the days of Hezekiah continues to be treated on two fronts: archaeology (Kleiman 2023a, who changes terminology from "reform" to "de facto centralization") and biblical exegesis (Edelman 2008; Herzog 2010; Pakkala 2010).[24] Regarding archaeology, also note that finds in the gate of Lachish were interpreted as relating to the Hezekiah reform (Ganor and Kreimerman 2019); however, I support the different interpretation of the finds by Sabine Kleiman (2020). The date when the Motza temple went out of use has not yet been clarified. In any event, the discussions referred to above do not call for a radical change in the views expressed in this chapter.

5. For updates on scribal activity in Judah, see chapters 12 and 13.

6. It has recently been suggested that the fortification unearthed on the eastern slope of the southeastern ridge, above the Gihon Spring (Vukosavović, Chalaf, and Uziel 2021), dates earlier in the eighth century than conventionally assumed, perhaps to the "later years" of Uzziah (Regev et al. 2024). Two arguments have been raised to support this claim. The first argument is that the construction of this fortification occurred after an earthquake documented in Room 17130 in Area U (Regev et al. 2024; see also Chalaf and Uziel 2018; Uziel and Chalaf 2021). This turbulence is identified with the event mentioned in Amos 1:1, traditionally

---

24. I avoid dealing here with Josianic times and with theories of cult centralization in the Persian period. I see the latter as part of the "Persian period fad" that is devoid of any reality on the ground (see in general ch. 23 below).

placed in 760 BCE. But this anchor is not firm, since it depends on the interpretation of the biblical verse and the dates of the reign of Uzziah and Jeroboam II, who are mentioned in it. Regarding the latter, both monarchs seem to have had co-regencies in the later years of their reigns, meaning that the earthquake may also be dated somewhat later than 760 BCE. Moreover, the architectural connection between Room 17130 and the city wall is not straightforward (see Vukosavović, Chalaf, and Uziel 2021, fig. 2). The second argument for dating the fortification earlier than usually proposed is the absence of stamped *lmlk* storage jars in a fill below a street pavement on the outer side of the fortification (Uziel et al. 2023). These impressions appear in the last third of the eighth century BCE. Evidently, this, too, is not a firm dating anchor, as the material in the fill gives nothing but a *terminus post quem* for dating the street. All things considered, the precise dating of the city wall in the second half of the eighth century BCE must be left to historical considerations.

16

The Settlement History of Jerusalem in the Eighth and Seventh Centuries BCE

In this chapter I deal with three issues related to Iron IIB–C Jerusalem: (1) the question of the beginning of settlement activity in the southwestern hill (the Jewish and Armenian Quarters of the modern Old City. (2) the forces behind the dramatic demographic growth in the late Iron IIB; and (3) the transition from the Iron IIB to the Iron IIC in the seventh century BCE. With regard to number 2, I repeat some of the issues discussed in chapter 14 and at the same time present new ideas.

In 2007 Nadav Na'aman published a comprehensive article on the history of Jerusalem in the Iron II. I differ from Na'aman on three themes, in which he argues that:

1. The expansion from the City of David to the southwestern hill (the Jewish and Armenian Quarters) was a gradual process that started as early as the ninth century BCE.
2. Jerusalem's population growth stemmed first and foremost from economic possibilities that opened up to Judah in the course of the eighth century BCE and later from the influx of refugees from the Shephelah after the Sennacherib devastation of the region in 701 BCE.
3. In the second half of the seventh century BCE, the population of Jerusalem decreased; when the geo-political tensions eased, many of the refugees returned to their hometowns in the Shephelah.

We are at odds not only in detail but also in methods, representing two different approaches to the reconstruction of the history of ancient Israel in biblical times. Na'aman's view of the history of Jerusalem is based primarily on his interpretation of the textual evidence—biblical and extrabiblical—rejecting the archaeological evidence if it negates what he reads in the texts. I would argue that the textual material, important as it may be, leaves many gaps in our knowledge and a broad area for interpretation; I therefore reconstruct the history of Jerusalem primarily according to the archaeological material, and only then do I turn to the textual data. In what follows I wish to clarify why the latter method is preferable.

When Did Jerusalem Expand to the Southwestern Hill?

The key to resolving this question is the date of two Judahite pottery assemblages that were best defined at Lachish. The first, of Level IV, represents the later phase of the Iron IIA (Mazar and Panitz-Cohen 2001, 273–76; Herzog and Singer-Avitz 2004), while the second, of Level III, characterizes the destruction layers caused in the course of the Sennacherib campaign in 701 BCE.[1]

Na'aman is correct in arguing that the assemblage of Lachish III was probably dominant during a meaningful part of the eighth century BCE *before* the Sennacherib campaign; this is evident from the fact that at Arad it appears in three strata (X–VIII), the latest of which (VIII) came to an end in 701 BCE (Singer-Avitz 2002, 159–80). And it probably continued into the early part of the seventh century BCE (already Finkelstein 1994). The dating of the Lachish IV assemblage (and its parallels, such as Beersheba V and Arad XI) to the mid- to second half of the ninth century BCE has been confirmed by ^{14}C results from Stratum IV at Tell eṣ-Ṣafi in the Shephelah. The nine measurements from this stratum (Sharon et al. 2007, 39, 44) provide an average uncalibrated date of 2707±27, which translates into a calibrated range of 895–820 BCE. Historically, it seems safe to assume that the destruction of this stratum was inflicted by Hazael, king of Damascus, sometime in the second half of the ninth century BCE

---

1. For a detailed discussion of the two assemblages, see Zimhoni 1997; 2004a, 1643–1788; 2004b, 1789–1899.

(Maeir 2004). The combination of the ^{14}C results and the historical argument restricts the date of destruction of Tell eṣ-Ṣafi IV to 842–820 BCE (Finkelstein and Piasetzky 2007).

The crucial question for this discussion is the date of *transition* from the assemblage of Lachish IV to that of Lachish III. Many scholars have placed it in the first half of the eighth century BCE (e.g., Zimhoni 1997, 172–73; Ussishkin 2004e, 83), while Fantalkin and I suggested dating it to circa 800 BCE (Fantalkin and Finkelstein 2006, 22–24). Seven measurements from the destruction of Beth-shemesh 3, a stratum that features transitional Iron IIA/Iron IIB pottery forms, provided an average ^{14}C date of 2505±30.[2] Due to the nature of the calibration curve, this translates into a broad 1 σ absolute date of 766–745 BCE (10.5 percent probability), 688–664 (10.4 percent), and 647–551 (47.2 percent). The two latter can be eliminated because they postdate the historical date for the Lachish III assemblage (701 BCE; Finkelstein and Piasetzky 2007). In any event, Beth-shemesh 3 shows that the Lachish III assemblage cannot predate the 760s BCE. In other words, the Lachish IV pottery may have still been in use in the early eighth century BCE.

Regarding the southwestern hill in Jerusalem, Na'aman asserts:

> Keeping in mind that only a small part of the Western Hill has been excavated, it is possible that the settlement began in areas that have not yet been unearthed. Moreover, the continued habitation of Jerusalem over thousands of years, the strength of its settlement in the eighth-seventh centuries B.C.E., and the continued occupation of the site until the destruction in 587/586, mean that pottery vessels from the early stages settlement had scattered in all directions and are therefore absent from the site's destruction stratum. We must also keep in mind that even in the excavations in the City of David, very little pottery from Iron Age I–IIA has been found, though there is no doubt that the city was inhabited, if partially. Finally, Avigad and Geva ... reported that four building stages preceded the construction of the Broad Wall; and isolated early Iron Age II sherds were found scattered in the Western Hill.... Thus, settlement of the Western Hill might have begun as early as the late ninth century B.C.E. (Na'aman 2007, 27)

---

2. For this stratum and its pottery, see Bunimovitz and Lederman 2006, 419–20; for the ^{14}C dates, see Sharon et al. 2007, 40, 44.

None of these arguments withstands scrutiny.

1. *Only a small part of the western hill has been excavated.* This is not so. Large parts of the southwestern hill were excavated—in the Jewish Quarter, the Armenian Quarter, the Citadel, and Mount Zion—and none produced Iron IIA finds (see map in Geva 2000). It can no longer be argued that future excavations may reveal the desired finds; after years of thorough excavation, the burden of proof rests on whoever argues against these facts.

2. *The Iron IIA pottery was scattered and disappeared.* Pottery does not vanish. Every dig of a multiperiod site reveals sherds of the early phases of activity in its later assemblages. They find their way there in brick material, fills, and the like. At Megiddo, for instance, Early Bronze I sherds are found even in Stratum IVA of the Iron IIB. Moreover, in a multiperiod site, sherds of all periods of activity can in most cases be found even in a surface survey. The idea that the Iron IIA sherds vanished negates all that we know about field archaeology.[3]

3. *In the City of David, too, only a limited amount of Iron I–IIA pottery could be found.* Indeed, even in this case of a small and poor settlement, the early pottery is present. It did not vanish.

4. *Four settlement phases predate the construction of the late eighth-century city wall* (Avigad and Geva 2000, 72–73, plan 2.1). These are phases in the growth of the settlement on the southwestern hill, not real strata, and therefore this argument is meaningless. The four phases could have developed during forty years of activity but also in ten years. Since the city wall was built at the very end of the eighth century BCE, between the death of Sargon II and the Sennacherib campaign (below), even a longer period of habitation represented by the four phases would not necessarily predate the mid-eighth century BCE.[4]

5. *A few Iron IIA finds were retrieved in the Jewish Quarter.* The publication speaks about a few sherds from the Middle Bronze and the Iron IIA.

---

3. Na'aman's example from Tel Miqne-Ekron (2007, 26) does not apply to our case. Pottery from the earliest occupation level of the lower city there has not yet been published, so one cannot discuss its precise foundation date.

4. The absence of *lmlk* seal impressions in the phases that predate the construction of the city wall (Na'aman 2007, 47–48) does not contribute to the dating of the first occupation on the southwestern hill, as they were uncovered in a limited area; in such a case, the negative evidence is dubious.

The excavators unanimously argued that there was no settlement activity on the southwestern hill in these periods. These sherds found their way to the southwestern hill with fill debris or as a result of agricultural activity of people who lived in the City of David (De Groot, Geva, and Yezerski 2003, 16; Avigad and Geva 2000, 81). A good parallel can be found in the archaeology of Jerusalem in the Persian period. There is a consensus among scholars that at that time the settlement was small and poor and that it was restricted to the City of David (Finkelstein 2008b). Still, a few Persian period sherds and coins found their way to the southwestern hill; they were probably brought there during work in the fields or in fill debris that was deposited in the course of the great building activities of the Hasmoneans and Herod the Great (Geva 2003, 525).

To make a long story short, the southwestern hill was not inhabited during the ninth century, and this probably holds true also for the early eighth century BCE.

Na'aman expands his view regarding the growth of Jerusalem to the entire land of Judah:

> The picture of the kingdom of Judah experiencing dramatic growth at the end of the eighth century should be replaced with one of a steady, slow growth during the ninth, and a momentum of settlement, construction and development during the eighth century. (Na'aman 2007, 47)

This statement, too, is negated by the archaeological finds. Although a few centers in the upper Shephelah and Beersheba Valley reveal early signs of public building activity in the Lachish IV phase in the history of the Southern Kingdom (Finkelstein 2001), the number of settlements in Judah remained limited and the population scarce, and there is no sign of economic prosperity. Archaeological surveys have recorded only thirty-four Iron IIA sites in the highlands south of Jerusalem and twenty-one sites in the Shephelah (see updates in ch. 14). This was the situation circa 800 BCE, if not somewhat later. In the late eighth century, the number of sites grew to 122 in the highlands south of Jerusalem and 276 in the Shephelah (Ofer 1994, 104–5; Dagan 1992). Even if one were to claim that a few sites from the Lachish IV phase have not been detected for this or that reason and that the eighth century sites are easier to trace, the picture is clear: the "great leap forward" in Judah began and accelerated during the eighth century.

But how can we pinpoint this commencement of prosperity during the eighth century BCE in Jerusalem in particular and Judah in general? There are no minute ceramic differences within the Lachish III phase (because there are no destruction layers in Judah except for those inflicted by Sennacherib in 701 BCE), so the only clue archaeology can offer is the ^{14}C results for Beth-shemesh 3, which places the upper limit of the Lachish III pottery no earlier than 765 BCE (see above). For a more accurate date one needs to turn to historical considerations. Judah is located in a remote corner of the Levant, with no economic resources such as ore and far from the harbors and the international road of the coastal plain. Therefore, in contrast to the Northern Kingdom, in the early phase of its history Judah remained a tribal society with limited population and almost no real urban centers. Judah could not have taken a meaningful step forward before it was directly incorporated as a vassal state into the global economy of the Assyrian Empire. Only then could it begin to profit from the Assyrian-led Arabian trade and its demand for olive oil, and only as a result of this would its capital begin to develop into a real metropolis. In short, contra Na'aman, there is no economic reason for a significant demographic growth in Judah and Jerusalem before the 730s BCE.[5]

Did Refugees from Israel come to Judah?

Na'aman rejects the proposal that the dramatic demographic growth in Jerusalem and Judah in the late eighth century resulted from the move-

---

5. Na'aman's assertion that Judah remained outside the borders of the Assyrian Empire (2007, 46) may be correct politically and administratively but certainly not economically. I agree with Na'aman (2007, 30–31) that Hezekiah did not try to involve Judah in the territories north of Judah. This confirms with my view that the pan-Israelite idea emerged only after the arrival of Israelite refugees in Judah. At that time this ideology addressed the situation within Judah. Only in the late seventh century BCE, in the days of Josiah and after the withdrawal of Assyria, did the pan-Israelite ideology receive its territorial aspect, which addressed the question of the territories of the then long-destroyed Northern Kingdom. Even at that time it was not fulfilled on the ground (for the possibility that the united-monarchy concept first emerged in Israel in the first half of the eighth century, see ch. 11).

ment of refugees from the territory of the Northern Kingdom after it was taken over by Assyria.[6] First, Na'aman claims that in the ancient Near East clear understandings existed between states, and even more so between empires and vassal states, about repatriating refugees to their homelands. He further argues that the Assyrian interest must have been to prevent a mass departure of refugees from the territory of vanquished Israel. Second, Na'aman argues that there is no evidence, textual or archaeological, for such a population movement.

Regarding the issue of repatriation of refugees, most if not all of the examples cited by Na'aman are not relevant to our case. Some of them concern the second millennium BCE, and most of them do not deal with war refugees who fled their homes but rather with problematic elements (some of them individuals) who endangered the interests of empires. Na'aman argues that empires could control their borders and hence could have prevented mass movements of people; this is partly true (depending on the landscape), but our case deals with people who fled during war, before the situation stabilized. In any event, Na'aman agrees that "there is evidence of refugees moving into the empire from outside.... There are some testimonies to the movement of refugees from the territory of the empire into Shubria and Urartu, two kingdoms to the north of Assyria" (2007, 34). Moreover, the Assyrian sources mention "the flight of inhabitants upon the arrival of the Assyrian army, but such flights usually occurred in mountainous regions and frontiers" (2007, 36). This is exactly the case under discussion: refugees fleeing from the advancing Assyrian army in a mountainous frontier area. Na'aman finds it possible that "an unknown number of inhabitants from Israel fled to Judah immediately after the Assyrian conquest, but after a while, when conditions stabilized and the anxieties abated, no doubt most of them returned to their homes and communities, and only a few remained in Judah" (2007, 36); we do not argue about the very notion of escape, then, but rather about the number of people who fled.

Na'aman brings in two cases to demonstrate the problems caused by the escape of people from one country to another: the Apiru and the settlement of the Sea Peoples, both in the second millennium BCE (Na'aman 2007, 36). I find it difficult to understand how the phenomenon of the

---

6. Broshi 1974; Schniedewind 2004, 94–95; ch. 15 above.

Apiru—gangs of uprooted elements who engaged in robbery and extortion and thus endangered the interests of the great powers—relates to the settlement of thousands of war refugees in Jerusalem and in the smaller towns and villages of Judah in the late eighth century BCE. Further, what is the relevance of the great crisis that took place in the entire eastern Mediterranean at the end of the Late Bronze Age for understanding a strictly local event: the movement of refugees from southern Samaria to Judah, a distance of several kilometers?[7]

Na'aman rightly points to the differences between Israel and Judah and questions whether the latter would have been willing to accept a large number of refugees who could have destabilized it. But at that time Judah experienced its early steps toward full statehood and did not have the power and means to prevent such a movement. A fully organized and well-administered state in Judah is an *outcome* of the processes that took place in the late eighth century BCE.[8]

Na'aman claims that there is no clue in the Bible for a torrent of refugees that came to Judah from the territory of vanquished Israel. In fact, Schniedewind pointed out just such clues (Schniedewind 2004, 94–95), but Na'aman rejects them all, some with no convincing reason (Na'aman 2007, 36–37). In addition, both Schniedewind and Silberman and I proposed that a change in the demographic structure of Judah, from a strictly Judahite society to a mixed Judahite-Israelite population, may explain how and why northern texts found their way into the biblical codex. I refer to materials such as the Jacob cycle, the Exodus story, the Book of Saviors in Judges, the Saul cycle, the Elijah-Elishah cycle, and northern prophetic works. Finally, why dismiss the theory that Deuteronomistic ideas origi-

---

7. Historical comparisons should be sought in similar circumstances, time, and location. The examples presented by Na'aman deviate from this rule in two of these factors, if not in all of them. I would mention a comparison that fits both the location and the circumstances, though not the time: the flooding of the Hashemite kingdom of Jordan with Palestinian refugees in 1948.

8. I agree with Na'aman that Israel and Judah were very different entities (Finkelstein 1999). One may ask, then, what could have been the advantages for Israelite villagers to flee to the south. The answer is that in pre-Deuteronomistic times the two kingdoms also had much in common (e.g., in their cult) and that we are dealing with similar landscapes and subsistence base of highlands horticulture. One can further argue that there were lineage connections between clans in southern Israel and northern Judah.

nated in the north (e.g., Nicholson 1967)? In any event, Na'aman (2007, 40) in the same breath speaks of "thousands of refugees" who came to Jerusalem from the Shephelah following the Sennacherib devastation there; the evidence in the Bible for this movement of people, if it exists at all, is far weaker than that for Israelites who settled in Judah.

Na'aman raises a list of archaeological arguments against the idea of Israelite refugees in Judah (Na'aman 2007, 37).

1. *There is no clue for northern elements (Baal names and names ending with* yahu*) in private names mentioned in the epigraphic corpus from Judah.* The problem is that we know about such northern elements in private names first and foremost from the Samaria ostraca, which date to the first half of the eighth century BCE, and from the Kuntillet 'Ajrud inscriptions, which also predate the last third of the eighth century BCE (contra Singer-Avitz 2006, 196–228). The only names in the epigraphic corpus from Judah that can safely be dated to the first half of the eighth century are Shebnayau servant of 'Uzziyau and Abiyau servant of 'Uzziyau; all three, including the name of the king of Judah, end with the northern *yau*.[9] Names ending with *yahu* appear in Judah as early as the late eighth century, mainly in private names on *lmlk* storage jars, but the bulk of the epigraphic material from the Southern Kingdom dates to the late seventh and early sixth centuries BCE. Three additional comments are in place here. (a) Private names on *lmlk* storage jars and on seals and seal impressions belonged to high officials in the administration of Judah, and one may wonder if refugees who came from rural parts of southern Israel could have climbed to the top echelons of the Judahite bureaucracy in the short period of less than twenty years. (b) The time that passed between the early eighth and late seventh century could have seen changes in the language and/or writing in Judah. (c) Regarding the corpus of names of the late seventh/early sixth centuries, one can assume that descendants of Israelite families had already taken Judahite names or written their names in a Judahite form.

---

9. Avigad and Sass 1997, 50–51. Ostracon 69 from Arad, which carries "... yahu" names, was attributed by the excavators to Stratum X, which dates to the mid-eighth century BCE (Singer-Avitz 2002, 159–80). However, the stratigraphy of Arad is quite problematic, and it is doubtful that one can build an argument on a single find from this site. The Tel Dan inscription from the second half of the ninth century BCE mentions [Ahaz]yahu king of Judah.

2. *No influence of north Israelite material culture can be traced in late eighth-century BCE Judah.* This is not so. Judahite olive-oil production was industrialized in the late eighth century (Eitan-Katz 1994), probably as a result of adaptation of technology that had been popular in the Northern Kingdom before its demise.[10] Singer-Avitz (1999, 12) pointed out northern elements in the pottery of late eighth-century Beersheba. Square bone seals that were popular in eighth-century Israel appear in Judah in the seventh century BCE, and the same holds true for limestone cosmetic bowls (Brandl 2006, 427–28 and personal communication). Alertness to this issue will undoubtedly yield other examples in the future. In any event, it is doubtful that one could anticipate tracing characteristic Israelite finds in late eighth-century Judah. (a) As far as I can judge, most refugees who came to Judah originated from the southern part of Israel. The pottery of this region is similar to that which characterizes Judah, and one can safely assume that this is also the case regarding other elements of the material culture. (b) Refugees who originated from the rural sector did not bring with them prestige items, those items that could have distinguished them from their fellow Judahites. (c) "National" or regional characteristics in the material culture of the southern Levant appear mainly in the seventh century BCE (Stern 2001, 130–215, 237–94; for Judah, see Kletter 1999).

3. Regarding the evidence for settlement and demographic depletion in southern Samaria in the Iron II/Persian period transition, depletion that was caused in my view by the movement of refugees to Judah during the Assyrian takeover, Na'aman argues that *similar processes can be traced in other parts of the highlands, for instance, in northern Samaria and Judah.* Concerning northern Samaria, Na'aman bases his argument on Zertal's interpretation of the results of his survey of this region. Zertal's (2003, 396) calculations are founded on a few pottery forms that he dated to the seventh century BCE; however, most of these are present in the eighth century, too. Therefore, his main, if not only, criterion is the appearance of the wedge-shaped decorated bowl, which he proposed associating with Mesopotamian deportees who were settled by the Assyrians in the territory of conquered Israel (Zertal 1989, 77–84). Without dealing with the validity of this identification, I would only note that the appearance or lack of a single pottery form in survey sites—many of which yielded a

---

10. On the northern devices, see Eitam 1987, 23–27.

limited number of sherds—may be random and therefore misleading. The numbers given by Zertal are therefore questionable. The straightforward evidence that emerges from his survey in northern Samaria indicates that (to differ from southern Samaria) the region did not experience a dramatic decrease in the number of sites between the late Iron II and the Persian period.[11] Moreover, in the Shechem syncline, for instance, a certain increase in the number of sites has been recorded (Zertal 1992, 54–56). In the entire region there was a decrease in the built-up area (which represents population), but it was mild relative to what emerges from the survey in southern Samaria. Na'aman's comparison of the situation in southern Samaria to that in Judah is irrelevant, because we all agree that Judah suffered a major settlement and demographic crisis as a result of the Babylonian destruction. Evidently, the highlands territory to the north of Judah did not suffer such devastation.

Beyond these details remains the simple riddle that Na'aman fails to resolve: What brought about the dramatic population growth in Jerusalem and Judah in the eighth century BCE? Even if one accepts, only for the sake of argument, his proposal that this growth started in the early eighth century, the numbers do not fit what we know about natural demographic growth in the ancient world. The latter cannot explain an increase from approximately one thousand to ten thousand people in Jerusalem, the growth from 34 small Iron IIA settlements to 122 larger Iron IIB (eighth-century) settlements in the highlands of Judah, and the increase from 21 Iron IIA to 275 or more Iron IIB settlements in the Shephelah.[12]

Na'aman (2007, 40) proposes that a torrent of "thousands of refugees" arrived in Jerusalem from all over the kingdom of Judah (that is, mainly from the Shephelah) as a result of the Sennacherib devastation in 701 BCE. But this hypothesis does not explain the growth of the Judahite capital in the second half of the eighth century. Had we accepted this theory, we should have continued the same line of thought and date the construction of the huge city wall unearthed in the southwestern hill to the early seventh century BCE, when Judah was an obedient vassal of Assyria. Needless to say, this is unacceptable. The Jerusalem city wall could have been built only in the short period of time between Sargon II's death on

---

11. For details, see ch. 15 above.
12. For the highlands, see Ofer 1994, 104–5; for the Shephelah, Dagan 1992 (updates in ch. 14).

the battlefield in 705 and Sennacherib's campaign in 701 BCE. Only then could Judah have undertaken such a bold step against Assyrian suzerainty.

Was There a Demographic Decrease in Jerusalem and Judah in the Second Half of the Seventh Century BCE?

Na'aman argues that, in the seventh century, "the kingdom of Judah had fewer settlements, a smaller population, and reduced economic capacity compared with the flourishing, densely populated kingdom it had been at the end of the eighth century, on the eve of Sennacherib's campaign" (2007, 40). This observation, central to his reconstruction of the history of Jerusalem and Judah in late monarchic times, is correct for the Shephelah and wrong for all other parts of the southern kingdom: the Beersheba Valley, the Judean Desert, the highlands, and Jerusalem and its environs.

In speaking about the seventh century, Na'aman refers to its later part. His discussion of the settlement shrinkage at that time is based on the differences between the pottery assemblages of Lachish III and Lachish II (Zimhoni 2004b). It seems that the former was still dominant at the beginning of the seventh century (Finkelstein 1994; Finkelstein and Na'aman 2004), but, with no destruction layers during the seventh century, it is difficult to fix the date of transition between the two horizons. Still, it seems reasonable to place it around the middle of that century.

A study of the settlement processes that took place in late monarchic Judah calls for a regional approach, according to the classical geographical niches of the kingdom; in biblical terms, these are the Shephelah, the Negev (Beersheba Valley), the desert (Judean Desert), the hill country, and, of course, Jerusalem and its environs.

There can be no doubt that the Shephelah experienced a severe crisis as a result of the Sennacherib assault in 701 BCE; from both settlement and demographic perspectives, the Shephelah, which had been taken from Judah and given to the Philistine cities, did not recover even when it was returned to Judahite hands, probably in the days of Manasseh in the first half of the seventh century BCE (Finkelstein 1994; Finkelstein and Na'aman 2004); in fact, it did not recover until the fall of Judah in the early sixth century. The archaeological survey indicates a decrease from circa 275 sites in the eighth century to 85 in the late seventh century BCE; the overall built-up area, which can be translated into population estimates, shrank to about one third of what it had been in the late eighth century (Dagan 2004, 2681–82). The settlement crisis in the Shephelah is manifested mainly in the rural sector, but it can also be traced in some urban sites: excavations show that towns such as Tell Beit-Mirsim, Beth-shemesh, Tel Halif, and Tel Eton were abandoned before the appearance of the Lachish II pottery assemblage.

The situation in the Beersheba Valley is utterly different. Most large sites, such as Tel ʿIra, Tel Malḥata, and Aroer, flourished in both the eighth and seventh centuries BCE (Singer-Avitz 1999, 56–57; Thareani-Sussely 2007). Only Tel Beersheba was abandoned in the late eighth century. But other sites, such as the forts of Tel Masos, and Horvat Uza, were established in the seventh century. It seems, therefore, that the Judahite Negev, which was also hit by Sennacherib in 701 BCE, recovered during the seventh century. A certain rearrangement of the settlement system, but no crisis similar to the one inflicted on the Shephelah, can be detected.

The Judean Desert experienced a settlement expansion in the seventh century BCE. In fact, many of the sites—both along the coast of the Dead Sea and in the Buqeiah—were established in the second half of the seventh century (Stager 1976; Bar-Adon 1989).

The situation in the hill country is more complex. The most detailed study of the settlement processes that took place in the highlands to the south of Jerusalem was conducted by Ofer. He proposed that the settlement system in this area reached its peak prosperity in the late eighth century and that a certain decline took place in the seventh century. Although the number of settlements did not change significantly, the total built-up area—that is, population—shrank by about a third (Ofer 1994, 106). Ofer sought the reason for this decline in the Sennacherib campaign, which in his view also affected the southern hill country.

This observation is based on shaky ground. First, the idea about Sennacherib destructions in the highlands is a speculation based on excavation at a single site—Khirbet Rabud south of Hebron (Ofer 1993b, part 4:15)—where the evidence comes from a very limited probe (Kochavi 1974, 13). In any event, Khirbet Rabud was inhabited in the seventh century, too.[13] Second, most other excavated sites in the southern highlands

---

13. Ofer says that other sites were "expected to have been destroyed in the course of the Sennacherib campaign." He summarizes that "for the time being it is preferable to hypothesize that the highlands of Judah experienced a considerable

reveal uninterrupted settlement continuity from the eighth to the seventh centuries BCE. Third, Ofer's built-up area calculations include contested variables (e.g., Finkelstein 1994, 175). Fourth, Ofer inflated the number of eighth-century sites by speculating (with no real basis) that some of the seventh-century sites were established a short time before Sennacherib's campaign. Fifth, there is no evidence—in the Bible or in the Assyrian records—that Sennacherib attacked the southern hill country.

In the highlands to the north of Jerusalem, as well as in the vicinity of the capital, settlement activity intensified in the seventh century. This is clear in the case of central sites such as Tell en-Naṣbeh and Gibeon, which reached their peak prosperity at that time, as well as in the case of the system of farms that developed around Jerusalem (Faust 1997; Feig 2000).

As for Jerusalem, the theory on demographic decline in the seventh century is based on two locations: the abandonment of the "quarter" on the eastern slope of the City of David and the desertion of isolated houses (possibly farms) that seem to have been located to the north of the Iron Age city wall, in today's Christian Quarter (Ariel and De Groot 2000, 164; Geva 2003b, 207–8). The City of David and the intramural parts of the southwestern hill do not exhibit a consequential demographic decline (Geva 2003a, 522). In any event, even if there was a certain weakening of settlement activity in the city, it was compensated by the meaningful growth in the rural sector around it.[14]

Conclusion

In the case of Jerusalem and Judah in the eighth and seventh centuries BCE, archaeology speaks loud and clear. (1) The expansion of the city to the southwestern hill and the settlement prosperity in the Judahite coun-

---

though not total devastation in the course of the Sennacherib campaign" (Ofer 1993b, part 4:15).

14. Na'aman (2007, 42–43) brings the biblical numbers of deportees from Jerusalem in the early sixth century BCE as supporting evidence that at that time the population of the city was already depleted. The opposite is true; assuming that the numbers in Kings and Jeremiah refer to the ruling elite, the groups that were deported by the Babylonians, a number of a few thousand attests to a large and prosperous city.

tryside did not start before the middle of the eighth century and reached their peak in the last third of that century. (2) The population growth in Jerusalem and Judah was so dramatic that it cannot be explained as representing a gradual, natural growth. Remote, mountainous Judah does not offer any economic advantage that could have attracted people from neighboring regions. Therefore, the only way to interpret the demographic transformation of Judah is on the background of the incorporation of the kingdom into the Assyrian world economy and the wave of refugees that came from the Northern Kingdom after the Assyrian takeover. The results of the archaeological surveys and information about the places where the Assyrians settled deportees from Mesopotamia seem to indicate that many of the Israelite refugees who settled in Judah originated from southern Samaria.

Whoever argues that the population explosion in Jerusalem was the result of a torrent of refugees who arrived from the Shephelah following the Sennacherib devastation in 701 BCE and that these refugees returned to their hometowns a while later (Na'aman 2007, 40) faces three problems. First, this means that the city wall unearthed in the southwestern hill was built in the days of Manasseh, with Assyrian consent. Second, such a claim disconnects the growth in Jerusalem from that in the entire territory of Judah, because there can be no doubt that the Shephelah reached its peak prosperity *before* the Sennacherib campaign. Such a theory, even if possible archaeologically (the pottery of Lachish III continued to dominate the Judahite repertoire in the early seventh century), is untenable historically. Third, if this had been the case, we would have seen a settlement recovery in the Shephelah during the seventh century BCE.

17

The Finds from the Rock-Cut Pool in Jerusalem and the Date of the Siloam Tunnel: An Alternative Interpretation

> In the next two chapters I consider two well-known features of material culture in late monarchic Jerusalem: remains around the Gihon Spring and the phenomenon of seal impressions on handles of storage jars. Here I deal with the date of the Siloam Tunnel, pointing to the connection between the hewing of this water system, the urban space of Jerusalem, and the date of the fortification that surrounded the city.

In a 2011 *Tel Aviv* article, Ronny Reich and Eli Shukron presented new archaeological data from the area of the Gihon Spring in Jerusalem. They interpreted them as indication that the Siloam Tunnel and the Siloam Inscription date to the late ninth or early eighth century—earlier than their generally accepted date in the late eighth century BCE.

Reich and Shukron's chain of reasoning proceeds as follows:

- The Middle Bronze Rock-Cut Pool (fig. 17.1)[1] near the Gihon Spring—and together with it the rock-cut Channel II that ran from the spring to the south along the eastern side of the Kidron Valley (fig. 17.2)—continued to function until the hewing of the Siloam Tunnel.

---

1. The floor of the Rock-Cut Pool (for this large feature, see pictures and detailed description in Reich 2011) is several meters higher than the Gihon Spring (Reich 2011, 200; Reich and Shukron 2011, 152 fig. 4 = fig. 17.3 here), hence it could serve to collect water from the slope, not from the spring. This issue is beyond the scope of the current chapter.

Fig. 17.1. The Rock-Cut Pool near the Gihon Spring (courtesy of the Ronny Reich and Eli Shukron expedition to the City of David; photograph by V. Naikhin).

- Tunnel IV, which starts in the Round Chamber hewn at the bottom of the Rock-Cut Pool (figs. 17.2 and 17.3), was cut in order to facilitate the work on the northern segment of the Siloam Tunnel. A panel near the entrance from the Round Chamber to Tunnel IV (fig. 17.3) could have been prepared in order to receive another Siloam Inscription, commemorating the construction. Once the Siloam Tunnel was completed and connected to the spring, Tunnel IV became obsolete.
- At a certain point thereafter, the Rock-Cut Pool was deliberately filled with debris, and an Iron IIB house was built over this fill. The fill covered the entrance to Tunnel IV.
- The latest pottery in the fill under the house must postdate the cutting of Tunnel IV, that is, the cutting of the Siloam Tunnel. This latest pottery parallels the finds that characterize Stratum XIII of the Yigal Shiloh excavations in the City of David, which date to the late Iron IIA in the late ninth or early eighth century BCE (De Groot and Fadida 2011), hence the Siloam Tunnel could not have been cut later than this date.

Reich and Shukron thus conclude that the Siloam Tunnel was hewn in the time of King Jehoash in the late ninth century BCE. They maintain that the Siloam Inscription, which commemorates the cutting of the tunnel, should be "reevaluated" accordingly.

The importance of this issue for the study of the archaeology and history of Jerusalem in particular and Judah in general encouraged me to take a close look at the finds and their interpretation.

Problems with the New Theory

There are three major problems with the new theory (Reich and Shukron 2011). The first stems from the urban development of the city. There was logic in cutting the over 500-meter-long tunnel under the City of David ridge only after the city expanded to the southwestern hill and was surrounded by a city wall. When this transpired, the cutting of the tunnel enabled: (1) water from the spring to be brought to a pool in the southern tip of the Tyropoeon Valley, *within* the fortified city (fig. 17.4); (2) the inhabitants of the new quarters of the southwestern hill, especially its

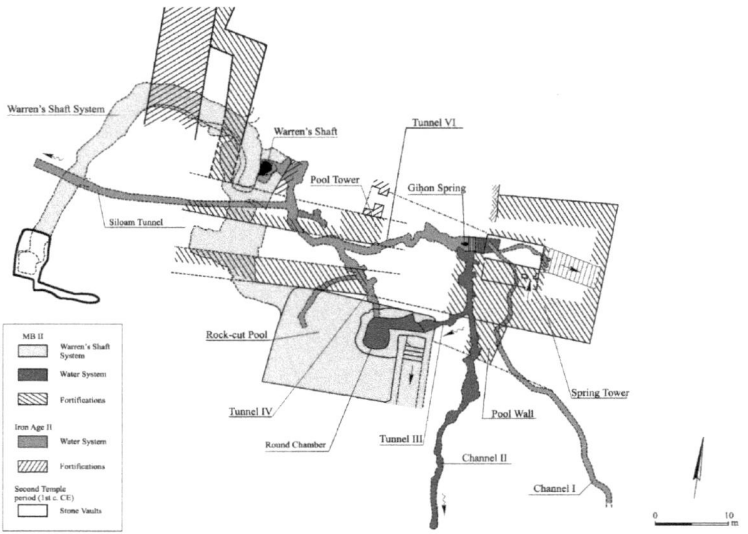

Fig. 17.2. The area of the Gihon Spring, marking the features mentioned in this chapter (Reich and Shukron 2011, 149; courtesy of the authors).

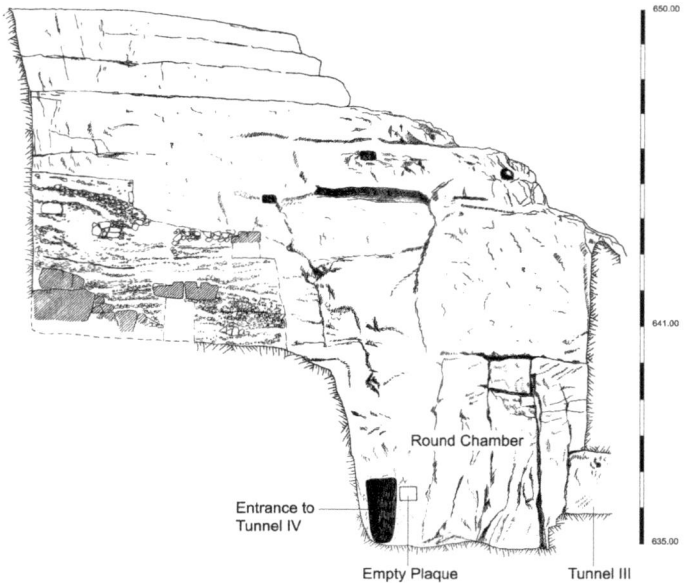

Fig. 17.3. Cross-section through the Rock-Cut Pool and the Round Chamber, showing entrance to Tunnel IV and empty panel on its right-hand side (Reich and Shukron 2011, 152; courtesy of the authors).

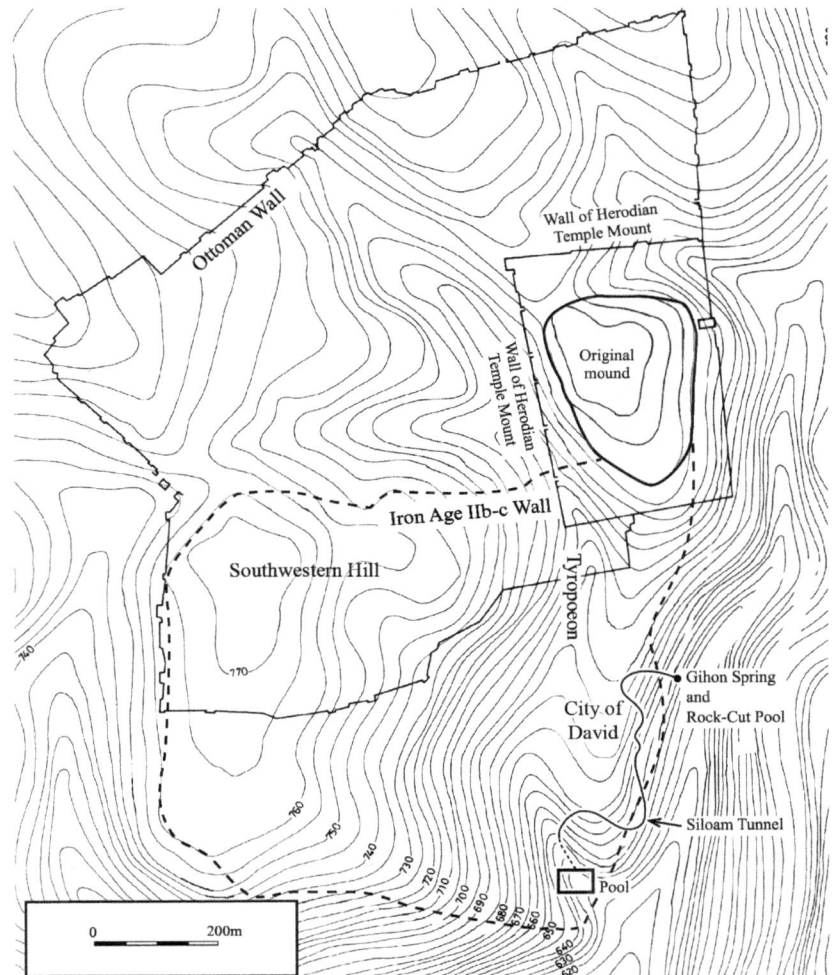

Fig. 17.4. Map of Iron Age Jerusalem.

southeastern slope, to be provided with easy access to water (fig. 17.4). In other words, had the Siloam Tunnel been cut before the city expanded and was surrounded by a city wall, the water would have been taken from one unprotected spot to another unprotected spot outside of the settlement.[2]

---

2. Several scholars (Ussishkin 1995; Knauf 2001a; Dalley 2004) suggested that the tunnel was cut in order to water an Assyrian-style royal garden at the meeting of the Kidron and the Tyropoeon. But for this a simple built tunnel on the side of

The expansion of Jerusalem to the southwestern hill and the erection of the Iron Age fortification took place in the Iron IIB. No pre-Iron IIB pottery (representing a settlement) has been found in the southwestern hill (Geva 2003a; ch. 16 above [contra Na'aman 2007]), and in all its sectors the fortification was found associated with Iron IIB finds (e.g., Shiloh 1984, 28; Geva 2003a, 514–16; Reich and Shukron 2008a). Radiocarbon results indicate that the Iron IIA/IIB transition should be dated sometime in the first half of the eighth century BCE (Finkelstein and Piasetzky 2010). Historical considerations seem to show that the expansion of the city and the construction of the city wall took place in the second half of the eighth century (e.g., Broshi 1974; Avigad 1983, 55–57; Reich and Shukron 2003; ch. 15 above). This means that the *earliest* possible date for the construction of the Siloam Tunnel is around the middle of the eighth century BCE.

The second obstacle has to do with radiocarbon dates. A piece of wood and a short-lived plant extracted from the early plaster in the pool provided a ^{14}C date in the eighth–seventh centuries BCE (Frumkin, Shimron, and Rosenbaum 2003). The absence of spring-water sedimentary layer between the early plaster and the rock-cut floor of the tunnel indicates that the plastering took place immediately after the hewing of the system (Frumkin, Shimron, and Rosenbaum 2003). These data do not comply with dating the tunnel in the ninth century BCE.

The third problem is the date of the Siloam Inscription. Fixing the cutting of the tunnel as suggested by Reich and Shukron means that the Siloam Inscription, too, should probably be redated to the late ninth or early eighth centuries BCE.[3] However, paleographically (that is, with no historical considerations), there must be a time interval of at least several decades between the earliest monumental alphabetic inscriptions in the Levant, such as the Mesha and Tel Dan Stelae, which date to the late ninth century (in general, Sass 2005, 83; for Mesha, Lemaire 2007; regarding the ceramic evidence for Dan, Arie 2008), and the Siloam Inscription. This would hardly allow dating the latter before the middle of the eighth cen-

---

the Kidron or a straight rock-cut tunnel from the spring to the south (e.g., reusing Tunnel II of the Middle Bronze Age) would have sufficed.

3. Theoretically, one could argue that the Siloam Inscription was added to a preexisting tunnel. This is unlikely for several reasons, among them the empty panel at the entrance from the Round Chamber to Tunnel IV, which was probably meant to receive a similar inscription.

tury (again, strictly paleographically; better later, e.g., Rollston 2003, 165; and see discussion in Vaughn 1999a, 58–60).[4]

Do the Finds Require the New Dating?

Do the new finds from Reich and Shukron's excavations near the Gihon Spring stand against this logic? Assuming that Tunnel IV and the panel in the Round Chamber indeed belong to the phase of construction of the Siloam Tunnel, the key for answering this question is the date of the finds from the fill-debris laid in order to prepare the area for the construction of the house in the out-of-use Rock-Cut Pool. Singer-Avitz (2012) has now shown that the pottery assemblage from the fill includes (in addition to Bronze Age and Iron I items) both Iron IIA and Iron IIB forms, the latter belonging to the Lachish Level III repertoire that dates to the late eighth century BCE. Keel (2012) states that the glyptic finds from the fill also date to different periods, until the middle of the eighth century BCE.[5] Since we are dealing here with a fill, the early sherds, even if they constitute the majority of the finds, have no bearing on fixing the time when the fill was put in the pool. The date of deposition depends on the *latest* pottery items from the fill, even if they constitute a small minority of the assemblage. Wheel-burnished bowls mentioned by De Groot and Fadida (2011, 161) indicate that the fill was laid in the Iron IIB (Singer-Avitz 2012). The absence in the fill of other typical Iron IIB types, such as closed cooking pots and *lmlk* storage jars, including stamped *lmlk* handles (De Groot and Fadida 2011), can be explained in two ways.

1. The fill was laid in an early phase of the Iron IIB, before the introduction of the *lmlk* storage jars and closed cooking pots.[6] According to this scenario, the Siloam Tunnel could have been cut in the middle of the

---

4. I wish to thank my friend Benjamin Sass for discussing this issue with me.
5. His down-dating of the latest finds from ca. 800 to the middle of the eighth century BCE expressed in an email message dated 3 November 2012.
6. The absence of early *lmlk* storage jar (for this type see, e.g., Shai and Maeir 2003) is in any event a problem; perhaps this type was not popular in the highlands in the Iron IIA.

eighth century, even in the 730s or 720s BCE, but not in the latest years of the century (for the lack of *lmlk* jars in the fill assemblage).

2. The volume of earth in the fill and the fact that it is not stratified (Singer-Avitz 2012) hint that it was not simply shoveled into the pool from its immediate surroundings, as argued by the excavators (Reich and Shukron 2011). Rather, it must have been brought from somewhere else in the vicinity, possibly an old city dump or the slope of the old mound of Jerusalem.[7] In this case, the finds represent the specific location from which earth was brought—nothing more, nothing less. The presence of Bronze Age items in the fill (Reich and Shukron 2011, 160) points in this direction. According to this scenario, the latest sherds represent the *earliest* possible date of deposition. The *actual* date of deposition should be fixed between the date of these latest sherds and the date of the material found on the floor of the house that was built over the fill.

Continuing this line of thought, the next question to ask is: Until when was Iron IIB pottery (found on the floor of the house) produced? Based on the evidence from Lachish, the conventional wisdom is to fix this date at 701 BCE, the year of Sennacherib's campaign to Judah (implied, for instance, in Ussishkin 2011). This is not necessarily the case. We know well the pottery assemblages of Lachish III (Iron IIB) and Lachish II (Iron IIC), which represent the Sennacherib 701 BCE and the Babylonian 586 BCE destructions, respectively. But for the lack of destruction layers between these two dates, we have no clue regarding the date of transition between these two assemblages. There is no reason to propose that the Iron IIB assemblage was replaced in the morning after the Sennacherib campaign. Indeed, it seems that this happened during the first half of the seventh century BCE (Finkelstein 1994; Finkelstein and Na'aman 2004; Lipschits et al. 2011; ch. 18 below). This means that the construction of the house in the Rock-Cut Pool, and thus the laying of the fill below it (see scenario 2 above), could have taken place in the early seventh century BCE.

---

7. I refer to the southeastern slope of the Temple Mount, situated about 200 m to the north of the Gihon Spring; for location of the Bronze and Iron I–IIA mound of Jerusalem on the Temple Mount, see ch. 2 above.

Discussion

The following scenario for the phases of construction in the Rock-Cut Pool and its vicinity seems to me to be the most logical one.

The old mound of Jerusalem was located on the Temple Mount, and activity on the City of David ridge (the southeastern hill of Jerusalem) was restricted to the area around the Gihon Spring (ch. 2 above). Starting in the middle of the eighth century BCE, and mainly in the last third of that century, Jerusalem grew dramatically to both the south (the City of David ridge) and southwest (the southwestern hill, that is, the Jewish and Armenian Quarters of the Old City). This was a result of the incorporation of Judah into the Assyrian world economy and the flow of refugees from the Northern Kingdom after 720 BCE (ch. 15 above). Once the new quarters became densely settled, they were surrounded by a massive fortification. The Siloam Tunnel was then cut in order to bring water to a pool in the southern tip of the Tyropoeon Valley (probably under the Roman Siloam Pool [Reich 2011, 225–44]), close to the new neighborhoods of the southwestern hill. In other words, the tunnel was not necessarily cut in preparation for an Assyrian assault, and hence there is no need to calculate how long it took to finish the project vis-à-vis the advance of the Assyrian army (Sneh, Weinberger, and Shalev 2010).

In a somewhat later phase of the Iron IIB, either in the last years of the eighth century or in the early seventh century BCE, the Rock-Cut Pool was filled with debris in preparation for the construction of a house. At this stage there was no need to continue keeping the entrance from the Rock-Cut Pool to Tunnel IV open. The volume of the fill and the sensitivity of this spot—near the water source of the city—speak against interpreting the construction of the house in the pool as a private endeavor (contra Reich and Shukron 2011, 153). It was probably built by the Jerusalem authorities in connection with the administration of the spring, hence the fill for the construction could have been brought from anywhere—even farther away from this spot. It is possible that the debris was taken from the slope of the original mound of Jerusalem somewhat to the north of the spring. There is no way to know if the latest finds in this debris—dating to the Iron IIB—represent the moment of deposition or whether they date a while before this action took place. They provide only a *terminus post quem* for the placing of the fill.[8]

---

8. In the same logic, the latest pottery in the fill provides a *terminu ante quem* for the many iconic but un-inscribed bullae found in this fill (Reich, Shukron, and

Summary

The scenario suggested above adheres well to what we know about the expansion of the urban space of Jerusalem, the date of the fortification that surrounded the city, and the conventional date assigned to the Siloam Tunnel—all in the last decades of the eighth century BCE. It also adheres to the conventional paleographic date assigned to the Siloam Inscription.

Addendum

Gadot (2022) has recently revived Knauf's proposal (2001) to date the cutting of the Siloam Tunnel to the days of Manasseh, in the first half of the seventh century BCE. According to Gadot, the hewing of the tunnel was part of an Assyrian-influenced royal gardening project rather than an endeavor aimed at bringing water to the city in times of siege. Gadot rightly argues that the exposure of the monumental seventh-century buildings at Mordot Arnona and Armon HaNatziv, as well as remains of what seems to be a royal garden in Ein el-Jowiezeh in Nahal Refaim (ch. 22 below), strengthens this possibility.

Lernau 2007; Keel 2012). These bullae, some of which have signs of papyrus on their back, are important for the study of the spread of writing and bureaucracy in Iron Age Jerusalem (see chs. 12–13).

18

Comments on the Date of Late Monarchic Judahite Seal Impressions

> Of all the territorial kingdoms of the southern Levant, seal impressions on handles of storage jars are unique to Judah. In this chapter I review the question of dating the two best known of these finds: the *lmlk* and rosette impressions. They are essential in any discussion of Jerusalem and Judah in the eighth–seventh centuries BCE

Oded Lipschits, Omer Sergi, and Ido Koch (2010, 2011) proposed a new reconstruction of the history of late monarchic Judahite seal impressions. They divided the impressions into four chronological phases:

(1) early *lmlk* impressions, between circa 730 and 701 BCE, with strong distribution in both the Shephelah and the highlands;
(2) late *lmlk* impressions in the early seventh century (already Grena 2004, 338), with distribution mainly in the highlands;
(3) concentric incisions (about half of them on late *lmlk* handles; Lipschits, Sergi, and Koch 2010, 31) replacing the *lmlk* system in the mid-seventh century BCE; and
(4) rosette impressions in the last third of the seventh century and early sixth century BCE.

Ussishkin (2011) contested this new scheme, adhering to the conventional dating of both early and late *lmlk* seal impressions in the short period before the Sennacherib campaign against Judah in 701 BCE (see Ussishkin 1976, 2004d).

This debate has far-reaching implications for the history of Judah in particular and the region in general in the late Iron II, circa 730–586 BCE. In what follows I wish to comment on methodological issues related to the debate over the date of the *lmlk* seal impressions and then deal with the date of appearance of the rosette seal impressions (fig. 18.1).

The Date of the *lmlk* Seal Impressions and the Transition from the Lachish III to the Lachish II Pottery Horizons

My interest is in several methodological issues related to the dating of late Iron II sites and finds. I leave it to Lipschits, Sergi, and Koch (2011) to struggle with the details of Ussishkin's arguments.

Ussishkin makes a case against the idea of two pre-701 BCE phases in the early *lmlk* system (four-winged Types Ia and Ib versus two-winged Type IIa), contending that they were all found in the destruction layer of Level III at Lachish, which dates to 701 BCE. But this issue cannot be resolved at Lachish, which has only a single Iron IIB stratum. In other words, Level III at the site covers the entire time span from the beginning of the Iron IIB in the first half of the eighth century (Finkelstein and Piasetzky 2010) to its demise as a result of the Sennacherib assault. Evidently, in a situation such as this, *all* pre-701 impressions will be found in the final destruction layer. The only Judahite sites that revealed strata prior to the late eighth-century Iron IIB are Beersheba (Stratum III), Arad (Strata IX and X; Herzog 2002a; Singer-Avitz 2002), Aroer (Stratum IV; Thareani 2011, 2), and possibly Tel Eton (Katz and Faust 2012). None of the impressions from the first two sites was found in the earlier Iron IIB strata, although the number of items is too limited to draw firm conclusions. A four-winged impression found in Stratum IV at Aroer (Thareani 2011, 225) seems to support Lipschits, Sergi, and Koch contra Ussishkin. No *lmlk* impressions have thus far been found in the Iron IIB destruction layer uncovered at Tel Eton, located near Lachish (Katz and Faust 2012). If this indicates that the conflagration is a result of a pre-Sennacherib Assyrian campaign (one of the possibilities proposed by Katz and Faust 2012), it may support Ussishkin contra Lipschits, Sergi, and Koch.

Lipschits, Sergi, and Koch (2010) date the Types IIb, IIc, and X II *lmlk* seal impressions to the early seventh century BCE because none were

18. Comments on the Date of Late Monarchic Judahite Seal Impressions   273

Fig. 18.1. Judahite, Yehud, and Judean seal impressions (photograph courtesy of Oded Lipschits).

found in a 701 destruction layer. Ussishkin contests this argument. His review of sites where these types appear does not resolve the problem, as they did not produce evidence for a distinction between the eighth and seventh centuries BCE; evidently, this is so because there is no 701 destruction horizon in the highlands.

Ussishkin dates the Iron IIB and Iron IIC pottery assemblages with his excavations at Lachish in mind, where Level III of the Iron IIB was destroyed in 701 BCE and Level II of the Iron IIC was annihilated in the early sixth century. However, neither Lachish nor any other site in Judah supplies evidence for the date of transition between these two assemblages. There is no reason to assume that the Lachish III repertoire ceased to exist as a result of the 701 BCE events, which means that the transition took place sometime in the course of the seventh century BCE. Moreover, there is no reason to argue that the entire Lachish III pottery assemblage was replaced by the Lachish II forms all at once. On the contrary, transitions in pottery traditions were gradual in the Levant and other places and could take a significant amount of time. Hence the fact that Lachish III ceramic forms were found in the Buqeiah Valley in the Judean Desert does not mean that these sites date to the eighth century BCE. Had the sites there been established, for example, in the early seventh century and continued to function with no disturbance until circa 600 BCE, their pottery would include both Lachish III and Lachish II forms. Therefore, the appearance of the two-winged Type IIa or IIb handle there does not necessarily indicate a date in the eighth century BCE. The same holds true for Ein Gedi. I see no clear-cut evidence that Ein Gedi was inhabited in the eighth century BCE.

All this culminates in the case of Horvat Shilhah, where a Type IIb *lmlk* impression was found with a Lachish II pottery assemblage. Assuming that the site was established in the seventh century, at the time of transition from the Lachish III to the Lachish II pottery horizons, and functioned during the time of the Lachish II repertoire, there is no need for deus ex machina explanations à la Mazar, Amit, and Ilan (1996, 208–9, that the handle belonged to an old jar that had been stored in Jerusalem for decades and was then brought to Horvat Shilhah) or Ussishkin (2011, 229, that the handle had already been collected in antiquity as a souvenir and was then thrown away at the site). In fact, Horvat Shilhah is possibly the most important site for this discussion: rather than viewing the Type IIb *lmlk* seal impression found there as "problematic" because "it was found in a context at least 80 years later than the assumed time of its manufacture" (Ussishkin 2011, 230), the site should be seen, to differ from most sites in the highlands of Judah, as a single-period settlement that supplies the smoking gun for the dating of the late *lmlk* impressions in the seventh century BCE.

Ussishkin's closing remark on the issue of the sites in the highlands, that "in many of those 'hill-country sites' handles bearing *lmlk* stamps of the suggested 'earlier' types were uncovered as well, many of them in the same context with the handles bearing stamps of the suggested 'later' types" (Ussishkin 2011, 230), encapsulates the problem: with no 701 destruction layer in the highlands, late eighth-century houses could have continued to be in use in the early seventh century BCE and later.

Ussishkin interprets several Type IIb handles found on the surface at Lachish as originating from Level III (that is, before 701 BCE), because following the destruction of this layer Lachish remained "desolate and abandoned until the foundation of Level II more than half a century later" (Ussishkin 2011, 231) and because when the Level II settlement was established, the *lmlk* impressions had already gone out of use. But

18. Comments on the Date of Late Monarchic Judahite Seal Impressions 275

as shown elsewhere (Finkelstein and Na'aman 2004), Lachish may have provided clues for an ephemeral early seventh-century reoccupation. An intermediate phase (Locus 4021) was discerned in the gate area, on top of the destruction and collapse of Level III and under the Level II fortification; several tombs may also belong to this phase (Ussishkin 2004e, 90–91; 2004a, 652–53). These remains may represent either squatters who returned to the ruined site shortly after 701 BCE or an early phase of reoccupation in the first half of the seventh century, before the construction of the new fortification system in the days of Level II. The pottery of this intermediate phase in the gate area belongs to the Lachish III repertoire. The Type IIb impressions found on the surface at Lachish could have originated from this intermediate phase. The same holds true for the concentric incisions from Lachish—also found on the surface of the site. The fact that *all* Type IIb impressions and concentric incisions from Lachish were found on the surface and not in the 701 destruction debris is telling.

Ussishkin points to the private seal impressions of Nera son of Shebna, which were found in sealed 701 destruction layers at Lachish and Beth-shemesh and with a Type IIb *lmlk* seal impression from Ramat Rahel. This, too, does not advance his case. If one assumes that this official functioned in the Judahite bureaucratic apparatus between, say, 705 and 690 BCE, the problem is resolved.[1]

Ostensibly, Ussishkin has a strong argument regarding the workshops that produced the *lmlk* storage jars: since all *lmlk* storage jars were manufactured in the upper Shephelah (Goren and Halperin 2004, 2556), how is it that the late *lmlk* vessels were produced there after the area had been taken from Judah and handed over to the Philistine city-states? However, I see no difficulty here. The long-lived Shephelah workshop(s) could have continued to manufacture *lmlk* jars after 701 BCE, especially if these jars served Judah's role in the Assyrian economic and administration system. After all, both the late Iron II Philistine cities of the Shephelah and Judah functioned under Assyrian domination.

To sum up this methodological discussion:

---

1. The storage jar with a Nera son of Shebna seal impression from Jerusalem (Avigad and Barkay 2000, 247–48) could have been incised with a concentric sign many years after its manufacture.

- Lachish cannot attest to the beginning of the *lmlk* system because it has only one stratum for the entire Iron IIB, so all pre-701 BCE impressions are found there together, in the final destruction layer.
- The transition from the Lachish III to the Lachish II pottery traditions occurred gradually, during the first half of the seventh century.
- Weak activity at Lachish in the first half of the seventh century may account for the Type IIb and concentric incisions found on the surface of the site.
- The Buqeiah sites, Ein Gedi, and Horvat Shilhah may have been established in the early seventh century, and settlements there continued as late as 586 BCE.
- Nera son of Shebna could have served in the administration of Judah in the very late eighth and very early seventh century BCE, hence his impressions are found both in 701 BCE destruction layers and on a Type IIb impression from Ramat Rahel.
- The pottery workshop/s in the Shephelah could have continued to produce *lmlk* jars in the early seventh century BCE, under Assyrian rule.

The Date of the Rosette Seal Impressions and the Archaeology of the Days of Manasseh

Based on their dating of the rosette seal impressions to the last third of the seventh century BCE, Lipschits, Sergi, and Koch dismissed the idea of a Judahite recovery in the Shephelah and Beersheba Valley in the days of Manasseh (for this, see Finkelstein 1994; Knauf 2005; Finkelstein and Silberman 2006a, 171–77; Thareani-Sussely 2007; Faust 2008). They suggest that the "meagre number of early seventh-century stamped jar handles found in the Judahite Shephelah and in the Beersheba-Arad Valleys indicates a decline in the royal economic activity ... during the days of Manasseh. The fact that almost all of the stamped or incised jar handles dated to the first half of the seventh century BCE were found in and around Jerusalem ... is an indication of the weakness of the monarchic administration at that time" (Lipschits, Sergi, and Koch 2011, 26).

Whether the distribution of the seal impressions indeed indicates strength of activity even in the periphery of the kingdom, in every period, can be debated. Assuming (for the sake of discussion) that this is so, whether the Lipschits, Sergi, and Koch statement is correct or not seems to depend on the date when the rosette impressions—which ostensibly signal stronger involvement in the Shephelah, Beersheba Valley, and Judean Desert than before (table 18.2)—were introduced into the bureaucratic system of the kingdom.

Several scholars limited the date of the rosette seal impressions to the last years of the kingdom of Judah (Cahill 1995, 2000, 2003b; Ussishkin 2004e, 109–11). Their main argument was that rosette seal impressions were found in destruction layers dated to the Babylonian assaults in the closing years of the seventh century (Cahill: Tel Batash) and the early sixth century BCE (Ussishkin: Jerusalem and Lachish). But Koch and Lipschits rightly noted (2010, 15) that the evidence cited by Cahill and Ussishkin provides only a datum for the *end* of use of the rosette seal impressions, not their introduction into the Judahite administrative system.

Aharoni (1964, 35) noted that no rosette seal impression was found under the floor of the Stratum VA building at Ramat Rahel. However, the date of construction of the building is dependent on these rosette impressions (Lipschits et al. 2011, 34; for the possibility that it was erected during the period of Assyrian rule in Judah, see Na'aman 2001a; Finkelstein 2011e). Hence, this is a circular argument that does not tell us much about when the rosette seal impressions were introduced into the Judahite system.

Na'aman (1991, 31) pointed out the similarity between the distribution of the rosette seal impressions and the list of Judahite towns in Josh 15, the latter conventionally dated to the time of Josiah (Alt 1925; Na'aman 1991). But the origin of the reality depicted in the list—in the time of Josiah or earlier—depends on archaeological considerations, mainly the date of transition from the Lachish III to the Lachish II pottery horizons. In other words, the list may indeed represent the time of Josiah, but it does not necessarily mark the *beginning* of Judahite (re)settlement of the regions represented in it. So this argument, too, does not help in establishing the date of introduction of the rosette system into the administration of Judah.

In addition to accepting the arguments raised by Aharoni and Na'aman (above), Koch and Lipschits (2010, 15) introduced three arguments of their own in support of their dating of the rosette seal impressions to the last third of the seventh century and the early sixth century.

(1) A rosette seal impression was apparently found in Stratum 11 in the City of David (Cahill 2000, 92); this predates Stratum 10, the layer that was destroyed in 586 BCE (Shiloh 1984, 18–19; for reservations regarding the stratigraphic affiliation of this seal impression, see Cahill 2000, 98).

(2) The large number of types and subtypes of the seals used in this system (four and twenty-four respectively, twenty-eight seals in total [see a larger number in Cahill 2000, 103], a greater number than that used for the *lmlk* impressions; Koch and Lipschits 2010, 34) attests to a long period of use.

(3) On the other hand, Lipschits, Sergi, and Koch (2011, 9) say that the number of late *lmlk* handles indicates that this system was used for a longer time than that of the concentric and rosette impressions, which in their opinion pushes the rosette system to the last third of the seventh century.

Points 1 and 2 attest to a long use of the rosette system. Point 3 cannot serve as an anchor for dating the appearance of the rosette seal impressions, as there is no clear correlation between the length of use of a given stamp system and the number of impressed handles found (table 18.1).

Table 18.1. The different seal impressions: number of items and supposed length of use

	Early *lmlk*[2]	Late *lmlk*[2]	Concentric[2]	Rosette	*yhd*	*yrslm*
Number of items	823	488	285	224	570[3]	104[4]
Use (years)[5]	30	40	20	45	350	50

---

2. The unidentified *lmlk* impressions were divided between the early and late *lmlk* groups according to the relative numbers of the identified items; *lmlk* handles with concentric circles were counted only in the concentric incisions column (Lipschits, Sergi, and Koch 2011, 10).

3. Vanderhooft and Lipschits 2007, 14.

4. Bocher and Lipschits 2011.

5. According to Lipschits, Sergi, and Koch 2011; Vanderhooft and Lipschits 2007.

18. Comments on the Date of Late Monarchic Judahite Seal Impressions

It is obvious, then, that archaeology does not supply unequivocal evidence for the date of introduction of the rosette impressions to the bureaucratic system of Judah. Establishing this date depends on circumstantial evidence and broader archaeological and historical considerations. The following arguments are relevant.

(1) As observed by Lipschits, Sergi, and Koch, a large number of seals (with a large number of types and subtypes) were used in this system.

(2) As noted by them, a rosette impression seems to have been found in Stratum 11 in the City of David (Stratum 11 or 10, according to Cahill 2000, 98). It is noteworthy that the subsequent layer, which came to an end in 586 BCE, had more than one phase. This is probably the reason why Shiloh dated Stratum 11 to the "mainly mid-seventh century" (1984, 3). The continuity of occupation in Jerusalem may, in fact, put the beginning of Stratum 11 even earlier, in this case depending on the date of transition from the Lachish III to the Lachish II pottery horizons.

(3) Koch and Lipschits (2010, 14) note that 30 of the 224 rosette impressions were found in 586 BCE destruction layers. Had these impressions been in use only close to 586 BCE, the percentage of the handles found in these layers would have been higher.

(4) With no precise archaeological pegs, one can turn to historical logic: it is difficult to imagine that Judahite activity in the Beersheba Valley remained weak during the years of prosperity of the Assyrian-led Arabian trade in the early to mid-seventh century BCE (see table 18.2 below for the rise in the number of impressions in the south in the rosette system phase).

Table 18.2: Number and percent of impressions in three Judahite regions

	Early *lmlk* (without Lachish)	Late *lmlk*	Concentric	Rosette
Beersheba Valley				
number	8	4	2	11
percent	2.7%	1%	0.7%	4.9%
Shephelah				
number	96	7	5	46
percent	32%	1.7%	1.7%	20.5%
Judean Desert				
number	—	2	2	12
percent	—	0.5%	0.7%	5.4%

Taking all this into account, the appearance of the rosette seal impressions can be dated to anytime in the not too early and not too late seventh century. The time of Josiah is no better than the later days of Manasseh, for example, circa 660 or 650 BCE. This seems to be supported by additional pieces of information.

The appearance of two late *lmlk* seal impressions in the Buqeiah sites indicates that they were established in the early seventh century, probably in order to try to supplement the grain needs of the kingdom following the fall of the Shephelah (Finkelstein 1994). The same holds true for the Beersheba Valley, which also yielded late *lmlk* and concentric impressions. The small number of impressions found in these regions is understandable if one relates the impressed storage jars to oil (and wine?) production. Certain activity in the Shephelah in the early seventh century is evident from both the distribution of late *lmlk* impressions and concentric incisions (table 18.2) and from the archaeological evidence (Finkelstein and Na'aman 2004). However, it is possible that a more significant Judahite recovery in the Shephelah started somewhat later, during the time of the rosette system. This seems to have taken place in the second quarter of the seventh century, in the days of King Manasseh.

19
Mozah, Nephtoah, and Royal Estates in the Jerusalem Highlands

In the following two chapters, I consider the economy of Jerusalem and Judah under Assyrian domination. Here I discuss the long-term phenomenon of royal estates in the vicinity of the city, which can possibly be traced as early as the Late Bronze Age and continued until Roman times. Special attention is given to the situation in the Iron IIB–C.

This chapter deals with the identification of two biblical places in the vicinity of Jerusalem and with the long-term phenomenon of royal estates in this region. Although at times hypothetical, the overall picture that emerges helps to clarify issues related to the history, economy, and geographical history of the Jerusalem countryside.[1]

Mozah

Tel Moza (Khirbet Mizzah, the ruins of the village of Qaluniya) is a 1.0–1.5 hectare site located in the narrow valley of Nahal Soreq, 6 kilometers west of the Old City of Jerusalem (G.R. 1656 1335; fig. 19.1). The vicinity of the site is characterized by narrow ridges with steep slopes and winding wadis, typical of the highlands west of Jerusalem. Topographically the site extends on a lower slope, near the wadi bed; hence, although it is a multi-period settlement, it does not bear the typical silhouette of a mound. Two springs are located in its immediate vicinity. The terrain around the site

This chapter was originally coauthored with Yuval Gadot.

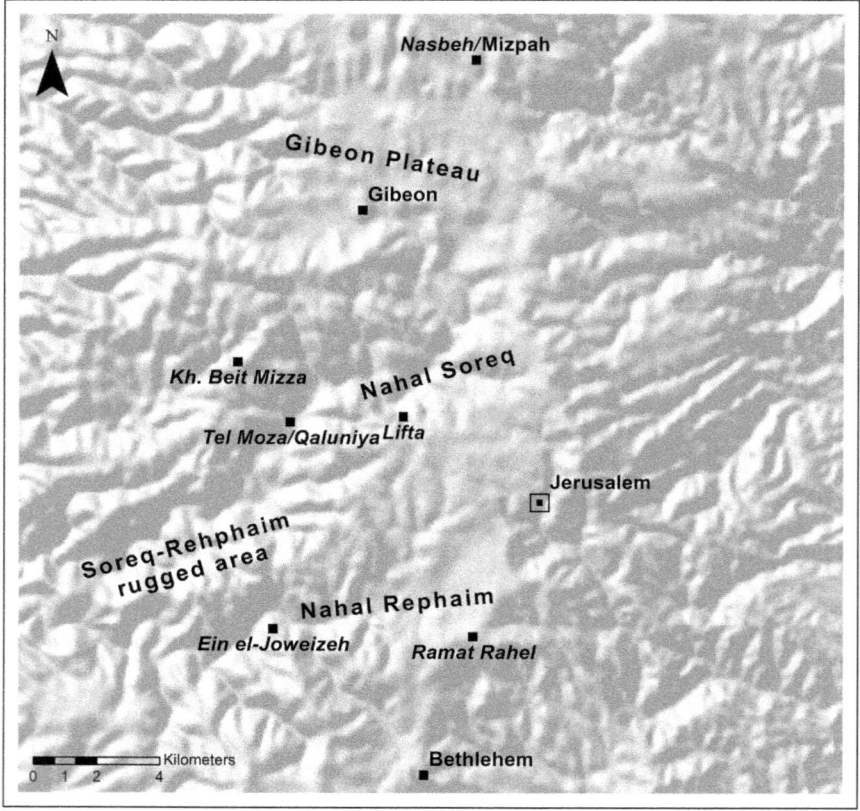

Fig. 19.1. The Jerusalem highlands

enables mainly horticulture cultivation,[1] but at an air distance of 1 kilometer to the east Nahal Soreq widens to form a small valley suitable for growing grain.

Tel Moza was excavated by the Israel Antiquities Authority in 1993 and 2002–2003 (Greenhut and De Groot 2009) and again in 2012–2013

---

1. Note the dramatic difference in land use in the 1940s between the hilly area west of Jerusalem, including Qaluniya, and the Gibeon Plateau. The average ratio between land devoted to plantations and cereal growing in the former was ca. 70:30 and in the latter 20:80 (Government of Palestine 1945). In the case of Qaluniya, the air distance between these agricultural landscapes is circa 5 kilometers!

(Kisilevitz 2013; for previous explorations, see summary in Greenhut and De Groot 2009, 4–6; 2008, 1958). Early activity at the site dates to the Neolithic period, Early Bronze IA, Middle Bronze, and Late Bronze Ages (sherds only for the latter). The Iron Age settlement covers the (late?) Iron I and the Iron IIA–C. Meager finds from the Hellenistic and Byzantine periods were exposed, as well as medieval remains. The negative evidence is also significant: no remains from the Babylonian or Persian periods or from the Roman era were found in the excavations. The most noteworthy finds dating to the Iron Age are the remains of an Iron IIA shrine (Kisilevitz 2013) and an elaborate system of stone-built silos, which, together with some prestige items, caused Greenhut and De Groot (2009, 225–26) to interpret the site as an administrative center that supplied food to Jerusalem.

The modern name, Tel Moza, stems from biblical Mozah, a place mentioned in the group of western Benjaminite towns (Josh 18:26) together with Gibeon, Ramah, Beeroth, Mizpeh, Chephirah, and Kiriath-jearim (the latter also appears in the northern highlands district of Judah [Josh 15:60]). A person Moza is mentioned in the genealogies of Caleb (1 Chr 2:46) and Benjamin (1 Chr 8:36; 9:42). Three or four Aramaic letters that appear on seal impressions probably dating to the Babylonian period are understood as the toponym Mozah and interpreted as representing vessels that originated from an estate that delivered its agricultural output to Mizpah (Avigad 1958; Naveh 1970, 58–59; Zorn, Yellin, and Hayes 1994). The end character in the toponym is either ה or א, in the latter case possibly meaning outlet of a source of water. The Mishnah (Sukkah 4:5) mentions Motza as a place "below Jerusalem." The Talmud identifies it with Colonia and interprets the name as signaling the special status of the inhabitants, who were exempt from royal taxes (b. Sukkah 45a).

Mozah has been identified by most scholars with the village of Qaluniya (and hence the Hebrew name of the site: Tel Moza; detailed discussion and bibliography in Greenhut and De Groot 2009, 3–4; Tsafrir, Di Segni, and Green 1994, 105) for the following reasons:

- the preservation of the Hebrew in the Arabic name of the site: Khirbet Mizzah;
- the location not far from the Benjamin-Judah border as described in Josh 15:8–9; 18:15–16, and in the context of the second Benjaminite district (Josh 18:25–28); and

- the link made in the Talmud between Motza and Colonia. Josephus (*B.J.* 7.6.6) reports that following the destruction of Jerusalem Vespasian settled eight hundred veterans in a place called Emmaus 30 stadia from Jerusalem. The distance fits the site of Qaluniya (Tel Moza), which stems from Colonia (for the confusion regarding the toponym Emmaus, see Fischer, Issac, and Roll 1996, 223–24).

Greenhut and De Groot summarized that, "in view of our recent excavations here, there is no doubt that biblical Moza is to be identified with Qaluniya" (2009, 3). We beg to differ.

- With the exception of Chephirah (Kiriath-jearim is also mentioned in Judah), the identified towns of the second (western) Benjaminite district are located in the Gibeon–Mizpah Plateau, including its southern edge (fig. 19.1). Indeed, geographic logic puts the line dividing the towns of Benjamin and Judah between the plateau and the hilly area to its south, with the northern tributaries of Nahal Soreq serving as dividing landmarks. Although Qaluniya/Tel Moza is close to the southern end of the plateau, it is located deep in the rugged area west of Jerusalem; this is no classical territory of Benjamin.
- The absence of finds from the Babylonian and Persian periods and the meager finds from the Hellenistic period seem to negate its identification with *mwsh* of the Babylonian period seal impressions and Moza of the genealogy of Benjamin.
- The absence of Roman remains makes the identification of Qaluniya proper with the place where Vespasian settled eight hundred of his veterans difficult.

Still, biblical Mozah should be sought in a place not too far from Qaluniya. This is so because of the preservation of the name: Khirbet Mizzah and nearby Khirbet Beit Mizza (below). Also, assuming that the *mwsh*-sealed storage jars delivered wine and/or olive oil, suitable terrace land for viniculture and oleiculture is found on the southern or western edges of the Gibeon Plateau. The combination of these considerations would fit a site in the vicinity to the north and especially topographically higher than Qaluniya, closer to the edge of the plateau.

Another site that seems to preserve the name Mozah is Khirbet Beit Mizza, situated circa 2 kilometers to the north of Qaluniya and 150 meters higher (G.R. 1652 1349; fig. 19.2). Although not far from Qaluniya, Khirbet Beit Mizza is located in a different ecological niche: higher up and near the southern margin of the Benjamin Plateau. The survey of this site, estimated as 1 hectare in size, yielded Iron Age, Persian, Hellenistic, and Roman pottery (Feldstein et al. 1993, 222). Indeed, this place was identified with Mozah by Kallai-Kleinman (1953, 112). A closer and bigger site, covering an area of more than 2 hectares, is Ein Hamevaser (Ein el-Joz, according to the PEF; G.R. 1650 1341), which lies circa 100 m higher than Qaluniya; the survey here yielded a more significant number of Iron Age sherds (Feldstein et al. 1993, 222–23; Greenhut and De Groot 2009, 225). If Qaluniya indeed stems from Colonia, the latter should be sought at a Roman period site close by.

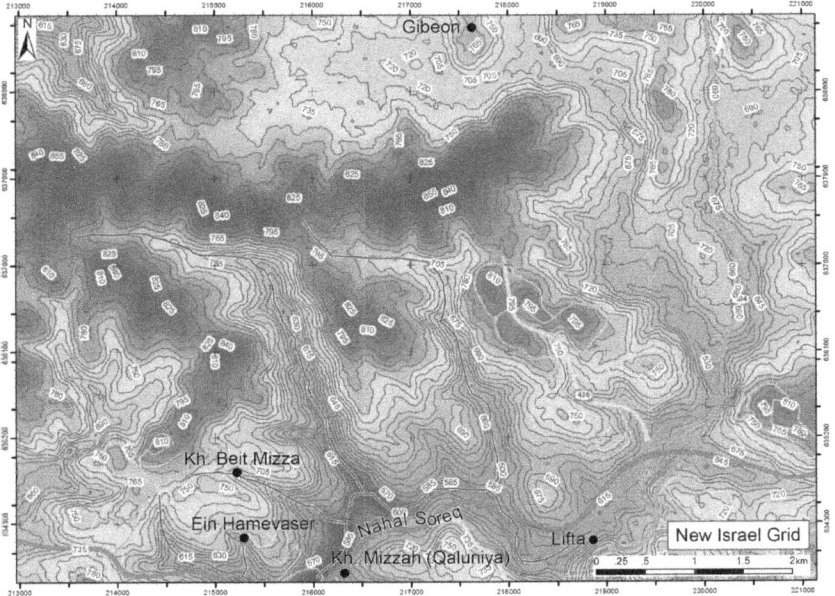

Fig. 19.2. Map of the vicinity of Tel Moza/Qaluniya; note the topographical differences between the area of Nahal Soreq and the Gibeon Plateau

Nephtoah

This leaves Qaluniya, an important Iron II mound near Jerusalem, unidentified. It is, of course, possible, that the town located here is not mentioned in the Bible, especially since the northernmost strip in the list of Judahite towns includes only two toponyms (Josh 15:60: Kiriath-jearim = Deir el-Azar and the enigmatic Rabbah; Kallai 1986, 394; Na'aman 1991, 10). Still, there is another possibility. A place named "spring of the Waters of Nephtoah" (מעין מי נפתוח) is mentioned twice in the Bible, both times in the description of the border between the allotments of Judah and Benjamin (Josh 15:9; 18:15). The name must refer to the spring of a town named Nephtoah, similar to waters of Merom (Josh 11:5, 7) and waters of Megiddo (Judg 5:19). The sequence of places referred to in Joshua puts this place west or northwest of Jerusalem, between the capital and Kiriath-jearim (Kallai 1968; 1986, 121–22). The shared identification is with the village of Lifta, 3 kilometers air distance to the east of Qaluniya (G.R. 1687 1336), which seems to preserve the ancient name. The Survey of Jerusalem mentions "various surveys" that were conducted in the 1960s and 1970 "at the site and its vicinity," which revealed Iron II sherds (Kloner 2003, 89). However, to the best of our knowledge Lifta does not have Iron Age remains. Only further field research can clarify this issue; in any event, the possibility that Nephtoah was located at Qaluniya and that the ancient name shifted a distance of a few kilometers to the east, along the same valley, cannot be brushed aside.

Another clue may help clarify this issue. The combination "spring of the Waters of Nephtoah" is unique and awkward. This toponym could be expected to read either "spring of Nephtoah" (e.g., spring of Tappuah [עין תפוח] [Josh 17:7]) or "Waters of Nephtoah" [מי נפתוח] e.g., waters of Merom]). Based on Papyrus Anastasi 3, which mentions the arrival at Sile of a military official from the "Wells of Merenptah … which is on the mountain ridge" (Wilson 1969, 258), scholars proposed to interpret the place name "spring of the Waters of Nephtoah" as a corruption of "Waters of Me[r]neptah" (e.g., Wilson 1969, 258 n. 6; Aharoni 1979, 184; discussion in Kallai 1968). This interpretation may sound simplistic, as a place named Waters of Merenptah that is "on the mountain ridge" could be located anywhere in Canaan. However, based on the descriptions in the Amarna tablets, an Egyptian fort in the highlands part of Canaan can be expected mainly near the two restless city-states of Jerusalem and

Shechem. Qaluniya is one of a few sites in the vicinity of Jerusalem that yielded Late Bronze finds (Greenhut and De Groot 2009, 217); it sits on a good supply of water and not far from arable land. Hence, although impossible to prove, the possibility that Qaluniya is the location of the Late Bronze Waters of Merenptah = biblical Nephtoah is stronger than perceived at first glance.

Royal Estates in the Highlands of Jerusalem

The discussion above calls attention to the long-term phenomenon of royal or temple estates in the highlands near Jerusalem. With the term *estate* we refer to large plots of land belonging to a political institution and administrated by a bureaucratic center, as opposed to lands that were given to farmers as tenants, to be cultivated in return for a share of the crops.

Royal/temple estates characterized the ancient Egyptian and, to a certain extent, Mesopotamian economies (Janssen 1979; Heltzer 1979; Yoffee 1995; Garcia 2014). Information regarding estates in the Levant is patchy. However, taking a long-term perspective (as practiced for other characteristics related to the environment and territorial administration), the fragmentary pieces of evidence from different periods create a more coherent picture.

Wine and olive oil from the highlands were not only of central importance in the subsistence patterns of the local population but also among the most valuable commodities that Canaan/ancient Israel could offer to neighboring arid regions, including Egypt in the south and Assyria in the north. Egypt's dependence on secondary products of the Levantine highlands horticulture is evident starting in the Early Bronze I (Finkelstein and Gophna 1993; van den Brink and Levy 2002). The two most important centers for this economic activity were Shechem (later Samaria) and Jerusalem.[2] Both feature evidence for the existence of royal estates under local or foreign administrations (for the Samaria ostraca, see, e.g., Rainey 1967; Lemaire 1977, 67–81; Aharoni 1979, 364–67; Niemann 2008, 250).

---

2. Until the Hellenistic and Roman (possibly already Persian) periods, the Galilee, especially its upper part, was more wooded and less settled and cultivated than the central highlands (Frankel 2001, 126).

In the case of Jerusalem, the earliest possible (admittedly hypothetical) clue for an agricultural estate comes from the late thirteenth-century BCE Merenptah text mentioned above. That the Egyptians exploited large plots of lands through a system of royal or temple estates is known from other regions in Canaan. EA 365 describes activities preformed in an estate at Shunem in the Jezreel Valley; it may possibly hint at another estate in the vicinity of Jaffa in the central coastal plain. Na'aman proposed that large plots of land located in the fertile Jezreel Valley were torn from the territories of Canaanite city-states and governed by the administrative center of Beth-shean (Na'aman 1981, 177–80). One of us suggested that another system of estates, which were administered by the Egyptian center of Jaffa, was established along the Yakron and Ayalon Rivers (Gadot 2010). The Egyptian estate network in Canaan reached its zenith during the days of the Twentieth Dynasty. A chain of small estates was established along the main wadis in the southern coastal plain: Nahal Besor (Tell el-Farʿah South, Qubur el-Walaydah, and Tel Jemmeh), Nahal Gerar (Tel Seraʿ, Tel Haror), and Nahal Lachish (Tel Mor) (Martin 2011, 248; Lehmann et al. 2010, 147–49). Bowls made in Egyptian style were used as tokens for rations brought from the estates or given to the workers, as can be deduced from the hieratic inscriptions written on them (e.g., Wimmer 2012; Wimmer and Lehmann 2014). The southern Egyptian estates were governed by Gaza, possibly under the auspices of the temple of Amun there (Wimmer 2012, 488). The question of an Egyptian stronghold near Jerusalem should be evaluated against this background. Such a place could have been engaged not only in maintaining the Egyptian grip over the highlands but also in supplying horticulture products—wine and olive oil—to Egypt.

Evidence for the early phases of the Iron Age is lacking. The Sheshonq I campaign is perceived as an attempt at long-term political and economic domination; one may wonder if the historically unusual Egyptian penetration into the highlands north of Jerusalem (Beth-horon, Gibeon, Zemaraim, and possibly also Kiriath-jearim, mentioned in the list of towns conquered) was not related to, among other reasons, attempts to take over the horticulture industry of the region. In a slightly later date—in the late Iron IIA (ninth century BCE)—a temple was built at the site of Tel Moza (Kisilevitz 2013); it is possible that this temple inherited the plots of land that had previously belonged to Egyptian rule.

More is known about the Iron IIB–C, between the mid-eighth and early sixth centuries BCE, when Jerusalem grew dramatically in size and population. The large number of stone-lined silos unearthed at Qaluniya (Tel Moza) seems to indicate that the site served as a royal granary: a major collection and distribution center for agricultural output in the vicinity of the capital. Its economy "was based on the marketing of agricultural produce to the urban center at Jerusalem" (Greenhut and De Groot 2009, 219; see also 225–27). Stamped jar handles of the *lmlk* and rosette types, so characteristic of Judah's administration in late monarchic times, are nearly absent there (only two *lmlk* stamp impressions, nine incised concentric circles, and four rosette stamp impresions were found; Greenhut and De Groot 2009, 129–33). Since these jars are usually associated with wine and olive oil, it seems that at least in this period the site served mainly for the collection and redistribution of grain. A recent study of the faunal assemblage from Tel Moza shows a high percentage of cattle raising (ca. 30 percent), a pattern typical of sites invested in grain economy, where cattle are used for ploughing. Dry farming could have been practiced mainly in the small valley in Nahal Soreq to the east of the site. The results of this study also hint that Tel Moza was a supplier of sheep to Jerusalem (Sapir-Hen, Gadot, and Finkelstein 2016).

Regarding Judah in the Iron IIB, most intriguing are the *lmlk* seal impressions that carry the enigmatic toponym *mmst*. Scholars debated whether *mmst* was an epithet for Jerusalem (Ginsberg 1948, 20–21, who read it as an assimilation of *mmšlt* = administration, government) or a town that does not appear in the Bible (most significantly, it is absent from the detailed late seventh-century list of Judahite towns in Josh 15) and extrabiblical sources. Various views were expressed to explain this absence: that the site had been destroyed in the course of the Sennacherib campaign in 701 BCE and was not inhabited later (Na'aman 1991, 26–27) or that it was a royal estate rather than a regular town (Fox 2000, 227–35). Scholars proposed locations north of Jerusalem (Welten 1969, 147–56; Lemaire 1975), the Rephaim Valley (Lipschits, Sergi, and Koch 2010, 21), which was an important center of agricultural activity near the capital city (Gadot 2015), or, more specifically, Ramat Rahel (Barkay 2006, 43). We suggest that *mmst*, which may indeed stem from *mmšlt*, was the name of the *system* of royal estates in the vicinity of Jerusalem, to the west and southwest of the city.

A recent study of the site of Ein el-Joweizeh in the Rephaim Valley, 8 kilometers southeast of Jerusalem (Ein Mor and Ron 2013) may shed light on the nature of these estates. The site includes a rock-cut tunnel aimed at increasing the yield of the spring and a springhouse decorated with a Proto-Ionic capital; originally there must have been a pair (or more) of capitals in the structure. The site dates to the later phases of the Iron Age. These remains seem to represent a royal garden, possibly part of a royal estate (Ein Mor and Ron 2013, 105). The estate's output—mainly wine and olive oil (the stepped landscape around Ein el-Joweizeh best fits horticultural activity)—could have been used by the royal family and their entourage, as well as for payment of taxes to the Assyrian overlords. The site and its layout could have been inspired by Assyrian royal gardens such as the one described in the Ashurbanipal relief from Nineveh (Dalley 1993 and bibliography).

The phenomenon of rock-cut tunnels aimed at increasing the yield of springs is characteristic of the Jerusalem highlands (Ron 1985). They make one component in an irrigation and intensive cultivation system. As the level of ground water dropped, these tunnels constantly had to be cut deeper into the rock. This procedure resulted in long and winding tunnels that are difficult to date. The evidence from Ein el-Joweizeh indicates that the technique had been known already in late monarchic times; thus many if not most of these spring systems may date to the later phases of the Iron Age (Ein Mor and Ron 2013, 102, 106; they were used and expanded, of course, in later periods). This should not come as a surprise in view of the dramatic growth of Jerusalem, the need to pay taxes to Assyria, and the fact that contemporary developed hydraulic technology is known from Jerusalem, Suba, and Ramat Rahel (Ein Mor and Ron 2013, 102–3; Gross, Gadot, and Lipschits 2014).

The long-term phenomenon of royal estates in the vicinity of Jerusalem continued after the Babylonian destruction. The *mwsh* seal impressions should apparently be dated to this period (Avigad 1958; Naveh 1970, 58–59; Zorn, Yellin, and Hayes 1994). The letters in the impression, reading *mwsh*, have been understood as the toponym Mozah and interpreted as an estate that served the local and possibly imperial administration. Seal impressions on storage jars mean shipment of liquids, in the case of the area of Jerusalem most probably wine and olive oil. Most *mwsh* seal impressions were found at Mizpah, the administrative center of the province, which means a change in the delivery of commodities like this after 586 BCE from Jerusalem to the new center. During the Persian period, Ramat Rahel, now a large, well-planned edifice surrounded by a royal garden, served as a collection center for horticulture products, as is evident from the hundreds of jar handles stamped with Yehud stamp impressions found at the site (Lipschits, Gadot, and Langgut 2012).[3] The phenomenon of seal impressions continued in the late Persian and Hellenistic periods, in the early fourth/third and second centuries BCE (Groups 13–15 in Lipschits and Vanderhooft 2011 and Groups 16–17 plus the *yrslm* impressions, respectively). One wonders if, similar to the earlier *mmst*, the title *yrslm* is not a general appellation to estates in the vicinity of Jerusalem.

The settlement of Roman army veterans by Vespasian west of Jerusalem, probably in the vicinity of Qaluniya, may also be connected (similar to what we suggested above for the Egyptian New Kingdom) both to the need to pacify and dominate Judea and to extract taxes from imperial estates.

Addendum

For an updated discussion of the seventh-century activity in the highlands of Jerusalem, see Gadot 2022.

---

3. But note residues of mead discovered in stamped Yehud storage jars from Ramat Rahel (Namdar et al. 2021).

20

The Unique Specialized Economy of Judah under Assyrian Rule and Its Impact on the Material Culture of the Kingdom

---

Here I conclude the discussion of the Iron IIB by linking the Assyrian domination over Judah, its impact on the kingdom's economy, and its influence on Judahite material culture. Emphasis is given to the geography of the kingdom, which enabled specialization in its different regions, in turn leading to the development of unique, advanced administrative apparatus.

Introduction

The geography of Judah is unique among the territorial kingdoms of the Levant. Judah stretches over four different geographical units: the highlands, the Shephelah (hilly lowlands), the Beersheba Valley, and the Judean Desert, including the shores of the Dead Sea (fig. 20.1). This division is recognized in the biblical text, first and foremost in the list of towns in Josh 15. The four units differ in their rock formations, topography, climate, and hence vegetation. As a result, they offer distinct subsistence opportunities that resulted in different settlement patterns. Intensive archaeological exploration allows reconstructing the settlement activity and economic base of each of the four geographical units and investigating its impact on the history and unique material culture of the kingdom. In what follows

---

This chapter was originally coauthored with Yuval Gadot and Dafna Langgut.

we focus on the economy of Judah in the Assyrian century in its history, circa 730–630 BCE.

Below we clarify our basic attitude to issues that are central to the reconstruction of the settlement, demographic, and subsistence patterns in Judah.

Chronology. We use a chronological outline that is radiocarbon-based for the early phases of the Iron Age (see, e.g., Finkelstein and Piasetzky 2015) and historically/culturally based for the later phases (in which radiocarbon cannot be used due to the Hallstatt plateau). We date the Iron I from the late twelfth century to around the middle of the tenth century BCE, the early Iron IIA until the very early ninth century; the late Iron IIA until the early eighth century, the Iron IIB until sometime in the first half to the middle of the seventh century BCE, and the Iron IIC thereafter, until 586 BCE.

Territorial expansion of Judah. Until the late Iron IIA the territory of Judah covered mainly the southern highlands, meaning that its extent was not different from that of the Late Bronze city-state of Jerusalem. Judah expanded to the Shephelah in the late Iron IIA, either before or after the destruction of Gath in the years following the middle of the ninth century BCE (Na'aman 2013a; Fantalkin and Finkelstein 2006; Sergi 2013, respectively). Here we focus on the Judahite, that is, eastern part of the Shephelah, acknowledging that several of the patterns observed below can also be identified in its western sector, which was dominated by Gath and later Ekron. Judah expanded to the Beersheba Valley around the middle of the ninth century, with the decline of the Tel Masos desert polity (Finkelstein 2014d).

Settlement patterns.[1] The Judean Highlands, characterized by rocky terrain, was sparsely settled until the late Iron IIA, which features the first demographic expansion south of Jerusalem. Settlement activity grew dramatically in the Iron IIB and continued uninterrupted in the Iron IIC. Similar patterns were identified in the settlement history of the kingdom's capital Jerusalem. The Shephelah was sparsely settled in the Iron I and early Iron IIA; activity grew in the late Iron IIA and peaked in the Iron IIB. Sennacherib's 701 BCE campaign caused severe devastation, but the

---

1. By *settlement patterns* we refer to sedentary activity; it goes without saying that the Beersheba Valley and the Judean Desert were also inhabited by pastoral nomads.

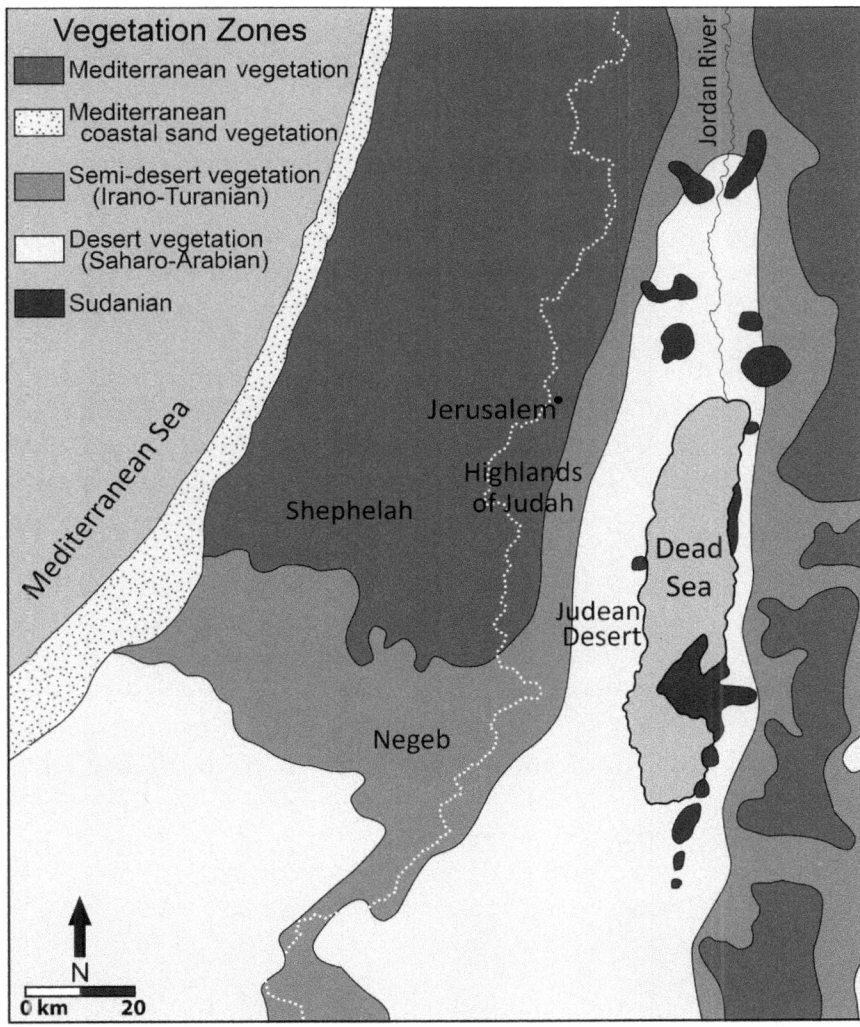

Fig. 20.1. The four geographical units and vegetation zones in Judah (for the latter, after Zohari 1962). The watershed is represented by a white dashed line.

region gradually recovered, although the settlement pattern changed: activity in the Iron IIC concentrated more in the main towns than in small villages and isolated farmhouses. Iron IIA activity in the Beersheba Valley was limited to several central sites, such as Tel Beersheba and the fort of Arad. Settlement activity in the region expanded in the Iron IIB and continued in the Iron IIC. Significant activity in the Judean Desert and the shores of the Dead Sea can be observed only in the Iron IIB–C (for all this, see ch. 15 above, with references).

Demographic growth in Judah. The dramatic growth in size and number of inhabitants of Jerusalem and in the settlement activity in the highlands and the Shephelah was probably the result of two factors. The first was the incorporation of the kingdom as a vassal into the Assyrian global system. In my view, the second was the migration of Israelites after the takeover of Israel by Assyria in 732–720 BCE (ch. 14 above, with references to previous studies).

Climate. The high-resolution, well-dated pollen records from the Sea of Galilee and the Dead Sea (Langgut et al. 2015) show a severe dryness phase circa 1250–1100 BCE, followed by an increase in arboreal percentages, representing humid conditions, between circa 1100–750 BCE (Langgut, Finkelstein, and Litt 2013). The latter phase covers most of the Iron I and Iron IIA. In circa 750–586 BCE (most of the Iron IIB and the Iron IIC), the region experienced moderate climatatic conditions (Finkelstein and Langgut 2018). These trends have recently been evaluated vis-à-vis oscillations in the settlement patterns along the fringe areas in the south and east of the southern Levant. The results show that climate is only one of the factors that influenced settlement and economic processes in the region in the Bronze and Iron Ages (Greener, Finkelstein, and Langgut 2018).

Terracing. Terraces cover over 60 percent of the landscape in the Jerusalem Highlands (Ron 1977) and considerable parts of the Judean Highlands farther to the south. Their construction resulted in a significant rise in the carrying capacity of these areas. Dating the terraces by conventional archaeological tools is difficult. A recent Optically Stimulated Luminescence (OSL) dating of soil supported by terrace walls shows that terracing became a meaningful component of agricultural activity in the region in the Hellenistic period. It has also been demonstrated that vast terracing is the product of land-management policies that engage large workforces (Elgart-Sharon, Porat, and Gadot 2020). Regarding the Iron Age, possible evidence for sporadic terracing was recorded at Nahal Shmuel northwest of Jerusalem (see below), but as a rule it seems that the dominant cultivation method was based on stone clearance and the exploitation of soil pockets between rock outcrops.

Terminology. The term *late Iron Age*, which is used below for Judah, signals the main part of the Iron IIB and the Iron IIC, meaning between circa 730 BCE and the destruction of the kingdom in 586 BCE. In other words, we refer to the Assyrian century in the history of Judah and the years that followed the withdrawal of Assyria from the region.

By *traditional Mediterranean economy*, we refer to the risk-reducing, self-sufficient subsistence economy of mixed dry farming, horticulture, and animal husbandry. The people of the Middle East have had the knowhow to engage in all three avenues of subsistence and to change the balance between them according to shifting historical, economic, and climatic conditions. By *specialized economy* we mean subsistence of a given area based mainly (but never solely) on a single crop. This was a high-risk/high-gain system that depended on the existence of regional markets and, equally significant, a strong centralized government that could react quickly to changing conditions, among them droughts.

Economic Patterns in the Late Iron Age

The Highlands

We start with the area west of Jerusalem, which has been intensively investigated and can therefore serve as an illustration for the highlands part of the kingdom. We will then comment on the broader picture of the highlands south of the city.

The site of ancient Jerusalem is located east of the highlands watershed, on the fringe of the Judean Desert (fig. 20.1). The immediate surroundings of the city are largely characterized by inhospitable, arid (in the east), and rocky terrain; few settlement sites from any period have been recorded in this area (Gadot 2015). The situation further to the west is different. This part of the hill country is dominated by two major valleys—the Soreq and the Rephaim—that merge circa 10 kilometers to the southwest of Jerusalem. Together with their tributaries, they served as the "food basket" of the city (Edelstein and Gibson 1982). Parts of these valleys feature rich alluvial soil suitable for dry farming, while the slopes could be used for vine and olive orchards; small springs located along their course could have been used for watering crops that required irrigation.

The late Iron Age marks an extraordinary intensification of rural activity in the Soreq and Rephaim Valleys (Gadot 2015). Sixty-five sites have been recorded in previous publications, and a few more have been excavated since then (e.g., Storchan 2015, 2017). The accumulated data allow reconstructing the subsistence base of at least some of the sites and establishing the hierarchy between them. The system can be described as four-tiered: (1) large sites that demonstrate signs of administrative function; (2) villages; (3) isolated buildings or farms; and (4) production spots such as winepresses not related to habitation sites.

West of Jerusalem, tier 1 is characterized by Tel Moza. Here thirty-seven large granaries were unearthed (Greenhut and De Groot 2009) that could store large quantities of grain from fields in the broad valley of the Soreq slightly to the northeast of the site. The fauna of the site also hints at its role in supplying animal products to the capital (Sapir-Hen, Gadot, and Finkelstein 2016). The limited number of handles with stamp impressions indicates that storing liquids, most probably wine or oil, was not an important component of the site's economy. Although slightly outside of the niche discussed here, the monumental, palatial center of Ramat Rahel should also be listed. While not a single silo was found there, and with animal economy typical of a consumer (to differ from production) site, the high number of stamped storage jars handles indicates Ramat Rahel's role as a collection center for taxes in kind (Lipschits et al. 2016).

Tier 2 constitutes villages such as Khirbet el-Burj and 'Alona to the northwest and Khirbet er-Ras to the southwest of Jerusalem. They feature large structures that were either built one next to the other or at some distance from each other (Weksler-Bdolah 1997 for 'Alona; Gadot 2015 for Khirbet er-Ras) and are surrounded by rock-cut agricultural installations, mainly winepresses.

Thirty-three sites may be classified as farms or single buildings (tier 3). They are not uniform in their ground plan; some were built just to fit the topography, while others were preplanned (Gadot and Bocher 2018). One example, unique in its size and number of rooms, is the Storeroom Building, part of a cluster of structures located along the upper Soreq Valley (Gadot et al. 2019). Other examples have a large courtyard in the front, surrounded by two or three wings (see, e.g., the building in Mamilla, immediately west of the boundary of Iron IIB–C Jerusalem; Amit 2011). The distribution of these structures all along the tributaries of the Rephaim and Soreq Valleys demonstrates the strong farming activities that took place in this region.

The main agro-production installations (tier 4) documented along the Rephaim and Soreq Valleys and their tributaries are the rock-cut winepresses that are found both inside settlements and in the countryside. Greenberg and Cinamon (2006) listed thirty-five Iron Age winepresses in the Rephaim Valley. Table 20.1 presents an updated count that includes similarly dated winepresses found along the Soreq Valley, as well as newly published ones from the Rephaim Valley. All in all, the number now stands at fifty-seven installations.

Table 20.1: Excavated and surveyed late
Iron Age winepresses along the Rephaim and Soreq Valleys

Site	Number	Valley	Reference
Rogem Ganim	8	Rephaim	Greenberg and Cinamon 2006
Giveat Massuah	5	Rephaim	Ovadiah 1994
Beit Safafa	4	Rephaim	Feig 2003
Manahat	16	Rephaim	Greenberg and Cinamon 2006
Khirbet er-Ras	2	Rephaim	Gadot 2015
Emeq Lavan	3	Rephaim	Storchan 2015
Ein Lavan	1	Rephaim	Baruch 2007
Nahal Draga	3	Kidron	Brzaily pers. comm.
Har Homa	1	Kidron	Sulimani 2012
Pisgat Zeev	1	Zimri	Meitilis 1992
Tell el-Ful	1	Soreq	Landes-Nagar 2014
Ramot Shlomo	1	Soreq	Storchan 2017
Ramot Forest	3	Soreq	Davidovich et al. 2006, Site 14/26
Nahal Shmuel	5	Soreq	see below
'Alona	2	Soreq	Weksler-Bdolah 1997
Wadi Ein Karem	1	Soreq	Gadot pers. comm.

Iron Age winepresses seem to feature one or two niches carved into the back wall of the treading surface (Amit and Yezerski 2001; for this type, see fig. 20.2). Excavation conducted by Gadot at Khirbet er-Ras seems to have unearthed direct evidence for this dating. Two winepresses were found at the site, both associated with late Iron Age structures. Especially apparent was the connection between Winepress I, which has a curved niche in its back wall, and Building II; the western external wall of the building also served the winepress (fig. 20.3), proving that the two were built together. An assemblage of at least twenty-three holemouth jars was found in the room just east of this winepress (Freud 2018, pl. 79). These jars, conclusively dated to the Iron IIC, were probably used to store wine produced at the site.

An illuminating example of the specialized wine industry in the highlands west of Jerusalem has been studied by Gadot and Langgut along the eastern slope of Nahal Shmuel. The slopes here were only sporadically terraced. Instead, intensive stone-clearance activities created small and shallow soil pockets between outcrops of limestone rock formations. More than fifty heaps of stones in various shapes and sizes were documented in a survey of the site. One of these was sampled using the OSL dating technique. The result shows that the soil at its base had last been exposed to sunlight 2,400+160 years ago, a date that fits the era after the Babylonian conquest until the early Hellenistic period. Five rock-cut winepresses, with rectangular niches fitted into their carved back wall, were also documented at the site. Remains of at least four stone-built structures were traced between the many stone piles. One such structure, located at mid-slope, was excavated. It is a rectangular platform measuring approximately 4.5 by 6.5 meters, made of large field stones, with no evidence for floor or partition walls. The structure was apparently used as a watchtower (for parallels in the traditional agriculture in the highlands in recent generations, see Ron 1977). The pottery found in the fill of the structure dates to the Iron IIC.

The Nahal Shmuel eastern slope was adapted in the Iron IIC to growing grapes for wine production. The grapes were planted in soil pockets between rock outcrops. We assume that the grapes were not trellised; rather, they were cultivated on the ground (see a picture from the early twentieth century in fig. 20.4). This cultivation method is more common in traditional agriculture when growing grapes for wine production, since contact with the ground promotes fruit ripening due to the heat. The small stone-built structures served as watchtowers and possibly also as temporary shelters for equipment and products, as well as to guard the area (for the Hellenistic–early Roman period in the western Samaria Highlands, see

20. The Unique Specialized Economy of Judah

Fig. 20.2. Iron Age winepress in the Jerusalem highlands characterized by the two small niches that were etched in the vertical rock wall at the back of the treading surface. The niches may have been used to install a wooden beam that was employed for secondary pressing of the crushed grapes.

Fig. 20.3. Winepress I and the southwest room of Building II at Khirbet er-Ras

Fig. 20.4. Harvesting of grapes in soil pockets in the Hebron hill country (early twentieth century). Grapes grown on the ground ripen early, at the beginning of the summer. In the background to the left one sees a watchtower located at midslope and a stone pile (Ayalon 2012, 95).

Applebaum, Dar, and Safrai 1978; for recent centuries in the highlands, see Ron 1977). An interesting textual reference to this kind of viticulture in the highlands can be found in Isa 5:1–2.

The Nahal Shmuel plots were part of a much larger wine industry. Rock-cut, jar-shaped cellars were found in clusters at several Iron Age sites in the Benjamin Plateau slightly to the north. The largest concentration, with as many as sixty-three cellars, was found at Gibeon (Pritchard 1964, 1–8). Pritchard interpreted them as storage facilities for aging wine. Twenty-four such cellars were found at the site of Khirbet el-Burj, located on a high hill overlooking Nahal Shmuel 2 kilometers from the winepresses described above (De Groot and Weinberg-Stern 2013). It seems that this site was the collection center for wine grown along the slopes of Nahal Shmuel and other nearby tributaries of the Soreq.

Contrary to the high number of winepresses found in the highlands west of Jerusalem, the number of Iron Age olive presses in this area is small. One such installation was found on the City of David ridge within a rock-cut room that was possibly used for cult activities during the early eighth century BCE. Three installations were found in villages surrounding the city.[2]

The spring system of Ein el-Joweizeh in the Rephaim Valley represents another aspect of activity in the Jerusalem Highlands. Water was directed via a long rock-cut and built tunnel into a collecting pool, from where it was probably channeled to irrigated plots on terraces below the

---

2. For the City of David, see Szanton 2013; for el-Burj, De Groot and Weinberg-Stern 2013; for Abu Shawan, Baruch 2007; for 'Alona, Weksler-Bdolah 1997.

spring. The monumentality of the spring house, which was equipped with stone-carved decorated capital (Ein Mor and Ron 2016), indicates that it was part of a public enterprise, possibly a royal estate in the style of an Assyrian *bitanu*. Indeed, the Ein el-Joweizeh setting may be compared to Assyrian reliefs depicting royal gardens (for the latter, see Asadpour 2018). Ein el-Joweizeh provides evidence that the method of rock-cut tunnels aimed at enlarging the flow of water from springs, which is typical of the highlands west of Jerusalem, was developed in the late Iron Age (Yechezkel and Frumkin 2019), hence other royal estates may have existed in this region.

The situation in the Judean hill country to the south of Jerusalem is less clear, due to the relative dearth of archaeological information. High altitude makes the Hebron area nonconducive to olive horticulture; hence this area was probably devoted to grape growing (for olive-tree habitat requirements, see Zinger 1985; Finkelstein and Langgut 2018). Indeed, this has been the situation in the region in recent generations. The reference to Ziph as one of the four toponyms in the *lmlk* seal impressions hints at the possibility of a royal estate south of Hebron. The Dead Sea Zeelim palynological record exhibits a significant decrease in olive pollen in the late Iron Age compared to the Iron I, probably indicating shrinkage of olive horticulture in the lower elevations of the southern highlands (Finkelstein and Langgut 2018; see fig. 20.5). Interestingly, grape pollen, which is usually underrepresented in palynological spectra, begins to appear in the Ein Gedi pollen diagram at the later stage of the eighth century BCE (Litt et al. 2012). Low arboreal values in the Dead Sea pollen records (Zeelim and Ein Gedi) during the Iron Age II do not reflect diminishing precipitation, as sediments along the lake were embedded in high lake levels (Langgut et al. 2014; Kagan et al. 2015). Rather, this must reflect the peak of settlement and agricultural activity, meaning massive deforestation in the Judean Highlands in the Iron IIB–C (Ofer 1994; ch. 15 above) in preparation of land for cultivation.

The Shephelah

While the archaeological and palynological evidence point to the expansion of viticulture in the Judean Highlands, a different picture emerges from the Shephelah. Large-scale olive horticulture in this part of the kingdom during the late Iron Age is evident by the widespread occurrence

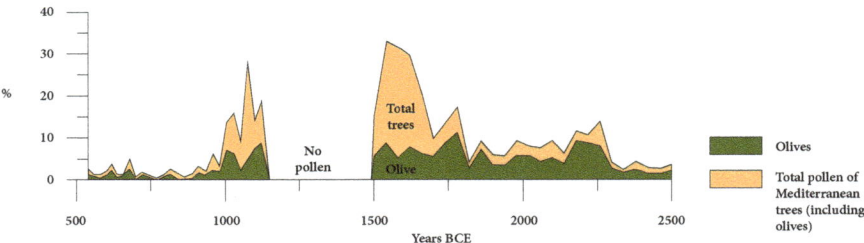

Fig. 20.5. Simplified pollen diagrams of the Dead Sea (Zeelim) record presenting paleoenvironmental reconstruction for the circa 2500–500 BCE time interval (after Finkelstein and Langgut 2018, fig. 2b)

of olive-oil installations.[3] Olive-oil presses are usually located not too far from the orchards in order to save the need to transport the raw material and as the oil extraction should take place no more than forty-eight hours after harvest, in order to avoid bitterness of the fruit.

To date, the earliest evidence of intensive olive-oil production in the Shephelah is attested at Tell eṣ-Ṣafi/Gath in the western (non-Judahite) sector of the region (Maeir, Welch, and Eniukhina 2020). Several such installations dating to the late Iron IIA were found in the lower city, indicating that much of this part of the settlement was dedicated to the production of olive oil. The takeover of the region by Assyria dramatically boosted its olive-oil industry. An unprecedentedly large olive-oil facility dated to the late Iron Age was identified at Tel Miqne-Ekron, also in the western Shephelah. Exhibiting over 115 installations, it is described as the largest olive-oil industry in antiquity (Gitin 1997; Eitam 1996). Additional evidence for olive-oil production in this part of the region during the late Iron Age was documented at Tel Batash, where excavations revealed several olive presses similar to those found at Tel Miqne-Ekron (A. Mazar 1997b, 1:262–63).

---

3. Studies of pollen in the Dead Sea do not testify to the Shephelah olive industry because pollen grains do not pass the barrier created by the massive block of the Judean Highlands (Finkelstein and Langgut 2018). Mid- to late Holocene palynological records west of the watershed are not available. Identification of charcoal assemblages from sites in the Shephelah is also challenging, since in most cases Iron Age strata were grouped together without attention to the subphases of the period (Liphschitz 2007).

Evidence of large-scale specialized olive oil production is also found at Judahite sites in the eastern Shephelah, which date to the Iron IIB before the Sennacherib campaign in 701 BCE. We refer to the olive presses found in the relevant layers at Tell Beit Mirsim and Beth-shemesh (Eitam 1979; Bunimovitz and Lederman 2009, respectively). Whether this industry developed with the incorporation of Judah as a vassal into the Assyrian economy in 732 BCE or commenced in a slightly earlier phase of the eighth century BCE is impossible to say with the data at hand. The large number of *lmlk* storage jars retrieved from Level III at Lachish (Lipschits, Sergi, and Koch 2011, 10) may also be related to the extensive olive-oil production in the Judahite Shephelah, suggesting royal control over olive-oil distribution. The Sennacherib Lachish relief, in which one of the most common plants can possibly be identified as an olive tree (Amar 1999), may provide another testimony for the cultural landscape of the Shephelah.

The town on the mound of Beth-shemesh was destroyed in 701 BCE (Bunimovitz and Lederman 2016, 70). Recent salvage excavations conducted immediately to the east of the tell revealed settlement activity in the later phase of the Iron Age (Haddad, Ben-Ari, and De Groot 2020). Extensive olive-oil production is evident from fourteen olive-oil presses (Z. Lederman, pers. comm.; Maeir, Welch, and Eniukhina 2020; Gross 2021). The Judahite olive orchards of the time must have sent their yields to be pressed both locally and in the central facility at Tel Miqne-Ekron.

The classic olive-orchard regions in the southern Levant are the Samaria Highlands and western Galilee (for recent generations, see Government of Palestine 1942–1943). The archaeological surveys show that the northern part of the former region did not suffer demographic decline after 720 (Zertal 1990), while settlement activity in its southern part, closer to the border of Judah, may have deteriorated (chs. 14 and 15 above). The shift to large-scale olive horticulture in the Shephelah in the late Iron Age, under Assyrian hegemony, seems to have been the result of an imperial decision. Production in the highlands, away from the main arteries of the southern Levant, was not convenient. Northern regions could have supplied enough oil to Assyria itself, and hence it is possible that the Shephelah industry, close to the main highway of the coastal plain, was directed at the market in Egypt.

Needless to say, not every plot in the Shephelah was devoted to olive orchards. This region was the breadbasket of Judah, and certain areas must have been devoted to dry farming, to supply grain for the locals, as well as for the growing population in Jerusalem in particular and the highlands in general.

The Beersheba Valley and the Judean Desert/Oases

Expansion of settlement activity in the Beersheba Valley was closely related to the prosperity of the Assyrian-dominated Arabian trade.[4] In the period discussed here, the main route of the Arabian trade passed along the Edomite highlands and then led, via the Beersheba Valley, to the Mediterranean coast. Buseirah in the highlands of Edom was probably the center of Assyrian administration in the region, featuring Assyrian-style architecture (e.g., Bennett 1982). The forts at Ein Hazeva and possibly Khirbet en-Nahas, seemingly garrisoned by local people, including Judahites (Na'aman 2001a), guarded the sector of the road where it crossed the Arabah Valley.[5] Remains of massive Iron Age brick architecture discovered in the area of the bedouin market in modern Beersheba (Fabian and Gilʻad 2010) may hint at the existence of an Assyrian center aimed at administering the valley. The fort at Kadesh-barnea, which was also manned by locals, including Judahites (Na'aman 2001a), may have served to block the western Arabian trade route, which led via northeastern Sinai and which was too remote (in the "deep" desert) for the Assyrians to control efficiently. In view of these observations, it is reasonable to suggest that the Beersheba Valley economy was "specialized" in services given to those who moved along the Arabian trade route. The inhabitants of the Judahite towns such as Tel ʻIra and Tel Beersheba could also have engaged in animal husbandry and opportunistic dry farming (the latter based on the precipitation in a given year). But they were not dependent on the grain from their vicinity; at least in dry years, grain must have been supplied by other regions of the kingdom, such as the Shephelah.

Parts of the Judean Desert, such as the Buqeiah Valley, could also have been exploited for opportunistic dry farming (for sites there, see Cross

---

4. Needless to say, transportation of Arabian goods to the Levant via the desert commenced in earlier phases of the Iron Age, if not before. This is seemingly hinted by the site of Kuntillet ʻAjrud, dated to the first half of the eighth century BCE.

5. For the date of the fort at Khirbet en-Nahas, see different opinions in Levy et al. 2004, 2016 versus Finkelstein and Piasetzky 2006a.

20. The Unique Specialized Economy of Judah

and Milik 1956). More important, the southern Jordan Valley and Dead Sea area—specifically, the oases of Jericho and Ein Gedi—were devoted to the cultivation of the Judean date palm and possibly exotic plants for the perfume industry such as the balsam tree. These crops require a special habitat characterized by high temperatures and very low humidity.

The archaeobotanical evidence points to the cultivation of date palms in this area since the Chalcolithic period (Zohary and Spiegel-Roy 1975). The Bible refers to Jericho as "the city of palms" (Deut 34:3) and draws a connection between Ein Gedi and palms (2 Chr 20:2).[6] By the fifth century BCE, Herodotus singles out the "Syrian" date (probably referring to the Judean variety) as being of the highest quality, with storage capability (*Hist.* 2.6.2); the latter quality must have added to its economic utility and trade value. Theophrastus, writing at the end of the fourth century BCE, remarks that Coele-Syria palms grow at the lowest part of the valley that extends from Syria to the Red Sea, where the soil is salty and where they are watered by the abundant natural springs (*Hist. plant.* 2.6.2, 5, 8). There can be little doubt that he refers to the area of Jericho and Ein Gedi. Theophrastus, too, notes the storing quality of these dates.

The question of cultivation of exotic plants such as the balsam for the perfume industry in this region is more enigmatic, since no botanical remains of such plants have been found. The balsam is frequently listed by ancient authors alongside the date palm as being a significant agricultural product unique to the Dead Sea area.[7] Especially noteworthy is Theophrastus, because of his specific interest in botany and for being the earliest among these authors (fourth to early third century BCE). Considering the data presented above for the Judah-Arabia connection, the Assyrian century is the most logical pre-Theophrastus time to be measured for the

---

6. Today date palms are artificially pollinated. Once the yellow dust from a male date palm is shaken above the flowers of a female tree, the fruit yield increases. It seems that the Assyrians were already aware of this method: a relief in the palace of Ashurnasirpal II shows a winged god dusting palm flowers with pollen; a similar motif is repeated in a number of other Assyrian reliefs.

7. Theophrastus, *Hist. plant.* 9.6.1–4; Diodorus Siculus, *Bibl. hist.* 2.48.9; 19.98; Strabo, *Geogr.* 16.2.41; 17.1.15; Pompeius Trogus (apud Justin), *Hist. Phil.* 36.3.1–7; Dioscorides Pedanius, *Mat. med.* 1.19.1; Pliny the Elder, *Nat.* 12.111; Tacitus, *Hist.* 4.6.1. Josephus says that it was introduced to the region as a gift to King Solomon by the queen of Sheba (*A.J.* 8.6.6).

introduction of large-scale cultivation of exotic plants to the region. We therefore suggest that Assyria made the oases of Jericho and Ein Gedi centers for cultivation of the globally appreciated Judean date palms and exotic plants that were brought from Arabia.

Another unique product of the Dead Sea region is bitumen.[8] This key resource could have been exported to Egypt by the coastal trading route.[9]

Discussion

Based on the data presented above, we suggest that the economy of Judah was transformed under Assyria (and initiated by the empire) from traditional Mediterranean subsistence to a sophisticated, region-based, specialized economy. As a compliant vassal, Judah benefited from the opportunities offered by the globalized economy of the empire.[10] The empire influenced every aspect of life in the kingdom; this can be observed in privately owned objects such as seals (Winderbaum 2012), in architecture (Ussishkin 1995; Gadot and Bocher 2018), in cult and religion (e.g., Ornan 2005), in the composition of texts (e.g., Van Seters 1990), and, perhaps most important, in administration.

---

8. In the Near East, bitumen can originate from five major areas: the city of Hit and surroundings and Mosul in modern Iraq; the area of southwestern Iran; the Dead Sea (Connan and Van de Velde 2010); and Abu Durba and Gebel Zeit on the shores of Egypt's Gulf of Suez (Harrell and Lewan 2002). Natural asphalt from the Dead Sea could be gathered from the deposits on the shore of the lake or occasionally during periods of intensification in seismic activity, when it was found floating on the water surface.

9. Although the Gulf of Suez seeps were much closer to Egypt, it seems that the ancient Egyptians favored the Dead Sea bitumen. This is perhaps due to its semisolid nature, which enabled it to be more portable. Additionally, the Dead Sea area was linked to Egypt by a well-established coastal trading route, whereas bitumen from the Gulf of Suez would have to be brought either across the rugged mountains of the Eastern Desert or up the Gulf of Suez by a circuitous route as long as the direct one from the Dead Sea (Harrell and Lewan 2002).

10. For the impact of Assyria on Judah, see, e.g., Na'aman 1995b; Thareani 2016; Koch 2018. Contra, e.g., Stager 1996; Faust 2021, who contest the theory regarding the impact of Assyria on Judah.

The stage setting for these developments was the unique geographical background of Judah, which is characterized by varied topography and climate, on the one hand, and access to international roads in the south and west, on the other.

Under Assyria, the kingdom exploited each of its special ecological niches in an optimal way. Cultivation in the highlands west of Jerusalem specialized in viticulture; judging from the palynological record of the Dead Sea (Finkelstein and Langgut 2018), this must also have been the situation in the Judean Hill Country south of the city. The Gibeon Plateau to the north of the capital was probably devoted to grain growing and, in part, to viticulture. At least a portion of the viticulture operation northwest, west, and southwest of Jerusalem seems to have been practiced in royal estates (ch. 19 above).

The Shephelah was divided between dry farming and olive orchards aimed at the oil industry. The latter was managed by the Assyrians, with production directed mainly at Egypt.

The economy of the Negev (Beersheba Valley) towns and forts was based on services given to the transportation of goods along the Arabian trade route: protection of movement along the southern fringe of Judah and providing supplies to travelers passing through. Several archaeological finds back this description, among them the khan unearthed at Aroer (Thareani-Sussely 2007), South Arabian inscriptions discovered at this site (Thareani 2011, 228; and in Jerusalem, Shiloh 1987b), and reference to the "towns of Judah" in a South Arabian inscription dated to circa 600 (Lemaire 2012), probably echoing a situation that started before, during the Assyrian century. In the biblical text, the participation of Judah in the Arabian trade under Assyrian hegemony is probably represented by the tale of the queen of Sheba's visit to King Solomon in Jerusalem (Finkelstein and Silberman 2006a, 167–71).

The economy of the Judean Desert focused on animal husbandry and the opportunistic growing of grain in the Buqeiah Valley. More important to the economy, however, was the date-palm industry and (possibly) growing balsam in the oases of Ein Gedi and Jericho. The qualities of these plants are clear: the former a delectable (and, perhaps more important, storable) fruit; the latter a fragrant medicinal resin. Based on historical sources, the Judean dates and balsam attained world reputation no later than the middle of the first millennium BCE, and it is only logical to suggest that the origin of this phenomenon was in the late Iron Age under

Assyria. Bitumen is another unique product of the Dead Sea region that could have been exported via the coastal trading route.

The unique economic system of Judah in the Assyrian century and thereafter, until the destruction of the kingdom, may explain some of the most characteristic features of the material culture of the kingdom, as well as the historical background of a key biblical text.

The first is the system of seal impressions and incisions on handles of storage jars, unique to the Southern Kingdom. We refer to the early *lmlk* impressions of the late eighth century, the late *lmlk* impressions of the early seventh century, the concentric incisions of the seventh century, and the rosette impressions of the late seventh century and early sixth centuries BCE (Lipschits, Sergi, and Koch 2011; Lipschits 2021). Scholars proposed that this system was related to the Assyrian rule over Judah (e.g., Lipschits, Sergi, and Koch 2010, 7). However, of all the Levantine kingdoms that were under Assyrian domination, Judah is the only one where such impressions/incisions appear. Above we demonstrated the unique, sophisticated specialized economy of Judah under Assyria. This system seems to have stimulated the development of advanced administration, including the collection of liquid commodities (wine, oil, and other beverages) as tax to be paid to Assyria and support of the palace and temple in the capital. No less important, in a situation of risky specialized economy, resourceful control over the products ensured quick reaction in times of crisis such as sudden droughts. The development of a unique specialized economy—not known in other kingdoms in the region—and singular system of impressing storage jars can hardly be seen as coincidence; the impression/incision system was probably connected to the control over the economy of the kingdom. The system of weights, also unique to Judah (Kletter 1998), is probably another manifestation of the particular specialized economy of the Southern Kingdom.

Another obvious feature of the material culture of Judah between the late eighth and early sixth centuries BCE is the dramatic dissemination of writing, which is especially expressed in the large number of ostraca and inscribed bullae (Faigenbaum-Golovin et al. 2016; Shaus et al. 2020; ch. 12 above). Most Judahite ostraca were found in the arid part of the kingdom, in the Beersheba Valley (e.g., Na'aman 2015). However, Edom and Moab, also characterized by arid areas, did not produce a similar number of ostraca. Today, bullae are identified in wet sifting, which is practiced in Israel but seemingly not in Jordan. Still, even before the introduction of this method, the number of bullae in Judah was far larger than in other kingdoms in the region. This phenomenon, too—the expansion of writing in the administration of the kingdom—unparalleled in the neighboring kingdoms, may be at least partly connected to the unique structure of the specialized Judahite economy. The risky system demanded organization of markets, transportation, and exchange and thus sophisticated bureaucracy.

On the side of the biblical text, attention should be given to the list of towns of Judah in Josh 15. The towns are grouped according to the kingdom's four geographical areas: Negev (Beersheba Valley), hill country, Shephelah, and desert (Judean Desert). In modern scholarship, the list is interpreted as depicting the administration of the kingdom in the days of King Josiah, in the second half of the seventh century (Na'aman 1991). However, we should ask: Why is the time of Josiah depicted and not the days of Manasseh in the first half of the seventh century, the peak period of Judah under Assyrian domination? The affiliation of the list with the days of Josiah is based mainly on the archaeology of sites mentioned in it, which seem to have been established in the Iron IIC (Na'aman 1991). Yet the Iron IIB/C transition occurred sometime in the first half to the middle of the seventh century, meaning in the time of Manasseh. Even if the composition comes from the days of Josiah, the organization of the kingdom into districts, emphasizing its geographical division, must have been put in place in the Assyrian century in the history of Judah and related to the unique specialized economy of the kingdom at that time.

Summary

Late Iron Age Judah features several unique phenomena among the territorial kingdoms of the southern Levant, stemming from each other:

- The geographical background: division into four distinctive regions, described in the Bible as highlands, Shephelah, Negev (the Beersheba Valley), and desert (the Judean Desert and shore of the Dead Sea).
- Economic specialization in these regions, focusing on viticulture in the highlands, olive-oil industry in the Shephelah, services to the Arabian trade route in the Beersheba Valley, and a date and

(possibly) exotic-plant industry in the oases of Jericho and Ein Gedi, with animal husbandry and dry farming practiced in all niches.
- Advanced administration apparatus to oversee centralized storage and distribution of agricultural products, represented by seal impressions and incisions on handles of storage jars, inscribed bullae, inscribed weights, and the dramatic expansion of literacy far beyond the capital of the kingdom.

The geographical background is a given, but it was not exploited in the same way in the early days of Judah, in the Iron IIA. The transformation of the kingdom from typical mixed Mediterranean subsistence agriculture to high-risk/high-gain specialized, region-based economy, which called for the development of elaborate administration, was an outcome of the incorporation of Judah as a vassal into the Assyrian global economy, in fact, probably an initiative of the empire.

Part 5
The Iron IIC

21

The Acts of Solomon:
The Impact of Jeroboam II of Israel and Manasseh of Judah

> In this part of the book, I discuss the seventh century BCE. Here I propose that the Book of the Acts of Solomon was composed in the days of King Manasseh, incorporating realities of both Manasseh's day and earlier ones that originated from eighth-century BCE Israel.

Three different Solomons appear on the stage of 1 Kings. The first comes into view in 1 Kgs 1–2, at the end of the Succession History; he is a somewhat passive figure dominated by his mother Bathsheba who ascends the throne and purges his enemies. The second is the great Solomon of 1 Kgs 3–10: the idyllic, wise monarch, builder of the temple, great trader with far-off lands, peaceful ruler of his vast kingdom. Parts of these chapters were described as deriving from a text described as the "the Book of the Acts of Solomon" (1 Kgs 11:41). The third Solomon is the old, somewhat pathetic and sinful sovereign of 1 Kgs 11 whose apostasy leads to the division of the illustrious united monarchy. It is impossible to reconcile these accounts, especially the last two, as characteristic of a single individual, so we can safely assume that they represent layers of the text that come from different periods and concerns. The Succession History, or Court History, has in several places an "ambiance" that is probably influenced by the time of Jeroboam II in Israel in the first half of the eighth century BCE (Sergi 2017b). About fifteen years ago, Neil Silberman and I suggested that this text was composed in the days of Hezekiah in the late eighth century BCE, against the background of dramatic demographic transformations in Jerusalem in particular and in Judah in general following the fall of the Northern Kingdom (Finkelstein and Silberman 2006a, 121–49; ch. 15

above). The section 1 Kgs 11:1–10 (or 13) is typically Deuteronomistic in theology and language; it is an "answer" to the chapters on the great Solomon, a sort of a warning about the outcome of globalization and success.[1] If this comes from the hands of the Josianic author in the late seventh century, the second Solomon, that of 1 Kgs 3–10, is "trapped" into the time slot between the late eighth century and the late seventh century. This makes sense considering what we know about the ability to compose literary texts in Judah (ch. 12 above).

But what is the background for the Book of the Acts of Solomon, and what was the reason for its composition? To answer these questions, I wish to concentrate here on key episodes in 1 Kgs 3–10.[2] The following notions stand behind what follows.

1. The description of a glamorous united monarchy is not historical; rather, it describes a great kingdom to be. It comes from the pens of the Josianic Deuteronomistic Historian and is based on memories of the realities of Israel (the Northern Kingdom) in the early eighth century (Finkelstein 2020d).
2. There is no evidence of writing in Judah before the late eighth century BCE. The earliest literary texts known from Israel—the Tell Deir ʿAlla and Kuntillet ʿAjrud plaster inscriptions—date to the first half of the eighth century (and in any event not before 800 BCE); the earliest such text from Judah is Ostracon 1 from Horvat Uza in the Negev (Beit-Arieh 1993; Naʾaman 2013b), which dates to the seventh century BCE. The beginning and dissemination of writing in Judah was influenced by the incorporation of the kingdom into the Assyrian administration and the impact of Israel and Israelites on the Southern Kingdom (chs. 20 and 14).
3. I am exceedingly doubtful about the possibility of composition of elaborate texts in Persian period Yehud (ch. 23).

Naʾaman has recently dealt with the Acts of Solomon (Naʾaman 2019), using as support the background of ancient Near Eastern records, and

---

1. This is one reason of many why the Solomon account in Kings is not a Josianic composition (contra Knauf 1991).

2. I will not deal with the gigantic body of literature on Solomon in the Bible, including discussions of his wisdom and the construction of the temple.

suggested dating this supposed text to the last years of the eighth century BCE. I wish to take a different approach; episodes that may be understood as originating from the Acts of Solomon include specific geographical or thematic references that can be studied against archaeological findings and the shifting historical realities of the Iron Age. Studying them can illuminate the stage setting behind the description of Solomon in 1 Kgs 3–10.

The Stage Setting of the Acts of Solomon

I suggest that the Acts of Solomon include references to realities of two periods: the prosperity of the Northern Kingdom in the days of Jeroboam II in the first half of the eighth century BCE; and the days of Manasseh in Judah in the first half of the seventh century BCE.

Solomon and Jeroboam II

Hazor, Megiddo, and Gezer. The first verse to discuss is the famous 1 Kgs 9:15, recounting Solomon's building of Hazor, Megiddo, and Gezer (for the latter also 9:17). These three cities never belonged to Judah, not even Gezer. Rather, they were the most important lowlands administrative centers in Israel: Hazor in the upper Jordan Valley, Megiddo in the Jezreel Valley, and Gezer in the coastal plain, in the southwestern sector of the kingdom's territory. The three prospered in the days of the Omride dynasty in the first half of the ninth century and under the later Nimshides in the first half of the eighth century. Megiddo seems to have experienced an occupational hiatus in the last decades of the ninth century, and Hazor was probably under Damascene rule at that time. After 732 BCE, Israel lost control of all three. Therefore, regarding 1 Kgs 9:15, I propose to put the spotlight on the early Iron IIB in the first half of the eighth century. Hazor prospered at that time (Stratum VII). At Megiddo (Stratum IVA) two stable compounds were constructed (more below), together with an elaborate four-chambered gate, a city wall, a water system, and an administrative center (Building 338). Gezer was fortified with the Outer Wall. I would therefore argue that the reference to these three cities in 1 Kgs 9:15 preserves the memory of their golden age in the days of Jeroboam II.

Baalath. Another town mentioned as having been built by Solomon is Baalath (1 Kgs 9:18). A place named Baalath also appears in the list of towns of the tribe of Dan, in a group together with Eltekeh and Gibbethon (Josh 19:44). Eltekeh and Gibbethon are located on the coastal plain, in the area of modern Rehovot and Ramle (for the possible identifications, see the entries in *ABD*). My recent excavations (with Thomas Römer and Christophe Nicolle of the Collège de France) at Kiriath-jearim in the highlands, to the east of this area, revealed evidence of monumental building activity at the site in the first half of the eighth century BCE (summary in Finkelstein, Römer, and Nicolle 2020). Kiriath-jearim is also known in the Bible as Kiriath-baal and Baalah, so it is tempting to identify Baalath of 1 Kgs 9:18 with this place.[3] Note that three of the places referred to in 1 Kgs 9 as having been built by Solomon—Gezer, Beth-horon (the two appear together in v. 17), and Baalath (whether at Kiriath-baal/Kiriath-jearim or somewhere near Ramle)—create a group on the border between Israel, Judah, and Ashdod. An obvious difficulty in this identification is the listing of Baalath as a Danite town with Eltekeh and Gibbethon—both on the coastal plain—while Kiriath-baal/Kiriath-jearim is a Benjaminite/Judahite town in the highlands. However, a connection between the tribe of Dan and Kiriath-jearim is made in Judg 18:12. Also note the link between Kiriath-jearim and the Danite towns of Zorah and Eshtaol, located in the Shephelah north of Beth-shemesh, in the genealogies of Judah (1 Chr 2:53). If the Danite list is a late addition to the Josianic list of towns of Judah,[4] its author may have added Baalath out of confusion.[5]

Horses, stables, and chariots. Horses, stables, and cities of chariots feature several times in the Acts of Solomon (1 Kgs 5:6 [Eng. 4:26]; 9:19, 22; 10:26). Moreover, Solomon trades Egyptian horses to the kingdoms of the north (10:28–29). The only possible background for this description is in the early Iron IIB, in the first half of the eighth century. I refer to the seventeen stables in two groups uncovered in Stratum IVA at Megiddo, which effectively turned Megiddo, an administrative city in the fertile Jezreel Valley, into a center of horse industry. The horses were probably

---

3. This possibility is also discussed in Cogan 2001, 302; Shipp 2011, 210.
4. On the tribal list of Dan in relation to the towns of Judah, see detailed discussion in Na'aman 1991.
5. Tamar "in the wilderness" is mentioned in the same breath with Baalath (v. 18). The identification of this place is not clear (summary in Ahituv 1982), but activities of Jeroboam II in the desert at Kuntillet 'Ajrud and possibly the head of the Gulf of Aqaba (Finkelstein 2014a) should be noted.

brought from Egypt, bred and trained at Megiddo, and then sold to the powers of the period, first and foremost the Assyrian Empire; this seems to have been one of the major sources for the prosperity of Israel at that time (Cantrell and Finkelstein 2006). Level III at Lachish also seems to feature a set of stables (Ussishkin 2004e, 86–87; 2004c, 831–34); the early days of this layer were probably around the middle of the eighth century BCE. There are strong reasons to argue that, following the victory of Joash over Amaziah (the chronistic verses in 2 Kgs 14:11–13), Israel dominated, if not ruled over, Judah, hence the construction of the stables at Lachish can possibly be understood as a northern endeavor.[6] Based on the Megiddo evidence, the historical king of horses and stables was Jeroboam II; he is the prototype for the description of Solomon as the king who traded Egyptian horses to the north.

The Solomonic districts. The reality behind the list of Solomonic districts in 1 Kgs 4 has been debated. Several scholars adhered to the biblical tradition, dating the list to the tenth century BCE.[7] With the dismissal of the historicity of the united monarchy and the realization that there is no evidence for Hebrew writing in Israel and Judah before circa 800 BCE, it has become clear that this theory should be rejected. Accordingly, Na'aman interpreted the list as reflecting the Assyrian province system in the region in the late eighth century BCE (Na'aman 2001b). He considered the possibility that the Assyrians inherited the district system of the Northern Kingdom but finally dismissed it because of the appearance of the region of Argob (in the Bashan), "which was a Damascene territory in the early first millennium BCE" (Na'aman 2001b, 432).

This is not a strong argument, as the expansion of Israel to the Bashan is hinted at in the reference to Karnaim in Amos 6:13. The list in 1 Kgs 4 speaks about a territory from the land of Benjamin in the south to Naphtali in the north in Cisjordan, and from the border of Moab near the northern tip of the Dead Sea in the south to the Bashan in the north in Transjordan. The only historical fit for this territory is the Northern Kingdom in

---

6. A building identified as a stable has recently been unearthed in Level 3 at Beth-shemesh (Zvi Lederman, pers. comm.). This layer was probably destroyed in the 765–745 BCE time slot (Finkelstein and Piasetzky 2007). Already in the years before this event, Beth-shemesh could have been ruled by Israel.

7. Niemann 1997; Kamlah 2001, in the footsteps of Alt 1953, 76–89; see the history of research in Ash 1995.

the first half of the eighth century. Three points are of importance: (1) the expansion of Israel to the northern upper Galilee and Dan in the upper Jordan Valley occurred in this period (e.g., Arie 2008); (2) the *mishor* in northern Moab, which was conquered by the Omrides and lost to Mesha, is indeed missing from the list; (3) the southern Bashan, apparently conquered by Jeroboam II (Amos 6:13) is included. Hence the list in 1 Kgs 4 is based on the administrative division of Israel in the days of Jeroboam II (see also Lee Sak 2023).

Na'aman, following others, interpreted 1 Kgs 4:19 in the list as referring to the district of Judah (Na'aman 2001b, 422–23, with references). This likewise fits the first half of the eighth century, following the defeat of Amaziah at the hands of Joash in the battle of Beth-shemesh. That Joash "broke down the wall of Jerusalem" (2 Kgs 14:13) probably means the subjugation of the Southern Kingdom. The list may therefore portray the united monarchy ideology in Israel: all the territory of the two Hebrew kingdoms "from Dan to Beersheba" (for Solomon, see 1 Kgs 5:5 [Eng. 4:25]) ruled by an Israelite king from Samaria.[8] The description of the rule of Solomon over the people of Israel "from Lebo Hamath to the Brook of Egypt," that is, from the Valley of Lebanon to Nahal Besor in the area of Gaza, also fits this period, assuming that in the south Jeroboam inherited the territory that had been ruled by Hazael in the decades before his own reign.

King Hiram of Tyre and the land of Cabul. The relationship of Solomon with Hiram king of Tyre is central to the Acts of Solomon. A historical Hiram of Tyre is mentioned in the Assyrian records from the days of Tiglath-pileser III; he came to the throne circa 739 BCE (Na'aman 2019, 80). Based on the Tyrian king list recounted by the second-century BCE historians Menander and Dius, who are cited by Josephus (*C. Ap.* 1.113–115, 117–119), this Hiram is labeled Hiram II, while Hiram of the days of Solomon is labeled by scholars Hiram I. Most scholars accepted the latter as a historical figure (Na'aman 2019, with references). However, this is a circular argument, as Menander and Dius could have taken his name, and his "early" association, from the biblical episode regarding the relationship of Solomon with a Hiram of Tyre.

---

8. Finkelstein 2020d. Note that the Northern Kingdom's expansion to Dan took place in the early eighth century (e.g., Arie 2008).

The eighth-century Hiram came to the throne several years after the death of Jeroboam and ruled in the period of the decline in the power of the Northern Kingdom. Indeed, the episode of the land of Cabul (1 Kgs 9:11–14) may reflect this phase in the history of Israel. In any event, the use of his name comes from Israelite memories of the eighth century BCE.

Pharaoh's daughter. Let me speculate on another matter. According to 1 Kgs 3–10, Solomon married a daughter of a pharaoh (3:1; 7:8; 9:16, 24). One wonders about the origin of this tradition, utterly out of context for small, powerless Judah. Of course, the reference to Solomon's marriage to the daughter of a pharaoh may have entered only in order to boost the stature of late monarchic Judah. But what about Israel? Jeroboam I is said to have fled to Egypt (1 Kgs 11:40), and the LXX (3 Kgdms 12e) says that he married an Egyptian princess.[9] Is it possible that Jeroboam I stands here for Jeroboam II, who could have married an Egyptian princess in order to strengthen his economic endeavors, first and foremost his equine business (see above)?[10]

Solomon and Manasseh

Two episodes in the Acts of Solomon refer to the role of Judah in Arabian trade: the visit of the queen of Sheba to Jerusalem (1 Kgs 10:1–13); and the building of ships "at Ezion-geber, which is near Eloth on the shore of the Red Sea" (9:26) and the trade expedition to Ophir. Scholars have suggested dating these texts to the Persian period (de Pury 2003; Römer 2008, 128–29, Lipinski 2010; Na'aman 2019, 78 n. 16). I see no historical logic for a Yehud author to include these materials in his work.[11] Rather, I suggest that the reality behind them is the participation of Judah in the Arabian trade endeavor as a vassal of the Assyrian Empire. I refer to the Assyrian century in the region, from 732 BCE to the withdrawal of Assyria from the area circa 630 BCE. Of course, trade expeditions could have continued to operate in the later decades of the seventh century and early sixth century BCE. Evidence for this scenario is abundant: the Assyrian (or Assyrian-initiated) constructions

---

9. On the possibility that the LXX preserves an old, pre-Deuteronomistic tradition, see Schenker 2000.

10. On the play between Jeroboam I and II, see Römer 2017.

11. I see little evidence for the composition of biblical texts in Persian period Jerusalem (see ch. 23 in this volume).

of forts in the south, at Hazeva and Tell el-Kheleifeh; the Assyrian-influenced edifices at Buseirah in the highlands of Edom, probably the headquarters of their activity in the south; Neo-Assyrian records referring to Arabian queens; South Arabian inscriptions found at Aroer and Jerusalem (Thareani 2011, 228; Shiloh 1987b, respectively); and, last but not least, the mention of the "towns of Judah" in a Sabaean inscription, probably dating to circa 600 BCE (Lemaire 2012).

The reference to Ezion-geber should be understood against the same background. There are two possible locations at the head of the Gulf of Aqaba for Ezion-geber and Eilat/Eloth: the fort at Tell el-Kheleifeh and the site of historical Aqaba. The earliest activity at the former is seemingly a small early eighth-century fort (Finkelstein 2014a); the main phase of activity there should be dated to the late eighth and seventh centuries BCE (Pratico 1993). No Iron Age remains have thus far been found at Aqaba.

But when during the Assyrian century is the best stage setting for the two episodes, and when and why was the Acts of Solomon composed? Archaeology and historical circumstances cannot supply the answer. One needs to turn back to the broader logic of the biblical text and the goals of the author.

The Historical and Ideological Stage Setting behind the Acts of Solomon

Two factors are essential for understanding the motivation behind the composition of the Book of the Acts of Solomon. The first is the migration of large groups of Israelites to Judah after 720 BCE; the second is the ideological struggles within Judah, which find expression in the tension between the two presentations of Solomon: the positive in the Acts of Solomon; and the negative in 1 Kgs 11.[12] Against this background, I propose that three ideas stand behind the presentation of the king in the Acts of Solomon.

---

12. See Morton Smith's description (1971) of two parties in late-monarchic Jerusalem—Yahwistic and syncretistic.

1. Justification of international commerce. This is expressed in the episodes on horse trading, the relationship with Phoenicia, and participation in Arabian trade. The internationalization of Judah in these activities is then condemned in the Deuteronomistic 1 Kgs 11. The lesson is clear: international relations, openness to neighbors, and its resulting economic prosperity leads to intermarriage, which in turn results in apostasy and disaster.
2. Competition with the memories of the great Jeroboam II of Israel, brought to Judah by Israelites after 720 BCE. Many of those who moved to Judah probably belonged to the upper echelon of Israelite society, among them the literati, who feared deportation. They must have brought with them Israelite traditions that were later incorporated into the Judahite texts. These included not only tales such as the Jacob cycle and heroic feats in Judges but also royal traditions, among them the memory of the great Jeroboam II, in whose time Israel flourished as never before and de facto ruled over the territories and people of the two Hebrew kingdoms. The Acts of Solomon is a "reminder" that there was a great king in Jerusalem before Jeroboam II who prospered economically and ruled over the territory of the two Hebrew kingdoms combined, from Dan to Beersheba.
3. Connected to number 2 is the preservation of the northern idea of a united monarchy in reverse—ruled by a Davidic king from Jerusalem. The Judahite pan-Israelite idea must have emerged following the fall of the Northern Kingdom, in the days of Hezekiah, and was preserved and probably elaborated through to the days of Josiah.

The king under whose reign all three concerns find their place is Manasseh, who ruled in Jerusalem for fifty-five years. He was a compliant vassal of Assyria, and during his rule the participation of Judah in southern trade reached its peak. Judah prospered as never before, thanks to this openness to the lands around it. The description of Solomon as a great merchant blessed by God was aimed to give him legitimacy in the eyes of the Deuteronomistic camp. Recent finds in the vicinity of Jerusalem demonstrate that Manasseh was also engaged in significant building activities (ch. 22 below), and under his reign the proportion of Israelites in the population of Judah swelled. No less important, the description of Solomon as a world-class monarch—similar to an Assyrian king—provided Judah with a glorious past and a sense of importance (Römer 2008) relative to the real great Israelite kingdom—the Northern Kingdom in the days of the Omrides and Jeroboam II.

Finally, dating the Acts of Solomon to the days of Manasseh also makes sense regarding the sequence of the three Solomons in 1 Kings: the Succession History before, perhaps in the days of Hezekiah, and the sinful king after, in the days of Josiah.

22

The Sites of Mordot Arnona and Armon HaNatziv on the Southern Outskirts of Jerusalem: An Alternative Archaeological and Historical Interpretation

In this chapter I put the spotlight on monumental building activity on the southern outskirts of Jerusalem in the days of King Manasseh (the first half to the middle of the seventh century) and on the first evidence for King Josiah's reform that followed.

The late Iron II sites of Mordot Arnona (Hebrew: the slope of the [modern] Arnona neighborhood) and Armon HaNatziv (Hebrew: governor's residency) are located in close proximity to each other on the ridge of the British Mandatory Government House, on the southern outskirts of Jerusalem (fig. 22.1). The two sites and nearby Ramat Rahel were active in approximately the same period, the seventh century BCE, and show resemblances in architecture (especially Armon HaNatziv and Ramat Rahel) and in features of administration (Mordot Arnona and Ramat Rahel). The two new digs (Mordot Arnona and Armon HaNatziv), as well as the older one (Ramat Rahel), shed important light on the material culture and history of late monarchic Judah. Preliminary reports on the results of these excavations, including historical interpretation of the finds, have recently been published.[1] In what follows, I will present an alternative archaeological and historical interpretation of the remains.

---

1. Sapir et al. 2022 for Mordot Arnona; Billig, Freud, and Bocher 2022 for Armon HaNatziv.

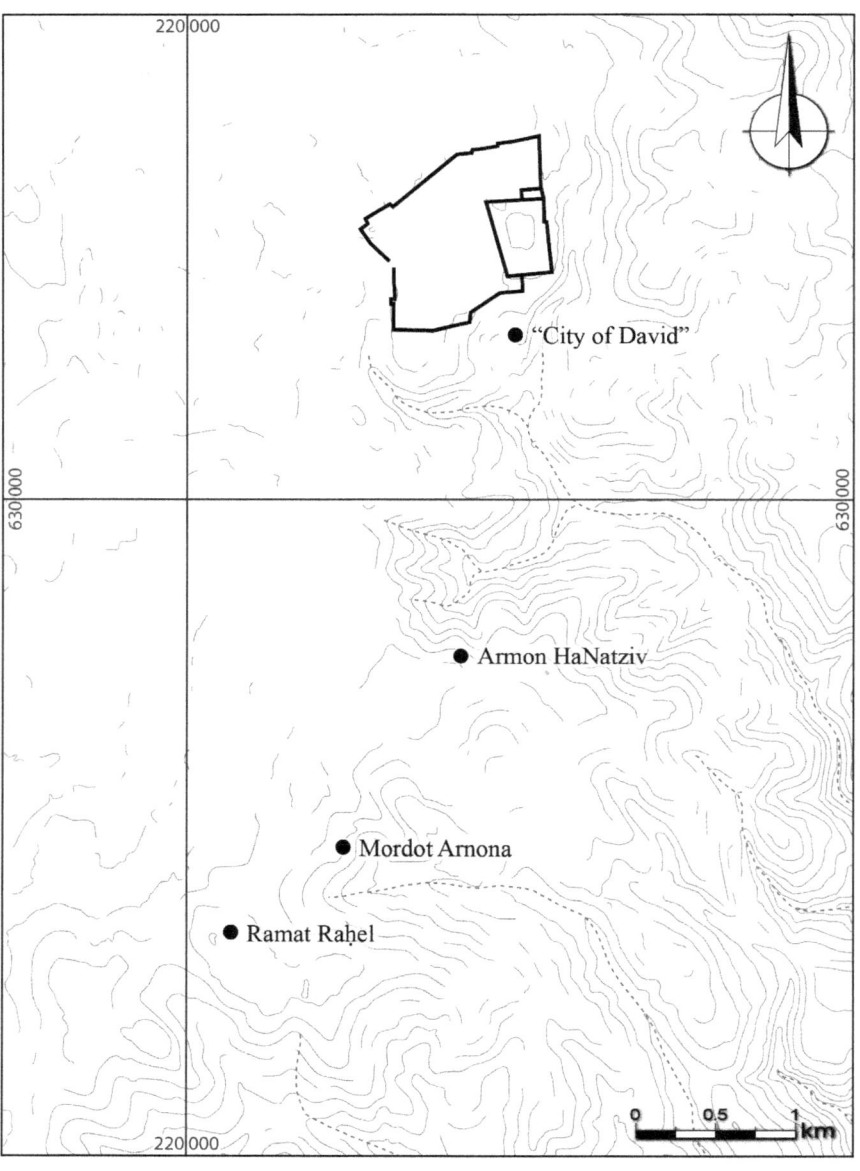

Fig. 22.1. Map indicating the location of the sites discussed in this chapter (based on Sapir et al. 2022, fig. 1).

Mordot Arnona

The site is located about 1 kilometer to the northeast of Ramat Rahel, on the upper eastern slope of the ridge (fig. 22.1). Its importance is in the remains of monumental walls established on bedrock, the huge stone heap, and the exceptional number of late monarchic Judahite seal impressions. Regarding this site, I suggest an alternative interpretation of its construction phases.

The Excavators' Description and Interpretation

The information on the results of the excavation is spread in different parts of the excavators' report (Sapir et al. 2022), sometimes with data on a given phase appearing in the description of another phase and in some cases with the information presented only in the discussion. Hence, I will first summarize the excavators' interpretation consistently (and concisely).

Area A at the site (Sapir et al. 2022, fig. 5), the main focus of the excavation, is described as featuring nine construction phases, covering the centuries from the Iron IIA to the late Roman period. I will deal here mainly with the most significant four: Phases 6c–a, dated to the Iron IIB–C (Phase 6d is represented by a rock-cut pit of the Iron IIA); and Phase 5, dated to the sixth to fourth centuries BCE.

Phase 6c includes elements that preceded the construction of a big stone heap. It features a quarry that supplied stones for the construction of the monumental building of Phase 6b, the presumed building that existed on a platform on top of the stone heap. The excavators refer to the possible existence of a monumental structure in this phase that was dismantled prior to the construction of the stone heap. Another feature of this phase is a layer of soil uncovered between the stone heap and Wall 2017. A similar layer was found above bedrock, below Building 2474 of Phase 6a (Sapir et al. 2022, 43). It contained late Iron IIB pottery. Phase 6c is also associated with private seal impressions and early *lmlk* seal impressions. It was therefore built in the late eighth century and dismantled at the end of that century or the early seventh century.

Phase 6b is characterized by the most prominent feature of the site: a very large stone heap (fig. 22.2) that was surrounded by stone walls and hence was seemingly well-planned. It covered an area of 0.4 hectares.[2] The

---

2. According to Sapir et al. 2022, fig. 5, 60 meters on a north–south axis.

excavation of large parts of the stone heap exposed three walls: 2017, 2121, and 2772. Wall 2017, established on bedrock, was found on the western side of the stone heap and is described as marking its western boundary. Monolithic limestones, which could be assigned to Phase 6c, were incorporated in Wall 2017 "in secondary use" (Sapir et al. 2022, 40; see fig. 7). Wall 2021 in the north, also established on bedrock, was covered by the stone heap. Part of this wall was built over Wall 2772, which was part of the stone heap. These walls seem to have had a supportive function: to stabilize the stone heap. The excavators suggested that a large platform was built on top of the stone heap. Its foundations are made of two parallel walls in its north and south (2334, 2220 and 2502, 2503 respectively) and three walls in the east (2224, 2276, and 2757). Only small wall stabs were preserved in the west, a sector that was damaged by quarrying activity in later periods.[3] According to the excavators, the walls, which were founded on bedrock (fig. 22.3), were dug *into* the stone heap. They were built of large stones, which seem similar to those that made up part of Wall 2017. Ashlars were placed at the ends of the walls. The foundation was sealed by a layer of white chalk. A monumental building was constructed on the platform, that is, on top of the stone heap. A fill of brown soil found in the space between the double walls (probably referring to Walls 2334 and 2220 and Walls 2502 and 2503) contained a rich assemblage of pottery dating to the early days of the Iron IIC, as well as a large number of *lmlk* jar handles, "mainly of the later types," and handles incised with concentric circles. The latter are dated to the middle of the seventh century BCE.[4] For the excavators, all this means that the monumental structure that was built on top of the platform (that is, on top of the stone heap) should be dated to the late Iron IIB/early Iron IIC in the first half of the seventh century.

Phase 6a features two longitudinal structures built on the stone heap on its western edge. Building 2881 was constructed over Wall 2017, and its foundations are dug into the stone heap (Sapir et al. 2022, fig. 5). The fill in the foundation trenches of this building contained a rich pottery assemblage from the later part of the Iron IIC, with *lmlk* seal impressions, mainly of the later types, and handles with concentric circles. The excavators mention that this phase also yielded four handles with rosette seal impressions.

---

3. For the walls, see Sapir et al. 2022, fig. 5.
4. The second third of the seventh century in Lipschits 2021, 121.

22. The Sites of Mordot Arnona and Armon HaNatziv

Fig.22.2. The Mordot Arnona stone heap, looking northwest (Sapir et al. 2022, fig. 6; photo by Alexander Wiegmann, Israel Antiquities Authority, courtesy of the Israel Antiquities Authority).

Fig. 22.3. Mordot Arnona, the monumental building of my Period 3 (Sapir et al. 2022, fig. 8; photo by Assaf Peretz, Israel Antiquities Authority, courtesy of the Israel Antiquities Authority).

Another building (2474) destroyed part of Wall 2017 as well as the western edge of the stone heap; its foundations reached bedrock. This phase dates to the Iron IIC in the late seventh–early sixth centuries BCE.

Phase 5 includes walls built into the stone heap, some with foundations on bedrock; they are located above the eastern sector of the well-built walls of Phase 6b and to their east (upper right side of Sapir et al. 2022, fig. 5; see fig. 11). Also belonging to this phase are several activity spots, including patches of floors and two *tabuns* found in situ. The pottery associated with this phase dates to the sixth to fourth centuries BCE. One early *yhwd* and two middle *yhud* seal impressions were also found (Sapir et al. 2022, table 2).

The excavators underlined the exceptional number of seal impressions that were found at the site, especially of the early and late *lmlk* types and handles incised with concentric circles. Accordingly, they propose that the site played a role in the Judahite administration. They compared Mordot Arnona to nearby Ramat Rahel and suggested that, in their early history, the sites complemented each other (Sapir et al. 2022, 49).

An Alternative Interpretation

I will start with three major issues that are essential for understanding and interpreting the site:

1. As there is no real stratigraphy here in the sense of floors connecting to walls with complexes built one on top of the other, and since there are no pottery assemblages on floors, much of the description in the excavators' article—and admittedly also below—is interpretational.
2. Related to the first issue, most contexts in this dig should be considered as fills and hence must be dated according to the latest items found in them.
3. The stone heap is an important feature of the site and central to the excavators' interpretation. According to them, it was piled as a foundation for a monumental structure. However, no monumental structure can be built over a stone heap (especially when bedrock can easily be reached for laying foundations). Such a building would collapse after several winters due to erosion. In fact, I see evidence of monumental building activity under the stone heap but nowhere on top of it.

With this in mind, I wish to present an alternative interpretation for Mordot Arnona. In order to avoid confusion with the excavators' description of phases of construction, I will refer below to periods.

Period 3. A monumental rectangular structure was built on bedrock.[5] It is circa 25 meters long on the (short?) northeast–southwest axis (to compare, the largest Iron IIB–C known in Jerusalem, the Royal Building in the Ophel, is 18 meters on the short axis; Mazar and Mazar 1989, plan 7). Its walls are built of impressive large stones, some of them ashlars. Since only part of the large stone heap of Period 2 (below) was removed (see Sapir et al. 2022, fig. 5), there is no information about Period 3 construction farther to the east and southeast. The area to the west of the remains is badly damaged by activity in later periods (Sapir et al. 2022, fig. 3). This monumental building can be dated according to the material in the brown fill between the parallel walls, which contained an assemblage of pottery belonging to the early days of the Iron IIC, as well as a large quantity of *lmlk* stamped jar handles, mainly of the later types, and handles incised with concentric circles. Evidently, the latter handles provide the *terminus post quem* for the construction of the building: sometime in the second third of the seventh century BCE.[6]

Period 2: A huge stone heap was piled (Sapir et al. 2022, fig. 6; fig. 22.2 here), with much effort, in order to bury the monumental structure. Much of the monumental building was intentionally dismantled before the stones were piled. Several walls (2017, 2021, 2772) served to delimit the stone heap and support it. Large stones in Wall 2017 (Sapir et al. 2022, figs. 7, 10) were probably robbed from the dismantled monumental building of Period 3. The soil layer that runs against Wall 2017 as well as above bedrock under Building 2474 could have been part of the construction of Period 1 or was laid as a constructional fill in Period 2; in the latter case, it provides the earliest possible date for the construction of the stone heap. The excavators do not provide data on pottery and other items found in the stone heap. To the best of my understanding, the finds described as coming from the foundation trenches of Buildings 2881 and 2474, which were dug into the stone heap, in fact, represent material from the stone heap. These finds date to the later part of the Iron IIC (the late seventh and

---

5. Sapir et al. 2022, fig. 8 (fig. 22.3 here); shown in the northeastern sector of Sapir et al. 2022, fig. 5.
6. For their date, see Lipschits 2021, 121.

early sixth centuries BCE). They include *lmlk* seal impressions, mainly of the later types, and concentric circles. Four rosette seal impressions mentioned by the excavators as belonging to Phase 6a (to which they date Buildings 2881 and 2474) must have originated from the stone heap. They fit the dating of the pottery to the later phase of the Iron IIC. The relatively small number of rosette seal impressions (compared, for instance, to their number at nearby Ramat Rahel; Sapir et al. 2022, table 2) may hint at dating the piling of the stone heap to the early days of their use, not too late in the second half of the seventh century.[7]

Period 1 features relatively poor construction over and into the stone heap. This period is represented by Buildings 2881 and 2474, built over Wall 2017, and walls to the east of the monumental structure of Period 3 (see Sapir et al. 2022, fig. 11). There is no spatial connection between these elements, and all that can be said is that they were constructed on top of the stone heap, not necessarily in a single activity. Pottery and seal impressions associated with several patches of floors and two *tabun*s date this activity to the sixth to fourth centuries BCE. The layer of white chalk identified on the stone heap and associated by the excavators with Phase 6b may also belong to this period.

To summarize my interpretation of Mordot Arnona:

- Period 3: Large monumental building with foundations on bedrock, constructed around the middle (or second third) of the seventh century BCE.
- Period 2: Intentional dismantling of the monumental structure and piling of a huge stone heap in the late seventh century BCE.
- Period 1: Poor walls and several activity spots on top of the stone heap, sixth to fourth centuries BCE.

Armon HaNatziv

The site is located on the upper, northern slope of the British Government House, on the southern outskirts of Jerusalem (fig. 22.1). It commands a sweeping view of the Old City, the Temple Mount, and the City of David

---

7. On the chronology of the rosette impressions, see summary in Lipschits 2021, 116–21; regarding the date of the rosette impressions, see ch. 18 above.

22. The Sites of Mordot Arnona and Armon HaNatziv

Fig. 22.4. Monumental architectural elements from Armon HaNatziv (courtesy of the Israel Antiquities Authority; photograph by Shai Halevi).

ridge. The site of Mordot Arnona is located circa 1.5 kilometers to its southwest. The importance of Armon HaNatziv is in the unique collection of monumental architectural elements—the most elaborate ever found in Judah (fig. 22.4). Below I suggest an alternative explanation for the location of the original building and hence the nature of the site. I also deal with the date of its abandonment.

The Excavators' Description and Interpretation

The excavation area, with shallow accumulation of earth, measures only circa 15 by 20 meters, probably part of a far larger site. The main remains include a wall, two trenches neatly cut in the rock, a quarry, a winepress, a cistern, and a latrine (Billig, Freud, and Bocher 2022, figs. 2–3).

Single-course Wall 21 is interpreted as the western boundary of the complex. Beautifully cut Trenches 22 and 23, 1.5 meters deep and 1 meter wide, are described as foundation trenches for the northern boundary wall, the stones of which were robbed in antiquity. The trenches were found filled with stone fragments, including carved stones, some of them with remains of paint, as well as fragments of window frames and balustrades. Remains of a quarry and several installations, including a winepress (Floor 26 and a Vat 19), were cleared in the southern sector of the excavated area.

A pile of ashlars (including beautifully carved capitals) and fieldstones, some burnt, and an iron plow blade, were found on the plastered floor.

A square stone, interpreted as a latrine, was found west of the southern part of the plastered floor. A large number of pottery sherds and animal bones was found in a fill under the installation. Soil samples collected from the stone provided evidence of parasite eggs, raising the possibility that the stone was part of a septic pit (Langgut and Billig 2021; Langgut 2022). Samples from this context also revealed pollen grains of ornamental trees, fruit trees, and water plants.

The earliest pottery types found at the site are typical of both the end of the eighth and the early seventh centuries BCE; they represent the *terminus post quem* for the establishment of the site probably during the first part of the seventh century BCE. Most of the pottery collected at the site dates to the second half of the seventh and the beginning of the sixth centuries BCE. The excavators associated the abandonment of the site with the Babylonian assault on Jerusalem.

The excavators describe the site as representing a lavish Iron IIC building and a lush garden. The building included beautiful architectural elements: volute capitals, fragments of window frames and balustrades, and fragments of painted construction stones. It functioned for a short period of time and went out of use during the early sixth century BCE.

Unlike the nearby sites of Mordot Arnona and Ramat Rahel, there were no Judahite seal impressions at the site, seemingly indicating that it did not serve as a central storage facility or as an administrative center.

An Alternative Interpretation

There is no indication of a monumental building in the excavated area. First, Wall 21 does not fit a boundary wall of a luxurious building with beautifully decorated stone elements. It is certainly lesser in quality than the Period 3 walls in Mordot Arnona and walls at Ramat Rahel. Second, the two well-cut, narrow trenches do not look like foundation trenches: they are too narrow and too deep, and there is no indication in them of construction blocks. Also, had they accommodated a wall, one would have to assume that it had been removed and the trenches filled with architectural elements in a short time span.

In fact, all in situ finds at the site hint solely at agricultural activity. I refer to the cistern, quarry, winepress, and rock-cut cave for storage, in a way also to the plow blade found at the site and the pollen evidence from the latrine pit (Billig, Freud, and Bocher 2022, 14). It seems that this area served as part of a farm or a garden. Stones similar to the one identified as a latrine were found in other places, and their function is disputed.[8] Langgut's work hints that, at least in the case of Armon HaNatziv, it indeed served as such (Langgut and Billig 2021; Langgut 2022); however, there are other ways to interpret the finds (Kleiman 2023b).

The luxurious building probably stood to the south, on the summit of the hill, where the British Government House was built in the 1930s. I propose that it served as a countryside villa, or an estate; based on the "latrine," a certain cult function is also possible (Kleiman 2023b). The building overlooked the Old City of Jerusalem, including the Temple Mount, in the north and the Judean Desert in the east. It dates to the first half of the seventh century BCE. It was then intentionally demolished, and at least part of its architectural elements were buried on the slope, in an agricultural area, perhaps the garden of the villa. The two trenches may have been cut in order to accommodate the demolished elements, some of which were treated respectfully. If so, the circumstances of the demise of this building do not fit the Babylonian assault. Rather, the dismantling of the building was part of cultural and historical changes in Judah in the late seventh century.

Historical and Biblical Comments

The Armon HaNatziv–Ramat Rahel ridge south of Jerusalem and the area of Nahal Refaim to its west feature intensive activity in the later phases of the Iron Age, which may have started in the late eighth century BCE but peaked in the terminal Iron IIB and the early phase of the Iron IIC—the first half to middle of the seventh century. The area includes four monumental sites: Ramat Rahel, Mordot Arnona, Armon HaNatziv, and Ein el-Jowiezeh. Remains of an elaborate spring house were explored in the latter, probably part of a royal estate (Ein Mor and Ron 2016). Less monumental farmhouses were part of the system (Gadot 2015), possibly—and

---

8. Discussion with references in Langgut and Billig 2021; Billig, Freud, and Bocher 2022, 14; and Kleiman 2023b.

not fully understandably—also the tumuli that characterize the ridge to the north of Nahal Refaim.

There is a resemblance between the architectural elements from Ramat Rahel and Armon HaNatziv (in a way, also from Ein el-Jouweizeh, despite the little that we know about it) and a likeness between Ramat Rahel and Mordot Arnona in the ashlar masonry and abundance of seal impressions. This shows the chronological and functional relationship of the four sites.

The exceptional monumentality of the remains (and the prevalence of royal seal impressions) indicates that the sites discussed here were state- (royally) sponsored, and their date hints that they were related to the Assyrian domination of Judah.[9] From the historical-biblical perspective, the main phase of activity in this area should be dated to the time of King Manasseh, who ruled in Jerusalem for fifty-five years in the first half to the middle of the seventh century (698–642 BCE) and in whose time Judah was fully incorporated into the Assyrian imperial economy and was influenced by Assyrian culture, including cult and religious traits (Ornan 2005).

The full nature of the royal activity under Assyrian sponsorship southwest of Jerusalem is difficult to assess, but it seems that the different monumental elements known in this area were all connected. Perhaps one can identify this large royal complex with the place named *mmst*, the fourth of the toponyms that appear on the royal *lmlk* stamp impressions (together with Hebron, Ziph, and Socoh). Many years ago Ginsberg suggested reading the name as a shortened version of the word *mmšlt*, that is, government, administration (Ginsberg 1948); if so, in this context it should be understood as the governmental system in charge of the Assyrian-related royal estate(s) rather than the government of the kingdom (see ch. 19 above).

Among the monuments, the somewhat easier to explain are Ramat Rahel and Ein el-Joweizeh. Ramat Rahel—probably to be identified with Beth-haccerem (Lipschits and Na'aman 2020)—seems to have served as the main administrative center of the system. Ein el-Joweizeh functioned as a royal garden, perhaps similar to the one described in Assyrian reliefs in the days of Ashurbanipal at Nineveh (Albenda 1976, fig. 4). The stone capital found at nearby Ein Hannia[10] may have originated from Ein el-Joweizeh or may represent a similar site.

---

9. For the impact of Assyria on the economy of Judah, see ch. 20 above.
10. Yuval Baruch and Irena Zilberbord, personal communication.

The original building that stood at Armon HaNatziv may have served as a royal villa, with architectural elements not too different from those known in Phase I at Ramat Rahel (below). Considering its date of construction—in the first half of the seventh century BCE—the original site may be identified with גן עזא, mentioned as the house (palace) and place of burial of two Judahite monarchs: Manasseh and his son Amon:[11]

> Manasseh slept with his ancestors and was buried in the garden of his house, in the garden of Uzza. His son Amon succeeded him. … Now the rest of the acts of Amon that he did, are they not written in the Book of the Annals of the Kings of Judah? He was buried in his tomb in the garden of Uzza; then his son Josiah succeeded him. (2 Kgs 21:18, 25–26 NRSVue)

According to the usual formula, the Davidic kings were buried "in the city of David," meaning somewhere within the urban complex of Jerusalem or immediately outside it (the eastern slope of the Temple Mount seems to be the most logical location). The reference to the garden of Uzza seems to indicate a place outside of the city. Note that the genealogy in 1 Chr 7:8 links the name Uzza with the village of Manahat, located circa 5 kilometers to the west of Armon HaNatziv.

The nature of the early seventh-century BCE ashlar-built structure at Mordot Arnona (my Period 3 above) is not clear, and there is hardly a way to reconstruct it. On one hand, the large number of Judahite seal impressions points to an administrative function; on the other hand, the ferocity with which it was destroyed and covered by a large stone heap may hint at a cult function, too.

The book of 2 Kings details the cult reform that was ostensibly carried out in Judah in general and in Jerusalem in particular by Josiah, the grandson of Manasseh and son of Amon. Josiah's reform has been a central topic in the discussion of the history of Judah and biblical historiography of the late monarchic and later periods (e.g., Eynikel 1996; Sweeney 2001 and bibliography). Archaeology fell short of supplying evidence for the Josianic reform. In fact, archaeology provided better clues for the centralization of

---

11. To the best of my knowledge, the first to suggest this identification in public was Yuval Gadot, in a lecture in the fourteenth conference on the archaeology of Jerusalem and its environs, October 2021.

cult in Judah under Hezekiah (ch. 15 above). The only clue for the Josianic activity is circumstantial: the decline of Bethel in the Iron IIC (Finkelstein and Singer-Avitz 2009). The data from the new digs—at Mordot Arnona and Armon HaNatziv—seem to provide a more direct clue for actions taken in Judah in the days of King Josiah. I refer to the elimination of monuments, civic and possibly also cultic, that were erected in the days of Manasseh. The monumental ashlar structure at Mordot Arnona was buried under a huge stone heap, and a monumental structure, which probably stood on the summit of the British Government House hill, was dismantled and its blocks buried on the slope, perhaps even desecrated (depending on how one interprets the parasite eggs on the "latrine"). The ferocity of the action fits the zeal described in Kings in relation to actions undertaken by Josiah.

Two contemporary biblical verses may be related to the decommissioning of the two sites. About Josiah, 2 Kgs 23:13 says:

ואת־הבמות אשר על־פני ירושלם אשר מימין להר־המשחית אשר בנה שלמה מלך־ישראל לעשתרת שקץ צידנים ולכמוש שקץ מואב ולמלכם תועבת בני־עמון טמא המלך:

The king defiled the high places that were east of Jerusalem, to the south of the Mount of Destruction, which King Solomon of Israel had built for Astarte the abomination of the Sidonians, for Chemosh the abomination of Moab, and for Milcom the abomination of the Ammonites. (NRSVue)[12]

Jeremiah (51:25) says:

הנני אליך הר המשחית נאם־יהוה המשחית את־כל־הארץ ונטיתי את־ידי עליך וגלגלתיך מן־הסלעים ונתתיך להר שרפה:

I am against you, O destroying mountain, says the LORD, that destroys the whole earth; I will stretch out my hand against you and roll you down from the crags and make you a burned-out mountain. (NRSVue)

The geographical description is straightforward: The high places in question overlook Jerusalem, located south of הר המשחית. Perhaps both sites discussed in this chapter are mentioned here: Har Hamashkhit may refer (apologetically) to the site that was located where the British Government

---

12. The phrase הר המשחית can be translated Mount of Destruction or Mount of Corruption

House stands today—the original structure of Armon HaNatziv, which was dismantled with its blocks thrown to the northern slope of the hill; the high places are located south of this spot. Mordot Arnona may be one of them.

Another toponym that may be related to the sites east of Nahal Refaim is Baal-perazim. The descriptions in Josh 15:8 and 18:16 anchor the valley of Rephaim with today's Nahal Refaim, and 2 Sam 5:18, 22 refers to the Philistine camp in the valley of Rephaim. Verse 20 in the same chapter says: "So David came to Baal-perazim, and David defeated them there. He said, 'The Lord has burst forth against my enemies before me like a bursting flood.' Therefore that place is called Baal-perazim" (NRSVue). This may be the Deuteronomistic author's way of legitimizing a Baal toponym in the vicinity of Jerusalem. Whether Isa 28:21 relates to the same place as a location of a foreign cult is difficult to say.

One question remains open: How is it that Mordot Arnona and Armon HaNatziv were abolished and Ramat Rahel survived? This question is difficult to answer because the chronology of the different phases at Ramat Rahel rests on little solid data. The spotlight should be placed here on Phase I, which apparently included a tower in the western part of the site and several other structures found under the floor of Phase II (Lipschits et al. 2011, 12). The construction style of the tower is different from the palace of Phase II. The monumental capitals and other architectural elements found at Ramat Rahel originated from Phase I (Lipschits et al. 2011, 20; Gadot and Lipschits 2016, 719). Phase I can be dated according to pottery found in the fill under the thick courtyard floor of Phase II and circumstantial evidence based on the pottery and seal impressions found at the site. The construction of this phase was dated by the recent excavators to the late eighth or first half of the seventh century BCE (Lipschits, Gadot, and Oeming 2020, 477) and its abandonment to the late seventh century (Gadot et al. 2020, 28). In the same breath, the excavators state that Phase I continued "at least until the mid-seventh century BCE, and perhaps even longer, towards the beginning of the last third of that century" (Lipschits, Gadot, and Oeming 2020, 477). The latter date comes from the finds under the floor of Courtyard 380 of Phase II (Lipschits et al. 2011, 13). The latest pottery items in this fill belong to the Iron IIC in the late seventh century BCE, but no rosette seal impressions, typical of this phase in the history of Judah, were found. This can be a coincidence or a sign that the floor was laid before rosette storage jars started to break. In light of the finds at Mordot Arnona and Armon

HaNatziv, I suggest that Phase I at Ramat Rahel was built in the first half of the seventh century, in the days of King Manasseh, and decommissioned during the days of Josiah in the late seventh century. The administrative nature of the site was maintained in the transition from Phase I to Phase II, but the details of its nature in Phase I remain vague.

Conclusion

Two monumental sites were built on the ridge of the British Government House on the southern outskirts of Jerusalem in the first half of the seventh century, the days of King Manasseh: the elaborate Period 3 building at Mordot Arnona and the original villa, which probably stood on the summit of the Government House hill. Both were decommissioned in the late seventh century, possibly in actions taken by King Josiah, as described in 2 Kgs 23. In fact, this may be the first direct clue to the Josianic cult reform. Mordot Arnona, which served administrative and possibly cultic functions, was dismantled and buried under a big stone heap, and the Armon HaNatziv building, a royal villa that may have had a cultic component, was destroyed and its architectural elements thrown in a garden/farming area on the northern slope of the hill. Ramat Rahel may show a certain resemblance: Phase I, with architectural elements that resemble those at Armon HaNatziv, was also constructed in the first half of the seventh century and decommissioned in the late seventh century BCE.

Addendum

Parallel to this chapter, Na'aman (2023) also discusses the sites of Mordot Arnona and Armon HaNatziv. Similar to my reconstruction, he identifies Mordot Arnona as one of the high places referred to in 2 Kgs 23:13–14, attributes its construction to Manasseh, and sees its obliteration as the result of Josiah's cult reform. In contrast to my view that the architectural elements retrieved at Armon HaNatziv originated from a royal villa with a possible cultic component on the summit of the hill, Na'aman proposes that they were brought from the demolished cult place at Mordot Arnona.

Part 6
The Dark Age and Recovery

23

Jerusalem and Judah 600–200 BCE: Implications for Understanding Pentateuchal Texts

---

The more than four centuries between the destruction of Jerusalem by the Babylonians in 586 BCE and the rise of the Hasmoneans in the second century BCE are crucial for understanding the Bible and the development of Judaism. On the one hand, scholars ascribe a large number of biblical texts to this period; on the other hand, the material evidence is meager at best. Here I present the archaeological record for the Persian and early Hellenistic periods and deal with its significance. I avoid going into details, as they are discussed in my book, *Hasmonean Realities behind Ezra, Nehemiah, and Chronicles*, published by SBL Press in 2018.

Several decades ago archaeology played a major role in pentateuchal research, mainly in attempts to locate the *Sitz im Leben*, the single historical period, for the patriarchs (Albright 1961; Gordon 1964; de Vaux 1978, 161–287). The failure (and, one must say today, naïveté) of this endeavor, and the realization that the texts are mulilayered and do not represent a single period of authorship, left archaeology outside the modern pentateuchal research arena. This was a mistake (already Thompson 1974; Van Seters 1975), because archaeology does have the capacity to shed light on the historical realities behind biblical texts; in the case of the Pentateuch, this means the historical background behind the authors rather than the historicity of the stories. In fact, archaeology can even help in identifying different layers of authorship. I therefore suggest that the future of research into the evolution of biblical texts is in collaboration between specialists in text analysis and archaeology (Finkelstein and Römer 2014a, 2014b, 2016) and in the introduction of computer-science methods into biblical studies (e.g., Yoffe et al. 2023).

This chapter is therefore divided into two. In the first part I wish to survey archaeological data on Jerusalem and Judah in the later phases of the Iron Age and the Babylonian, Persian, and early Hellenistic periods. In the second part I attempt to demonstrate possible implications of these data for understanding the historical background in the compilation of several pentateuchal texts. As an introduction, let me emphasize two points: First, my intention is *not* to give an overall exposé of the archaeology of Judah/Yehud/Judea (for this, see, e.g., parts in Stern 2001); I will introduce some finds that seem to be applicable to topics discussed in this volume. Second, although my title refers to the period of circa 600–200 BCE, as I am a devotee of the long-term approach, I will discuss a somewhat broader time span that starts with the collapse of the Northern Kingdom in 720 BCE and possibly ends in the second century BCE.

The Data

The Iron IIB–C

As far as I can judge, the most important issue here is the settlement patterns. The number of sites in the Judean Highlands in the late Iron IIA (until the early eighth century) can be estimated at about eighty. The peak prosperity of Judah commenced in the Iron IIB, in the late eighth century, and continued in the Iron IIC, in the late seventh century BCE, with over 120 sites and dense population in the entire area, including the semiarid south Hebron Hills. The Shephelah, which suffered a major blow from Sennacherib's 701 BCE campaign, partially recovered in the Iron IIC, although on a smaller scale and in a different pattern than previously. The Beersheba Valley also reached a settlement peak in the Iron IIB–C (for all this, see an updated discussion in ch. 14 above). Farther south, until the withdrawal of Assyria from the region in circa 630–625 BCE, Judahites probably served in Assyrian forts (or Assyrian-dominated strongholds) along desert routes such as Ein Hazeva and Kadesh-barnea. Archaeological finds, especially at Kadesh-barnea, as well as information in the Arad ostraca regarding movement of troops and shipping of commodities in the south, show that Judah and Judahites continued to be present in the arid areas south of the Beersheba Valley even after the retreat of Assyria from the region (e.g., Cohen and Bernick-Greenberg 2007).

Regarding Jerusalem, I first wish to draw attention to the proposal that the core of the ancient city is located under the Temple Mount and that the City of David cannot be regarded as the tell of ancient Jerusalem (ch. 2 above). This theory resolves some of the most tantalizing problems in the archaeology and history of Jerusalem, first and foremost the lack of evidence for activity in the City of David ridge in periods for which habitation in Jerusalem is securely attested in textual evidence, such as the Amarna letters (see discussion in Na'aman 1996). Accordingly, the mound on the Mount was the location of ancient Jerusalem of the Bronze Age and the early phases of the Iron Age. The city started expanding to the south, to the upper part of the City of David ridge, in an advanced stage of the late Iron IIA, that is, the late ninth century BCE (chs. 7–9 above). The "great leap forward" in Jerusalem took place in a relatively short period of time in the eighth century BCE, when it grew to cover the entire area of the City of David ridge as well as the Western Hill, today's Armenian and Jewish Quarters (e.g., Reich and Shukron 2003; Geva 2003b). This means growth from circa 8.5 hectares to over 60 hectares in a matter of several decades (fig. 23.1).

The reason for the sudden, dramatic population growth in Jerusalem in particular and Judah in general has been debated. Neil Silberman and I (ch. 15 above), following scholars such as Broshi (1974), Schniedewind (2004), and Van der Toorn (1996, 339–72), suggested interpreting this phenomenon against the background of migration of Israelites to Judah after 720 BCE. Nadav Na'aman opposed this view (2007; for a rejoinder, see ch. 16 above), and he has recently published another article on the matter (Na'aman 2014a). In my answer I updated the demographic data on Jerusalem and Judah and dealt with material culture indications for movement of Israelites to Judah (see ch. 14 above; see also below).

Highly important for the study of the Pentateuch is the expansion of writing. Benjamin Sass and I recently investigated the pre-eighth-century BCE linear alphabetic inscriptions from the Levant (Finkelstein and Sass 2013). We especially emphasized the stratigraphy and relative chronology of the contexts where the inscriptions were found and translated this into absolute chronology using the massive information from recent radiocarbon studies (Sharon et al. 2007; Toffolo et al. 2014). We showed that there are no inscriptions in the territories of Israel and Judah before the later phase of the late Iron IIA, in the late ninth century BCE. It is clear that

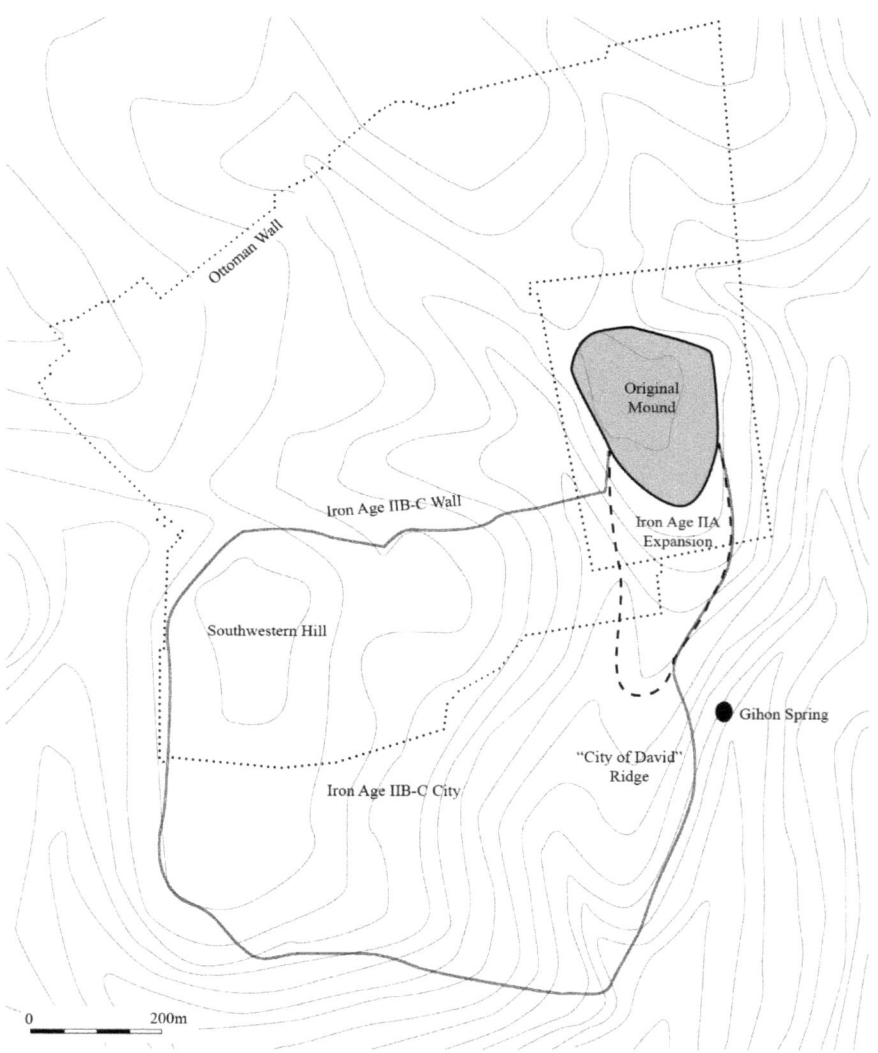

Fig. 23.1. Expansion of Jerusalem during the Iron Age

writing spread only in the eighth century—in the first half of the century in Israel and in the second half in Judah. Complex literary works appear for the first time in Israel in the early eighth century, at Deir ʿAlla and Kuntillet ʿAjrud (for the latter, see Ahituv, Eshel, and Meshel 2012, 105–20; Naʾaman 2012a). This is the basic evidence. Regarding interpretation, Sass thinks that writing on papyri must have been present in the administration of the territorial kingdoms, especially Israel, starting in the first half of the ninth century. This is possible, but I prefer to see evidence for this theory, if not in the form of papyri, then in the expansion of other media of writing such as bullae and seals. For now this evidence is lacking.

In any event, the main expansion of scribal activity and literacy in Judah came in the seventh century BCE. Most corpora of ostraca—Arad, Lachish, Uza, Malḥata, Kadesh-barnea—belong to this period (e.g., Ahituv 2008; see ch. 12 above). The spread of literacy is also attested in the proliferation of seals and seal impressions; it is noteworthy that a large corpus of bullae from Jerusalem, dated slightly earlier, circa 800 BCE, is not inscribed (Reich, Shukron, and Lernau 2007). The seventh century BCE is the moment when Judah becomes what one can describe as a writing society beyond the circles of temple and palace in the capital. This was probably an outcome of the century (ca. 730–630 BCE) when Judah was dominated by Assyria and was incorporated into the sphere of the Assyrian global economy, administration, and culture.

This is supported by a new study. A research group at Tel Aviv University is working on digital methods of comparing handwriting.[1] The mathematicians on the team developed a method that has recently helped to check the number of (writing) "hands" in the Arad ostraca. We found evidence for several writers; the information in the texts of the examined ostraca discloses that literacy infiltrated to the smallest forts in the Beer-heba Valley and all the way down the bureaucratic ladder. There is no need to emphasize the importance of this information for the themes discussed here; suffice it to say that the recognition of the power of writing infiltrated all echelons of the Judahite administration, far beyond temple and palace (see summary of this study in Faigenbaum-Golovin et al. 2021).

The Babylonian, Persian, and Early Hellenistic Periods

The archaeology of the Babylonian period is difficult to isolate and study. This is due to its short duration and because the finds are difficult to distinguish from those of the earlier Iron IIC and the later Persian period. Still, there are

---

1. For previous achievements of this group, see summary in Faigenbaum-Golovin et al. 2015.

several issues concerning the Babylonian period that can be emphasized in regard to what is being discussed here.

I begin with the destruction of Jerusalem; a thorough investigation of the data from the many fields of excavations there seems to indicate that destruction by fire is evident only in areas close to the Temple Mount and the Gihon Spring;[2] with the exception of one place (Geva and Avigad 2000b, 134, 155), there is almost no sign of conflagration and/or assemblage of broken vessels on floors on the Western Hill (e.g., Geva and Avigad 2000a, 42; Geva and Avigad 2000c, 215). Rural sites in the vicinity of Jerusalem also show no signs of major destruction (e.g., A. Mazar 1981, 237; Mazar, Amit, and Ilan 1984, 241; Edelstein 2000, 57). Although it is clear that the city *was* devastated—most of its sectors feature a long occupational gap— there are clues in some places of meager activity immediately after 586 BCE (Barkay 2003, 27). There is yet another piece of evidence for continuity of certain activity in Jerusalem after Nebuchadnezzar's assault; I refer to the *mwsh* and lion seal impressions found in Jerusalem, which make the link in the bureaucratic sequence of Judah–Yehud, between the Iron Age rosette impressions and the Persian period early Yehud impressions. In other words, they probably represent the administration of the province after 586 BCE (Zorn, Yellin, and Hayes 1994; Lipschits 2005, 149–52). The City of David features several *mwsh* impressions and a large number of lion impressions; the latter make up a large part of the assemblage in the entire region.[3] Since not a single Babylonian period building was found in the City of David ridge, activity must have focused on the core of the city: the Temple Mount. There is simply no other way to understand these finds. Note that no *mwsh* and lion impressions were found south of Ramat Rahel, probably indicating that the province stretched over the limited area from Mizpah in the north to Ramat Rahel in the south (more below).

This brings me to a site outside of Yehud but of great importance for the discussion here: Bethel. Several years ago Lily Singer-Avitz and I revisited the finds retrieved from this site, both in the published report and unpublished, in storage in Jerusalem and Pittsburgh. The results of our investigation (Finkelstein and Singer-Avitz 2009) indicated that the set-

---

2. Barkay 2003, 27; details in Shiloh 1984, 14, 18–19, 29; Mazar and Mazar 1989, 16, 21, 43; Steiner 2001, 108–9, 114; evidence for destruction is limited south of the spring (De Groot 2012, 164).

3. In a seminar paper by my student Erin Hall.

tlement history of the site was not continuous, as held by the excavators (Kelso 1968). Rather, it was characterized by oscillations, with three phases of strong activity in the Iron I, Iron IIB, and Hellenistic (probably second century BCE) periods; two periods of decline in the late Iron IIA and the Iron IIC; and two periods of probable abandonment in the early Iron IIA and, most significantly, the Babylonian and Persian periods. This evidence cannot be brushed aside as stemming from deficiencies in the excavations, as significant sectors of the small mound—bigger than can be suggested at first glance—had been excavated (more below).

Turning to the Persian period, in Jerusalem evidence for activity comes primarily from the central sector of the City of David ridge, above the Gihon Spring. It is characterized mainly by a relatively large number of early Yehud seal impressions, most of which come from fills. Not a single building or a single floor has ever been found there or in any other place in ancient Jerusalem. The early Hellenistic period seems to feature a similar picture (summary in Finkelstein 2008b; for the data, see also Lipschits 2009). As in the case of the Babylonian impressions, the combination of these data—abundance of Yehud impressions and no architectural remains—must mean that the focus of the Persian period activity was in the old core of the city on the Temple Mount. Yet even here settlement activity must have been quite low, as only a limited number of Persian period sherds were found in the vicinity of the Temple Mount: in the sifting of debris from the area of the Al-Aqsa Mosque, the eastern slope of the Temple Mount, and the Ophel excavations south of the Temple Mount.[4]

In addition, no sign of a Persian period fortification was found in Jerusalem; as far as I can judge (Finkelstein 2008b), the description in Neh 3 echoes the construction of the First Wall by the Hasmoneans. The Nehemiah Memoir, which speaks in general about the deplorable state of Jerusalem and its fortifications, probably refers to the mound on the Temple Mount.

The territory of Persian period Yehud has traditionally been reconstructed according to the references to subdistricts of the province in Neh 3.[5] This, of course, is a circular argument because the background and

---

4. Barkay and Zweig 2006, 222; Dvira (Zweig), Zigdon, and Shilov 2011, 68; pers. comm. from Eilat Mazar, respectively.

5. For summaries of the different opinions, see Stern 1982, 247–49; Carter 1999, 79–80; Lipschits 2005, 168–74.

date of this list is far from decided. Further, as I have previously indicated (2008a), the lists of returnees in Ezra and Nehemiah cannot be of help either because the archaeology of the securely identified sites that are mentioned in them also hints at a Hellenistic period background.

Therefore, the only independent way to study the territorial extent of the province is to plot the distribution of the Yehud seal impressions (types 1–12 in Lipschits and Vanderhooft 2011). Indeed, the map does not fit the territory described in Neh 3. Yehud seems to have extended from Mizpah in the north to Ramat Rahel in the south, possibly slightly farther, though Beth-zur probably remained outside of it; and from Jericho and Ein Gedi in the east to the border of the Shephelah in the west, since no Yehud impressions were found in any of the sites of the upper Shephelah. In 2010 I assembled the archaeological data on the settlement patterns in this area in the Persian period. I estimated the total built-up area in Yehud at circa 60 hectares, which can be translated to approximately twelve thousand people—about half of the low numbers proposed previously (Finkelstein 2010b, compared to Carter 1999, 195–205; Lipschits 2003, 364). This estimate means a dramatic settlement and demographic decline compared to the situation in the Iron IIC. It runs counter to scholars who tend to belittle the scope of the catastrophe that befell Judah in 586 BCE (also Faust 2012; contra, e.g., Barstad 1996); it also supports the notion that the "return" to Yehud was more a trickle than a flood.

Ofer reported that in the Persian period the settlement system south of Hebron, beyond the border of Yehud, "almost died out" (1994, 106). The Beersheba Valley is almost devoid of evidence of habitation at that time,[6] and activity in the key sites in the desert south of the Beersheba Valley was also weak (Finkelstein 2015c). The same holds true for the Edomite Plateau (Bienkowski 2001). The low settlement system in the south is probably due to a phase of dry climate, as indicated by Dead Sea palynological research led by Tel Aviv University archaeobotanist Dafna Langgut and myself.

Regarding material culture, a crucial piece of evidence for the Babylonian and Persian periods has not been given sufficient attention. I refer to the disappearance of Hebrew writing from the archaeological record. Compared to the unprecedented prosperity in scribal activity and liter-

---

6. For instance, not a single Persian period site was found in the eastern part of the valley; see Beit-Arieh 2003, *12.

acy in the Iron IIC, which, as I have shown above, penetrated into the lowest echelons of the Judahite administration, the southern highlands in the Babylonian and Persian periods show almost no evidence of Hebrew inscriptions. In fact, the only (meager) evidence comes from the few *yhd* coins that date to the fourth century BCE, and coins can hardly attest to genuine scribal activity. This means that not a single inscription has been found for the period between 586 and circa 350 BCE: neither an ostracon, nor a seal, nor a seal impression, nor a bulla! This can hardly be a coincidence. I am not suggesting, of course, that the knowledge of writing Hebrew disappeared, but scribal activity declined—and significantly so.

Some Implications for Pentateuchal Studies

My observations below are based on archaeological and historical data and are limited to specific issues. Further, they are no more than illustrations; combining modern archaeological research with text analysis can lead to many more insights.

Chronologically, I should start with Bethel. Scholars suggested that the Bethel temple served as the "repository" and place of composition of northern biblical traditions such as the Jacob cycle and the Book of Saviors in Judges (Knauf 2006, 319–22). This proposed scribal activity should best be associated with the period of prosperity at Bethel in the Iron IIB in the eighth century. Archaeology cannot help in deciding between the years before or after the destruction of the Northern Kingdom. Historical considerations—the need to promote foundation myths of the north in times of reorganization of the kingdom under Jeroboam II—may favor the former possibility. The Deir 'Alla and Kuntillet 'Ajrud plaster texts—both affiliated with the north and dated to the first half of the eighth century—demonstrate that this is a viable possibility. The other side of this coin is no less important: scholars proposed that Bethel served as a prominent cult place and center of learning in the Babylonian period (Pakkala 2002; Blenkinsopp 2003; Knauf 2006; Gomes 2006). This idea is contradicted by the archaeological evidence, which shows weak activity in the late seventh and early sixth centuries and probably no activity in the Babylonian and Persian periods (Finkelstein and Singer-Avitz 2009).

Thomas Römer and I recently suggested, following de Pury and Blum (de Pury 2001; Blum 2012), that the early layer in the Jacob cycle originated relatively early in the Iron Age and was put in writing at Bethel at the early eighth century. In other words, the Northern Kingdom had an eponym ancestor tradition, first oral and then written. We added that this tradition developed in a restricted area in the Gilead: in the Jabbok basin and south of it; only later, in our view, in connection with reorganization of the kingdom in the days of Jeroboam II, it became a "national" myth of the north and was "moved" to Bethel (Finkelstein and Römer 2014b). These observations call attention to the south. In view of the settlement, demographic, and scribal prosperity in Judah in the Iron IIB-C, it is difficult to imagine that there were no southern shrines with competing traditions while the two Hebrew kingdoms lived side by side and then after the fall of Israel. This was one of the reasons Römer and I proposed that the original Abraham tradition developed in a cult place in the vicinity of Hebron, perhaps the holy oak of Mamre (Finkelstein and Römer 2014a). The original, Iron Age Mamre could have been a shrine connected to a sacred tree and/or grove. Considering that the place of memory of an ancestor is in many cases a shrine related to his grave, it is also possible that there was a burial tradition of Abraham in the area of Hebron already in monarchic times. Machpelah *asher al-penei Mamre* ("which is before Mamre," Gen 49:30) is a different story. The origin of this concept may be sought in the geopolitical situation of the Persian period, if not somewhat later: the original cult place (and possibly sacred tomb) was left outside of the province of Yehud, so a tradition developed according to which there was a Mamre somewhere at Hebron and a grave at Machpelah slightly to its north. Note that Herod the Great constructed two monuments: one for the tomb and another for the shrine.

Outside the Pentateuch and the genealogies in Chronicles, Isaac is mentioned independent of the patriarchal triad only in Amos 7:9, 16, where he seems to represent the south in opposition or parallel to the north. If the Isaac tradition indeed comes from the Beersheba Valley (Noth 1981b, 103-7), it must have originated in the Iron Age, because after 586 BCE the area was sparsely inhabited (possibly not inhabited at all) and far from Yehud. It is therefore plausible that there was a second ancestor figure in the south, possibly venerated in a sanctuary at Beersheba. In the seventh century Abraham may have had two "sons": Isaac in the Beersheba Valley and Ishmael in the areas farther south, in the "deep" desert (Finkelstein and Römer 2014a). This may depict realities of the time: Judahite settlement in the Beersheba Valley peaked in the late eighth and seventh centuries BCE; activity farther south characterizes the same period, when Judahites served in Kadesh-barnea and probably also in the Assyrian forts along the Arabian trade routes.

The possibility of the existence of an Iron II Abraham tradition in Judah raises the question of the merging of the late monarchic southern Abraham and older northern Jacob cycles into a single Judahite tradition. This, in turn, raises—yet again—the question of the "migration" of northern traditions to Judah.

There is no escape from the archaeological evidence of a dramatic demographic transformation in Judah in the second half of the eighth century and the early seventh century BCE (Broshi 1974; ch. 15 above; updated in ch. 14 above). This can in no way be explained as the result of natural population growth, economic prosperity, or intra-Judahite movement of people. I therefore insist that many of the new settlers in Jerusalem and the highlands of Judah originated in the territory of Israel, many of them from the southern Samaria highlands, where surveys demonstrate deterioration of settlement activity after 720 BCE. Appearance of items of north Israelite material culture in Judah starting in the late eighth century supports this historical reconstruction. I refer to stone installations for olive-oil extraction, northern pottery forms, ashlar masonry, Proto-Ionic capitals, longitudinal pillared buildings that served as stables, and rock-cut tombs. The number of Israelites in Judah was probably large enough to force biblical authors to be mindful of their most important traditions. Of course, some of these traditions could have reached Judah in later times; for instance, Israelite texts could have been preserved at Bethel and found their way to Jerusalem when Judah appropriated this shrine in the late seventh century. In any event, it is reasonable to assume that the merging of the Jacob and Abraham stories was undertaken after 720 BCE but before 586 BCE (Finkelstein and Römer 2014a).

The book of Numbers presents an intriguing case of centuries-old memories in a late composition. Archaeology and extrabiblical historical sources, most significantly the Mesha Stela, indicate that, although being the latest in the Pentateuch (Römer 2007), Numbers preserves shreds of Israelite traditions regarding the conquest of the *mishor* from a late Canaanite king who ruled from Heshbon, as well as "memories" about the existence of an early Moabite kingdom south of the Arnon River. These traditions can come only from the days of the Omrides—the only period when Israel ruled over territories in northern Moab (Finkelstein and

Römer 2016). If so, how and when did these traditions find their way to Judah and to a late text such as Numbers? The stories must have first been transmitted orally in the Northern Kingdom (they may have originated from the temple of YHWH at Nebo, referred to in the Mesha Inscription) and were probably put in writing in the first half of the eighth century. Promotion of memories of Israelite presence in northern Moab could have served northern territorial ambitions in the days of Jeroboam II; indeed, another layer in Numbers puts the border with Moab on the northern tip of the Dead Sea—in line with the situation in late monarchic times. The written early north Israelite traditions regarding Moab came to be known in Judah in the decades after 720 BCE, were preserved there in ways not disclosed to us, and still later were incorporated into Yehudite/early Judean works and given a southern orientation.

Regarding Transjordan in the book of Numbers, attention should also be given to the lists of towns built by the tribes of Gad and Reuben in Num 32:34–38. Five of the places mentioned are securely identified and supplied archaeological data: Dibon, Ataroth, Aroer, Heshbon and Nebo. They have produced rich Iron Age and Hellenistic finds but no Persian period material. This piece of evidence, too, cannot be brushed aside when dealing with the process of compilation of texts in the Pentateuch: we are facing either a memory of the situation in the later phases of the Iron Age or an old memory combined with a later situation.

Numbers brings me to the desert wanderings lists. This material has been the subject of intensive research, including issues of sources and redactions (e.g., Noth 1940; 1968, 242–46; Coats 1972; Davies 1983; Römer 2007). Scholars such as Noth, Fritz, and Davies assumed that the itineraries are based on early materials (Noth 1968, 243; 1981b, 224–27; Fritz 1970, 116–17; Davies 1983). If so, the period from which these toponyms originated can be located in two ways: the archaeology of sites that can be securely identified and possible knowledge of the southern deserts by biblical authors (for both, see in detail Finkelstein 2015c). For the latter, let me start with the period of the latest redaction(s) of the text by Priestly or post-Priestly scribes, then pull back chronologically. As I have indicated above, the sparsely settled and demographically depleted province of Yehud stretched no farther than Beth-zur in the south. There was no Jewish presence at that time in the southern Hebron Hills or the Beer-sheba Valley, and activity at the key sites in the south was weak. Under these circumstances, Priestly authors' knowledge of the southern desert must have been fragmentary at best. The toponyms that appear in the wandering narrative and itineraries can hardly represent Persian period realities.

In the closing decades of its history, after the Assyrian pullout, Judah was still strongly present in the Beersheba Valley. Farther to the southwest, finds at Kadesh-barnea indicate that the fort continued to function after Assyria's withdrawal, probably under Judahite auspices (Cohen and Bernick-Greenberg 2007). The Arad ostraca, dated circa 600 BCE, mention movement of units and shipment of commodities in the south, probably also beyond the Beersheba Valley (Aharoni 1981, 15).

The Assyrian century (ca. 730–630 BCE) evidenced the strongest Judahite activity in the southern desert. This was the time of peak prosperity in the Beersheba Valley. The towns and forts there, and especially markets and khans, were places where Judahite merchants and administrators met Edomites and Arabs from the desert (Thareani 2011, 301–7). Beyond the Beersheba Valley, the Assyrians controlled the desert trade routes from several pivotal strongholds that were probably manned by local people: Edomites, Arabs, and possibly also Judahites. Information about the south could also have been transmitted by Arab merchants who visited Jerusalem (Shiloh 1987a; Lemaire 2012). What is clear from this short review is that detailed knowledge of the south, accompanied by lists of toponyms, probably represents a pre-586 reality. Needless to say, the incorporation of this material into the biblical texts could have taken place later.

Much of what I discussed above indicates that the Pentateuch includes significant traditions that come from the Iron Age and that at least some of them were probably put in writing for the first time in the later phase of the Iron Age. This old material went through several stages of redaction in the Persian period and possibly even later, and much material was added at that time. But where was this done?

This question brings me to the issue of composition of biblical texts in Yehud of the Persian period, in fact, also Judea of early Hellenistic times. As I have already shown, there is almost no evidence for Hebrew writing in Yehud in circa 586–350 BCE and very little evidence until circa 200 BCE. This should come as no surprise: the destruction of Judah brought about the collapse of the kingdom's bureaucracy and deportation of many of the educated intelligentsia, the literati; the "vinedressers and tillers of the soil" (2 Kgs 25:12) who remained in the land were hardly capable of producing written documents. This should serve as a warning signal to those who tend to place much biblical material in Persian period Yehud. My humble advice is therefore twofold.

First, try to date as much material as possible to periods in Judah/Judea that demonstrate widespread scribal activity and literacy in all media and all forms of inscriptions, that is, the latest phase of the Iron Age and late Hellenistic period after circa 200 BCE. The latter possibility calls for a clarification: Is it possible that material was added to the Pentateuch as late as the second century BCE? A good example is the Melchizedek episode in Gen 14, which may be understood on the background of the Hasmonean period (Soggin 1995). The translation of the Torah into Greek is commonly supposed to have taken place during the third century BCE, and it may be difficult to imagine that the first Greek translation was based on a Hebrew text to which whole chapters were later added. On the other hand, it is also obvious that the translated Hebrew text was not yet considered as fixed and stable and that the Greek Torah text is the result of revisions that persisted into the Hasmonean period (Tilly 2005, 57–58, 81–87). So it is possible that, even after a first translation into Greek, short passages were added or revised (Finkelstein and Römer 2014a).

My second piece of advice is that, for the period in between circa 600 and 200 BCE, especially the Babylonian and Persian periods, one should place the compilation of as much material as possible in Babylonia (e.g., Albertz 2003), perhaps also in Egypt. Of course, I accept that there must have been continuity in production of literary works in Yehud; one can imagine, for instance, a secluded, educated priestly group near the temple. But even this is not an elegant solution, as I would have expected something to leak to daily life. In short, I, too, am tantalized by this fact and can only urge scholars not to ignore the archaeological evidence—despite the fact that at times it is mainly negative and even if it threatens to shatter slick, fad-driven theories.

Addendum

For an updated, detailed discussion of Jerusalem following the Babylonian conquest, see Shalom et al. 2019.

Part 7
Conclusions

24

Jerusalem and Empires: Long-Term Observations

In this concluding chapter, I return to the main question that I raised in the introduction to this book: the anomaly of Jerusalem. My goal is to explain how, in certain periods, Jerusalem grew to become the largest and most dominant city in the southern Levant.

Jerusalem is an anomaly. Important ancient cities prospered on international roads with strategic and economic significance, as seaports, as centers in areas of fertile land and abounding agricultural output, or near important natural resources.[1] Jerusalem had nothing of all this. It is located on the desert fringe, in the isolated southern highlands. It is not connected to a major international road; in fact, the only relatively important local west–east road, leading from the coast to Transjordan, passed slightly to its north, and roads from the south, aiming at northern Transjordan or the coast, could easily bypass it. Further, its agricultural land is limited: most of its hinterland is inhospitable, and arable land can be found only to its north or southwest (Gadot 2015). The only "natural resource"—wine and possibly oil from hilly areas to its west—could hardly compete with the same products in the highlands of Samaria to the north. So why in certain periods did Jerusalem become the largest and most prosperous city in the southern Levant? Late Bronze Age Hazor in a fertile valley, on the

---

1. Hosting an important temple is also a reason for prosperity, yet the development of an influential temple may be an outcome of the above-mentioned factors rather than a prime mover. In any event, in the case of Jerusalem the temple became an attraction for people beyond its immediate region only in Roman times.

international road to Syria and beyond, is easy to explain, as is Gaza as an outlet of the Arabian trade routes and Roman Caesarea or medieval Acco on the coast. But why, in the late eighth century, did Jerusalem become a city spread out over 60 hectares, when Ashdod, the most important coastal city of that time, was only half this size? The same can be asked about Jerusalem of the late Hellenistic and early Roman period. Finally, given Jerusalem's lack of visible resources, where did the capital for large-scale public works such as fortifications, monumental buildings, and water systems come from? In what follows I wish to provide a long-term, systemic answer to this question.

Preliminaries

In order to explain the Jerusalem Anomaly, I wish to deal with the period of time between the Late Bronze Age, more specifically the Amarna period in the fourteenth century BCE, and the First Jewish Revolt. This era is crucial for understanding the history of Jerusalem and Judah/Judea in particular and the southern Levant in general, because most of it involves local entities under the influence of neighboring superpowers. No such powers are known before the Late Bronze Age, and after the First Jewish Revolt and until modern times the region was *directly* ruled by great empires. This means that I will be treating a duration of about fifteen hundred years, which covers vital processes and events in the history of the city: the Egyptian rule in Canaan, the rise of the Davidic dynasty, Sennacherib's assault and the Babylonian destruction, the rise and rule of the Hasmonean dynasty, Herodian times and the destruction of the Second Temple.

Before presenting a short settlement history of Jerusalem, I wish to reiterate a crucial issue for understanding its settlement oscillations: the location of its original Bronze and Iron Age mound. Conventional wisdom maintains that the mound of Jerusalem should be sought on the southeastern ridge, known in archaeological research as the City of David (recently Gadot and Uziel 2017; Geva and De Groot 2017; and A. Mazar 2020). However, long periods in the history of Jerusalem—some of them well-attested in the textual record (e.g., the Amarna phase of the Late Bronze Age and the Persian and early Hellenistic periods; see, e.g., Na'aman 1996, 2010c; Finkelstein 2008b)—are represented only by a small number of sherds, with no evidence of building activity. In fact, even these scant finds are known only in the area above and slightly to the south of the Gihon Spring. Moreover, in pre-Roman times the southeastern ridge was fully inhabited only in the Iron IIB–C and the late Hellenistic periods; in all other periods—even those that provide evidence for building endeavors—activity was limited to the area of the Gihon Spring (the Middle Bronze) or the southern slope of the Temple Mount and the area of the spring (the Iron IIA).

There are additional problems in identifying the southeastern ridge as the mound of Bronze and Iron Age Jerusalem.

1. Although the eastern side of the ridge was protected by city walls in the Iron IIB–C and the late Hellenistic periods, no trace of any fortification has ever been found on its western side (Ussishkin 2006a).

2. The earliest remains in the northern sector of the City of David ridge date to the Iron IIA.[2] This means that for earlier periods the conventional theory results in an impossible layout of a city divided into two (the temple and the area of the spring), with a large empty space in its midst (recently Gadot and Uziel 2017; Geva and De Groot 2017; A. Mazar 2020).

3. Highland mounds were usually located in a dominating topographical point; the southeastern ridge is overlooked by higher ground on three sides.

4. The idea that in the Iron Age the Temple Mount—the elevated spot that is the easiest to protect—was occupied only by the temple and the Davidic dynasty's palace and that it featured large, empty spaces is influenced by what scholars know about the situation there in Herodian times and by today's landscape of the Haram al-Sharif platform. However, in the Bronze and Iron Ages no city in the Levant featured this layout; rather, temple and palace compounds formed one sector in densely inhabited capital towns.

In short, the southeastern ridge cannot be regarded as the original mound of ancient Jerusalem.

In view of these observations, the original mound of Jerusalem must have been located on the Temple Mount.[3] Similar to other hubs of Bronze

---

2. E. Mazar 2015b; Winderbaum 2022. See a thorough review in ch. 9 above.

3. Knauf 2000; ch. 2 above. Geva and De Groot (2017) raise two main objections to the mound on the Temple Mount proposal: (1) The project of sifting debris bulldozed by the Waqf from the area of Al-Aqsa Mosque yielded only a few pre-Iron II sherds (Barkay and Zweig 2006), and sherds collected from the eastern

Age city-states and Iron Age territorial kingdoms, this mound, which could have covered an area of 5 hectares (the size of the biggest tells in the highlands, such as Shechem), included both residential and public areas. This original mound was the heart of Jerusalem in the Bronze and Iron Ages. Before Roman times, the city expanded to cover both the southeastern ridge and the southwestern hill (the Jewish and Armenian Quarters of today's Old City and Mount Zion) only in the Iron IIB–C and the late Hellenistic periods and was then surrounded by fortifications.

A Brief Survey of Jerusalem's Settlement History

Having located the old tell on the Temple Mount, I now proceed with a brief survey of the settlement history of Jerusalem, that is, the extent of the city and the size of its population. Although I have already discussed many of these matters previously, it is essential to present this summary in order to draw conclusions regarding periods of prosperity and decline and their connection to imperial rule.

In the Early Bronze Age, the urban center of the southern highlands was located at Khirbet et-Tell (Ai) to the north of Jerusalem. The architectural evidence from Jerusalem's southeastern ridge is poor at best (summary in Maeir 2000), hence the settlement must have been located on the Temple Mount. This was also the hub of the Middle Bronze town. Major fortifications and water installations unearthed near the Gihon Spring were dated to this period.[4] These fortifications may have belonged to an extramural fortress that protected the water source. The Amarna letters of the fourteenth century BCE disclose that Jerusalem was the hub of

---

slope of the Temple Mount did not yield pre–Iron II items (Dvira [Zweig], Zigdon, and Shilov 2011). This is probably due to site formation processes and strong cover in the Iron II, early Roman, and later periods, as well as to the distance of the supposed mound from these spots. (2) Bedrock is exposed on the eastern slope and summit of the Temple Mount. This is no argument, as a similar situation is known in other highlands mounds, e.g., Tell en-Naṣbeh, Kiriath-jearim and Shiloh. For additional comments on Geva and De Groot's article, see Finkelstein 2023.

4. Reich 2011, 2018; Reich and Shukron 2004, 2010; contra Ussishkin 2016; Regev et al. 2017. I doubt if these fortifications extended further to the south, contra De Groot 2012, 144–49.

a city-state that ruled over the southern highlands. The town of this period also must have been located on the Temple Mount; in the City of David the finds are limited to a small number of sherds, retrieved mainly above the spring. The Iron I displays slightly stronger evidence (Shiloh 1984, 26; Steiner 2001, 24–41; E. Mazar 2009, 39–41), though still limited in scope.

The first significant change came in the Iron IIA, when the town expanded from the Temple Mount to the northern sector of the southeastern ridge. Remains of monumental structures, probably dating to this period, have been unearthed immediately to the south of the Al-Aqsa Mosque (E. Mazar 2015b; critical review in ch. 9 above) and above the Gihon Spring (E. Mazar 2007, 2009; dating according to chs. 7 and 8 above). Poorer remains were uncovered in the Givati Compound, to the west of the latter (Ben-Ami 2014). This means that the town almost doubled its size. The next, dramatic expansion of Jerusalem, in the Iron IIB, included both the southeastern and southwestern hills. Jerusalem now stretched over an area at least six times larger than the Iron IIA town and more than ten times larger than the original mound on the Temple Mount; this issue has been intensively discussed (Geva 2003b; Reich and Shukron 2003; ch. 15 above) and its reasons debated (recently Na'aman 2014a; ch. 14 above, with reference to previous studies). This "great leap forward" took place in the second half (or better, the last third) of the eighth century BCE. As a result, for almost a century and a half, until its destruction in 586 BCE, Jerusalem was the biggest city in the southern Levant.

Almost no architectural finds dating to the next 450 years, until the late second century BCE, have been uncovered in Jerusalem (Finkelstein 2008b). Pottery and seal impressions collected especially near the Gihon Spring indicate a certain activity. The same holds true for the Givati Compound, where recent fieldwork revealed evidence for limited activity in the early Persian period in the ruins of an elaborate Iron IIC building and remains dating to the second century (Shalev et al. 2020; review in Finkelstein 2023). A small settlement must have been located on the Temple Mount at that time, and this could have been the place referred to in the part of the book of Nehemiah known as the Nehemiah Memoir (the description of the city wall in Neh 3 represents later reality).[5] Jerusalem

---

5. Finkelstein 2008b; contra Lipschits 2012. For the possibility that the Nehemiah Memoir also exhibits Hasmonean realities, see Diaz Solano 2020.

grew again to encompass the southeastern and southwestern hills in the late Hellenistic period, under the Hasmoneans (Geva 2003a, 526–35), and was thereafter gradually fitted with monumental buildings, including the Herodian Temple Mount—probably the biggest single building project in the history of the region in antiquity.

Archaeology, then, shows that, in the millennium and a half discussed here, Jerusalem went through several dramatic oscillations of growth and decline. The written sources disclose that during most of this era Jerusalem was dominated by either foreign powers or by strong local Levantine forces. Regarding the former, there are two opposing situations: empires that brought about prosperity and those whose rule is characterized by decline. I therefore need to provide two explanations: for the Jerusalem anomaly and for the contradiction between two types of imperial rule.

Jerusalem and Empires

I now wish to integrate what we know from archaeology with the textual evidence. I am aware of the fact that this may create a bias for periods with no textual record or for which the historicity of the textual material is contested. Still, this part, too, is essential in order to reach the broader insights that are presented in the last part of this chapter.

Under Egyptian Rule (ca. 1450–1130 BCE)

Starting in the fifteenth century BCE, Jerusalem was under the hegemony of the Egyptian Empire. The Amarna tablets disclose interesting information about the status of the town. Jerusalem ruled over the entire southern highlands (Finkelstein 1996c; contra Na'aman 1992a; 2010d, 46), while Shechem dominated the hill country to its north. Abdi-heba, the local ruler, was involved in affairs far from Jerusalem (EA 288), which means that the town's influence was significant compared to its marginal location and minimal resources. Jerusalem attempted to expand to the west, into territories contested with Gezer, Gath, and perhaps also Lachish (Na'aman 2010d; ch. 4 above). In parallel, Labayu of Shechem tried to extend his rule into the Jezreel Valley to its north. At first glance, the threats caused by Jerusalem and Shechem to the Egyptian interests in

Canaan look analogous; however, the Egyptian authorities' reaction was not similar. While in the north they eliminated Labayu and prepared for a military expedition to pacify the country, in the south Abdi-heba was not punished.

In a previous article (ch. 4 above) I reconstructed two coalitions in the south of Canaan, with Egypt backing the city-states of the Shephelah. Looking at the evidence afresh, I now suggest a somewhat different scenario, in which Jerusalem was, in fact, of pivotal importance for Egyptian rule. This is hinted at in the letters of Abdi-heba referring to the existence of an Egyptian stronghold and garrison in Jerusalem (EA 285–287, 289) and in his intimate relationship with Egyptian "commissioners" in Canaan (Na'aman 2010d). Note that in EA 289 Abdi-heba compares Jerusalem to Gaza, the center of Egyptian rule in Canaan. One could add expressions such as "I am a soldier for the king" (EA 285) or "neither my father nor my mother put me in this place, but the strong arm of the king" (EA 286, 287, 288); they can be read as literary formulae (Moran 1975; Na'aman 2010d) but may at the same time hint that Abdi-heba was indeed a servant of Egyptian interests. It is also possible that Egypt established a stronghold in the highlands immediately to the west of Jerusalem (ch. 19 above). The intimate relationship with Egypt would explain why the pharaohs did not intervene against Jerusalem's expansion attempts to the west. In short, the strength of remote and poor Jerusalem in the Amarna period stemmed from its close connection with the Egyptian administration in Canaan. This, in turn, may have stemmed from its location: blocking Shechem in the north and guarding the approach to the desert in the south.

The Amarna correspondence illuminates only a few decades in the fourteenth century BCE, but it is logical to assume, though impossible to prove, that the situation of Jerusalem serving the Egyptian empire continued until the withdrawal of Egypt from Canaan in the late twelfth century BCE. The reference to the "Wells of Merneptah … which is on the mountain ridge" in Papyrus Anastasi 3 (Wilson 1969, 258), if indeed pointing to a place in the vicinity of Jerusalem (ch. 19 above), may support this hypothesis.

Who Is in Charge (ca. 1130–880 BCE)?

We know nothing about the Iron I, neither from archaeology nor from the written sources. The Sheshonq I topographical list, inscribed in the second half of the tenth century and summarizing his campaign in Canaan, does not mention Jerusalem or any other town in Judah. On the other hand, it seems to hint at the existence of a center of power in the Gibeon Plateau to the north. Rather than assuming that Judah paid taxes to Egypt at Gibeon (e.g., Kitchen 1986, 447), a theory that stemmed from the idea of a great united monarchy in the decades before the Sheshonq I campaign, this seems to hint that Jerusalem had no importance at that time or that it cooperated with the pharaoh. In the latter scenario, the rise of the Southern Kingdom was, in fact, the result of renewed imperial Egyptian interests in Canaan. Until the campaign, Jerusalem could have been dominated by the above-mentioned north Israelite territorial entity that had its hub in the area of Geba-Gibeon. Whether this was so depends on the historical value of the biblical verses reporting King Saul's presence at Adullam and the Valley of Elah (ch. 5 above).

From the biblical record alone, it is difficult to reconstruct the status of Jerusalem in the days of the early kings of Judah; if the account in 1 Kgs 15:17, 22 regarding the conflict between Baasha and Asa has any historical value, it may hint that already before the Omrides Judah had been subject to Israelite pressure.

Local Powers (ca. 880–730 BCE)

During the Omride dynasty rule in the north (884–842 BCE), Jerusalem was under the hegemony of Israel. The dominance of Israel is expressed in the biblical account of Ahab and Jehoshaphat, as well as Joram and Ahaziah, the latter supported by the Tel Dan Stela; these biblical accounts, even if redacted centuries later, originated from northern prophetic circles before the fall of the north. The royal marriage of the Israelite princess Athaliah to a Davidic king was an Israelite attempt to appropriate Judah from within (e.g., Miller and Hayes 2006, 303–4); the account on the murder of the Davidide heirs to the throne by Athaliah should also be seen in this light.[6]

---

6. Miller and Hayes (2006, 320–23) proposed that the northern Joram and southern Jehoram who ruled in approximately the same years could have been one and the same person—a complete takeover of Judah by Israel in the middle of the ninth century BCE.

For the four decades following Damascus's victory over Israel at Ramoth-gilead in 841 BCE, hegemony over Jerusalem shifted from the Omrides to Aram. Hazael's destruction of Gath in the west and the decline of the copper-related "Masos chiefdom" in the south opened the way for Judah's expansion to the Shephelah and Beersheba Valley (Fantalkin and Finkelstein 2006; Fantalkin 2008; Sergi 2013; Finkelstein 2014d). This is apparently the time when Jerusalem expanded from the mound on the Temple Mount southward, in the direction of the Gihon Spring. Monumental buildings seem to have been constructed in the eastern sector of the Ophel[7] and slightly to the south, above the spring. The rise of an administration system more sophisticated than before is expressed in the large number of iconic but uninscribed bullae that date to the later phase of the late Iron IIA (Reich, Shukron, and Lernau 2007), in the late ninth century BCE or circa 800 BCE. All this means that the first significant growth of Jerusalem as well as territorial expansion of Judah took place under Damascene hegemony and Damascene-related economic prosperity. Judah was made the guardian of Aram's interests in the south, controlling the incipient Arabian trade and promoting Cypriot copper supply by blocking transportation of Arabah copper to the coast.[8]

With the decline of Damascus in the days of Adad-nirari III, Israel reexerted its hegemony over Judah in the days of Joash and Jeroboam II. This is expressed in the chronistic account of the defeat of Amaziah at the hands of Joash at Beth-shemesh and the resulting takeover of Jerusalem (2 Kgs 14:11b–15), as well as in the construction of the summit compound at Kiriath-jearim in the days of Jeroboam II (Finkelstein and Römer 2020; ch. 11 above). Another archaeological clue comes from the finds at Kuntillet ʿAjrud, which also seem to depict Israelite hegemony over Judah in the first half of the eighth century BCE (various chapters in Meshel 2012; Ornan 2015).

---

7. E. Mazar 2015b. The remains date to the Iron IIA, probably to the later phase of the period; see ch. 9 above.

8. On the southern trade prior to the eighth century, see Liverani 1992; Jasmin 2005.

The Assyrian Century (ca. 730–630 BCE)

Under Assyrian domination, Jerusalem and Judah prospered as never before. The details have been discussed at length (e.g., Geva 2003b; Reich and Shukron 2003; chs. 15 and 19 above); suffice it to say that in a matter of a few decades the territory of the city expanded from less than 10 to 60 hectares, and the population grew accordingly. Similar processes took place in the countryside of Judah, both in the highlands and the Shephelah.

This period, too, discloses a clear difference in the policy of the suzerain toward the highlands polity. The territory of Israel had much to offer economically: vast, fertile valleys, horticulture in the highlands, a major prospering seaport at Dor, control over the international road to Egypt, the horse industry at Megiddo, and, not to be downplayed, human resources. Further, because of its strategic location, at Samaria, as much as in Damascus, the threat of rebellion carried with it serious implications. Hence Tiglath-pileser III and his successors opted for conquest, deportations, and direct rule in the territories of the Northern Kingdom. Judah was poor enough so as not to whet the Assyrian appetite; it was also remote and weak enough not to pose a threat. Hence it survived as a client-state of Assyria, something of an outpost designed to serve the political and economic concerns of the empire (for the economy, see ch. 20). In the west, pre-701 Judah with its strong Shephelah population could serve Assyrian interests on the outskirts of the border with Egypt. In the south, Assyria, with the help of Judah, blocked the western desert road from the Gulf of Aqaba to the Mediterranean and promoted the alternative Arabian trade route along the Edomite Plateau and the Beer-sheba Valley. There can be no doubt, then, that the prosperity of Jerusalem was Assyria-inspired. It is noteworthy that even the 701 uprising did not motivate Assyria to remove Judah from the map. The fact that, unlike the Shephelah, the Beersheba Valley survived as Judahite territory indicates that Judahite rule in this area was of the highest economic importance to Assyria. This is well attested by the system of Assyrian fortresses in the south, which were probably operated on a daily basis by Judahite and Edomite troops (Na'aman 2001a, 267–68).

The impact of Assyria on the Judahite vassal kingdom can be seen in different facets, such as in economic regional specialization and the ensuing development of an advanced bureaucratic system (ch. 20 above), in participation of Judah in the above-mentioned Assyrian control system in the south, in certain domains of material culture (e.g., Winderbaum 2015), and, of course, in aspects of the biblical text. Recent discoveries in the Jerusalem highlands hint at the existence there of royal gardens that seem to have been influenced by similar places in Assyria (Ein Mor and Ron 2013).

Centuries of Decline (ca. 630–130 BCE)

Some scholars suggested a certain decline in Jerusalem in the Iron IIC (Geva 2003a, 522–23; for Judah, see Ofer 1994, 106), which can be translated as relating to the decades after the Assyrian withdrawal from the region. I doubt if the archeological data support this idea (ch. 16 above); the phenomenon of a large city with significant population continued for a few decades under the domination of Egypt's Twenty-Sixth Dynasty and until the Babylonian destruction.

A period of decline that lasted for over four centuries followed. Some evidence of activity has been detected in post-586 destruction Jerusalem (Barkay 2003; Shalev et al. 2020), but the overall picture is that of desolation; textually we know that the center of power shifted to Mizpah. Even when the hub of Yehud returned to Jerusalem, the picture drawn by archaeology is that of sparse activity. Almost no Persian and early Hellenistic architectural remains have been uncovered, and the evidence for settlement activity is limited to pottery and seal impressions in the vicinity of the spring and slightly to its south. Regardless of its date of composition, the Nehemiah Memoir on the deplorable situation of the town (without the description of the building of the wall in Neh 3) probably relates to the old tell. The sherd evidence from the eastern slopes of the Temple Mount (Dvira [Zweig], Zigdon, and Shilov 2011), as well as from the sifting project of earth bulldozed by the Waqf from the area of the Al-Aqsa Mosque (Barkay and Zweig 2006), hint that even in the old mound activity was weak.

During this entire period Yehud/early Judea was ruled by strong superpowers: Babylonia, Achaemenid Persia, and Ptolemaic Egypt. Obviously, unlike the Assyrians before them and the Romans later, they did not promote Jerusalem as an important city. The reason must have stemmed from different geopolitical preferences of the overlords: Babylonia opted for destruction and devastation, with certain emphasis on Transjordan and possibly diversion of the Arabian trade routes via Mesopotamia and Syria to the coast of the Levant, while the Achaemenids and Ptolemies invested much of their efforts along the coast (Lipschits 2006).

Renewed Prosperity (ca. 130 BCE–70 CE)

In the following two centuries, from the Hasmoneans until the Jewish Revolt, Jerusalem was back as the most important city in the southern Levant. The Hasmonean uprising started in a small Judea that covered a territory in the highlands between Mizpah and Beth-zur.[9] The Hasmoneans then brilliantly exploited rivalries in the Seleucid kingdom in order to gain territory. Growth was gradual; first the Seleucids conceded territories in southern Samaria to Jonathan, and Simeon took over Gezer and Jaffa, meaning the creation of an outlet to the sea. The great leap forward for Judea took place in the days of John Hyrcanus, when the Hamsonean state stretched from northern Samaria to the south Hebron Hills and the Beersheba Valley, and slightly later, when the Galilee was also annexed to their state (Avi-Yonah 1977, 52–76). There were some deliberations regarding the date of construction of the First Wall in Jerusalem, that is, the regrowth of the city to its size in the Iron IIB–C (Geva 2003a, 533–34). Such a large-scale construction project requires significant resources, including a workforce, and I cannot see such wealth in Judea before the territorial expansion in the days of Hyrcanus. Moreover, from a historical viewpoint the fortification of Jerusalem must have been a reaction to the surprise attack of Antiochus VII Sidetes in the early days of Hyrcanus. This dating may be supported by recent discoveries. If the Hellenistic fortification, including the impressive glacis, unearthed in the Givati Compound indeed belongs to the Hellenistic Acra, and the towers discovered long ago on the eastern slope were part of this citadel (Ben-Ami and Tchekhanovets 2015; Zilberstein 2019), then the First Wall is later than this citadel, which was taken over by Simeon in 141 BCE.

With the conquest of Samaria by John Hyrcanus and more so the conquest of the Galilee by Aristobulus I, Hasmonean Jerusalem ruled over much of the territory of the ancient kingdoms of Israel and Judah combined, which gave it significant economic and geopolitical clout. The several decades between the days of Hyrcanus and the takeover by Pompey the Great were the only "independent" days of Jerusalem as a major city, when it was not dominated by stronger powers.

---

9. Similar to that of Yehud in the Persian period; see Finkelstein 2010b.

The rest—Judea as a vassal of Rome until the destruction in 70 CE—is well known. There is no need to elaborate here, except perhaps to recall the impact of Roman culture on its client kingdom, stronger, but not dissimilar in nature, than that of Assyria several centuries before.

The following table summarizes the history of Jerusalem vis-à-vis the great empires and the local Levantine powers between the Amarna period and the First Jewish Revolt.

Approximate date	Suzerain		Jerusalem
	Empire	Local power	
1450–1130 BCE	Egypt		mound on the Temple Mount; strong territorial influence in Canaan
1130–880 BCE	Possible involvement of Egypt (Shehsonq I)	Egypt? Israel?	mound on the Temple Mount
880–840 BCE		Israel	mound on the Temple Mount
840–800 BCE		Damascus	expansion in the direction of the Gihon Spring
800–730 BCE		Israel	
730–630 BCE	Assyria		large city, including the southwestern hill
630–586 BCE	Egypt, Babylonia		
586–130 BCE	Babylonia, Persia, Ptolemaic Egypt, Seleucids		sparse activity; mound on the Temple Mount
130–63 BCE	Independent of direct foreign power		large city, including the southwestern hill
63 BCE–70 CE	Rome		same as before plus expansion to the north

Jerusalem, Empires, and Local Powers: A Systemic Approach

From the point of view of location and resources, Jerusalem is a marginal phenomenon. It could prosper almost only as a vassal serving stronger powers. Catering to such forces—empires or local Levantine suzerains—was indeed the destiny of the city in almost all of the roughly millennium and a half discussed here.

Empires that dominated the Levant were of diverse nature and interests and ruled in different geopolitical circumstances. Accordingly, two—Assyria and Rome—promoted Jerusalem, while others—Babylonia, Achaemenid Persia, and Ptolemaic Egypt—neglected it.

Egypt—another empire that exploited Jerusalem to advance its goals in Canaan in the Late Bronze Age—did not bring about the same prosperity as Assyria and Rome. Indeed, the different nature of New Kingdom Egypt and Assyria as dominating empires can be detected in diverse aspects of material culture and in the textual record. Evidence has recently been traced for advanced, standardized, and specialized economy in the Assyrian century that did not exist in the period of Egyptian rule in Canaan (Finkelstein et al. 2011; Sapir-Hen, Gadot, and Finkelstein 2014; ch. 20 above). One can argue that, economically, Assyria's impact was closer in nature to Rome's than to Egypt's.

Prosperity under Assyria and Rome meant strong foreign impact in every aspect of life in Jerusalem and Judah/Judea. Empires are by definition multicultural, as they rule over diverse territories and populations. By contrast, an isolated, demographically homogenous, ideologically motivated, and tribal-in-nature place such as Jerusalem is monocultural. When these opposites meet, the inevitable result is a disastrous clash: cultural and political resistance, revolt, and destruction. This cycle is true for the Sennacherib campaign on Judah and, of course, for the First Jewish Revolt. This and the misconception of geopolitical situations by the leadership of isolated Judah brought about the catastrophes of the Sennacherib campaign, the killing of Josiah at Megiddo, and the Babylonian destruction.

The importance of Jerusalem as a servant of empires and strong local forces was mainly in its location on the southern fringe: controlling the most important outlet of the Arabian trade routes, preventing desert groups from raiding the sedentary land, and playing the role of a buffer polity near the border of Egypt. Hence empires that considered the desert fringe and border with Egypt important preferred Jerusalem over Samaria as a client-state. Stripped of fertile valleys and the coast, Samaria had less to offer to their interests.

Left to struggle on the scene of the Levant without imperial protection in the Iron IIA and the early Iron IIB, Jerusalem and Judah could not but be dominated by the two stronger local powers that competed for hegemony in the region: Israel and Damascus. Both seem to have exploited

24. Jerusalem and Empires: Long-Term Observations

Jerusalem somewhat similarly to the great empires: to serve their interests along the outlets of the southern trade routes. This is evident especially in the expansion of Judah to the Shephelah and Beersheba Valley in the late Iron IIA under Damascene hegemony and from the role played by Judah under Israelite auspices in the south in the early Iron IIB, as expressed in the finds of Kuntillet ʿAjrud (various studies in Meshel 2012).

The only period of local strength in Jerusalem, when it was not dominated by an empire or local Levantine polity, was that of the Hasmoneans—about sixty years between the days of John Hyrcanus and the takeover of the region by Pompey the Great. Similar to other phenomena in the history of the Levant—for instance, Amurru of the Late Bronze Age and many centuries later Fakhr ed-Din in the early Ottoman period, both in the mountains of Lebanon, and Dahr el-Umar in the lower Galilee (Marfoe 1979; Goren, Finkelstein, and Naʾaman 2003)—the Hasmoneans exploited a unique geopolitical moment in order to expand from the highlands to the lowlands, including the coast, and create a powerful territorial kingdom. In fact, for sixty years in the late Hellenistic period Jerusalem played a role in the southern Levant similar to that of Samaria and Damascus in the Iron Age IIA.

In periods in which the region was ruled by empires that had lesser interest in the desert fringe and the border with Egypt, Jerusalem lost its importance and retreated to the status of a small town controlling limited territory in the southern highlands. In fact, the standing of Jerusalem in the Persian and early Hellenistic periods was perhaps the norm—what can be expected from the local resources without serving as a client of a stronger force.

Works Cited

Aharoni, Miriam. 1981a. "Inscribed Weights and Royal Seals." Pages 126–27 in *Arad Inscriptions*, by Yohanan Aharoni. Judean Desert Studies. Jerusalem: Israel Exploration Society.

———. 1981b. "The Pottery of Strata 12–11 of the Iron Age Citadel at Arad" [Hebrew]. *ErIsr* 15:181–204.

Aharoni, Yohanan. 1964. *Excavations at Ramat Raḥel: Seasons of 1961 and 1962*. Rome: Università degli studi, Centro di studi.

———. 1968a. "Arad: Its Inscriptions and Temple." *BA* 31:1–32.

———. 1968b. "Negev, ha'Negev" [Hebrew]. *Encyclopaedia Biblica* 5:749–52.

———. 1969. "Rubute and Ginti-kirmil." *VT* 19:141–44.

———. 1971. "The Hebrew Inscriptions." Pages 71–78 in *Beer-sheba I: Excavations at Tel Beer-sheba, 1969–1971 Seasons*. Edited by Yohanan Aharoni. Tel Aviv: Tel-Aviv University Institute of Archaeology.

———. 1974. "The Horned Altar at Beersheba." *BA* 37:2–23.

———. 1975a. "Excavations at Tel Beer-sheba, Preliminary Report of the Fifth and Sixth Seasons, 1973–1974." *TA* 2:146–68.

———. 1975b. *Investigations at Lachish: The Sanctuary and the Residency (Lachish V)*. Tel Aviv: Gateway.

———. 1976. "Nothing Early and Nothing Late: Rewriting Israel's Conquest." *BA* 39:55–76.

———. 1979. *The Land of the Bible: A Historical Geography*. Philadelphia: Westminster.

———. 1981. *Arad Inscriptions*. Judean Desert Studies. Jerusalem: Israel Exploration Society.

———. 1986. *Arad Inscriptions* [Hebrew]. Jerusalem: Bialik.

Ahituv, Shmuel. 1982. "Tamar" [Hebrew]. *EncBib* 8:607–8.

———. 1984. *Canaanite Toponyms in Ancient Egyptian Documents*. Jerusalem: Magnes; Leiden: Brill.

———. 2008. *Echoes from the Past: Hebrew and Cognate Inscriptions from the Biblical Period.* Jerusalem: Carta.

Ahituv, Shmuel, Ether Eshel, and Ze'ev Meshel. 2012. "The Inscriptions." Pages 73–142 in *Kuntillet ʿAjrud (Ḥorvat Teman): An Iron Age II Religious Site on the Judah-Sinai Border*, by Ze'ev Meshel. Edited by Liora Freud. Jerusalem: Israel Exploration Society.

Ahlström, Gösta W. 1993. *The History of Ancient Palestine from the Palaeolithic Period to Alexander's Conquest.* JSOT 146. Sheffield: JSOT Press.

Albenda, Pauline. 1976. "Landscape Bas-Reliefs in the *Bīt-Ḥilāni* of Ashurbanipal." *BASOR* 224:49–72.

Albertz, Rainer. 2003. *Israel in Exile: The History and Literature of the Sixth Century B.C.E.* Translated by David Green. SBLStBL 3. Atlanta: Society of Biblical Literature.

Albright, William F. 1930–1931. "Excavations at Jerusalem." *JQR* 21:163–68.

———. 1932. *The Excavation of Tell Beit Mirsim I: The Pottery of the First Three Campaigns.* AASOR 12. New Haven: American Schools of Oriental Research.

———. 1943. *The Excavation of Tell Beit Mirsim III: The Iron Age.* AASOR 21–22. New Haven: American Schools of Oriental Research.

———. 1958. "Was the Age of Solomon without Monumental Art?" *ErIsr* 5:1*–9*.

———. 1961. "Abraham the Hebrew: A New Archaeological Interpretation." *BASOR* 163:36–54.

Alexandre, Y. 2002a. "A Fluted Bronze Bowl with a Canaanite-Early Phoenician Inscription from Kefar Veradim." Pages 65–74 in *Eretz Zafon: Studies in Galilean Archaeology*. Edited by Zvi Gal. Jerusalem: Israel Antiquities Authority.

———. 2000b. "The Iron Age Assemblage from Cave 3 at Kefar Veradim." Pages 53–63 in *Eretz Zafon: Studies in Galilean Archaeology*. Edited by Zvi Gal. Jerusalem: Israel Antiquities Authority.

Alt, Albrecht. 1925. "Judas Gaue unter Josia." *PJb* 21:100–116.

———. 1928. "Das Taltor von Jerusalem." *PJb* 24:74–98.

———. 1939. "Erwägungen über die Landnahme der Israeliten in Palästina." *PJb* 35:8–63.

———. 1953. *Kleine Schriften zur Geschichte des Volkes Israel II.* Munich: Beck.

Amar, Zohar. 1999. "Agricultural Produces in the Lachish Relief" [Hebrew]. *BetM* 159:350–56.

Amit, David. 2009. "Water Supply to the Upper City of Jerusalem during the First and Second Temple Periods in Light of the Mamilla Excavations" [Hebrew]. *NSAJR* 3:94–108.

———. 2011. "First and Second Temple Period Discoveries near the Mamilla Pool in Jerusalem." *Qad* 44:29–39.

Amit, David, and Irit Yezerski. 2001. "An Iron Age II Cemetery and Wine Presses at an-Nabi Danyal." *IEJ* 51:171–193.

Applebaum, Shimon, Shimon Dar, and Zeev Safrai. 1978. "The Towers of Samaria." *PEQ* 110:91–100.

Arie, Eran. 2008. "Reconsidering the Iron Age II Strata at Tel Dan: Archaeological and Historical Implications." *TA* 35:6–64.

Ariel, Donald T., and Alon De Groot, 2000. "The Iron Age Extramural Occupation at the City of David and Additional Observations on the Siloam Channel." Pages 155–69 in *Extramural Areas*. Vol. 5 of *Excavations at the City of David 1978–1985 Directed by Yigal Shiloh*. Edited by Donald T. Ariel. Qedem 40. Jerusalem: Institute of Archaeology, Hebrew University.

Ariel, Donald T., and Jodi Magness. 1992. "Area K: Stratigraphic Report." Pages 63–97 in *Stratigraphical, Environmental, and Other Reports*. Vol. 3 of *Excavations at the City of David 1978–1985 Directed by Yigal Shiloh*. Edited by Alon De Groot and Donald T. Ariel. Qedem 33. Jerusalem: Institute of Archaeology, Hebrew University.

Arnold, Patrick M. 1990. *Gibeah: The Search for a Biblical City*. JSOTSup 79. Sheffield: JSOT Press.

Asadpour, Ali. 2018. "Phenomenology of Garden in Assyrian Documents and Reliefs; Concepts and Types." *The Monthly Scientific Journal of Bagh-e Nazar* 15:55–66.

Ash, Paul S. 1995. "Solomon's? District? List." *JSOT* 67:67–86.

Astour, Michael C. 1966. "Political and Cosmic Symbolism in Genesis 14 and Its Babylonian Sources." Pages 65–112 in *Biblical Motifs: Origins and Transformations*. Edited by Alexander Altmann. Cambridge: Harvard University Press.

Auld, A. Graeme, and Craig Y. S. Ho. 1992. "The Making of David and Goliath." *JSOT* 56:19–39.

Avigad, Nahman. 1958. "New Light on the MṢH Seal Impressions." *IEJ* 8:113–19.

———. 1983. *Discovering Jerusalem*. Nashville: Nelson.

———. 1986. *Hebrew Bullae from the Time of Jeremiah: Remnants of a Burnt Archive*. Jerusalem: Israel Exploration Society.

Avigad, Nahman, and Gabriel Barkay. 2000. "The *lmlk* and Related Seal Impressions." Pages 243–66 in *Architecture and Stratigraphy, Areas A, W and X-2*. Vol. 1 of *Jewish Quarter Excavations in the Old City of Jerusalem*. Edited by Hillel Geva. Jerusalem: Israel Exploration Society.

Avigad, Nahman, and Hillel Geva. 2000. "Area A—Stratigraphy and Architecture: Iron Age II Strata 9–7." Pages 44–82 in *Architecture and Stratigraphy, Areas A, W and X-2*. Vol. 1 of *Jewish Quarter Excavations in the Old City of Jerusalem*. Edited by Hillel Geva. Jerusalem: Israel Exploration Society.

Avigad, Nahman, and Benjamin Sass. 1997. *Corpus of West Semitic Stamp Seals*. Jerusalem: Israel Exploration Society; Institute of Archaeology, the Hebrew University of Jerusalem.

Avi-Yonah, Michael. 1977. *The Holy Land from the Persian to the Arab Conquests (536 B.C. to A.D. 640): A Historical Geography*. Grand Rapids: Baker.

Ayalon, Etan. 2012. *Images from the Land of the Bible: People, Life and Landscapes, 1898–1946*. Exhibition catalog. Eretz Israel Museum, Tel Aviv.

Bahat, Dan. 1980. *Jerusalem: Selected Plans of Historical Sites and Monumental Buildings*. Jerusalem: Ariel.

Bar-Adon, Pesach. 1989. *Excavations in the Judean Desert* [Hebrew]. 'Atiqot 9. Jerusalem: Israel Antiquities Authority.

Barkay, Gabriel. 2000. "The Necropoli of Jerusalem in the First Temple Period" [Hebrew]. Pages 233–70 in *The History of Jerusalem: The Biblical Period*. Edited by Shmuel Ahituv and Amihai Mazar. Jerusalem: Yad Izhaq Ben-Zvi.

———. 2003. "The King's Palace and 'The House of the People' in Jerusalem at the Time of the Babylonian Conquest" [Hebrew]. *New Studies on Jerusalem* 9:21–28.

———. 2006. "Royal Palace, Royal Portrait? The Tantalizing Possibilities of Ramat Rahel." *BAR* 32.5:34–44.

Barkay, Gabriel, and Zachi Zweig. 2006. "The Project of Sifting Soil from the Temple Mount: Preliminary Report" [Hebrew]. *New Studies on Jerusalem* 11:213–37.

———. 2007. "New Data in the Sifting Project of the Soil from the Temple Mount: Second Preliminary Report" [Hebrew]. Pages 27–68 in *City of David: Studies of Ancient Jerusalem; The Eighth Annual Conference*. Edited by Eyal Meiron. Jerusalem: Megalim.

Barstad, Hans M. 1996. *The Myth of the Empty Land: A Study in the History and Archaeology of Judah during the "Exilic" Period.* Oslo: Scandinavian University Press.

Baruch, Yuval. 2007. "A Farmstead from the End of the Iron Age and Installations at the Foot of Khirbat Abu Shawan" [Hebrew]. *'Atiqot* 56:25–55.

Beit-Arieh, Itzhaq. 1993. "A Literary Ostracon from Horvat 'Uza." *TA* 20:55–63.

———. 1999. "Stratigraphy and Historical Background." Pages 170–78 in *Tel 'Ira: A Stronghold in the Biblical Negev.* Edited by Itzhaq Beit-Arieh. Monograph Series of the Institute of Archaeology Tel Aviv University 15. Tel Aviv: Emery and Claire Yass Publications in Archaeology, Institute of Archaeology, Tel Aviv University.

———. 2003. *Archaeological Survey of Israel, Map of Tel Malhata (144).* Jerusalem: Israel Antiquities Authority.

———. 2007. "Epigraphic Finds." Pages 122–87 in *Ḥorvat 'Uza and Ḥorvat Radum: Two Fortresses in the Biblical Negev.* Edited by Itzhaq Beit-Arieh. Monograph Series of the Institute of Archaeology, Tel Aviv University 25. Tel Aviv: Emery and Claire Yass Publications in Archaeology.

Ben-Ami, Doron. 2014. "Notes on the Iron IIA Settlement in Jerusalem in Light of Excavations in the Northwest of the City of David." *TA* 41:3–19.

Ben-Ami, Doron, and Yana Tchekhanovets. 2008. "The Contribution of the Excavations at the 'Givati Parking Lot' to the Study of the History of the Early Settlement in the City of David" [Hebrew]." Pages 97–112 in *City of David: Studies of Ancient Jerusalem; The Ninth Annual Conference.* Edited by Eyal Meiron. Jerusalem: Megalim.

———. 2010. "The Extent of Jerusalem during the Iron Age IIA" [Hebrew]. *NSAJR* 4:67–73.

———. 2015. "The Seleucid Fortification System in the Givati Parking Lot, City of David" [Hebrew]. *NSAJR* 9:313–22.

———. 2016. "'Then They Built Up the City of David with a High, Strong Wall and Strong Towers, and It Became Their Citadel' (I Maccabees 1:33)." *City of David Studies of Ancient Jerusalem* 11:19–29.

Ben-Dor Evian, Shirly. 2011. "Shishak's Karnak Relief: More Than Just Name Rings." Pages 1–22 in *Egypt, Canaan and Israel: History, Imperialism, Ideology and Literature; Proceedings of a Conference at the*

University of Haifa, 3–7 May 2009. Edited by Shay Bar, Dan'el Kahn, and J. J. Shirley. Leiden: Brill.

Bennett, Crystal-M. 1982. "Neo-Assyrian Influence in Transjordan." *Studies in the History and Archaeology of Jordan* 1:181–87.

Ben-Shlomo, David, and Emanuel Eisenberg. 2017. *The Tel Hevron 2014 Excavations: Final Report*. Ariel: Ariel University Press.

Bezzel, Hannes. 2015. *Saul: Israels König in Tradition, Redaction und früher Rezeption*. FAT 97. Tübingen: Mohr Siebeck.

Bienkowski, Piotr. 1991. *Treasures from an Ancient Land: The Art of Jordan*. Stroud, Gloucestershire: Sutton.

———. 2001. "New Evidence on Edom in the Neo-Babylonian and Persian Periods." Pages 198–213 in *The Land That I Will Show You: Essays in the History and Archaeology of the Ancient Near East in Honour of J. Maxwell Miller*. Edited by J. Andrew Dearman and M. Patrick Graham. JSOTSup 343. Sheffield: Sheffield Academic.

———. 2002. *Busayra: Excavations by Crystal-M. Bennett, 1971–1980*. Oxford: Oxford University Press.

Billig, Ya'akov, Liora Freud, and Efrat Bocher. 2022. "A Luxurious Royal Estate from the First Temple Period in Armon ha-Natziv, Jerusalem." *TA* 49:8–31.

Blenkinsopp, Jospeh. 1974. "Did Saul Make Gibeon His Capital?" *VT* 24:1–7.

———. 2003. "Bethel in the Neo-Babylonian Period." Pages 93–107 in *Judah and the Judeans in the Neo-Babylonian Period*. Edited by Oded Lipschits and Joseph Blenkinsopp. Winona Lake, IN: Eisenbrauns.

Blum, Erhard. 2012. "The Jacob Tradition." Pages 181–211 in *The Book of Genesis: Composition, Reception, and Interpretation*. Edited by Craig A. Evans, Joel N. Lohr, and David L. Petersen. VTSup 152. Leiden: Brill.

Boaretto, Elisabetta, Israel Finkeltsein, and Ruth Shahack-Gross. 2010. "Radiocarbon Results from the Iron IIA Site of Atar Haroa in the Negev Highlands and Their Archaeological and Historical Implications." *Radiocarbon* 52:1–12.

Bocher, Efrat. 2021. "The Fortifications on the Eastern Slopes of the City of David in Areas A and J: A Reappraisal" [Hebrew]. *NSAJR* 14:39–52.

Bocher, Efrat, and Oded Lipschits. 2011. "Initial Conclusions from the Study of the *YRSLM* Stamp Impressions on Jar Handles" [Hebrew]. *New Studies on Jerusalem* 17:199–217.

Brandl, Baruch. 2006. "Two Stamped Jar Handles." Pages 426–29 in *Megiddo IV: The 1998–2002 Seasons*. Edited by Israel Finkelstein, David Ussishkin, and Baruch Halpern. Monograph Series of the Institute of Archaeology Tel Aviv University 24. Tel Aviv: Emery and Claire Yass Publications in Archaeology.

Braun, Roddy L. 1977. "A Reconsideration of the Chronicler's Attitude toward the North." *JBL* 96:59–62.

Brink, Edwin C. M. van den, and Thomas E. Levy, eds. 2002. *Egypt and the Levant: Interrelations from the Fourth through the Early Third Millennium BCE*. London: Leicester University Press.

Broshi, Magen. 1974. "The Expansion of Jerusalem in the Reigns of Hezekiah and Manasseh." *IEJ* 24:21–26.

Broshi, Magen, and Israel Finkelstein. 1992. "The Population of Palestine in Iron Age II." *BASOR* 287:47–60.

Bunimovitz, Shlomo. 1992 "The Middle Bronze Age Fortifications in Palestine as a Social Phenomenon." *TA* 19:221–34.

———. 1994. "The Problem of Human Resources in Late Bronze Age Palestine and Its Socioeconomic Implications." *UF* 26:1–20.

Bunimovitz, Shlomo, and Zvi Lederman. 2001. "The Iron Age Fortifications of Tel Beth Shemesh: A 1990–2000 Perspective." *IEJ* 51:121–47.

———. 2006. "The Early Israelite Monarchy in the Sorek Valley: Tel Beth-Shemesh and Tel Batash (Timnah) in the Tenth and Ninth Centuries BCE." Pages 407–27 in *"I Will Speak the Riddles of Ancient Times": Archaeological and Historical Studies in Honor of Amihai Mazar*. Edited by Aren Maeir and Pierre de Miroschedji. Winona Lake, IN: Eisenbrauns.

———. 2009. "The Archaeology of Border Communities: Renewed Excavations at Tel Beth-Shemesh, Part 1: The Iron Age." *NEA* 72:114–42.

———. 2016. *Tel Beth-Shemesh: A Border Community in Judah; Renewed Excavations 1990–2000; The Iron Age*. 2 vols. Monographs of the Institute of Archaeology Tel Aviv University 34. Winona Lake, IN: Eisenbrauns.

Bunimovitz, Shlomo, Zvi Lederman, and Eleni Hatzaki. 2013. "Knossian Gifts? Two Late Minoan IIA Cups from Tel Beth-shemesh, Israel." *The Annual of the British School at Athens* 108:51–66.

Burke, Aaron J., Martin Peilstöcker, Amy Karoll, George A. Pierce, Krister Kowalski, Nadia Ben-Marzouk, Jacob C. Damm, Andrew J. Danielson, Heidi D. Fessler, Brett Kaufman, Krystal V. L. Pierce, Felix Höflmayer, Brian N. Damiata, and Michael Dee. 2017. "Excavations of the New

Kingdom Fortress in Jaffa, 2011–2014: Traces of Resistance to Egyptian Rule in Canaan." *American Journal of Archaeology* 121: 85–133.

Cahill, Jane M. 1995. "Rosette Stamp Impressions from Ancient Judah." *IEJ* 45:230–52.

———. 2000. "Rosette-Stamped Handles." Pages 85–108 in *Inscriptions*. Vol. 6 of *Excavations at the City of David 1978–1985 Directed by Yigal Shiloh*. Edited by Donald T. Ariel. Qedem 41. Jerusalem: Institute of Archaeology, the Hebrew University of Jerusalem.

———. 2003a. "Jerusalem at the Time of the United Monarchy: The Archaeological Evidence." Pages 13–80 in *Jerusalem in Bible and Archaeology: The First Temple Period*. Edited by Andrew G. Vaughn and Ann E. Killebrew. SymS 18. Atlanta: Society of Biblical Literature.

———. 2003b. "Rosette Stamp Seal Impressions." Pages 85–98 in *The Finds from Areas A, W and X-2, Final Report*. Vol. 2 of *Jewish Quarter Excavations in the Old City of Jerusalem*. Edited by Hillel Geva. Jerusalem: Israel Exploration Society.

Campbell, Edward F. 1964. *The Chronology of the Amarna Letters: With Special Reference to the Hypothetical Coregency of Amenophis III and Akhenaten*. Baltimore: Johns Hopkins University Press.

Cantrell, Deborah O., and Israel Finkelstein. 2006. "A Kingdom for a Horse: The Megiddo Stables and Eight Century Israel." Pages 643–65 in *Megiddo IV: The 1998–2002 Seasons*. Edited by Israel Finkelstein, David Ussishkin, and Baruch Halpern. Monograph Series of the Institute of Archaeology Tel Aviv University 24. Tel Aviv: Emery and Claire Yass Publications in Archaeology.

Carr, David M. 1996. *Reading the Fractures of Genesis: Historical and Literary Approaches*. Louisville: Westminster John Knox.

Carter, Charles E. 1999. *The Emergence of Yehud in the Persian Period: A Social and Demographic Study*. JSOTSup 294. Sheffield: Sheffield Academic.

Chalaf, Ortal, and Joe Uziel. 2018. "Beyond the Walls: New Findings on the Eastern Sope of the City of David and Their Significance for Understanding the Urban Development of Late Iron Age Jerusalem." *City of David Studies of Ancient Jerusalem* 13:17*–32*.

Coats, George W. 1972. "The Wilderness Itinerary." *CBQ* 34:135–52.

Cogan, Mordechai. 2001. *I Kings: A New Translation with Introduction and Commentary*. AB 10. New York : Doubleday.

Cohen, Rudolph, and Hannah Bernick-Greenberg. 2007. *Excavations at*

Kadesh Barnea (Tell el-Qudeirat) 1976–1982. IAA Reports 34. Jerusalem: Israel Antiquities Authority.

Connan, Jacques, and Thomas van de Velde. 2010. "An Overview of Bitumen Trade in the Near East from the Neolithic (c. 8000 BC) to the Early Islamic Period." *Arabian Archaeology and Epigraphy* 21:1–19.

Cotton, Hannah M., Leah Di Segni, Werner Eck, Benjamin Isaac, Alla Kushnir-Stein, Haggai Misgav, Jonathan Price, and Ada Yardeni, eds. 2010. *1–704*. Part 1 of *Jerusalem*. Vol. 1 of *Corpus Inscriptionum Iudaeae/Palaestinae*. Berlin: De Gruyter.

Cross, Frank M. 1967. "The Origin and Early Evolution of the Alphabet." *ErIsr* 8:8*–24*.

Cross, Frank M., Jr., and Józef T. Milik. 1956. "Explorations in the Judaean Buqê'ah." *BASOR* 142:5–17.

Crowfoot, John W., and Gerald M. Fitzgerald. 1929. *Excavations in the Tyropoeon Valley, Jerusalem, 1927*. Palestine Exploration Fund Annual 1927. London: Palestine Exploration Fund.

Dagan, Yehuda. 1992. "The Shephelah during the Period of the Monarchy in Light of Archaeological Excavations and Survey" [Hebrew]. MA thesis, Tel Aviv University.

———. 2000. "The Settlement in the Judean Shephela in the Second and First Millennia B.C.: A Test Case of Settlement Processes in a Geographical Region" [Hebrew]. PhD diss., Tel Aviv University.

———. 2004. "Results of the Survey: Settlement Patterns in the Lachish Region." Pages 2674–92 in vol. 5 of *The Renewed Archaeological Excavations at Lachish (1973–1994)*, by David Ussishkin. Monograph Series of the Institute of Archaeology Tel Aviv University 22. Tel Aviv: Institute of Archaeology of Tel Aviv University.

———. 2011. "Tel Azekah: A New Look at the Site and Its 'Judean' Fortress." Pages 71–86 in *The Fire Signals of Lachish: Studies in the Archaeology and History of Israel in the Late Bronze Age, Iron Age, and Persian Period in Honor of David Ussishkin*. Edited by Israel Finkelstein and Nadav Na'aman. Winona Lake, IN: Eisenbrauns.

Dalley, Stephanie. 1993. "Ancient Mesopotamian Gardens and the Identification of the Hanging Gardens of Babylon Resolved." *Garden History* 21:1–13.

———. 2004. "Recent Evidence from Assyrian Sources for Judaean History from Uzziah to Manasseh." *JSOT* 28:387–401.

Davidovich, Uri, Yoav Farhi, Shlomo Kol-Yaakov, Misgav Har-Peled, Dalit Weinblatt-Krauz, and Yoav Alon. 2006. "Salvage Excavation at Ramot

Forest and Ramat Bet-Hakerem: New Data Regarding Jerusalem's Periphery during the First and Second Temple Periods" [Hebrew]. *New Studies on Jerusalem* 11:35–112.

Davies, Graham I. 1983. "The Wilderness Itineraries and the Composition of the Pentateuch." *VT* 33:1–13.

De Groot, Alon. 2012. "Discussion and Conclusions." Pages 141–84 in *Area E: Stratigraphy and Architecture*. Vol. 7A of *Excavations at the City of David 1978–1985 Directed by Yigal Shiloh*. Edited by Alon De Groot and Hannah Bernick-Greenberg. Qedem 53. Jerusalem: Institute of Archaeology, Hebrew University.

De Groot, Alon, and Hannah Bernick-Greenberg, eds. 2012. *Area E: Stratigraphy and Architecture*. Vol. 7A of *Excavations at the City of David 1978–1985 Directed by Yigal Shiloh*. Qedem 53. Jerusalem: Institute of Archaeology, Hebrew University.

De Groot, Alon, D. Cohen and A. Caspi. 1992. Area A1." Pages 1–29 in *Stratigraphical, Environmental, and Other Reports*. Vol. 3 of *Excavations at the City of David 1978–1985 Directed by Yigal Shiloh*. Edited by Alon De Groot and Donald T. Ariel. Qedem 33. Jerusalem: Institute of Archaeology, Hebrew University.

De Groot, Alon, and Atalya Fadida. 2010. "The Ceramic Assemblage from the Rock Cut Pool beside the Gihon Spring" [Hebrew]. *NSAJR* 4:53–60.

———. 2011. "The Pottery Assemblage from the Rock-Cut Pool Near the Gihon Spring." *TA* 38:158–66.

De Groot, Alon, Hillel Geva, and Irit Yezerski. 2003. "Iron Age II Pottery." Pages 1–49 in *The Finds from Areas A, W and X-2, Final Report*. Vol. 2 of *Jewish Quarter Excavations in the Old City of Jerusalem*. Edited by Hillel Geva. Jerusalem: Israel Exploration Society.

De-Groot, Alon, and Michal Weinberg-Stern. 2013. "Wine, Oil and Gibeonites: Iron II–III at Kh. el-Burj Northern Jerusalem" [Hebrew]. *New Studies on Jerusalem* 19:95–102.

Diaz Solano, Mila A. 2020. "Nehemiah, the Yehudites and Their Enemies: Characters in the Making; A Diachronic Study of 2 Esd 11:1–12:20; 14:1–17:5 // Neh 1:1–2:20; 3:33–7:5. PhD. diss., École biblique et archéologique française de Jérusalem.

Dietrich, Walter. 2007. *The Early Monarchy in Israel: the Tenth Century B.C.E.* Translated by Joachim Vette. BibEnc 3. Atlanta: Society of Biblical Literature.

Dobbs-Allsopp, F. W., J. J. M. Roberts, C. L. Seow, and R. E. Whitaker. 2005. *Hebrew Inscriptions: Texts from the Biblical Period of the Monarchy with Concordance*. New Haven: Yale University Press.

Dodson, Aidan M. 2000. "Towards a Minimum Chronology of the New Kingdom and Third Intermediate Period." *The Bulletin of the Egyptological Seminar* 14:7–18.

Dothan, Trude, and Seymour Gitin. 1993. "Miqne, Tel (Ekron)." *NEAEHL* 3:1051–59.

———. 2008. "Miqne, Tel (Ekron)." *NEAEHL* 5:1952–58.

Driver, Samuel R. 1913. *Notes on the Hebrew Text and the Topography of the Books of Samuel*. Oxford: Clarendon.

Dvira (Zweig), Zachi, Gal Zigdon, and Lara Shilov. 2011. "Secondary Refuse Aggregates from the First and Second Temple Periods on the Eastern Slope of the Temple Mount." *New Studies on Jerusalem* 17:63–106.

Edelman, Diana Vikander. 1985. "The 'Ashurites' of Eshbaal's State (2 Sam. 2.9)." *PEQ* 117:85–91.

———. 1988. "Saul's Journey through Mt. Ephraim and Samuel's Ramah (1 Sam. 9:4–5, 10:2–5)." *ZDPV* 104:44–58.

———. 1991. *King Saul in the Historiography of Judah*. JSOTSup 121. Sheffield: JSOT Press.

———. 1992. "Saul." *ABD* 5:989–99.

———. 1996. "Saul ben Kish in History and Tradition." Pages 142–59 in *The Origins of the Ancient Israelite States*. Edited by Volkmar Fritz and Philip R. Davies. JSOTSup 228. Sheffield: Sheffield Academic.

———. 2008. "Hezekiah's Alleged Cultic Centralization." *JSOT* 32:395–434.

Edelstein, Gershon. 2000. "A Terraced Farm at Er-Ras." *'Atiqot* 40:39–63.

Edelstein, Gershon, and Shimon Gibson. 1982. "Ancient Jerusalem's Rural Food Basket." *BAR* 8.4:46–55.

Edenburg, Cynthia, and Reinhard Müller, eds. 2015a. *Deuteronomy: A Judean or Samari(t)an Composition. Perspectives on Deuteronomy's Origins, Transmission and Reception*. HBAI 4.

Edenburg, Cynthia, and Reinhard Müller. 2015b. "A Northern Provenance for Deuteronomy? A Critical Review." *HBAI* 4:148–61.

Ehrlich, Carl S., with Marsha C. White, eds. 2006. *Saul in Story and Tradition*. FAT 47. Tübingen: Mohr Siebeck.

Ein Mor, Daniel, and Zvi Ron. 2013. "An Iron Age Royal Tunnel Spring in the Region of Nahal Rephaim" [Hebrew]. *NSAJR* 7:85–109.

———. 2016. "Ain Joweizeh: An Iron Age Royal Rock-Cut Spring System in the Naḥal Refa'im Valley, Near Jerusalem." *TA* 43:127–146.
Eisenberg, Emanuel, and David Ben-Shlomo, eds. 2017. *The Tel Hevron 2014 Excavations: Final Report*. Ariel: Ariel University Press.
Eitam, David. 1979. "Olive Presses of the Israelite Period." *TA* 6:146–55.
———. 1987. "Olive Oil Production during the Biblical Period." Pages 16–36 in *Olive Oil in Antiquity: Israel and Neighboring Countries from the Neolithic to the Early Arab Period*. Edited by Michael Heltzer and David Eitam. Haifa: Dagon Museum.
———. 1996. "The Olive Oil Industry at Tel Miqne–Ekron during the Late Iron Age." Pages 167–98 in *Olive Oil in Antiquity: Israel and Neighboring Countries from the Neolithic to the Early Arab Period*. Edited by Michael Heltzer and David Eitam. Padova: Sargon.
Eitan-Katz, Hayah. 1994. "Specialized Economy of Judah in the Eighth–Seventh Centuries BCE" [Hebrew]. MA thesis, Tel Aviv University.
Elgart-Sharon, Yelena, Naomi Porat, and Yuval Gadot. 2020. "Land Management and the Construction of Terraces for Dry Farming: The Case of the Soreq Catchment, Israel." *OJA* 39:274–89.
Eshel, Hanan, Jodi Magness, and Eli Shenhav. 2000. "Khirbet Yattir, 1995–1999: Preliminary Report." *IEJ* 50:153–68.
Eynikel, Erik. 1996. *The Reform of King Josiah and the Composition of the Deuteronomistic History*. OtSt 33. Leiden: Brill.
Fabian, Peter, and Yitzhak Gil'ad. 2010. "Beer Sheva (Compound C)." *ESI* 122. http://tinyurl.com/SBLPressIFa1.
Faigenbaum-Golovin, Shira, Arie Shaus, Barak Sober, Yana Gerber, Eli Turkel, Eli Piasetzky, and Israel Finkelstein. 2021. "Literacy in Judah and Israel: Algorithmic and Forensic Examination of the Arad and Samaria Ostraca." *NEA* 84:148–58.
Faigenbaum-Golovin, Shira, Arie Shaus, Barak Sober, Israel Finkelstein, David Levin, Murray Moinester, Eli Piasetzky, and Eli Turkel. 2015. "Computerized Paleographic Investigation of Hebrew Iron Age Ostraca." *Radiocarbon* 57:317–25.
Faigenbaum-Golovin, Shira, Arie Shaus, Barak Sober, David Levin, Nadav Na'aman, Benjamin Sass, Eli Turkel, Eli Piasetzky, and Israel Finkelstein. 2016. "Algorithmic Handwriting Analysis of Judahite Military Correspondence Sheds Light on Composition of Biblical Texts." *Proceedings of the National Academy of Sciences* 113:4664–69.
Faigenbaum-Golovin, Shira, Arie Shaus, Barak Sober, Eli Turkel, Eli Piasetzky, and Israel Finkelstein. 2020. "Algorithmic Handwriting Analysis

of the Samaria Inscriptions Illuminates Bureaucratic Apparatus in Biblical Israel." *PLoS ONE* 15(1): e0227452.

Fantalkin, Alexander. 2008. "The Appearance of Rock-Cut Bench Tombs in Iron Age Judah as a Reflection of State Formation." Pages 17–44 in *Bene Israel: Studies in the Archaeology of Israel and the Levant during the Bronze and Iron Ages in Honour of Israel Finkelstein*. Edited by Alexander Fantalkin and Assaf Yassur-Landau. CHANE 31. Leiden: Brill.

Fantalkin, Alexander, and Israel Finkelstein. 2006. "The Sheshonq I Campaign and the Eighth-Century BCE Earthquake: More on the Archaeology and History of the South in the Iron I–IIA." *TA* 33:18–42.

———. 2017. "The Date of Abandonment and Territorial Affiliation of Khirbet Qeiyafa: An Update." *TA* 44:53–60.

Fantalkin, Alexander, and Oren Tal. 2009. "Re-discovering the Iron Age Fortress at Tell Qudadi in the Context of Neo-Assyrian Imperialistic Policies." *PEQ* 141:188–206.

Faust, Avraham. 1997. "The Impact of Jerusalem's Expansion in the Late Iron Age on the Forms of Rural Settlement in Its Vicinity" [Hebrew]. *Cathedra* 84:53–62.

———. 2008. "Settlement and Demography in Seventh-Century Judah and the Extent and Intensity of Sennacherib's Campaign." *PEQ* 140:168–94.

———. 2010. "The Large Stone Structure in the City of David." *ZDPV* 124:116–30.

———. 2012. *Judah in the Neo-Babylonian Period: The Archaeology of Desolation*. ABS 18. Atlanta: Society of Biblical Literature.

———. 2021. *The Neo-Assyrian Empire in the Southwest: Imperial Domination and Its Consequences*. Oxford: Oxford University Press.

Faust, Avraham, and Hayah Katz, H. 2012. "Survey, Shovel Tests and Excavations at Tel 'Eton: On Methodology and Site History." *TA* 39:158–85.

Feig, Nurit. 2000. "The Environs of Jerusalem in the Iron Age II" [Hebrew]. Pages 387–409 in *The History of Jerusalem: The Biblical Period*. Edited by Shmuel Ahituv and Amihai Mazar. Jerusalem: Yad Izhaq Ben-Zvi.

———, 2003. "Excavations at Beit Safafa: Iron Age II and Byzantine Agricultural Installations South of Jerusalem." *'Atiqot* 44:191–238.

Feldstein, A., G. Kidron, N. Hanin, Y. Kamaisky, and David Eitam. 1993. "Southern Parts of the Maps of Ramallah and el-Bireh and Northern Part of the Map of 'Ein Kerem" [Hebrew]. Pages 133–264 in *Archeological Survey of the Hill Country of Benjamin*. Edited by Israel Finkelstein and Yitzhak Magen. Jerusalem: Israel Antiquities Authority. English summaries: 28*–47*.

Finkelstein, Israel. 1988. *The Archaeology of the Israelite Settlement*. Jerusalem: Israel Exploration Society.

———. 1992a. "*Ḥorvat Qiṭmīt* and the Southern Trade in the Late Iron Age II." *ZDPV* 108:156–70.

———. 1992b. "Middle Bronze Age 'Fortifications': A Reflection of Social Organization and Political Formations." *TA* 19:201–20.

———. 1994. "The Archaeology of the Days of Manasseh." Pages 169–87 in *Scripture and Other Artifacts: Essays on the Bible and Archaeology in Honor of Philip J. King*. Edited by Michael D. Coogan, J. Cheryl Exum, and Lawrence E. Stager. Louisville: Westminster John Knox.

———. 1995. *Living on the Fringe: The Archaeology and History of the Negev, Sinai and Neighbouring Regions in the Bronze and Iron Ages*. Monographs in Mediterranean Archaeology 6. Sheffield: Sheffield Academic.

———. 1996a. "The Archaeology of the United Monarchy: An Alternative View." *Levant* 28:177–87.

———. 1996b. "The Philistine Countryside." *IEJ* 46:225–42.

———. 1996c. "The Territorio-Political System of Canaan in the Late Bronze Age." *UF* 28:221–55.

———. 1999. "State Formation in Israel and Judah: A Contrast in Context, A Contrast in Trajectory." *NEA* 62:35–52.

———. 2001. "The Rise of Jerusalem and Judah: The Missing Link." *Levant* 33:105–15.

———. 2002a. "Chronology Rejoinders." *PEQ* 134:118–29.

———. 2002b. "The Philistines in the Bible: A Late-Monarchic Perspective." *JSOT* 27:131–67.

———. 2006a. "The Last Labayu: King Saul and the Expansion of the First North Israelite Territorial Entity." Pages 171–77 in *Essays on Ancient Israel in Its Near Eastern Context: A Tribute to Nadav Na'aman*. Edited by Yairah Amit, Ehud Ben Zvi, Israel Finkelstein, and Oded Lipschits. Winona Lake, IN: Eisenbrauns.

———. 2006b. "Shechem in the Late Bronze Age." Pages 349–56 in *Timelines: Studies in Honour of Manfred Bietak*. Edited by Ernst Czerny et al. OLA 149. Leuven: Peeters.

———. 2008a. "The Archaeology of the List of Returnees in Ezra and Nehemiah." *PEQ* 140:7–16.

———. 2008b. "Jerusalem in the Persian (and Early Hellenistic) Period and the Wall of Nehemiah." *JSOT* 32:501–20.

———. 2008c. "The Settlement History of Jerusalem in the Eighth and Seventh Centuries BCE." *RB* 115:499–515.

———. 2010a. "A Great United Monarchy? Archaeological and Historical Perspectives." Pages 3–28 in *One God – One Cult – One Nation: Archaeological and Biblical Perspectives*. Edited by Reinhard G. Kratz and Hermann Spieckermann. BZAW 405. Berlin: De Gruyter.

———. 2010b. "The Territorial Extent and Demography of Yehud/Judea in the Persian and Early Hellenistic Periods." *RB* 117:39–54.

———. 2011a. "The 'Large Stone Structure' in Jerusalem: Reality versus Yearning." *ZDPV* 127:1–10.

———. 2011b. "Observations on the Layout of Iron Age Samaria." *TA* 38:194–207.

———. 2011c. "Saul, Benjamin and the Emergence of 'Biblical Israel': An Alternative View." *ZAW* 123:348–67.

———. 2011d. "Tell el-Umeiri in the Iron I: Facts and Fiction." Pages 113–28 in *The Fire Signals of Lachish: Studies in the Archaeology and History of Israel in the Late Bronze Age, Iron Age, and Persian Period in Honor of David Ussishkin*. Edited by Israel Finkelstein and Nadav Na'aman. Winona Lake, IN: Eisenbrauns.

———. 2011e. "Tell el-Ful Revisited: The Assyrian and Hellenistic Periods (with a New Identification)." *PEQ* 143:106–18.

———. 2012a. "Comments on the Date of Late-Monarchic Judahite Seal Impressions." *TA* 39:203–11.

———. 2012b. "The Great Wall of Tell en-Nasbeh (Mizpah), The First Fortifications in Judah and 1 Kings 15:16–22." *VT* 62:14–28.

———. 2013a. "The Finds from the Rock-Cut Pool in Jerusalem and the Date of the Siloam Tunnel: An Alternative Interpretation." *Semitica et Classica* 6:279–84.

———. 2013b. *The Forgotten Kingdom: The Archaeology and History of Northern Israel*. ANEM 5. Atlanta: Society of Biblical Literature.

———. 2013a. "Geographical and Historical Realities behind the Earliest Layer in the David Story." *SJOT* 27:131–50.

———. 2014a. "The Archaeology of Tell el-Kheleifeh and the History of Ezion-geber/Elath." *Sem* 56:105–36.

———. 2014b. "Settlement Patterns and Territorial Polity in the Transjordanian Highlands in the Late Bronze Age." *UF* 45:143–59.

———. 2014c. "The Shephelah and Jerusalem's Western Border in the Amarna Period." *Egypt and the Levant* 24:265–74.

———. 2014d. "The Southern Steppe of the Levant ca. 1050–750 BCE: A Framework for a Territorial History." *PEQ* 146:89–104.

———. 2015a. "The Expansion of Judah in II Chronicles: Territorial Legitimation for the Hasmoneans?" *ZAW* 127:669–95.

———. 2015b. "Migration of Israelites into Judah after 720 BCE: An Answer and an Update." *ZAW* 127:188–206.

———. 2015c. "The Wilderness Narrative and Itineraries and the Evolution of the Exodus Tradition." Pages 39–54 in *Israel's Exodus in Transdisciplinary Perspective: Text, Archaeology, Culture, and Geoscience*. Edited by Thomas E. Levy, Thomas Schneider, and William H. C. Propp. Quantitative Methods in the Humanities and Social Sciences. New York: Springer.

———. 2016. "Jerusalem and Judah 600–200 BCE: Implications for Understanding Pentateuchal Texts." Pages 3–18 in *The Fall of Jerusalem and the Rise of the Torah*. Edited by Peter Dubovský, Dominik Markl, and Jean-Pierre Sonnet. FAT 107. Tübingen: Mohr Siebeck.

———. 2017. "A Corpus of North Israelite Texts in the Days of Jeroboam II?" *HBAI* 6:262–89.

———. 2019. "Between Jeroboam and Jeroboam: Israelite Identity Formation." Pages 139–55 in *Research on Israel and Aram: Autonomy, Independence and Related Issues, Proceedings of the First Annual RIAB Center Conference, Leipzig, June 2016*. Edited by Angelika Berlejung and Aren M. Maeir. ORA 34. Tubingen: Mohr Siebeck.

———. 2020a. "The Emergence and Dissemination of Writing in Judah." *Semitica and Classica* 13:269–82.

———. 2020b. "Jeroboam II in Transjordan." *SJOT* 34:19–29.

———. 2020c. "Jeroboam II's Temples." *ZAW* 132:250–65.

———. 2020d. "Northern Royal Traditions in the Bible and the Ideology of a 'United Monarchy' Ruled from Samaria." Pages 113–26 in *Stones, Tablets, and Scrolls: Periods of the Formation of the Bible*. Edited by Peter Dubovský and Federico Giuntoli. Archaeology and Bible 3. Tübingen: Mohr Siebeck.

———. 2020e. "Saul and Highlands of Benjamin Update: The Role of Jerusalem." Pages 33–56 in *Saul, Benjamin, and the Emergence of Monarchy in Israel: Biblical and Archaeological Perspectives*. Edited by Joachim J. Krause, Omer Sergi, and Kristin Weingart. AIL 40. Atlanta: SBL Press.

———. 2020f. "Was There an Early Northern (Israelite) Conquest Tradition?" Pages 211–21 in *Eigensinn und Entstehung der Hebräischen Bibel Erhard Blum zum siebzigsten Geburtstag*. Edited by Joachim J. Krause, Wolfgang Oswald, and Kristin Weingart. FAT 136. Tübingen: Mohr Siebeck.

———. 2022. "The Iron Age Complex in the Ophel in Jerusalem: A Critical Analysis." *TA* 49:191–204.

———. 2023. "Jerusalem's Settlement History: Rejoinders and Updates." Pages 753–69 in *"And in Length of Days Understanding" (Job 12:12): Essays on Archaeology in the Eastern Mediterranean and Beyond in Honor of Thomas E. Levy*. Edited by Erez Ben-Yosef and Ian W. N. Jones. Interdisciplinary Contributions to Archaeology. Cham: Springer.

Finkelstein, Israel, and Alexander Fantalkin. 2012. "Khirbet Qeiyafa: An Unsensational Archaeological and Historical Interpretation." *TA* 39:38–63.

Finkelstein, Israel, Alexander Fantalkin, and Eli Piasetzky. 2008. "Three Snapshots of the Iron IIA: The Northern Valleys, the Southern Steppe and Jerusalem." Pages 32–44 in *The Archaeology*. Vol. 1 of *Israel in Transition: From Late Bronze II to Iron IIA (c. 1250–850 BCE)*. Edited by Lester L. Grabbe. LHBOTS 491. New York: T&T Clark.

Finkelstein, Israel, and Yuval Gadot. 2015. "Mozah, Nephtoah and Royal Estates in the Jerusalem Highlands." *Semitica et Classica* 8:227–34.

Finkelstein, Israel, Yuval Gadot, and Dafna Langgut. 2022. "The Unique Specialised Economy of Judah under Assyrian Rule and Its Impact on the Material Culture of the Kingdom." *PEQ* 154:261–79.

Finkelstein, Israel, and Ram Gophna. 1993. "Settlement, Demographic, and Economic Patterns in the Highlands of Palestine in the Chalcolithic and Early Bronze Periods and the Beginning of Urbanism." *BASOR* 289:1–22.

Finkelstein, Israel, Ze'ev Herzog, Lily Singer-Avitz, and David Ussishkin. 2007. "Has the Palace of King David in Jerusalem Been Found?" *TA* 34:142–64.

Finkelstein, Israel, and Assaf Kleiman. 2019. "The Archaeology of the Days of Baasha?" *RB* 126:277–96.

Finkelstein, Israel, Ido Koch, and Oded Lipschits. 2011. "The Mound on the Mount: A Solution to the 'Problem with Jerusalem'?" *JHS* 11. doi.org/10.5508/jhs.2011.v11.a12.

Finkelstein, Israel, and Dafna Langgut. 2018. "Climate, Settlement History and Olive Cultivation in the Iron Age Southern Levant." *BASOR* 379:153–69.

Finkelstein, Israel, and Zvi Lederman. 1993. "Area H–F: Middle Bronze III Fortifications and Storerooms." Pages 49–64 in *Shiloh: The Archaeology of a Biblical Site* Edited by Israel Finkelstein. Monograph Series of the Institute of Archaeology, Tel Aviv University 10. Tel Aviv: Tel Aviv University.

Finkelstein, Israel, Zvi Lederman, and Shlomo Bunimovitz. 1997. *Highlands of Many Cultures: The Southern Samaria Survey; The Sites*. Monograph Series of the Institute of Archaeology Tel Aviv University 14. Tel Aviv: Institute of Archaeology of Tel Aviv University.

Finkelstein, Israel, and Oded Lipschits. 2010. "Omride Architecture in Moab: Jahaz and Ataroth." *ZDPV* 126:29–42.

———. 2011. "The Genesis of Moab." *Levant* 43:139–52.

Finkelstein, Israel, and Nadav Na'aman. 2004. "The Judahite Shephelah in the Late Eighth and Early Seventh Centuries BCE." *TA* 31:60–79.

———. 2005. "Shechem of the Amarna Period and the Rise of the Northern Kingdom of Israel." *IEJ* 55:172–93.

Finkelstein, Israel, Christophe Nicolle, and Thomas Römer. 2018 "Les fouilles archéologiques à Qiryath Yéarim et le récit de l'arche d'alliance." *CRAI* 162:983–1000.

Finkelstein, Israel, and Eli Piasetzky. 2006a. "^{14}C and the Iron Age Chronology Debate: Rehov, Khirbet en-Nahas, Dan and Megiddo." *Radiocarbon* 48:373–386.

———. 2006b. "The Iron I–IIA in the Highlands and Beyond: ^{14}C Anchors, Pottery Phases and the Shoshenq I Campaign." *Levant* 38:45–61.

———. 2007. "Radiocarbon Dating and Philistine Chronology with an Addendum on el-Ahwat." *Egypt and the Levant* 17:74–82.

———. 2009. "Radiocarbon-Dated Destruction Layers: A Skeleton for Iron Age Chronology in the Levant." *OJA* 28:255–74.

———. 2010. "Radiocarbon Dating the Iron Age in the Levant: A Bayesian Model for Six Ceramic Phases and Six Transitions." *Antiquity* 84:374–85.

———. 2011. "The Iron Age Chronology Debate: Is the Gap Narrowing?" *NEA* 74:50–54.

———. 2015. "Radiocarbon Dating Khirbet Qeiyafa and the Iron I–IIA Phases in the Shephelah: Methodological Comments and a Bayesian Model." *Radiocarbon* 57:891–907.

Finkelstein, Israel, and Thomas Römer. 2014a. "Comments on the Historical Background of the Abraham Narrative: Between 'Realia' and 'Exegetica.'" *HBAI* 3:3–23.

———. 2014b. "Comments on the Historical Background of the Jacob Narrative in Genesis." *ZAW* 126:317–38.

———. 2016. "Early North Israelite 'Memories' on Moab." Pages 711–27 in *The Formation of the Pentateuch: Bridging the Academic Cultures of Europe, Israel, and North America*. Edited by Jan Christian Gertz, Bernard M. Levinson, Dalit Rom-Shiloni, and Konrad Schmid. FAT 111. Tübingen: Mohr Siebeck.

———. 2019a. "Kiriath-jearim and the List of Bacchides Forts in 1 Maccabees 9:50–52." *NSAJR* 13:7*–17*.

———. 2019b. "Kiriath-jearim, Kiriath-baal/Baalah, Gibeah: A Geographical-History Challenge." Pages 211–22 in *Writing, Rewriting and Overwriting in the Books of Deuteronomy and the Former Prophets. Essays in Honor of Cynthia Edenburg*. Edited by Ido Koch, Thomas Römer, and Omer Sergi. Leuven: Peeters.

———. 2020. "The Historical and Archaeological Background behind the Old Israelite Ark Narrative." *Bib* 101:161–85.

Finkelstein, Israel, Thomas Römer, and Christophe Nicolle. 2020. "Archaeological Excavations at Kiriath-jearim and the Ark Narrative in the Books of Samuel." Pages 313–31 in *The Mega Project at Motza (Moẓa): The Neolithic and Later Occupations up to the Twentieth Century*. Edited by Hamoudi Khalaily, Amit Re'em, Jacob Vardi, and Ianir Milevski. Jerusalem: Israel Antiquities Authority.

Finkelstein, Israel, Thomas Römer, Christophe Nicolle, Zachary C. Dunseth, Assaf Kleiman, Juliette Mas, J. and Naomi Porat. 2018. "Excavations at Kiriath-jearim Near Jerusalem, 2017: Preliminary Report." *Semitica* 60:31–83.

Finkelstein, Israel, and Benjamin Sass. 2013. "The West Semitic Alphabetic Inscriptions, Late Bronze II to Iron IIA: Archeological Context, Distribution and Chronology." *HBAI* 2:149–220.

———. 2021. "The Exceptional Concentration of Inscriptions at Iron IIA Gath and Rehob and the Nature of the Alphabet in the Ninth Century BCE." Pages 127–73 in *Oral et ecrit dans l'Antiquite orientale: Les processus de redaction et d'edition; Actes du colloque organise par le College de France, Paris, les 26 et 27 mai 2016*. Edited by Thomas Römer, Hervé Gonzalez, Lionel Marti, and Jan Rückl. Leuven: Peeters.

Finkelstein, Israel, and Neil Asher Silberman. 2006a. *David and Solomon: In Search of the Bible's Sacred Kings and the Roots of Western Tradition.* New York: Free Press.

———. 2006b. "Temple and Dynasty: Hezekiah, the Remaking of Judah and the Rise of the Pan-Israelite Ideology." *JSOT* 30:259–85.

Finkelstein, Israel, and Lily Singer-Avitz. 2009. "Reevaluating Bethel." *ZDPV* 125:33–48.

Finkelstein, Israel, Elena Zapassky, Yuval Gadot, Daniel M. Master, Lawrence E. Stager, and Itzhak Benenson. 2011. "Phoenician 'Torpedo' Amphoras and Egypt: Standardization of Volume Based on Linear Dimensions." *Egypt and the Levant* 21:249–59.

Fischer, Moshe, Benjamin H. Issac, Israel Roll. 1996. *Roman Roads in Judaea II: The Jaffa-Jerusalem Roads.* BAR international series 628. Oxford: Tempus Reparatvm.

Fleming, Daniel A. 2012. *The Legacy of Israel in Judah's Bible: History, Politics, and the Reinscribing of Tradition.* Cambridge: Cambridge University Press.

Fox, Nili Sacher. 2000. *In the Service of the King: Officialdom in Ancient Israel and Judah* Cincinnati: Hebrew Union College Press.

Frankel, Rafi. 2001. *Settlement Dynamics and Regional Diversity in Ancient Upper Galilee: Archaeological Survey of Upper Galilee.* Jerusalem: Israel Antiquities Authority.

Freud, Liora. 2018. "Judahite Pottery in the Transitional Phase between the Iron Age and the Persian Period: Jerusalem and Environs" [Hebrew]. PhD diss., Tel Aviv University.

Fried, Lisbeth S. 2002. "The High Places (Bamôt) and the Reforms of Hezekiah and Josiah: An Archaeological Investigation." *JAOS* 122:1–29.

Fritz, Volkmar. 1970. *Israel in der Wüste: Traditionsgeschichtliche Untersuchung der Wüstenüberlieferung des Jahwisten.* Marburg: Elwert.

———. 1975. "Erwägungen zur Siedlungsgeschichte des Negeb in der Eisen I Zeit (1200–1000 v. Chr. im Lichte der Ausgrabungen auf der Khirbet el-Mšāš." *ZDPV* 91:30–45.

———. 1994. *Das Buch Josua.* HAT 7. Tübingen: Mohr Siebeck.

Frumkin, Amos, Aryeh Shimron, and Jeff Rosenbaum. 2003. "Radiometric Dating of the Siloam Tunnel, Jerusalem." *Nature* 425:169–71.

Gadot, Yuval. 2010. "The Late Bronze Egyptian Estate at Aphek." *TA* 37:48–66.

———. 2015. "In the Valley of the King: Jerusalem's Rural Hinterland in the Eighth–Fourth Centuries BCE." *TA* 42:3–26.

———. 2015. "In the Valley of the King: Jerusalem's Rural Hinterland in the Eighth–Fourth Centuries BCE." *TA* 42:3–28.

———. 2022. "Jerusalem, the Reign of Manasseh and the Assyrian World Order." Pages 145–61 in *Jerusalem and the Coastal Plain in the Iron Age and Persian Periods: New Studies on Jerusalem's Relations with the Southern Coastal Plain of Israel/Palestine (c. 1200–300 BCE)*. Edited by Felix Hagemeyer. Research on Israel and Aram in Biblical Times 4. Tübingen: Mohr Siebeck.

Gadot, Yuval, and Efrat Bocher. 2018. "The Introduction of the 'Open-Courtyard Building' to the Jerusalem Landscape and Judean-Assyrian Interaction." Pages 205–28 in *Archaeology and History of Eighth-Century Judah*. Edited by Zev Farber and Jacob L. Wright. ANEM 23. Atlanta: SBL Press.

Gadot, Yuval, Efrat Bocher, Liora Freud, and Yiftah Shalev. 2023. "An Early Iron Age Moat in Jerusalem between the Ophel and the Southeastern Ridge/City of David." *Tel Aviv* 50:147–70.

Gadot, Yuval, Liora Freud, Manfred Oeming, and Oded Lipschits. 2020. "The Renewed Excavations by the Tel Aviv—Heidelberg Expedition." Pages 22–34 in *Ramat Raḥel IV: The Renewed Excavations by the Tel Aviv-Heidelberg Expedition (2005-2010); Stratigraphy and Architecture*. Edited by Oded Lipschits, Manfred Oeming, and Yuval Gadot. Monograph Series of the Institute of Archaeology, Tel Aviv University 39. University Park: Penn State University Press.

Gadot, Yuval, and Oded Lipschits. 2016. "Summary and Conclusions." Pages 715–24 in *Ramat Raḥel III: Final Publication of Aharoni's Excavations (1954, 1959-1962)*. Edited by Oded Lipschits, Yuval Gadot, and Liora Freud. Monograph Series of the Institute of Archaeology, Tel Aviv University, 35. Winona Lake, IN: Eisenbrauns.

Gadot, Yuval, Sivan Mizrahi, Liora Freud, and David Gellman. 2019. "What Kind of Village Is This? Buildings and Agroeconomic Activities Northwest of Jerusalem during the Iron IIB–C Period." Pages 89–118 in *The Last Century in the History of Judah: The Seventh Century BCE in Archaeological, Historical and Biblical Perspectives*. Edited by Filip Čapek and Oded Lipschits. AIL 37. Atlanta: SBL Press.

Gadot, Yuval, and Joe Uziel. 2017. "The Monumentality of Iron Age Jerusalem Prior to the Eighth Century BCE." *TA* 44:123–40.

Ganor, Saar, and Igor Kreimerman. 2019. "An Eighth-Century BCE Gate Shrine at Tel Lachish, Israel." *BASOR* 381:211–36.

Garcia, Juan Carlos Moreno. 2014. "Recent Developments in the Social and Economic History of Ancient Egypt." *Journal of Ancient Near Eastern History* 1:231–61.

Garfinkel, Yosef, Saar Ganor, and Michael G. Hasel. 2011. "Khirbet Qeiyafa and the Rise of the Kingdom of Judah" [Hebrew]. *ErIsr* 30:174–194.

Gazit, Dan, and Ram Gophna. 1993. "An Unfortified Late Bronze Age Site at Gerar: Survey Finds" [Hebrew]. *'Atiqot* 22:15–19.

Geva, Hillel. 1979. "The Western Boundary of Jerusalem at the End of the Monarchy." *IEJ* 29:84–91.

———. 1983. "Excavations in the Citadel of Jerusalem, 1979–1980: Preliminary Report." *IEJ* 33:55–71.

———. 1993. "A Summary of Twenty-Five Years of Archaeological Research in Jerusalem: Achievements and Evaluations" [Hebrew]. *Qad* 101–102:2–24.

———. 2000. "General Introduction to the Excavations in the Jewish Quarter." Pages 1–30 in *Architecture and Stratigraphy, Areas A, W and X-2*. Vol. 1 of *Jewish Quarter Excavations in the Old City of Jerusalem*. Edited by Hillel Geva. Jerusalem: Israel Exploration Society.

———. 2003a. "Summary and Discussion of Findings from Areas A, W and X-2." Pages 501–52 in *The Finds from Areas A, W and X-2, Final Report*. Vol. 2 of *Jewish Quarter Excavations in the Old City of Jerusalem*. Edited by Hillel Geva. Jerusalem: Israel Exploration Society.

———. 2003b. "Western Jerusalem at the End of the First Temple Period in Light of the Excavations in the Jewish Quarter." Pages 183–208 in *Jerusalem in Bible and Archaeology: The First Temple Period*. Edited by Andrew G. Vaughn and Ann E. Killebrew. SymS 18. Atlanta: Society of Biblical Literature.

———. 2006. "The Settlement on the Southwestern Hill of Jerusalem at the End of the Iron Age: A Reconstruction Based on the Archaeological Evidence." *ZDPV* 122:140–50.

———. 2014. "Jerusalem's Population in Antiquity: A Minimalist View." *TA* 41:131–60.

Geva, Hillel, and Nahman Avigad. 2000a. "Area A: Stratigraphy and Architecture, Introduction." Pages 37–43 in *Architecture and Stratigraphy, Areas A, W and X-2*. Vol. 1 of *Jewish Quarter Excavations in the Old City of Jerusalem*. Edited by Hillel Geva. Jerusalem: Israel Exploration Society.

———. 2000b. "Area W: Stratigraphy and Architecture." Pages 131–98 in *Architecture and Stratigraphy, Areas A, W and X-2*. Vol. 1 of *Jewish*

Quarter Excavations in the Old City of Jerusalem. Edited by Hillel Geva. Jerusalem: Israel Exploration Society.

———. 2000c. "Area X-2: Stratigraphy and Architecture." Pages 199–240 in *Architecture and Stratigraphy, Areas A, W and X-2*. Vol. 1 of *Jewish Quarter Excavations in the Old City of Jerusalem*. Edited by Hillel Geva. Jerusalem: Israel Exploration Society.

Geva, Hillel, and Alon De Groot. 2017. "The City of David Is Not on the Temple Mount After All." *IEJ* 67:32–49.

Gibson, Shimon, and David M. Jacobson. 1996. *Below the Temple Mount in Jerusalem: A Sourcebook on the Cisterns, Subterranean Chambers and Conduits of the Haram al-Sharif*. BAR International Series 637. Oxford: BAR.

Ginsberg, H. L. 1948. "MMŠT AND MṢH." *BASOR* 109:20–22.

Gitin, Seymour. 1997. "The Neo-Assyrian Empire and Its Western Periphery: The Levant, with a Focus on Philistine Ekron." Pages 77–103 in *Assyria 1995: Proceedings of the Tenth Anniversary Symposium of the Neo-Assyrian Text Corpus Project, Helsinki, September 7–11, 1995, Helsinki*. Edited by Simo Parpola and Robert M. Whiting. Helsinki: Neo-Assyrian Text Corpus Project.

———. 2003. "Neo-Assyrian and Egyptian Hegemony over Ekron in the Seventh Century BCE: A Response to Lawrence E. Stager." *ErIsr* 27:55–61.

Golub, Mitka R. 2017. "Israelite and Judean Theophoric Personal Names in the Hebrew Bible in the Light of the Archaeological Evidence." *Ancient Near Eastern Studies* 14:35–46.

———. 2018. "Aniconism and Theophoric Names in Inscribed Seals from Judah, Israel and Neighbouring Kingdoms." *TA* 45:157–69.

Gomes, Jules Francis. 2006. *The Sanctuary of Bethel and the Configuration of Israelite Identity*. BZAW 368. Berlin: De Gruyter.

Gophna, Ram, and Yosef Porath. 1972. "The Land of Ephraim and Manasseh" [Hebrew]. Pages 196–241 in *Judaea, Samaria and the Golan Archaeological Survey 1967–1968*. Edited by Moshe Kochavi. Jerusalem: Carta.

Gordon, Cyrus H. 1964. "Biblical Customs and the Nuzu Tablets." Pages 21–33 in *The Biblical Archaeologist Reader Volume 2*. Edited by Edward F. Campbell and David Noel Freedman. Garden City, NY: Doubleday.

Goren, Yuval, Israel Finkelstein, and Nadav Na'aman. 2003. "The Expansion of the Kingdom of Amurru according to the Petrographic Investigation of the Amarna Tablets." *BASOR* 329:2–11.

———. 2004. *Inscribed in Clay: Provenance Study of the Amarna Letters and Other Ancient Near Eastern Texts*. Monograph Series of the Institute of Archaeology, Tel Aviv University 23. Tel Aviv: Emery and Claire Yass Publications in Archaeology.

Goren, Yuval, and Netta Halperin, N. 2004. "Selected Petrographic Analyses." Pages 2553–68 in vol. 5 of *The Renewed Archaeological Excavations at Lachish (1973–1994)*, by David Ussishkin. Monograph Series of the Institute of Archaeology of Tel Aviv University 22. Tel Aviv: Emery and Claire Yass Publications in Archaeology.

Government of Palestine. 1942–1943. *Census of Olive Oil Production*. Special Bulletin 8. Jerusalem: Government of Palestine.

———. 1945. *Village Statistics, April 1945*. Jerusalem: Government of Palestine.

Greenberg, Raphael, and Gilad Cinamon. 2006. "Stamped and Incised Jar Handles from Rogem Ganim and Their Implications for the Political Economy of Jerusalem, Late Eighth–Early Seventh Centuries BCE." *TA* 33:227–43.

Greener, Aaron, Israel Finkelstein, and Dafna Langgut. 2018. "Settlement Oscillations along the Desert Fringes of the Southern Levant: Impact of Climate versus Economic and Historical Factors." *UF* 49:195–226.

Greenhut, Zvi, and Alon De Groot. 2008. "Moza." *NEAEHL* 5:1958–61.

———. 2009. *Salvage Excavations at Tel Moza: The Bronze and Iron Age Settlements and Later Occupations*. Jerusalem: Israel Antiquities Authority.

Grena, George M. 2004. *Lmlk—A Mystery Belonging to the King*. Redondo Beach, CA: 4000 Years of Writing History.

Gross, Boaz. 2021. "The Other Side of Beth Shemesh: Salvage Archaeology Exposes Deep History of Famed Biblical Site." *Bible History Daily*. https://tinyurl.com/SBLPress9033c8.

Gross, Boaz, Yuval Gadot, and Oded Lipschits. 2014. "The Ancient Garden at Ramat Rahel and Its Water Installations." Pages 93–114 in *Cura aquarum in Israel II: Water in Antiquity; Proceedings of the Fifteenth International Conference on the History of Water Management and Hydraulic Engineering in the Mediterranean Region, Israel, 14–20 October 2012*. Edited by Christoph Ohlig and Tsevikah Tsuk. Siegburg: DWhG.

Guillaume, Philippe. 2008. "Jerusalem 720–705 BCE: No Flood of Israelite Refugees." *SJOT* 22:195–211.

Gunkel, Hermann. 1901. *Genesis*. HKAT. Göttingen: Vandenhoeck & Ruprecht.

Haddad, Elie, Nathan Ben-Ari, and Alon De Groot. 2020. "A Century Old Enigma: The Seventh-Century BCE Settlement at Tel Beth Shemesh (East)." *IEJ* 70:173–88.

Halpern, Baruch. 1981. "Sacred History and Ideology: Chronicles' Thematic Structure—Identification of an Earlier Source." Pages 35–54 in *The Creation of Sacred Literature: Composition and Redaction of the Biblical Text*. Edited by Richard Elliott Friedman. Berkeley: University of California Press.

———. 1991. "Jerusalem and the Lineages in the Seventh Century BCE: Kinship and the Rise of Individual Moral Liability." Pages 11–107 in *Law and Ideology in Monarchic Israel*. Edited by Baruch Halpern and Deborah W. Hobson. JSOTSup 124. Sheffield: JSOT Press.

———. 2001. *David's Secret Demons: Messiah, Murderer, Traitor, King*. Grand Rapids: Eerdmans.

Handy, Lowell K. 1988. "Hezekiah's Unlikely Reform." *ZAW* 100:111–15.

Haran, Menahem. 1978. *Temples and Temple-Service in Ancient Israel: An Inquiry into the Character of Cult Phenomena and the Historical Setting of the Priestly School*. Oxford: Clarendon.

Harrell, James A., and Michael Lewan. 2002. "Sources of Mummy Bitumen in Ancient Egypt and Palestine." *Archaeometry* 44:285–293.

Hasel, Michael G., Yosef Garfinkel, and Shifra Weiss. 2017. *Socoh of the Judean Shephelah: The 2010 Survey*. Winona Lake, IN: Eisenbrauns.

Heltzer, Michael. 1979. "Royal Economy in Ancient Ugarit." Pages 459–96 in vol. 2 of *State and Temple Economy in the Ancient Near East: Proceedings of the International Conference Organized by the Katholieke Universiteit Leuven from the 10th to the 14th April 1978*. Edited by Edward Lipinski. 2 vols. OLA 5–6. Leuven: Departement Oriëntalistiek.

Herzog, Ze'ev. 1997. *Archaeology of the City: Urban Planning in Ancient Israel and Its Social Implications*. Monograph Series of the Institute of Archaeology of Tel Aviv University 13. Tel Aviv: Emery and Claire Yass Archaeology Press.

———. 2001. "The Date of the Temple at Arad: Reassessment of the Stratigraphy and the Implications for the History of Religion in Judah." Pages 156–78 in *Studies in the Archaeology of the Iron Age in Israel and Jordan*. Edited by Amihai Mazar. JSOTSup 331. Sheffield: Sheffield Academic.

———. 2002a. "The Fortress Mound at Tel Arad: An Interim Report." *TA* 29:3–109.

———. 2002b. "Water Supply at Tel Beersheba" [Hebrew]. *Qad* 35:87–101.

———. 2010. "Perspectives on Southern Israel's Cult Centralization: Arad and Beer-sheba." Pages 169–99 in *One God – One Cult – One Nation: Archaeological and Biblical Perspectives*. Edited by Reinhard G. Kratz and Hermann Spieckermann. BZAW 405. Berlin: De Gruyter.

———. 2016. "Topography and Stratigraphy." Pages 15–29 in *Beer-sheba III: The Early Iron IIA Enclosed Settlement and the Late Iron IIA-Iron IIB Cities*. Edited by Ze'ev Herzog and Lily Singer-Avitz. Monograph Series of the Institute of Archaeology, Tel Aviv University 33. Winona Lake, IN: Eisenbrauns.

Herzog, Ze'ev, Miriam Aharoni, Anson F. Rainey, and Shmuel Moshkovitz. 1984. "The Israelite Fortress at Arad." *BASOR* 254:1–34.

Herzog, Ze'ev, Anson F. Rainey, and Shmuel Moshkovitz. 1977. "Stratigraphy at Beersheba and the Location of the Sanctuary." *BASOR* 225:49–58.

Herzog, Ze'ev, and Lily Singer-Avitz. 2004. "Redefining the Centre: The Emergence of State in Judah." *TA* 31:209–44.

———. 2011. "Iron Age IIA Occupational Phases in the Coastal Plain of Israel." Pages 159–74 in in *The Fire Signals of Lachish: Studies in the Archaeology and History of Israel in the Late Bronze Age, Iron Age, and Persian Period in Honor of David Ussishkin*. Edited by Israel Finkelstein and Nadav Na'aman. Winona Lake, IN: Eisenbrauns.

Hizmi, Hananya. 1993. "Southern Part of the Map of Beit Sira." Pages 97–131 in *Archeological Survey of the Hill Country of Benjamin*. Edited by Israel Finkelstein and Yitzhak Magen. Jerusalem: Israel Antiquities Authority. English summaries: 23*–28*.

Hubbard, R. Pearce S. 1966. "The Topography of Ancient Jerusalem." *PEQ* 98:130–54.

Hutzli, Jürg. 2011. "The Meaning of the Expression 'ir dāwīd in Samuel and Kings." *TA* 38:167–78.

Isser, Stanley. 2003. *The Sword of Goliath: David in Heroic Literature*. SBLStBL 6. Atlanta: Society of Biblical Literature.

Jamieson-Drake, David W. 1991. *Scribes and Schools in Monarchic Judah: A Socio-archeological Approach*. SWBA 9. Sheffield: Almond.

Janssen, Jac J. 1979. "The Role of the Temple in the Egyptian Economy during the New Kingdom." Pages 509–15 in vol. 2 of *State and Temple Economy in the Ancient Near East: Proceedings of the International*

Conference Organized by the Katholieke Universiteit Leuven from the 10th to the 14th April 1978. Edited by Edward Lipinski. 2 vols. OLA 5–6. Leuven: Departement Oriëntalistiek.

Japhet, Sara. 1985. "The Historical Reliability of Chronicles: The History of the Problem and Its Place in Biblical Research." *JSOT* 33:83–107.

———. 1989. *The Ideology of the Book of Chronicles and Its Place in Biblical Thought*. BEATAJ 9. Frankfurt am Main: Lang.

———. 1993. *I and II Chronicles: A Commentary*. OTL Louisville: Westminster/John Knox.

Jasmin, Michael. 2005. "Les conditions d'émergence de la route de l'encens à la fin du IIe millénaire avant notre ère." *Syria* 82:49–62

Kagan, Elisa Joy, Dafna Langgut, Elisabetta Boaretto, Frank Harald Neumann, and Mordechai Stein. 2015. "Dead Sea Levels during the Bronze and Iron Ages." *Radiocarbon* 57:237–52.

Kaiser, Otto. 2011. "Der historische und der biblische König Saul (Teil I)." *ZAW* 122:520–45.

———. 2012. "Der historische und der biblische König Saul (Teil II)." *ZAW* 123:1–14.

Kallai, Zecharia. 1968. "Nephtoah, Mei Nephtoah" [Hebrew]. *EncBib* 5:904–5.

———. 1976. "Ramah, 4" [Hebrew]. *EncBib* 7:375.

———. 1986. *Historical Geography of the Bible: The Tribal Territories of Israel*. Jerusalem: Magnes.

Kallai, Zecharia, and Hayim Tadmor. 1969. "Bit Ninurta = Beth Horon - On the History of the Kingdom of Jerusalem in the Amarna Period" [Hebrew]. *ErIsr* 9:138–47.

Kallai-Kleinman, Zecharia. 1953. "Topographical Problems in the Land of Benjamin" [Hebrew]. *ErIsr* 2:108–12.

Kamlah, Jens. 2001. "Die Liste der Regionalfürsten in 1 Kön 4, 7–19 als historische Quelle für die Zeit Salomos." *BN* 106:57–78.

Katz, Hayah. 2001. "Main Aspects in the Economy of Judah during the Ninth–Beginning of the Sixth Centuries BCE" [Hebrew]. Ph.D. diss., Bar Ilan University.

———. 2008. *"A Land of Grain and Wine ... A Land of Olive Oil and Honey": The Economy of the Kingdom of Judah* [Hebrew]. Jerusalem: Yad Ben Zvi.

Katz, Hayah, and Avraham Faust. 2012. "The Assyrian Destruction Layer at Tel ʿEton." *IEJ* 62:22–53.

———. 2014. "The Chronology of the Iron Age IIA in Judah in the Light of Tel 'Eton Tomb C3 and other Assemblages." *BASOR* 371:103–127.

Keel, Othmar. 2012. "Paraphernalia of Jerusalem Sanctuaries and Their Relation to Deities Worshiped Therein during the Iron Age IIA–C." Pages 317–42 in *Temple Building and Temple Cult: Architecture and Cultic Paraphernalia of Temples in the Levant (2.–1. Mill. B.C.E.); Proceedings of a Conference on the Occasion of the Fiftieth Anniversary of the Institute of Biblical Archaeology at the University of Tübingen (28–30 May 2010)*. Edited by Jens Kamlah. Wiesbaden: Harrassowitz.

———. 2015. "Glyptic Finds from the Ophel Excavations 2009–2013." Pages 475–530 in vol. 1 of *The Ophel Excavations to the South of the Temple Mount 2009–2013: Final Reports*, by Eilat Mazar. Jerusalem: Shoham.

Kelso, James L. 1968. *The Excavation of Bethel (1934–1960)*. AASOR 39. Cambridge: American Schools of Oriental Research.

Kempinski, Aharon, Orna Zimhoni, Erel Gilboa, and Nahum Rösel. 1981. "Excavations at Tel Masos 1972, 1974, 1975" [Hebrew]. *ErIsr* 15:154–80.

Kenyon, Kathleen M. 1963. "Excavations in Jerusalem, 1962." *PEQ* 95:7–21.

———. 1965. "Excavations in Jerusalem, 1964." *PEQ* 97:9–20.

———. 1966. "Excavations in Jerusalem, 1965." *PEQ* 98:73–88.

———. 1974. *Digging Up Jerusalem*. London: Benn.

Keys, Gillian. 1996. *The Wages of Sin: A Reappraisal of the 'Succession Narrative'*. JSOTSup 221. Sheffield: Sheffield Academic.

Kisilevitz, Shua. 2013. "Ritual Finds from the Iron Age at Tel Motza" [Hebrew]. *NSAJR* 7:38–46.

Kitchen, Kenneth A. 1973. *The Third Intermediate Period in Egypt, 1100–650 B.C.* Warminster: Aris & Phillips.

———. 1986. *The Third Intermediate Period in Egypt, 1100–650 B.C.* 2nd ed. Warminster: Aris & Phillips.

Kleiman, Assaf. 2015. "A Late Iron IIA Destruction Layer at Tel Aphek in the Sharon Plain." *TA* 42:177–232.

———. 2017. "A North Israelite Royal Administrative System and Its Impact on Late-Monarchic Judah." *HBAI* 6:354–71.

———. 2021. "The Date of the Ophel Pithos Inscription: An Archaeological Perspective." *ZDPV* 137:167–79.

Kleiman, Sabine. 2020. "The Iron IIB Gate Shrine at Lachish: An Alternative Interpretation." *TA* 47:55–64.

———. 2023a. "The End of Cult Places in 8th Century Judah: Cult Reform or de facto Centralization?" Pp. 249–66 in *Temples, Synagogues, Churches, and Mosques: Sacred Architecture in Palestine from the Bronze Age to Medieval Times*. Edited by Jens Kamlah and Markus Witte. Wiesbaden: Harrassowitz.

———. 2023b. "Interpreting Ancient Artefacts: The Case of the So-Called 'Toilet Seats' from Iron Age Judah." Pages 77–93 in *Studies in the History and Archaeology of Ancient Israel and Judah*. Edited by Ido Koch and Omer Sergi. Archaeology and Bible 7. Tübingen: Mohr Siebeck.

Kletter, Raz. 1998. *Economic Keystones: The Weight System of the Kingdom of Judah*. JSOTSup 276. Sheffield: Sheffield Academic.

———. 1999. "Pots and Polities: Material Remains of Late Iron Age Judah in Relation to Its Political Borders." *BASOR* 314:19–54.

Kletter, Raz, and Etty Brand. 1998. "A New Look at the Iron Age Silver Hoard from Eshtemoa." *ZDPV* 114:139–54.

Kloner, Amos. 1984. "Reḥov Hagay." *ESI* 3:57–59.

———. 2003. *Survey of Jerusalem: The Northwestern Sector, Introduction and Indices*. Jerusalem: Israel Antiquities Authority.

Knauf, Ernst Axel. 1988. *Midian: Untersuchungen zur Geschichte Palästinas und Nordarabiens am Ende des 2. Jahrtausends v. Chr*. Wiesbaden: Harrassowitz.

———. 1991. "King Solomon's Copper Supply." Pages 167–86 in *Phoenicia and the Bible*. Edited by Edward Lipiński. OLA 44. Leuven: Peeters.

———. 1995. "Edom: The Social and Economic History." Pages 93–117 in *You Shall Not Abhor an Edomite for He Is Your Brother: Edom and Seir in History and Tradition*. Edited by Diana Vikander Edelman. ABS 3. Atlanta: Scholars Press.

———. 2000. "Jerusalem in the Late Bronze and Early Iron Ages: A Proposal." *TA* 27:75–90.

———. 2001. "Hezekiah or Manasseh? A Reconsideration of the Siloam Tunnel and Inscription." *TA* 28:282–87.

———. 2001. "Saul, David, and the Philistines: From Geography to History." *BN* 109:15–18.

———. 2003. "Who Destroyed Beersheba II?" Pages 181–95 in *Kein Land für sich allein: Studien zum Kulturkontakt in Kanaan, Israel/Palästina und Ebirnâri für Manfred Weippert zum 65. Geburtstag*. Edited by Ulrich Hübner and Ernst Axel Knauf. Fribourg: Universitätsverlag; Göttingen: Vandenhoeck & Ruprecht.

———. 2005. "The Glorious Days of Manasseh." Pages XX in Grabbe, L.L., ed. *Good Kings and Bad Kings: The Kingdom of Judah in the Seventh Century BCE.* Edited by XX. London: 164–188.

———. 2006. "Bethel: The Israelite Impact on Judean Language and Literature." Pages 291–349 in *Judah and the Judeans in the Persian Period.* Edited by Oded Lipschits and Manfred Oeming. Winona Lake, IN: Eisenbrauns.

Knudtzon, J. A. 1915. *Die el-Amarna Tafeln: Mit Einleitung und Erläuterungen.* Leipzig: Hinrichs.

Koch, Ido. 2012. "The Geopolitical Organization of the Judean Shephelah during the Iron Age I–IIA (1150–800 BCE)" [Hebrew]. *Cathedra* 143:45–64.

———. 2017. "Kiriath-Jearim." *EBR* 15:344.

———. 2018. "Introductory Framework for Assyrian-Levantine Colonial Encounters." *Sem* 60:367–96.

Kochavi, Moshe. 1969. "Excavations at Tel Esdar" [Hebrew]. *'Atiqot* 5:14–48.

———. 1972. The Land of Judah" [Hebrew]. Pages 17–89 in *Judaea, Samaria and the Golan, Archaeological Survey 1967–1968.* Edited by Moshe Kochavi. Jerusalem: Carta.

———. 1974. "Khirbet Rabud = Debir." *TA* 1:2–33.

———. 1989. "The Identification of Zeredah, Home of Jeroboam Son of Nebat, King of Israel" [Hebrew]. *ErIsr* 20:198–201.

Landes-Nagar, Annette. 2014. "Jerusalem, Tell el-Ful." *ESI* 126. http://tinyurl.com/SBLPressIFa2.

Langgut, Dafna. 2022. "Mid-Seventh Century BC Human Parasite Remains from Jerusalem." *International Journal of Paleopathology* 36:1–6.

Langgut, Dafna, and Ya'akov Billig. 2021. "Remains of Tapeworms from Iron Age II at Armon Ha-Naziv" [Hebrew]. *NSAJR* 14:101–110.

Langgut, Dafna, Israel Finkelstein, and Thomas Litt. 2013. "Climate and the Late Bronze Collapse: New Evidence from the Southern Levant." *TA* 40:149–75.

Langgut, Dafna, Frank Harald Neumann, Mordechai Stein, Allon Wagner, Elisa Joy Kagan, Elisabetta Boaretto, and Isrel Finkelstein. 2014. "Dead Sea Pollen Record and History of Human Activity in the Judean Highlands (Israel) from the Intermediate Bronze into the Iron Ages (~2500–500 BCE)." *Palynology* 38:1–23.

Langgut Dafna, Israel Finkelstein, Thomas Litt, Frank Harald Neumann, and Mordechai Stein. 2015. "Vegetation and Climate Changes during the Bronze and Iron Ages (~3600–600 BCE) in the Southern Levant Based on Palynological Records." *Radiocarbon* 57:217–35.

Lee Sak, Yitzhak. 2023. "The Solomonic Districts and the Nimshide Dynasty Administrative System in the Southern Levant." *Religions* 14:598. https://doi.org/10.3390/rel14050598.

Lehmann, Gunnar, Steven A. Rosen, Angelika Berlejung, Bat-Ami Neumeier, and Hermann M. Niemann. 2010. "Excavations at Qubur al-Walaydah, 2007–2009." *Die Welt des Orients* 40:137–59.

Lemaire, André. 1973. "L'ostracon 'Ramat-Négeb' et la topographie historique du Négeb." *Sem* 23:11–26.

———. 1975. "Mmst = Amwas, vers la solution d'une énigme de l'épigraphie hébraïque." *RB* 82:15–23.

———. 1977. *Les ostraca*. Vol. 1 of *Inscriptions hébraïques*. Paris: Cerf.

———. 1978. "Les ostraca paleo-Hebreux des fouilles de L'Ophel." *Levant* 10:156–60.

———. 1985. "Les inscriptions de Deir 'Alla et la littérature araméenne antique." *CRAI* 129:270–85.

———. 2004. "Ostraca and Incised Inscriptions." Pages 2099–2132 in vol. 4 of *The Renewed Archaeological Excavations at Lachish (1973–1994)*, by David Ussishkin. Monograph Series of the Institute of Archaeology of Tel Aviv University 22. Tel Aviv: Emery and Claire Yass Publications in Archaeology.

———. 2006. "La datation des rois de Byblos Abibaal et Élibaal et les relations entre l'Égypte et le Levant au Xe siècle av. notre ère." *CRAI* 150:1697–1715.

———. 2007. "The Mesha Stele and the Omri Dynasty." Pages 135–44 in *Ahab Agonistes: The Rise and Fall of the Omri Dynasty*. Edited by Lester L. Grabbe. LHBOTS 421. London: T&T Clark.

———. 2012. "New Perspectives on the Trade between Judah and South Arabia." Pages 93–110 in *New Inscriptions and Seals Relating to the Biblical World*. Edited by Meir Lubetski and Edith Lubetski. ABS 19. Atlanta: Society of Biblical Literature.

———. 2015. "Levantine Literacy ca. 1000–750 BCE." Pages 1–45 in *Contextualizing Israel's Sacred Writings: Ancient Literacy, Orality, and Literary Production*. Edited by Brian B. Schmidt. AIL 22. Atlanta: SBL Press.

Levy, Thomas E., Russell B. Adams, Mohammad Najjar, Andreas Hauptmann, James D. Anderson, Baruch Brandl, Mark A. Robinson, and Thomas Higham. 2004. "Reassessing the Chronology of Biblical Edom:

New Excavations and ^{14}C Dates from Khirbat en-Nahas (Jordan)." *Antiquity* 78:865–79.
Levy, Thomas E., Thomas Higham, Christopher Bronk Ramsey, Neil G. Smith, Erez Ben-Yosef, Mark Robinson, Stefan Münger, Kyle Knabb, Jürgen P. Schulze, Mohammad Najjar, and Lisa Tauxe. 2008. "High-Precision Radiocarbon Dating and Historical Biblical Archaeology in Southern Jordan." *PNAS* 105:16460–65.
Levy, Thomas E., Mohammad Najjar, Thomas Higham, Yoav Arbel, Adolfo Muniz, Erez Ben-Yosef, Neil G. Smith, Marc Beherec, Aaron Gidding, Ian W. Jones, Daniel Frese, Craig Smitheram II, and Mark Robinson. 2016. "Excavations at Khirbet en-Nahas, 2002–2009: An Iron Age Copper Production Center in the Lowlands of Edom." Pages 89–245 in vol. 1 of *New Insights in the Iron Age Archaeology of Edom, Southern Jordan: Surveys, Excavations and Research from the University of California, San Diego and Department of Antiquities of Jordan, Edom Lowlands Regional Archaeology Project (ELRAP)*. Edited by Thomas Evan Levy, Mohammad Najjar, and Erez Ben-Yosef. Los Angeles: Cotsen Institute of Archaeology Press, University of California.
Liphschitz, Nili. 2007. *Timber in Ancient Israel: Dendroarchaeology and Dendrochronology*. Monograph Series of the Institute of Archaeology of Tel Aviv University 26. Tel Aviv: Emery and Claire Yass Publications in Archaeology, Institute of Archaeology, Tel Aviv University.
Lipinski, Edward. 2000. *The Aramaeans: Their Ancient History, Culture, Religion*. OLA 100. Leuven: Peeters.
———. 2010. "Hiram of Tyre and Solomon." Pages 251–72 in *The Book of Kings: Sources, Composition, Historiography and Reception*. Edited by André Lemaire and Baruch Halpern. VTSup 129. Leiden: Brill.
Lipschits, Oded. 2003. "Demographic Changes in Judah between the Seventh and the Fifth Centuries B.C.E." Pages 323–76 in *Judah and the Judeans in the Neo-Babylonian Period*. Edited by Oded Lipschits and Jospeh Blenkinsopp. Winona Lake, IN: Eisenbrauns.
———. 2005. *The Fall and Rise of Jerusalem: Judah under Babylonian Rule*. Winona Lake, IN: Eisenbrauns.
———. 2006. "Achaemenid Imperial Policy, Settlement Processes in Palestine, and the Status of Jerusalem in the Middle of the Fifth Century B.C.E." Pages 19–52 in *Judah and the Judeans in the Persian Period*. Edited by Oded Lipschits and Manfred Oeming. Winona Lake, IN: Eisenbrauns.

———. 2007. "Who Financed and Who Arranged the Building of Jerusalem's Walls? The Sources of the List of The Builders of the Walls (Nehemiah 3:1–32) and the Purposes of Its Literary Placement within Nehemiah's Memoirs" [Hebrew]. Pages 73–90 in *Shai le-Sara Japhet: Studies in the Bible, Its Exegesis and Its Language*. Edited by Moshe Bar-Asher, Dalit Rom-Shiloni, Emanuel Tov, and Nili Wazana. Jerusalem: Mosad Bialik.

———. 2009. "Persian Period Finds from Jerusalem: Facts and Interpretations." *JHS* 9:article 20. https://doi.org/10.5508/jhs.2009.v9.a20.

———. 2012. "Nehemiah 3:Sources, Composition, and Purpose." Pages 73–99 in *New Perspectives on Ezra-Nehemiah: History and Historiography, Text, Literature, and Interpretation*. Edited by Isaac Kalimi. Winona Lake, IN: Eisenbrauns Eisenbrauns.

———. 2021. *Age of Empires: The History and Administration of Judah in the Eighth–Second Centuries BCE in Light of the Storage-Jar Stamp Impressions*. University Park, PA: Eisenbrauns; Tel Aviv: Emery and Claire Yass Publications in Archaeology, The Institute of Archaeology, Tel Aviv University.

Lipschits, Oded, Yuval Gadot, Benjamin Arubas, and Manfred Oeming. 2011. "Palace and Village, Paradise and Oblivion: Unraveling the Riddles of Ramat Raḥel." *NEA* 74:2–49.

———. 2016. *What Are the Stones Whispering? Ramat Raḥel: 3,000 Years of Forgotten History*. Winona Lake, IN: Eisenbrauns.

Lipschits, Oded, Yuval Gadot, and Dafna Langgut. 2012. "Ramat Rahel during the Babylonian and Persian Periods: The Archaeology of a Royal Edifice." *Transeu* 41:57–79.

Lipschits, Oded, Yuval Gadot, and Manfred Oeming. 2012. "Tel Azekah 113 Years After: Preliminary Evaluation of the Renewed Excavations at the Site." *NEA* 75:196–207.

———. 2020. "Deconstruction and Reconstruction: Reevaluating the Five Expeditions to Ramat Raḥel." Pages 476–91 in *Ramat Raḥel IV: The Renewed Excavations by the Tel Aviv-Heidelberg Expedition (2005–2010); Stratigraphy and Architecture*. Edited by Oded Lipschits, Manfred Oeming, and Yuval Gadot. Monograph Series of the Institute of Archaeology, Tel Aviv University 39. University Park: Penn State University Press.

Lipschits, Oded, and Ido Koch. 2010. "The Final Days of the Kingdom of Judah in Light of the Rosette-Stamped Jar Handles" [Hebrew]. *Cathedra* 137:7–26.

Lipschits, Oded, and Nadav Na'aman. 2020. "The Ancient Name of the Site." Pages 8–13 in *Ramat Raḥel IV: The Renewed Excavations by the Tel Aviv-Heidelberg Expedition (2005–2010); Stratigraphy and Architecture*. Edited by Oded Lipschits, Manfred Oeming, and Yuval Gadot. Monograph Series of the Institute of Archaeology, Tel Aviv University 39. University Park: Penn State University Press.

Lipschits, Oded, Omer Sergi, and Ido Koch. 2010. "Royal Judahite Jar Handles: Reconsidering the Chronology of the *lmlk* Stamp Impressions." *TA* 37:3–32.

———. 2011. "Judahite Stamped and Incised Jar Handles: A Tool for Studying the History of Late Monarchic Judah." *TA* 38:5–41.

Lipschits, Oded, and David S. Vanderhooft. 2007. "Jerusalem in the Persian and Hellenistic Periods in Light of the *Yehud* Stamp Impressions." *ErIsr* 28:106–15.

———. 2011. *The Yehud Stamp Impressions: A Corpus of Inscribed Impressions from the Persian and Hellenistic Periods in Judah*. Winona Lake, IN: Eisenbrauns.

Litt, Thomas, Christian Ohlwein, Frank H. Neumann, Andreas Hense, and Mordechai Stein. 2012. "Holocene Climate Variability in the Levant from the Dead Sea Pollen Record." *Quaternary Science Reviews* 49:95–105.

Liverani, Mario. 1992. "Early Caravan Trade between South-Arabia and Mesopotamia." *Yemen* 1:111–15

Lowery, R. H. 1991. *The Reforming Kings: Cults and Society in First Temple Judah*. JSOTSup 120. Sheffield: JSOT Press.

Macalister, R. A. S., and J. Garrow Duncan. 1926. *Excavations on the Hill of Ophel, Jerusalem, 1923–1925*. Palestine Exploration Fund Annual 4. London: Palestine Exploration Fund.

Maeir, Aren M. 2000. "Jerusalem before King David: An Archaeological Survey from Protohistoric Times to the End of the Iron Age I" [Hebrew]. Pages 33–66 in *The History of Jerusalem: The Biblical Period*. Edited by Shmuel Ahituv and Amihai Mazar. Jerusalem: Yad Izhaq Ben-Zvi.

———. 2001. "The Philistine Culture in Transformation: A Current Perspective Based on the Results of the First Seasons of Excavations at Tell es-Safi/Gath" [Hebrew]. Pages XX in Maeir, A.M. and Baruch, E. eds. *Settlement, Civilization and Culture, Proceedings of the Conference in Memory of David Alon*. Ramat Gan: 111–129.

———. 2004. "The Historical Background and Dating of Amos VI 2:An Archaeological Perspective from Tell eṣ-Ṣafi/Gath." *VT* 54:319–334.

———. 2012. "The Tell es-Safi/Gath Archaeological Project 1996–2010: Introduction, Overview and Synopsis of Results." Pages 1–88 in *Text*. Part 1 of *Tell es-Safi/Gath I: The 1996–2005 Seasons*. Edited by Aren M. Maeir. ÄAT 69. Wiesbaden: Harrassowitz.

Maeir, Aren M. and Carl S. Ehrlich. 2001. "Excavating Philistine Gath." *BAR* 27.6:22–31.

Maeir, Aren M. and Esther Eshel. 2014. "Four Short Alphabetic Inscriptions from Iron Age IIa Tell eṣ-Ṣafi/Gath and Their Contribution for the Development of Literacy in Iron Age Philistia and Environs." Pages 69–88 and 205–10 in *"See, I Will Bring a Scroll Recounting What Befell Me" (Ps 40:8), Epigraphy and Daily Life from the Bible to the Talmud Dedicated to the Memory of Professor Hanan Eshel*. Edited by Esther Eshel and Yigal Levin. JAJSup 12. Göttingen: Vandenhoeck & Ruprecht.

Maeir, Aren M., Eric L. Welch, and Maria Eniukhina. 2020. "A Note on Olive Oil Production in Iron Age Philistia: Pressing the Consensus." *PEQ* 152:1–16.

Manor, Dale W. 2016. "A Priest House at Beth-shemesh? An Incised *qdš* Bowl." Pages 470–79 in vol. 2 of *Tel Beth-shemesh: A Border Community in Judah; Renewed Excavations 1990–2000; The Iron Age*. Edited by Shlomo Bunimovitz and Zvi Lederman. Monograph Series of the Institute of Archaeology, Tel Aviv University 34. Tel Aviv: Emery and Claire Yass publications in archaeology; Winona Lake, IN: Eisenbrauns.

Marfoe, Leon. 1979. "The Integrative Transformation: Patterns of Sociopolitical Organization in Southern Syria." *BASOR* 234:1–42.

Martin, Mario A. S. 2011. *Egyptian-Type Pottery in the Late Bronze Age Southern Levant*. Vienna: Verlag der Österreichische Akademie der Wissenschaften.

Martin, Mario A. S., and Israel Finkelstein. 2013. "Iron IIA Pottery from the Negev Highlands: Petrographic Investigation and Historical Implications." *TA* 40:6–45.

Mattingly, Gerald L. 1992. "Amalek." *ABD* 1:169–71.

Mazar, Amihai. 1981. "The Excavations at Khirbet Abu et-Twein and the System of Iron Age Fortresses in Judah." *ErIsr* 15:229–49.

———. 1997a. "Iron Age Chronology: A Reply to I. Finkelstein." *Levant* 29:155–65.

———. 1997b. *Timnah (Tel Batash) I: Stratigraphy and Architecture*. 2 vols. Qedem 37. Jerusalem: Hebrew University, Institute of Archaeology.

———. 2005. "The Debate over the Chronology of the Iron Age in the Southern Levant: Its History, the Current Situation, and a Suggested Resolution." Pages 15–30 in *The Bible and Radiocarbon Dating: Archaeology, Text and Science*. Edited by Thomas E. Levy and Tom Higham. London: Equinox.

———. 2006a. "Iron Age Inscriptions." Pages 505–13 in *From the Late Bronze Age IIB to the Medieval Period*. Vol. 1 of *Excavations at Tel Beth-Shean 1989–1996*, by Amihai Mazar. Jerusalem: Israel Exploration Society; The Institute of Archaeology, The Hebrew University of Jerusalem.

———. 2006b. "Jerusalem in the 10th Century B.C.E.: The Glass Half Full." Pages 255–72 in *Essays on Ancient Israel in Its Near Eastern Context: A Tribute to Nadav Na'aman*. Edited by Yairah Amit, Ehud Ben Zvi, Israel Finkelstein, and Oded Lipschits. Winona Lake, IN: Eisenbrauns.

———. 2010. "Archaeology and the Biblical Narrative: The Case of the United Monarchy." Pages 29–58 in *One God – One Cult – One Nation: Archaeological and Biblical Perspectives*. Edited by Reinhard G. Kratz and Hermann Spieckermann. BZAW 405. Berlin: De Gruyter.

———. 2011. "The Iron Age Chronology Debate: Is the Gap Narrowing? Another Viewpoint." *NEA* 74:105–11.

———. 2020. "Jerusalem in the Tenth Cent. B.C.E.: A Response." *ZDPV* 136:139–51.

Mazar, Amihai, David Amit, and Zvi Ilan. 1984. "The 'Border Road' between Michmash and Jericho and Excavations at Horvat Shilhah" [Hebrew]. *ErIsr* 17:236–50.

———. 1996. "Hurvat Shilhah: An Iron Age Site in the Judean Desert." Pages 193–211 in *Retrieving the Past: Essays on Archaeological Research and Methodology in Honor of Gus W. Van Beek*. Edited by Joe D. Seger. Winona Lake, IN: Eisenbrauns.

Mazar, Amihai, and Ehud Netzer. 1986. "On the Israelite Fortress at Arad." *BASOR* 263:87–91.

Mazar, Amihai, and Nava Panitz-Cohen. 2001. *Timnah (Tel Batash) II: The Finds from the First Millennium BCE; Text*. Qedem 42. Jerusalem: Institute of Archaeology, Hebrew University of Jerusalem.

Mazar, Benjamin. 1957. "The Campaign of Pharaoh Shishak to Palestine." Pages 57–66 in *Volume du Congrès International pour l'étude de l'Ancien Testament: Strasbourg 1956*. Edited by G. W. Anderson, P. A.

H. de Boer, Millar Burrows, Henri Cazelles, E. Hammershaimb, and Martin Noth. VTSup 4. Leiden: Brill.

———. 1971. *The Excavations in the Old City of Jerusalem near the Temple Mount: Preliminary Report of the Second and Third Seasons 1969–1970.* Jerusalem: Institute of Archaeology, Hebrew University.

Mazar, Eilat. 1997. "Excavate King David's Palace!" *BAR* 23.1:50–57, 74.

———. 2006a. "Did I Find King David's Palace?" *BAR* 32 16–27, 70.

———. 2006b. "The Fortifications of Jerusalem in the Second Millennium BCE in Light of the New Excavations in the City of David" [Hebrew]. *New Studies on Jerusalem* 12:21–28. English abstract on 8*–9*.

———. 2006c. "It Looks Like King David's Palace" [Hebrew]. *New Studies on Jerusalem* 11:7–16.

———. 2006d. "The Solomonic Wall in Jerusalem." Pages 775–86 in *"I Will Speak the Riddles of Ancient Times": Archaeological and Historical Studies in Honor of Amihai Mazar.* Edited by Aren Maeir and Pierre de Miroschedji. Winona Lake, IN: Eisenbrauns.

———. 2007. *Preliminary Report on the City of David Excavations 2005 at the Visitors Center Area.* Jerusalem: Shalem.

———. 2009. *The Palace of King David: Excavations at the Summit of the City of David; Preliminary Report of Seasons 2005–2007.* Jerusalem: Shoham.

———. 2011. *Discovering the Solomonic Wall in Jerusalem: A Remarkable Archaeological Adventure.* Jerusalem.

———. 2015. "The Solomonic (Early Iron Age IIA) Royal Quarter in the Ophel." Pages 459–74 in vol. 1 of *The Ophel Excavations to the South of the Temple Mount 2009–2013: Final Reports*, by Eilat Mazar. Jerusalem: Shoham.

Mazar, Eilat, David Ben-Shlomo, and Shmuel Ahituv. 2013. "An Inscribed Pithos from the Ophel, Jerusalem." *IEJ* 63:39–49.

Mazar, Eilat, and Tzachi Lang. 2018. "The Fortified Enclosure at the Ophel—The 'Far House': Architecture and Stratigraphy." Pages 325–93 in vol. 2 of *The Ophel Excavations to the South of the Temple Mount 2009–2013: Final Reports*, by Eilat Mazar. 2 vols. Jerusalem: Shoham.

Mazar, Eilat, and Reut Livyatan Ben-Arie. 2015. "Hebrew and Nonindicative Bullae." Pages 299–362 in vol. 1 of *The Summit of the City of David Excavations 2005–2008: Final Report*, by Eilat Mazar. Jerusalem: Shoham.

———. 2018. Hebrew Seal Impressions (Bullae) from the Ophel (Area A2009)." Pages 247–79 in vol. 2 of *The Ophel Excavations to the South of the Temple Mount 2009–2013: Final Reports*, by Eilat Mazar. 2 vols. Jerusalem: Shoham.

Mazar, Eilat, and Benjamin Mazar. 1989. *Excavations in the South of the Temple Mount: The Ophel of Biblical Jerusalem*. Qedem 29. Jerusalem: Institute of Archaeology, the Hebrew University of Jerusalem.

Mazar, Eilat, and Jonathan R. Morgan. 2018. "The Pottery from the Ophel, L09–421b (Area A2009)." Pages 225–42 in vol. 2 of *The Ophel Excavations to the South of the Temple Mount 2009–2013: Final Reports*, by Eilat Mazar. 2 vols. Jerusalem: Shoham.

McCarter, P. Kyle. 1980a. *I Samuel: A New Translation with Introduction, Notes and Commentary*. AB 8. Garden City, NY: Doubleday.

———. 1980b. "The Apology of David." *JBL* 99:489–504.

McKay, J. W. 1973. *Religion in Judah under the Assyrians, 732–609 BC*. SBT 2/26. Naperville, IL: Allenson.

McKinny, Chris, Oron Schwartz, Gabriel Barkay, Alexander Fantalkin, and Boaz Zissu. 2018. "Kiriath-Jearim (Deir el-ʿÂzar): Archaeological Investigations of a Biblical Town in the Judaean Hill Country." *IEJ* 68:30–49.

Meitilis, Itzhak. 1992. "Jerusalem, Wadi Zimra." *ESI* 10:125–27.

Mendel-Geberovich, Anat, Ortel Chalaf, and Joe Uziel. 2020. "The People behind the Stamps: A Newly-Found Group of Bullae and a Seal from the City of David, Jerusalem." *BASOR* 384:159–82.

Meshel, Zeʾev. 2012. *Kuntillet ʿAjrud (Ḥorvat Teman): An Iron Age II Religious Site on the Judah-Sinai Border*. Edited by Liora Freud. Jerusalem: Israel Exploration Society.

Millard, Alan R. 1989. "Does the Bible Exaggerate King Solomon's Golden Wealth?" *BAR* 15.3:20–34.

———. 2009. "The Armor of Goliath." Pages 337–43 in *Exploring the Longue Durée: Essays in Honor of Lawrence E. Stager*. Edited by J. David Schloen. Winona Lake, IN: Eisenbrauns.

———. 2012. "Scripts and Their Uses in the Twelfth–Tenth Centuries BCE." Pages 405–12 in *The Ancient Near East in the Twelfth–Tenth Centuries BCE: Culture and History; Proceedings of the International Conference Held at the University of Haifa, 2–5 May, 2010*. Edited by Gershon Galil, Ayelet Leyinzon-Gilboʿa, Aren M. Maeir, and Danʾel Kahn. Münster: Ugarit-Verlag.

Miller, J. Maxwell, and John H. Hayes. *A History of Ancient Israel and Judah*. 2nd ed. Louisville: Westminster John Knox, 2006.

Miller, Patrick D., and J. J. M. Roberts. 1977. *The Hand of the Lord: A Reassessment of the "Ark Narrative" of 1 Samuel*. Baltimore: Johns Hopkins University Press.

Moran, William L. 1975. "The Syrian Scribe of the Jerusalem Amarna Letters." Pages 146–66 in *Unity and Diversity: Essays in the History, Literature and Religion of the Ancient Near East*. Edited by Hans Goedicke and J. J. M. Roberts. Baltimore: Johns Hopkins University Press.

———. 1992. *The Amarna Letters*, Baltimore: Johns Hopkins University Press.

Mowinckel, Sigmund. 1964. *Studien zu dem Buche Ezra-Nehemia*. Skrifter utgitt av det Norske videnskaps-akademi i Oslo 2. Oslo: Universitetsforlaget.

Mullins, Robert A., and Amihai Mazar. 2007. "Area R: The Stratigraphy and Architecture of the Middle and Late Bronze Ages; Strata R-5-R-1." Pages 39–241 in *The Middle and Late Bronze Age Strata in Area R*. Vol. 2 of *Excavations at Tel Beth-Shean 1989–1996*. Edited by Amihai Mazar, A. and Robert A. Mullins. Jerusalem: Israel Exploration Society; The Institute of Archaeology, The Hebrew University of Jerusalem.

Naʾaman, Nadav. 1975. "The Political Disposition and Historical Development of Eretz-Israel according to the Amarna Letters" [Hebrew with English abstract]. PhD diss., Tel Aviv University.

———. 1979. "The Origin and Historical Background of Several Amarna Letters." *UF* 11:673–84.

———. 1980. "The Inheritance of the Sons of Simeon." *ZDPV* 96:136–52.

———. 1981. "Economic Aspects of the Egyptian Occupation of Canaan." *IEJ* 31:172–85.

———. 1986. "Ḫabiru and Hebrews: The Transfer of a Social Term to the Literary Sphere." *JNES* 45:271–88.

———. 1990a. "The Kingdom of Ishbaal." *BN* 54:33–37.

———. 1990b. "On Gods and Scribal Traditions in the Amarna Letters." *UF* 22:247–55.

———. 1991. "The Kingdom of Judah under Josiah." *TA* 18:3–71.

———. 1992a. "Canaanite Jerusalem and Its Central Hill Country Neighbours in the Second Millennium B.C.E." *UF* 24:275–91.

———. 1992b. "The Pre-Deuteronomistic Story of King Saul and Its Historical Significance." *CBQ* 54:638–58.

———. 1994. "The 'Conquest of Canaan' in the Book of Joshua and in History." Pages 218–81 in *From Nomadism to Monarchy: Archaeological and Historical Aspects of Early Israel*. Edited by Israel Finkelstein. and

Nadav Na'aman. Jerusalem: Yad Izhak Ben-Zvi; Israel Exploration Society; Washington, DC: Biblical Archaeology Society.

———. 1995a. "The Debated Historicity of Hezekiah's Reform in the Light of Historical and Archaeological Research." *ZAW* 107:179–95.

———. 1995b. "Province System and Settlement Pattern in Southern Syria and Palestine in the Neo-Assyrian Period." Pages 103–15 in *Neo-Assyrian Geography*. Edited by Mario Liverani. Rome: Università di Roma, Dipartimento di scienze storiche, archeologiche e antropologiche dell'Antichità.

———. 1996. "The Contribution of the Amarna Letters to the Debate on Jerusalem's Political Position in the Tenth Century B.C.E." *BASOR* 304:17–27.

———. 1997. "The Network of Canaanite Kingdoms and the City of Ashdod." *UF* 29:599–626.

———. 1999. "No Anthropomorphic Graven Image: Notes on the Assumed Anthropomorphic Cult Statues in the Temples of YHWH in the Preexilic Period." *UF* 31:391–415.

———. 2000a. "Rubutu/Aruboth." *UF* 32:373–83.

———. 2000b. "The Egyptian Canaanite Correspondence." Pages 125–38 in *Amarna Diplomacy: The Beginning of International Relations*. Edited by Raymond Cohen and Raymond Westbrook. Baltimore: Johns Hopkins University Press.

———. 2001a. "An Assyrian Residence at Ramat Raḥel?" *TA* 28:260–80.

———. 2001b. "Solomon's District List (1 Kings 4:7–19) and the Assyrian Province System in Palestine." *UF* 33:419–36.

———. 2002a. "The Abandonment of Cult Places in the Kingdoms of Israel and Judah as Acts of Cult Reform." *UF* 34:585–602.

———. 2002b. "In Search of Reality behind the Account of David's Wars with Israel's Neighbours." *IEJ* 52:200–224.

———. 2003. "Ostracon No. 40 from Arad Reconsidered." Pages 199–204 in *Saxa loquentur: Studien zur Archäologie Palästinas/Israels; Festschrift für Volkmar Fritz zum 65. Geburtstag*. Edited by Cornelis Gijsbert den Hertog, Ulrich Hübner, and Stefan Münger. AOAT 302. Münster: Ugarit-Verlag.

———. 2007. "When and How Did Jerusalem Become a Great City? The Rise of Jerusalem as Judah's Premier City in the Eighth-Seventh Centuries B.C.E." *BASOR* 347:21–56.

———. 2008. "In Search of the Ancient Name of Khirbet Qeiyafa." *JHS* 8:article 21. https://doi.org/10.5508/jhs.2008.v8.a21.

———. 2009a. "The Growth and Development of Judah and Jerusalem in the Eighth Century BCE: A Rejoinder." *RB* 116:321–35.

———. 2009b. "Saul, Benjamin and the Emergence of 'Biblical Israel.'" *ZAW* 121:211–24, 335–49.

———. 2010a. "The Date of the List of Towns That Received the Spoil of Amalek (1 Sam 30:26–31)." *TA* 37:175–87.

———. 2010b. "David's Sojourn in Keilah in Light of the Amarna Letters." *VT* 60:87–97.

———. 2010c. "Does Archaeology Really Deserve the Status of a 'High Court' in Biblical and Historical Research?" Pages 165–83 in *Between Evidence and Ideology: Essays on the History of Ancient Israel Read at the Joint Meeting of the Society for Old Testament Study and the Oud Testamentisch Werkgezelschap, Lincoln, July 2009*. Edited by Bob Becking and Lester L. Grabbe. OtSt 59. Leiden: Brill.

———. 2010d. "Jerusalem in the Amarna Period." Pages 31–48 in *Jérusalem antique et médiévale: Mélanges en l'honneur d'Ernest-Marie Laperrousaz*. Edited by Caroline Arnould-Béhar and André Lemaire. Collection de la Revue des études juives 52. Paris: Peeters.

———. 2011. "The Shephelah according to the Amarna Letters." Pages 281–300 in *The Fire Signals of Lachish: Studies in the Archaeology and History of Israel in the Late Bronze Age, Iron Age, and Persian Period in Honor of David Ussishkin*. Edited by Israel Finkelstein and Nadav Na'aman. Winona Lake, IN: Eisenbrauns.

———. 2012a. "The Inscriptions of Kuntillet 'Ajrud through the Lens of Historical Research." *UF* 43:1–43.

———. 2012b. "Khirbet Qeiyafa in Context." *UF* 42:497–526.

———. 2013a. "The Kingdom of Judah in the Ninth Century BCE: Text Analysis versus Archaeological Research." *TA* 40:247–76.

———. 2013b. "A Sapiential Composition from Horvat 'Uza." *HBAI* 2:221–33.

———. 2014a. "Dismissing the Myth of a Flood of Israelite Refugees in the Late Eighth Century BCE." *ZAW* 126:1–14.

———. 2014b. "Jebusites and Jabeshites in the Saul and David Story-Cycles." *Bib* 95:489–92.

———. 2015. "Literacy in the Negev in the Late Monarchical Period." Pages 47–70 in *Contextualizing Israel's Sacred Writings: Ancient Literacy, Orality, and Literary Production*. Edited by Brian B. Schmidt. AIL 22. Atlanta: SBL Press.

———. 2017. "Memories of Monarchical Israel's in the Narratives." *HBAI* 6:308–28.

———. 2019. "Hiram of Tyre in the Book of Kings and in the Tyrian Records." *JNES* 78:75–85.

———. 2021. "New Light on Six Inscriptions from Arad." *TA* 48:213–35.

———. 2023. "The High Places Which Are in Front of Jerusalem" (2 Kings 23:13): A Proposed Identification." *IEJ* 73:212–26.

Naʾaman, Nadav, and Ran Zadok. 1988. "Sargon II's Deportations to Israel and Philistia." *JCS* 40:36–46.

———. 2000. "Assyrian Deportations to the Province of Samaria in the Light of the Two Cuneiform Tablets from Tel Hadid." *TA* 27:159–88.

Namdar, Dvory, Oded Lipschits, Liora Freud, and Yuval Gadot. 2021. "Organic Content of Persian YHWD-Stamped Storage Jars." Pages 121–30 in *Ramat Raḥel VI: The Renewed Excavations by the Tel Aviv–Heidelberg Expedition (2005–2010); The Babylonian-Persian Pit*, by Oded Lipschits, Liora Freud, Manfred Oeming, and Yuval Gadot. Monograph Series of the Sonia and Marco Nadler Institute of Archaeology 40. Tel Aviv: The Institute of Archaeology of Tel Aviv University; University Park, PA: Eisenbrauns.

Naveh, Joseph. 1970. *The Development of the Aramaic Script*. Jerusalem: Israel Academy of Sciences and Humanities.

———. 1978. "Some Considerations on the Ostracon from Izbet Sartah." *IEJ* 28:21–35.

———. 1982. *Early History of the Alphabet: An Introduction to West Semitic Epigraphy and Palaeography*. Jerusalem: Magnes.

———. 2000. "Hebrew and Aramaic Inscriptions." Pages 1–14 in *Inscriptions*. Vol. 6 of *Excavations at the City of David 1978–1985 Directed by Yigal Shiloh*. Edited by Donald T. Ariel. Qedem 41. Jerusalem: Institute of Archaeology, the Hebrew University of Jerusalem.

Nicholson, Ernest W. 1967. *Deuteronomy and Tradition*. Oxford: Blackwell.

Niemann, Hermann Michael. 1997. "The Socio-political Shadow Cast by the Biblical Solomon." Pages 252–99 in *The Age of Solomon: Scholarship in the Turn of the Millennium*. Edited by Lowell K. Handy. SHANE 11. Leiden: Brill.

———. 2008. "A New Look at the Samaria Ostraca: The King-Clan Relationship." *TA* 35:249–66.

Nihan, Christoph. 2006. "Saul among the Prophets (1 Sam 10:10–12 and 19:18–24): The Reworking of Saul's Figure in the Context of the Debate on 'Charismatic Prophecy' in the Persian Era." Pages 88–118 in *Saul in Story and Tradition*. Edited by Carl S. Ehrlich, with Marsha C. White. FAT 47. Tübingen: Mohr Siebeck.

Noth, Martin. 1938a. *Das Buch Josua*. HAT 7. Tübingen: Mohr Siebeck.

———. 1938b. "Grundsätzliches zur geschichtlichen Deutung archäologischer Befunde auf dem Bodem Palästinas." *PJb* 37:7–22.

———. 1940. "Der Wallfahrtsweg zum Sinai (Nu 33)." *PJb* 36:5–28.

———. 1968. *Numbers: A Commentary*. OTL. Philadelphia: Westminster.

———. 1981a. *The Deuteronomistic History*. JSOTSup 15. Sheffield: JSOT Press.

———. 1981b. *A History of Pentateuchal Traditions*. Chico, CA: Scholars Press.

Ofer, Avi. 1993a. "The Highland of Judah during the Biblical Period." PhD diss., Tel Aviv University.

———. 1993b. "Hebron." *NEAEHL* 2:606–9.

———. 1994. "'All the Hill Country of Judah': From Settlement Fringe to a Prosperous Monarchy." Pages 92–121 in *From Nomadism to Monarchy: Archaeological and Historical Aspects of Early Israel*. Edited by Israel Finkelstein. and Nadav Na'aman. Jerusalem: Yad Izhak Ben-Zvi; Israel Exploration Society; Washington, DC: Biblical Archaeology Society.

Oredsson, Dag. 2000. *Moats in Ancient Palestine*. ConB 48. Stockholm: Almqvist & Wiksell.

Oren, Eliezer D. 1982. "Ziklag: A Biblical City on the Edge of the Negev." *BA* 45:155–66.

———. 1993. "Sera', Tel." *NEAEHL* 4:1329–35.

Ornan, Tallay. 2005. *The Triumph of the Symbol: Pictorial Representation of Deities in Mesopotamia and the Biblical Image Ban*. OBO 213. Fribourg: Academic Press; Göttingen: Vandenhoeck & Ruprecht.

———. 2015. "Drawings from Kuntillet 'Ajrud" [Hebrew]. Pages 44–68 in *To YHWH of Teman and His Asherah: The Inscriptions and Drawings from Kuntillet 'Ajrud ('Horvat Teman') in Sinai*. Edited by Shmuel Ahituv and Esther Eshel. Jerusalem: Israel Exploration Society.

Ottosson, Magnus. 1979. "Fortifikation och Tempel: En studie I Jerusalems topografi." *Religion och Bibel* 38:26–39.

———. 1989. "Topography and City Planning with Special Reference to Jerusalem." *TTKi* 4:263–70.

Ovadiah, Ruth. 1993. "Jerusalem, Giv'at Massu'a" [Hebrew]. *ESI* 12:64–69.

Pakkala, Juha. 2002. "Jeroboam's Sin and Bethel in 1 Kgs 12:25–33." *BN* 112:86–93.

———. 2010. "Why the Cult Reforms in Judah Probably Did Not Happen." Pages 201–35 in *One God – One Cult – One Nation: Archaeological and Biblical Perspectives*. Edited by Reinhard G. Kratz and Hermann Spieckermann. BZAW 405. Berlin: De Gruyter.

Panitz-Cohen, Nava. 2006. "The Pottery of Strata XII–V." Pages 9–150 in *Timnah (Tel Batash) III: The Finds from the Second Millennium BCE*. Edited by Nava Panitz-Cohen and Amihai Mazar. Qedem 45. Jerusalem: Institute of Archaeology, Hebrew University of Jerusalem.

Porat, Naomi, Uri Davidovich, Yoav Avni, Gideon Avni, and Yuval Gadot. 2018. "Using OSL to Decipher Past Soil History in Archaeological Terraces, Judean Highlands, Israel." *Land Degradation and Development* 29:643–50.

Porten, Bezalel. 1996. *The Elephantine Papyri in English: Three Millennia of Cross-Cultural Continuity and Change*. DMOA 22) Leiden: Brill.

Porzig, Peter. 2009. *Die Lade Jahwes im Alten Testament und in den Texten vom Toten Meer*. BZAW 397. Berlin: De Gruyter.

Pratico, Gary D. 1993. *Nelson Glueck's 1938–1940 Excavations at Tell el-Kheleifeh: A Reappraisal*. ASOR Archaeological Reports 3. Atlanta: Scholars Press.

Pritchard, James B. 1964. *Winery, Defenses, and Soundings at Gibeon*. Philadelphia: University Museum, University of Pennsylvania.

Pury, Albert de. 2001. "Situer le cycle de Jacob: Quelques réflexions, vingt-cinq ans plus tard." Pages 213–41 in *Studies in the Book of Genesis: Literature, Redaction and History*. Edited by André Wénin. BETL 155. Leuven: Peeters.

———. 2003. "Salomon et la reine de Saba: L'analyse narrative peut-elle se dispenser de poser la question du contexte historique?" Pages 213–38 in *La Bible en récits: L'exégèse biblique à l'heure du lecteur*. Edited by Daniel Marguerat. Monde de la Bible 48. Geneva: Labor et Fides.

Pury, Albert de, and Thomas Römer, T. 2000. *Die Sogenannte Thronfolgegeschichte Davids: Neue Einsichten und Anfragen*. OBO 176. Fribourg: Universitätsverlag; Göttingen: Vandenhoeck & Ruprecht.

Rad, Gerhard von. 1966. *The Problem of the Hexateuch and Other Essays*. Translated by E. W. Trueman Dicken. Edinburgh: Oliver & Boyd.

Rainey, Anson F. 1967. "The Samaria Ostraca in the Light of Fresh Evidence." *PEQ* 99:32–41.

———. 1975. "The Identification of Philistine Gath: A Problem in Source Analysis for Historical Geography." *ErIsr* 12:63*–76*.

———. 1976. "Ramat-negev, Ramoth-negev" [Hebrew]. *EncBib* 7:298–99.

———. 1977. "Three Additional Hebrew Ostraca from Tel Arad." *TA* 4:97–104.

———. 1994. "Hezekiah's Reform and the Altars at Beer-sheba and Arad." Pages 333–54 in *Scripture and Other Artifacts: Essays on the Bible and Archaeology in Honor of Philip J. King*. Edited by Michael D. Coogan, J. Cheryl Exum, and Lawrence E. Stager. Louisville: Westminster John Knox.

———. 1997. "The Chronicles of the Kings of Judah: A Source Used by the Chronicler." Pages 30–72 in *The Chronicler as Historian*. Edited by M. Patrick Graham. JSOTSup 238. Sheffield: Sheffield Academic.

———. 2003. "Some Amarna Collations." *ErIsr* 27:192*–202*.

———. 2012. "Possible Involvement of Tell es-Safi (Tel Zafit) in the Amarna Correspondence." Pages 133–40 in vol. 1 of *Tell es-Safi/Gath I: The 1996–2005 Seasons*. Edited by Aren M. Maeir. 2 vols. ÄAT 69. Wiesbaden: Harrassowitz.

Redford, Donald B. 1973. "Studies in Relations between Palestine and Egypt during the First Millennium B.C." *JAOS* 93:3–17.

———. 1992. *Egypt, Canaan and Israel in Ancient Times*. Princeton: Princeton University Press.

Regev, Johanna, Yuval Gadot, Helena Roth, Joe Uziel, Ortal Chalaf, Doron Ben-Ami, Eugenia Mintz, Lior Regev, and Elisabetta Boaretto. 2021. "Middle Bronze Age Jerusalem: Recalculating Its Character and Chronology." *Radiocarbon* 63:853–83.

Regev, Johanna, Yuval Gadot, Joe Uziel, Ortal Chalaf, Yiftah Shalev, Helena Roth, Nitsan Shalom, Nahshon Szanton, Efrat Bocher, Charlotte L. Pearson, David M Brown, Eugenia Mintz, Lior Regev, and Elisabetta Boaretto. 2024. "Radiocarbon Chronology of Iron Age Jerusalem Reveals Calibration Offsets and Architectural Developments." *Proceedings of the National Academy of Sciences of the United States of America*.

Regev, Johanna, Joe Uziel, Nahshon Szanton, and Elisabetta Boaretto. 2017. "Absolute Dating of the Gihon Spring Fortifications, Jerusalem." *Radiocarbon* 59:1171–93.

Reich, Ronny. 2000. "The Topography and Archaeology of Jerusalem in the First Temple Period" [Hebrew]. Pages 93–130 in *The History of*

Jerusalem: The Biblical Period. Edited by Shmuel Ahituv and Amihai Mazar. Jerusalem: Yad Izhaq Ben-Zvi.

———. 2011. *Excavating the City of David: Where Jerusalem's History Began*. Jerusalem: Israel Exploration Society.

———. 2018. "The Date of the Gihon Spring Tower in Jerusalem." *TA* 45:114–19.

Reich, Ronny, and Eli Shukron. 2000. "City-Walls and Water Channels from the Middle Bronze II and Late Iron Age in the City of David: New Evidence from the 2000 Season" [Hebrew]. *New Studies on Jerusalem* 6:5–8.

———. 2003. "The Urban Development of Jerusalem in the Late Eight Century B.C.E." Pages 209–18 in *Jerusalem in Bible and Archaeology: The First Temple Period*. Edited by Andrew G. Vaughn and Ann E. Killebrew. SymS 18. Atlanta: Society of Biblical Literature.

———. 2004. "The History of the Gihon Spring in Jerusalem." *Levant* 36:211–23.

———. 2007. Some New Insights and Notes on the Cutting of the Siloam Tunnel" [Hebrew]." Pages 133–61 in *City of David: Studies of Ancient Jerusalem; The Eighth Annual Conference*. Edited by Eyal Meiron. Jerusalem: Megalim.

———. 2008a. "The Date of City-Wall 501 in Jerusalem." *TA* 35:114–22.

———. 2008b. "The History of the Archaeological Excavations in the City of David (1867–2007)" [Hebrew]. Pages 13–42 in *City of David: Studies of Ancient Jerusalem; The Ninth Annual Conference*. Edited by Eyal Meiron. Jerusalem: Megalim.

———. 2009. The Recent Discovery of a Middle Bronze II Fortification in the City of David, Jerusalem" [Hebrew]. Pages 13–34 in *City of David: Studies of Ancient Jerusalem; The Tenth Annual Conference*. Edited by Eyal Meiron. Jerusalem: Megalim.

———. 2010. "A New Segment of the Middle Bronze Fortification in the City of David." *TA* 37:141–53.

———. 2011. "The Date of the Siloam Tunnel Reconsidered." *TA* 38:147–57.

Reich, Ronny, Eli Shukron, and Omri Leranu. 2007. "Recent Discoveries in the City of David, Jerusalem." *IEJ* 57:153–69.

Reinmuth, Titus. 2003. *Der Bericht Nehemias: Zur literarischen Eigenart, traditionsgeschichtlichen Prägung und innerbiblischen Rezeption des Ich-Berichts Nehemias*. OBO 183. Fribourg: Universitätsverlag; Göttingen: Vandenhoeck & Ruprecht.

Rendsburg, Gary A., and William M. Schniedewind. 2010. "The Siloam Tunnel Inscription: Historical and Linguistic Perspectives." *IEJ* 60:188–203.
Renz, Johannes. 1995. *Text und Kommentar*. Vol. 1 of *Die Althebräischen Inschriften*. Darmstadt: Wissenschaftliche Buchgesellschaft.
Richelle, Matthieu. 2016. "Elusive Scrolls: Could Any Hebrew Literature Have Been Written Prior to the Eighth Century BCE?" *VT* 66:556–94.
Ritmeyer, Leen. 1992. "Locating the Original Temple Mount." *BAR* 18.2:24–45, 64–65.
Robker, Jonathan Miles. 2012. *The Jehu Revolution: A Royal Tradition of the Northern Kingdom and Its Ramifications*. BZAW 435. Berlin: De Gruyter.
Rofé, Alexander. 1987. "The Battle of David and Goliath: Folklore, Theology, Eschatology." Pages 117–51 in *Judaic Perspectives on Ancient Israel*. Edited by Jacob Neusner, Baruch Levine, and Ernest S. Frerichs. Philadelphia: Fortress.
Rollston, Christopher A. 2003. "Non-provenanced Epigraphs I: Pillaged Antiquities, Northwest Semitic Forgeries, and Protocols for Laboratory Tests." *Maarav* 10:135–93.
———. 2017. "Epigraphic Evidence from Jerusalem and Its Environs at the Dawn of Biblical History: Methodologies and a Long Durèe Perspective." *NSAJR* 11:7–20.
Römer, Thomas. 2007. "Israel's Sojourn in the Wilderness and the Construction of the Book of Numbers." Pages 419–45 in *Reflection and Refraction: Studies in Biblical Historiography in Honour of A. Graeme Auld*. Edited by Robert Rezetko, Timothy H. Lim, and W. Bryan Aucker. VTSup 113. Leiden: Brill.
———. 2008. "Salomon d'après les Deutéronomistes: Un roi ambigu." Pages 98–130 in *Le Roi Salomon: Un héritage en question. Hommage à Jacques Vermeylen*. Edited by Claude Lichtert and Dany Nocquest. Brussels: Lessius.
———. 2017. "How Jeroboam II became Jeroboam I." *HBAI* 6:372–82.
Römer, Thomas, and Albert de Pury. 2000. "Deuteronomistic Historiography (DH): History of Research and Debated Issues." Pages 24–141 in *Israel Constructs Its History: Deuteronomistic Historiography in Recent Research*. Edited by Albert de Pury, Thomas Römer, and Jean-Daniel Macchi. JSOTSup 306. Sheffield: Sheffield Academic.
Ron, Zvi. 1977. "Stone Huts as an Expression of Terrace Agriculture in the Judean and Samarian Hills" [Hebrew]. PhD diss., Tel Aviv University.

———. "Development and Management of Irrigation Systems in Mountain Regions in the Holy Land." *Transactions of the Institute of British geographers* 10:149–69.
Rost, Leonhard. 1982. *The Succession to the Throne of David*. Sheffield: Almond. Translation of *Die Überlieferung von der Thronnachfolge Davids*. Stuttgart: Kohlhammer, 1926.
Roth, Helena, Yuval Gadot, and Dafna Langgut. 2019. "Wood Economy in Early Roman Period Jerusalem." *BASOR* 382:71–87.
Rowley, H. H. 1962. "Hezekiah's Reform and Rebellion." *BJRL* 44:395–431.
Rowton, Michael B. 1976. "Dimorphic Structure and the Problem of the Apiru-Ibrim." *JNES* 35:13–20.
Sapir, Naria, Nathan Ben-Ari, Liora Freud, and Oded Lipschits. 2022. "History, Economy and Administration in Late Iron Age Judah in Light of the Excavations at Mordot Arnona, Jerusalem." *TA* 49:32–53.
Sapir-Hen, Lidar, Yuval Gadot, and Israel Finkelstein. 2014. "Environmental and Historical Impacts on Long Term Animal Economy: The Southern Levant in the Late Bronze and Iron Ages." *JESHO* 57:703–44.
Sapir-Hen, Lidar, Yuval Gadot, and Israel Finkelstein. 2016. "Animal Economy in a Temple City and Its Countryside: Iron Age Jerusalem as a Case Study." *BASOR* 375:103–18.
Sass, Benjamin. 1993. "The Pre-exilic Hebrew Seals: Iconism vs. Aniconism." Pages 194–256 in *Studies in the Iconography of Northwest Semitic Inscribed Seals: Proceedings of a Symposium Held in Fribourg on April 17–20, 1991*. Edited by Benjamin Sass and Christoph Uehlinger. OBO 125. Fribourg: Universitätsverlag; Göttingen: Vandenhoeck & Ruprecht.
———. 2005. *The Alphabet at the Turn of the Millennium: The West Semitic Alphabet ca. 1150–850 BCE; The Antiquity of the Arabian, Greek and Phrygian Alphabets*. Tel Aviv: Emery and Claire Yass Publications in Archaeology.
———. 2017. "The Emergence of Monumental West Semitic Alphabetic Writing, with an Emphasis on Byblos." *Sem* 59:109–41.
Sass, Benjamin, and Israel Finkelstein. 2016. "The Swan-Song of Proto-Canaanite in the Ninth Century BCE in Light of an Alphabetic Inscription from Megiddo." *Semitica et Classica* 9:19–42.
Schäfer-Lichtenberger, Christa. 1995. "Beobachtungen zur Ladegeschichte und zur Komposition der Samuelbücher." Pages 323–38 in *Freiheit und Recht: Festschrift für Frank Crüsemann zum 65. Geburtstag*. Edited

by Christof Hardmeier, Rainer Kessler, and Andreas Ruwe. Gütersloh: Gütersloher Verlagshaus.

Scheffler, Eben. 2000. "Saving Saul from the Deuteronomist." Pages 263–71 in *Past, Present, Future: The Deuteronomistic History and the Prophets*. Edited by Johannes C. de Moor and Harry F. van Rooy. OtSt 44. Leiden: Brill.

Schenker, Adrian. 2000. "Jeroboam and the Division of the Kingdom in the Ancient Septuagint: LXX 3 Kingdoms 12.24 a–z, MT 1 Kings 11–12; 14 and the Deuteronomistic History." Pages 214–57 in *Israel Constructs Its History: Deuteronomistic Historiography in Recent Research*. Edited by Albert de Pury, Thomas Römer, and Jean-Daniel Macchi. JSOTSup 306. Sheffield: Sheffield Academic.

———. 2008. "Jeroboam's Rise and Fall in the Hebrew and Greek Bible." *JSJ* 39:367–73.

Schneider, Thomas. 2010. "Contributions to the Chronology of the New Kingdom and the Third Intermediate Period." *Egypt and the Levant* 20:373–403.

Schniedewind, William M. 1998. "The Geopolitical History of Philistine Gath." *BASOR* 309:69–77.

———. 2003. "Jerusalem, the Late Judaean Monarchy and the Composition of the Biblical Texts." Pages 375–93 in *Jerusalem in Bible and Archaeology: The First Temple Period*. Edited by Andrew G. Vaughn and Ann E. Killebrew. SymS 18. Atlanta: Society of Biblical Literature.

———. 2004. *How the Bible Became a Book: The Textualization of Ancient Israel*. Cambridge: Cambridge University Press.

Schütte, Wolfgang. 2012. "Wie wurde Juda israelisiert?" *ZAW* 124:52–72.

———. 2016. *Israels Exil in Juda: Untersuchungen zur Entstehung der Schriftprophetie*. OBO 279. Fribourg: Academic Press; Göttingen: Vandenhoeck & Ruprecht.

Seger, Joe D. 1993. "Ḥalif, Tel." *NEAEHL* 2:553–59.

Sergi, Omer. 2012. "The Rise of Judah in the Ninth Century BCE: Archaeological, Historical and Historiographical Perspectives." PhD diss., Tel Aviv University.

———. 2013. "Judah's Expansion in Historical Context." *TA*: 226–46.

———. 2017a. "The Emergence of Judah as a Political Entity between Jerusalem and Benjamin." *ZDPV* 133:1–23.

———. 2017b. "The United Monarchy and the Kingdom of Jeroboam II in the Story of Absalom and Sheba's Revolts (2 Samuel 15–20)." *HBAI* 6:329–53.

———. 2020. "On Scribal Tradition in Israel and Judah and the Antiquity of the Historiographical Narratives in the Hebrew Bible." Pages 275–99 in *Eigensinn und Entstehung der Hebräischen Bibel: Erhard Blum zum siebzigsten Geburtstag*. Edited by Joachim J. Krause, Wolfgang Oswald, and Kristin Weingart. FAT 136. Tübingen: Mohr Siebeck.

Shahack-Gross, Ruth, Elisabetta Boaretto, Dan Cabanes, Ofir Katz, and Israel Finkelstein. 2014. "Subsistence Economy in the Negev Highlands: The Iron Age and the Byzatine/Early Islamic Period." *Levant* 46:98–117.

Shai, Itzhack, and Aren M. Maeir. 2003. "Pre-*lmlk* Jars: A New Class of Iron Age IIA Storage Jars." *TA* 30:108–23.

Shalev, Yiftah, Nitsan Shalom, Efrat Bocher, and Yuval Gadot. 2020. "New Evidence on the Location and Nature of Iron Age, Persian and Early Hellenistic Period Jerusalem." *TA* 47:149–72.

Shalom, Nitsan, Yiftah Shalev, Josef (Joe) Uziel, Ortal Chalaf, Oded Lipschits, Elisabetta Boaretto, and Yuval Gadot. 2019. "How Is a City Destroyed? New Archaeological Data on the Babylonian Campaign to Jerusalem" [Hebrew]. *NSAJR* 13:229–48.

Sharon, Ilan, Ayelet Gilboa, A. J. Timothy Jull, and Elisabetta Boaretto. 2007. "Report on the First Stage of the Iron Age Dating Project in Israel: Supporting a Low Chronology." *Radiocarbon* 49:1–46.

Shaus, Arie, Yana Gerber, Shira Faigenbaum-Golovin, Barak Sober, Eli Piasetzky, and Israel Finkelstein. 2020. "Forensic Document Examination and Algorithmic Handwriting Analysis of Judahite Biblical Period Inscriptions Reveal Significant Literacy Level." *Plos One* 9 September 2020. https://doi.org/10.1371/journal.pone.0237962.

Shavit, Alon. 1992. "The Ayalon Valley and Its Vicinity during the Bronze and Iron Ages" [Hebrew with English abstract]. MA thesis, Tel Aviv University.

Shiloh, Yigal. 1984. *Excavations at the City of David I: 1978–1982: Interim Report of the First Five Seasons*. Qedem 19. Jerusalem: Institute of Archaeology, Hebrew University.

———. 1987a. "South Arabian Inscriptions from the City of David, Jerusalem." *PEQ* 119:9–18.

———. 1987b. "South Arabian Inscriptions of the Iron Age II from Jerusalem" [Hebrew]. *ErIsr* 19:288–94.

Shipp, R. Mark. 2011. "Baalah." *EBH* 3:210–11.

Shoham, Yair. 2000. "Hebrew Bullae." Pages 29–57 in in *Inscriptions*. Vol. 6 of *Excavations at the City of David 1978–1985 Directed by Yigal Shiloh*.

Edited by Donald T. Ariel. Qedem 41. Jerusalem: Institute of Archaeology, the Hebrew University of Jerusalem.

Singer, Itamar. 1991. "A Concise History of Amurru." Pages 134–95 in vol. 2 of *Amurru Akkadian: A Linguistic Study*. Edited by Shlomo Izre'el. 2 vols. HSS 40–41. Atlanta: Scholars Press.

———. 1993. "The Political Organization of Philistia in Iron Age I." Pages 132–41 in *Biblical Archaeology Today, 1990: Proceedings of the Second International Congress on Biblical Archaeology; Pre-congress Symposium, Supplement*. Edited by Avraham Biran and Joseph Aviram. Jerusalem: Israel Academy of Sciences and Humanities.

Singer-Avitz, Lily. 1999. "Beersheba—A Gateway Community in Southern Arabian Long-Distance Trade in the Eighth Century B.C.E." *TA* 26:3–74.

———. 2002. "Arad: The Iron Age Pottery Assemblages." *TA* 29:110–214.

———. 2006. "The Date of Kuntillet 'Ajrud." *TA* 33:196–228

———. 2010. "The Relative Chronology of Khirbet Qeiyafa." *TA* 37:79–83.

———. 2012. "The Date of the Pottery from the Rock-Cut Pool Near the Gihon Spring in the City of David, Jerusalem." *ZDPV* 128:10–14.

———. 2016. "Pottery from Strata III–I: The Iron IIB Period." Pages 583–991 in *Beer-sheba III: The Early Iron IIA Enclosed Settlement and the Late Iron IIA-Iron IIB Cities*. Edited by Ze'ev Herzog and Lily Singer-Avitz. Monograph Series of the Institute of Archaeology, Tel Aviv University 33. Winona Lake, IN: Eisenbrauns.

Smith, Morton. 1971. *Palestinian Parties and Politics That Shaped the Old Testament*. New York: Columbia University Press.

Sneh, Amihai, Ram Weinberger, and Eyal Shalev. 2010. "The Why, Now and When of the Siloam Tunnel Reevaluated." *BASOR* 359:57–65.

Soggin, J. A. 1995. "Abraham and the Eastern Kings: On Genesis 14." Pages 283–91 in *Solving Riddles and Untying Knots: Biblical, Epigraphic, and Semitic Studies in Honor of Jonas C. Greenfield*. Edited by Ziony Zevit, Seymour Gitin, and Michael Sokoloff. Winona Lake, IN: Eisenbrauns.

Sulimani, Gideon. 2012. "Jerusalem, Har Homa." *ESI* 124. http://tinyurl.com/SBLPressIFa3.

Stager, Lawrence E. 1976. "Farming in the Judean Desert." *BASOR* 221:145–58.

———. 1996. "Ashkelon and the Archaeology of Destruction: Kislev 604 BCE." *ErIsr* 25:61*–74*.

Steiner, Margreet L. 1994. "Re-dating the Terraces of Jerusalem." *IEJ* 44:13–20.

———. 2001. *The Settlement in the Bronze and Iron Ages.* Vol. 3 of *Excavations by Kathleen M. Kenyon in Jerusalem 1961–1967.* Copenhagen International Series 9. Sheffield: Sheffield Academic.

———. 2003. "The Evidence from Kenyon's Excavations in Jerusalem: A Response Essay." Pages 347–63 in *Jerusalem in Bible and Archaeology: The First Temple Period.* Edited by Andrew G. Vaughn and Ann E. Killebrew. SymS 18. Atlanta: Society of Biblical Literature.

Steiner, Richard C. 1991. "The Aramaic Text in Demotic Script: The Liturgy of a New Year's Festival Imported from Bethel to Syene by Exiles from Rash." *JAOS* 111:362–63.

Stern, Ephraim. 1982. *Material Culture of the Land of the Bible in the Persian Period, 538–332 B.C.* Jerusalem: Israel Exploration Society; Warminster: Aris & Phillips.

———. 2001. *The Assyrian, Babylonian, and Persian Periods (732–332 B.C.E.).* Vol. 2 of *Archaeology of the Land of the Bible.* New York: Doubleday.

Storchan, Benyamin. 2015. "Jerusalem, Emeq Lavan." *ESI* 127. http://tinyurl.com/SBLPressIFa4.

———. 2017. "Jerusalem, Ramat Shelomo." *Hadashot Arkheologiyot* 129. http://tinyurl.com/SBLPressIFa5.

Swanson, Kristin A. 2002. "A Reassessment of Hezekiah's Reform in Light of Jar Handles and Iconographic Evidence." *CBQ* 64:460–69.

Sweeney, Deborah. 2004. "The Hieratic Inscriptions." Pages 1601–17 in vol. 3 of *The Renewed Archaeological Excavations at Lachish (1973–1994),* by David Ussishkin. Monograph Series of the Institute of Archaeology of Tel Aviv University 22. Tel Aviv: Emery and Claire Yass Publications in Archaeology.

Sweeney, Marvin A. 2001. *King Josiah of Judah: The Lost Messiah of Israel.* Oxford: Oxford University Press.

———. 2007. "A Reassessment of the Masoretic and Septuagint Versions of the Jeroboam Narratives in 1 Kings/3 Kingdoms 11–14." *JSJ* 38:165–95

Szanton, Nahshon. 2013. "The Rock-Cut Rooms and Cave 1: Evidence for Cultic Activity along the City of David's Eastern Slope in the Iron Age II" [Hebrew]. *New Studies on Jerusalem* 19:67–93.

Talshir, Zipora. 1993. *The Alternative Story of the Division of the Kingdom: 3 Kingdoms 12:24a–z.* Jerusalem Biblical Studies 6. Jerusalem: Simor,

Tappy, Ron E. 2008. "Zayit, Tel." *NEAEHL* 5:2082–83.

Thareani, Yifat. 2011. *Tel ʿAroer: The Iron Age II Caravan Town and the Hellenistic-Early Roman Settlement; The Avraham Biran (1975–1982)*

and Rudolph Cohen (1975–1976) Excavations. Jerusalem: Hebrew Union College.

———. 2016. "The Empire and the 'Upper Sea': Assyrian Control Strategies along the Southern Levantine Coast." *BASOR* 375:77–102.

Thareani-Sussely, Yifat. 2007. "The 'Archaeology of the Days of Manasseh' Reconsidered in the Light of Evidence from the Beersheba Valley." *PEQ* 139:69–77.

Thompson, Thomas L. 1974. *The Historicity of the Patriarchal Narratives: The Quest for the Historical Abraham*. BZAW 133. Berlin: De Gruyter.

Throntveit, Mark A. 2003. "The Relationship of Hezekiah to David and Solomon in the Books of Chronicles." Pages 105–21 in *The Chronicler as Theologian, Essays in Honor of Ralph W. Klein*. Edited by M. Patrick Graham, Steven L. McKenzie, and Gary N. Knoppers. JSOTSup 331. London: T&T Clark.

Tilly, Michael. 2005. *Einführung in die Septuaginta*. Darmstadt: Wissenschaftliche Buchgesellschaft.

Toffolo, Michael B., Eran Arie, Mario A. S. Martin, Elisabetta Boaretto, and Israel Finkelstein. 2014. "Absolute Chronology of Megiddo, Israel, in the Late Bronze and Iron Ages: High-Resolution Radiocarbon Dating." *Radiocarbon* 56:221–44.

Toorn, Karel van der. 1993. "Saul and the Rise of the Israelite State Religion." *VT* 43:519–42.

———. 1996. *Family Religion in Babylonia, Ugarit, and Israel: Continuity and Changes in the Forms of Religious Life*. SHANE 7. Leiden: Brill.

Torrey, Charles C. 1896. *The Composition and Historical Value of Ezra-Nehemiah*. BZAW 2. Giessen: Ricker.

Tov, Emanuel. 1985. "The Composition of 1 Samuel 16–18 in the Light of the Septuagint Version." Pages 97–130 in *Empirical Models for Biblical Criticism*. Edited by Jeffrey H. Tigay. Philadelphia: University of Pennsylvania Press.

Tsafrir, Yoram, Leah Di Segni, and Judith Green. 1994. *Tabula imperii Romani Judaea Palestina: Erez Israel in the Hellenistic, Roman and Byzantine periods*. Jerusalem: Israel Academy of Sciences and Humanities.

Tsuk, Tsvika. 2008. "'And Brought the Water to the City' (2 Kings 20:20): Water Consumption in Jerusalem in the Biblical Period" [Hebrew]. *New Studies on Jerusalem* 14:107–19.

Tufnell, Olga. 1953. *Lachish III (Tell ed Duweir): The Iron Age*. London: Oxford University Press.

Ussishkin, David. 1976. "Royal Judean Storage Jars and Private Seal Impressions." *BASOR* 223:1–13.

———. 1977. "The Destruction of Lachish by Sennacherib and the Dating of the Royal Judean Storage Jars." *TA* 4:28–60.

———. 1982. *The Conquest of Lachish by Sennacherib*. Tel Aviv: Tel Aviv University, Institute of Archaeology.

———. 1983. "Excavations at Tel Lachish 1978–1983: Second Preliminary Report." *TA* 10:97–175.

———. 1988. "The Date of the Judaean Shrine at Arad." *IEJ* 38:142–57.

———. 1993. *The Village of Silwan: The Necropolis from the Period of the Judean Kingdom*. Jerusalem: Israel Exploration Society.

———. 1995. "The Water Systems of Jerusalem during Hezekiah's Reign." Pages 289–307 in *Meilenstein: Festgabe für Herbert Donner zum 16. Februar 1995*. Edited by Manfred Weippert and Stefan Timm. Wiesbaden: Harrassowitz.

———. 1996. "Excavations and Restoration Work at Tel Lachish 1985–1994: Third Preliminary Report." *TA* 23:3–60.

———. 2003a. "Jerusalem as a Royal and Cultic Center in the 10th-8th Centuries B.C.E." Pages 529–38 in *Symbiosis, Symbolism, and the Power of the Past: Canaan, Ancient Israel, and Their Neighbors from the Late Bronze Age through Roman Palaestina*. Edited by William G. Dever and Seymour Gitin. Winona Lake, IN: Eisenbrauns.

———. 2003b. "The Level V 'Sanctuary' and 'High Place' at Lachish." Pages 205–11 in *Saxa loquentur: Studien zur Archäologie Palästinas/Israels; Festschrift für Volkmar Fritz zum 65. Geburtstag*. Edited by Cornelis Gijsbert den Hertog, Ulrich Hübner, and Stefan Münger. AOAT 302. Münster: Ugarit-Verlag.

———. 2003c. "Solomon's Jerusalem: The Text and the Facts on the Ground." Pages 103–15 in *Jerusalem in Bible and Archaeology: The First Temple Period*. Edited by Andrew G. Vaughn and Ann E. Killebrew. SymS 18. Atlanta: Society of Biblical Literature.

———. 2004a. "Area GE: The Inner City-Gate." Pages 624–89 in vol. 2 of *The Renewed Archaeological Excavations at Lachish (1973–1994)*, by David Ussishkin. Monograph Series of the Institute of Archaeology of Tel Aviv University 22. Tel Aviv: Emery and Claire Yass Publications in Archaeology.

———. 2004b. "Area GW: The Outer City-Gate." Pages 535–623 in vol. 2 of *The Renewed Archaeological Excavations at Lachish (1973–1994)*, by David Ussishkin. Monograph Series of the Institute of Archaeology of

Tel Aviv University 22. Tel Aviv: Emery and Claire Yass Publications in Archaeology.

———. 2004e. "Area Pal.: The Judean Palace-Fort." Pages 768–870 in vol. 1 of *The Renewed Archaeological Excavations at Lachish (1973–1994)*, by David Ussishkin. Monograph Series of the Institute of Archaeology of Tel Aviv University 22. Tel Aviv: Emery and Claire Yass Publications in Archaeology.

———. 2004c. "The Royal Judean Storage Jars and Seal Impressions from the Renewed Excavations." Pages 2133–47 in vol. 4 of *The Renewed Archaeological Excavations at Lachish (1973–1994)*, by David Ussishkin. Monograph Series of the Institute of Archaeology of Tel Aviv University 22. Tel Aviv: Emery and Claire Yass Publications in Archaeology.

———. 2004d. "A Synopsis of the Stratigraphical, Chronological and Historical Issues." Pages 50–119 in vol. 1 of *The Renewed Archaeological Excavations at Lachish (1973–1994)*, by David Ussishkin. Monograph Series of the Institute of Archaeology of Tel Aviv University 22. Tel Aviv: Emery and Claire Yass Publications in Archaeology.

———. 2006a. "The Borders and *De Facto* Size of Jerusalem in the Persian Period." Pages 147–66 in *Judah and the Judeans in the Persian Period*. Edited by Oded Lipschits and Manfred Oeming. Winona Lake, IN: Eisenbrauns.

———. 2006b. "Sennacherib's Campaign to Philistia and Judah: Ekron, Lachish, and Jerusalem." Pages 338–57 in *Essays on Ancient Israel in Its Near Eastern Context: A Tribute to Nadav Na'aman*. Edited by Yairah Amit, Ehud Ben Zvi, Israel Finkelstein, and Oded Lipschits. Winona Lake, IN: Eisenbrauns.

———. 2009. "The Temple Mount in Jerusalem during the First Temple Period: An Archaeologist's View." Pages 473–83 in *Exploring the Longue Durée: Essays in Honor of Lawrence E. Stager*. Edited by J. David Schloen. Winona Lake, IN: Eisenbrauns.

———. 2011. "The Dating of the *lmlk* Storage Jars and Its Implications: Rejoinder to Lipschits, Sergi and Koch." *TA* 38:220–40.

———. 2016. "Was Jerusalem a Fortified Stronghold in the Middle Bronze Age? An Alternative View." *Levant* 48:135–51.

Uziel, Joe, and Ortal Chalaf. 2021. "Archaeological Evidence of an Earthquake in the Capital of Judah." *City of David Studies of Ancient Jerusalem* 16:51*–64*.

Uziel, Joe, and Aren M. Maeir. 2005. "Scratching the High Surface of Gath: Implications of the Tell es-Safi/Gath Surface Survey." *TA* 32:50–75.

Uziel, Joe, Helena Roth, Ortal Chalaf, and Filip Vukosavović. 2023. "Jerusalem's Eastern Fortifications in Light of New Discoveries" [Hebrew]. *NSAJR* 16:87–102.

Uziel, Joe, and Nahshon Szanton. 2015. "Recent Excavations near the Gihon Spring and Their Reflection on the Character of Iron II Jerusalem." *TA* 42:233–50.

———. 2017. "New Evidence on Jerusalem's Urban Development in the Ninth Century BCE." Pages 429–40 in *Rethinking Israel: Studies in the History and Archaeology of Ancient Israel in Honor of Israel Finkelstein*. Edited by Oded Lipschits, Yuval Gadot, and Matthew J. Adams. Winona Lake, IN: Eisenbrauns.

Vainstub, Daniel. 2017. "A Hebrew Seal and Ostracon Fragment." Pages 395–400 in *The Tel Hevron 2014 Excavations: Final Report*. Edited by Emanuel Eisenberg and David Ben-Shlomo. Ariel: Ariel University Press.

Vainstub, Daniel, and David Ben-Shlomo. 2016. "A Hebrew Seal and an Ostracon from Tel Hebron." *IEJ* 66:151–60.

Van Seters, John. 1975. *Abraham in History and Tradition*. New Haven: Yale University Press.

———. 1990. "Joshua's Campaign of Canaan and Near Eastern Historiography." *SJOT* 4:1–12.

Vanderhooft, David, and Oded Lipschits. 2007. "A New Typology of the Yehud Stamp Impressions." *TA* 34:12–37.

Vaughn, Andrew G. 1999a. "Palaeographic Dating of Judaean Seals and Its Significance for Biblical Research." *BASOR* 313:43–64.

———. 1999b. *Theology, History, and Archaeology in the Chronicler's Account of Hezekiah*. ABS 4. Atlanta: Scholars Press.

Vaux, Roland de. 1978. *The Early History of Israel*. Philadelphia: Westminster.

Vincent, Louis-Hugues. 1912. *Jerusalem: Recherches de Topographie, d'archeologie et d'histoire*. Paris: Gabalda.

Vos, Jacobus Cornelis de. 2003. *Das Los Judas: Über Entstehung und Ziele der Landbeschreibung in Josua 15*. VTSup 95. Leiden: Brill.

Vukosavovic, Filip, Ortal Chalaf, and Joe Uziel. 2021. "'And You Counted the Houses of Jerusalem and Pulled Houses Down to Fortify the Wall' (Isaiah 22:10): The Fortifications of Iron Age II Jerusalem in Light of New Discoveries in the City of David." *NSAJR* 14:1*–16*.

Warren, Charles, and C. R. Conder. 1884. *The Survey of Western Palestine III: Jerusalem*. London: Palestine Exploration Fund.
Weber, Martin. 2017. "Two (?) Lion Reliefs from Iron Age Moab: Further Evidence for an Architectural and Intellectual Koiné in the Levant?" *BASOR* 377:85–106.
Weinfeld, Moshe. 1964. "Cult Centralization in Israel in the Light of a Neo-Babylonian Analogy." *JNES* 23:202–12.
Weippert, Manfred. 1971. *The Settlement of the Israelite Tribes in Palestine*. London: SCM.
Weksler-Bdolah, Shlomit. 1997. "Alona." *ESI* 19:68*–70*.
Welten, Peter. 1969. *Die Königs-Stempel: Ein Beitrag zur militärpolitik Judas unter Hiskia und Josia*. ADPV. Wiesbaden: Harrassowitz.
White, Marsha. 2000. "'The History of Saul's Rise': Saulide State Propaganda in 1 Samuel 1–14." Pages 271–92 in *"A Wise and Discerning Mind": Essays in Honor of Burke O. Long*. Edited by Saul M. Olyan and Robert C. Culley. BJS 325. Providence, RI: Brown University.
Wightman, G. J. 1993. *The Walls of Jerusalem: from the Canaanites to the Mamluks*. Mediterranean Archaeology Supplement 4. Sydney: Meditarch.
———. 2022. "The Disappearing Walls of Jerusalem? Observations on the Bronze and Iron Age Fortifications and Waterworks on the East Slope of the City of David." *Levant* 54:230–46.
Williamson, Hugh G. M. 1977. *Israel in the Books of Chronicles*. Cambridge: Cambridge University Press.
———. 1991. "The Temple in the Books of Chronicles." Pages 15–31 in *Templum amicitiae: Essays on the Second Temple Presented to Ernst Bammel*. Edited by William Horbury. JSNTSup 48. Sheffield: JSOT Press.
Wilson, Charles W., and Charles Warren. 1871. *The Recovery of Jerusalem: A Narrative of Exploration and Discovery in the City and the Holy Land*. London: Bentley.
Wilson, John A. 1969. "Historical Texts." Pages 227–64 in *Ancient Near Eastern Texts Relating to the Old Testament*. Edited by James B. Pritchard. 3rd ed. Princeton: Princeton University Press, 1969), .
Wimmer, Stefan J. 2012. "Hieratic Inscriptions from Tell es-Safi/Gath." Pages 485–89 in vol. 1 of *Tell es-Safi/Gath: The 1996–2005 Seasons*. Edited by Aren M. Maeir. ÄAT 69. Munich: Harrassowitz.
Wimmer, Stefan J., and Gunnar Lehmann. 2014. "Two Hieratic Inscriptions from Qubur el-Walaydah." *Egypt and the Levant* 24:343–48.

Winderbaum, Ariel. 2012. "Assur in Jerusalem: New Glyptic Evidence of the Assyrian Influence on Jerusalem" [Hebrew]. *NSAJR* 6:83–104.

———. 2015. "The Iconic Seals and Bullae of the Iron Age." Pages 363–419 in vol. 1 of *The Summit of the City of David Excavations 2005–2008: Final Reports*. Edited by Eilat Mazar. Jerusalem: Shoham.

———. 2021. "The Iron IIA Pottery Assemblages from the Ophel Excavations and Their Contribution to the Understanding of the Settlement History of Jerusalem." 2 vols. PhD diss., Tel Aviv University.

———. 2022. "Jerusalem's Growth in Light of the Renewed Excavations in the Ophel." *TA* 49:149–90.

Yadin, Azzan. 2004. "Goliath's Armor and Israelite Collective Memory." *VT* 54:373–95.

Yadin, Yigael. 1965. "A Note on the Stratigraphy of Arad." *IEJ* 15:180.

Yadin, Yigael, Yohanan Aharoni, Ruth Amiran, Trude Dothan, Immanuel Dunayevski, and Jean Perrot. 1960. *Hazor II: An Account of the Second Season of Excavations, 1956*. Jerusalem: Magnes.

Yechezkel, Azriel, and Amos Frumkin. 2019. "Spring Tunnels in Ancient Israel and the Jerusalem Hills: Physical, Geographical and Human Aspects" [Hebrew]. *Horizons in Geography* 96:154–80.

Yeivin, Zeev. 1990. "The Silver Hoard from Eshtemoa" [Hebrew]. *'Atiqot* 10:43–56.

Yezerski, Irit. 2013. "Iron Age Burial Customs in the Samaria Highlands." *TA* 40:72–98.

Yoffe, Gideon, Axel Bühler, Nachum Dershowitz, Israel Finkelstein, Eli Piasetzky, Thomas Römer, and Barak Sober. 2023. "A Statistical Exploration of Text Partition Into Constituents: The Case of the Priestly Source in the Books of Genesis and Exodus." Pages 1918–40 in *Findings of the Association for Computational Linguistics: ACL 2023*. Edited by Anna Rogers, Jordan Boyd-Graber, and Naoaki Okazaki. Toronto: Association for Computational Linguistics. https://aclanthology.org/2023.findings-acl.121.pdf.

Yoffee, Norman. 1995. "Political Economy in Early Mesopotamian States." *Annual Review of Anthropology* 24:281–311.

Younger, K. Lawson, Jr. 2003. "The Great 'Summary' Inscription." COS 2.118E:296–97.

Zadok, Ran. 1986. Review of *The History of Eretz Israel I: Introductions; The Early Period*, ed. Israel Eph'al. *ZDPV* 102:179–80.

Zertal, Adam. 1989. "The Wedge-Shaped Decorated Bowl and the Origin of the Samaritans." *BASOR* 276:77–84.

———. 1990. "The Pahwah of Samaria (Northern Israel) during the Persian Period. Types of Settlement, Economy, History and New Discoveries." *Transeu* 3:9–15.

———. 1992. *The Manasseh Hill Country Survey: The Shechem Syncline* [Hebrew]. Haifa: University of Haifa.

———. 1993. "The Mount Manasseh (Northern Samaria Hills) Survey." *NEAEHL* 4:1311–12.

———. 1996. *The Manasseh Hill Country Survey: The Eastern Valleys and the Fringes of the Desert* [Hebrew]. Haifa: University of Haifa.

———. 2003. "The Province of Samaria (Assyrian Samerina) in the Late Iron Age (Iron Age III)." Pages 377–412 in *Judah and the Judeans in the Neo-Babylonian Period*. Edited by Oded Lipschits and Joseph Blenkinsopp. Winona Lake, IN: Eisenbrauns.

Ziffer, Irit, Shlomo Bunimovitz, and Zvi Lederman. 2009. "Divine or Human? An Intriguing Late Bronze Age Plaque Figurine from Tel Beth-Shemesh." *Egypt and the Levant* 19:333–41.

Zilberstein, Ayala. 2019. "'On Your Walls, City of David': The Line of the Western Fortification of the City of David during the Hellenistic Period in Light of New Finds." *NSAJR* 13:31–50.

Zimhoni, Orna. 1985. "The Iron Age Pottery of Tel 'Eton and Its Relation to the Lachish, Tell Beit Mirsim and Arad Assemblages." *TA* 12:63–90.

———. 1997. *Studies in the Iron Age Pottery of Israel: Typological, Archaeological and Chronological Aspects*. Tel Aviv: Institute of Archaeology.

———. 2004a. "The Pottery of Levels V and IV and Its Archaeological and Chronological Implications." Pages 1643–1788 in vol. 4 of *The Renewed Archaeological Excavations at Lachish (1973–1994)*, by David Ussishkin. Monograph Series of the Institute of Archaeology of Tel Aviv University 22. Tel Aviv: Emery and Claire Yass Publications in Archaeology.

———. 2004b. "The Pottery of Levels III and II." Pages 1789–1899 in vol. 4 of *The Renewed Archaeological Excavations at Lachish (1973–1994)*, by David Ussishkin. Monograph Series of the Institute of Archaeology of Tel Aviv University 22. Tel Aviv: Emery and Claire Yass Publications in Archaeology.

Zinger, Avraham. 1985. *Olive Cultivation* [Hebrew]. Tel Aviv: Ministry of Agriculture.

Zohary Daniel, and Pinhas Spiegel-Roy. 1975. "Beginnings of Fruit Growing in the Old World." *Science* 187:319–27.

Zohary, Michael. 1962. *Plant Life of Palestine: Israel and Jordan.* New York: Ronald.

Zorn, Jeffrey R. 2010. "Reconsidering Goliath: An Iron Age I Philistine Chariot Warrior." *BASOR* 360:1–22.

Zorn, Jeffrey R., Joseph Yellin, and John Hayes. 1994. "The $m(w)ṣh$ Stamp Impressions and the Neo-Babylonian Period." *IEJ* 44:161–83.

Ancient Sources Index

Amarna Letters		EA 370	47
EA 64	38	**Hebrew Bible**	
EA 229	35, 38		
EA 250	43	Genesis	
EA 271	43	14	356
EA 273	34, 36–37, 40, 129	14:18	90
EA 274	34, 40, 42, 129	49:30	352
EA 275	34, 37		
EA 276	34, 37	Numbers	
EA 277	34	32:34–38	354
EA 278	36–37		
EA 279	39	Deuteronomy	
EA 280	39	34:3	307
EA 281	43		
EA 283	43	Joshua	
EA 284	43	10	91
EA 285	365	11:5	286
EA 285–287	365	11:7	286
EA 286	365	15	41, 130, 277, 289, 311
EA 287	39, 44, 365	15:8	339
EA 288	35, 43–44, 364–65	15:8–9	283
EA 289	39, 43, 365	15:9	286
EA 290	40–41	15:9–10	149
EA 292	43	15:22	138
EA 298	43–45	15:30	139
EA 306	43	15:37	41
EA 314	37	15:41	41
EA 316	37	15:42	138
EA 319	35, 38	15:60	149, 283, 286
EA 333	35, 38	18:14	149
EA 335	35, 37, 43	18:14–15	149
EA 365	288	18:15	286
EA 366	37, 41, 43	18:15–16	283
EA 367	47	18:16	339

Joshua (cont.)		26:3	130–31
18:23	230	27:6	129
18:25–28	283	30	127–29, 138, 143
18:26	283	30:7–82	129
18:28	150	30:26–31	129, 137, 139
19:4	139	30:28	130
19:50	55	30:30	130
21:21	55		
		2 Samuel	
Judges		2:6	161, 163
1:8	91	2:9	52, 57, 60
1:16	138	5:1	74
4:5	55	5:6–9	91
5:19	286	5:11	91
10:1	55	5:17	92
18:12	318	5:17–25	129
		5:18	339
1 Samuel		5:22	339
1:1	55	6	161–62
1:4b	149	6:2	149
4–6	161	6:3	150
4:1	160–61, 163	8:16	167
5	235	9–20	238
6	149	10:5	54
7:1	149, 150, 160–61, 163	13:3	54
9:4a	55	21:15–22	54, 129
9:4–5	55	21:16	130
11:8	57	21:18	130
13:3	59	21:19	56, 130
13:17	55	23:8–21	54, 129
16–1 Kgs 2	238	23:14	54, 59, 136
16:14–2 Sam 5	238		
17:1	136	1 Kings	
17:1–3	56	1–2	238, 315
17:1–4	130	3–10	315–17, 321
17:8–11	130, 145	3:1	321
17:52	133, 145	4	319–20
21:19	130	4:10	40
22:1–2	129	4:13	125
22:5	129, 131	4:19	320
23	129–30, 141	5:5	320
23:13	135	5:6	318
23:19	53, 130	6–8	162–63
24:1–2	53	7:8	321
26:1	130–31	8	162

9	318	8:36	283
9:11–14	321	9:42	283
9:15	317	11:4–7	91
9:16	321	11:4–8	91
9:18	317–18	11:13	136
9:19	318	13:6	149–50
9:22	318		
9:24	321	2 Chronicles	
9:26	321	20:2	307
10:1–13	321	30:1	237
10:26	318	35:3	162
11	315, 322–23		
11:1–10	316	Isaiah	
11:40	321	5:1–2	302
11:41	315	28:21	339
12:25	55		
15:16–22	68	Jeremiah	
15:17	366	51:25	338
15:22	366		
18:3–4	236	Hosea	
		4:15	150
2 Kings		10:15	150
2	238	12:1	223
12	161		
12:18–19	15	Amos	
12:19	143	1:1	223
14:9–10	223	3:13	319
14:11–13	57, 119, 160, 182, 319	5:5	150
14:11b–15	367	5:11	223
14:13	15, 23, 320	6:4–6	223
17:24	230	6:13	320
18:3–4	231	7:9	352
21	337	7:16	352
23	340		
23:13	338	**Deuterocanonical Books**	
23:13–14	340		
25:12	355	1 Maccabees	
		11:34	55
Nehemiah			
3	15, 23–24, 91, 349–50, 363, 369	**Dead Sea Scrolls**	
1 Chronicles		4QSam	149
2:46	283		
2:53	318		
7:8	337		

New Testament

Matthew
  27:57   55

John
  19:38   55

Other Sources

Diodorus Siculus, *Bibliotheca historica*
  2.48.9   307

Eusebius, *Onomasticon*
  48.24   147

Herodotus, *Historiae*
  2.6.2   307

Josephus, *Antiquitates judaicae*
  8.6.6   307
  17.10.9   42

Josephus, *Bellum judaicum*
  2.5.1   42
  7.6.6   284

Josephus, *Contra Apionem*
  1.113–115   320
  117–119   320

Rabbinic Works
  m. Sukkah 4:5   283
  b. Sukkah 45a   283

Pliny the Elder, *Naturalis historia*
  12.111   307

Pompeius Trogus, *Historiae Philippicae Epitoma*
  36.3.1–7   307

Strabo, *Geographica*
  16.2.41   307
  17.1.15   307

Taʿanach Tablet
  1:26   40

Tacitus, *Historiae*
  4.6.1   307

Theophrastus, *Historia plantarum*
  2.6.2   307

Place Names Index

Abu Durba, 308
Abu Shawan, 302
Achshaph, 44
Acco, 44–45, 56–57, 360
Adadah, 138
Adullam, 52, 129, 132–33, 135, 366
Aḥṭiruna, 35, 38
Aijalon Valley, 36, 41, 133, 141. *See also* Ayyaluna
'Alona, 298–99, 302
Amman, 38
Amurru, 42, 45, 56, 373
Anaharath, 44
Aqaba, Gulf, 318, 322, 368
Arabah, 139, 143, 145, 306, 367
Arad, 138, 169, 171–76, 178, 193, 222, 224, 231–33, 235, 246, 253, 295, 344
  inscription, 171–73, 178, 182–83, 185, 188–90, 193
  ostraca, 168–73, 178, 190, 192, 244, 347, 355
  fortification, 143, 171
  sanctuary, 232
  strata/layers, 15, 121, 131, 139, 169–71, 174, 246, 272
Aram, 367
'Ar'ara, Khirbet (or Arair), 138. *See also* Aroer
Argob, 319
Arimathea, 55
Armon HaNatziv, 270, 325–26, 332, 333, 335–40

Arnon River, 55, 353
Aroer, 138, 224, 257, 272, 309, 322, 354
Aruboth, 40
Ashdod, 37, 43–44, 132, 161, 204, 226, 318, 360
Ashkelon, 37, 44
Ataroth, 38, 354
Atarus, Khirbet, 93
Athach, 131
Atlit, 18
Avva/Avvim, 230
Ayalon River, 288
Ayyaluna (biblical Aijalon), 36–37, 39–41, 129, 140. *See also* Aijalon Valley
Azekah, 130, 133–34, 136, 145
Baalah. *See* Baalath
Baalath, 149–50, 161, 317–18. *See also* Kiriath-jearim
Baal-perazim, 339
Bashan, 45, 319, 320
Batash, Tel, 47, 277, 304
Beeroth, 283
Beersheba, Tel, 20, 24, 82, 119, 121, 125, 131, 139, 143, 162, 168, 171–75, 178–79, 216, 222, 224, 231, 233–35, 243, 254, 257, 272, 295, 306, 320, 323, 352
  fortification, 125, 131, 143, 224, 298
  osatraca, 174–75, 178–79
Beersheba Valley, 15, 22, 69, 127, 131–32, 134–35, 138, 142–44, 167, 173–74, 177, 179, 213, 222, 224–27, 249, 256–57, 276–77, 279–80, 293–95, 306, 309,

---

For kingdoms, empires, and territories, see also the subject index.

Beersheba Valley (cont.)
   311, 344–45, 347, 350, 352, 355, 367–68, 370, 373
Beer-sheva, Tell, 138
Beirut, 36
Beit ʿAnat, 41
Beit Mirsim, Tell, 138, 177, 216, 225–26, 228, 257, 305
Beit Mizza, 284–85. *See also* Mozah
Beit Safafa, 299
Beit Ur el-Tahta, 41
Besor, Nahal, 143, 288, 320
Beth-aven, 150
Beth-dagon, 41
Bethel, 16, 55, 63, 67–68, 138, 141, 150, 161, 181, 204, 218, 230–31, 236–37, 241, 338, 348, 351–53
Bethesda Valley, 19
Beth-haccerem, 336
Beth-horon, 41, 288, 318. *See also* Bit-NIN.URTA
Bethlehem, 54, 56, 59, 63, 67, 136–37, 141, 144
Beth-shean, 45, 47, 52, 179, 288
Beth-shean Valley, 36, 44
Beth-shemesh, 15, 34, 36, 38, 46, 48, 121, 132–33, 161, 168–69, 171, 177, 200, 205, 213, 222, 224, 226, 228, 247, 250, 257, 275, 305, 318–20, 367
Beth-zur, 41, 63, 354, 370
Bezek, 57
Bit-NIN.URTA, 40–42
Bor-ashan (Ashan), 138
Buqeiah, 257, 273, 276, 280, 306, 309
Burj, Khirbet el- (Horvat Tittora), 42, 298, 302
Buseirah, 159, 306, 322
Byblos, 201
Byzantium, 218
Cabul, land of, 320–21
Caesarea, 360
Carmel, 137, 139. *See also* Kirmil, Khirbet
Chephirah, 283–84
Chouf Mountains of Lebanon, 46

Cisjordan, 160, 319
coastal plain, 37, 45, 57, 147, 250, 288, 305, 317–18
   southern coastal plain, 36–37, 43, 45, 288
Colonia, 283–85. *See also* Motza; Moza, Tel
Cyprus/Cypriot, 143, 367
Damascus/Damascene, 15–16, 50, 69, 131, 143–44, 180, 246, 317, 319, 367–68, 371–73
Dan, Tel, 161–62, 243, 318, 320, 323
   inscription/stela, 15, 253, 266, 366
   tribe, 318
Dawwara, Khirbet, 55, 58, 136
Dead Sea, 142, 160, 257, 293, 296, 303–4, 307–11, 319, 350, 354
Deir ʿAlla, Tell, 177, 181, 346
   inscription/text, 316, 351
Deir el-Azar, 147–50, 288. *See also* Kiriath-jearim
Dibon, 354
Dor, 45, 368
Dothan Valley, 40
Ein el-Jowiezeh, 270, 285, 289–90, 302–3, 335–36
Ein Gedi, 137, 274, 276, 303, 307–9, 311, 350
Ein Hania, 336
Ein Hazeva, 306, 344
Ein Karem, Wadi, 299
Ekron, 54, 131, 133, 141–42, 226, 294. *See also* Miqne, Tel/Ekron
Elah Valley, 51–53, 56, 127, 130, 133, 136, 141, 366
Elephantine, 15
Eloth, 321
Eltekeh, 318
Emmaus, 284
Esdar, Tel, 138
Eshtaol, 133, 318
Eshtemoa, 137, 176. *See also* Samuʿ, es-
Eton, Tel, 38, 106, 138, 257, 272
Ezion-geber, 322
Farʿah North, Tell el-, 53

Far'ah South, Tell el-, 288
Feinan, Wadi, 142, 180
Ful, Tell el-, 51, 299
Galilee, 287, 305, 320, 373
   Sea of Galilee, 296
Gath (Gimtu) 15, 34, 36-40, 42-44, 48, 53-54, 56, 59, 69, 129, 131-35, 137, 139-44, 170, 176, 198, 200, 205, 239, 294, 304, 364, 367. See also Ṣafi, Tell eṣ-
Gaza, 36, 38, 288, 320, 360, 365
Geba, 51, 54, 59
   Geba/Gibeah, 51, 54-55
   Geba-Gibeon, 366
Gerar, Nahal, 288
Gezer (Gazru) 34, 36-38, 40-45, 48, 140, 230, 317, 318, 364, 370
Gibbethon, 318
Gibeah, 55, 150. See also Geba; Gibeon; Kiriath-jearim
Gibeon, 51, 54-55, 58-59, 135-36, 140, 142, 258, 283-84, 288, 302, 366
   Gibeon-Bethel, 50, 54, 142
   Gibeon-Gibeah, 127, 135, 140-41, 145
   Gibeon-Gibeah-Bethel, 140-41
   Gibeon-Mizpah, 284
   Plateau, 52-53, 56, 58, 282, 284-85, 309, 366
Gihon Spring, 5-7, 9, 13-15, 20, 22, 25, 31-32, 63, 68, 71, 95, 107, 119, 124-26, 177, 207, 213, 225, 243, 261-64, 267-69, 348-49, 361-63, 367, 371
   Gihon Spring Tower, 30, 32, 65-66, 68, 124
Gilboa, 52, 57
Gilead, 51-52, 58, 136, 352
Giloh, 73, 77
Ginti, 40
Ginti-Kirmil, 42, 44
Gob, 130-31, 133
Hachilah, 130
Hadid, Tel, 230
Halif, Tel, 47, 139, 257
Hama, 17
Hamashkhit, Har, 338

Hamideh, Khirbet (Bir el-Hilu), 40
Haror, Tel, 288
Hazeva, 322
Hazor, 9, 44, 179, 216, 223, 317
Hebron (Tell Rumeida) 16, 68, 136-39, 141, 143-44, 150, 175, 213, 257, 301, 303, 336, 350, 352
   Hebron Highlands, 40, 53, 56, 131-32
   Hebron Hills, 127, 131, 134, 140-41, 143, 344, 354, 370
Hereth, 131
Heshbon, 353-54
Horesh, 130
Hormah, 139
Horvat Shilhah, 274, 276
Horvat Uza, 181, 257, 316
'Ira, Tel, 173, 224, 257, 306
Izbet Sartah, 197, 200
Jaba, 51, 54
Jabbok River, 51-52, 58, 136, 142, 352
Jabesh, 51, 57
Jaffa, 34, 45, 47, 288
Jebus(ite), 53, 56, 96
Jemmeh, Tel, 288
Jericho, 307-9, 311, 350
Jerusalem
   Acra, 107, 370
   Al-Aqsa Mosque, 67, 349, 361, 363, 369
   Armenian Quarter, 6, 10, 23, 208, 245, 248, 269, 345, 362. See also Jerusalem: southwestern hill
   Burnt Room House, 82
   Citadel, 248
   City of David, 9-18, 20-25, 29, 31, 63-64, 67, 71, 73, 76, 79, 84, 90-93, 95-97, 99, 107, 109, 119, 125, 176, 178, 206-7, 213, 222-25, 245, 247-49, 258, 262-63, 269, 277, 279, 302, 332, 337, 345, 348-49, 360-63. See also Jerusalem: southeastern hill
   destruction of, 19, 74, 109, 124, 284, 343, 348
   expansion of, 19-20, 24-25, 44, 48, 63, 68, 124, 213, 266, 294, 346, 363

Jerusalem (cont.)
  Givati Parking Lot (Compound), 7–8, 11, 25, 32, 67, 107, 112, 124, 126, 213, 370
  HaGai (el-Wad), 23
  Haram al-Sharif, 16, 19, 207, 361
  Jewish Quarter, 23, 248. See also Jerusalem: southwestern hill
  Kenyon's excavation areas, 11, 13, 64, 80, 84, 90
  Large Stone Structure, 7, 65, 67–68, 71–80, 84–86, 88, 90, 92, 95–96, 98–101, 104–6, 124, 126. See also Jerusalem: visitors center
  Maccabean Tower, 72–73
  mound of, 9–10, 24, 124, 206–7, 212–13, 242, 268–69, 360–61. See also Jerusalem: Temple Mount
  Mount of Olives, 20
  Mount Zion, 208, 248, 362. See also Jerusalem: southwestern hill
  Old City, 4, 6, 20, 23, 208, 245, 268–69, 281, 332, 334–35, 362
  Ophel, 5–8, 11, 23, 25, 71, 79, 90, 109–26, 170, 177, 197–98, 200, 213, 331, 349, 367
  Shiloh's excavation areas, 13–14, 21–22, 30, 64, 67, 72–73, 77–79, 82, 90, 97, 101, 106, 175, 213, 263
  Siloam, 226
    Inscription, 168, 178, 180, 208, 261, 263, 266
    Pool, 13, 269
    Rock-Cut Pool, 261–64, 267–69
    Round Chamber, 263–64, 266–67
    Tunnel, 168, 225–26, 261, 263–64, 266–67, 269–70
  Stepped Stone Mantle, 14, 64, 80–82, 84, 95, 96
  Stepped Stone Structure, 14, 22–23, 63–65, 67–68, 71–73, 77, 80–81, 83–84, 86, 95–97, 99, 101–4, 107, 124, 126, 213, 224
  southeastern hill (or ridge) 5, 7–9, 16, 20–23, 25, 32, 63, 67, 77, 125–26,

Jerusalem: southeastern hill (cont.)
  206–8, 211, 213, 269, 360–63. See also Jerusalem: City of David
  southwestern hill (Jewish and Armenian Quarters), 4, 10, 20, 23, 25, 125, 204, 208, 211, 214, 245, 247–49, 255, 258, 263, 266, 269, 362–64, 371
  Temple Mount, 5–8, 10–11, 13, 16–25, 32, 56, 63, 67–68, 71, 79, 90, 93, 119, 124–25, 207–8, 213–14, 219, 242, 268–69, 332, 335, 337, 344, 348–49, 361–63, 367, 369, 371
  Herodian Temple Mount, 16, 109
  Tyropoeon Valley, 7, 11–12, 19, 90, 207, 263, 265, 269
  visitors center, 13, 14, 21, 22, 25, 67, 126
Jezreel Valley, 36, 44, 46, 57, 59, 93, 136, 229, 288, 317–18, 364
Jordan River, 38, 51, 135, 141, 252
Jordan Valley, 307, 317, 320
Kadesh-barnea, 173, 306, 344, 347, 353, 355
Karmelo (Carmel), 139
Karmil, Khirbet el-, 137. See also Carmel
Karnaim, 319
Kefar Veradim, 170, 197, 200–201
Keilah (biblical), 39–40, 42, 129, 132, 134–35, 140–41. See also Qeltu
Kerak, 18
Kheleifeh, Tell el-, 322
Kidron Valley, 9, 12, 19, 23, 118, 261, 265–66, 299
Kiriath-arba, 150. See also Hebron.
Kiriath-jearim, 57, 147–50, 153, 155, 159–63, 162, 182, 283–84, 286, 288, 318, 362, 367. See also Baalath; Deir el-Azar; Qaryat el'Inab (Abu-Gosh)
Kirmil, Khirbet, 137
Kuntillet ʿAjrud, 57, 171, 173, 177, 179, 181, 197, 253, 306, 316, 318, 346, 351, 367, 373
Lachish (Lakisha) 9, 15, 17–20, 24, 34, 37–38, 41–44, 48, 106, 119, 121–22,

Place Names Index

Lachish (cont.)
125, 132–33, 141, 168, 170–71, 173–79, 206, 210, 213–14, 217, 222–27, 231, 233–35, 243, 246–47, 249–50, 256–57, 259, 267–68, 272–77, 279–80, 305, 319, 347, 364
Lebanon, 56, 320, 373
Lebo Hamath, 320
Libnah, 133
Lifta, 286
Lod (Diospolis), 149
Luz, 150. See also Bethel
Machpelah, 352
Malḥata, Tel, 173, 257, 347
Mamre, 352
Manahat, 299, 337
Manḥatu, 43
Maon (Khirbet Main) 137, 137
Maresha, 133
Masos, Tel, 56, 131, 137, 139, 142–44, 257, 294, 367
Megiddo, 3, 9, 17–18, 44, 59, 106, 121, 170, 195–96, 201, 216–17, 223, 248, 286, 317–18, 368
Merenptah, Waters of, 286–87, 365. See also Nephtoah
Merom, 286
Mesha, 320
Mesopotamia, 45, 229–30, 254, 259, 287, 369
Michmash, 51
Migdal-gad, 41
Miqne/Ekron, Tel, 47, 248, 304–5
Mizpah (Tell en-Naṣbeh) 15, 20, 22, 24, 283, 290, 350, 369–70
Mizpeh, 283
Mizzah, Khirbet, 283–84. See also Moza, Tel
Monastery of Eliazar, 149. See also Kiriath-jearim
Mor, Tel, 288
Mordot Arnona, 270, 325–27, 329–35, 337, 339, 340
Moresheth-gath (biblical). See Murshati
Motza, 243, 284. See also Moza, Tel

Mount Lebanon, 45, 46
Moza, Tel, 281–85, 288–90, 296. See also Colonia; Qaluniya; Mizzah, Khirbet
Mozah (biblical). See Moza, Tel
Muḫḫazu, 44–45
Murabaʿat, Wadi, 179
Murshati, 35, 37, 43
Nahas, Khirbet en-, 306
Naphtali, 319
Naṣbeh, Tell en,- 55, 69, 258, 362
Nebo, 354
Negev, 138–39, 142–43, 167, 176, 256, 309, 311, 316
Nentisha, 43
Nephtoah, 286. See also Merenptah, Waters of
Nile Delta, 44
Nineveh, 290, 336
Ophir, 321
Ophrah, 55, 230
Orontes Valley, 45
Penuel, 161
Philistia, 131, 161, 204, 239
Phoenicia, 216, 323
Pihilu (Pehel) 44
Qaluniya, 281–87, 289, 291. See also Moza, Tel
Qaryat el ʿInab (Abu-Gosh) 149. See also Kiriath-jearim
Qeiyafa, Khirbet, 51–52, 56, 58–59, 127, 133, 136, 145, 198, 200–201
Qeltu, 39, 40–42, 129, 132, 134–35, 140–41. See also Keilah (biblical)
Qubur el-Walaydah, 288
Rabbah, 286
Rabud, Khirbet, 257
Racal, 139
Raddana, Khirbet, 136
Ramah, 55, 283
Ramallah, 58
Ramathaim, 55
Ramath-negeb, 138, 173. See also ʿIra, Tel
Ramat Rahel, 216, 275–77, 290–91, 298, 325, 327, 330, 332, 334–37, 339–40, 348, 350

Ramle, 318
Ramoth-gilead, 367
Rantis, 55
Ras, Khirbet er-, 298–99, 301
Ras Karkar, 55
Red Sea, 307, 321
Refaim, Nahal, 270, 335–36, 339
Reḥob (Tel Reḥov), 3, 44, 106, 141, 198, 200
Rephaim Valley, 289, 296, 299, 302
Rogem Ganim, 299
Rubutu, 39–41, 140
Ṣaffa, 42
Ṣafi, Tell eṣ-, 15, 35, 37, 43, 106, 170, 176, 198, 205, 223, 246–47, 304. See also Gath (Gimtu)
Salem, 90
Samaria, 9, 16, 17, 20, 116, 130, 209, 212, 215–17, 219, 223, 229, 228–30, 236, 241–42, 254–55, 259, 287, 320, 370, 372–73
    Highlands, 300, 305, 353, 359
    ostraca, 171, 179, 223, 253, 287
Samu', es- 137, 176. See also Eshtamoa
Sappho of Josephus, 42
Ṣapuma, 40, 42, 129, 140
Ṣarḥa, 36, 37, 41, 129, 133, 140. See also Zorah (biblical)
Sera', Tel, 133, 288
Sha'alim, 55
Shalisha, 55
Sharon, 45
Sheba, 307, 321
Shechem (Tell Balatah) 16–17, 22, 30, 32, 34, 43–45, 48, 53, 55, 57–60, 67–68, 142, 207, 216, 229–30, 255, 287, 362, 364–65
Sheikh Madhkur esh-, 133
Shephelah, 15, 22, 33–36, 38–42, 44, 46, 48, 52–53, 56, 59, 69, 91, 127, 129, 132–35, 140–45, 177, 204, 206, 209–16, 218, 223–28, 231, 245–46, 249, 253, 255–57, 259, 271, 275–77, 280, 293–94, 296, 303–5, 309, 311, 318,

Shephelah (cont.)
    344, 350, 365, 367–68, 373
    city-states, 38, 43, 140
Shiloh, 30, 57, 67, 72, 160–61, 163, 362
Shimon, 44
Shmuel, Nahal, 296, 299, 300, 302
Shubria, 251
Shunem, 288
Sile, 286
Silu, 43
Simeon, 139
Sinai, 306
Siphmoth, 131
Socoh, 130, 133–34, 136, 145, 336
Soreq, Nahal, 36, 281–82, 284–85, 289
Soreq Valley, 41, 133, 133, 135, 141, 297–99, 302
Suba, 290
Suez, Golf, 308
Syria, 45, 360, 369
    Coele-Syria, 307
Ta'anach, 40
Tamar, 318
Taiyiba et-, 67
Tell, Khirbet et- (Ai), 53, 55, 58, 136, 362
Tianna, 43
Tubeiqah, Khirbet et-, 41
Tyre, 91
Urartu, 251
Uzza, garden of, 337, 347
Yalo, 41
Yarkon River, 45, 288
Yatir, Khirbet, 138
Yavne-Yam, 45
Yemini, 55
Yokneam, Tel, 44
Yurza, 37, 43–44
Zayit, Tel, 35, 37, 43, 47, 198
Zedek Valley, 21, 77
Zeelim, 303
Zemaraim, 230, 288
Zeredah, 55
Zif, Tell, 137
Ziph (Khirbet Ziph) 137, 303, 336

Ziklag, 129, 132–35, 139, 143
Zorah (biblical), 318. *See also* Ṣarḥa
Zuph, 55

Personal Names Index

Abdi-Ashtarti (of Gath), 34, 37–38, 43, 45
Abdi-Heba (of Jerusalem), 11, 39–42, 45, 364–65
Abdina, 35, 38
Abibaal, 200
Abinadab, 161
Abiyau, 253
Abner, 238
Abraham, 204, 352–53
Absalom, 238
Adad-nirari III, 367
Adoni-zedek, 91
Ahab, 366
Ahaz, 226, 236, 253
Ahaziah, 366
Ahiram, 200
Alexander Jannaeus, 74, 86
Amasa, 238
Amaziah, 182, 223, 319–20, 367
Amon, 337
Antiochus VII Sidetes, 370
Aristobolus I, 370
Asa, 366
Ashurbanipal, 290
Ashurnasirpal II, 307, 336
Athaliah, 366
Aziru (of Amurru), 45, 56
Baasha, 366
Ba'lu-danu (of Gezer), 34
Bathsheba, 315
Belit-labi'at, 34, 36, 40–42
Ben Sira, 16
Byzas (of Megara), 218
Caleb, 283
Dahr el-Omar, 45, 56–57, 373

David, 11, 53, 56, 58–60, 74, 91–92, 96, 109, 128–32, 135–37, 139–44, 161–63, 167, 199, 204, 237–41, 339
    narrative, 40, 128–29, 145
    stories, 51, 53, 56, 127, 129–30, 132, 134, 143–44, 204
Diodorus Siculus, 307
Dioscorides Pedanius, 307
Dius, 320
Eleazar, 149, 161
Elhanan (David's warrior), 56, 123
Eliashib, 171, 186, 188, 191
Elibaal, 200
Elijah-Elisha cycle, 252
Eusebius, 149
Fakhr ed-Din, 46, 56, 373
Hazael, 15, 50, 69, 131–32, 143–44, 170, 180, 246, 320, 367
Herod the Great, 352
Herodotus, 307
Hezekiah, 162–63, 231–34, 236–38, 243, 250, 315, 323–24, 338
Hiram (of Tyre), 91, 320–21
Hiram I, 320
Hiram II, 320
Isaac, 352
Ishbaal, 52, 59
Ishmael, 352
Jacob, 182, 204, 252, 323, 351, 353
Jehoash, 15, 50, 263
Jehoram, 366
Jehoshaphat, 366
Jeremiah, 258
Jeroboam, 321
Jeroboam I, 55, 58–60, 161, 176, 321

Jeroboam II, 50, 52, 57, 60, 160–61, 163, 182, 223, 243–44, 315, 317–21, 323–24, 351–52, 354, 367
Joash, 15, 23, 50, 125, 160, 182, 223, 319–20, 367
John Hyrcanus, 370, 373
Jonathan, 370
Joram, 59, 366
Josephus, 284, 307, 320
Joshua, 91, 286
Josiah, 162–63, 231–32, 250, 277, 280, 311, 323–25, 337–38, 340, 372
Labayu, 37, 39, 43, 52, 57, 364–65
Manasseh, 256, 259, 270, 276, 280, 311, 315–16, 323–25, 336–38, 340
Melchizedeck, 90
Menander, 320
Merenptah, 288
Milkilu, 34, 36, 39–40, 42–43
Nebuchadnezzar, 348
Nehemiah, 74, 111
Nera, 275–76
Osorkon I, 200–201
Pliny the Elder, 307
Pompeius Trogus, 307
Pompey, 370, 373
Pu-Baʻlu (of Yurza), 37
Sargon II, 132, 248, 255
Saul, 49–59, 128–29, 131, 135–36, 141, 161, 204, 238, 252, 366
  house of, 49, 60, 141, 145
Sennacherib, 133, 139, 160, 206, 208–11, 215, 223, 225, 227, 232, 234–35, 237, 245–46, 248, 250, 253, 255–59, 268, 271–72, 289, 294, 305, 344, 360, 372
Shebna, 275–76
Shebnayau, 253
Shema (servant of), 176
Sheshonq I, 50–52, 58–59, 74, 127, 135–36, 141–42, 144, 200–201, 288, 365–66, 371
Shipṭi-Baʻlu (of Lachish), 34–35, 38
Shubandu, 37
Shuwardata, 34, 36–37, 39–41, 43
Simeon, 370

Solomon, 11, 59, 162, 167, 196, 199, 237–39, 241, 307, 309, 315–18, 320–24, 338
  Acts of Solomon, book of the, 315–18, 320–24
  Solomonic, 40, 64, 90, 199, 239–40, 319
Strabo, 307
Tacitus, 307
Tagi, 39, 41, 42
Tiglath-pileser III, 226, 320, 368
Theophrastus, 307
Thutmose III, 40
Turbazu, 35, 37, 43
Uriah the Hittite, 91, 238
Uzziah, 176, 178, 180, 182, 223–24, 244
Uzziyau, 176, 253
Vespasian, 284, 291
Yabni-Ilu, 34
Yaḥzib-Hadda, 34–37, 43
Yapaḥu, 34, 45
Yidia, 37
Zimreddi, 34, 37–38, 43

Subject Index

Achaemenid Persia, 369, 372
alphabetic writing, 133, 195–96, 198, 200–201, 266, 345. *See also* inscriptions
Amalek, 127, 129, 132, 137, 139, 143
Amarna, 135, 200, 225
    archive, 14, 33–34, 36, 39–43, 46, 48–49, 129, 140, 286, 365
    period, 15, 33–34, 38–40, 46–47, 52, 56–57, 207, 345, 360, 362, 364–65, 371
Ammon(ite), 51, 55, 338
Amun, temple of, 288
Annals of the Kings of Judah, 337
Arabia(n), 226, 308
Arabs, 355
    inscriptions, 309, 322
    queens, 322
    trade, 159, 226, 306, 309–10, 321, 323, 353, 360, 367–69, 372
Arameans, 15
Apiru, 40–42, 45, 53, 58, 127, 129, 131, 137, 139–42, 144, 251–52
ark of the covenant, 149–50, 160–63
    narrative, 133, 147, 149, 160–61, 163
Assyria(n), 23, 50, 132, 143, 159–60, 174, 180, 182, 204, 210–12, 215, 217, 221, 226–30, 233–34, 236–37, 242–43, 250–51, 254, 256, 258–59, 265, 269–70, 272, 275–77, 279, 281, 287, 290, 293–94, 296–97, 303, 305–7, 308–12, 316, 319–22, 324, 336, 344–45, 347, 353, 355, 368–69, 371–72
    administration, 182, 306, 316
    Assyrian-led Arabian trade, 180, 250, 279

Assyria(n) (*cont.*)
    culture, 336
    economy, 226, 228, 242, 259, 269, 305, 312, 336, 347, 372
    Empire, 250, 319, 321
    Neo-Assyrian, 322
Astarte, 338
Baal, 149–50, 200, 253, 339
Babylonia(n), 230, 255, 258, 268, 277, 283–84, 300, 334, 343–44, 347–51, 356, 360, 369, 372
    conquest, 300, 356
    destruction, 109, 255, 290, 360, 369, 372
    Empire, 356, 369, 371–72
    impressions, 349
Benjamin, land of, 55, 149, 162, 283–86, 319
    Benjaminite, 283, 318
    district, 283–84
    highlands, 49–50, 130, 230
    Plateau, 63, 68, 285, 302
    tribe, 149, 159
Bronze Age, 11, 17, 60, 76, 90, 92, 107, 117, 124, 141, 147, 206–8, 267–68, 296, 345, 360–62
    Early Bronze, 53, 76, 125, 150, 248, 283, 287, 362
    Middle Bronze, 3, 9, 13–14, 20–22, 24, 29–32, 65–66, 73, 76–77, 90–91, 114, 122, 207, 248, 261, 283, 361–62
    Late Bronze, 10, 13–16, 20, 22, 24, 33–34, 38, 41–42, 46–47, 49, 56, 64, 73, 76–77, 91, 104, 129, 133–34,

Subject Index 449

Bronze Age: Late Bronze (cont.)
    140–41, 143, 158, 195, 197, 199–201, 207, 213, 222, 252, 281, 283, 294, 359–60, 372–73
bulla, 14, 68, 80, 85, 99, 168, 177–79, 209, 269–70, 310–12, 347, 351, 367
Canaan(ite), 14–15, 33–37, 44–47, 50–52, 57, 59, 91, 127, 136–37, 140, 142, 231, 286–88, 353, 360, 365–66, 371–72
    city-states, 14–15, 34, 92, 136, 288
    Proto-Canaanite inscriptions, 167, 170, 176, 199, 201
Chalcolithic, 73, 76, 307
Chemosh, 338
chronology, 3, 50–51, 58–59, 77–78, 82, 99, 110, 127, 145, 168, 178, 196–97, 205, 223, 232, 294, 332, 339
Dagon, 161
Davidic dynasty, 49, 57, 142, 144, 204, 219, 231, 237–42, 323, 337, 360–61, 366
Delphi oracle, 218
Deuteronomistic, 16, 50, 53, 55–56, 60, 91, 128, 130, 217, 223, 237–38, 240, 252, 316, 323, 339
    pre-Deuteronomistic, 49–54, 58, 60, 128, 144, 240, 252, 321
digital elevation model, 151, 153, 155, 158
Edom(ite), 159, 175, 179, 226, 306, 310, 322, 368
    Plateau, 350, 368
Egypt(ian), 40, 42–48, 51–52, 54, 57–60, 136, 142, 204, 287–88, 305, 308–9, 318–19, 321, 356, 364–66, 368–69, 371–73
    Brook of Egypt, 320
    Empire, 364, 371
    New Kingdom, 46, 291, 372
    ruler/pharaoh, 34, 39, 42, 45–48, 58–59, 140, 142, 321, 360, 365–66
    Twenty-First Dynasty, 57, 288
    Twenty-Second Dynasty, 57–58, 136
    Twenty-Sixth Dynasty, 369
Ephraim, highlands of, 55, 212
exodus (story), 252

First Temple period, 114
Greek, 218, 356
ground-penetrating radar, 155
Hasmonean, 24, 46, 72, 74, 80, 84–86, 90, 96, 99, 107, 160, 243, 249, 343, 349, 356, 360, 363–64, 370, 373
Hebrew, 79, 129, 169–71, 173–74, 178–80, 190, 193, 200–201, 283, 319, 325
Hellenistic period, 11, 17, 20, 23–24, 32, 46, 78, 85, 92–93, 96, 98, 100, 102, 104, 107, 111, 139, 159, 171–72, 183, 187, 190, 193, 234, 283–85, 287, 291, 296, 300, 349–50, 354, 370
    early, 10, 13–14, 16–17, 23–24, 84, 150, 207, 343–44, 349, 355, 360, 369, 373
    late, 3, 9, 11, 13, 19–21, 24–25, 72, 74, 84, 86, 90, 92, 96, 101, 107, 151, 156–59, 207–8, 356, 360–64, 373
Herodian, 10, 16–20, 80, 84, 98–99, 104, 207, 249, 360–61
impressions, seal
    ḥmš, 137–38, 176
    lion, 348
    lmlk, 79, 168, 177–78, 180, 187, 193, 206, 226, 243, 248, 253, 267–68, 271–72, 275–76, 278, 280, 289, 303, 305, 310, 327–28, 330–32, 336
    mmšlt (*mmst*), 289, 291, 336
    mwsh, 284, 290, 348
    rosette, 271–72, 276–80, 289, 328, 332, 339
    Yehud, 348–50
    yhd, 278, 351
    yhud/yhwd, 16, 330
    yhw, 16, 208–9
    yrslm, 278, 291
    yw, 209
inscriptions, 37, 43, 133, 138, 161, 167–68, 170–73, 175–83, 187–92, 194–201, 209, 224, 253, 266, 288, 309, 316, 345, 351, 356
    Arad, 171, 172, 172, 178, 182, 183, 189, 190, 193
    Aramaic, 185, 190, 192, 283

inscriptions (cont.)
  Beth-shean, 179
  Dan, Tel, 15, 253
  Deir ʿAlla, Tell, 177
  Gath, 170
  Hazor, 179
  Hebrew, 137–38, 167, 170–71, 176, 195, 200, 351
  Izbet Sartah, 197
  Kefar Veradim, 170
  Kuntillet ʿAjrud, 173, 177, 179, 181, 316
  Lachish, 170
  Megiddo, 170
  Mesha, 180, 266, 353–54
  monumental, 168, 178, 200, 226
  Ophel, 170, 197–98
  Proto-Canaanite, 167, 176, 199, 201
  royal, 181, 200
  Sabaean, 322
  Ṣafi, Tell eṣ-, 170, 176
  Siloam, 168, 178, 180, 208, 261, 263, 266, 270
  South Arabian, 309, 322
Iron Age, 11, 15–19, 30, 33–34, 37, 46, 64, 66–68, 90, 96, 98, 102, 104, 106–7, 109, 113, 116–19, 124–25, 128, 136–38, 141, 144–45, 147, 150, 158, 168, 196, 206–8, 211, 216, 258, 266, 270, 283, 285–86, 288, 290, 294, 296–97, 299, 301–2, 304–6, 309, 317, 335, 344–46, 348, 352, 354–56, 360–62
  early Iron Age, 16
  late Iron Age, 300, 303–5, 311
  Iron I, 10, 13–14, 22–24, 48–49, 51, 54, 56, 63–64, 67, 73, 76–78, 91, 96, 99, 104–6, 122, 125–26, 131–33, 137–38, 140–41, 144–45, 157, 195, 197, 199, 200, 213, 221, 225, 267, 283, 294, 296, 349, 363, 365
    early Iron I, 56, 77, 197
    middle Iron I, 77, 197
    late Iron I, 50, 55, 63, 77, 84, 92, 127, 131, 136–37, 139, 141, 198
  Iron I–II, 68, 123

Iron Age (cont.)
  Iron I–IIA, 134, 139, 180, 196, 198–200, 247–48, 268
  Iron II, 30, 32, 68, 82, 99, 109, 133–34, 145, 178, 205, 210–11, 225, 247, 254, 285–86, 303, 362
    late Iron II, 11, 13, 20, 80, 82, 85, 99, 101–2, 114, 117, 119, 210, 229, 255, 272, 275, 325
  Iron IIA, 3, 10–11, 14–16, 22–25, 49, 63–66, 68, 71, 74, 78–79, 81–82, 84–86, 93, 96, 99, 101, 104–7, 110, 112, 114–18, 124, 126–27, 131–35, 133, 137–39, 143–45, 150, 157, 171, 176, 178–79, 183, 195, 197–99, 201, 205, 207, 209, 213–16, 227, 229, 246, 248–49, 255, 267, 283, 288, 295–96, 312, 327, 345, 353, 361, 363, 367, 372–73
    early Iron IIA, 10, 50–51, 55–56, 63, 77, 84, 92, 105, 110, 120–25, 127, 135–36, 138–39, 141, 143, 169, 197, 199, 200, 213, 221, 225, 294, 349
    late Iron IIA, 14–15, 19, 22, 24, 65–68, 78, 82, 92–93, 96, 105, 110, 121–25, 131, 138, 168–70, 176–77, 179, 181, 197, 200–201, 205, 211, 214, 216, 219, 222–23, 235, 263, 288, 294, 304, 344–45, 349, 367, 373
    late Iron IIA1, 131, 135, 139, 143
    late Iron IIA2, 131, 139
  Iron IIA–B, 14, 138, 205, 215, 217
  Iron IIA–C, 283
  Iron IIB, 3, 14–15, 19–20, 23–25, 29–30, 52, 74, 79, 84–86, 105–6, 110, 117, 119–21, 124–25, 147, 156–58, 170, 172, 178–79, 183, 187–90, 192–95, 205–12, 214–18, 245, 248, 255, 263, 266–69, 272–73, 276, 289, 294–97, 305, 335, 344, 349, 351, 363

Subject Index

Iron Age: Iron IIB (cont.)
    early Iron IIB, 158–59, 168, 179, 181–82, 199, 214, 216, 317–18, 372–73
    late Iron IIB, 245, 327, 328
  Iron IIB–C, 6, 9, 11, 13, 18, 20, 29, 110, 115–18, 124, 145, 150, 174–75, 179, 188, 194, 205, 208, 216, 245, 281, 288, 296, 298, 303, 311, 327, 331, 344, 352, 361–62, 370
  Iron IIC, 64, 110, 112, 115, 119, 138–39, 156–58, 168, 172, 174, 177–78, 183, 185–89, 192, 194, 205–6, 209, 214, 245, 273, 294–97, 300, 311, 328, 330–32, 334–35, 338–39, 344, 347, 349–51, 363, 369
    early Iron IIC, 328
Islamic, 11, 20, 151
Israel, 48–50, 52, 57–58, 60, 92, 110, 121, 125, 130, 137–38, 147, 150, 159–63, 171, 177, 179–82, 199–200, 204–5, 209–10, 214–15, 217–219, 223, 228, 231, 236–38, 240–41, 243, 250–51, 252, 254, 287, 315–18, 320–23, 345–47, 352–53, 366, 368, 370–71
Israelite, 52–53, 58, 130, 136, 142, 160–62, 176, 181–82, 203–5, 208–11, 215–16, 218–19, 228–31, 237–38, 240, 242–43, 250, 252–53, 259, 316, 320–24, 345, 353–54, 366–67, 373
  north Israelite, 49, 52, 58–59, 127, 135–37, 141–43, 162, 167, 180–81, 236, 242
Jewish Revolt, 160, 360, 370–72
Josianic authors, 162–63, 316, 337–38, 340
Judah, 3, 15, 23–24, 48–50, 53, 56–60, 64–65, 91, 109, 121–22, 125, 127–31, 133, 142–43, 147, 149, 159–62, 167–68, 170–71, 175–77, 179–82, 195, 200, 203–6, 209–10, 212–13, 215–19, 221–28, 230–31, 234–37, 239–43, 245, 249–56, 258–59, 263, 268–69, 272, 276–77, 279, 281, 283–84, 286, 289, 291, 293–97, 305, 308–9, 311–12,

Judah (cont.)
  315–24, 333, 336–38, 344–47, 350–51, 353, 355, 360, 366–68, 373
  highlands of, 53, 129, 135, 141, 211, 214–15, 218, 224, 255, 257, 274, 294, 304, 359
Judahite, 15, 19, 41, 50–53, 59, 128–30, 132, 139, 167, 171, 176–77, 204, 209, 213, 215, 218, 226–28, 231, 234, 237–40, 242–43, 246, 252–54, 256, 271, 273, 275–77, 280, 286, 289, 294, 306, 310–11, 318, 323, 325, 327, 334, 344, 347, 352–53, 355, 368
  kingdom, 68, 160, 163, 167, 212, 221, 228, 249, 256
  literacy, 167–68, 174, 182, 217–18
  Negev, 257
Judaism, 343
Judea, 291, 355–56, 360, 369–72. *See also* Yehud
Judean, 219, 273, 307
  Desert, 256–57, 273, 277, 280, 293, 294, 296, 297, 307, 309, 311, 335
  Highlands, 129, 131, 140, 147, 294, 296, 303, 309
Levant, 16–17, 22, 55, 104–5, 109, 143, 147, 167, 180, 195–96, 198–200, 207, 216, 250, 254, 266, 271, 273, 287, 293, 305–6, 310, 345, 361, 364, 369, 370–73
  southern, 296, 359–60, 373
Levites, 162
Mediterranean, 226, 252, 297, 304, 306, 308, 312, 368
Milcom, 338
Mishnah, 283
Moab(ite), 18, 55, 93, 168, 180, 310, 319–20, 338, 353–54
monarchy, united, 50, 52, 57–58, 60, 63, 109, 142, 145, 147, 162–63, 167, 182, 199–200, 219, 224, 237–38, 241–43, 250, 315–16, 319–20, 323, 366
Ninurta, 41
Northern Kingdom, 23, 46, 55, 69, 121, 128–30, 142, 147, 160, 163, 173, 179, 203, 211, 216, 221, 223, 226, 228, 230,

Northern Kingdom (cont.)
  236, 242, 250–51, 254, 259, 269, 315–21, 323–24, 344, 351–52, 354, 368
Omride(s), 50, 131, 196, 317, 320, 324, 353, 366–67
Optical Stimulated Luminescence (OSL), 158–60, 296, 300
ostraca, 79, 116, 168–83, 188, 190, 192, 197, 216, 200, 223–24, 226, 253, 287, 310, 316, 344, 347, 351, 355
Ottoman, 55–57, 373
palace, 14, 17, 19, 24, 74, 92, 175, 207, 235–36, 307, 310, 337, 339, 347
  Davidic dynasty's, 16, 22, 24, 71, 361
  King David's, 11, 91, 92
paleography, 170, 178–79, 182, 185, 187, 189, 193, 194, 196–97, 266–67, 270
palynology, 303–4, 309, 350
papyri, 177, 179–81, 230, 270, 286, 347
  Papyrus Amherst, 63, 230
  Papyrus Anastasi, 3, 286, 365
patriarchal narratives, 90, 204
Persian period, 10–11, 13–17, 23–24, 74, 84, 150, 192, 197, 207, 229–30, 234, 243, 249, 254–55, 283–85, 287, 290–91, 316, 321, 343–44, 347–52, 354–56, 360, 363, 369, 371–73
petrography, 33, 36–38, 176
Philistine, 92, 136, 139, 141, 161, 238, 339
  city-states, 54, 56, 59, 132, 133, 256, 275. *See also* Place Names Index: Gath; Ekron
  garrison, 54, 58, 136
  people, 128–30, 136, 160–61
Phoenicia(n), 74, 200, 216, 323
Proto-Ionic capital, 84, 216, 290, 353
Ptolemaic, 16, 369, 371–72
radiocarbon, 3, 6, 30, 32, 59, 65–66, 77, 79, 96, 105–6, 110, 125, 139, 157, 168–69, 196, 199, 205, 266, 294, 345
  ^{14}C, 77, 125, 126, 205, 246–47, 250, 266
refugees, 204, 208, 211–12, 215, 227–28, 230, 240–42, 245, 250–55, 259, 269
ritual bath (*mikveh*), 74, 80, 85–86

Roman period, 9, 11, 13, 21, 74, 84–86, 92, 98, 149, 151, 156–60, 192, 207, 269, 281, 283–85, 287, 291, 300, 327, 359–62, 369, 371
  early Roman, 11, 13, 21, 74, 85–86, 98, 151, 156–59, 300, 360, 362
sanctuary, 160, 183, 188, 191, 231–36
  Arad, 232
  ark, of the, 163
  Beersheba, 233, 352
  Bethel, 231
  Juhadite, 234
  Kiriath-jearim, 161
  Shiloh, 160
Saulides, Saulide territory, 52, 54–55, 58, 238, 240
Saviors, Book of, 252, 351
scribe(s), 35, 57, 162–63, 167, 179, 197, 199, 208, 352, 354
  activity, 130, 167, 181, 195, 199–201, 224, 239–40, 242–43, 347, 350–51, 356
Sea Peoples, 251
seals, 79, 168, 176, 177–80, 187, 206, 209, 224, 226, 248, 253, 261, 275, 271–80, 283–84, 289–91, 303, 310, 312, 327–28, 330, 332, 334, 336–37, 339, 347351, 363, 369. *See also* impressions, seal
Seleucid(s), 16, 107, 160, 370–71
Septuagint, 58, 58
shrine, 150, 163, 181, 218, 232–37, 242, 352–53, 283
  Bethel, 181
  Judahite, 235
  Kiriath-jearim, 163
  Lachish "Solar Shrine" 234
Southern Kingdom, 130, 142–43, 176, 180–82, 225, 249, 253, 256, 310, 316, 320, 366
Talmud, 283–84
temple, 3, 16–17, 19, 24, 41, 135, 150, 160–63, 204, 207, 219, 236–38, 241–43, 287–88, 310, 315–16, 347, 351, 356, 359, 361

temple (cont.)
    Amun, 288
    Bethel, 236–37, 241, 351
    Jerusalem, 231, 237, 242, 371
    Motza, 243, 288
    Solomon, 238, 316
    YHWH, 354
Torah, 356
trade, 44–45, 143, 159, 180–81, 217, 226, 242, 250, 306–7, 309, 311, 321, 323, 353, 355, 360, 367–69, 367, 372
Transjordan, 38, 45, 142, 168, 319, 354, 359, 369
united monarchy. *See* monarchy, united
West-Semitic, 41, 199, 201
Yahwistic, 162, 322
Yehud, 16, 273, 290–91, 316, 321, 344, 348, 350, 352, 354–56, 369–70
YHWH, 129, 150, 160–62, 354

www.ingramcontent.com/pod-product-compliance
Lightning Source LLC
Chambersburg PA
CBHW062025290426
44108CB00025B/2781